Youard

Karl Engeroff — Cicely Lovelace-Käufer

AN ENGLISH-GERMAN DICTIONARY OF IDIOMS

KARL ENGEROFF — CICELY LOVELACE-KÄUFER

An English-German Dictionary of Idioms

Idiomatic and Figurative English Expressions with German Translations

MAX HUEBER VERLAG

5. Auflage

4. 3. 2. | Die letzten Ziffern
1983 82 81 80 79 | bezeichnen Zahl und Jahr des Druckes.
Alle Drucke dieser Auflage können nebeneinander benutzt werden.

Umschlaggestaltung: Erich Hölle, Otterfing
Druck und Bindung: Ludwig Auer, Donauwörth · Printed in Germany
ISBN 3 19 00.6217 X

VORWORT

To have (to put) all one's eggs in one basket, alles auf eine Karte setzen. Abertausende von festen Wendungen solcher Art bieten sich uns in der Muttersprache an. Gern und unbefangen benutzen wir sie bei jeder Gelegenheit, ohne uns etwas dabei zu denken. In der Unterhaltung stellen sie sich von selbst ein; sie fließen in die Feder, wenn wir Briefe schreiben.

Sobald wir aber argwöhnen, daß der vorgeprägte Formelschatz unserer Muttersprache nicht genau das ausdrückt, was wir persönlich sagen wollen, fangen wir an, unsere sprachliche Unschuld zu verlieren. In diese unbequeme und heilsame Wandlung vom naiven zum bewußten Gebrauch der Sprache wird jeder hineingezwungen, der eine fremde Sprache gründlich lernen möchte. Er wird sehr bald merken, daß nur wenige feste Wendungen seiner eigenen Sprache, wörtlich in die Fremdsprache übersetzt, dort einen befriedigenden oder gar entsprechenden Sinn ergeben. Er muß sich also den für den rechten Verkehrston so notwendigen Formelschatz der Fremdsprache neu aneignen. Das wortwörtliche Übersetzen aus der Muttersprache führt in die Irre.

Wer allerdings viele Monate in einer fremden Sprachwelt untertauchen kann und dort von früh bis spät dem fremden Idiom ausgesetzt ist, wird bei einiger Sprachbegabung einen Schatz von Wendungen für die wichtigsten Sprech- und Schreibsituationen instinktiv übernehmen. Jeder andere ist auf ein Studium der fremdsprachlichen Wendungen angewiesen. Für ein solches Studium des Englischen gibt es eine Reihe kleinerer Nachschlagewerke der Idiomatik. Bisher fehlte aber ein Werk, das einen sehr großen Teil der gegenwärtig gebräuchlichen Wendungen des Englischen verzeichnet, ihren stilistischen Anwendungsbereich bestimmt und eine treffende deutsche Entsprechung danebensetzt.

Kollege Engeroff hat sich dieser Aufgabe unterzogen. Er brachte alle Voraussetzungen dafür mit. Die Sprache seiner Mutter war Englisch, seine Muttersprache Deutsch. Als Universitätslektor und Studienrat war er gleichermaßen erfahren in der Sprachpädagogik der Universität und der Höheren Schule. Er zog jeden, dem er ein Urteil zutraute, ins Gespräch über sein jeweils letztes Problem der Verdeutschung eines englischen Ausdrucks, und es war schwer, dem von seiner Aufgabe Besessenen zu entkommen. Es sollte ihm nicht vergönnt sein, sein Buch selbst fertigzustellen. Aus dem Kreise seiner Gewährspersonen hat sich Cicely M. Käufer bereitgefunden, die Arbeit zu Ende zu führen, die einzelnen Artikel für den Druck durchzusehen und das Manuskript neu zu schreiben, ein schwieriges Unterfangen, höchst mühselig und undankbar. Cicely M. Käufer ist in England geboren und aufgewachsen. Ihr englisches Sprachbewußtsein sagt ihr, welche Wendungen heute noch üblich sind. Andererseits lebt sie so lange als Frau eines Deutschen in Westdeutschland, daß ihr auch die deutschen Entsprechungen der englischen Wendungen vertraut sind. Es ist also ein Glücksfall, daß auch der Abschluß des Buches von einer sachkundigen Persönlichkeit geleistet wurde, die zweisprachig ist.

Ich habe einige Wochen mit den Druckfahnen gearbeitet. Die einzelnen englischen Wendungen sind leicht aufzufinden, da sie im jeweiligen Artikel alphabetisch angeordnet sind. Nicht immer gibt es eine entsprechende feste Wendung im Deutschen. Wir müssen uns dann mit einer deutschen Umschreibung des Ausdrucks begnügen. Jedenfalls aber kommen die deutschen Entsprechungen dem Ideal sehr nahe, daß sie auf derselben stilistischen Ebene liegen wie die englischen Ausdrücke. Der besondere Vorzug des vorliegenden Werkes liegt darin, daß es sehr reichhaltig ist, nur heute gebräuchliche englische Wendungen enthält und ihre richtige Verwendung sowohl durch eine ihrer Stilebene entsprechende deutsche Übertragung wie auch durch die üblichen Zeichen (sl. usw.) angibt.

Universitätsprofessor Dr. Wolfgang Schmidt-Hidding, Bonn

Verwendete Abkürzungen

a. = adjective	*Adjektiv, Eigenschaftswort*
abbr. = abbreviated	*abgekürzt*
adv. = adverb	*Adverb, Umstandswort*
arch. = archaic	*archaisch, altertümlich, veraltet*
art. = article	*Artikel*
aux. = auxiliary	*Hilfs-, zusätzlich*
colloq. = colloquial	*umgangssprachlich*
conj. = conjunction	*Konjunktion, Bindewort*
contempt. = contemptuously	*verachtend, verächtlich, geringschätzig*
Dan. = Daniel	*Daniel*
dat. = dative	*Dativ, Wem-Fall*
def. = definite	*bestimmt*
Eccl. = Ecclesiastes	*der Prediger Salomo*
esp. = especially	*speziell, besonders, hauptsächlich*
euphem. = euphemism	*Euphemismus, Beschönigung*
Exod. = Exodus	*2. Buch Moses*
Ezek. = Ezekiel	*Hesekiel*
facet. = facetious	*scherzhaft, witzelnd, witzig*
fam. = familiar	*familiär, vertraulich*
fig. = figurative	*figürlich, bildhaft*
gen. = genitive	*Genitiv, Wes-Fall*
Gen. = Genesis	*1. Buch Moses*
gym. = gymnastics	*Gymnastik, Turnerei*
herald. = heraldry	*Heraldik, Wappenkunde*
Hos. = Hosea	*Hosea*
hunt. = hunting	*Jagd*
indef. = indefinite	*unbestimmt*
int. = interjection	*Interjektion, Ausrufswort*
iron. = ironical	*ironisch, gegenteilig*
Is. = Isaiah	*Jesaja*
j., j.es, j.em, j.en	*jemand, jemandes, jemandem, jemanden*
joc. = jocular	*scherzhaft, launig*
lat. = Latin	*Latein(isch)*
leg. = legal	*juristisch*
math. = mathematics	*Mathematik*
Matt. = Matthew	*Matthäus*
mil. = military	*militärisch*
n. = noun	*Nomen, Substantiv, Hauptwort*
naut. = nautical	*nautisch, seemännisch*
nav. = navigation	*Schiffahrtskunde*
neg. = negation	*Negation, Verneinungswort*
n. pr. = proper noun (name)	*Eigenname*

orig. = originally	*ursprünglich*
parl. = parliamentary	*parlamentarisch*
Pet. = Peter	*Epistel Petri*
pl. = plural	*Plural, Mehrzahl*
poet. = poetical	*poetisch, dichterisch*
p. p. = past participle	*Partizip Perfekti, Mittelwort der Vergangenheit*
pred. = predicative	*prädikativ*
pref. = prefix	*Präfix, Vorsilbe*
prep. = preposition	*Präposition, Verhältniswort*
pron. = pronoun	*Pronomen, Fürwort*
prov. = proverb	*Sprichwort*
Ps. = Psalms	*der Psalter*
Rev. = Revelation	*Offenbarung Johannes*
Rom. = Romans	*Römerbrief*
Sam. = Samuel	*Buch Samuelis*
sl. = slang	*Slang, Argot, Vulgärsprache*
U. S. = United States	*(Vereinigte Staaten von) Amerika*
v. = verb	*Verbum, Tätigkeitswort*
v. aux. = auxiliary verb	*Hilfsverbum, Zeitwort*
v. i. = intransitive verb	*intransitives Verbum, Zeitwort*
v. refl. = reflexive verb	*reflexives, rückbezügliches Verbum, Zeitwort*
v. tr. = transitive verb	*transitives Verbum, Zeitwort*
vulg. = vulgar	*vulgär, gewöhnlich, gemein*

A

a (an) indef. art.: ∾ few *einige, ein paar;* ∾ good deal, ∾ good many *ziemlich viel(e);* ∾ great deal, ∾ great many *sehr viel(e);* many ∾ *manche(r), manches;* such ∾ one *ein solcher, eine solche, ein solches;* he is ∾ teacher *er ist Lehrer;* he died ∾ hero *er starb als Held;* eight hours ∾ day *acht Stunden täglich;* so much ∾ day *soviel pro Tag;* once ∾ day *einmal am Tage;* it costs ∾ shilling ∾ pound *es kostet einen Schilling das Pfund;* this is as large ∾ box as that *diese Dose ist ebenso groß wie jene;* he recognised how great ∾ man Cromwell was *er erkannte, was Cromwell für ein großer Mann war;* so great ∾n effort *eine so große Anstrengung;* too strict ∾ teacher *ein zu strenger Lehrer;* too heavy ∾n expense *eine zu große Ausgabe;* 'wot are you ∾-doin' of? (cockney dialect) *was machst du?;* the bells are ∾-ringing (old-fash.) *die Glocken läuten („sind am Läuten")*

A 1 a.: it is ∾ (colloq.) *es ist I A, erstklassig, prima*

aback adv.: to be taken ∾ *bestürzt, überrascht, verblüfft werden*

ABC n.: the ∾ of a subject *die Anfangsgründe eines Faches;* as easy as ∾ *kinderleicht;* an ∾ *(Eisenbahn) ein alphabetischer Fahrplan*

abeyance n.: the matter is in (has fallen into) ∾ *die Sache ruht zeitweise, ist in der Schwebe*

abide I. v.i.: I ∾ by what I have said *ich bleibe bei meiner Aussage;* I shall ∾ by my promise *ich werde mein Versprechen halten;* to ∾ (by) the consequences *die Folgen auf sich nehmen;* ∾ with us, good Lord! *bleibe bei uns (stehe uns bei), Herr!* — **II.** v.tr.: we can't ∾ this man (colloq.) *wir können diesen Menschen nicht ausstehen*

ability n.: to the best of one's ∾ *nach besten Kräften;* to have the ∾ to manage a business (to pay one's bills, to pass an examination) *fähig (in der Lage) sein, ein Geschäft zu führen (seine Rechnungen zu bezahlen, eine Prüfung zu bestehen);* he has (he is possessed of) great abilities *er hat hohe geistige Anlagen*

able a.: an ∾-bodied seaman (abbr. A. B.) *ein Vollmatrose;* get-at-∾ *erreichbar*

abomination n.: to hold something in ∾ *etwas verabscheuen;* their behaviour was an ∾ *ihr Benehmen war ein Greuel (eine Gemeinheit);* he is my pet ∾ (colloq.) *er ist mir zuwider*

about I. adv.: all ∾ *rings herum;* a great many people are ∾ *sehr viele Leute sind auf den Beinen;* he is somewhere ∾ *er ist irgendwo in der Nähe;* what are you ∾ there? *was machst (treibst, tust) du da?;* it was ∾ midnight *es war gegen (ungefähr) Mitternacht;* I am ∾ sick of it *ich habe es nachgerade satt;* it is much ∾ my size *es ist ungefähr meine Größe;* to be ∾ to do something *im Begriff (gerade dabei) sein, etwas zu tun;* to bring ∾ *zustande bringen;* to bring a person ∾ *j.en ins Leben (zum Bewußtsein) zurückbringen;* to carry ∾ with one *mit sich herumtragen;* to come ∾ *sich ereignen;* he followed me ∾ *er folgte mir überall hin nach;* I do not get ∾ much *ich komme nicht viel herum;* he can get ∾ again *er ist wieder auf den Beinen (nach einer Krankheit);* rumours are getting ∾ *Gerüchte sind im Umlauf (verbreiten sich);* to get a thing the wrong way ∾ *etwas verkehrt machen;* to go ∾ *umhergehen;* to go ∾ to do a thing *sich bemühen, etwas zu tun;* to hang ∾ (colloq.) *herumstehen;* do you know your way ∾ here? *kennen Sie sich hier aus? finden Sie sich hier zurecht?;* mind what you are ∾ *nimm dich in acht!;* the ship put ∾ *das Schiff wendete (drehte);* to put a tale ∾ *eine Geschichte in Umlauf setzen;* I was much put ∾ *ich wurde in große Aufregung versetzt;* a round∾ way, a long way ∾ *ein Umweg;* to send a person to the right-∾ *j.en hinauswerfen (fortjagen);* turn ∾ is fair play (prov.) *eine Liebe ist der anderen wert;* right ∾ turn (milit.) *(macht) kehrt!* — **II.** prep.: to beat ∾ the bush *wie eine Katze um den heißen Brei gehen;* well, what ∾ it? *nun, wie steht's damit?;* be quick ∾ it *mach schnell damit!;* the objects ∾ us *die Gegenstände um uns herum;* I have no cash ∾ me *ich habe kein Kleingeld bei mir;* there is nothing good ∾ him *an ihm ist nichts Gutes;* he has his wits ∾ him *er hat seine fünf Sinne zusammen (beieinander);* what have you come ∾? *was führt Sie her?;* a man ∾ Town *ein eleganter, gewandter Typ;* go ∾ your business *kümmere dich um deine Angelegenheiten;*

scher' dich weg!; to go ∾ one's work *sich an die Arbeit machen;* I'll see ∾ it *ich werde es schon besorgen (regeln);* to send a person ∾ his business *j.em heimleuchten, die Tür weisen;* ∾ my Father's business *in Sachen meines Vaters*

above I. adv.: see ∾ *siehe oben;* as was stated (remarked) ∾ *wie oben angeführt (bemerkt) wurde;* the ∾-cited *(besser:* the foregoing, preceding) passages *die oben angeführten Stellen;* the ∾-quoted prices *die oben zitierten Preise;* over and ∾ *noch dazu, überdies, obendrein;* the powers ∾ *die himmlischen Mächte.* — **II.** prep.: ∾ all (things) *vor allem, vor allen Dingen;* he is ∾ doing that *er ist darüber erhaben;* she is ∾ taking advice *sie ist zu stolz, (einen) Rat anzunehmen;* that is ∾ me, ∾ my understanding *das ist mir zu hoch, das geht über meinen Verstand;* to be ∾ oneself *außergewöhnlich gut aufgelegt sein;* to be ∾ a person *j.em überlegen sein;* she can't get ∾ C (Music) *sie kommt nicht über das (hohe) C hinaus;* the Rhine ∾ Remagen *der Rhein stromaufwärts von Remagen;* to keep one's head ∾ water *den Kopf über Wasser halten;* to be ∾ ground *noch am Leben sein;* ∾ a mile *mehr als eine Meile;* ∾ a year *(für) länger als ein Jahr;* ∾ board *offen und ehrlich*

Abraham n.pr.: to sham ∾ *Krankheit (Not, Unkenntnis) vortäuschen, den kranken Mann spielen*

abreast adv.: to be ∾ of the times *mit der Zeit Schritt halten, auf dem laufenden bleiben;* the horsemen rode four ∾ *die Reiter ritten zu vieren nebeneinander.*

abroad adv.: he has gone ∾, he lives ∾ *er ist ins Ausland gereist, er lebt im Ausland;* the schoolmaster is ∾ *Bildung verbreitet sich überall;* to be all ∾ (colloq.) *seiner Sache nicht sicher, verwirrt, auf dem Holzwege sein;* the oarsmen were all ∾ *die Ruderer waren ganz aus dem Takt;* there is a report (rumour) ∾ *es geht das Gerücht (um);* I don't know how the secret got ∾ *ich weiß nicht, wie das Geheimnis ruchbar wurde (herauskam)*

absence n.: ∾ of mind *Zerstreutheit, geistige Abwesenheit;* he was conspicuous by his ∾ *er glänzte durch Abwesenheit;* we have leave of ∾ *wir haben Urlaub;* in ∾ of any proof *in Ermangelung jeglichen Beweises*

absent a.: ∾-minded *zerstreut, geistesabwesend;* the ∾ party is always to blame *die Abwesenden haben immer unrecht;* long ∾, soon forgotten (prov.) *aus den Augen, aus dem Sinn*

abuse I. [əˈbjuːz] v.tr.: he ∾s his authority *er mißbraucht seine Autorität;* he ∾d my confidence *er täuschte (schändete) mein Vertrauen;* she ∾d her neighbour *sie beschimpfte ihren Nachbarn;* he ∾d the secret *er verriet das Geheimnis;* I was ∾d right and left *ich wurde tüchtig ausgeschimpft.* — **II.** [əˈbjuːs] n.: it is a crying ∾ *es ist ein grober Mißbrauch;* I heard a lot of ∾ *ich hörte viele Schimpfworte;* to have recourse to ∾ *sich aufs Schimpfen verlegen*

abusive a.: to use ∾ language *Schimpfworte gebrauchen*

accede v.i.: to ∾ to a thing *in eine Sache einwilligen;* to ∾ to an opinion *einer Meinung beistimmen;* to ∾ to a party *einer Partei beitreten;* to ∾ to an office *ein Amt antreten;* to ∾ to the throne *den Thron besteigen*

accident n.: by ∾ *zufälligerweise;* a chapter of ∾s *der unvorhergesehene Verlauf der Ereignisse;* he met with an ∾ *er verunglückte, ihm stieß ein Unfall zu*

accord n.: to be of (at) ∾ with *übereinstimmen mit;* with one ∾ *einstimmig, einmütig;* of one's own ∾ *freiwillig, von selbst, aus eigenem Antrieb, unaufgefordert*

accordance n.: in ∾ with *gemäß, zufolge (dat.)*

according prep.: ∾ to all accounts *nach allen Berichten;* to cut one's coat ∾ to one's cloth *sich nach der Decke strecken;* it's all ∾ (as you take it) (colloq.) *es kommt ganz darauf an, wie man es nimmt*

account I. n.: according to the latest ∾s *nach den letzten Berichten;* to give an ∾ of a thing *über etwas Bericht erstatten;* to give an ∾ of oneself *sich ausweisen;* he gave a good ∾ of himself *er hatte guten Erfolg; er führte sich gut ein, er bewährte sich;* to balance (to square) ∾s *ein Konto saldieren, ausgleichen;* to cast ∾s *rechnen, aufrechnen;* to clear an ∾ *eine Rechnung bezahlen;* to close an ∾ *eine Rechnung abschließen;* to draw on (upon) an ∾ *auf ein Konto ziehen, trassieren;* to have a current (running) ∾ *ein laufendes Konto haben;* to keep ~s *Rechnungsbücher führen;* to make up an ~ *eine Rechnung auf-, zusammenstellen;* on ~ rendered *laut erhaltener Rechnung;* outstanding ~s *ausstehende Rechnungen;* he has overdrawn his ~ *er hat sein Konto überzogen;* to pay on ~ *auf Abschlag zahlen, eine Anzahlung machen;* to put down to (to charge to) a person's ~ *j.es Konto belasten, auf j.es Rechnung setzen;* to run up an ~ *auf Kredit kaufen, anschreiben lassen;* to send in one's ~ *seine Rechnung einreichen;* to settle (to square) an ~ *eine Rechnung bezahlen, begleichen;* to bring (to call) a person to ~ *j.en zur Rechenschaft (Verantwortung) ziehen;* to find one's ~ in a thing *durch eine Sache profitieren, aus einer Sache Nutzen ziehen;* gone to his ~ *vor Gottes Richterstuhl getreten;* the great ~ *das jüngste Gericht;* to lay one's ~ with a thing *auf eine Sache rechnen, sie erwarten;* to leave out of ~ *außer Betracht lassen;* to make ~ of *hochschätzen;* to make no ~ of *kein Aufheben (Wesen) von etwas machen;* on no ~ *auf keinen Fall, um keinen Preis;* that is of no ~ *das ist belanglos;* on ~ of *wegen, um ... willen;* on one's own ~ *auf eigene Rechnung und Gefahr;* person (thing) of ~, held in ~ *wichtige, geschätzte Person (Sache);* to render (an) ~ of *Rechenschaft ablegen über;* to settle an old ~ *eine alte Rechnung begleichen, sich rächen;* short ~s make long friends (prov.) *glatte Rechnung erhält die Freundschaft;* to square ~s with a person *sich an j.em rächen;* to take ~ of a person (thing) *j.en (etwas) bemerken, beachten;* to take into ~ *in Betracht ziehen;* to turn to ~ *verwerten, zunutze machen.* — **II.** v.tr.: I ~ him a hero, wise, to be guilty *ich halte ihn für einen Helden, für klug, für schuldig;* it is ~ed bad taste *es gilt als schlechter Geschmack;* to be little ~ed of *wenig geachtet sein.* — **III.** v.i.: how do you ~ for it? *wie erklärst du dir das?;* he could not ~ for the money *er konnte keine Rechenschaft über den Verbleib des Geldes geben;* there is no ~ing for tastes *über (den) Geschmack läßt sich nicht streiten*

ace n.: within an ~ of *um ein Haar, beinahe;* to bate an ~ *j.em einen kleinen Vorsprung geben;* to have an ~ in the hole *noch einen Trumpf in der Hand haben;* to serve an ~ (tennis) *mit dem Aufschlag einen Punkt gewinnen;* an air-~ *ein hervorragender Kampfflieger;* a bridge-~, a jazz-~ *ein erstklassiger Bridge-, Jazzspieler*

ache I. v.i.: he is aching to do it *er brennt darauf, es zu tun.* — **II.** n.: to have a head~, a tooth~ *Kopf-, Zahnschmerzen haben;* it's not my head~ (sl.) *das soll meine Sorge nicht sein*

acquaint v.tr.: to ~ oneself with the rules *sich über die Regeln informieren;* to ~ someone (of) with the news *j.em eine Nachricht mitteilen;* to be ~ed with a thing *etwas kennen;* we are ~ed *wir kennen uns;* to become ~ed with something *etwas kennenlernen*

acquaintance n.: on closer (with longer) ~ *bei näherer (längerer) Bekanntschaft;* to make someone's ~ *j.en kennenlernen*

acquit v.tr.: to ~ a debt *eine Schuld abtragen;* to ~ someone of an offence *j.en von einer Beschuldigung freisprechen;* to ~ someone of a duty *j.en von einer Pflicht entbinden;* to ~ oneself well (ill) *sich gut (schlecht) machen, eine Sache gut (schlecht) erledigen*

across I. prep.: to come (to run) ~ a person, a thing *j.en zufällig treffen, auf etwas stoßen;* a strange idea came ~ my mind *ein seltsamer Gedanke ging mir durch den Kopf;* to put it ~ a person (sl.) *mit j.em abrechnen, ihm betrügerisch etwas aufdrängen, aufbinden, ihn täuschen, hintergehen;* she lives ~ the way *sie wohnt gegenüber.* — **II.** adv.: he got his jokes ~ (colloq.) *er hatte Erfolg mit seinen Witzen;* to put a thing ~ *eine Sache erklären, glücklich durchführen*

act I. n.: he was in the very ~ of packing *er war mitten beim (im) Packen;* he was caught in the (very) ~ *er wurde auf frischer Tat ertappt;* to put on an ~ (sl.) *j.em etwas vorspielen;* an ~ of God *höhere Gewalt;* I deliver this as my ~ and deed *ich erkläre hiermit feierlich.* — **II.** v. tr.: to ~ a part *eine Rolle spielen; etwas vormachen, -heucheln;* to ~ a play *ein Stück aufführen.* — **III.** v.i.: to ~ as an interpreter *als Dolmetscher dienen;* to ~ up to a principle *nach einem Grundsatz handeln;* to ~ upon a suggestion *eine Anregung befolgen;* this remedy ~s (up)on the nerves *dieses Mittel wirkt auf die Nerven;* to ~ well by a person *gut an j.em handeln*

acting a.: ∾ commanding officer *zeitweilig mit dem Oberbefehl betrauter Offizier;* ∾ consul *Konsulatsverweser;* ∾ manager *geschäftsführender Direktor;* ∾ partner *tätiger Teilhaber*

action n.: he is a man of ∾ *er ist ein Mann der Tat;* to bring (to enter, to lay) an ∾ against a person *eine Klage anstrengen gegen j.en;* to go into ∾ *in den Kampf ziehen;* to be killed in ∾ *in der Schlacht (im Kampf) fallen;* to set in ∾ *in Tätigkeit setzen, in Gang bringen;* he suited the ∾ to the words *er ließ die Tat dem Worte folgen;* suit the ∾ to the word, the word to the ∾ (Hamlet III, 2, 19) *paßt die Gebärde dem Wort, das Wort der Gebärde an (Schlegel);* to take ∾ against a person (a matter) *gegen j.en (eine Sache) Schritte unternehmen*

ad lib. a. (colloq.): an ∾ remark *eine unüberlegte Bemerkung, eine Bemerkung aus dem Stegreif*

Adam n.pr.: ∾'s ale (wine) *Trinkwasser, Gänsewein;* I don't know him from ∾ (colloq.) *ich habe keine Ahnung, wer er ist;* the old ∾ *der alte Adam, die menschliche Schwäche*

add v.tr.: to ∾ insult to injury *eine Sache noch schlimmer machen;* ∾ed to which *wozu noch kommt;* an ∾ed interest *ein erhöhtes, verstärktes Interesse;* to ∾ to the confusion *die Verwirrung (das Durcheinander) erhöhen (vermehren)*

address I. n.: a person of good ∾ *eine geschickte (gewandte) Person;* to deliver an ∾ *eine Ansprache halten;* to pay one's ∾es to a person *j.em den Hof machen.* — **II.** v.tr.: to ∾ a person *j.en anreden;* to ∾ the ball (golf) *den Ball richten, zielen (Golfspiel)*

administer I. v.tr.: to ∾ the cane to a boy *einen Jungen verprügeln;* to ∾ law *Recht sprechen;* to ∾ an oath (to someone) *(j.em) einen Eid abnehmen;* to ∾ a plaster *ein Pflaster auflegen;* to ∾ a rebuke, a blow, etc. *einen Tadel erteilen, einen Schlag usw. versetzen.* — **II.** v.i.: to ∾ to a person's comfort *zu j.es Bequemlichkeit beitragen*

admit I. v.tr.: he will not ∾ it *er gibt es nicht zu;* this ticket ∾s one to all the concerts *dieses Billet ist für alle Konzerte gültig;* to ∾ a person into one's confidence *j.en ins Vertrauen ziehen;* to ∾ a person to a privilege *j.em ein Vorrecht einräumen.* — **II.** v.i.: that ∾s of doubt *das läßt sich bezweifeln*

admittance n.: no ∾ *Eingang (Zutritt) verboten!*

ado n.: I shall make no more ∾ about it *ich werde kein Aufhebens mehr davon machen, werde darüber schweigen;* Much Ado about Nothing (Shakespeare) *Viel Lärm um Nichts;* without further ∾ *ohne weitere Umstände*

adrift adv.: to be all ∾ *nicht aus noch ein wissen;* to cut a boat ∾ *ein Boot loswerfen, treiben lassen;* the buoy cut ∾ *die Boje riß sich los;* he has cut ∾ *er hat allen Halt verloren;* to cut oneself (a person) ∾ from a thing *sich (j.en) von etwas absondern;* to set a rumour ∾ *ein Gerücht in Umlauf bringen, in die Welt setzen;* to turn a person ∾ *j.en sich selbst überlassen, ihn seinem Schicksal preisgeben, ihn fortjagen*

advance I. n.: in ∾ *im voraus;* to ask for an ∾ *um einen Vorschuß bitten;* to make ∾s to a person *j.em Entgegenkommen zeigen, Avancen machen.* — **II.** v.tr.: to ∾ a claim *Anspruch erheben;* to ∾ money *Geld vorstrecken;* ∾d in years (age) *in vorgerücktem Alter*

advantage n.: to follow up an ∾ *einen Vorteil ausnutzen;* to have the ∾ of a person *j.em gegenüber im Vorteil sein;* you have the ∾ of me *ich habe nicht die Ehre, Sie zu kennen;* to play upon ∾ *beim Spiel betrügen;* that frock sets her off to ∾ *das Kleid steht ihr gut;* to take ∾ of a person *j.en übervorteilen, übers Ohr hauen;* to take a person at ∾ *j.en überraschen;* to turn a thing to one's private ∾ *etwas für Privatzwecke ausbeuten*

affair n.: ∾s of state *Staatsangelegenheiten;* a man of many ∾s *ein vielbeschäftigter Mann;* as ∾s stand *wie die Dinge stehen (liegen);* at the head of ∾s *an der Spitze der Regierung (des Unternehmens);* to have an ∾ with someone (colloq.) *eine Liebelei mit j.em haben;* a big ∾ *eine wichtige Angelegenheit;* that is not my ∾ *das ist nicht meine Sache, das geht mich nichts an;* that is a put-up ∾ *das ist eine abgekartete Sache*

affect[1] v.tr.: he ∾s the philosopher *er gebärdet sich als Philosoph;* he ∾s interest *er heuchelt Interesse;* he ∾s a limp *er stellt* *sich hinkend;* he ∾s a red tie *er trägt gern einen roten Schlips*

affect[2] v.tr.: a disease ∾ed the herd *eine Seuche befiel die Herde;* it does not ∾ me in the least *es berührt mich nicht im geringsten*

afford v.tr.: to ∾ an opportunity, a satisfaction *eine Gelegenheit, Freude, Befriedigung bieten;* I can ill ∾ it *ich kann es mir schlecht leisten*

affront n.: to feel it an ∾ *es als Beleidigung empfinden;* to pocket (to swallow) an ∾ *eine Beleidigung einstecken;* to put ∾ upon (to offer an ∾ to) a person *j.en beleidigen, beschimpfen*

afloat adv. and pred. a.: a rumour is ∾ *es geht das Gerücht;* to get (to set) ∾ *(ein Schiff) flottmachen;* to keep ∾ (fig.) *sich über Wasser halten;* to set a report ∾ *eine Nachricht in Umlauf bringen*

afore adv.: the ∾mentioned (∾named, ∾said) people *die vorerwähnten, vorgenannten Leute;* with malice ∾thought *mit bösem Vorbedacht;* ∾time *ehemals, früher*

afraid pred. a.: I am ∾ to meet (of meeting) him *ich fürchte, ihn zu treffen;* I am ∾ lest I should meet him (that I will meet him) *ich fürchte, daß ich ihn treffen werde;* I'm ∾ (colloq.) *etwa: ich bedauere, muß leider zugeben;* I'm ∾ I'm late *ich komme leider wohl etwas spät;* I'm ∾ there's no beer left *es ist leider kein Bier mehr da*

after I. prep.: ∾ hours *nach Ladenschluß, Polizeistunde;* what are you ∾? (colloq.) *was willst du, was suchst du?;* ∾ all, he is my brother *er ist schließlich mein Bruder;* he consented ∾ all *er gab am Ende noch zu;* ∾ a fashion *einigermaßen;* ∾ this fashion *auf diese Weise;* a garden ∾ my own heart *ein Garten, wie ich ihn liebe;* to look ∾ someone *für j.en sorgen;* to hanker ∾ a thing *sich nach etwas sehnen.* — **II.** n. (colloq.): what is there for ∾s? *was gibt's als Nachtisch?*

again adv.: ∾ and ∾, time and ∾ *immer wieder;* ever and ∾, now and ∾ *gelegentlich, ab und zu;* as much ∾ *noch einmal soviel;* half as much ∾ *anderthalbmal soviel;* this coat ∾ is not so warm *dieser Mantel ist, andrerseits, nicht so warm*

against I. prep.: ∾ my sister's visit *in Erwartung des Besuches meiner Schwester;* he ran ∾ his school friend *er traf zufällig seinen Schulkameraden;* over ∾ the hospital *gegenüber dem Krankenhaus;* ∾ a rainy day *für die Zeit der Not;* to be up ∾ it (colloq.) *in Schwierigkeiten sein;* I am ∾ vegetarian diet *ich bin gegen vegetarische Kost.* — **II.** conj.: be ready ∾ he calls *sei bereit, wenn er ruft*

age n.: ∾ of consent *sechzehn Jahre;* ∾ of discretion (legal) *über 14 Jahre;* over ∾ *über das vorgeschriebene Lebensalter;* under ∾ *unmündig;* green old ∾ *rüstiges Alter;* Ice ∾ *Eiszeit;* tender ∾ *Kindesalter;* with ∾ *mit den Jahren;* to come of ∾ *mündig, großjährig werden;* I had to wait for ∾s (colloq.) *ich mußte eine Ewigkeit warten*

agenda n.: to be on the ∾ *auf der Tagesordnung stehen*

ago adv.: long ∾ *vor langer Zeit;* how long is that ∾? *wie lange ist das her?;* five years ∾ *vor fünf Jahren*

agog pred. a.: they were all ∾ to do it *sie brannten darauf, es zu tun;* they were all ∾ with excitement *sie waren in fieberhafter Aufregung*

agony n.: the ∾ column (colloq.) *Anzeigenspalte in der Zeitung über vermißte Verwandte, Freunde, Verluste usw.;* in an ∾ of confusion *in äußerster Verwirrung;* to be in the agonies of death *mit dem Tode ringen;* an ∾ of grief (of sorrow) *ein schweres Herzeleid;* an ∾ of suspense *eine quälende Ungewißheit, „schwebende Pein";* an ∾ of tears *ein Tränenstrom;* to pile up (on) the ∾ *in Sensation machen, gruselig schildern*

agree v.i.: these two colours do not ∾ *diese beiden Farben passen nicht zueinander;* I cannot make these figures ∾ *ich kann diese Zahlen nicht in Übereinstimmung bringen;* I ∾ to your proposal *ich stimme deinem Vorschlag zu (bei);* they ∾d upon the terms *sie einigten sich über die Bedingungen;* the food (air, climate, wine) does not ∾ with him *das Essen (die Luft, das Klima, der Wein) bekommt ihm nicht*

agreeable a.: she has an ∾ manner *sie hat eine gefällige, liebenswürdige Art;* I am ∾ to your suggestion *ich bin mit Ihrem Vorschlag einverstanden;* ∾ to all experience *im Einklang (in Übereinstimmung) mit aller Erfahrung*

ahead adv. & pred. a.: there is a car ∾ of us *ein Auto ist vor uns;* to get ∾ of a person *j.en überholen, überflügeln;* go ∾! *vorwärts!;* go ∾ with your job *mach' voran mit deiner Arbeit;* straight ∾ *gerade aus*

aid I. v.tr.: to ∾ a person in a matter (to do, in doing, a thing) *j.em bei einer Sache helfen, ihm helfen, etwas zu tun;* to ∾ and abet a crime *einem Verbrechen Beistand (Vorschub) leisten.* — **II.** n.: by the ∾ of a person *mit j.es Hilfe;* in ∾ of a cause *zum Besten, zugunsten einer Sache;* to come to a person's ∾ *j.em zu Hilfe kommen;* to give (to lend) a person ∾ *j.em Hilfe leisten;* ∾s and appliances *Hilfsmittel*

aim I. v.tr.: to ∾ a pistol at a person *eine Pistole auf j.en richten;* that is ∾ed at you *das ist auf dich gemünzt.* — **II.** v.i.: what are you ∾ing at? *worauf willst du hinaus?;* they ∾ed at getting a full house *sie zielten darauf, ein volles Haus zu bekommen;* to ∾ at perfection *nach Vollkommenheit streben.* — **III.** n.: to gain (to miss) one's ∾ *sein Ziel (seinen Zweck) erreichen, verfehlen;* to take ∾ at a thing *auf (nach) etwas zielen*

air[1] **I.** n.: these opinions are in the ∾ *diese Ansichten liegen in der Luft (sind noch unsicher);* to be quite in the ∾ *völlig in der Luft hängen;* to beat the ∾ *sich erfolglos bemühen;* to build castles in the ∾ *Luftschlösser bauen;* to clear the ∾ *die Luft reinigen;* to be on the ∾ *im Rundfunk gehört werden;* to get a breath of fresh ∾ *frische Luft schöpfen;* to give someone the ∾ (sl.) *j.em den Laufpaß geben;* to go up in the ∾ (colloq.) *sich über etwas aufregen; hochgehen;* to take ∾ *bekannt werden, Verbreitung gewinnen;* to take the ∾ (old fash.) *an die Luft gehen;* to tread (to walk) on ∾ *im siebenten Himmel sein;* hot ∾ *viel Gerede, nur um Eindruck zu machen;* in the open ∾ *unter freiem Himmel;* to be ∾-borne *in der Luft fliegen;* the school is ∾-conditioned *die Schule hat eine Klimaanlage;* to be ∾-minded *sich der Bedeutung der Luftfahrt bewußt sein;* an ∾-liner *ein Verkehrsflugzeug;* an ∾-raid *ein Luftangriff;* an ∾-raid warning *Fliegeralarm;* ∾-raid protection (abbr. A.R.P.) *Luftschutz.* — **II.** v.tr.: to ∾ the beds *die Betten lüften;* he is always ∾ing his grievances *er beklagt sich immer, er bringt dauernd seine Beschwerden öffentlich vor*

air[2] n.: with a sad ∾ *mit trauriger Miene;* she gives herself ∾s, ∾s and graces *sie tut sehr vornehm, sie spielt sich auf*

alarm n.: an ∾ (alarum)-clock *eine Weckuhr, ein Wecker;* all these ∾s (alarums) and excursions *das ganze Geschrei und Getue;* to beat (to sound) an (the) ∾ *Alarm schlagen (blasen);* to cause ∾ *Unruhe erregen;* to give (to raise) the ∾ *das Alarmzeichen geben;* to raise a false ∾ *blinden Alarm schlagen;* to take ∾ at a thing *über etwas in Angst (Unruhe) geraten*

alarmist n.: he is an ∾ *er ist ein Bangemacher, Schwarzseher;* this ∾ letter *dieser alarmierende (beunruhigende) Brief*

Alec(k) n.: a smart ∾ *ein Alleswisser, (derb:) Klugscheißer*

alert n.: to be on the ∾ *wachsam (auf dem Posten, auf der Hut) sein;* to sound (to give) the ∾ *Fliegeralarm geben*

alive a. & pred. a.: ∾ and kicking (sl.) *wohl und munter;* I am fully ∾ to the necessity of doing something *ich bin mir der Notwendigkeit, etwas zu tun, vollkommen bewußt;* the house is ∾ with cats *das Haus wimmelt von Katzen;* to keep ∾ *am Leben (er)halten, nicht ausgehen lassen, nähren (Feuer, Haß usw.);* to look ∾ *sich beeilen, sich sputen;* man ∾! (colloq.) *Mensch!;* any man ∾ *jeder auf der Welt*

all I. a.: ∾ day *den ganzen Tag;* ∾ England *ganz England;* ∾ kinds of *jede Art von;* ∾ his life *sein ganzes Leben;* ∾ men *alle Menschen;* ∾ the others *alle anderen;* beyond ∾ question, ∾ doubt *ganz außer Frage (Zweifel);* with ∾ speed *in aller (mit größter) Geschwindigkeit;* ∾ the time *die ganze Zeit (über).* — **II.** n.: ∾ are agreed *alle stimmen überein;* ∾ of it *das Ganze;* ∾ of us (you, them); we (you, they) ∾ *wir (ihr, sie) alle;* that is ∾ *das ist alles;* he lost his ∾ *er verlor sein ganzes Hab und Gut;* it is ∾ but fair *es ist alles andere als gerecht;* ∾ in ∾ *alles in allem;* did you speak at ∾? *hast du überhaupt gesprochen?;* not at ∾ *durchaus (überhaupt) nicht;* one and ∾, ∾ and sundry *alle miteinander;* ∾ along of (sl.) *wegen (Gen.), dank (Dat.);* that's ∾ very fine (very well) *das ist alles gut und schön;* it is ∾ one to me *es ist mir alles eins (einerlei, gleich);* when ∾ is said and done *letzten Endes;* ∾ my eye and Betty Martin (colloq.) *Quatsch!*

— **III.** adv.: ∾ along *die ganze Zeit;* ∾ the better *um so besser;* ∾ in a blaze *lichterloh;* ∾ clear! *(Luftschutz) Entwarnung, (Seemannssprache) alles klar!;* ∾ covered with mud *ganz mit Schlamm bedeckt;* ∾ hot and bothered (colloq.) *aufgeregt, nervös;* ∾-in policy *Versicherung gegen alle Risiken;* ∾-in wrestling *Ringkampf ohne Einschränkungen;* I'm ∾ in (colloq.) *ich bin erschöpft (erledigt);* I feel ∾-overish (colloq.) *mir ist nicht gut (ich fühle mich krank);* ∾-set (colloq.) *fertig! los!;* I ∾ but succeeded *es gelang mir beinahe (fast);* it is ∾ but impossible *es ist fast unmöglich;* that's Jack ∾ over *das sieht Hans ähnlich!;* everything is ∾ right *es ist alles in Ordnung;* ∾ right *ganz richtig, in Ordnung, schon gut!;* ∾ right (iron.), you'll be sorry for that *na schön, das wirst du noch bereuen;* he won the race ∾ the same *trotz alledem gewann er das Rennen;* ∾ the same, I wish you hadn't done it *nichtsdestoweniger, ich wünschte, du hättest es nicht getan;* if it's ∾ the same to you *wenn es Ihnen nichts ausmacht;* ∾ of a sudden, ∾ at once *plötzlich, auf einmal;* ∾ too soon *allzubald, allzufrüh;* he is not quite ∾ there (colloq.) *er ist nicht ganz bei Trost;* this year's programme of events is an ∾-time high (∾-time low) (sl.) *das Programm der Veranstaltungen in diesem Jahr übertrifft alles (war noch nie so schlecht);* he is an ∾-round sportsman *er ist ein vielseitiger Sportsmann;* excuse my disturbing you. Not at ∾! *entschuldigen Sie die Störung, bitte. Das macht nichts;* ∾'s well that ends well (prov.) *Ende gut, alles gut;* ∾ cry and no wool *viel Geschrei und wenig Wolle, viel Lärm um nichts;* in ∾ conscience *entschieden, ohne Zweifel;* ∾ the world and his wife *eine Menge Leute*

allergic a.: I am ∾ to cats (colloq.) *ich habe eine Abneigung gegen Katzen*

allow I. v.tr.: to ∾ a thing to be *zugeben, daß etwas ist;* his firm ∾s him 4 weeks' holiday a year *seine Firma gibt ihm jährlich 4 Wochen Urlaub.* — **II.** v.i.: you must ∾ for the bad season *du mußt auf die schlechte Jahreszeit Rücksicht nehmen;* you must ∾ for the wind *du mußt den Wind berechnen;* it ∾s of no excuse *es ist nicht zu entschuldigen*

allowance n.: the daily ∾ of grog *die tägliche Grogration;* his father makes him an ∾ *sein Vater gewährt ihm einen Zuschuß;* to make ∾ for *in Anschlag bringen, Rücksicht nehmen auf*

alone pred. a. & adv.: to leave (to let) ∾ *in Ruhe lassen, allein lassen;* let ∾ the expense *ganz abgesehen von den Kosten;* man shall not live by bread ∾ (Luke, IV, 4) *der Mensch soll nicht vom Brot allein leben;* he ∾ remained *er allein blieb übrig;* not ∾, but *nicht nur, sondern auch*

along adv. & prep.: to carry ∾ *weiterführen;* come ∾ *vorwärts! mach schnell!;* to get ∾ well *gut vorwärts kommen, gute Fortschritte machen;* he came ∾ with his brother *er kam und sein Bruder auch;* they get ∾ well together (with each other) *sie vertragen sich gut;* you must get ∾ without my help *du mußt ohne meine Hilfe auskommen;* get ∾ with you *fort mit dir! Unsinn!;* to go ∾ *dahin-, weitergehen;* I knew it all ∾ *ich wußte es die ganze Zeit über;* all ∾ of (sl.) *wegen (Gen.), dank (Dat.)*

aloof adv. & pred. a.: to stand (to keep, to hold) ∾ *sich fern (abseits) halten;* the wind sprang ∾ *der Wind sprang nach der Windseite (luvwärts) um*

amends n.: to make ∾ for a thing *etwas wiedergutmachen, ersetzen*

amiss adv. & pred. a.: it is not ∾ *es ist nicht unpassend;* what's ∾ with that? *was ist daran auszusetzen?;* to come (to happen) ∾ *ungelegen, in die Quere kommen;* to take a thing ∾ *etwas übelnehmen*

anchor n.: the ∾ comes home *der Anker reißt sich los;* to cast (to drop) anchor *Anker werfen;* the ship drags her ∾, the ∾ drags *das Schiff schleppt den Anker, treibt vor Anker;* to lay an ∾ to windward *Sicherheitsmaßregeln ergreifen;* to ride at ∾ *vor Anker liegen;* to weigh (to slip) ∾ *den Anker lichten*

angel n.: it was agreed that he should act as ∾ to the enterprise *es wurde vereinbart, daß er das Unternehmen finanzieren sollte;* ∾s on horseback *Austern in Speckscheiben gebraten;* to entertain an ∾ unawares (Heb. XIII, 2) *ohne Wissen einen Engel beherbergen; j.em, der sich später als gewichtige Person herausstellt, einen Dienst erweisen;* visits, like those of ∾s, short and far between *kurze und seltene Besuche (gesagt von selten vorkommenden angenehmen Dingen)*

angle n.: I am trying to get an ∾ on the political situation (colloq.) *ich versuche, einen Begriff von der politischen Lage zu bekommen;* seen from this ∾ *von diesem Standpunkt aus gesehen*

another I. a.: are you of ∾ mind? *bist du anderer Meinung?;* that's ∾ thing altogether *das ist etwas ganz anderes;* will you have ∾ cup of tea? *wollen Sie noch eine Tasse Tee?;* I'll wait ∾ day or two *ich warte noch ein paar Tage;* he is ∾ Solomon *er ist ein zweiter Salomon.* — **II.** pron.: to help one ∾ *einander helfen;* one after ∾ *eine (-r, -s) nach der (dem) anderen;* they were taken for one ∾ *man hielt den einen für den anderen; sie wurden verwechselt;* give him such ∾ *gib ihm noch so eins;* if we take them one with ∾ *wenn man die Dinge nimmt, wie sie fallen;* A: you're an ass. B: you're ∾ (vulg.) *A: du bist ein Esel. B: du auch*

answer I. v.tr.: to ∾ the door, the bell *die Tür beim Klopf- oder Klingelzeichen öffnen;* the ship ∾s the helm *das Schiff gehorcht dem Steuer;* to ∾ (to) my hopes, your description *meinen Hoffnungen, deiner Beschreibung entsprechen;* to ∾ a letter *einen Brief beantworten;* to ∾ my purpose *meinen Zweck erfüllen.* — **II.** v.i.: that will not ∾ *das wird es nicht tun;* he always ∾s back *er gibt immer Widerworte;* I will not ∾ for his safety *ich verbürge mich nicht für seine Sicherheit;* to ∾ to the name of Tom *auf den Namen ‚Tom' hören*

anvil n.: to be on the ∾ *in Arbeit, in Vorbereitung, in Erwägung gezogen sein;* between the hammer and the ∾ *zwischen Hammer und Amboß, in großer Bedrängnis (sein)*

anxiety n.: to be in ∾ about a thing *in Sorge um etwas sein;* an ∾ to please *ein eifriger Wunsch zu gefallen*

anxious a.: to be ∾ about a thing *sich um etwas Sorgen machen;* to be ∾ to do a thing *begierig sein, etwas zu tun;* it was an ∾ time *es war eine bange Zeit*

any I. pron.: I cannot see ∾ difference *ich kann keinen Unterschied sehen;* have you ∾ paper? *hast du etwas Papier? (= denn ich habe keins);* have you ∾ more pins? *hast du noch mehr Nadeln?;* were there ∾ students there? *waren irgendwelche Studenten dort?;* ∾ doctor will tell you *jeder Arzt wird dir sagen;* I don't know ∾ of them *ich kenne keinen von ihnen;* ∾ of these books *irgendeins von diesen Büchern;* at ∾ time *zu jeder Zeit;* in ∾ place *überall;* under ∾ circumstances *unter allen Umständen;* he is as clever as ∾(one) *er ist so klug wie nur irgendeiner;* in ∾ case *auf jeden Fall.* — **II.** adv.: is he ∾ the better for it? *geht es ihm deshalb irgendwie besser?;* I am not ∾ the wiser *ich bin ebenso klug wie vorher;* I will not do it ∾ more *ich will's nicht wieder tun;* I cannot wait ∾ longer *ich kann (durchaus) nicht länger warten;* ∾ time (day) *zu jeder Zeit, an jedem beliebigen Tage.* — ∾ more for ∾ more? (colloq.) *will noch j. (etwas essen)?;* I'm not having (taking) ∾ (sl.) *ich will nichts damit zu tun haben;* it didn't hurt him ∾ (U.S. sl.) *es hat ihm überhaupt nicht wehgetan (nicht geschadet)*

anybody n.: if he wishes to be ∾ *wenn er eine Person von Bedeutung sein will;* a bunch of anybodies *ein Haufen gewöhnlicher Leute.* — **II.** pron.: has ∾ else written? *hat sonst noch jemand geschrieben?*

anyhow I. adv.: she cleans the house just ∾ *sie putzt das Haus sehr nachlässig;* she does her work ∾ *sie arbeitet nachlässig;* my hair is all ∾ *mein Haar ist ganz in Unordnung.* — **II.** conj.: ∾, I shall do it *immerhin, ich werde es tun*

anything pron. & n.: for ∾ I know *soviel ich weiß;* is there ∾ to be seen? *gibt's etwas zu sehen?;* if he had been ∾ of a man *wenn er nur halbwegs ein Mann gewesen wäre;* I cannot do ∾ in the matter *ich kann in der Angelegenheit nichts unternehmen;* I wouldn't do that for ∾ *ich würde das um keinen Preis tun;* I am as wet as ∾ *ich bin vollkommen durchnäßt;* she is ∾ but rich *sie ist alles andere als reich;* he is capable of ∾ *er ist zu allem fähig;* he is a little better, if ∾ *ihm geht's ein wenig besser, wenn von Besserung überhaupt die Rede sein kann;* he ran like ∾ *er lief wie besessen (toll)*

anyway adv. & conj. = ‚anyhow'

apart adv.: joking ∾ *Scherz beiseite;* that is a matter ∾ *das ist eine Sache für sich*

ape I. n.: to play the ∾ *nachäffen;* to lead ∾s in hell *als alte Jungfer sterben;* to say an ∾'s paternoster *vor Kälte mit den Zähnen schnattern, klappern.* — **II.** v.tr.: to ∾ *nachäffen*

appeal v.i.: an advertisement which ∾s to the eyes *eine Reklame, welche das Auge anspricht;* to ∾ against a sentence *gegen ein Urteil Berufung einlegen;* to ∾ to the country *an die Wählerschaft des Landes appellieren*

appearance n.: to all ∾ *allem Anschein nach;* to judge by ∾s *nach dem Äußeren zu urteilen;* to put in an ∾ *in Person erscheinen;* to save (to keep up) ∾s *den Schein wahren;* ∾s are against him *der Schein ist gegen ihn;* default of ∾ *Nichterscheinen vor Gericht*

appetite n.: to have a voracious ∾ *einen wahren Heißhunger haben;* to (after) one's ∾ *gerade, wie es einem gefällt;* a good ∾ is the best sauce (prov.) *Hunger ist der beste Koch;* ∾ is concealed under the teeth *der Hunger (Appetit) kommt beim Essen*

apple n.: the ∾ of discord *der Zankapfel;* to upset a person's ∾-cart (colloq.) *j.es Pläne durchkreuzen;* an ∾-pie bed *ein Budenzauber, bei dem die Bettücher so kurz gefaltet werden, daß man sich nicht hineinlegen kann;* in ∾-pie order (colloq.) *in größter Ordnung;* ∾ sauce (sl.) *Schmeichelei*

apply I. v.i.: ∾ in writing (in your handwriting) *reichen Sie ein schriftliches (eigenhändig geschriebenes) Gesuch ein;* room to let, ∾ within *Zimmer zu vermieten, Auskunft im Hause;* to ∾ for work *um Arbeit nachsuchen;* this applies to you *das gilt dir, betrifft dich.* — **II.** v.tr.: to ∾ one's mind to study *fleißig studieren;* he applied the money to his own use *er verwandte das Geld zu seinem eigenen Nutzen;* to ∾ a remedy (a rule) *ein Mittel (eine Regel) anwenden*

appro (colloq. = approbation, approval) n.: on ∾ *zur Ansicht*

apron n.: he is tied to his mother's ∾-strings *er ist ein Muttersöhnchen*

apt a.: it was a very ∾ remark *es war eine sehr treffende Bemerkung;* he is very ∾ at mathematics *er ist ein guter Mathematiker;* every one is ∾ to make mistakes *jeder kann sich irren;* he is ∾ to take offence *er nimmt leicht etwas übel (krumm)*

Arab n.: a street ∾ *ein obdachloses Straßenkind*

argue I. v.tr.: it ∾s him an honest man *es beweist, daß er ein ehrlicher Mann (Mensch) ist;* to ∾ a point of law *eine Rechtsfrage erörtern;* to ∾ a matter away (off) *eine Sache hinwegdisputieren;* to ∾ a person into (out of) an action *j.en durch Argumente zu einer (gegen eine) Handlungsweise überreden;* to ∾ the hind leg off a donkey (colloq.) *j.en tot und lebendig reden.* — **II.** v.i.: to ∾ about a matter *eine Angelegenheit erörtern;* to ∾ against a decision *Einwendungen gegen eine Entscheidung machen;* to ∾ for mitigation of punishment *für Strafmilderung eintreten;* to ∾ with a person *mit j.em argumentieren (disputieren)*

arm n.: the ∾ of the law *die Macht des Gesetzes;* to keep at ∾'s length *sich (dat.) vom Leibe halten;* to work at ∾'s length *ungeschickt (unvorteilhaft) arbeiten;* to make a long ∾ (colloq.) *den Arm nach etwas ausstrecken;* a child in ∾s *ein Kind, das noch nicht laufen kann;* to welcome with open ∾s *herzlich willkommen heißen*

arms n.: a man of ∾ *ein Ritter;* a coat of ∾ *Wappen, Wappenschild;* fire ∾ *Feuerwaffen;* small-∾ *Handfeuerwaffen;* a stand of ∾ *eine vollständige Soldatenausrüstung;* shoulder ∾ *Gewehr umhängen!;* slope ∾ *das Gewehr über!;* ground ∾ *Gewehr ab!;* pile ∾ *setzt die Gewehre zusammen!;* unpile ∾ *Gewehr in die Hand!;* by force of ∾ *mit bewaffneter Hand, mit Waffengewalt;* to be up in ∾ *in Harnisch (Aufruhr) geraten*

arrange I. v.tr.: to ∾ a dispute *einen Streit beilegen, schlichten;* to ∾ a time *eine Zeit festsetzen, verabreden;* to ∾ troops for battle *Truppen in Schlachtordnung aufstellen;* it was ∾d that we should go *es wurde vereinbart (verabredet, ausgemacht), daß wir gehen sollten.* — **II.** v.i.: I ∾d to be there in time *ich traf Vorkehrungen (ich unternahm Schritte, richtete mich ein), (um) rechtzeitig dort zu sein;* I shall ∾ about it *ich werde dafür sorgen;* I shall ∾ for a dance-band *ich werde für eine Tanzkapelle sorgen;* he ∾d for a reporter to be there *er sorgte dafür, daß ein Reporter (Berichterstatter) dort war;* to ∾ with a person about (to do) a thing, that a thing should be done *sich mit j.em über etwas verständigen*

arrangement n.: to come to an ∾ *zu einem Vergleich kommen;* to enter into (to make) an ∾ with a person *mit j.em ein Übereinkommen (eine Übereinkunft) tref-*

fen; to make ~s *Vorkehrungen treffen;* pianoforte ~ *Klavierauszug*

arrest I. v.tr.: to ~ attention *die Aufmerksamkeit fesseln;* to ~ judgement *ein Gerichtsverfahren nach erfolgtem Urteil wegen Irrtums einstellen.* — **II.** n.: to be under ~ *in Haft sein*

arrive v.i.: he has ~d *er ist jetzt ein berühmter (gemachter) Mann;* to ~ at a conclusion *zu einem Schluß kommen;* to ~ upon the scene *auf dem Schauplatz erscheinen*

art n.: to be ~ and part in a thing *an einer Sache teilhaben*

as adv., conj. & rel. pron.: ~ for example *wie zum Beispiel;* ~ a rule *in der Regel;* ~ follows *wie folgt;* ~ usual *wie gewöhnlich;* just ~ *genau so wie;* he spoke ~ a friend *er sprach als Freund;* ~ she is not yet ready *da sie noch nicht fertig ist;* ~ old ~ *so alt wie;* ~ far ~ I can go *so weit wie ich gehen kann;* ~ good ~ *so gut wie;* such men ~ Caesar *solche Männer wie Cäsar;* he's ~ good ~ his word *er ist ein Mann von Wort;* I thought ~ much *das dachte ich mir;* ~ near ~ makes no difference (colloq.) *beinahe, nur mit ganz geringem Unterschied;* ~ quick ~ lightning *blitzschnell;* such ~ need our help *diejenigen, welche unsere Hilfe nötig haben;* one day, ~ the sun shone *eines Tages, als die Sonne schien;* I was so tired, ~ not to be able to stand *ich war so müde, daß ich nicht mehr stehen konnte;* be so kind ~ to give me a chair *seien Sie so gut, mir einen Stuhl zu geben;* put on your coat, so ~ to keep warm *ziehen Sie sich Ihren Mantel an, um warm zu bleiben;* ~ from Ist January 1958 *vom 1. Januar 1958 an;* ~ regards to *was anbelangt (betrifft);* ~ well *ebenfalls;* ~ yet *bisher, bis jetzt;* he said nothing ~ to when he would come *er sagte nichts über den Zeitpunkt seiner Ankunft*

ashamed pred. a.: I am ~ to do it *es widerstrebt mir (ich geniere mich), es zu tun;* to be ~ of a person (of a thing) *sich j.es (einer Sache) schämen;* you ought to be (to feel) ~ of yourself *du solltest dich schämen*

aside adv.: to lay (to set) ~ *beiseitelegen, verwahren;* he has put a tidy sum ~ *er hat eine hübsche Summe zurückgelegt (gespart);* to speak ~ *halblaut flüstern (beiseite sprechen)*

ask I. v.tr.: to ~ the banns *kirchlich aufbieten;* to ~ a person's permission, a person for permission *j.en um Erlaubnis bitten;* to ~ a person a question, a question of a person *an j.en eine Frage stellen (richten);* to ~ pardon *um Verzeihung bitten;* ~ no questions and you will be told no lies (colloq.) *wer viel fragt, erhält viel (falsche) Antworten;* ~ him to come in *bitten Sie ihn einzutreten;* to ~ one's way *nach dem Wege fragen;* to ~ the time *sich nach der Zeit erkundigen.* — **II.** v.i.: to ~ about a thing *sich nach etwas erkundigen;* he ~ed after your health *er erkundigte sich nach deiner Gesundheit;* to ~ for *bitten um, fragen nach;* it ~s for attention *es verlangt Aufmerksamkeit;* he is ~ing for it (colloq.) *er fordert es geradezu heraus;* it is there for the ~ing *es ist auf Verlangen umsonst zu haben;* there is no harm in ~ing *fragen schadet nichts, man darf doch mal fragen;* ~ me another (colloq.) *ich weiß es nicht (als Antwort auf eine dumme Frage);* he has ~ed me out for the evening *er hat mich eingeladen, mit ihm abends auszugehen;* that's ~ing (colloq.) *sei nicht (so) neugierig!*

askance adv.: to look ~ at; to eye (to view) ~ *scheel ansehen, mit Mißtrauen, Verachtung betrachten*

ass I. n.: to make an ~ of oneself (colloq.) *sich blamieren, sich lächerlich machen.* — **II.** v.i.: to ~ about (sl.) *Blödsinn machen*

assault n.: to carry by ~ *im Sturm nehmen;* ~ and battery *tätliche Beleidigung*

assurance n.: to make ~ double sure (Macbeth, IV, 1) *jeden möglichen Zweifel beheben*

astray adv.: to go ~ *irregehen, verloren gehen;* to lead ~ *irreführen, verleiten*

asunder adv.: to come (to tear) ~ *in Stücke auseinanderfallen, -reißen*

attach v.tr. & i.: he is deeply ~ed to her *er hat sie sehr lieb;* no blame ~es to him *ihn trifft keine Schuld;* he ~ed a special meaning to my words *er hat meinen Worten einen besonderen Sinn beigemessen;* to ~ *gerichtlich mit Beschlag belegen*

attendance n.: a furnished room with ~ *ein möbliertes Zimmer mit Bedienung;* medical ~ *ärztliche Behandlung;* to be in ~ on *diensttuend;* Lady in ~ *Hofdame;*

hours of ∾ *Dienststunden;* late ∾ *Zuspätkommen (zum Dienst);* to dance ∾ (up)on a person *um j.en herumscharwenzeln;* ∾ at church, at a lecture *Kirchenbesuch, Besuch einer Vorlesung;* list of ∾s *Präsensliste;* people in ∾ *die Wartenden*

attention n.: ∾! *stillgestanden!;* I am all ∾ *ich bin ganz Ohr;* may I call (draw) your ∾ to it? *darf ich dich darauf aufmerksam machen?;* to catch a person's ∾ *j.es Aufmerksamkeit erregen;* to come to (to stand at) ∾ *eine militärische Haltung annehmen, stillstehen;* to give (to pay) ∾ to a thing *einer Sache Aufmerksamkeit (Beachtung) schenken;* to pay one's ∾s to a person *j.em den Hof machen*

attitude n.: an ∾ of mind *eine Geisteshaltung;* to strike an ∾ *eine theatralische Haltung annehmen*

attorney n.: a power of ∾ *eine Vollmacht*

autocade n.: an ∾ *eine Autoschlange (vgl. Kavalkade)*

avail I. v.tr.: to ∾ a person to do a thing *j.em helfen, etwas zu tun;* to ∾ oneself of a thing *sich einer Sache bedienen, von etwas Gebrauch machen.* — **II.** v.i.: what does it ∾ to do so? *was nützt es, das zu tun?* — **III.** n.: to be of (of little, of no) ∾ *von Nutzen (von geringem Nutzen, nutzlos) sein;* to little ∾ *mit geringem Erfolg;* it was without ∾ *es war vergeblich, ohne Erfolg*

average n.: on the (an) ∾ *im Durchschnitt;* to strike the ∾ *den Durchschnitt nehmen*

awake pred. a.: to be wide ∾ *hell wach sein;* to be ∾ to a fact *einer Sache bewußt sein, sie durchschauen*

away adv.: ∾ with it *fort damit!;* to clear ∾ *den Tisch abdecken;* far and ∾ the best *bei weitem das beste;* to let oneself be carried ∾ *sich fortreißen lassen;* fire ∾ (colloq.) *schieß' los! fang' an!;* to fool ∾ the time *die Zeit vertrödeln, verplempern;* to get ∾ *entkommen, starten;* to get ∾ from *entschlüpfen;* to get ∾ with it (colloq.) *Erfolg bei seinem Bemühen haben; ungestraft (ungeschoren) davonkommen;* get ∾ with you! *mach', daß du fortkommst!;* to give oneself ∾ *sich verraten;* he is ∾ *er ist fort, verreist;* to idle ∾ one's time *die Zeit vertrödeln;* laugh ∾! *lach' nur!;* to make ∾ with something *etwas abschaffen, fortschaffen;* to make (to do) ∾ with oneself *sich (dat.) das Leben nehmen;* to peg ∾ at something *beharrlich an etwas arbeiten;* he put ∾ a whole loaf of bread *er verdrückte ein ganzes Brot;* right ∾! *sofort!;* to run ∾ *fortlaufen;* to run ∾ with *durchbrennen mit;* to while the time ∾ *die Zeit verbringen;* to work ∾ *drauf losarbeiten*

awe I. n.: to stand in ∾ of *Respekt haben, sich fürchten vor.* — **II.** a.: ∾-struck *von Ehrfurcht (Scheu) ergriffen*

awry adv.: to go (to run, tread, step, walk) ∾ *irren (von Personen), schiefgehen (von Sachen);* to look ∾ *schielen, scheel ansehen;* to tread the shoe ∾ *vom Wege der Tugend abweichen, einen Fehltritt tun*

axe n.: to hang up one's ∾ *die Arbeit an den Nagel hängen, sich zur Ruhe setzen;* to have an ∾ to grind *Privatinteressen verfolgen;* to lay (to set) the ∾ to a thing *die Axt an etwas legen;* to put the ∾ in the helve *eine Schwierigkeit lösen;* the ∾ *Sparmaßnahmen, besonders der öffentlichen Hand*

ay n.: the ∾es have it *die Mehrzahl ist dafür (für den Antrag)*

aye adv.: for ∾ *für immer, auf ewig*

B

baby n.: a ∾-car (colloq.) *ein Kleinauto;* a cry-∾ *ein kleiner Schreihals, ein Heulfritze, eine Heulsuse;* to hold (to carry) the ∾ (colloq.) *eine (unerwünschte) Verantwortung übernehmen, für etwas geradestehen müssen;* you're a regular ∾ *du bist ein richtiger Kindskopf;* a ∾-farmer *j., der Kinder in Pflege nimmt;* a ∾-grand *ein Stutzflügel;* a ∾-sitter *j., der in Abwesenheit der Eltern bei den Kindern bleibt;* a ∾-snatcher (colloq.) *eine Frau, die einen viel jüngeren Mann heiratet*

back I. n.: full-∾; half-∾ *(Fußball) Verteidiger; Läufer;* the Backs *die hinter den Colleges in Cambridge liegenden Gärten;* ∾ and belly *Kleidung und Nahrung;* he was at the ∾ of it *er stand dahinter, unterstützte die Sache;* in the ∾ of the car *auf dem Rücksitz des Wagens;* on the ∾ of it *noch dazu, außerdem;* he was on his ∾ for weeks *er war wochenlang bettlägerig, lag steif;* to break a person's ∾ *j.en über-*

lasten, -bürden, zugrunde richten; to break the ∾ of a task *das Schwerste (Schlimmste) hinter sich bringen;* the ship broke her ∾ *das Schiff brach entzwei;* to do something behind his ∾ (when his ∾ is turned) *etwas hinter seinem Rücken tun;* that book has a ∾ to it *ich werde dir das Buch leihen, du mußt es aber wiederbringen;* they were fighting with their ∾s to the wall *sie waren in großer Bedrängnis (in die Enge getrieben);* to give (to make) a ∾ for a person *sich beim Bockspringen bücken;* to have a ∾ equal to the burden *eine Last tragen können;* to have a person on one's ∾ *j.en auf dem Hals haben;* to put (to get, to set) a person's ∾ up *j.en erbosen, aufregen, reizen;* to see the ∾ of a person *j.en loswerden;* to turn one's ∾ upon a person, upon a thing *j.em, einer Sache den Rücken kehren, davonlaufen; j.en, eine Sache im Stich lassen.* — **II.** a.: ∾ to ∾ houses *kleine, enggebaute Slumwohnungen;* a ∾-bencher, see 'bench'; ∾-room boys *Erfinder, Techniker, die hinter der Szene wichtige Arbeit leisten;* to the ∾bone *durch und durch, bis auf die Knochen;* ∾-chat (sl.) *Gegenbeschuldigungen, gegenseitige Anpöbelungen;* to slip in by (through) a ∾door *durch ein Hintertürchen hineinschlüpfen;* ∾-fire *Frühzündung;* the word is a ∾ formation *das Wort ist eine Rückbildung;* to keep in the ∾ground *sich im Hintergrunde halten;* he has a good ∾hand (tennis) *er hat einen guten Rückhandschlag;* a ∾hand blow, a ∾hander *ein indirekter, unerwarteter Schlag, Angriff;* ∾log of work, orders *rückständige Arbeit, Bestellungen;* the ∾most row *die hinterste Reihe;* a ∾ number of a periodical *eine alte Nummer einer Zeitschrift;* he is a ∾ number (colloq.) *er ist rückständig (hinter dem Mond zurück);* the ∾ rent *die rückständige Miete;* ∾-scratching *kriecherische Schmeichelei;* to take a ∾ seat *bescheiden in den Hintergrund treten;* he fell on his ∾side *er fiel auf den Hintern.* — **III.** adv.: ∾ and forth *hin und her;* ∾ home in America (U.S.) *bei uns zu Hause in Amerika;* ∾ of the house (U.S.) *hinter dem Hause;* the house stands well ∾ from the road *das Haus liegt weit ab von der Straße;* I've been doing that for years ∾ *das tue ich schon seit Jahren, jahrelang;* it comes ∾ to me *es kommt mir wieder ins Gedächtnis;* to fall ∾ *zurücktreten, -bleiben;* to fall ∾ upon a person (thing) *auf j.en (eine Sache) zurückkommen; zu j.em (einer Sache) Zuflucht nehmen;* to get ∾ home safely *sicher (glücklich) nach Hause zurückkommen;* to get one's (some of one's) own ∾ (sl.) *sich rächen;* to go ∾ from (upon) one's word *sein Wort brechen, nicht halten;* to put (to set) the clock ∾ *die Uhr zurückstellen, die Geschichte zurückschrauben;* to put ∾ to harbour *in den Hafen zurückkehren;* to ∾bite a person *j.en verleumden;* to ∾slide into sin *wieder in Sünde verfallen.* — **IV.** v.tr.: to ∾ a bill *einen Wechsel gegenschreiben (indossieren);* to ∾ a car into the garage *ein Auto rückwärts in die Garage fahren (setzen);* to ∾ a horse *ein Pferd besteigen; auf ein Pferd setzen (wetten);* to ∾ a person (up) *j.en unterstützen, ihm die Stange halten.* — **V.** v.i.: to ∾ down (colloq.) *einen Anspruch aufgeben, klein beigeben, kneifen;* the room ∾s on to the garden *das Zimmer liegt hinten nach dem Garten zu;* to ∾ out of (away from) an affair, a promise *sich aus (von) einer Sache (von einem Versprechen) zurückziehen*

bacon n.: to bring home the ∾ (sl.) *Erfolg in seinem Tun haben; den Vogel abschießen;* to save one's ∾ *sich in Sicherheit bringen, mit heiler Haut davonkommen*

bad I. a.: I am in his ∾ books *ich bin bei ihm schlecht angeschrieben;* it was not ∾ *es war ganz gut;* that is too ∾ *das ist zu dumm, zu arg;* he made ∾ blood between them *er hat sie gegen einander aufgehetzt;* a ∾ coin *eine falsche Münze;* a ∾ debt *eine nicht eintreibbare Schuld;* he's a ∾ egg, a ∾ hat, a ∾ lot (sl.) *er ist ein übler Kunde (Bursche, Kerl);* that is ∾ form *das schickt sich nicht;* with ∾ grace *widerwillig;* to use ∾ language *fluchen, zoten;* to have ∾ luck *Unglück (Pech) haben;* to be ∾ for one's health *der Gesundheit unzuträglich (schädlich) sein;* he made a ∾ shot at it *er hat schlecht geraten;* to feel ∾ about a thing *sich über etwas ärgern;* to go (to turn) ∾ *schlecht werden, verderben;* to be taken ∾ (sl.) *schlecht, krank werden.* — **II.** n.: things are going from ∾ to worse *es wird immer schlimmer, wir kommen aus dem Regen in die Traufe;* he is £ 500 to the ∾ *er hat ein Defizit von 500 Pfund;* to go to the ∾ *in schlechte Gesellschaft (auf Abwege) geraten; völlig verdorben werden;* to take the ∾ with the good *sich mit allem abfinden*

badly adv.: to need (to want) a thing ∾; to be ∾ in need (in want) of a thing *etwas dringend benötigen;* he is ∾ off *er ist arm dran;* he is ∾ off for books *es fehlt ihm sehr an Büchern*

bag I. n.: with ∾ and baggage *mit Sack und Pack;* the whole ∾ of tricks (sl.) *jeder Kniff, der ganze Kram;* he is a mere ∾ of bones *er ist ein wahres Gerippe;* to give a person the ∾ to hold *j.en beschäftigen, um sich selbst aus dem Staube machen zu können;* I've got that in the ∾ (colloq.) *das habe ich so gut wie sicher (wie in der Tasche);* to let the cat out of the ∾ *ein Geheimnis ausplappern, die Katze aus dem Sack lassen;* to make a good ∾ *gute Jagdbeute machen;* he has ∾s of money (sl.) *er ist unwahrscheinlich reich;* to remain in the bottom of the ∾ *als letztes Hilfsmittel bleiben, die letzte Rettung sein;* to wear flannel ∾s (sl.) *eine Flanellhose tragen.* — **II.** v.tr.: they ∾ged the whole lot *sie haben alles eingesackt (geklaut);* I ∾, ∾s I, first turn (school sl.) *ich komm' zuerst dran! Erster!;* he has ∾ged all the cake *er hat den ganzen Kuchen geklaut*

bail I. n.: a magistrate accepts (admits to, allows, holds to, takes) ∾ *ein Richter läßt Bürgschaft zu;* to be (to become, to go) ∾ for a person *für j.en Bürgschaft leisten, bürgen, Kaution stellen;* to forfeit one's ∾ *durch Nichterscheinen vor Gericht der gestellten Kaution verlustig gehen;* to give leg ∾ *Fersengeld geben;* to release on ∾ *gegen Bürgschaft freilassen;* to save (to surrender to) one's ∾ *sich dem Gericht wieder stellen.* — **II.** v.tr.: to ∾ a person out *j.en durch Bürgschaft aus der Haft befreien*

bait I. n.: to rise to (to swallow, to take) the ∾ *sich ködern lassen, auf den Leim gehen.* — **II.** v.tr.: bear-, Jew-∾ing *Bären-, Judenhetze*

bake v.tr.: he is only half-∾d *er ist ein unreifer, geistig minderwertiger Bursche*

baker n.: pull devil, pull ∾ *eine Ermunterung für beide Parteien;* a ∾'s dozen *13 Stück*

balance I. n.: the ∾ of power in Europe *das europäische Gleichgewicht;* the ∾ of trade *die Handelsbilanz;* upon a fair ∾ *nach reiflicher Überlegung;* to adjust the ∾ *das Gleichgewicht herstellen;* to be in the ∾ *in der Schwebe sein;* to have a ∾ in (to) one's favour *etwas gut haben;* to hold the ∾ *das Zünglein an der Waage bilden;* to keep the ∾ after paying a bill *den Rest des Geldes nach Bezahlung einer Rechnung für sich behalten;* to lose one's ∾ *das Gleichgewicht verlieren;* to strike a ∾ *die Bilanz ziehen;* to throw a person off his ∾ *j.en aus dem Gleichgewicht bringen;* to tip (to turn) the ∾ *den Ausschlag geben.* — **II.** v.tr.: to ∾ accounts *ein Konto saldieren, ausgleichen;* to ∾ one thing against another *eine Sache gegen eine andere abwägen;* the expenses ∾ the receipts *Ausgaben und Einnahmen decken sich.* — **III.** v.i.: the account ∾s *die Bilanz (Rechnung) stimmt*

bald a.: as ∾ as a coot *(Wasserhuhn) ratzekahl, so kahl wie eine Billardkugel;* to go ∾-headed at something (sl.) *für eine Sache alles ohne Rücksicht auf die Folgen einsetzen*

bale v.i.: to ∾ out *vom Flugzeug mit Fallschirm abspringen, „aussteigen“*

ball n.: the ∾ is with you *die Reihe ist an dir, du bist dran;* to catch the ∾ at the bound *die Gelegenheit beim Schopfe fassen;* to have the ∾ at one's feet *Herr der Lage sein;* to keep up the ∾, to keep the ∾ rolling *das Gespräch im Gang halten;* to open the ∾ *den Reigen eröffnen;* to set the ∾ rolling *eine Sache in Gang setzen;* to take the ∾ before the bound *etwas überstürzt (übereilt) tun (machen);* a ∾ of Fortune *ein Spielball des Glückes;* he won't play ∾ (Amer.) *er will nicht mitmachen;* the three golden ∾s *das Zeichen eines Leihhauses*

bally *(entstanden aus Aussprache von* bl — y = bloody). **I.** a. (sl.): the whole ∾ lot *der ganze Kram (Salat);* it is a ∾ nuisance *es ist verflucht lästig;* the ∾ radio makes such a noise *das verfluchte Radio macht so viel (so einen) Krach.* — **II.** adv. (sl.): I'm too ∾ tired *ich bin verflucht müde*

balmy see 'barmy'

bamboozle v.tr.: (sl.): he ∾d me into doing it *er beschwatzte mich dazu, es zu tun;* to ∾ a person out of a thing *j.en um etwas beschwindeln*

bandbox n.: he looked as if he came out of a ∾ *er sah aus wie aus dem Ei gepellt*

bandwagon n.: she got on the ∾ about votes for women *sie war für das Frauenwahlrecht sehr aktiv*

bandy I. v.tr.: to ∾ words with someone *einen kurzen, scharfen Wortwechsel mit j.em haben;* to ∾ a tale about *eine Geschichte herumtragen;* to have one's name bandied about *der Gegenstand eines Tratsches oder einer unfreundlichen Kritik sein.* — **II.** a.: ∾-legs *O-Beine*

bang I. v.tr.: to ∾ the bush *alles Dagewesene übertreffen;* to ∾ the door to *die Tür zuknallen.* — **II.** v.i.: the door ∾s to *die Tür knallt zu.* — **III.** n.: to go off with a ∾ *mit lautem Knall explodieren.* — **IV.** adv.: it went ∾ *es explodierte, knallte;* ∾ on! (sl.) *alles in Ordnung (alles O.K.)!*

bank I. v.tr.: to ∾ one's money *sein Geld auf die Bank bringen;* to ∾ up the fire *das gut gestochte (geschürte) Feuer zudecken, damit es lange anhält.* — **II.** v.i.: to ∾ upon a person (thing) *seine Hoffnungen auf j.en (eine Sache) setzen.* — **III.** a.: a ∾-holiday *ein (offizieller) Bankfeiertag*

banker n.: let me be your ∾ *erlauben Sie mir, daß ich Ihnen das Geld leihe (gebe)*

banns n.pl.: to ask (to call, to publish, to put up) the ∾ *kirchlich aufbieten;* to forbid the ∾ *Einspruch gegen die Eheschließung erheben*

bar I. n.: the D.S.O. (Distinguished Service Order) with ∾ *der Verdienstorden mit Spange;* at the ∾ of public opinion *vor der Schranke der öffentlichen Meinung;* the ∾ sinister (herald.) *Querbalken am Schild als Zeichen der Unehelichkeit;* the horizontal ∾ *das Reck;* to be called to the ∾ *als Barrister (Rechtsanwalt) zugelassen werden;* to have a drink at the ∾ *an der Theke eins (einen) trinken;* to play a few ∾s *einige Takte spielen;* the ∾-keeper (-man, -tender) *der Büffetier;* the ∾-maid *das Büffetfräulein.* — **II.** v.tr.: to ∾ a person (sl.) *j.en ablehnen, nicht ausstehen (nicht leiden, nicht riechen) können;* ∾ring that *mit Ausnahme davon;* the law ∾s the use of weapons *das Gesetz verbietet den Gebrauch von Waffen;* to ∾ the way *den Weg versperren;* to ∾ a person out *j.en aussperren;* to ∾ a passage up *einen Durchgang vergittern (verrammeln)*

barefaced a.: a ∾ lie *eine unverhüllte (unverschämte, schamlose) Lüge*

bargain I. n.: into the ∾ *obendrein, noch dazu;* it was a good (bad) ∾; a chance ∾ *es war ein guter (schlechter) Kauf; ein Gelegenheitskauf;* to make the best of a bad ∾ *sich so gut wie möglich aus einem schlechten Handel ziehen; gute Miene zum bösen Spiel machen;* to close (to strike) a ∾ *ein Geschäft abschließen;* to drive a hard ∾ with *streng handeln mit.* — **II.** v.i.: to stand to one's ∾ *(sein) Wort halten;* to ∾ with a person for a thing *mit j.em um etwas feilschen;* that was more than I ∾ed for *das habe ich nicht erwartet; damit bin ich schön hereingefallen*

barge I. n.: to have a ∾ with someone (sl.) *ein Wortgefecht mit j.em haben;* I would not touch him with a ∾-pole (colloq.) *ich würde ihn nicht mit einer (Feuer)zange anfassen, ich ekele mich vor ihm.* — **II.** v.i. (sl.): to ∾ about *herumbummeln, -strolchen;* to ∾ against a person *j.en zufällig treffen;* excuse my barging into your conversation *entschuldigt, wenn ich mich so in eure Unterhaltung einmische*

bark I. n.: his ∾ is worse than his bite; ∾ing dogs seldom bite (prov.) *Hunde, die bellen, beißen nicht (Sprichw.).* — **II.** v.tr.: to ∾ out an order *einen Befehl herausbellen, -schreien.* — **III.** v.i.: I was ∾ing the whole night (sl.) *ich habe die ganze Nacht gehustet;* to ∾ up the wrong tree *auf falscher Fährte, auf dem Holzweg sein;* to ∾ at the moon *aussichtslos auf etwas schimpfen, den Mond anbellen*

barmy a.: he is ∾ on the crumpet (sl.) *er hat einen Vogel, er hat sie nicht alle beisammen (beieinander), er ist nicht richtig im Dach-, Oberstübchen*

barrel n.: a ∾-organ *eine Drehorgel;* a ∾-vault *ein Tonnengewölbe;* lock, stock, and ∾ *alles in allem; die ganze Geschichte*

barrelled p.p.: a double-∾ compliment *ein zweifelhaftes Kompliment;* a double-∾ gun *eine Doppelflinte;* a double-∾ name *ein Doppelname*

basket n.: it was the pick of the ∾ *es war das beste von allen, das beste Stück, das beste Pferd im Stall;* to have (to put) all one's eggs in one ∾ *alles auf eine Karte setzen;* to be left in the ∾ *vernachlässigt (nicht berücksichtigt) werden*

bat¹ n.: to do a thing off one's own ∾ *etwas selbständig tun;* to keep a straight ∾ *aufrecht (ehrlich) handeln*

bat² n.: he went off at a rare ∾ *er sauste los, er legte ein schnelles Tempo vor*

bat³ n.: he is as blind as a ∾ *er ist stockblind;* he has ∾s in the belfry, is ∾ (colloq.) *er hat einen Vogel (einen Sparren, einen Spleen)*

bat⁴ v.tr.: I never ∾ted an eyelid (colloq.) *ich habe kein Auge zugetan; ich zeigte keine(rlei) Überraschung; ich habe mit keiner Wimper gezuckt*

batch n.: I got a whole ∾ of letters *ich bekam einen ganzen Stoß Briefe*

bate¹ v.tr.: to ∾ an ace *eine Kleinigkeit nachlassen;* with ∾d breath *mit verhaltenem Atem;* not to ∾ a jot of a thing *keinen Deut von etwas ablassen*

bate², bait n.: he was in an awful ∾ (sl.) *er hatte eine furchtbare Wut*

bath I. n.: to take a ∾ every morning *jeden Morgen ein Wannenbad nehmen, sich baden;* to take sun-∾s in the summer *im Sommer Sonnenbäder nehmen;* to use a ∾-chair *einen Rollstuhl benutzen;* to take the ∾s *eine Badekur machen.* — **II.** v.i.: to ∾ *baden.* — **III.** v.tr.: to ∾ a child, one's dog *ein Kind, seinen Hund baden*

bathe I. n.: to take a ∾ *ein Bad im Freien nehmen;* to find a bathing beach *einen Badestrand finden;* the bathing costume *der Badeanzug;* to enjoy sunbathing *gern Sonnenbäder nehmen.* — **II.** v.tr.: to be ∾d in tears *in Tränen schwimmen;* to ∾ a place with Eau-de-Cologne *eine Stelle mit Kölnisch Wasser baden.* — **III.** v.i.: to go bathing *schwimmen gehen*

battery n.: assault and ∾ *tätliche Beleidigung;* to mask one's batteries *seine Absichten verschleiern;* she turned my ∾ against me *sie hat mich mit meinen eigenen Argumenten geschlagen*

battle I. n.: the ∾ is to the strong *der Sieg liegt bei den Starken;* youth is half the ∾ *jung sein ist ein großer Vorteil;* it was a pitched ∾ *es war eine regelrechte Schlacht;* to accept (to offer, to refuse) ∾ *eine Schlacht annehmen (-bieten, verweigern);* to do ∾ for a cause *um eine Sache kämpfen;* to give (to join) ∾ *eine Schlacht liefern;* a ∾-royal *eine heftige (kräftige) Auseinandersetzung.* — **II.** v.i.: to ∾ against (with) difficulties *mit Schwierigkeiten kämpfen;* to ∾ for a cause *um eine Sache kämpfen*

batty a. (sl.): he is ∾ *er ist verrückt, er hat einen Hau (Spleen, Sparren, Vogel)*

bay n.: to hold (to keep, to set) at ∾ *hinhalten, in Schach halten;* to stand (to be) at, to turn to ∾ *sich zur Wehr setzen*

be v.i. & aux.: to ∾ or not to ∾ (Hamlet) *Sein oder Nichtsein;* he lived to ∾ (to become) famous *er wurde am Ende berühmt;* he waited to ∾ admitted *er wartet darauf, eingelassen zu werden;* do not ∾ long *bleib' (mach') nicht lange!;* there he is at it again *da macht er es schon wieder!;* he is always at me to do it *er redet mir immer zu, es zu tun;* he is always at me for not doing so *er macht mir immer Vorwürfe, daß ich es nicht getan habe;* what is that to you? *was geht das dich an?;* what are you at (after, about) there? *was macht ihr da?;* it is for you to say (to do that) *du mußt es sagen; es ist deine Sache, das zu tun;* it was not to ∾ *es sollte nicht sein;* what are we to do? *was sollen wir tun?;* he was to have played *er hatte spielen sollen;* that is to say *das heißt;* to ∾ in a matter *an einer Sache beteiligt sein;* he is in for trouble *er wird Schwierigkeiten bekommen;* ∾ it so (so ∾ it) *so sei es;* let it ∾ so *laß es so sein;* if that ∾ so *wenn das der Fall ist;* the ∾-all and end-all *das ein und alles;* the to-∾ *die Zukunft;* if it were not for me *ohne mich, ohne mein Dazutun;* I am ordered *mir wird befohlen;* I am ∾ing fetched at 6 o'clock *ich werde um 6 Uhr abgeholt;* ∾ing scolded is not pleasant *ausgeschimpft zu werden, ist nicht angenehm;* who else is ∾ing invited? *wer wird sonst noch eingeladen?;* he is to go *er muß gehen;* it is to ∾ had *es ist zu haben;* this house is to (∾) let *dieses Haus ist zu vermieten;* it is to ∾ hoped *es ist zu hoffen;* he is sleeping *er schläft (noch);* the book is ∾ing printed *das Buch ist (noch) im Druck;* for the time ∾ing *vorläufig;* to call into ∾ing *ins Leben rufen;* the house is no more *das Haus besteht nicht mehr;* there is *es gibt;* it is not in him *es steckt nicht in ihm;* it is five years since she wrote *es ist fünf Jahre her, daß (seit) sie schrieb;* he had been to the cinema *er war ins Kino gegangen;* has anyone been? (colloq.) *ist j. hier gewesen?;* you have been and spilt the milk (vulg.) *da hast du doch wirklich die Milch verschüttet!;* now you've been and gone and done it! (vulg.) *da hast du (et)was Nettes angerichtet!;* the dog is my brother's *der Hund gehört meinem Bruder;* how much are these shoes? *was kosten diese*

Schuhe?; he is a has-been *seine Glanzzeit ist vorüber;* the might-have-beens *die verpaßten Gelegenheiten;* he is a would-∾ philosopher *er möchte gern als Philosoph gelten;* ∾ your age! (colloq.) *sei nicht so kindisch! denk' vernünftig!*

bead n.: to draw a ∾ on a thing *auf etwas zielen;* to tell (to count) one's ∾s *den Rosenkranz beten*

beak n.: to appear before the ∾ (sl.) *vor dem Richter, Lehrer (Schulsprache) erscheinen*

beam I. n.: to be on (off) the ∾ (colloq.) *auf dem richtigen, falschen Wege sein;* to be on one's ∾ends (colloq.) *in Gefahr, in Verlegenheit sein;* to kick the ∾ *zu leicht befunden, besiegt werden;* to be broad in the ∾ (colloq.) *weit um die Hüften sein.* — **II.** v.i.: to ∾ on a person *j.en strahlend anlächeln, -lachen.* — **III.** v.tr.: to ∾ a radio programme *eine Rundfunkübertragung an eine bestimmte Empfangsstation senden;* to ∾ a ship, a plane *ein Schiff, Flugzeug mittels Radar entdecken*

bean n.: well, old ∾ (sl.) *na, mein Lieber, alter Bursche!;* to be full of ∾s, ∾-fed *voller Lebenslust, guter Dinge sein;* to give a person ∾s (sl.) *j.en verprügeln, ausschimpfen;* I haven't a ∾ *ich bin völlig abgebrannt (ohne Geld);* to know how many ∾s make five *wissen, wo Barthel den Most holt;* to spill the ∾s (sl.) *eine Sache verraten (ausplappern); die Katze aus dem Sack lassen;* a ∾-feast, ∾o (sl.) *das jährliche Fest des Arbeitgebers für seine Arbeiter; ein Freudenfest*

bear[1] I. v.tr.: I had to ∾ the brunt of it *ich hatte den schwersten Stand, ich litt am meisten darunter;* to ∾ a child *ein Kind gebären;* he was born *er wurde geboren;* to ∾ a person company *j.em Gesellschaft leisten;* that does not ∾ comparison with *das hält keinen Vergleich aus mit;* to ∾ a grudge against a person, a person a grudge *einen Groll gegen j.en hegen, j.en auf dem Strich haben;* to ∾ a hand in a thing *an etwas teilnehmen, mithelfen;* I cannot ∾ him *ich kann ihn nicht ausstehen (leiden, riechen);* to grin and ∾ it *gute Miene zum bösen Spiel machen;* to ∾ a thing in mind *etwas im Gedächtnis behalten, es nicht vergessen, es berücksichtigen;* to ∾ oneself well *sich halten, sich gut betragen;* to ∾ a part in a thing *an etwas Anteil haben;* his language won't ∾ repeating *seine unpassenden Worte lassen sich nicht wiederholen;* ∾ round to the left behind the church *wenden Sie sich nach links hinter der Kirche;* to ∾ witness of a thing *von etwas Zeugnis ablegen;* to ∾ away the bell *erster sein, den Preis davontragen;* to be borne away by a feeling *von einem Gefühl fort-, hingerissen werden:* it was borne in upon me *es wurde mir klar;* to ∾ out a statement *eine Behauptung bestätigen.* — **II.** v.i.: to ∾ down upon a thing *auf etwas losfahren, -segeln, -fliegen;* the tax ∾s hard upon poor people *die Steuer lastet schwer auf armen Leuten;* to bring to ∾ on a thing *etwas zur Geltung bringen, auf eine Sache einwirken lassen;* that does not ∾ on the subject *das hat mit dem Thema nichts zu tun;* to ∾ up *nicht verzweifeln;* to ∾ up against adversity *sich gegen (ein) Mißgeschick behaupten;* to ∾ with a person *mit j.em Geduld (Nachsicht) haben*

bear[2] I. n.: like a ∾ with a sore head *wie ein alter Brummbär;* a ∾-garden *eine lärmende Versammlung;* a ∾-leader *ein Bären-, Fremdenführer;* to play the ∾ with a thing *großen Schaden unter etwas anrichten.* — **II.** v.tr.: to ∾ the market *auf Baisse spekulieren*

beard v.tr.: to ∾ the lion in his den (W. Scott, Marmion, canto 6, 14) *sich in die Höhle des Löwen begeben*

bearing n.: what is the ∾ of this on the argument? *was hat das mit dem Argument zu tun?;* to consider a thing in all its ∾s *etwas nach allen Seiten hin erwägen;* he has lost his ∾s *er hat sich verirrt, er weiß nicht, wo er ist (steht);* to take one's ∾s *sich orientieren*

beastly I. a. (sl.): it's a ∾ shame *es ist eine Affenschande.* — **II.** adv. (sl.): it is ∾ hard *es ist verflucht (verteufelt, verdammt) schwer*

beat I. v.tr.: to ∾ the air *offene Türen einrennen; sich unnütz, überflüssigerweise bemühen;* to ∾ a person black and blue *j.en grün und blau schlagen;* to ∾ one's brains *sich (dat.) den Kopf zerbrechen;* that ∾s cockfighting *das übertrifft alles, das schießt den Vogel ab;* to ∾ a person hollow *j.en bei weitem übertreffen, ihn vollständig schlagen;* ∾ it (colloq.) *hau ab! verdufte!;*

to ∾ a retreat *zum Rückzug blasen (trommeln); sich aus dem Staube machen;* to ∾ a tattoo *den Zapfenstreich schlagen;* to ∾ the devil's tattoo *ungeduldig mit den Fingern auf dem Tisch trommeln;* to ∾ time *den Takt schlagen;* to ∾ down the price *den Preis herunterdrücken;* to ∾ a thing into a person's head *j.em etwas einhämmern (einbleuen);* to ∾ up eggs *Eier schlagen;* to ∾ up a person *j.en fürchterlich verprügeln;* to ∾ up a person's quarters *j.en aufsuchen;* to ∾ up recruits *Rekruten werben;* I am dead ∾ *ich bin völlig erschöpft;* off the ∾en track *in (auf) einem weniger bekannten Gebiet (geogr. od. übertragen).* — **II.** v.i.: to ∾ about the bush *wie die Katze um den heißen Brei gehen;* to ∾ at the door *an die Tür klopfen.* — **III.** n.: the ∾ of the pulse *der Pulsschlag;* the policeman is on his ∾ *der Schutzmann macht seine Runde;* to be out of ∾ *aus dem Takt sein*

beauty n.: ∾ is but skin(-)deep (prov.) *man kann nicht nach dem Äußeren urteilen;* you're a ∾! *du bist mir ein Netter!;* that's the ∾ of it *das ist das Schöne daran;* ∾-sleep *der Schlaf vor Mitternacht*

beck n.: to be at a person's ∾ and call *auf j.es Wink und Ruf bereit sein;* to have a thing at one's ∾ *etwas zur Verfügung haben*

bed I. n.: she was brought to ∾ of a boy *sie gebar einen Sohn;* to get out of ∾ on the wrong side *mit dem falschen (verkehrten, linken) Bein zuerst aus dem Bett steigen (zuerst aufstehen), den ganzen Tag übel gelaunt sein;* to die in one's ∾ *aus natürlichen Gründen (eines natürlichen Todes) sterben;* to keep to ∾ *das Bett hüten;* to lie in the ∾ one has made *die Folgen einer Handlung tragen, „liegen (schlafen), wie man sich bettet";* to put to ∾ *ins (zu) Bett bringen, legen;* to take to one's ∾ *sich wegen Krankheit ins Bett legen;* in the twinkling of a ∾post *im Augenblick, im Nu;* between you and me and the ∾post *im Vertrauen, unter uns gesagt;* to be ∾ridden *bettlägerig sein;* life is no ∾ of roses *das Leben ist nicht leicht;* let's get down to ∾rock *gehen wir der Sache (den Dingen) auf den Grund!;* a good ∾side manner *ein taktvolles, Vertrauen erweckendes Benehmen eines Arztes am Krankenbett;* a ∾-sitter (∾-sitting-room) *ein Wohn- und Schlafzimmer;* to have a ∾sore *sich wund gelegen haben;* a hot∾ of vice *eine Brutstätte des Lasters.* — **II.** v.tr.: to ∾ out the dahlias *die Dahlien auspflanzen.* — **III.** v.i.: to ∾ down for the night *schlafen gehen*

bee n.: as busy as a ∾ *so emsig wie eine Biene;* to have a ∾ in one's bonnet *an (unter) einer fixen Idee leiden, eine Grille (einen Spleen, Sparren) haben;* to put a ∾ in a person's bonnet *j.em Raupen in den Kopf setzen;* to make a ∾-line for a thing *auf dem nächsten (kürzesten) Wege, schnurgerade (-stracks) auf etwas losgehen;* a spelling-∾ *ein Wettstreit im Buchstabieren schwieriger Wörter*

beef I. n.: put some ∾ into it (colloq.) *streng' dich (etwas) an!* — **II.** v.i.: he is always ∾ing about how much he has to do (sl.) *er klagt immer über viele Arbeit (wieviel er zu tun hat)*

beefy a.: a ∾ man *ein strammer Bursche*

beer n.: life is not all ∾ and skittles (prov.) *das Leben ist nicht nur eitel Lust und Freude;* to chronicle small ∾ (Othello, II, 1) *Lappalien als wichtig darstellen;* to think no small ∾ of it *eine hohe Meinung von etwas haben*

beetle I. n.: as blind as a ∾ *stockblind;* a ∾-brain *ein Dummkopf;* ∾-browed *mit buschigen Brauen, finster blickend;* a ∾-crusher (sl.) *ein großer Stiefel (Fuß), eine Quadratlatsche;* ∾-eyed *kurzsichtig.* — **II.** v.i.: to ∾ off *abhauen, weggehen*

before I. adv.: long ∾ *lange vorher;* why did you not say so ∾? *warum hast du das nicht früher gesagt?* — **II.** prep.: to bow ∾ authority *sich der Obrigkeit beugen;* the question ∾ us *die uns vorliegende Frage;* to sail ∾ the mast *einfacher Matrose sein.* **III.** conj.: look ∾ you leap (prov.) *erst wäge, dann wage;* it was not long ∾ he knew *es dauerte nicht lange, bis er erfuhr;* I would die ∾ I lied *lieber stürbe ich, als daß ich die Unwahrheit sagte*

beforehand adv.: to be ∾ with *zuvorkommen;* to be ∾ with the world *in guten Verhältnissen leben*

beg I. v.tr.: I ∾ your pardon *ich bitte um Verzeihung;* I ∾ your pardon? *wie beliebt? wie bitte?;* to ∾ the question *der Hauptfrage ausweichen; etwas Umstrittenes als ausgemachte Tatsache hinstellen;* to ∾ one's way *sich durchbetteln;* to ∾ someone off *j.en losbitten.* — **II.** v.i.: I ∾ to differ from you *Sie gestatten wohl, daß ich anderer Ansicht bin;* I ∾ to inform you *ich gestatte mir, Ihnen mitzuteilen;* the situation is going a-∾ging *die Stelle will niemand haben*

beggar I. n.: he's an awful ∾ (colloq.) *er ist ein furchtbarer Kerl;* he's a nice little ∾ (colloq.) *er ist ein netter kleiner Bengel;* ∾s must not be choosers *arme Leute dürfen nicht wählerisch sein;* if wishes were horses, ∾s would ride (prov.) *vom Wünschen ist noch keiner reich geworden (bes. zu j.em gesagt, der Unerreichbares erhofft).* — **II.** v.tr.: it ∾s all description *es spottet jeder Beschreibung*

begin v.tr. & i.: to ∾ with, I must say *erstens einmal (zunächst einmal) muß ich sagen;* he began the world as errand-boy *er fing als Laufjunge an*

behalf n.: on (in) my ∾, in a person's ∾, on (in) ∾ of *im Namen von, um — willen, zugunsten von*

behaviour n.: to be on one's good ∾ *sich gut aufführen*

behind prep.: ∾ the scenes *hinter den Kulissen;* ∾ time *unpünktlich;* ∾ the times *veraltet, altmodisch;* to fall ∾ *im Rückstand bleiben;* to go ∾ a person's words *nach geheimen Motiven suchen; zu erfahren suchen, was hinter den Worten steckt;* to put ∾ one *sich weigern, etwas zu berücksichtigen;* stay ∾ after the others leave *bleib' noch (hier), wenn die andern weggehen*

behindhand pred. a.: to be ∾ with *im Rückstande sein mit*

being n.: in ∾ *bestehend, lebend;* to call into ∾, to give ∾ to *ins Leben rufen;* to come into ∾ *entstehen;* a human ∾ *ein Mensch*

belfry n.: he has bats in the ∾ *er hat einen Vogel (einen Sparren im Kopf)*

belief n.: beyond ∾ *erstaunlich;* easy of ∾ *glaubhaft;* it staggers ∾ *es ist äußerst unerwartet;* I have no great ∾ in this treatment *ich glaube nicht, daß diese Behandlung mir helfen wird;* to the best of my ∾ *nach meiner festen (besten) Überzeugung*

bell I. n.: to answer the ∾ *die Tür öffnen (aufmachen);* as clear as a ∾ *glokkenrein;* as sound as a ∾ *gesund wie ein Fisch im Wasser, kerngesund;* to bear (to carry) away (off) the ∾ *erster sein, den Preis davontragen;* to curse a person with ∾, book, and candle *j.en feierlich exkommunizieren, j.en mit Verwünschungen überhäufen.* — **II.** v.tr.: to ∾ the cat *der Katze die Schelle umhängen; freiwillig Schwieriges unternehmen; eine Sache harmlos machen*

belt I. n.: to hit below the ∾ *einen Tiefschlag führen, unfair kämpfen;* to produce on the conveyer-∾ *am laufenden Band herstellen;* to tighten one's ∾ *sich (dat.) den Riemen enger schnallen.* — **II.** v.tr.: to ∾ someone *j.en verhauen*

bench n.: to be raised to the ∾ *zum Richter (oder Bischof) ernannt werden;* to be a back-∾er *als weniger bedeutendes Mitglied des englischen Unterhauses auf einer rückwärtigen Bank sitzen;* the front ∾ *die vorderste, für Minister und ehemalige Minister reservierte Bank im englischen Unterhaus*

bend I. n.: to give a ∾ to a thing *etwas biegen;* she is round the ∾ (colloq.) *sie ist verrückt (verblödet);* to go (out) on a ∾ (colloq.) *eine Sauferei mitmachen;* the ∾ sinister, see 'bar'. — **II.** v.tr.: to ∾ an ear *j.en gnädig anhören (ihm gnädig zuhören);* she implored him on her ∾ed knees *sie flehte ihn kniefällig an;* to ∾ a person to (before) one's will *j.en seinem Willen unterwerfen;* to ∾ one's steps (one's way) to a place *seine Schritte lenken (seinen Weg einschlagen) nach einem Orte;* I am not bent that way *ich habe keine derartige Neigung;* he is bent on mischief *er führt Böses im Schilde;* he is bent on reaching the top of the mountain *er ist fest entschlossen, die Bergspitze zu erreichen.* — **III.** v.i.: it will not ∾ *es läßt sich nicht biegen*

benefit I. n.: a maternity ∾ *eine Wöchnerinnenbeihilfe;* to give a person the ∾ of the doubt *im Zweifelsfalle die günstigere Auslegung annehmen* (lat. in dubio pro reo); he had no end of a ∾ finding the right house *er hatte eine verflixte Arbeit (Mühe), das richtige Haus zu finden;* ∾ of clergy (leg.) *Vorrecht der Geistlichen, den weltlichen Gerichtshöfen nicht unterworfen zu sein;* ∾ night *Benefizvorstellung zugunsten eines (oder mehrerer) Schauspieler(s).* — **II.** v.i.: we ∾ed by your advice *wir zogen Nutzen aus Ihrem Rat*

bent n.: to the top of one's ∾ *nach Herzenslust*

berth n.: he has a good ∾ *er hat eine gute Stelle;* to give a wide ∾ to a person (to a thing) *einen großen Bogen um j.en (um etwas) schlagen, j.em (etwas) aus dem Wege gehen*

beside prep.: to be ∾ oneself with joy *außer sich vor Freude sein;* that is ∾ the point (mark) *darum handelt es sich hier nicht, das hat nichts mit der Sache zu tun*

besides I. adv.: ∾, I told you so *ich habe es dir überdies gesagt;* I gave him money ∾ *ich gab ihm noch Geld obendrein.* — **II.** prep.: ∾ being a fool, he is also a nuisance *nicht nur daß er ein Narr ist, er fällt einem auch noch lästig;* there was another visitor ∾ me *außer mir war noch ein Besucher da*

best I. a. & adv.: at ∾ *im günstigsten Falle, allenfalls;* his Sunday ∾ *seine Sonntagskleider;* the ∾-abused book of the year (colloq.) *das am heftigsten geschmähte Buch des Jahres;* she is his ∾ girl *sie ist sein Schatz;* the ∾ man at a wedding *der Brautführer bei einer Hochzeit;* the ∾ part of the week *der größere Teil der Woche;* to the ∾ of my power *soweit es in meiner Macht liegt;* to the ∾ of my knowledge *nach meinem besten Wissen;* to the ∾ of my recollection *soviel ich mich erinnere;* the book was a ∾ seller (colloq.) *das Buch war ein Reißer, Verkaufsschlager;* he can do it with the ∾ *er kann es so gut wie irgendein anderer;* he did it for the ∾ *er tat es in bester Absicht;* to give a person ∾ *sich geschlagen geben;* I had ∾ not to do it *ich täte es am besten nicht;* to have the ∾ of it *am besten dabei wegkommen;* to make the ∾ of a bad job *gute Miene zum bösen Spiel machen;* to make the ∾ of things *vorliebnehmen, sich zufrieden geben;* to put one's ∾ leg (foot) foremost *sich sehr beeilen, die Beine in die Hand nehmen;* the ∾ is the enemy of the good (prov.) *das Bessere ist der Feind des Guten; das Streben nach Vollkommenheit hemmt oft den Fortschritt;* he stayed the ∾ part of the afternoon (colloq.) *er ist fast den ganzen Nachmittag geblieben;* dressed in one's ∾ bib and tucker *im Sonntagsstaat.* — **II.** v.tr.: do you think I've ∾ed you? *glaubst du, ich hätte dich übers Ohr gehauen?*

bet I. v.tr. & i.: to ∾ one's bottom dollar *sein letztes Geld auf etwas setzen;* you ∾! *aber sicher! na und ob!* — **II.** n.: to lay (to make) a ∾ *eine Wette machen, wetten*

better I. a. & adv.: to become (to get, to grow) ∾ and ∾ *immer besser werden;* upon ∾ acquaintance *bei näherer Bekanntschaft;* it goes against my ∾ feelings *es geht mir gegen den Strich;* my ∾ half *meine bessere Hälfte, meine Frau;* to be ∾ off *besser dran, wohlhabender sein;* for the ∾ part *zum größten Teil;* she is no ∾ than she should be *mit ihrer Tugend ist es nicht weit her;* to be ∾ than one's word *mehr tun, als man versprochen hat;* the ∾ the day, the ∾ the deed *je schöner der Tag, desto besser die Tat (als Antwort auf den Vorwurf „du sollst den Sonntag nicht entehren, entheiligen");* ∾ late than never *besser spät als niemals (als Antwort darauf);* ∾ never late *besser nie spät;* I feel ∾ *ich fühle mich besser;* all the ∾, so much the ∾ *um so besser;* six feet high and ∾ *sechs Fuß hoch und darüber;* to go one ∾ *eins mehr bieten, überbieten;* you had ∾ not do that *das läßt du lieber bleiben;* I know ∾ than to do that *ich bin nicht so töricht, das zu tun;* I think ∾ of him than to believe that *ich habe eine bessere Meinung von ihm, als daß ich glauben könnte, daß;* to think ∾ of it *es sich anders überlegen.* — **II.** n.: one's ∾s *Leute höheren Ranges;* for ∾ (or) for worse *auf Glück und Unglück (Formel bei der Trauung); auf Gedeih und Verderb;* a change for the ∾ *eine Wendung zum Besseren;* to get the ∾ of a person *j.en besiegen, übertreffen.* — **III.** v.tr.: to ∾ oneself *sich bessern, eine höhere Stellung (höheren Lohn, höheres Gehalt) bekommen*

Betty Martin n.pr.: that's all my eye and ∾ *das ist Unsinn (dummes Zeug, Quatsch)*

between I. prep.: ∾ cup and lip *zwischen Lipp' und Kelchesrand, zwischen Erwartung und Erfüllung (gibt es manche Enttäuschung);* ∾ the devil and the deep sea *zwischen zwei Feuern, in großer Verlegenheit, in verzweifelter Lage;* ∾ ourselves, ∾ you and me *unter uns, im Vertrauen;* they shared the bread ∾ them *sie teilten das Brot unter einander;* we had only a shilling ∾ us *wir hatten zusammen nur einen Schilling;* ∾ whiles, times *zwischendurch, dann* *und wann;* ∾ wind and water *an einer verwundbaren (verfänglichen) Stelle;* betwixt and ∾ *in der Mitte zwischen beiden; weder ... noch ...* — **II.** adv.: few and far ∾ *vereinzelt, dünn gesät;* the space ∾ *der Zwischenraum*

beware v.i.: ∾ of pickpockets *vor Taschendieben wird gewarnt*

beyond I. prep.: ∾ dispute *außer allem Zweifel;* ∾ measure, expectation *über die Maßen, über Erwarten;* you have succeeded ∾ me *du hast mehr Glück gehabt als ich;* his behaviour puts him ∾ the pale *sein Benehmen schließt ihn von (aus) der guten Gesellschaft aus;* ∾ possibility *unmöglich;* ∾ all praise *über alles Lob erhaben;* ∾ all price *unbezahlbar;* it's ∾ me *es geht über meinen Verstand.* — **II.** n.: the ∾ *das Jenseits;* the back of ∾ *der abgelegenste Winkel der Erde*

bib n.: she was dressed in her best ∾ and tucker *sie trug ihren feinsten Staat*

bid I. v.tr. & i.: to ∾ against *überbieten (auch beim Kartenspiel), den Preis in die Höhe treiben;* to ∾ the banns *das Brautpaar kirchlich aufbieten;* to ∾ one's beads *den Rosenkranz beten;* to ∾ defiance *Trotz bieten;* he ∾s fair to become a great man *er verspricht, ein großer Mann zu werden;* to ∾ goodnight, farewell *Gute Nacht, Lebewohl sagen;* do as you are bidden *tu', was man dir gesagt hat.* — **II.** n.: he made a ∾ for popularity *er bemühte sich, sich beliebt zu machen*

bide v.tr.: I can ∾ my time *ich kann ruhig abwarten*

big I. a.: ∾ with child; ∾ with young *schwanger (in Hoffnung, in Umständen); trächtig;* he is a ∾wig, a ∾-bug, a ∾ noise, a ∾-pot (sl.) *er ist ein großes Tier (eine hohe Persönlichkeit);* to get (to grow) too ∾ for one's boots (sl.) *eingebildet werden.* — **II.** adv.: to go over ∾ *einschlagen, einen großen Erfolg haben;* to look (to talk) ∾ *sich dicke tun, angeben*

bill[1] I. n.: to fill the ∾ *in den Kram passen;* to foot the ∾ *die Rechnung (Zeche) bezahlen;* to run up a ∾ *eine Rechnung anwachsen (auflaufen) lassen, Schulden machen;* he gave me a ∾ of exchange *er stellte mir einen Wechsel aus;* what is on the ∾ of fare? *was steht auf der Speisekarte (fig.: auf dem Programm)?;* a clean ∾ of health *eine Bescheinigung über einwandfreien Gesundheitszustand;* stick no ∾s! *Plakate anschlagen verboten!* — **II.** v.tr.: he was ∾ed to appear as Hamlet *nach dem Theaterzettel sollte er den Hamlet spielen*

bill[2] v.i.: to ∾ and coo *schnäbeln und girren, sich verliebt benehmen*

billet I. n.: he is looking for a ∾ *er sieht sich nach einer Stellung um;* the soldier was not in his ∾ *der Soldat war nicht in seinem Quartier;* every bullet has its ∾ (prov.) *jede Kugel hat ihre Bestimmung, d. h. nur der vom Schicksal Bestimmte wird getroffen.* — **II.** v.tr.: we have an officer and ten men ∾ed on us *wir haben einen Offizier und zehn Mann als Einquartierung*

billingsgate n.: ∾ *Pöbelsprache (des Londoner Fischmarktes);* to talk ∾ (vulg.) *Schimpfreden halten*

billy-(h)o n. (colloq.): they are fighting like ∾ *sie kämpfen (schlagen sich) wie toll;* it's raining like ∾ *es regnet Bindfäden*

bind v.tr.: safe (fast) ∾, safe (fast) find (prov.) *sicher verwahrt, schnell gefunden;* to ∾ a bargain *ein Geschäft festmachen;* to ∾ a boy apprentice *einen Jungen in die Lehre geben;* we agree to ∾ the insurance rates *wir verpflichten uns (wir garantieren), die Versicherungsprämien nicht zu erhöhen;* to ∾ a person down to secrecy *j.en zum Schweigen verpflichten;* to ∾ up wounds *Wunden verbinden;* he ∾s the whole time (sl.) *er klagt (knatscht) die ganze Zeit;* I'll be bound (for it) *ich bürge dafür, ich mache mich anheischig;* where are you bound for? *wohin gehst du?;* I was bound rigid (sl.) *ich langweilte mich zu Tode;* you are not bound to do so *du bist nicht verpflichtet, es zu tun;* he is bound to win *er gewinnt todsicher;* the accused was bound over to keep the peace *der Angeklagte wurde unter Bürgschaft verpflichtet, sich friedfertig zu benehmen;* he was bound over for two years *er erhielt eine Bewährungsfrist von zwei Jahren;* she is quite bound up in her children *sie geht völlig in ihren Kindern auf, sie lebt nur für ihre Kinder;* to be bound up with a thing *mit etwas verbunden sein, in Zusammenhang stehen;* it is my bounden duty *es ist meine Pflicht und Schuldigkeit;* the harbour is ice-bound *der Hafen ist vereist (zugefroren)*

bird I. n.: a ∾ of passage *j., der unseßhaft (immer unterwegs) ist, ein Zugvogel;* a ∾ of ill omen *j., der stets schlechte Nachrichten bringt, ein Unglücksbote;* a gaol-∾ *ein Gewohnheitsverbrecher, Zuchthäusler;* a little ∾ told me *das hat mir ein Vögelchen zugeflüstert;* an old ∾ *ein vorsichtiger Patron, Schlauberger;* a ∾ in the hand is worth two in the bush (prov.) *ein Sperling in der Hand ist besser (mehr wert) als eine Taube auf dem Dache;* ∾s of a feather flock together (prov.) *gleich und gleich gesellt sich gern;* it is a dirty ∾ that fouls its own nest (prov.) *ein garstiger Vogel, der sein eigenes Nest beschmutzt; man soll über seine eigene Familie (sein Vaterland) nicht übelreden;* the early ∾ catches the worm (prov.) *Morgenstunde hat Gold im Munde;* an early ∾ *ein Frühaufsteher;* fine feathers make fine ∾s (prov.) *Kleider machen Leute;* to give a person the ∾, to get the ∾ (sl.) *j.en auspfeifen; ausgepfiffen werden;* to kill two ∾s with one stone *zwei Fliegen mit einer Klappe schlagen;* as seen from a ∾'s-eye view *aus der Vogelschau gesehen.* — **II.** a.: ∾-witted *flatterhaft*

birth n.: by ∾ *von Geburt;* to give ∾ to *gebären, zur Welt bringen, hervorbringen;* the small boy was in his ∾day suit *der kleine Junge war nackt (nackig, ein Nacktfrosch)*

biscuit n.: that takes the ∾ (colloq.) *das übertrifft alles*

bishop n.: the ∾ has set his foot in it (Swift) *der Inhalt der Schüssel war angebrannt*

bit[1] n.: to draw the ∾ *die Zügel anziehen, die Eile mäßigen;* to take the ∾ between one's teeth *störrisch, aufsässig werden*

bit[2] n.: a dainty ∾, a tit-∾ *ein Leckerbissen;* ∾ by ∾ *allmählich;* he is a ∾ of a coward *er ist ein wenig feige;* it was every ∾ as good *es war genau so gut;* not a ∾ of it *keine Spur, ganz und gar nicht;* he did his ∾ during the war *er hat während des Krieges seinen Teil getan;* to give a person a ∾ of one's mind *j.em die Meinung sagen, den Marsch blasen;* just wait a ∾ *wart' mal eben, einen Augenblick*

bite I. v.tr. & i.: the biter bit *der betrogene Betrüger;* were you bitten? *bist du beschwindelt worden (hereingefallen)?;* to ∾ on the bullet *in den sau(e)ren Apfel beißen;* to ∾ the dust (the ground) *ins Gras beißen;* to ∾ off more than one can chew *sich (dat.) zuviel vornehmen (zumuten);* he had his head bitten off *er bekam ordentlich den Kopf gewaschen;* to be bitten with a fixed idea *von einer fixen Idee besessen sein;* once bitten, twice shy (prov.) *(ein) gebranntes Kind scheut das Feuer;* to ∾ one's thumbs at a person *j.en höhnisch herausfordern, ihn verhöhnen.* — **II.** n.: to have a ∾ and a sup *einen Happen essen*

black I. a.: as ∾ as pitch (as my hat, as night) *kohlrabenschwarz;* a ∾-coat worker *ein Kopfarbeiter;* a ∾-letter day *ein Unglückstag;* ∾ Maria *Wagen zum Transport von Gefangenen;* I am deep in his ∾ books *ich bin bei ihm sehr schlecht angeschrieben;* I must have it in ∾ and white *ich will (muß) es schwarz auf weiß haben (sehen);* to give a person a ∾ eye *j.em ein blaues Auge schlagen;* to paint a thing ∾ *etwas in ungünstigem Lichte darstellen;* a ∾guard *ein Lump, gemeiner Kerl;* a ∾leg *ein Schwindler (bes. beim Pferderennen), ein Streikbrecher.* — **II.** v.tr.: to ∾ out a word *ein Wort schwarz ausstreichen;* to ∾ out the windows *die Fenster verdunkeln;* the ∾-out *die Verdunkelung (Luftschutz).* — **III.** v.i.: to ∾ out *zeitweilig blind werden, das Bewußtsein (das Gedächtnis) verlieren*

blackball v.tr.: he was ∾ed from the Carlton Club *seine Mitgliedschaft bei C.C. wurde abgelehnt*

blackmail v.tr.: to ∾ a person *von j.em Geld erpressen*

blame I. v.tr.: I don't ∾ you *ich mache dir keinen Vorwurf;* who is to ∾? *wer ist Schuld daran?* — **II.** n.: to cast (to lay, to put) the ∾ on a person *j.em die Schuld zuschieben;* no ∾ attaches to you *dich trifft keine Schuld*

blank I. a.: to look ∾ *verdutzt aussehen;* leave three lines ∾ *laß drei Zeilen frei;* a ∾-cartridge *eine Platzpatrone, eine leere Drohung;* to give someone a ∾ cheque *j.em freie Hand geben (lassen);* a ∾ verse *Blankvers (reimloser jambischer Vers).* — **II.** n.: to draw a ∾ *eine Niete ziehen;* to leave a ∾ *eine freie Stelle lassen;* his memory (his mind) is a ∾ *er hat sein Gedächtnis verloren;* I asked him point-∾ *ich fragte ihn ins Gesicht (geradeheraus)*

blanket n.: a wet ∾ *ein Dämpfer, kalter Wasserstrahl; ein Spielverderber (Miesmacher);* to be born on the wrong side of the ∾ *außerehelich geboren sein*

blast I. n.: winter's chilly ∾ *des Winters eisiger Hauch;* at the first ∾ of the trumpet *beim ersten Trompetenstoß;* the ∾-furnace is in (out of) ∾ *der Hochofen ist an-, ausgeblasen;* to be in full ∾ *in voller Tätigkeit sein;* to sound a ∾ *einen Tusch blasen.* — **II.** v.tr.: O ∾! *ei verflucht!;* ∾ed hopes *vereitelte Hoffnungen;* to ∾ a person's reputation *j.en um seinen guten Namen bringen*

blaze[1] I. n.: in a ∾ of passion *in einem leidenschaftlichen Zornesausbruch;* in the ∾ of publicity *im vollen Licht der Öffentlichkeit;* go to ∾s (sl.) *geh zum Teufel!;* what the ∾s do you want? (sl.) *was willst du denn zum Teufel?;* he ran like ∾(s) (sl.) *er lief wie der Teufel (was das Zeug hielt).* — **II.** v.i.: to ∾ away at a thing *begeistert an einer Sache arbeiten;* to ∾ up *in Flammen, in Wut ausbrechen;* a blazing indiscretion *eine Taktlosigkeit sondergleichen;* a blazing scent (hunting) *eine frische Witterung, warme Fährte (Jägersprache).* — **III.** v.tr.: to ∾ a trail *eine Bahn brechen*

blaze[2] v.tr.: the news was ∾d abroad *die Nachricht wurde überall ausposaunt*

bleed I. v.i.: I had to ∾ for it *ich mußte dafür bluten (Haare lassen).* — **II.** v.tr.: to ∾ a person *j.en zur Ader lassen, schröpfen;* we were bled white *wir wurden bis zum Weißbluten ausgepreßt*

bleeding I. n.: ∾ at (from, of) the nose *Nasenbluten.* — **II.** a. (vulg. euphem. for bloody): a ∾ nuisance *eine verfluchte Schweinerei*

bless v.tr.: (God) ∾ me, my life, my soul! *du meine Güte! du lieber Himmel!;* well I'm blest! *da bin ich aber platt!;* I haven't a penny to ∾ myself with *ich besitze keinen roten Heller;* to ∾ one's stars *sich glücklich schätzen*

blessedness n.: to be in a state of single ∾ (joc. cf. M.N.D. I, 1, 78) *im ledigen Stande (Junggeselle,-in) sein*

blessing n.: a ∾ in disguise *eine unangenehme aber heilsame Erfahrung, ein Glück im Unglück, eine verkappte Wohltat;* to ask a ∾ *das Tischgebet sprechen;* what a ∾ that you came *welch ein Glück, daß du kamst!*

blighter n.: (colloq.) a ∾ *ein Kerl (Bursche, Lump)*

Blighty n. (army sl.): to return to ∾ *nach England zurückkehren;* to get a ∾ one *einen Heimatschuß bekommen*

blimey int. (vulg.): ∾! (= God blind me!) *Gott straf' mich! wahrhaftig!*

Blimp n.pr.: Colonel ∾ *Typ eines älteren konservativen (stockpatriotischen) Engländers, Ultrakonservativer*

blind I. a.: love is ∾ (prov.) *Liebe macht blind;* as ∾ as a bat (mole); stone-∾ *stockblind;* a ∾ alley *eine Sackgasse;* a ∾-alley occupation *eine aussichtslose Beschäftigung;* to be ∾, ∾ to the world; ∾-drunk (sl.) *sternhagelvoll sein;* to be ∾ of (in) one eye *auf e i n e m Auge blind sein;* to turn a ∾ eye to a thing *etwas nicht sehen wollen;* to go ∾ *blind werden;* to go it ∾ *blind draufloswirken;* a ∾ letter *ein Brief mit mangelhafter oder unleserlicher Anschrift;* the children played ∾-man's buff *die Kinder spielten ‚Blinde Kuh';* a ∾man's holiday *Zwielicht, Abenddämmerung;* ∾ radio *Radio ohne Fernsehen;* he attacked me on my ∾ side *er griff mich an meiner schwachen Seite an;* none so ∾ as those that will not see (prov.) *niemand ist so blind wie der, welcher nicht (ein)sehen will;* to have the ∾-staggers (colloq.) *vollkommen blau sein;* that is her ∾ spot *in dieser Beziehung ist sie unvernünftig, von allen guten Geistern verlassen;* a ∾-worm *eine Blindschleiche.* — **II.** v.tr.: to ∾ a person *j.en blenden, des Augenlichts berauben; täuschen;* to ∾ a person to a thing *j.en für etwas blind machen.* — **III.** v.i.: the motorist went ∾ing along (sl.) *der Autofahrer sauste rücksichtslos daher.* — **IV.** n.: among the ∾ the one-eyed is king (prov.) *unter den Blinden ist der Einäugige König;* a Venetian ∾ *eine Jalousie;* his enthusiasm was only a ∾ *sein Eifer war nur ein Vorwand (eine Tarnung)*

blindfold I. v.tr.: to ∾ a person *j.em die Augen verbinden;* he tried to ∾ me with his talk *er versuchte, mich mit seinem Gerede zu blenden.* — **II.** adv.: I could do it ∾ *ich könnte es mit verbundenen Augen tun*

blink I. v.tr.: to ∾ the facts *die Tatsachen nicht sehen wollen.* — **II.** v.i.: it's a ∾ing shame *es ist eine Sünde und Schande;* (∾ing vulg. euphem. for 'bloody')

blister I. n.: to raise a ∾ *eine Blase ziehen.* — **II.** v.tr.: to ∾ a person (sl.) *j.en bestrafen, verhauen*

blitz I. n.: I was in London during the ∾ *ich war in London während der Luftangriffe.* — **II.** v.tr.: our house was ∾ed *unser Haus wurde von einer Bombe getroffen*

block I. n.: he is a chip of the old ∾ *er ist der leibhafte Vater (ganz der Vater), „der Apfel fällt nicht weit vom Stamm";* to cut ∾s with a razor *seinen Geist an etwas verschwenden;* they dropped a few ∾-busters *sie warfen ein paar Bezirksbomben (Wohnblockknacker) ab;* he is a ∾head *er ist ein Dummkopf;* to write in ∾ letters *in Druckschrift schreiben.* — **II.** v.tr.: to ∾ in, out *in Umrissen skizzieren (entwerfen)*

blockade n.: a paper ∾ *eine erklärte, aber nicht durchgeführte Blockade;* to raise the ∾ *die Blockade aufheben;* to run the ∾ *die Blockade brechen*

bloke n. (sl.): I don't know the ∾ *ich kenne den Kerl nicht;* the ∾ (Navy sl.) *der Kapitän*

blood n.: ∾ is thicker than water (prov.) *Blutsverwandtschaft ist das stärkste Bindemittel;* his ∾ was up *sein Blut geriet in Wallung, es kochte in ihm;* in cold ∾ *kaltblütig, gefaßt;* in hot (warm) ∾ *in der Hitze, Erregung, im Zorn;* a prince of the ∾ royal, of the ∾ *ein Prinz aus königlichem Geblüt;* he is a young ∾ *er ist ein junger Stutzer;* you can't get ∾ out of a stone (prov.) *man kann kein Mitleid (Geld) von Mitleidlosen (Geizigen, Armen) bekommen;* to let ∾ *zur Ader lassen;* that will make (breed) bad ∾ *das wird böses Blut machen;* to make a person's ∾ boil *j.es Unwillen (Zorn) erregen;* to make a person's ∾ creep (run cold) *j.em das Blut in den Adern erstarren lassen;* that runs in the ∾ *das steckt im Blute, liegt in der Familie;* to shed (to spill) ∾ *Blut vergießen;* with ∾shot eyes *mit blutunterlaufenen Augen;* a ∾-and-thunder story, a ∾ curdler *eine Schauergeschichte, eine Geschichte von Mord und Totschlag;* ∾ sports *die Jagd*

bloody a. & adv.: a ∾-minded tyrant *ein blutgieriger Tyrann;* ∾ (in foul language = damned, or ∾ as mere intensive) *in gemeiner Sprache = verdammt, oder einfaches Intensivum;* he is a ∾ ass *er ist ein verdammter Esel;* not a ∾ one *kein einziger, kein Schwein*

bloom n.: to take the ∾ off a thing *einer Sache den Glanz nehmen*

bloomer n. (sl.): I made a terrible ∾ *ich habe einen furchtbaren Bock geschossen*

blooming a. (vulg. euphem. for 'bloody'): the whole ∾ lot *die ganze Blase, der ganze Salat, der ganze Kram (Krempel, Plunder)*

blossom v.i.: he ∾ed out into a statesman *er entwickelte sich zu einem Staatsmann*

blot I. n.: a ∾ on his scutcheon *eine Schande für seinen Leumund.* — **II.** v.tr.: to ∾ out a memory *eine Erinnerung auslöschen;* to ∾ one's copybook (colloq.) *einen schlechten Eindruck machen, einen Bock schießen*

blotto a. (sl.): he is ∾ *er ist betrunken*

blow[1] I. v.tr.: O ∾! (sl.) *ei verflucht!;* well I'm ∾ed (sl.) *na so was! da bin ich aber platt! hast du Worte!;* I'll be ∾ed if I do so (sl.) *ich lasse mich hängen, ehe ich das tue;* to ∾ an accomplice (sl.) *einen Mitschuldigen verraten (verpfeifen);* to ∾ the expense (sl.) *nicht auf die Kosten sehen;* to ∾ the gaff (sl.) *ein Geheimnis preisgeben;* to ∾ a kiss *eine Kußhand zuwerfen;* to ∾ one's nose *sich (dat.) die Nase putzen;* to ∾ one's own trumpet (horn) *sein eigenes Lob singen;* to ∾ off steam *überschüssige Kraft loswerden;* to ∾ out one's brains *sich (dat.) eine Kugel durch den Kopf jagen;* the bridge was ∾n up *die Brücke wurde in die Luft gesprengt;* he blew me up sky high (sl.) *er putzte mich fürchterlich herunter.* — **II.** v.i.: a fuse ∾s *eine Sicherung schlägt durch;* to ∾ great guns *gewaltig stürmen;* to ∾ hot and cold *bald so, bald so sprechen; den Mantel nach dem Winde hängen;* excuse my ∾ing in like this (sl.) *entschuldige, wenn ich so hereinschneie;* the clouds will soon ∾ over *die Wolken verziehen sich bald.* — **III.** n.: to get a ∾ of fresh air *an die frische Luft gehen, frische Luft schöpfen;* we had a ∾-out (sl.) *wir haben uns (dat.) den Bauch voll gefressen*

blow² **n.:** to come to (to exchange) ∾s *handgemein werden;* to deal a person a ∾ *j.em einen Schlag versetzen;* to get in a ∾ *einen Schlag erfolgreich anbringen;* to stop a ∾ *einen Schlag parieren (abwehren);* to strike a ∾ against a thing *einen Schlag gegen etwas führen, sich einer Sache widersetzen;* to strike a ∾ for a person *für j.en eintreten*

blower n. (sl.): I got it over the ∾ *ich habe es durchs Telefon erfahren*

blue I. a.: a ∾-eyed boy *ein Liebling, Günstling;* a ∾ ruin *ein totaler Zusammenbruch;* true-∾ *absolut treu, loyal;* to look ∾ *mißvergnügt, niedergeschlagen aussehen;* things look ∾ *die Aussichten sind trübe;* he is a ∾ conservative *er ist stockkonservativ;* he is in a ∾ funk (sl.) *er hat eine Mordsangst (einen Mordsbammel);* once in a ∾ moon *(einmal) alle Jubeljahre, nur alle Jubeljahre einmal;* to cry ∾ murder *Zeter und Mordio schreien;* he ran like ∾ murder *er lief, was das Zeug hielt;* to sport the ∾ ribbon *das Blaue Kreuz tragen, Mitglied des Mäßigkeitsvereins sein.* — **II.** n.: a bolt from the ∾, out of the ∾ *ein Blitz aus heiterem Himmel, völlig unerwartet;* he got his ∾ *er wurde in die Universitätsmannschaft gewählt;* the man in ∾ *der Schutzmann, Polizist;* the ∾s *die englische Leibgarde zu Pferde;* the dark (the light) ∾s *die Vertreter (Anhänger) der Universität Oxford bzw. Cambridge bei Sportveranstaltungen;* to be in the ∾s (to have the ∾ devils) *in gedrückter Stimmung sein, Trübsal blasen.* — **II.** v.tr.: to ∾ one's money (sl.) *sein Geld verprassen (verwichsen)*

blunder I. v.tr.: to ∾ away a thing *etwas vergeuden, verschwenden;* to ∾ out a word *mit einem Worte herausplatzen.* — **II.** v.i.: to ∾ about (along, on) *blindlings dahertappen;* to ∾ upon a thing *zufällig auf etwas stoßen*

blurt v.tr.: to ∾ out a thing *mit etwas herausplatzen, mit der Tür ins Haus fallen*

blush I. v.i.: he did not ∾ to own *er schämte sich nicht, zuzugeben.* — **II.** n.: at the first ∾ *auf den ersten Blick;* to put a person to a ∾ *j.en erröten machen*

blushing: ∾ honours (Shakespeare, Henry VIII) *öffentliche Auszeichnungen*

bo, boo, boh int.: he can't (he daren't) say ∾ to a goose *er ist äußerst scheu und ängstlich, er tut den Mund nicht auf*

board I. n.: the ∾ of directors *der Aufsichtsrat;* ∾ and lodging *Kost und Logis;* the Board of Trade *das Handelsministerium;* separation from bed and ∾ *Trennung von Bett und Tisch (Tisch und Bett);* a groaning ∾ *eine reichbesetzte Tafel;* to sweep the ∾ *alle Einsätze gewinnen, einen Bombenerfolg haben;* to tread (to walk) the ∾s *Schauspieler(in) sein;* to act above ∾ *offen und ehrlich handeln;* the mast went by the ∾ *der Mast ging über Bord;* to be bound in ∾s *in Pappband gebunden, kartoniert sein;* to be on the ∾s *Schauspieler(in) sein;* to go on ∾ (a∾) (ship) *an Bord gehen.* — **II.** v.tr.: to ∾ a ship *an Bord gehen, ein Schiff entern;* the passage was ∾ed up *der Durchgang war mit Brettern verrammelt.* — **III.** v.i.: to ∾ with a person *bei j.em in Kost und Logis sein;* a ∾ing school *ein Internat (Pensionat);* to pay ∾-wages *Kostgeld zahlen*

boast I. n.: to make a ∾ of *prahlen mit.* — **II.** v.i.: to ∾ of something (of having something) *sich einer Sache rühmen (sich rühmen, etwas zu haben);* it's not much to ∾ of *es ist nicht sehr rühmenswert.* — **III.** v.tr.: he ∾ed only one shirt *er rühmte sich des Besitzes eines einzigen Hemdes;* not ∾ing a car, I shall go by train *in Ermangelung eines Autos, werde ich mit der Bahn fahren*

boat n.: to have an oar in everyone's ∾ *sich in jedermanns Angelegenheiten mischen;* we are all in the same ∾ *wir sind alle in der gleichen Lage;* they all row in the same ∾ *sie ziehen alle am gleichen Strang;* he's missed the ∾ *er hat die Gelegenheit verpaßt*

bob¹ v.tr.: she wears her hair ∾bed *sie trägt einen Bubikopf*

bob² I. v.i.: to ∾ up like a cork *immer wieder an die Oberfläche kommen, sich nicht unterkriegen lassen.* — **II.** v.tr.: to ∾ a curtsy *einen Knicks machen*

bob³ n.: a dry (a wet) ∾ *ein Schüler in Eton, der Rasensport (bzw. Wassersport) treibt;* Bob's your uncle! (sl.) *das geht in Ordnung!*

bob⁴ n. (sl.): that cost me five ∾ *das hat mich fünf Schillinge gekostet*

bobbish a. (colloq.) *munter, aufgeweckt, lebhaft*

bobtail n.: a ∾ *ein Stummelschwanz;* ragtag (tag-rag) and ∾ *Krethi und Plethi*

bodkin n.: to ride (to sit, to travel) ∾ *eingequetscht (eingezwängt) zwischen zwei anderen Personen fahren (sitzen, reisen)*

body n.: the ∾ politic *der Staat;* all in a ∾ *alle zusammen;* what is a ∾ to do? *was soll da einer tun?;* he is a good sort of ∾ *er ist ein guter Kerl;* he is a busy∾, see 'busy'; to keep ∾ and soul together *Leib und Seele zusammenhalten;* an able-bodied seaman, see 'able'

boil I. v.i.: to make the pot ∾, to keep the pot ∾ing *sich (dat.) den Lebensunterhalt verdienen; die Sache in Gang halten;* what does it all ∾ down to? *was kommt schließlich dabei heraus? was ist das Endergebnis?* — **II.** v.tr.: as tight as a ∾ed owl (sl.) *sternhagelvoll, blau wie ein Märzveilchen;* a ∾ed shirt *ein Frackhemd.* — **III.** n.: it is on the ∾ *es kocht;* to bring to the ∾ *zum Kochen bringen;* he is at ∾ing point *er ist nahe daran, seine Selbstbeherrschung zu verlieren, er ist auf dem Siedepunkt*

bold a.: as ∾ as brass *(so) frech wie Oskar;* a ∾ face *eine dreiste Miene;* in ∾ outline *in deutlichen Umrissen;* in ∾ type *in Fettdruck;* may I make so ∾ as to say *darf ich mich erdreisten (mir erlauben) zu sagen;* to make ∾ with a difficult task *sich an eine schwierige Aufgabe wagen*

bolster v.tr.: he ∾ed up his story with much pathos *er unterstützte (unterstrich) seine Geschichte mit viel Pathos*

bolt I. v.tr.: to ∾ the door *die Tür verriegeln;* to ∾ (down) one's food *das Essen hastig herunterschlingen;* to ∾ a person in, out *j.en ein-, aussperren;* a ∾ hole *ein Versteck, ein Ausweg;* ∾ upright *kerzengerade.* — **II.** v.i.: the horse ∾ed *das Pferd ging durch;* to ∾ away, off *eiligst davonstürzen (ausreißen, durchbrennen).* — **III.** n.: a ∾ from the blue *ein Blitz aus heiterem Himmel;* he has shot his ∾ *er hat sein Pulver verschossen;* a fool's ∾ is soon shot *Narrenwitz ist bald zu Ende;* to shoot a ∾ *einen Riegel vorschieben;* to make a ∾ for it *Reißaus nehmen*

bone I. n.: a ∾ of contention *ein Zankapfel;* to be ∾-lazy *äußerst faul, stinkfaul sein;* what's bred in the ∾ will come out in the flesh (prov.) *Art läßt nicht von Art;* to feel in one's ∾s *etwas (ganz sicher) ahnen;* I have a ∾ to pick with you *ich habe ein Hühnchen mit dir zu rupfen;* to have a ∾ in one's leg (colloq.) *zu bequem (zu faul) sein zu gehen (etwas zu tun);* he makes no ∾s of (about) saying, to say *er zögert (zaudert) nicht, macht kein Federlesen daraus zu sagen; er macht aus seinem Herzen keine Mördergrube;* he will never make old ∾s *er wird niemals alt werden;* to set a ∾ *einen Knochen einrichten;* to work oneself (one's fingers) to the ∾ for a person *sich für j.en abschinden.* — **II.** v.i.: to ∾ up on something (sl.) *etwas pauken*

booby n.: he is a ∾ *er ist ein blöder Kerl, ein Tölpel;* a ∾ prize *ein Trostpreis;* a ∾ trap *ein derber Streich (Schule), eine Minenfalle*

book I. n.: ∾-maker (bookie) *Buchmacher (beim Pferderennen);* ∾-lore *Wissen aus Büchern, Buchgelehrsamkeit;* ∾ of reference *Nachschlagewerk;* ∾-work *was man auswendig lernen kann;* by the ∾ *peinlich genau;* to be at one's ∾s *studieren, lernen, über seinen Büchern sitzen;* to be in a person's bad (black; good) ∾s *bei j.em schlecht (gut) angeschrieben sein (einen Stein im Brett haben);* to bring to ∾ *zur Rechenschaft ziehen;* to keep the ∾s *die Bücher führen;* to keep one's name on (to take one's name off) the ∾s of a society *Mitglied einer Gesellschaft bleiben, aus einer Gesellschaft austreten;* to know it like a ∾ *etwas ganz genau wissen;* to kiss (to swear on) the ∾ *bei der Bibel schwören;* it doesn't suit my ∾ *das paßt mir nicht;* to take a leaf out of a person's ∾ *j.en nachahmen, ihn zum Muster nehmen.* — **II.** v.tr.: I'm ∾ed *ich bin gefangen, ich kann nicht entkommen;* I'm ∾ed for tonight *heute abend bin ich besetzt;* I shall ∾ my luggage *ich gebe mein Gepäck auf;* to ∾ seats for the theatre *Theaterkarten im Vorverkauf besorgen;* the ∾ing-clerk *der Fahrkartenverkäufer;* the ∾ing office *der Fahrkartenschalter.* — **III.** v.i.: I shall ∾ through to London *ich löse eine Fahrkarte bis London durch*

boot I. n.: the ∾ of the car *der Kofferraum (eines Autos);* the ∾ is on the other leg *die Sache ist gerade umgekehrt;* like old ∾s (sl.) *ungeheuer, kolossal;* over shoes over ∾s *wenn schon denn schon;* to die in one's ∾s *nicht im Bett sterben, einen plötz-*

lichen, gewaltsamen Tod finden; to give (to get) the ∾ (sl.) *entlassen; entlassen werden;* to have one's heart in one's ∾s *das Herz in den Hosen haben;* a ∾jack *ein Stiefelknecht;* a ∾legger *ein Alkoholschmuggler;* a ∾licker *ein Speichellecker.* — **II.** v.tr. (sl.): to ∾ a person out *j.en hochkantig hinauswerfen, -schmeißen*

booty n.: to play ∾ *sich als Köder zur Ausplünderung eines Dritten benutzen lassen*

booze n. (sl.): to go on the ∾ *eine Bierreise machen, saufen, sumpfen*

bo-peep n.: to play ∾ *Versteck spielen*

bore I. n.: he is a terrible ∾ *er ist ein entsetzlich langweiliger Mensch.* — **II.** v.tr.: to ∾ a person stiff (sl.) *j.en tödlich langweilen*

born p.p. & a.: to be ∾ with a silver spoon in one's mouth, to be ∾ under a lucky star *ein Glückskind, ein Kind reicher Eltern sein;* I was not ∾ yesterday *ich bin nicht von gestern;* in all my ∾ days *in meinem ganzen Leben*

borne p.p. & a.: it was ∾ in upon me *es wurde mir ganz klar*

bosh I. n. & int. (sl.): he talks a lot of ∾ *er schwatzt eine Menge Blödsinn;* ∾! *Unsinn! Dummes Zeug! Quatsch!* — **II.** v.tr. (sl.): to ∾ a person *j.en zum Narren halten*

bosom n.: the wife of my ∾ *das Weib meines Herzens;* in the ∾ of one's family *im Schoße seiner Familie;* my ∾-friend *mein Busenfreund;* my ∾-secret *mein Herzensgeheimnis*

boss I. n.: he is my ∾ *er ist mein Chef.* — **II.** v.tr.: to ∾ the show *an der Spitze stehen, eine Sache (ein Geschäft) leiten, die Sache schmeißen.* — **III.** a. (sl.): ∾-eyed *schieläugig;* ∾y *herrisch*

botch n. & v.tr.: to make a ∾ of (to ∾) a thing *eine Sache verhunzen (verkorksen, vermasseln, verpfuschen)*

both a.: to make ∾ ends meet *mit seinen Einnahmen gerade auskommen, sich nach der Decke strecken;* you can't have it ∾ ways *du kannst es nicht einmal so und einmal so haben wollen*

bother I. v.tr.: I can't be ∾ed, ∾ my head with it now *ich kann mich jetzt nicht damit abgeben, meinen Kopf nicht darüber zerbrechen;* you mustn't ∾ him now *du darfst ihn jetzt nicht belästigen, stören;* ∾ it! ∾ation! *verflucht, zum Kuckuck nochmal!;* ∾ these flies! *diese verfluchten Fliegen!* — **II.** v.i.: don't ∾ *bemühe dich nicht.* — **III.** n.: it was an awful ∾ *es war eine furchtbare Schererei*

bottle[1] I. n.: to crack a ∾ *einer Flasche den Hals brechen;* to sell by the ∾ *flaschenweise verkaufen;* to bring up a child on the ∾ *ein Kind mit der Flasche großziehen;* to discuss a matter over a ∾ *etwas bei einer Flasche Wein besprechen;* the ∾-holder *der Sekundant beim Boxkampf;* a ∾-neck *ein Engpaß;* a ∾-party *eine Gesellschaft, zu der die Gäste die Getränke mitbringen;* a ∾-washer (fam.) *ein Faktotum.* — **II.** v.tr.: to ∾ up one's anger *seinen Zorn zurückhalten*

bottle[2] n.: to look for a needle in a ∾ of hay (in a haystack) *etwas vergeblich suchen*

bottom n.: prices have touched ∾ *die Preise haben den tiefsten Stand erreicht;* to knock the ∾ out of a thing *etwas gänzlich vernichten;* he is a kind man at ∾ *er ist im Grunde ein gütiger Mann;* to be at the ∾ of a thing *einer Sache zugrunde liegen;* from the ∾ of my heart *aus Herzensgrund, aus tiefstem Herzen;* to convey in British ∾s *auf britischen Schiffen befördern;* to stand on one's own ∾ *unabhängig sein, auf eigenen Füßen stehen;* to get (to go, to search) to the ∾ of a thing *einer Sache auf den Grund gehen;* to send to the ∾ *in den Grund bohren, versenken.* — **II.** a.: to bet one's ∾ dollar *sein letztes Geld auf etwas setzen;* to put away in the ∾ drawer *für die Aussteuer zurücklegen;* to put in the ∾ gear *den ersten Gang einschalten.* — **III.** v.tr.: to ∾ a chair *einen Stuhl mit einem Boden versehen;* to ∾ an argument upon a fact *ein Argument auf eine Tatsache stützen.* — **IV.** v.i.: the argument ∾s on it *das Argument stützt sich darauf*

bounce v.i.: he ∾d, came bouncing, into the room *er stürmte (platzte) ins Zimmer hinein;* she is a bouncing girl *sie ist ein strammes Mädchen;* the cheque ∾d *die Bank verweigerte die Annahme (Auszahlung; Einlösung) des Schecks*

bound[1] n.: to go beyond the ∾s of reason *alle Vernunft übersteigen;* to keep within ∾s *Maß halten;* to put (to set) ∾s to a thing *etwas in Schranken halten;* out of ∾s for troops *Zutritt für Soldaten verboten*

bound[2] n.: at a ∾ *mit einem Satze;* to advance by leaps and ∾s *sprunghaft steigen*

bound[3] a.: this ship is ∾ for Africa *dies Schiff fährt (ist bestimmt, ist unterwegs) nach Afrika;* homeward ∾ *auf der Heimreise begriffen;* I'll be ∾ *ich bin ganz sicher*

bound[4], bounden, p.p., see 'bind'

bow[1] n.: to bend (to draw) the ∾ *den Bogen spannen;* to draw one's ∾ at a venture *auf den Busch klopfen;* to draw the long ∾ *aufschneiden (übertreiben, flunkern);* to have two strings to one's ∾ *mehrere Eisen im Feuer haben, mehr als ein Mittel bereit haben (halten);* to make (to tie) a ∾ *eine Schleife knüpfen;* ∾-legs, -legged *O-Beine, O-beinig;* to ∾string a person (in Turkey) *j.en mit der seidenen Schnur erdrosseln;* a ∾ tie *eine Fliege (Schlips);* a ∾ window *ein Schmerbauch*

bow[2] I. v.i.: to ∾ to the inevitable *sich ins Unvermeidliche fügen;* he is only a ∾ing acquaintance *ich stehe mit ihm nur auf dem Grußfuß;* to ∾ down to a person *sich j.em beugen, unterwerfen;* to ∾ and scrape, to scrape and ∾ *Kratzfüße machen.* — **II.** v.tr.: to ∾ one's head *den Kopf neigen;* to ∾ the knee to a thing *sich in Ehrfurcht vor etwas beugen;* he is quite ∾ed down by the loss *der Verlust hat ihn ganz niedergebeugt, -gedrückt;* to ∾ a person in, out *j.en unter Verbeugungen hinein-, hinausbegleiten.* — **III.** n.: to give a ∾ *sich verbeugen; durch Neigen des Kopfes grüßen;* to make one's ∾ *sich zurückziehen; abtreten;* to make one's first ∾ *zum ersten Male auftreten*

bowl I. v.tr.: to ∾ down *umkegeln, umwerfen;* I was completely ∾ed over *ich war vollkommen außer Fassung gebracht (ich war erschlagen).* — **II.** v.i.: to ∾ along *dahinrollen, -fahren*

bow-wow n.: a big ∾ *ein großer Wauwau;* a (big) ∾ style *eine dogmatische, gebieterische Art zu sprechen (zu schreiben)*

box[1] I. n.: the ∾-office *die Theaterkasse;* a Christmas-∾ *ein Weihnachtsgeschenk;* ∾ing-day *der zweite Weihnachtstag;* the jury- (witness-)∾ *die Geschworenen-, Zeugenbank;* a shooting-∾ *eine Jagdhütte;* a strong-∾ *eine Geldkassette;* to be in the same ∾ *in gleich übler Lage sein;* to be in a tight ∾ *in Verlegenheit, in der Klemme sein;* to be in the wrong ∾ *auf dem Holzwege sein;* to get into the wrong ∾ *in des Teufels Küche geraten.* — **II.** v.tr.: to ∾ the compass *die Kompaßpunkte der Reihe nach nennen; sich gänzlich umstellen und auf den Ausgangspunkt zurückkommen (bei Argumenten, in der Politik usw.);* to ∾ **up** *zusammenpferchen, -quetschen*

box[2] n.: a ∾ on the ear *eine Ohrfeige*

boy n.: an old ∾ of our school *ein früherer Schüler unserer Anstalt;* well my (old) ∾! *na, mein Junge, alter Bursche!;* ∾s will be ∾s (prov.) *Jugend hat keine Tugend*

brace I. n.: a pair of ∾s *Hosenträger;* to splice the main ∾ (Navy) *Getränke an die Mannschaften austeilen; saufen.* — **II.** v.tr.: to ∾ one's energies (oneself) up to do a thing *seine Kräfte anspannen (sich aufraffen), etwas zu tun;* a bracing air *eine kräftigende, erfrischende Luft*

brain I. n.: to blow out one's ∾s *sich (dat.) eine Kugel durch den Kopf jagen;* to cudgel (to puzzle, to rack) one's ∾s about (over) a thing *sich (dat.) den Kopf über etwas zerbrechen;* to get (to have) a thing on the ∾ *nur für etwas Gedanken haben, auf etwas versessen sein;* to pick (to suck) a person's ∾s *die Ideen eines anderen verwerten;* this stroke of luck quite turned his ∾ *dieser Glücksfall verdrehte ihm ganz den Kopf, brachte ihn aus dem Häuschen;* to suffer from a ∾-fag *an nervöser Erschöpfung leiden;* the ∾-pan *der Schädel;* the ∾-sauce *die Intelligenz, der Verstand;* to suffer from a ∾-storm *an einer plötzlichen schweren geistigen Störung leiden;* a ∾s trust *ein Gehirntrust (eine Gruppe intelligenter, gut informierter Personen, die sich treffen und wichtige Fragen diskutieren);* a ∾ wave (colloq.) *ein plötzlicher, glücklicher Einfall.* — **II.** v.tr.: to ∾ a person *j.em den Schädel einschlagen*

branch n.: to destroy root and ∾ *mit Stumpf und Stiel ausrotten*

brand n.: to snatch (to pluck) the ∾ from the burning *j.en aus Gefahr retten;* ∾ *(bran)-new funkelnagelneu*

brass I. n.: the ∾ *die Blasinstrumente;* as bold as ∾ *frech wie Oskar;* to be lousy with ∾ (sl.) *stinkreich sein;* to make the

∾es shine *auf Hochglanz polieren, wienern.* — **II.** a.: I don't care a ∾ farthing *ich mache mir einen Dreck daraus;* a ∾ hat (army sl.) *ein höherer Offizier;* to get down to ∾ tacks (sl.) *zur Hauptsache kommen;* to part ∾ rags with a person (naut. sl.) *alle näheren Beziehungen zu j.em abbrechen.* — **III.** v.tr.: to be ∾ed off (sl.) *es satt haben;* to ∾ up (sl.) *bezahlen, blechen*

brassy a.: *frech, unverschämt*

brazen a. & v.tr.: a ∾-faced fellow *ein schamloser (unverschämter) Bursche;* to ∾ it out *sich (dat.) durch Unverschämtheit helfen*

breach n.: a custom more honoured in the ∾ than the observance (Hamlet, I, 4) *ein Gebrauch, gegen den zu verstoßen ehrenvoller ist, als ihn zu befolgen;* to batter in a ∾ *eine Bresche schlagen (schießen, legen);* to stand in the ∾ *in die Bresche springen;* a ∾ of close *das widerrechtliche Betreten fremden Besitztums;* a ∾ of confidence (of trust) *ein Vertrauensbruch;* a ∾ of promise *Nichterfüllung eines Eheversprechens*

bread n.: his ∾ is buttered on both sides *er ist gut daran, er hat eine einträgliche Stellung;* one man's ∾ (meat) is another man's poison (prov.) *was dem einen sin Uhl, is(t) dem annern sin Nachtigall;* to break ∾ *essen; am Abendmahl teilnehmen;* to cast one's ∾ upon the waters (cf. Eccles. XI, 1) *Gutes tun, ohne Dankbarkeit oder Vorteil zu erwarten;* to earn (to make) one's ∾ *sich (dat.) sein Brot verdienen;* to eat the ∾ of affliction *Kummer und Sorgen haben;* to eat the ∾ of idleness *auf der faulen Haut liegen;* to know on which side one's ∾ is buttered *sich auf seinen Vorteil verstehen; wissen, wo Barthel den Most holt;* to take the ∾ out of a person's mouth *j.en brotlos machen;* the ∾-basket (sl.) *der Magen;* a ∾-and-butter letter *ein Dankesbrief für erwiesene Gastfreundschaft;* a ∾-and-butter miss *ein Schulmädchen (Backfisch);* to quarrel with one's ∾ and butter *sich (dat.) selbst im Lichte stehen; den Ast absägen, auf dem man sitzt;* ∾ and cheese *einfache Kost, die nackten Lebensbedürfnisse;* ∾ and cheese and kisses *Armut durch Liebe versüßt;* ∾ and scrape *ein dünn beschmiertes Brot;* the ∾-winner *der Brotverdiener*

break **I.** v.tr.: I am broke, stony-broke (sl.) *ich bin pleite;* to ∾ the back (the neck) of a task, see 'back', 'neck'; to ∾ the bank *die Bank sprengen;* to ∾ a bottle with a person *mit j.em eine Flasche trinken;* to ∾ bounds *die erlaubten Grenzen überschreiten, über die Stränge schlagen;* to ∾ bread, see 'bread'; to ∾ butterflies (a butterfly) on the wheel *mit Kanonen nach Spatzen schießen;* to ∾ company, cover, (a) custom, (one's) faith, (a) fall, see 'company, cover, etc.'; to ∾ one's fast *sein Fasten brechen, frühstücken;* to ∾ the force of a blow *die Wucht eines Schlages abschwächen;* to ∾ a person's head *j.em den Schädel einschlagen;* to ∾ Priscian's head *grammatische Schnitzer machen;* to ∾ a person's heart *j.em das Herz brechen;* to ∾ a horse to the rein *ein Pferd zureiten;* to ∾ fresh ground *ein neues Gebiet erschließen;* to ∾ the ice *die anfängliche Schüchternheit (Zurückhaltung) überwinden;* to ∾ a journey *eine Reise unterbrechen;* to ∾ a knot *einen Knoten lösen;* to ∾ a lance for a person *für j.en eintreten; eine Lanze für j.en brechen;* to ∾ a lance with a person *sich mit j.em messen;* to ∾ the news to a person *j.em etwas schonend beibringen;* to ∾ an officer *einen Offizier verabschieden;* ∾ ranks! *weg(ge)treten!;* to ∾ a rebellion *einen Aufstand niederschlagen;* to ∾ a person's shins (sl.) *j.en anpumpen;* to ∾ squares; that ∾s no squares, see 'square'; to ∾ step *ohne Tritt marschieren;* to ∾ water *auftauchen, an die Oberfläche kommen (von Fischen);* — with prep. & adv.: to ∾ asunder *entzweibrechen;* to ∾ down *ein-, niederreißen; brechen, besiegen, zugrunde richten;* to ∾ in an animal *ein Tier zähmen, abrichten;* to ∾ in a door *eine Tür aufbrechen;* to ∾ into a house *in ein Haus einbrechen;* to ∾ into one's savings *seine Ersparnisse angreifen;* to ∾ a person of a habit *j.em etwas abgewöhnen;* to ∾ off a business *ein Geschäft aufgeben;* to ∾ off an engagement *ein Verlöbnis lösen;* to ∾ off negotiations *Verhandlungen abbrechen;* to ∾ a thing loose *etwas losbrechen;* to ∾ a thing open *etwas aufbrechen, erbrechen;* to ∾ small *in kleine Stücke brechen, klein stoßen;* to ∾ a thing to pieces *etwas in Stücke brechen;* to ∾ up *zerbrechen,-schlagen,-schmettern;* to ∾ up a crowd *eine Menge auseinandertreiben;* to ∾ up a meeting *eine Versammlung auflösen.* — **II.** v.i.: the ball ∾s *der Ball ändert beim Aufprallen auf den Boden seine Richtung;* the clouds ∾ *die Wolken teilen sich;* the day ∾s *der Tag bricht an;* a merchant ∾s *ein Kaufmann macht bankrott;* his voice ∾s *seine Stimme schlägt um, er ist im Stimmbruch;* the weather ∾s *das Wetter wird schlechter.* — with prep. & adv.: the prisoner broke away from the police *der Gefangene riß sich von der Polizei los;* the enemy broke away *der Feind ergriff die Flucht;* to ∾ down *zusammenbrechen;* our car broke down, we had a ∾down *wir hatten eine Panne;* to ∾ even *ohne Gewinn oder Verlust aus einer Sache herauskommen;* to ∾ forth *hervorbrechen;* the words broke from his lips *die Worte entfuhren seinen Lippen;* to ∾ free, hold, loose *ausbrechen, sich losreißen;* to ∾ in *einbrechen, eindringen;* to ∾ in upon a conversation *eine Unterhaltung unterbrechen;* they broke in upon the camp *sie fielen über das Lager her;* to ∾ into tears *in Tränen ausbrechen;* to ∾ off *abbrechen, aufhören;* his wound broke open *seine Wunde brach auf;* a rebellion broke out *ein Aufstand brach aus;* to ∾ out into lamentations *in Klagen ausbrechen;* to ∾ out into a rash *einen Ausschlag bekommen;* to ∾ through the lines *die Linien durchbrechen;* to ∾ to pieces *in Stücke zerfallen;* to ∾ up *aufbrechen, auseinandergehen;* school ∾s up next week *die Schulferien beginnen nächste Woche;* he is ∾ing up *es geht mit ihm zu Ende;* to ∾ with a person *mit j.em brechen, sich entzweien.* — **III.** n.: at the ∾ of day, at day∾ *bei Tagesanbruch;* without a ∾ *ohne Unterbrechung;* it was a bad ∾ *es war eine unglückliche Bemerkung, eine unüberlegte Tat;* to give a person a ∾ *j.em eine Chance (Möglichkeit) geben;* to have a ∾ of 15 minutes *eine Viertelstunde Pause haben;* to make a ∾ of 200 (billiards) *eine Serie von 200 machen;* to put ∾ on a ball *einem Balle Effet geben*

breaker n.: ∾s ahead! *Vorsicht! Gefahr droht!*

breast I. n.: to make a clean ∾ of it *offen bekennen, ein unumwundenes Geständnis ablegen.* — **II.** v.tr.: to ∾ a hill *einen Berg hinaufsteigen;* to ∾ the waves *gegen die Strömung schwimmen; Trotz bieten;* a double-∾ed coat *ein zweireihiger Rock*

breath n.: with bated ∾ *mit verhaltenem Atem;* to be out of (short of) ∾ *atemlos, außer Atem sein;* to catch (to hold) one's ∾ *den Atem anhalten;* to draw a deep ∾ *tief Atem holen;* to gasp for ∾ *nach Luft schnappen;* to gather (to get, to recover) one's ∾ *wieder zu Atem kommen;* to get a ∾ of fresh air *frische Luft schöpfen;* keep your ∾ to cool your porridge *schone deine Lunge, behalte deine Meinung für dich;* to save one's ∾ *die Lunge schonen, schweigen;* to say inconsistent things in one (in the same) ∾ *sich widersprechende Dinge in einem Atem, in demselben Atemzuge sagen;* to spend (to waste) one's ∾ *in den Wind reden;* to stop a person's ∾ *j.en ersticken;* to take ∾ *Atem schöpfen;* to talk below (under) one's ∾ *im Flüstertone reden*

breathe I. v.i.: to ∾ again freely *wieder frei aufatmen;* to ∾ upon *beflecken, besudeln.* — **II.** v.tr.: to ∾ wholesome air *gesunde Luft einatmen;* to ∾ fragrance *Duft ausströmen;* to ∾ one's last breath *den letzten Atemzug tun;* to ∾ new life into a thing *einer Sache neues Leben einhauchen;* to ∾ simplicity *Arglosigkeit an den Tag legen;* to ∾ vengeance *Rache schnauben;* to ∾ a wish *leise einen Wunsch äußern;* to ∾ a word into a person's ear *j.em ein Wort zuflüstern;* don't ∾ a word of it *verrate kein Sterbenswörtchen davon!*

breather n.: to take a ∾ (colloq.) *frische Luft schnappen*

brevity n.: ∾ is the soul of wit (Hamlet, II, 2) *in der Kürze liegt die Würze*

brew v.tr. & i.: you must drink as you have ∾ed *du mußt auslöffeln, was du dir eingebrockt hast;* there is something ∾ing *es braut sich da etwas zusammen*

brick n.: he is a ∾ (colloq.) *er ist ein ganz famoser Kerl;* like a cat on hot ∾s *wie auf heißen Kohlen, wie eine aufgeregte Glucke;* he came down on them like a ton (a hundred, a cartload) of ∾s *er putzte sie gewaltig herunter;* to drop a ∾ (sl.) *ins Fettnäpfchen treten;* to be up against a ∾ wall *nicht mehr weiter können;* to see through a ∾ wall *überschlau sein, das Gras wachsen hören;* to make ∾s without straw (Exod. V, 7) *ohne das nötige Material arbeiten müssen*

bridge n.: a ∾ of boats *eine Schiffsbrücke;* to build a ∾ of gold, a golden ∾ *eine goldene Brücke bauen;* to shoot a ∾ *unter einer Brücke durchfahren*

brief¹ I. v.tr.: to ∾ someone *j.em genaue Anweisungen geben, j.en genau vorbereiten, instruieren.* — **II.** n.: to hold a ∾ for someone *j.en vor Gericht vertreten;* to hold no particular ∾ for someone *für j.en nicht viel übrig haben;* to hold a watching ∾ for someone (legal) *j.es Interessen als Beobachter in einer Gerichtsverhandlung vertreten*

brief² I. a.: to be ∾ *sich kurz fassen.* — **II.** n.: in ∾ *kurz, mit kurzen Worten*

bright a.: as ∾ as a button, a new pin *blitzblank;* honour ∾! *auf Ehrenwort!*

bring I. v.tr.: to ∾ down the house *(Theater) die Zuhörer zu stürmischem Beifall hinreißen;* to ∾ home to a person *j.em nahebringen, eindringlich vorstellen;* to ∾ into line *j.en zwingen, sich nach gewissen Richtlinien zu richten, sich zu unterwerfen (zu gehorchen);* to ∾ into notice *bekanntmachen;* to ∾ into play *zur Wirkung bringen, einsetzen;* to ∾ into the world *zur Welt bringen;* to ∾ oneself to do a thing *sich überwinden, etwas zu tun;* to ∾ to subjection *unterwerfen;* to ∾ upon oneself *sich (dat.) etwas zuziehen;* to ∾ word *Nachricht bringen.* — with adv.: to ∾ about, forth, forward, etc., see 'about, forth, forward, etc.'; to ∾ a person in guilty *j.en (für) schuldig erklären;* to ∾ off a thing *etwas zustande bringen, erfolgreich durchführen;* to ∾ on a discussion *eine Diskussion herbeiführen;* to ∾ out details *Einzelheiten klar hervortreten lassen;* to ∾ out a girl *eine junge Dame in die Gesellschaft einführen;* to ∾ a person over (round) to one's opinion *j.en zu seiner Ansicht bekehren;* to ∾ a person round, to *j.en wieder zu(m) Bewußtsein bringen;* to ∾ up a child *ein Kind auf-, erziehen;* to ∾ up one's food *sich übergeben;* to ∾ up a matter *etwas vorbringen, zur Sprache bringen;* to ∾ up the rear *den Nachtrab (die Nachhut) bilden, der letzte sein;* to ∾ up short *kurz anhalten;* to be brought up against reality *sich plötzlich vor die Wirklichkeit gestellt sehen.* — **II.** v.i.: to ∾ to *beidrehen, anhalten (von Schiffen);* to ∾ up *vor Anker gehen*

brink n.: to be on the ∾ of discovery *unmittelbar vor der Entdeckung stehen;* to be on the ∾ of the grave *am Rande des Grabes sein;* to shiver on the ∾ *zaudern, unschlüssig sein*

bristle I. v.i.: to ∾ with difficulties *von Schwierigkeiten strotzen.* — **II.** n.: to set up a person's ∾s *j.es Zorn erregen, ihn in die Wolle bringen*

Bristol n.pr.: everything was shipshape and ∾ fashion *alles war in bester Ordnung*

broad a.: it is as ∾ as it is long *es ist gehuppt (gehüpft) wie gesprungen, Jacke wie Hose;* in ∾ daylight *bei hellem Tageslicht;* a ∾ hint *ein Wink mit dem Zaunpfahl;* the teacher was ∾-minded *der Lehrer war großzügig (weitherzig, tolerant, liberal);* adv.: ∾ly speaking *im allgemeinen*

broomstick n.: to be married (to jump) over the ∾ *in wilder Ehe leben*

broth n.: too many cooks spoil the ∾ (prov.) *viele Köche verderben den Brei*

brow n.: his tastes are low-∾ *sein Geschmack ist etwas ungebildet, er liebt das Volkstümliche (in Musik, Kunst usw.);* she is very high∾ *sie hat einen auserlesenen Geschmack, gehört zur Intelligenz;* to knit (to wrinkle) one's ∾s *die Stirn runzeln;* to clear up one's ∾ *ein heiteres Gesicht machen*

brown I. a.: as ∾ as a berry *kaffeebraun;* to be in a ∾ study *in Nachdenken versunken sein;* I've been done ∾ (sl.) *ich bin beschwindelt worden.* — **II.** v.tr.: to be ∾ed-off (sl.) *es dicke (satt) haben, die Nase voll haben.* — **III.** n.: to fire into the ∾ *(Vogeljagd) blindlings in eine Menge schießen*

brunt n.: I had to bear the ∾ of it *ich mußte den Hauptstoß aushalten, ich hatte den schwersten Stand, ich litt am meisten darunter*

brush I. n.: a picture from the same ∾ *ein Gemälde desselben Malers;* to have a ∾ with an opponent *einen kurzen, scharfen Zusammenstoß mit einem Gegner haben.* — **II.** v.tr.: to ∾ aside (away) objections *Einwendungen ignorieren (beiseiteschieben, abtun);* I must ∾ up my English *ich muß meine englischen Kenntnisse auffrischen.* — **III.** v.i.: to ∾ (up) against a person *j.en streifen, zufällig auf j.en stoßen;* to ∾ by a person *an j.em vorbeieilen*

bubbly n. (sl.) a glas of ∾ *ein Glas Sekt*

buck¹ v.t. & i. (sl.): to ∾ a person up *j.en ermutigen;* ∾ up! *mach schnell! Kopf hoch!;* he ∾s against doing it *er sträubt sich dagegen, es zu tun*

buck² n. (sl.): to pass the ∾ *j.em die Verantwortung zuschieben; j.en anführen;* none of your ∾! *kein Widerwort! halt's Maul!*

bucket n.: a drop in the ∾ *ein Tropfen auf den heißen Stein;* to kick the ∾ (sl.) *sterben, eingehen, verrecken;* it's coming down ∾s (colloq.) *es gießt in Strömen, es regnet Bindfäden*

buckle I. v.tr.: to ∾ on (up) a thing *etwas an-, zuschnallen.* — II. v.i.: to ∾ to (down to) work *sich eifrig an die Arbeit machen;* we all ∾d to with a will *wir gaben (machten) uns alle eifrig daran*

buckram n.: men in ∾, ∾ men (1 Henry IV, II, 4, 210-50) *Männer, die nur in der Phantasie leben*

bud n.: to nip in the ∾ *im Keime ersticken*

buffer n. (sl.): he is an old ∾ *er ist ein alter Tropf (Trottel)*

bug n.: he is a big ∾ (sl.) *er ist ein großes (hohes) Tier*

bugger n. (low colloq.): he's a funny ∾ *er ist ein komischer Bursche;* it's a ∾ of a hard job *es ist eine verteufelt schwere Arbeit;* that's ∾ed it *da! jetzt ist es im Eimer;* well, I'm ∾ed! *ich bin platt!;* ∾ off! *marsch! fort!*

bulge n.: to have (to get) the ∾ on a person (sl.) *j.em gegenüber im Vorteil sein; j.en übervorteilen*

build-up n. (colloq.): to give a person a ∾ *j.em durch Propaganda einen wichtigen Anschein geben*

bulk I. n.: the ∾ of the things *der größere Teil, die Mehrzahl der Dinge;* in ∾; by the ∾ *lose, unverpackt; in Bausch und Bogen;* to break ∾ *die Ladung zu löschen anfangen;* to load a ship in ∾ *ein Schiff mit Stürzgütern beladen;* to sell in ∾ *in großen Mengen verkaufen.* — II. v.i.: hunting ∾s large in his tale *die Jagd hat eine große Bedeutung (spielt eine große Rolle) in seiner Erzählung;* it ∾s up to a considerable sum *es schwillt zu einer beträchtlichen Summe an.* — III. v.tr.: to ∾ fish *Fische aufhäufen;* to ∾ tea (Customs) *beim Zoll das Gewicht des Tees durch Ausleeren aus der Kiste feststellen*

bull I. n.: a ∾ in a china-shop *ein Elefant im Porzellanladen;* a cock-and-∾ story *ein Ammenmärchen;* to take the ∾ by the horns *den Stier bei den Hörnern fassen;* a ∾'s-eye *ein Bullauge; eine Blendlaterne; ein Pfefferminzbonbon; das Zentrum einer Schießscheibe;* a ∾ party *eine Herrenpartie;* to score a ∾'s-eye *ins Schwarze treffen, eine Zwölf schießen.* — II. v.tr.: to ∾ the market *auf Hausse spekulieren*

bulldoze v.tr.: to ∾ someone *j.en einschüchtern, terrorisieren*

bullet n.: to bite on the ∾ *in den sau(e)ren Apfel beißen;* to stop a ∾ *totgeschossen werden;* ∾-proof *kugelfest*

bully¹ I. n.: he tried to come the ∾ over me *er versuchte, mich einzuschüchtern, mich zu tyrannisieren.* — II. v.tr.: to ∾ a person into (out of) doing a thing *j.en durch Drohungen (Einschüchterung) dazu zwingen, etwas zu tun (nicht zu tun)*

bully² I. a. (U.S. & colonial): it was a ∾ affair *die Sache war prima, ganz groß.* — II. interj.: ∾ for you! *bravo! das hast du gut gemacht!*

bully³ n.: ∾; ∾ beef *gesalzenes Rindfleisch in Büchsen*

bum I. n. (colloq.): he is a ∾ *er ist ein liederlicher Mensch, ein berufsmäßiger Faulenzer;* to go on the ∾ *schmarotzen.* — II. a. (U.S. colloq.): it is a ∾ affair *es ist eine minderwertige Sache.* — III. v.i. (U.S. colloq.): to ∾ *herumlungern, faulenzen*

bump I. v.tr.: to ∾ one's head against (on) a wall *mit dem Kopf gegen eine Wand stoßen;* to get ∾ed off (U.S. sl.) *gewaltsam beseitigt (ermordet) werden.* — II. v.i.: I ∾ed against him *ich stieß gegen ihn.* — III. n.: to come down with a ∾ *hart auf den Boden aufschlagen; unsanft aus einem Traum (einer Illusion) gerissen werden; wie aus allen Wolken fallen;* to have the ∾ for a thing *die Begabung für eine Sache haben;* to have a ∾ of locality *Orts-, Orientierungssinn besitzen;* to make a ∾ *beim Bootsrennen in Oxford und Cambridge mit dem Bug gegen das Heck des voranfahrenden Bootes anstoßen (als Zeichen des Überholens).* — IV. adv.: I came (went) ∾ against him *ich stieß heftig mit ihm zusammen*

bumper n.: a ∾ *ein volles Glas;* a ∾ attendance *ein ungewöhnlich großer (starker) Besuch;* a ∾ crop, harvest *eine reiche Ernte, eine Rekordernte*

bunch n.: he is the best of the ∾ *er ist der beste von allen, das beste Pferd im Stall*

bundle I. v.tr.: to ∾ a person away (off, out) *j.en schnell weg-, hinausbefördern.* — **II.** v.i.: to ∾ off, out *sich packen, sich wegmachen.* — **III.** n.: a ∾ from heaven (colloq.) *ein neugeborenes Kind*

bungle v.tr.: to ∾ a thing *etwas verkorksen (vermasseln, versieben)*

bungler n.: he is a ∾ *er ist ein Pfuscher, Stümper*

bunk v.i. & n. (sl.): to ∾, to do a ∾ *fortlaufen, ausreißen;* that is all ∾ *das ist alles leeres Geschwätz*

bunkum n. = 'bunk'

burn I. v.tr.: to ∾ one's boats (bridges) behind one *alle Brücken hinter sich abbrechen;* to ∾ one's fingers *sich die Finger verbrennen;* to ∾ the candle at both ends *seine Kräfte unnütz verschwenden, mit ihnen aasen;* a ∾t child dreads the fire (prov.) *(ein) gebranntes Kind scheut das Feuer; durch Schaden wird man klug;* to ∾ daylight (Shakespeare, Romeo) *ein Licht bei Tage brennen lassen;* the money ∾s a hole in his pocket *das Geld brennt ihm in der Tasche;* to ∾ the midnight oil *bis in die tiefe Nacht hinein arbeiten (lesen);* to ∾ the water *Lachse bei Fackelschein stechen;* I have ∾t up the papers *ich habe die Papiere verbrannt.* — **II.** v.i.: he has money to ∾ *er hat Geld im Überfluß (wie Heu);* my ears are ∾ing *meine Ohren klingen;* he is ∾ing with eagerness to do it *er brennt darauf, es zu tun;* it is a ∾ing shame *es ist eine Sünde und Schande;* the fire ∾t up *das Feuer flammte auf, verbrannte gänzlich;* to make a ∾t offering *ein Opfer bringen.* — **III.** n.: he received serious ∾s *er erhielt schwere Brandwunden*

burst I. v.tr.: a river ∾s its banks *ein Fluß durchbricht seine Dämme, tritt über die Ufer;* to ∾ one's buttons with food *essen, daß die Knöpfe abreißen;* to ∾ one's sides with laughing *vor Lachen platzen;* to ∾ a door open *eine Tür aufsprengen, aufreißen.* — **II.** v.i.: to ∾ in *herein-, hineinplatzen;* to ∾ into flame, tears *in Flammen, in Tränen ausbrechen;* to ∾ out laughing *in Lachen ausbrechen;* he ∾ out with the remark *er platzte mit der Bemerkung heraus;* to ∾ with pride *vor Stolz platzen;* to ∾ up *explodieren, platzen.* — **III.** n.: a ∾ of applause *ein Beifallssturm;* a sudden ∾ of flame *ein plötzlicher Flammenausbruch;* a ∾ of thunder *ein Donnerschlag;* a ∾-up *ein Zusammenbruch*

bury v.tr.: to ∾ one's head in the sand *den Kopf in den Sand stecken, Vogelstraußpolitik machen*

bus n.: to go by ∾, to ∾ it *mit dem Omnibus fahren;* to miss the ∾ (sl.) *eine Gelegenheit verpassen;* to take a ∾man's holiday *seine Ferien bei der gewohnten Tätigkeit verbringen*

bush n.: to beat about the ∾ *wie eine Katze um den heißen Brei gehen;* good wine needs no ∾ (prov.) *gute Ware lobt sich selbst;* to take to the ∾ (Australia) *Buschklepper werden*

bushel n.: to hide one's light (candle) under a ∾ *sein Licht unter einen Scheffel stellen;* to measure another's corn by one's own ∾ *von sich auf andere schließen*

business n.: the ∾ end of a tin tack *die Spitze eines Nagels;* to combine ∾ with pleasure *das Angenehme mit dem Nützlichen verbinden;* to do (to settle) a person's ∾ *j.em den Hals brechen;* to get down to ∾ *zur Sache kommen;* good ∾! *gut gemacht! bravo!;* to do a good stroke of ∾ *ein gutes Geschäft machen;* to go out of ∾ *ein Geschäft aufgeben;* to make a great ∾ of a thing *viel Aufhebens von einer Sache machen; viel Getue (Sums, Theater) um eine Sache machen;* to make it one's own ∾ *es sich (dat.) angelegen sein lassen;* he means ∾ *er meint es ernst;* mind your own ∾, go about your ∾ *kümmere dich um deine Angelegenheiten!;* he has no ∾ to do so *er hat kein Recht, das zu tun;* he has no ∾ to be here *er hat hier nichts zu suchen;* it is no ∾ of yours, it is none of your ∾ *es geht dich nichts an;* it was quite a ∾ *es war unerwartet schwierig;* to run (to carry on) a ∾ *ein Geschäft betreiben (leiten);* to send a person about his ∾ *j.em heimleuchten, die Tür weisen;* I am sick of the whole ∾ *ich habe die ganze Sache satt*

bust I. (colloq.) v.i.: to ∾ (up) *explodieren, platzen, zusammenbrechen.* — **II.** n.: to go ∾ *bankrott (pleite) machen;* to go on the ∾ *eine Bierreise machen, sumpfen;* it came to a ∾-up between them *sie bekamen miteinander Krach*

busy I. a.: as ∾ as a bee *emsig wie eine Biene;* to be ∾ at work *eifrig bei der Arbeit sein;* he was ∾ packing *er war mit Packen beschäftigt, er packte eifrig;* to be ∾ with a thing *mit einer Sache beschäftigt sein;* he is a ∾body *er mischt sich in alles ein; er ist ein Geschaftlhuber, ein Hans Dampf in allen Gassen;* he is ∾ idle *er verschwendet seine Energie an Kleinigkeiten;* ∾ as a hen with one chick *lächerlich ängstlich und umständlich.* — **II.** v.tr.: to ∾ oneself about (at, in, with doing) a thing *sich mit etwas beschäftigen.* — **III.** n.: he is a ∾ (sl.) *er ist ein Detektiv*

but I. adv.: she is ∾ a child *sie ist nur ein Kind;* he all ∾ did it *er brachte es beinahe fertig;* I can ∾ try *mehr als es versuchen, kann ich nicht;* it was ∾ yesterday *es war erst gestern.* — **II.** prep.: no man ∾ a fool could say so *nur ein Narr könnte das sagen;* no one ∾ me *keiner außer mir;* the last ∾ one *der vorletzte;* nothing ∾ patience *nichts als Geduld, nur Geduld.* — **III.** conj.: ten to one ∾ it was you *ich wette zehn gegen eins, daß du es warst;* what can he do ∾ confess? *was bleibt ihm anders übrig als einzugestehen?;* I cannot ∾ do it *ich kann nicht umhin, es zu tun;* it shall go hard ∾ I will get there *es müßte verteufelt zugehen, wenn ich nicht dorthin käme;* no one ∾ knows that it was so *jeder weiß, daß es so war;* no one ∾ I noticed it *keiner außer mir bemerkte es;* it never rains ∾ it pours (prov.) *ein Unglück kommt selten allein;* I don't deny (doubt) ∾ that it is so *ich leugne (zweifle) nicht, daß es so ist;* he is not such a fool ∾ (∾ that, ∾ what) he can see that *er ist nicht so töricht, daß er das nicht einsehen könnte;* I could never have done it ∾ for that *ich hätte es nicht tun können, wenn das nicht gewesen wäre;* it is hot, no doubt, ∾ then the heat is dry *es ist zweifellos heiß, aber andrerseits ist die Hitze trocken.* — **IV.** v.tr. & n.: ∾ me no ∾s *komm mir nicht mit deinem Aber*

butt[1] the ∾ of a cigar *der Zigarrenstummel;* the ∾-end *das dickere Ende; das Überbleibsel;* the ∾ of a rifle *der Gewehrkolben*

butt[2] n.: to be the ∾ of ridicule *Zielscheibe des Spottes sein*

butt[3] **I.** n.: to come full ∾ against a thing *heftig mit etwas zusammenstoßen.* — **II.** v.i.: excuse my ∾ing in *entschuldige, wenn ich mich einmische*

butter I. n.: he looks as if ∾ would not melt in his mouth *er sieht aus, als ob er kein Wässerchen trüben könnte;* you ∾-fingers! *du Taps, du läßt alles fallen!;* for other phrases see 'bread' *andere Wendungen unter 'bread'.* — **II.** v.tr.: fair words ∾ no parsnips (prov.) *Redensarten sind billig, schöne Worte machen den Kohl nicht fett;* to ∾ up *schmeicheln*

butterfly n.: to break a ∾ (to break butterflies) on the wheel *mit Kanonen nach Spatzen schießen*

button I. n.: as bright as a ∾ *blitzblank;* a boy in ∾s, a ∾s *ein Page, Diener in Livree;* he is a ∾ short (sl.) *bei ihm ist eine Schraube los;* to take a person by the ∾, to ∾hole a person *j.en beim Knopf halten, zum Zuhören zwingen, ihn sich (dat.) vorknöpfen;* you only need touch (press) the ∾, and the thing is done *du brauchst bloß auf den Knopf zu drücken, und die Sache ist gemacht.* — **II.** v.tr.: to ∾ up one's coat *den Rock zuknöpfen;* to ∾ up one's mouth *Stillschweigen bewahren.* — **III.** v.i.: the garment ∾s up on the left *das Kleidungsstück wird links geknöpft*

buy v.tr.: I'll ∾ it *ich gebe es auf, ich weiß es nicht (als Antwort auf Rätsel);* to ∾ a pig in a poke, see 'pig'; to ∾ off *loskaufen;* to ∾ someone out *j.en abfinden;* to ∾ someone over *j.en bestechen;* to ∾ up *aufkaufen*

buzz v.i.: ∾ off! (sl.) *hau ab! verdufte!*

by I. prep.: to come ∾ the nearest way *auf dem kürzesten Wege kommen;* he stood ∾ me *er stand mir bei;* close, hard ∾ *dicht, nahe bei;* to abide ∾ a decision *sich mit einer Entscheidung abfinden;* how did you come ∾ that? *wie bist du daran gekommen?;* ∾ oneself *allein;* ∾ the ∾, ∾ the way *nebenbei bemerkt;* to pass someone ∾ *an j.em vorbeigehen;* ∾ day *bei Tage;* to know ∾ heart *auswendig kennen;* to multiply, to divide ∾ 3 *mit 3 multiplizieren, durch 3 dividieren;* to lead ∾ the hand *an der Hand führen;* to set two people ∾ the ears *zwei Leute zum Streit aufhetzen;* side ∾ side *Seite an Seite;* to go (to be known) ∾ the name of Smith *Schmidt mit Namen;* to travel ∾ rail *mit der Bahn fahren;* ∾ all means *ja sicher, freilich;* ∾ no means *keineswegs;* ∾ birth *von Geburt;* ∾ blood *der Abstammung nach;* to live ∾ bread alone *von Brot allein leben;* his son ∾ his first wife *sein Sohn aus erster Ehe;* to begin, to end ∾ *beginnen, enden mit;* ∾ way of a joke *zum Scherz;* he is ∾ way of knowing everybody *er soll (angeblich) alle Welt kennen;* he is suspicious ∾ nature *er ist von Natur argwöhnisch;* ∾ chance *durch Zufall;* ∾ means of (∾ dint of) hard work *mittels schwerer Arbeit;* ∾ that time, ∾ then *bis dahin;* ∾ next week *bis spätestens nächste Woche;* ∾ now *mittlerweile, jetzt schon;* ∾ rights *von rechtswegen;* ∾ your leave *mit deiner Erlaubnis;* to judge ∾ appearances *nach dem Äußeren zu urteilen;* to sell ∾ the pound *pfundweise verkaufen;* ∾ the hour *stundenweise;* ∾ degrees, little ∾ little *allmählich;* to miss ∾ an inch *um einen Zoll verfehlen;* I did my duty ∾ him *ich habe meine Pflicht an ihm getan;* to swear ∾ vegetarianism *auf Pflanzenkost schwören.* — **II.** adv.: all that is gone ∾ *das ist alles vorbei;* to stand ∾ (for action) (Naut.) *sich bereithalten;* to put (to lay, to set) money ∾ *Geld (auf)sparen, beiseite legen;* taken ∾ and large *im großen und ganzen genommen*

by and by adv.: *später, nachher*

by-gone n.: let ∾s be ∾s *laß die Vergangenheit ruhen! Schwamm drüber! Strich darunter!*

by-word n.: to become a ∾ *ein warnendes Beispiel werden*

C

caboodle n. (sl.): the whole ∾ *die ganze Gesellschaft (Blase), der ganze Kram (Krempel, Salat)*

cackle n.: cut the ∾ (sl.) *hör auf mit dem Geschwätz!*

Caesar n.pr.: ∾'s wife *eine Person, die über jeden Verdacht erhaben sein sollte*

cagey a. (colloq.): a ∾ person *eine vorsichtige Person, die sich nichts vormachen läßt*

Cain n.pr.: to raise ∾ about a thing *wegen einer Sache einen Höllenlärm machen, gehörig Krach schlagen*

cake n.: a ∾ of soap *ein Stück Seife;* it is not all ∾s and ale *es ist nicht alles eitel Lust und Freude;* the land of ∾s *Schottland;* you can't eat your ∾ and have it (prov.) *man kann nicht zwei entgegengesetzte Sachen zugleich genießen; entweder — oder;* they sold like hot ∾s *sie gingen ab wie warme Semmeln;* that takes the ∾ (colloq.) *das übertrifft alles, das ist die Höhe!;* to get one's share of the ∾ *Erfolg haben*

calf n.: the cow is in (or: with) ∾ *die Kuh ist trächtig;* to eat the ∾ in the cow's belly *voreilig etwas annehmen, zu früh frohlocken;* to kill the fatted ∾ (Luke, IV, 23) *einen Festschmaus geben;* to slip the ∾ *zu früh kalben;* ∾-love *erste Neigung zwischen unreifen jungen Menschen*

call I. v.tr.: see 'account, attention, banns, etc.'; for many be ∾ed, but few chosen (Matthew, XX, 16) *denn viele sind berufen, aber wenige sind auserwählt;* to ∾ someone's bluff *j.en stellen, in die Enge treiben;* to ∾ a person names *j.en beschimpfen;* ∾ yourself a man! *das nennt sich ein Mann!;* not a moment to ∾ one's own *keinen Augenblick für sich;* I can't ∾ my soul my own *ich habe nicht die geringste Freiheit;* to ∾ someone over the coals *j.en zur Rechenschaft ziehen;* a much ∾ed-for commodity *eine vielbegehrte Sache;* that remark was not ∾ed for *das war eine unpassende (unnötige) Bemerkung;* — with adv.: to ∾ a person aside, away *j.en beiseiterufen; ab-, wegrufen;* to ∾ a person down (U.S.) *j.en tadeln;* to ∾ forth *hervorrufen;* to ∾ in silver coins *Silbermünzen einziehen;* to ∾ in a mortgage *eine Hypothek kündigen;* the match was ∾ed off *das Wettspiel wurde abgesagt (abgeblasen);* let's ∾ it square *laßt uns die Sache als erledigt betrachten;* when were you ∾ed up? *wann wurdest du zum Heeresdienst eingezogen?;* that ∾s up former times *das erinnert mich an frühere Zeiten.* — **II.** v.i.: did anybody ∾ in my absence? *ist j. während meiner Abwesenheit hier gewesen?* — with prep. & adv.: a ship ∾s at a port *ein Schiff läuft einen Hafen an;* that ∾s for strict measures *das verlangt strenge Maßnahmen;* the parcel will be ∾ed for *das Paket wird abgeholt werden;* to ∾ (in) on a person *bei j.em vorsprechen, j.em einen Besuch abstatten (machen);* to ∾ on a person to do a thing *j.en auffordern, etwas zu tun;* I feel ∾ed (up) on to do so *ich fühle mich verpflichtet, es zu tun;* to ∾ out for help *um Hilfe schreien;* to ∾ to a person *j.em zurufen.* —

III. n.: whose ∾ is it? *wer muß bieten (reizen)? (Bridgespiel)*; a house of ∾ *ein Absteigequartier;* there is no ∾ to blush *es liegt keine Veranlassung vor zu erröten;* there is no ∾ for straw hats *es ist (besteht) keine Nachfrage nach Strohhüten;* to be within ∾ *in Rufweite sein;* to feel (to hear) a ∾ *eine innere Berufung erleben;* to give a person a ∾ *j.en telef. anrufen;* he has no ∾ upon my time *er hat kein Anrecht auf meine Zeit;* to have the first ∾ on something *das Vorrecht auf etwas haben;* to make (to pay) a ∾ on a person *j.em einen kurzen Besuch abstatten (machen);* the actor took many ∾s *der Schauspieler hatte viele Vorhänge;* the ∾-over *(Schule) Verlesung der Namensliste*

calm a.: it's pretty ∾ of him (colloq.) *es ist unverschämt von ihm*

camel n.: to swallow a ∾ (Matthew, XXIII, 24) *etwas Unglaubliches schlucken;* it is the last straw that breaks the ∾'s back *noch ein Tropfen, und das Glas (Faß) fließt über; eine Vollbelastung kann keine weitere (wenn auch nur kleine) Belastung mehr ertragen (vertragen)*

camouflage v.tr.: to ∾ a thing *etwas tarnen*

camp I. n.: to break (to strike) ∾ *das Lager abschlagen;* to pitch a ∾ *ein Lager aufschlagen;* a ∾-bed *ein Feldbett;* a ∾-follower *ein Schlachtenbummler;* a ∾-stool *ein Klappstuhl.* — **II.** v.i.: to ∾ *zelten, kampieren*

campaigner n.: an old ∾ *ein Veteran; ein alter Praktikus; ein alter Fuhrmann*

can I. v.tr.: ∾ it (sl.) *halt's Maul! halt' den Rand!;* he is ∾ned (sl.) *er ist besoffen;* eat what you can and ∾ what you can't *iß, was du kannst, und mache ein, was du nicht essen kannst;* ∾ned music *Musik von Platten oder Bandaufnahmen.* — **II.** n.: I must carry the ∾ (sl.) *ich muß die Sache ausbaden;* to put in the ∾ (sl.) *ins Gefängnis werfen, einlochen;* to be in the ∾ (colloq.) *gebrauchsfertig sein*

candle n.: the ∾s were alight *die Kerzen brannten;* to burn the ∾ at both ends *spät aufbleiben und sehr früh aufstehen, zu wenig schlafen; mit der Gesundheit (seinen Kräften) aasen;* to curse a person with bell, book, and ∾, see 'bell'; to hide one's ∾ under a bushel *sein Licht unter einen Scheffel stellen;* to hold the ∾ to the devil *dem Teufel das Pferd satteln;* he can't (is not fit to) hold a ∾ to him *er kann ihm nicht das Wasser reichen;* to hold a ∾ to the sun *etwas Überflüssiges tun;* to sell by inch of ∾ *versteigern, wobei das letzte Angebot vor Erlöschen der Kerze den Zuschlag erhält;* the game is not worth the ∾ *die Sache lohnt nicht;* ∾-ends *wertlose Brocken*

canoe n.: to paddle one's own ∾ *sich aus eigener Kraft durchs Leben schlagen*

canter n.: to win in a ∾ *im Handgalopp gewinnen*

cap I. n.: with ∾ in hand *demütig, bescheiden, „mit dem Hute in der Hand (kommt man durch das ganze Land)“;* if the ∾ fits, put it on (wear it) (prov.) *wem der Schuh paßt, der ziehe ihn an; wen es juckt, der kratze sich; wenn eine auf andere gemünzte Kritik auch auf dich selbst paßt, so richte dich nach ihr;* she sets her ∾ at him *sie versucht, ihn zu angeln;* to throw one's ∾ over the windmill *jede Vorsicht (Vernunft) außer Acht lassen.* — **II.** v.tr.: to ∾ the climax (the globe) *alles Bisherige übertreffen;* to ∾ a person *vor j.em die Mütze ziehen;* I can ∾ that story *ich kann eine bessere Geschichte erzählen;* to ∾ verses *um die Wette Verse hersagen unter Berücksichtigung gewisser Vorschriften bezüglich Anfangsbuchstabe, Endreim usw.*

caper n.: to cut a ∾ *einen Luftsprung machen*

capful n.: a ∾ of wind *eine vorübergehende Brise*

capital I. a.: that's ∾ *das ist großartig (famos, prima);* we had some ∾ fun *wir amüsierten uns köstlich;* the ∾ sentence *das Todesurteil, die Todesstrafe.* — **II.** n.: to make ∾ out of a thing *aus etwas Kapital schlagen*

captain n.: a led ∾ *ein Schmeichler, Schmarotzer*

card n.: that is the ∾! *das ist das Richtige! so ist's richtig! das ist die Masche!;* it is on the ∾s *es ist wahrscheinlich, möglich;* he is a knowing ∾ (colloq.) *er ist ein Schlauberger;* to have a ∾ up one's sleeve *etwas in Reserve haben, noch einen Trumpf in der Hand haben;* to shuffle, to make (to cut, to deal) the ∾s *die Kar-*

ten mischen (abheben, austeilen); to throw up (or: in) one's ∾s *das Spiel verloren geben;* to speak by the ∾ (Hamlet, V, 1) *nach der Schnur sprechen (Schlegel); sich deutlich ausdrücken, es genau mit seinen Worten nehmen*

care I. n.: ∾ of (abbr. c/o) *per Adresse;* ∾ killed the cat (prov.), see 'cat'; that shall be my ∾ *das laß meine Sorge sein;* to take (to have a) ∾ *vorsichtig sein, sich vorsehen;* to take (to have the) ∾ of a thing *für etwas Sorge tragen, achtgeben auf etwas;* take ∾ of the pence and the pounds will take ∾ of themselves (prov.) *wer den Pfennig nicht ehrt, ist des Talers nicht wert;* he is well taken ∾ of *für ihn wird gut gesorgt;* to put in a ∾-taker *einen Verwalter einsetzen.* — **II.** v.tr.: I couldn't ∾ less (sl.) *das ist mir (doch) Wurst (Wurscht, ganz schnuppe);* I don't ∾ a damn (a doit, a farthing, two hoots, a pin, a straw, two straws) *ich mache mir nicht die Bohne (ich mache mir einen Dreck) daraus.* — **III.** v.i.: I don't ∾ *es ist mir einerlei; meinetwegen;* what do I ∾? *was kümmert es mich? was frage ich danach?;* for all you ∾ *was du dir schon daraus machst; wenn es nach dir ginge; deinetwegen;* I don't ∾ about going there *ich habe keine Lust, dahin zu gehen;* she doesn't ∾ for him *sie mag ihn nicht, hat nichts für ihn übrig;* the children are well ∾d for *die Kinder sind gut aufgehoben (versorgt);* I should not ∾ to be seen with him *ich möchte nicht mit ihm gesehen werden;* do you ∾ to try them? *möchtest du sie versuchen?;* I'm past caring about it now *jetzt bin ich soweit, daß es mir nichts ausmacht*

carpet n.: the matter is on the ∾ *die Sache steht auf dem Tapet, sie wird erörtert*

carriage n.: a ∾ and four *ein Vierspänner*

carry I. v.tr.: to ∾ all before one *auf der ganzen Linie siegen, einen überwältigenden Erfolg haben;* the speaker carried the audience with him *der Redner riß die Zuhörer mit fort;* to ∾ the battery at the point of the bayonet *die Batterie mit dem Bajonett erstürmen;* I must ∾ the baby (the can) (sl.) *ich muß die Sache ausbaden;* she carries herself well *sie hat eine gute Haltung;* to ∾ coals to Newcastle *Eulen nach Athen tragen;* his arguments ∾ conviction (weight) *seine Argumente wirken überzeugend;* to ∾ the day *den Sieg davontragen;* to ∾ a thing into effect, to excess, into execution, see 'effect, excess, execution'; to ∾ the joke too far *den Scherz zu weit treiben;* these provisions will ∾ me over Sunday *diese Lebensmittel reichen für mich über Sonntag;* to ∾ a motion, one's point, all sail, see 'motion, point, sail'; five and ∾ one *fünf hin und eins im Sinn (beim Addieren).* — with adv.: to ∾ about, along, see 'about, along'; to let oneself be carried away *sich fortreißen lassen;* that carries me back *das erinnert mich an frühere Zeiten;* to ∾ an item forward *einen Posten vortragen, übertragen;* she was carried off her feet *sie ließ sich hinreißen;* to be carried off by an illness *von einer Krankheit hingerafft werden;* they carried it off well *sie haben sich tapfer gehalten;* he is ∾ing on his father's business *er führt das väterliche Geschäft fort;* he carried on a long conversation *er führte eine lange Unterhaltung;* to ∾ out (through) a plan *einen Plan aus-, durchführen.* — **II.** v.i.: the sound carries many miles *man kann es meilenweit hören;* to fetch and ∾ *niedrige Arbeiten verrichten;* this pistol does not ∾ far *diese Pistole trägt nicht weit;* ∾ on! (colloq.) *mach' weiter! fahr' fort!;* don't ∾ on so (colloq.) *gehab' dich nicht so!;* he is ∾ing on with a girl *er hat ein Verhältnis mit einem Mädel;* this fruit will not ∾ well *dieses Obst wird unter dem Transport leiden*

cart I. n.: to put the ∾ before the horse *das Pferd beim Schwanze aufzäumen, etwas verkehrt anfangen;* to be in the ∾ (the soup) (sl.) *in Gefahr (in Schwierigkeiten) sein.* — **II.** v.tr.: to ∾ a thing about with one *etwas mit sich herumschleppen*

case n.: here is a ∾ in point *hier ist ein ganz ähnlicher Fall, ein typisches Beispiel;* it's a ∾ of who will hold out longest *es kommt darauf an, wer am längsten aushält;* just as the ∾ may be. *je nach den Umständen;* such is the ∾ with us *so steht es mit uns;* in any ∾ *auf jeden Fall;* to call a ∾ *einen Fall bei Gericht aufrufen;* to give the ∾ for (against) a person *für (gegen) j.en entscheiden;* to make out one's ∾ *seinen Fall (seine Sache) begründen, beweisen; sich zu verteidigen wissen*

cash I. n.: ∾ on delivery (abbr. C.O.D.) *gegen Nachnahme;* I am out of (short of)

∾ *ich habe kein Geld, ich bin knapp bei Kasse;* he is rolling in ∾ (colloq.) *er ist stinkreich;* to sell ∾ down *gegen Barzahlung verkaufen.* — **II.** a.: ∾-price *Barpreis (Preis bei Barzahlung).* — **III.** v.tr.: to ∾ a cheque *einen Scheck einwechseln;* to ∾ in one's checks (poker phrase) *sterben.* — **IV.** v.i.: to ∾ in on a thing (sl.) *aus einer Sache Nutzen ziehen (profitieren)*

cast I. v.tr.: to ∾ a column of figures *eine Zahlenreihe addieren;* to ∾ dust in somebody's eyes *j.em Sand in die Augen streuen;* to ∾ an eye on something *ein Auge auf etwas werfen (es betrachten, ansehen);* to ∾ a horoscope *ein Horoskop stellen;* to be ∾ in the same mould *aus demselben Holz geschnitzt sein;* the tree ∾s a shadow *der Baum wirft einen Schatten;* the horse ∾ a shoe *das Pferd verlor ein Hufeisen;* a snake ∾s its skin *eine Schlange häutet sich;* to ∾ a spell on a person *j.en behexen, bezaubern;* to ∾ a statue *eine Statue (Figur) gießen;* he ∾ it in my teeth *er hat mir einen Vorwurf daraus gemacht;* to ∾ a vote *eine Stimme abgeben;* the ∾ing vote *die entscheidende, ausschlaggebende Stimme;* to ∾ away *weg-, verwerfen;* a ∾away *ein Schiffbrüchiger;* to be ∾ down *niedergeschlagen, in schlechter Stimmung sein;* to ∾ off *abwerfen; verstoßen; beim Stricken Maschen abnehmen;* to ∾ in one's lot with a person *mit j.em das Schicksal teilen, gemeinsame Sache machen;* to ∾ up *in die Höhe werfen; durch Erbrechen von sich geben; zusammenrechnen.* — **II.** v.i.: to ∾ about for (how to do) a thing *umhersuchen, sich nach etwas umsehen; Mittel und Wege suchen, etwas zu tun;* to ∾ back to *zurückgehen, -greifen auf;* to ∾ loose from *sich loslösen von.* — **III.** n.: he has a ∾ in his (the) eye *er schielt etwas;* a ∾ of mind *eine Geistesart;* the ∾ of a play *die Rollenbesetzung eines Stückes*

caste n.: to lose ∾ *gesellschaftlich herabsinken;* a half-∾ *ein Mischling*

castle n.: an Englishman's house is his ∾ (prov.) *eines Engländers Haus ist seine Burg, d. h. niemand darf gewaltsam eindringen;* to build ∾s in the air, in Spain *Luftschlösser bauen*

cat n.: at night all ∾s are grey (prov.) *nachts sind alle Katzen grau; Schönes kann man nur bei Tageslicht sehen und von Häßlichem unterscheiden;* a ∾ may look at a king (prov.) *sieht doch die Katz' den Kaiser an (als Erwiderung auf die Frage einer hochmütigen Person, warum man sie ansehe);* a tame ∾ *eine gutmütige Person, die stets zu persönlichen Diensten bereit ist;* he is a ∾-burglar *er ist ein Fassadenkletterer;* the ∾-o'-nine-tails *die neunschwänzige Katze;* when the ∾ is away the mice will play (prov.) *wenn die Katze nicht zu Hause ist, tanzen die Mäuse über Tische und Bänke;* it is enough to make a ∾ laugh *man könnte sich einen Ast lachen;* to bell the ∾ *der Katze die Schelle umhängen; eine Sache harmlos machen;* to fight like Kilkenny ∾s *bis zur Vernichtung kämpfen;* to grin like a Cheshire ∾ *ständig und sinnlos grinsen;* care killed the ∾ (prov.) *vor Sorgen ist die Katze trotz ihres zähen Lebens umgekommen, d. h. mach' dir nichts daraus, sei fröhlich;* to lead a ∾-and-dog life *wie Hund und Katze (zusammen) leben;* to let the ∾ out of the bag *ein Geheimnis ausplappern, die Katze aus dem Sack lassen;* a ∾-nap *ein Nickerchen (Schläfchen) im Sitzen;* to play ∾'s-cradle *Fadenabnehmen spielen;* it is raining ∾s and dogs *es regnet Bindfäden (gießt in Strömen);* to shoot the ∾, to ∾ (sl.) *sich übergeben, kotzen;* to skin the ∾ (gym.) *den Kreuzaufzug machen;* there is no room to swing a ∾ *man kann sich hier kaum umdrehen;* to turn ∾ in pan *zur Gegenpartei übergehen;* like a ∾ on hot bricks *wie auf glühenden Kohlen, wie eine aufgeregte Glucke;* to wait for the ∾ to jump; to see which way the ∾ jumps; to follow the cult of the jumping ∾ *sehen, wie der Hase läuft;* to whip the ∾ (sl.) *sich betrinken; blauen Montag machen; knickerig sein; einen Schabernack spielen; als Schneider im Hause der Kundschaft arbeiten; alle Stiche beim Whist machen;* to use a person as a ∾'s-paw, to make a ∾'s-paw of a person *sich (dat.) von einem anderen die Kastanien aus dem Feuer holen lassen*

catch I. v.tr.: see 'attention, breath, cold, death, etc.'; to ∾ someone bending (napping) *durch die Unaufmerksamkeit des anderen einen Vorteil gewinnen;* to ∾ the Speaker's eye *im Unterhaus das Wort erhalten;* to ∾ one's finger in the door *sich (dat.) den Finger in der Tür klemmen;* to ∾ one's foot in a trap *mit dem Fuß in einer Falle hängen bleiben;* you will ∾ it when you come home *es setzt was, wenn du nach Hause kommst;* you will ∾ him at home *du triffst ihn noch zu Hause an;* ∾ me doing that *du kannst lange warten, bis ich das tue;* did you ∾ your train? *hast du deinen Zug noch erreicht?;* I did not ∾ a word *ich habe kein Wort mitbekommen (verstanden);* to ∾ a person out, to ∾ him in the act; to ∾ him red-handed *j.en bei einem Fehler, einem Unrecht ertappen, erwischen;* he caught up his bundle *er raffte sein Bündel auf;* to ∾ a person up, to ∾ up with a person *j.en einholen;* to ∾ up a habit *eine Gewohnheit annehmen;* to ∾ up the speaker *den Redner unterbrechen.* — **II.** v.i.: a ∾-as-∾-can wrestling bout *ein Ringkampf, bei dem alle Griffe erlaubt sind;* the bolt will not ∾ *der Riegel hält nicht;* the hind-wheel caught against the curbstone *das Hinterrad stieß gegen den Prellstein;* to ∾ at a straw *nach einem Strohhalm greifen;* her foot caught in her train *ihr Fuß verfing sich in ihrer Schleppe;* I don't quite ∾ on *ich verstehe nicht ganz, ich komme nicht ganz mit;* the tune caught on *die Melodie fand Anklang (schlug ein);* my coat caught on a nail *ich blieb mit dem Rock an einem Nagel hängen;* to ∾ up (on) to a thing *an etwas herankommen;* a ∾-word *ein Schlagwort.* — **III.** n.: it is only a ∾ *es ist nur eine Falle;* there is a ∾ in it *da steckt etwas dahinter, die Sache hat einen Haken;* there was a ∾ in his voice *seine Stimme stockte;* he is a good (or: safe) ∾ *er fängt Bälle gut; er ist ein Gewinn;* it is no ∾ *es ist ein schlechtes Geschäft;* she is no great ∾ *sie ist keine gute Partie.* — **IV.** a.: ∾-penny *etwas, das einem die Groschen aus der Tasche lockt*

cause I. n.: to fight for a good (just) ∾ *für eine gute (gerechte) Sache kämpfen;* to gain one's ∾ *obsiegen;* to give ∾ for (to do) a thing *zu etwas Anlaß geben;* to make common ∾ with a person *mit j.em gemeinsame Sache machen;* to plead a ∾ in court *eine Sache vor Gericht vertreten;* to show ∾ for a thing *die Gründe (Motive) für etwas angeben.* — **II.** v.tr.: to ∾ a disturbance *eine Störung verursachen;* to ∾ a person trouble *j.em Schwierigkeiten (Unannehmlichkeiten) bereiten;* to ∾ a person to do a thing *j.en veranlassen, etwas zu tun;* they ∾d him to be killed *sie ließen ihn töten*

caution I. n.: he is a ∾ (sl.) *er ist ein seltsamer, ulkiger Kerl;* to deposit ∾ money *eine Kaution hinterlegen;* he was dismissed with a ∾ *er wurde mit einer Verwarnung entlassen.* — **II.** v.tr.: to ∾ a person against doing a thing *j.en vor etwas warnen*

caviar(e) n.: ∾ to the general (Hamlet II, 2) *Kaviar fürs Volk*

cavil v.i.: to ∾ at (about) a thing *an etwas herumnörgeln*

ceiling n.: to hit the ∾ (sl.) *sehr böse werden, hochgehen;* the ∾-price *der Höchstpreis (der höchste Preis, der verlangt werden kann)*

centre I. n.: the ∾ of attraction *der Hauptanziehungspunkt;* the ∾ of gravity *der Schwerpunkt;* to come to a dead ∾ *auf (an) einen toten Punkt kommen.* — **II.** a.: to play ∾ forward *Mittelstürmer spielen.* — **III.** v.tr. & i.: to be ∾d, to ∾ (in, on, at, round, about) a thing *sich (in, auf, um, etwas) konzentrieren*

ceremony n.: no ∾! *keine Umstände! tun Sie sich keinen Zwang an!;* to stand upon ∾ *auf konventionelle Formen bestehen; Distanz wahren; sich zieren*

cert n. (sl.): it's a dead ∾ *es ist eine todsichere (bombensichere) Sache*

certain a.: a lady of a ∾ age *eine Dame gewissen Alters;* a ∾ cure for a thing *ein unfehlbares Heilmittel für (gegen) etwas;* a ∾ Jack Smith *ein gewisser Hans Schmidt;* to be (to feel) ∾ of a thing *einer Sache sicher sein, von etwas fest überzeugt sein;* it is ∾ to happen *es tritt bestimmt ein;* I do not know for ∾ *ich weiß nicht bestimmt (sicher);* under ∾ circumstances *unter (gewissen) Umständen;* to make ∾ of a thing *sich (dat.) etwas sichern, sich einer Sache vergewissern;* to take a thing as ∾ *etwas fest annehmen*

certainty n.: to (for) a ∾ *ganz bestimmt, ganz gewiß;* to bet on a ∾ *auf eine sichere Sache setzen (gewöhnlich unehrlich, mit geheimer Kenntnis des Ausgangs)*

chaff I. n.: he is not to be caught with ∾ *er läßt sich nicht auf den Leim locken.* — **II.** v.tr.: he was ∾ed about his hair *er wurde wegen seines Haares aufgezogen*

chair n.: to address the ∾ *sich an den Vorsitzenden wenden;* to leave the ∾ *die Sitzung schließen;* to take the ∾ *den Vor-*

sitz übernehmen, die Sitzung eröffnen; please take a ∾ *bitte nehmen Sie Platz;* the ∾ (Amer.) *der elektrische (Hinrichtungs-) Stuhl*

chalk I. n.: as like as ∾ and cheese *grundverschieden, ein Unterschied wie Tag und Nacht;* not by a long ∾ *noch lange nicht, bei weitem nicht;* to walk the ∾ *auf dem Kreidestrich gehen können, nüchtern sein.* — **II.** v.tr.: to ∾ it up for him *ihm Kredit geben, es ihm ankreiden*

chance I. n.: it is a ∾ to see Brussels *es ist eine gute Gelegenheit, Brüssel zu sehen;* by ∾ *zufällig, von ungefähr;* an even ∾ *ebensoviel Aussichten;* it was a happy ∾ *es war ein Glück;* a mere ∾ *ein reiner Zufall;* the ∾s are against it *die Wahrscheinlichkeit spricht dagegen;* the doctrine of ∾s *die Wahrscheinlichkeitsrechnung;* to look to (to have an eye to) the main ∾ *auf eigenen Vorteil bedacht sein;* a game of ∾ *ein Glücksspiel;* on the ∾ that *für den Fall, im Falle daß;* to go there on the ∾ of meeting him *hingehen auf gut Glück, daß man ihn trifft, in der leisen Hoffnung, ihn zu treffen;* to give a person a ∾ *es einmal versuchen mit j.em;* to leave to ∾ *dem Zufall überlassen;* he stands a good (or: fair) ∾ of getting it *er hat gute Aussichten, es zu bekommen;* I shall take my ∾ *ich lasse es darauf ankommen;* to take the best ∾ going *die beste Gelegenheit wahrnehmen, die sich bietet;* to take no ∾s with a thing *sich nicht den Gefahren einer Sache aussetzen.* — **II.** v.i.: it ∾d that *es traf zufällig zu;* he ∾d to do it *er tat es zufällig;* to ∾ upon a person, a thing *zufällig auf j.en, eine Sache stoßen.* — **III.** v.tr.: I'll ∾ my arm, I'll ∾ it (colloq.) *ich wage, riskiere es.* — **IV.** a.: a ∾ comer *ein unerwartet Kommender*

chancery n.: to be in ∾ (colloq.) *beim Boxkampf mit dem Kopf unter dem Arm des Gegners eingeklemmt sein; im Schwitzkasten sein*

change I. v.tr.: to ∾ one's condition *heiraten;* to ∾ hands *den Besitzer wechseln;* to ∾ one's mind (foot) *seine Ansicht (Meinung) ändern; sich anders besinnen, es sich (dat.) anders überlegen;* to ∾ one's note (tune) *einen anderen Ton anschlagen;* let us ∾ the subject *reden wir von etwas anderem;* to ∾ water into wine *Wasser in Wein verwandeln;* I should not like to ∾ places with him *ich möchte nicht mit ihm tauschen.* — **II.** v.i.: All ∾! *alle(s) umsteigen!;* you must ∾ at N. *du mußt in N. umsteigen;* I must go and ∾ *ich muß mich umziehen gehen;* to chop and ∾ *hin- und herschwanken, unentschlossen sein;* she has ∾d lately *sie hat sich in der letzten Zeit verändert (geändert).* — **III.** n.: to do something for a ∾ *etwas zur Abwechslung tun;* I could get no ∾ out of him *ich konnte ihn nicht übervorteilen;* you did not give me the right ∾ *du hast mir nicht richtig herausgegeben;* I have no ∾ about me *ich habe kein Kleingeld bei mir;* to ring the ∾s on a subject *ein Thema in der mannigfachsten Weise behandeln, dieselbe Sache in immer neuen Formen behandeln;* to take one's ∾ (the ∾) out of a person *sich an j.em rächen*

chapter n.: the ∾ of accidents *der unvorhergesehene Verlauf der Ereignisse;* to the end of the ∾ *bis ans Ende, in alle Ewigkeit;* to give ∾ and verse for a thing *etwas genau belegen*

character n.: in ∾ with *in Übereinstimmung, im Einklang mit;* out of ∾ *im Widerspruch, unvereinbar, unpassend;* to act out of ∾ *aus der Rolle fallen;* to appear in the ∾ of Hamlet *in der Rolle des Hamlet auftreten;* to give a person a ∾ *j.em ein Zeugnis ausstellen;* he's a ∾ *er ist spleenig (exzentrisch, wunderlich, ein Original)*

charge I. n.: at his own ∾ *auf seine eigenen Kosten;* no ∾, free of ∾ *kostenlos;* petty ∾s *Spesen;* to make a ∾ for something *etwas berechnen;* a teacher was in ∾ of the children *ein Lehrer hatte die Aufsicht über die Kinder;* the children were in ∾ of a teacher *die Kinder waren in der Obhut eines Lehrers;* to give a person in ∾ *j.en der Polizei übergeben;* to lay a crime to a person's ∾ *j.en eines Verbrechens beschuldigen;* to return to the ∾ *von neuem versuchen; ein Argument wiederaufnehmen;* to take ∾ of a thing *die Aufsicht (Verwaltung) über etwas übernehmen.* — **II.** v.tr.: the guns (the batteries) were ∾d *die Geschütze (die Batterien) waren geladen;* the water was ∾d with calcium *das Wasser enthielt Kalk;* to ∾ one's memory with a thing *sein Gedächtnis mit etwas belasten;* he ∾d me to do it *er befahl mir (beauftragte mich), es zu tun;* I ∾d myself with it *ich unternahm, es zu tun; ich über-*

nahm es selbst; to ∾ a man with a crime *j.en eines Verbrechens beschuldigen;* to ∾ a person a high price *j.em einen hohen Preis abfordern;* ∾ this bottle of wine to me *diese Flasche Wein geht auf meine Rechnung.* — **III.** v.i.: the cavalry ∾d *die Kavallerie attackierte (griff an)*

charity n.: ∾ begins at home (prov.) *jeder ist sich selbst der Nächste; das Hemd ist mir näher als der Rock;* as cold as ∾ *bitter wie das Brot der Barmherzigkeit;* Faith, Hope, and Charity *Glaube, Liebe, Hoffnung;* a sister of ∾ *eine barmherzige Schwester;* for ∾'s sake, for ∾ *um der Barmherzigkeit (Liebe) willen; um Gottes Lohn, umsonst;* he left his money for ∾ *er hat sein Geld für wohltätige Zwecke hinterlassen;* in (out of) pure ∾ *aus reiner Barmherzigkeit;* that is too bad, in all ∾ *das ist bei aller Nachsicht zu schlecht;* to dispense ∾ *milde Gaben verteilen;* he lives (he depends) on ∾ *er lebt von milden Gaben; er ist auf die Mildtätigkeit anderer angewiesen*

charm I. n.: to break the ∾ *den Zauber (Bann) brechen.* — **II.** v.tr.: he bears a ∾ed life *sein Leben ist gegen alles gefeit;* I shall be ∾ed to meet her *ich werde sehr erfreut sein, sie zu treffen*

chase n.: to be in ∾ of a thing, to have (to hold) a thing in ∾ *etwas verfolgen;* to give ∾ to an animal *Jagd machen auf ein Tier, einem Tier nachjagen;* to ride to the ∾ *auf die Jagd reiten;* a steeple∾ *ein Hindernisrennen;* a wild-goose ∾ *ein vergebliches (fruchtloses) Suchen*

chat I. n.: to come in (to drop in) for a ∾ *zu einem Plauderstündchen kommen;* to have a ∾ with a person *mit j.em plaudern (schwatzen);* hold your ∾! none of your ∾! (colloq.) *halt's Maul! keine Unverschämtheiten.* — **II.** v.i.: to ∾ with a person *mit j.em plaudern (schwatzen)*

chattel n.: all my goods and ∾s *mein ganzes Hab und Gut*

cheap a.: ∾ and nasty *billig und schlecht;* it was dirt ∾ *es war spottbillig;* I feel ∾ *ich fühle mich nicht ganz wohl; ich schäme mich;* to get off ∾ *leichten Kaufs, mit einem blauen Auge davonkommen;* to go ∾ *billig verkauft werden;* to hold ∾ *geringschätzen;* a holiday on the ∾ *ein billiger, sparsamer Urlaub;* to make oneself ∾ *sich wegwerfen*

check I. n.: to act as a ∾ upon, to hold (to keep) in ∾ *im Schach, im Zaume halten;* to cash (to hand, to pass) in one's ∾s (poker phrase) *sterben;* I have lost the ∾ for my coat *ich habe die Garderobennummer für meinen Mantel verloren.* — **II.** v.tr.: to ∾ a bill *eine Rechnung prüfen;* to ∾ oneself *plötzlich einhalten, sich anders besinnen;* to ∾ off a list *eine Liste als richtig befunden bezeichnen;* I must ∾ that up *der Sache muß ich nachgehen.* — **III.** interj.: ∾! *das stimmt genau!*

cheek I. n.: ∾ by jowl *dicht aneinander, in traulicher Gemeinschaft;* to one's own ∾ *ausschließlich für sich allein;* to have the ∾ to do a thing *die Frechheit (Unverschämtheit) haben (besitzen), etwas zu tun;* what ∾! *was für eine Unverschämtheit!;* to speak with one's tongue in one's ∾ *ironisch, unaufrichtig sprechen;* to turn (to offer) the other ∾ (Matthew, V, 39; Luke VI, 29) *den anderen Backen (auch die andere Backe) darbieten.* — **II.** v.tr.: to ∾ a person *gegen j.en (zu j.em) frech sein*

cheer I. n.: what ∾? *was gibt's? wie geht's?;* the fewer, the better ∾ *je weniger Leute, desto besser zu essen;* to be of good ∾ *guter Dinge (guten Mutes) sein;* to give three ∾s for a person *ein dreifaches Hoch auf j.en ausbringen;* ∾s (three ∾s)! *fein! prima!;* to make good ∾ *gut essen, schmausen.* — **II.** v.tr.: the cups that ∾ but not inebriate *der Tee;* to ∾ a person on to a thing *j.en zu etwas anspornen;* to ∾ a person up *j.en aufheitern (aufmuntern).* — **III.** v.i.: they ∾ed loudly *sie riefen laut Hurra;* ∾ up! *frischauf! nur Mut! lustig!*

cheeribye interj.: ∾! (colloq.) *auf Wiedersehen!*

cheerio interj. (colloq.): ∾! *prost! auf dein Wohl, zum Wohlsein!; auf Wiedersehen!*

cheese[1] n.: as like as chalk and ∾ *grundverschieden, ein Unterschied wie Tag und Nacht;* bread and ∾ *einfache Kost, die nackten Lebensbedürfnisse;* he is a ∾-paring fellow *er ist ein knickeriger (knauseriger) Kerl:* they are only ∾-parings *es sind nur wertlose Brocken;* hard ∾ (colloq.) *Pech!*

cheese[2] n.: that's the ∾! (sl.) *so ist's richtig! das ist die Masche!*

cheese[3] (sl.) **I.** v.tr.: ∾ it *hör auf! halt's Maul! halt den Rand!;* to be ∾d off *es* *satt, die Nase voll haben.* — **II.** n.: to get the ∾ *enttäuscht werden*

cheesy a.: it was a ∾ affair *es war eine schicke Sache;* he has ∾ feet (vulg.) *er hat Schweißfüße*

cherry I. n.: to make two bites at a ∾ *einen kleinen, nicht lohnenden Gegenstand verteilen; zwei Gänge für eine Arbeit tun, die leicht in einem einzigen zu machen wäre.* — **II.** a.: ∾ lips *rote Lippen*

Cheshire a.: to grin like a ∾ cat (Alice in Wonderland) *ständig und sinnlos grinsen*

chest n.: to get a thing off one's ∾ (sl.) *seinem Herzen Luft machen, sich etwas von der Seele reden;* to throw a ∾ *sich in die Brust werfen*

chestnut n.: to tell a ∾ (colloq.) *einen uralten Witz erzählen*

chew v.tr.: to ∾ the cud of reflection *über etwas nachsinnen;* to ∾ the fat (or: rag) (sl.) *schimpfen, nörgeln; auf einer alten Beschwerde herumreiten, meckern;* to bite off more than one can ∾ *sich (dat.) zuviel vornehmen (zumuten);* I feel like a ∾ed rag (sl.) *ich bin erschossen, todmüde*

chicken n.: don't count your ∾s before they are hatched (prov.) *man soll den Tag nicht vor dem Abend loben; man soll die Haut des Bären nicht verkaufen, bevor man ihn erlegt hat; frohlocke nicht zu früh!;* what he earns is mere ∾-feed *er verdient ein Minimum (ein elendes Gehalt);* ∾-hearted, ∾-livered *feige, furchtsam;* ∾-pox *Windpocken;* she's no ∾ (colloq.) *sie ist nicht mehr jung*

child n.: a burnt ∾ dreads the fire (prov.) *gebranntes Kind scheut das Feuer;* ∾ren· of Isaak Walton (author of „The Compleat Angler") *Leute, die Angelsport treiben, Angler;* from a ∾ *von Kindheit an;* she is with ∾ *sie ist in Hoffnung, in (anderen) Umständen;* to get with ∾ *schwängern;* it was ∾'s play *es war ein Kinderspiel, kinderleicht*

chill n.: his words cast a ∾ on (over) the assembly *seine Worte wirkten deprimierend auf die Versammlung;* to catch (to take) a ∾ *sich erkälten;* to take the ∾ off the claret *den Rotwein leicht anwärmen;* to be ∾ed to the bone *durchgefroren sein;* a ∾y room (reception) *ein (unangenehm) kaltes Zimmer (ein unfreundlicher, frostiger Empfang)*

Chiltern Hundreds n.: to apply for (to accept) the ∾ *einen Sitz im Unterhaus aufgeben*

chime v.i.: to ∾ in *sich in ein Gespräch einmischen;* to ∾ together with a person *mit j.em übereinstimmen*

chimney n.: he smokes like a ∾ *er raucht wie ein Schlot;* a ∾ hat, a ∾-pot hat *ein Zylinderhut, eine Angströhre*

chin n.: keep your ∾ up *Kopf hoch!;* to set ∾s wagging *ein Gerede aufbringen;* a ∾-wag *eine Plauderei*

chip I. n.: a ∾ of the old block *der leibhaftige Vater, ganz der Vater;* as dry as a ∾ *geschmacklos, uninteressant;* to have a ∾ on one's shoulder (colloq.) *besonders empfindlich, argwöhnisch sein.* — **II.** v.tr.: to ∾ someone *j.en aufziehen, hänseln.* — **III.** v.i.: to ∾ at someone *an j.em herumnörgeln;* he ∾ped in with the remark (sl.) *er mischte sich in das Gespräch mit der Bemerkung*

chisel v.tr.: (sl.): to ∾ a person *j.en betrügen, übers Ohr hauen*

chit n.: she is a ∾ of a girl *sie ist ein ganz junges Ding;* ∾-chat *Geplauder, Plauderei*

chock-a-block pred.a.: to be ∾ with *angefüllt, vollgepfropft sein mit*

choice n.: at ∾ *nach Belieben;* for ∾ *vorzugsweise, mit Vorliebe;* the girl of one's ∾ *die Auserwählte;* to have one's ∾ *die Wahl haben;* to have no ∾ but *nicht anders können als;* to make the ∾ of, to take one's ∾ *eine Auswahl treffen unter;* Hobson's ∾ *das nehmen, was übrig bleibt*

choke v.tr.: to ∾ down a thing *etwas herunterschlucken, ein Gefühl verheimlichen;* to ∾ off a person *j.en zwingen, seinen Versuch aufzugeben;* to get ∾d off (sl.) *einen gedeckelt, heruntergerissen bekommen;* to ∾ up *verstopfen;* to ∾ to death *erwürgen*

choose I. v.tr.: they chose him as guide *sie haben ihn als Führer gewählt.* — **II.** v.i.: to pick and ∾ *sorgfältig auswählen, mäkeln;* there's nothing to ∾ between them *es ist kein Unterschied zwischen ihnen;* just as you ∾ *wie du willst;* to do as one ∾s *tun, wie einem beliebt;* he cannot ∾ but *er kann nicht umhin, zu*

choosers n.: beggars must not be ∾s (prov.) *Bettler dürfen nicht wählerisch sein*

choosey a.: (colloq.) ∾ *wählerisch, anspruchsvoll*

chop[1] **I.** v.tr.: to ∾ away (down, off) with an axe *mit einer Axt abhauen;* to ∾ up wood *Holz kleinhacken.* — **II.** v.i.: to ∾ back *seine Richtung plötzlich ändern, einen Haken schlagen;* to ∾ in *sich in die Unterhaltung einmischen;* to ∾ up, out *an die Oberfläche kommen;* to ∾ upon a person *j.em plötzlich begegnen.* — **III.** n.: a ∾-house *ein billiges Speisehaus;* a mutton-∾ *ein Hammelkotelett*

chop[2] **I.** v.tr.: to ∾ logic *pedantisch disputieren.* — **II.** v.i.: to ∾ and change *hin- und herschwanken, unentschlossen sein;* to ∾ round, about (esp. of wind) *die Richtung plötzlich ändern*

chop[3], chap n.: to lick one's ∾s *sich (dat.) die Finger (Lippen) lecken;* to be ∾-fallen *ein langes Gesicht machen*

chop[4] (Anglo-Ind. & colloq.): first-, second-∾ *erst-, zweitklassig*

chow n.: rustle us some ∾ (sl.) *verschaffe uns etwas zu essen*

Christmas n.: ∾ comes but once a year *es ist nicht alle Tage Sonntag; nur einmal blüht im Jahr der Mai;* a ∾-box *ein Weihnachtsgeschenk;* ∾ Eve *Heiliger Abend;* Father ∾ *der Weihnachtsmann*

chuck I. v.tr. (colloq.): to ∾ away a chance *eine Gelegenheit verpassen, sich (dat.) eine Gelegenheit entgehen lassen;* ∾ **it** (sl.) *hör auf! halt's Maul! halt den Rand!;* to ∾ a person out *j.en hinauswerfen,-schmeißen;* to ∾ a person under the chin *j.em liebkosend unter das Kinn fassen;* to ∾ up the sponge *sich für besiegt erklären, die Sache aufgeben;* to ∾ work, a friend, one's job *die Arbeit, den Freund, seine Stelle (Stellung) aufgeben.* — **II.** n.: to get good ∾ (sl.) *gutes Essen bekommen;* hard ∾ *Schiffszwieback;* to give a person the ∾; to get the ∾ (sl.) *j.en entlassen; entlassen werden;* a ∾er out *ein Hinauswerfer (in einer Kneipe)*

chum I. n.: they are great ∾s *sie sind dicke Freunde.* — **II.** v.i.: to ∾ up with a person *mit j.em Freundschaft schließen*

chummy a.: *freundlich, befreundet*

chump n.: he is a ∾ (sl.) *er ist ein Narr;* to be off one's ∾ (colloq.) *von Sinnen (furchtbar aufgeregt) sein*

circle n.: to argue in a ∾ *einen Zirkelschluß machen;* to come round full ∾ *einen vollen Kreis beschreiben, sich einmal im Kreise drehen, an den Ausgangspunkt zurückkommen;* to run round in ∾s (colloq.) *viel Aufhebens mit wenig Erfolg machen;* to square the ∾ *das Unmögliche (die Quadratur des Kreises) versuchen*

circumstance n.: with great pomp and ∾ *mit großem Pomp und Gepränge;* without ∾ *ohne Formalitäten (ohne Umstände);* in (under) the ∾s *unter den obwaltenden Umständen;* under no ∾s *unter keinen Umständen;* under certain ∾s *unter (gewissen) Umständen;* he lives in good (bad, easy, reduced, straitened) ∾s *er lebt in guten (schlechten, angenehmen, zerrütteten, bedrängten) Verhältnissen;* extenuating ∾s *mildernde Umstände*

circumstancial a.: ∾ evidence *Indizienbeweis*

cissy, sissy n. (sl.): he is a ∾ *er ist ein Waschlappen (Schlappschwanz), ein weibischer Typ*

civil a.: keep a ∾ tongue in your head! *immer hübsch höflich bleiben!*

claim I. v.tr.: that ∾s attention *das verdient Beachtung;* he ∾s to be the owner *er behauptet, der Eigentümer zu sein.* — **II.** n.: to enter (to put forward, to put in) a ∾ for (to lay ∾ to) a thing *auf etwas Anspruch erheben;* to jump a ∾ *unrechtmäßig in den Besitz von etwas kommen;* to stake out a ∾ *neues Land abstecken; einen Anspruch erheben*

clap I. v.tr.: to ∾ eyes on a person *j.en zu sehen bekommen;* to ∾ one's hands *in die Hände klatschen;* to ∾ a pistol to a person's breast *j.em die Pistole auf die Brust setzen;* to ∾ spurs to a horse *einem Pferde die Sporen geben;* to ∾ a person into prison (colloq.) *j.en ohne weiteres ins Gefängnis (ins Loch) stecken;* to ∾ a person on the back *j.em auf den Rücken klopfen;* to ∾ on all sail *alle Segel setzen, sich beeilen;* to ∾ up a bargain *voreilig oder nachlässig ein Geschäft abschließen.* — **II.** v.i.: let us ∾ *laßt uns klatschen;* the door ∾ped to *die Tür schlug zu*

clap-trap n.: *(großes) Geschwätz, um Beifall zu ernten*

claret n.: he tapped his ∾ (sl.) *er schlug ihm auf die Nase, daß sie blutete*

class n.: in the same ∾ with *vom selben Jahrgang; gleichwertig mit;* she's no ∾ (fam.) *sie ist nicht vornehm*

claw I. n.: to get one's ∾s into a person *j.en heimtückisch anfallen;* to cut (to pare) a person's ∾s *j.en entwaffnen, unschädlich machen.* — **II.** v.tr.: ∾ me and I'll ∾ thee *Wurst wider Wurst; wie du mir, so ich dir*

clean I. a. & adv.: see 'breast, heel, slate, sweep'; to come ∾ (sl.) *alles eingestehen;* a ∾-cut face *ein scharfgeschnittenes Gesicht;* it is ∾ gone *es ist vollständig verschwunden (rein weg);* it is ∾ impossible *es ist glatt (rein) unmöglich;* he is ∾-shaven *er ist glattrasiert.* — **II.** v.tr.: to ∾ one's plate *seinen Teller leer essen;* to ∾ down a thing *etwas abbürsten, abschrubben;* to ∾ a person out *j.em den letzten Pfennig aus der Tasche ziehen;* to ∾ up a room *ein Zimmer gründlich reinigen.* — **III.** n.: give it a ∾ *mach' es sauber*

clear I. a.: that's as ∾ as anything *das ist so klar wie nur was;* the all-∾ *die Entwarnung nach Fliegeralarm;* the coast is ∾ *die Luft ist rein, es ist keine Gefahr vorhanden;* a ∾ case of fraud *ein offenbarer Fall von Betrug;* a ∾ conscience *ein reines Gewissen;* three ∾ days *drei volle Tage;* a ∾ profit *ein Reingewinn;* a man of ∾ sight *ein Mann von klarem Blick.* — **II.** adv.: a ∾-cut proposal *ein scharf umrissener Vorschlag;* to get ∾ away *ungehindert entkommen;* to get ∾ off *frei ausgehen, freigesprochen werden;* to go ∾ through *glatt durchgehen;* to keep ∾ of a thing *sich fern-, freihalten von etwas;* to shine ∾ *hell leuchten;* to speak loud and ∾ *laut und deutlich sprechen;* stand ∾ of the doors *nicht an den Türen stehen bleiben!* — **III.** v.tr.: to ∾ an account *eine Rechnung bezahlen;* to ∾ the air *die Luft reinigen;* to ∾ the decks for action *das Deck klar zum Gefecht machen;* to ∾ a dish *eine Schüssel leer machen;* to ∾ a hurdle *glatt über ein Hindernis springen;* to ∾ land *roden;* he ∾ed ten pounds *er hatte einen Reingewinn von zehn Pfund;* to ∾ a ship *die Ladung eines Schiffes löschen;* to ∾ one's throat *sich räuspern;* to ∾ the way *den Weg freimachen;* to ∾ a thing away (out of the way) *etwas wegräumen, aus dem Wege räumen;* to ∾ off debts *Schulden bezahlen, loswerden;* to ∾ out a cupboard *einen Schrank ausräumen;* to ∾ up a mystery *ein Geheimnis aufklären;* to ∾ up a room *ein Zimmer aufräumen.* — **IV.** v.i.: the fog has ∾ed away *der Nebel hat sich gelichtet;* the intruders ∾ed off, out *die Eindringlinge machten sich auf und davon;* ∾ out of the way *geh mir aus dem Weg! mach, daß du fortkommst!;* the weather has ∾ed up *das Wetter hat sich aufgeklärt.* — **V.** n.: to be in the ∾ (sl.) *Aktiva haben*

clearance n.: a ∾ sale *ein Räumungsausverkauf*

cleave I. v.tr.: to be in a cleft stick *in Verlegenheit (in der Klemme) sein;* to have a cleft palate *einen Wolfsrachen haben;* to show the cloven hoof *den Pferdefuß, sein wahres Gesicht zeigen.* — **II.** v.i.: to ∾ asunder, in two *aufspringen, bersten, sich spalten*

clergyman n.: a ∾'s throat *Rachenentzündung (durch vieles Sprechen);* a ∾'s week (fortnight) *ein Urlaub, der zwei (bzw. drei) Sonntage umfaßt*

clerical a.: a ∾ error *ein Schreibfehler*

clerk n.: a ∾ in holy orders *ein Kleriker (Geistlicher);* the Clerk of the Weather *der Wettergott*

clever a.: to be ∾ at doing a thing *gut verstehen, etwas zu tun;* ∾ ∾ *übergescheit, gerissen*

click I. v.tr.: they ∾ed their glasses together *sie stießen mit den Gläsern an;* to ∾ one's heels *die Hacken zusammenschlagen;* to ∾ one's tongue *mit der Zunge schnalzen.* — **II.** v.i.: to ∾ (sl.) *Glück haben, sein Ziel erreichen;* the two ∾ed (sl.) *die beiden verliebten sich ineinander*

climb I. v.tr.: to ∾ a tree *einen Baum hinaufklettern.* — **II.** v.i.: to ∾ down *herunterklettern; seine Ansprüche aufgeben, einen Rückzieher machen.* — **III.** n.: it was a steep ∾ *es war eine steile Kletterpartie (Kletterei, Kraxelei);* it was a ∾-down for him *er mußte einen Rückzieher machen*

clinch I. v.tr.: that ∾es the matter *damit ist die Sache entschieden.* — **II.** n.: the boxers were in a ∾ *die Boxer hatten sich umklammert*

clip v.tr.: to ∾ the wings of a person *j.em die Flügel beschneiden;* to ∾ one's words *die Silben verschlucken, abgehackt sprechen*

cloak n.: under the ∾ of *unter dem Vorwand von;* the ∾-room *die Garderobe; die Gepäckannahme und -ausgabe;* the ladies' ∾-room *die Damentoilette*

clock I. n.: like one o'∾ *glatt (ohne Verzögerung, rasch);* it is six o'∾ *es ist sechs Uhr;* what o'∾ is it? *wieviel Uhr ist es?;* I must set the ∾ *ich muß die Uhr stellen;* to work like ∾-work *regelmäßig, mechanisch arbeiten.* — **II.** v.i.: to ∾ in *die Kontrolluhr stechen*

clod n.: a ∾-hopper *ein Bauernlümmel*

close[1] **I.** a.: upon ∾r acquaintance *bei näherer Bekanntschaft;* ∾ air *drückende (schwüle) Luft;* to pay ∾ attention *gespannt zuhören;* to give ∾ chase to a person *j.en dicht verfolgen, ihm auf den Fersen sitzen;* as ∾ as a coffin *verschwiegen wie das Grab;* in ∾ combat *im Nahkampf;* to keep in ∾ confinement *in strenger Haft halten;* in ∾ conversation *in vertrautem Gespräch;* a ∾ crop of hair *kurzgeschnittenes Haar;* to be ∾ friends *vertraute (intime) Freunde sein;* to march in ∾ order *in geschlossener Ordnung marschieren;* he is as ∾ as an oyster *er ist äußerst zugeknöpft;* ∾ reasoning *bündige Beweisführung;* to bear ∾ resemblance to a person *große Ähnlichkeit mit j.em besitzen;* the ∾ season for game *die Schonzeit für Wild;* it was a ∾ shave for us *wir sind mit knapper Not entkommen;* to come to ∾ quarters *heftig aneinander geraten, handgemein werden.* — **II.** adv.: to be ∾ upon sixty *nahe an die Sechzig sein;* to draw ∾ to a person *dicht an j.en heranrücken;* to follow ∾ behind *dicht auf den Fersen folgen;* that happened ∾ upon my return *das geschah kurz nach meiner Rückkehr;* to keep (to lie) ∾ *geheimhalten, sich verbergen;* to keep a person ∾ *j.en knapp halten;* the train passes ∾ by our house *der Zug fährt dicht an unserem Hause vorbei;* to run a person ∾ *j.em dicht auf den Fersen sein; ihm Konkurrenz machen;* to sail ∾ to the wind *sich an der Grenze des Erlaubten (des Schicklichen) bewegen;* the door is not shut ∾ *die Tür ist nicht dicht (nicht fest) zu;* to sit (to stand) ∾ *dicht gedrängt sitzen (stehen);* a ∾-up *eine Großaufnahme (Film).* — **III.** n.: the ∾ of a cathedral *die Domfreiheit*

close[2] **I.** v.tr.: to ∾ an account (bargain) *eine Rechnung (ein Geschäft) abschließen;* to ∾ one's days *seine Tage beschließen;* to ∾ the door *die Tür schließen (zumachen);* behind ∾d doors *geheim, hinter verschlossenen Türen, unter Ausschluß der Öffentlichkeit;* to ∾ down the hatches *die Luken schließen.* — **II.** v.i.: the days are closing in *die Tage nehmen ab;* to ∾ in with an enemy *mit einem Feinde handgemein werden;* the waves ∾d over him *die Wellen schlugen über ihm zusammen;* to ∾ round the enemy *den Feind umzingeln;* to ∾ the door upon a person *die Tür hinter j.em zumachen, nichts mehr mit ihm zu tun haben wollen;* to ∾ with an offer *ein Anerbieten annehmen;* closing time *Laden-, Geschäftsschluß.* — **III.** n.: at the ∾ of the year *am Jahresschluß;* to bring to a ∾ *beendigen;* to come to a ∾ *zum Schluß kommen;* to draw to a ∾ *zu Ende gehen*

closet I. n.: a ∾ play *ein Lesedrama;* a ∾ strategist *ein Biertischstratege;* a china-∾ *ein Porzellanschrank;* a water-∾ *ein Klosett mit Wasserspülung.* — **II.** v.tr.: to be ∾ed (together) with a person *mit j.em eine geheime Besprechung hinter verschlossenen Türen führen*

clot (sl.) n.: a ∾ *eine dumme, einfältige Person, ein Tölpel*

cloth n.: the ∾ *die Geistlichkeit;* to cut one's coat according to one's ∾ *sich nach der Decke strecken;* to lay the ∾ *den Tisch decken*

clotted a.: ∾ cream *verdickte Sahne;* ∾ hair *verfilztes Haar;* that is ∾ nonsense *das ist völliger Unsinn*

cloud n.: every ∾ has a silver lining (prov.) *auch das Schlimmste hat ein Ende (kann Besseres bringen);* there was a ∾ on his brow *eine Wolke des Unmuts (Kummers) lag auf seiner Stirn;* to be in the ∾s *in den Wolken (in höheren Regionen) schweben;* his name is under a ∾ *sein Name ist in Verruf;* under the ∾ of night *unter dem Schutze der Nacht;* to cast a ∾ on (over) a thing *etwas trüben;* to lift the ∾ *das Dunkle lichten*

clover n.: to be (to live) in ∾ *im Überfluß leben, in der Wolle sitzen;* to go from ∾ to rye-grass *vom Pferd auf den Esel kommen (besonders von zweiten Ehen gesagt)*

club I. v.tr.: they ∾bed the money up (or: together) *sie brachten das Geld zusammen auf.* — **II.** v.i.: to ∾ together for joint action *sich zu gemeinsamem Handeln vereinigen;* we all ∾bed together *wir steuerten alle etwas bei.* — **III.** a.: ∾ land *das Gesellschaftsviertel von London, wo die bekannten Herrenklubs zu finden sind*

clue n.: I haven't a ∾, I'm ∾less (sl.) *ich habe keine Ahnung (keinen Schimmer)*

coach I. n.: to drive a ∾ and six (four) through an act of Parliament *ein Gesetz unwirksam machen;* to go to a ∾ *zum Repetitor (Einpauker) gehen;* he is a slow-∾ *er ist ein langsamer, schwerfälliger Mensch, ein Trödelfritze.* — **II.** v.tr.: to ∾ a person for an examination *j.en zum Examen einpauken.* — **III.** v.i.: in the old ∾ing days *in den Tagen der Postkutsche*

coal n.: to blow the ∾s of passion *eine Leidenschaft anfachen;* to call (to haul) a person over the ∾s *j.em einen scharfen Verweis (Rüffel) erteilen, ihn zur Rechenschaft ziehen, ihn abkanzeln;* to carry ∾s to Newcastle *Eulen nach Athen tragen; Überflüssiges, Unnützes tun;* to heap ∾s of fire on a person's head *feurige Kohlen auf j.es Haupt sammeln*

coast n.: the ∾ is clear *die Luft ist rein, es ist keine Gefahr vorhanden;* to hug the ∾ *sich dicht an der Küste halten*

coat n.: to cut one's ∾ according to one's cloth *sich nach der Decke strecken;* to dust a person's ∾ *j.em die Jacke voll hauen;* to trail one's ∾-tails (for somebody to tread on) *Streit anzufangen suchen, zum Kampf herausfordern;* to turn one's ∾ *abtrünnig werden, sich auf die andere Seite schlagen, den Mantel nach dem Winde hängen*

cobweb n.: to blow away the ∾s from one's brain *sich (dat.) einen klaren Kopf schaffen*

cock I. n.: he is ∾ of the roost (or: walk) *er dominiert, er ist Hahn im Korbe;* that ∾ won't fight *das geht nicht an, der Einwand zieht nicht;* they live like fighting ∾s *sie haben alles im Überfluß; sie leben wie Gott in Frankreich;* that beats ∾-fighting *das übertrifft alles, das ist großartig, das schießt den Vogel ab;* a ∾-and-bull story *ein Ammenmärchen;* ride a-∾-horse to Banbury Cross (nursery rhyme) *hoppe, hoppe, Reiter!;* to be ∾-sure about (of) a thing *etwas ganz sicher wissen;* to be ∾-a-hoop *beschwingt, in gehobener Stimmung sein.* — **II.** v.tr.: to ∾ the ears *die Ohren spitzen;* to ∾ one's eye at a person *j.en verschmitzt ansehen, ihm zublinzeln;* he is ∾-eyed (sl.) *er schielt; er ist blau;* to ∾ one's hat *den Hut keck aufs Ohr setzen;* to knock into a ∾ed hat *etwas zu Brei schlagen;* to ∾ one's nose *die Nase rümpfen;* to ∾ a snook *eine lange Nase machen;* to ∾ one's toes (sl.) *sterben*

Cocker n.pr.: according to ∾ *genau, korrekt; nach Adam Riese*

cockle n.: to warm the ∾s of a person's heart *j.en erfreuen;* a ∾-shell *ein sehr kleines Boot*

coco-, cocoa-, coker-nut n.: that accounts for the milk in the ∾ *daher der Name! das erklärt alles*

coffin n.: as close as a ∾ *verschwiegen wie das Grab;* to drive a nail into a person's ∾ *ein Nagel zu j.es Sarg sein;* a ∾-nail *ein Sargnagel (eine billige, schlechte Zigarette)*

coign n.: a ∾ of vantage (Macbeth, I, 6) *eine vorteilhafte Stellung*

coin I. n.: to pay a person in his own ∾ *Gleiches mit Gleichem vergelten, j.en mit gleicher Münze bezahlen.* — **II.** v.tr.: to ∾ money *leicht und schnell Geld verdienen;* to ∾ a word *ein Wort prägen*

cold I. a.: as ∾ as charity *bitter wie das Brot der Barmherzigkeit;* a ∾ comfort *ein schlechter (schwacher, magerer) Trost;* to have (to get) ∾ feet (sl.) *eine Heidenangst haben, kalte Füße bekommen;* ∾ pig (sl.) *kaltes Wasser, das auf einen Schläfer geschüttet wird, um ihn zu wecken;* to give the ∾ shoulder to a person, to ∾-shoulder a person *j.em die kalte Schulter zeigen;* to pour (to throw) ∾ water on a plan *von einem Vorhaben abraten (abschrecken);* to get a person ∾ (sl.) *j.en in seine Gewalt bekommen;* my blood runs ∾ *das Blut erstarrt mir in den Adern.* — **II.** n.: to catch (a) ∾ (a ∾ in the head) *sich erkälten, sich (dat.) einen Schnupfen holen;* to leave out in the ∾ *vernachlässigen, stiefmütterlich behandeln*

collar I. n.: to work against the ∾ *sich schwer anstrengen;* the ∾-bone *das Schlüsselbein;* ∾-work *harte (anstrengende) Arbeit.* — **II.** v.tr.: to ∾ a person *j.en beim Kragen packen;* to ∾ a thing (sl.) *sich (dat.) etwas aneignen*

colour n.: a man of ∾ *ein Neger;* to apply ∾s *Farben auftragen;* he is with the ∾s *er dient im Heere (ist Soldat);* the regimental ∾s, the stand of ∾s *die Regimentsfahne;* under ∾ of *unter dem Vorwand von;* to change ∾ *die Farbe wechseln;* to come off with flying ∾s *den Sieg davontragen, mit Ehren bestehen;* to give (to lend) ∾ to a thing *einer Sache den Anschein von Wahrscheinlichkeit geben;* to give a person his ∾s *j.en in eine repräsentative Sportmannschaft aufnehmen;* to have a ∾ *blühend aussehen;* to lower one's ∾s *die Fahne streichen;* to nail one's ∾ to the mast *standhaft bleiben;* to sail under false ∾s *unter falscher Flagge segeln;* to put false ∾s upon a thing *ein falsches Licht auf etwas werfen;* to see the ∾ of a person's money *von j.em eine Zahlung bekommen;* to see a thing in its true ∾s *etwas in wahrem Lichte sehen;* to show one's ∾s *Farbe bekennen;* to stick to one's ∾s *einer Sache treu bleiben*

colt n.: the old man has a ∾'s tooth *der alte Mann hat einen kindlichen Geschmack*

comb I. n.: to cut the ∾ of a person *j.en demütigen.* — **II.** v.tr.: to ∾ out *sieben, ausmustern (Mil.)*

come I. v.i.: ∾, ∾ now *sachte, sachte!;* first ∾, first served (prov.) *wer zuerst kommt, mahlt zuerst;* light ∾, light go (prov.) *wie gewonnen, so zerronnen;* in years to ∾ *in der Zukunft, in den kommenden Jahren;* he has ∾ to be a good driver *er ist ein guter Fahrer geworden;* how do you ∾ to be here? *wie kommt es, daß du hier bist?;* to ∾ to be used *allmählich gebraucht werden;* I have ∾ to believe *ich bin zu der Überzeugung gekommen;* he tried to ∾ the bully over me, see 'bully'; two years ∾ Christmas *Weihnachten ist es zwei Jahre her;* to ∾ a cropper (sl.) *einen schweren Sturz tun (hinschlagen); Mißerfolg haben;* it ∾s easy to him *es fällt ihm leicht;* that will ∾ expensive *das wird teuer werden;* the truth came home to him *er kannte die Wahrheit;* to ∾ to know a person (a thing) *j.en (etwas) kennenlernen;* to ∾ it too strong *übertreiben;* the laces have ∾ loose, untied *die Schuhriemen haben sich gelöst, sind aufgegangen;* to ∾ natural to a person *j.em ganz selbstverständlich sein;* to ∾ near to do a thing *etwas beinahe tun;* he is coming nineteen *er wird neunzehn;* it will ∾ right *es geht schon in Ordnung;* ∾ and see me *besuch' mich mal;* to ∾ short of a thing *einer Sache nicht entsprechen, hinter etwas zurückbleiben;* it has ∾ to stay *es ist etwas Dauerhaftes (Bleibendes);* to ∾ true *wahr werden, sich bewahrheiten;* are you coming my way? *hast du den gleichen Weg wie ich?;* a coming man *ein kommender Mann, einer, der Karriere machen wird;* no work came his way *er fand keine Arbeit.* — with prep.: to ∾ across a person (a thing) *j.en zufällig treffen (auf etwas stoßen);* ∾ along! *beeile dich! mach' schnell (fix)!;* to ∾ along the street *die Straße entlangkommen;* to ∾ at a thing *etwas erreichen, entdecken;* ∾-atable *erreichbar, zugänglich;* how did you ∾ by it? *wie bist du daran gekommen?;* he has ∾ for the luggage *er will das Gepäck abholen;* he ∾s from Greece *er stammt aus Griechenland;* to ∾ into force, a fortune, a person's head, play, sight, see 'force, fortune, head, play, sight'; nothing will ∾ of it *daraus wird nichts;* he ∾s of a good family *er kommt (stammt) aus einer guten Familie;* to ∾ off duty *vom Dienst abgelöst werden, mit dem Dienst fertig sein;* to ∾ (all) over queer (colloq.) *sich plötzlich schlecht fühlen;* to ∾ on one's head *auf den Kopf fallen;* a change came over him *es trat eine Änderung bei ihm ein;* to ∾ to blows, an end, grief, etc., see 'blow, end, grief, etc.'; it ∾s under his jurisdiction *es untersteht (es fällt unter seine) Rechtssprechung;* to ∾ (up)on the parish *Gemeindeunterstützung erhalten;* to ∾ upon a person *j.en überraschend angreifen;* to ∾ upon a thing *etwas zufällig finden, auf etwas stoßen.* — with adv.: to ∾ about, along, asunder, back, see 'about, along, asunder, back'; ∾ again! (colloq.) *sag' es bitte nochmal!;* to ∾ by *vorbeikommen;* to ∾ down handsomely *sich nobel zeigen;* to ∾ down a peg or two *einige Pflöcke zurückstecken, etwas kleinlaut werden;* to ∾ down upon a person *j.en anfahren, anschnauzen;* to ∾ down with a bump, see 'bump'; to ∾ down with the money *mit dem Geld herausrücken;* to ∾ forward with a proposal *mit einem*

Vorschlag hervortreten; ∾ in *herein!;* the socialists came in at the election *die Sozialisten kamen bei der Wahl an die Regierung;* to ∾ in third *als Dritter durchs Ziel gehen;* that will ∾ in useful *das kommt ja sehr gelegen, das kann ich gut gebrauchen;* to ∾ in for money *zu Geld kommen, Geld erben;* to ∾ in for a good thrashing *eine tüchtige Tracht Prügel erhalten;* where do I ∾ in? *wo bleibe ich? (wo bleiben meine Interessen?);* to ∾ near to a thing *mit einer Sache Ähnlichkeit haben;* the button has ∾ off *der Knopf ist abgegangen;* the match did not ∾ off *das Wettspiel fand nicht statt;* to ∾ off with a fine *mit einer Geldstrafe davonkommen;* to ∾ off with flying colours *den Sieg davontragen, mit Ehren bestehen;* to ∾ off a loser *bei etwas verlieren;* to ∾ off well (badly) *gut (schlecht) bei etwas fahren;* ∾ on! *vorwärts! mach schnell!;* the baby is coming on nicely *das Kindchen gedeiht gut, es macht sich;* the young lady has ∾ out *die junge Dame ist in die Gesellschaft eingeführt worden;* the miners have ∾ out *die Bergarbeiter sind in den Streik getreten;* the paper ∾s out once a month *die Zeitschrift erscheint einmal im Monat;* to ∾ out with a curse *mit einem Fluche herausplatzen;* to ∾ round *vorbeikommen, einen Besuch machen; sich erholen, wieder zu sich kommen;* summer has ∾ round again *es ist wieder Sommer geworden;* he came round to my opinion *er bekehrte sich zu meiner Ansicht;* the call came through *es wurde telephonisch durchgesagt;* to ∾ to *wieder zu sich kommen;* the tide is coming up *die Flut steigt;* to ∾ up against opposition *auf Widerspruch (Widerstand) stoßen;* to ∾ up for discussion *zur Diskussion kommen;* the water came up to his chin *das Wasser stieg ihm bis ans Kinn;* it did not ∾ up to my expectations *es entsprach nicht meinen Erwartungen;* to ∾ up to a person *an j.en herantreten;* to ∾ up with a person *j.en erreichen (einholen).* — **II.** n.: to make a ∾-back (colloq.) *die Macht oder Beliebtheit wiedergewinnen;* the to-∾ *die Zukunft;* it was a ∾-down *es war eine Erniedrigung, Blamage, ein Reinfall*

comfort n.: a cold ∾ *ein schlechter, magerer Trost;* creature ∾s, see 'creature'; to live in ∾ *ein behagliches Leben führen;* to take ∾ *sich trösten, Mut fassen;* to derive ∾ from *Trost finden in*

comic a.: a ∾ actor *ein Komiker;* a ∾ paper *ein Witzblatt;* it has its ∾ side *es hat seine heitere Seite*

comical a.: a ∾ actor *ein komischer, seltsamer Schauspieler;* to cut a ∾ figure *eine komische, lächerliche Figur abgeben*

comma n.: inverted ∾s *Anführungsstriche, Gänsefüßchen*

command I. n.: at ∾ *zur beliebigen Verfügung;* he has a great ∾ of language *er ist sehr redegewandt;* he has much money at his ∾ *er verfügt über viel Geld.* — **II.** v.i.: I am yours to ∾ *ich stehe Ihnen zur Verfügung (zu Diensten).* — **III.** v.tr.: the house ∾s a view of the river *von dem Haus aus überblickt man den Fluß;* he ∾s our respect *er flößt uns Achtung ein*

comment I. n.: to cause ∾ *Anlaß zur Kritik geben.* — **II.** v.i.: to ∾ upon a text *erklärende Bemerkungen zu einem Text geben;* to ∾ upon a thing *(ungünstige) Bemerkungen über etwas machen*

commit v.tr.: to ∾ a crime *ein Verbrechen begehen;* ∾ no nuisance! *Verunreinigung verboten!;* to ∾ oneself *sich verpflichten, sich binden, etwas zu tun; sich kompromittieren;* to ∾ suicide *Selbstmord begehen;* to ∾ for trial *dem Gericht zur Aburteilung überweisen;* to ∾ to the care (to the charge) of a person *j.es Fürsorge (Obhut) übergeben;* to ∾ to the deep *eine Leiche ins Meer versenken;* to ∾ to the earth (to the grave) *beerdigen;* to ∾ to the flames *den Flammen überliefern (übergeben);* to ∾ one's soul to God *seine Seele Gott befehlen;* to ∾ to memory *auswendig lernen;* to ∾ to oblivion *der Vergessenheit überantworten;* to ∾ to paper (to writing) *zu Papier bringen, auf-, niederschreiben*

common I. a.: to make ∾ cause with a person *mit j.em gemeinsame Sache machen;* to do by ∾ consent *mit allgemeiner Zustimmung tun;* it is a ∾ experience *es ist eine gewöhnliche (allgemeine) Erfahrung;* the Junior (Senior) Common Room (abbr.: J.C.R., S.C.R.) *der Aufenthaltsraum für Studenten (bzw. Dozenten) in einem College;* to be on ∾ ground *auf gleichen Voraussetzungen fußen;* ∾ ground *Gemeindeland;* the ∾ herd *das gemeine Volk;* ∾ Law *Gewohnheitsrecht* (ant.: Statute Law); the ∾ man *der Durchschnittsmensch;* in ∾

parlance *in einfachen Worten;* the Book of ∾ Prayer *Gebet- und Ritualbuch der anglikanischen Kirche;* of ∾ origin *vom selben Ursprung;* to have ∾ sense *gesunden Menschenverstand haben;* he is a ∾ soldier *er ist gemeiner Soldat;* it is ∾ talk *es ist allgemeines Stadtgespräch;* ∾ time *Viervierteltakt;* it is ∾ usage *es ist ein weitverbreiteter (Ge)brauch;* the ∾ voice *das Urteil aller, die Stimme des Volkes;* the ∾ weal (archaic) *das gemeine Wohl, Gemeinwohl;* ∾ or garden things *Feld-, Wald- und Wiesendinge.* — **II.** n.: a ∾ *Gemeindeland, ein offenes Gebiet, meistens Heide;* to be in ∾ with *in Übereinstimmung sein mit;* to have in ∾ with *gemein haben mit;* to be something out of the ∾ *etwas Außergewöhnliches sein;* to keep on short ∾s *bei schmaler Kost halten;* the ∾s *die Staatsbürger mit Ausnahme der Adeligen;* the House of Commons *das Unterhaus*

commute v.tr. & i.: work was ∾d for payment *Arbeit wurde an Stelle von Zahlung geleistet;* the punishment was ∾d into a fine *die Strafe wurde durch eine Geldbuße abgelöst;* he ∾s (he is a ∾r) between his work in the town and his home in the country *er pendelt zwischen seiner Arbeitsstätte in der Stadt und seinem Heim auf dem Lande hin und her*

company n.: two is ∾, three is none (a crowd) *der Dritte wirkt immer störend;* in ∾ with *in Gesellschaft, zusammen mit;* to be fond of ∾ *die Geselligkeit lieben;* to be good (bad) ∾ *ein angenehmer (langweiliger) Gesellschafter sein;* to break ∾ *auseinandergehen;* to get one's ∾ *Hauptmann werden;* to keep (to bear) a person ∾ *j.em Gesellschaft leisten;* he is keeping ∾ with her *er hat ein Verhältnis mit ihr;* to part ∾ with a person *sich von j.em trennen;* to see a great deal of ∾ *viele Gesellschaften geben, viel in Gesellschaft(en) gehen;* I sin in good ∾ *ich befinde mich in guter Gesellschaft, wenn ich das tue;* to weep for ∾ *zur Gesellschaft mitweinen*

compare I. v.tr.: the witness ∾d the noise to thunder *der Zeuge sagte, der Krach wäre einem Donnerschlage gleichgekommen;* the lecturer ∾d the British field-gun with the French *der Vortragende zog einen Vergleich zwischen dem britischen und französischen Feldgeschütz;* to ∾ notes with one another *untereinander die Meinungen austauschen.* — **II.** v.i.: no lady can ∾ with Sally *keine Dame kommt der Sarah gleich*

comparison n.: beyond all ∾ *unvergleichlich;* by ∾ *zum Vergleich, vergleichsweise;* in ∾ with *im Vergleich mit, verglichen mit;* to draw (to establish, to make) a ∾ *einen Vergleich anstellen (ziehen);* to bear (to challenge, to stand, to sustain) ∾ with a thing *einen Vergleich mit etwas aushalten*

compass n.: to box the ∾, see 'box'; to fetch (to go) a ∾ *einen Umweg machen*

competence, -cy n.: the ∾ of the court *die Zuständigkeit des Gerichts;* to have the ∾ for (to do) a task *die Befähigung (Fähigkeit) haben, etwas zu tun;* to have (to enjoy) a ∾ *sein Auskommen haben*

competent a.: the court is not ∾ *das Gericht ist nicht zuständig;* to be ∾ for (to do) a task *die Befähigung haben, etwas zu tun;* it was ∾ to him to refuse *er durfte sich weigern*

complain v.i.: to ∾ about (of) the cold *über die Kälte klagen;* he ∾s of a headache *er klagt über Kopfschmerzen;* to ∾ to the authorities *sich bei der Behörde beklagen;* it was ∾ed that *es wurde Klage geführt, daß*

compliment I. n.: in ∾ to a person *j.em zu Ehren, aus Höflichkeit gegen j.en;* with Mr. N.'s ∾s *mit den besten Empfehlungen (Grüßen) von Herrn N.;* with the ∾s of the season *mit den besten Wünschen zum Fest (Weihnachten, Neujahr, Ostern);* he did me the ∾ of saying *er erwies mir die Ehre zu sagen;* to fish for ∾s *sich selber herabsetzen, in der Hoffnung, gelobt zu werden;* give (present) my ∾s to your parents *empfehlen Sie mich Ihren Eltern;* to make (to pay) a ∾ to a person *j.em ein Kompliment machen;* to return the ∾ *das Kompliment erwidern;* to turn a ∾ *ein Kompliment elegant anbringen.* — **II.** v.tr.: to ∾ a person on a thing *j.en zu etwas beglückwünschen;* to ∾ a person with a thing *j.en mit etwas beehren*

complimentary a.: a ∾ speech *eine Lobrede;* ∾ tickets *Frei-, Ehrenkarten*

comply v.i.: to ∾ with the rules *sich an die Regeln halten;* to ∾ with a person's wishes *j.es Wünsche erfüllen*

compound a.: a ∾ fracture *ein komplizierter Bruch;* ∾ interest *Zinseszins*

conceit n.: in my own ∾ *meiner Meinung nach, in meinen Augen;* to be out of ∾ with a thing *einer Sache überdrüssig sein;* to put a person out of ∾ with a thing *j.em die Lust zu einer Sache nehmen;* to take the ∾ out of a person *j.en demütigen*

concern I. v.tr.: it does not ∾ me *es betrifft mich nicht, es geht mich nichts an;* to ∾ oneself with (in, about) a matter, to do a thing *sich um eine Angelegenheit kümmern;* to be ∾ed in an affair *mit einer Sache etwas zu tun haben, in eine Sache verwickelt sein;* as far as I am ∾ed *soweit es mich betrifft (angeht);* I am not ∾ed to do it *es ist nicht meine Sache, es zu tun;* your reputation is ∾ed *es handelt (dreht) sich um deinen Ruf; dein guter Ruf steht auf dem Spiele;* to be (to feel) ∾ed to hear (at hearing); ∾ed for (about) a person, a thing *beunruhigt (besorgt) sein zu hören; sich (dat.) Sorge machen (in Unruhe sein) um eine (wegen einer) Person, Sache;* a ∾ed air, look *eine besorgte Miene, ein besorgter Blick;* he said nothing ∾ing me *er sagte nichts über mich.* — **II.** n.: I'll make it my ∾ to do so *ich werde es mir angelegen sein lassen, es zu tun;* that is no ∾ of mine *das geht mich nichts an;* he had no ∾ in the crime *er war an dem Verbrechen nicht beteiligt;* his illness causes us deep ∾ *seine Krankheit macht uns große Sorge;* it is a flourishing (going) ∾ *es ist ein blühendes (gutgehendes) Geschäft;* to cut the whole ∾ *mit dem ganzen Kram nichts zu tun haben wollen;* he is always meddling in my ∾s *er mischt sich immer in meine Angelegenheiten*

concert ['kɔnsə:t, kən'sə:t] n. & v.tr.: to work in ∾ with a person *in Übereinstimmung mit j.em arbeiten;* they agreed upon ∾ed action *sie beschlossen, gemeinsam vorzugehen;* to be at ∾-pitch *in höchster Erwartung sein*

conclusion n.: to come to the ∾ that *zu der Ansicht gelangen, daß;* the meeting came to a ∾ *die Versammlung kam zum Abschluß;* it was a foregone ∾ that *es stand von vornherein fest, daß;* he jumped to a (wrong) ∾ *er hat voreilig (überstürzt) gefolgert, er hat falsch angenommen;* in ∾ *zum Schluß;* to try ∾s with a person *sich mit j.em messen*

condition n.: in ∾, out of ∾ *gesundheitlich (nicht) auf der Höhe;* she is in no ∾ to travel *sie ist nicht kräftig (gesund) genug, um zu verreisen;* a man in his ∾ of life *ein Mann in seiner gesellschaftlichen Stellung;* the dog is in good ∾ *der Hund ist in gutem Zustand;* she was allowed to go on ∾ (but it was made a ∾) that she returned early *sie durfte gehen unter der Bedingung, daß sie früh zurückkehrte;* on no ∾ *unter keinen Umständen;* under favourable ∾s *unter günstigen Bedingungen;* to change one's ∾ *heiraten*

confidence n.: a vote of no ∾ (parl.) *ein Mißtrauensvotum;* in strict ∾ *streng vertraulich;* with ∾ *zuversichtlich;* to give ∾ *Vertrauen einflößen;* to place (to put, to repose) one's ∾ *sein Vertrauen setzen auf;* to take someone into one's ∾ *j.en ins Vertrauen ziehen;* a ∾ man, ∾ trick *ein Bauernfänger, eine Bauernfängerei*

confine I. v.tr.: to ∾ a person *j.en einsperren;* to be ∾d of a child *von einem Kinde entbunden werden;* to ∾ oneself to a thing *sich auf etwas beschränken;* to be ∾d to one's room, bed *ans Zimmer gefesselt, bettlägerig sein.* — **II.** v.i. (rare): to ∾ with *angrenzen an*

confinement n.: after her ∾ *nach ihrer Niederkunft (Entbindung);* to place under ∾ *in Haft setzen*

confound v.tr.: I ∾ed her with her sister *ich habe sie mit ihrer Schwester verwechselt;* the news ∾ed me *die Nachricht verwirrte mich;* ∾ it! *hol's der Teufel! hol's der Henker!;* a ∾ed (∾edly) long time *eine verflixt lange Zeit*

confusion n.: ∾! *ei verflucht!*

conjure[1] v.tr.: to ∾ a person to do a thing *j.en beschwören, etwas zu tun*

conjure[2] **I.** v.tr.: to ∾ away *bannen, weghexen;* to ∾ up a ghost *einen Geist heraufbeschwören (zitieren).* — **II.** v.i.: he has a name to ∾ with *er hat einen Namen von gewaltigem Einfluß*

conjurer, -or n.: he is no ∾ *er hat das Pulver nicht erfunden*

conk I. n. (sl.): a ∾ *eine Nase.* — **II.** v.i. (sl.): the engine ∾ed out *der Motor versagte (blieb stehen, setzte aus)*

conscience n.: in all ∾! upon my ∾! *wahrhaftig! auf mein Wort!;* out of all ∾ *unbillig, unverschämt;* to have the ∾ to do something *sich (dat.) kein Gewissen daraus machen (die Frechheit haben), etwas zu tun;* ∾ money *aus Gewissensbedenken (-bissen) zurückerstattetes Geld;* a good ∾ is a soft pillow (prov.) *ein gutes Gewissen ist ein sanftes Ruhekissen*

consent n.: the age of ∾ *das Mündigkeitsalter;* by common ∾ *mit Zustimmung aller;* silence gives ∾ (prov.) *Schweigen ist auch eine Antwort, Wer schweigt, stimmt zu*

consequence n.: a man of ∾ *ein Mann von Bedeutung;* it is of no ∾ *es hat nichts auf sich, es macht nichts;* to take the ∾s *die Folgen tragen (auf sich nehmen)*

consider I. v.tr.: he does not ∾ the consequences *er denkt nicht an die Folgen, er überlegt nicht, was daraus werden könnte;* he ∾s going abroad *er erwägt eine Reise ins Ausland;* I ∾ him (to be) a scoundrel *ich halte ihn für einen Schurken;* I ∾ him to have acted nobly *ich finde, er hat edel gehandelt;* ∾ yourself under arrest *betrachten Sie sich als verhaftet;* ∾ yourself at home *tun Sie, als ob Sie zu Hause wären;* you ought to ∾ yourself lucky *du solltest dich glücklich schätzen;* it is my ∾ed opinion *es ist meine wohlüberlegte Meinung;* it is ∾ed bad taste *es gilt als abgeschmackt;* his youth ∾ed *in Anbetracht seiner Jugend;* that is not so bad, ∾ing (the circumstances), all things ∾ed *eine ganz gute Leistung, wenn man (die Umstände) in Betracht zieht.* — **II.** v.i.: he ∾ed (that) it would be better *er überlegte, daß es besser wäre;* I'll ∾ about it *ich will es mir mal überlegen, ich lasse es mir durch den Kopf gehen*

consideration n.: that is a ∾ *das ist ein Grund; das läßt sich hören;* with every ∾ *bei aller Rücksicht;* £ 5 are a great ∾ to a poor man *5 Pfund bedeuten sehr viel (sind keine Kleinigkeit) für einen armen Mann;* in ∾ of *in Anbetracht von;* money is of no ∾ *auf Geld wird nicht gesehen, der Preis spielt keine Rolle;* he is an author of some ∾ *er ist ein Schriftsteller von einiger Bedeutung;* on (under) no ∾ *unter keinen Umständen;* your proposal is under ∾ *Ihr Vorschlag wird erwogen;* to bring before a person's ∾ *j.es Erwägung anheimstellen;* he will do it for a ∾ *er tut es gegen Entgelt;* to give ∾ to a thing *eine Sache erwägen;* to have no ∾ for old age *keine Rücksicht auf das Alter nehmen;* to take into ∾, to leave out of ∾ *(nicht) in Betracht (Erwägung) ziehen; (nicht) berücksichtigen*

conspicuous a.: he made himself ∾ *er machte sich verdächtig (benahm sich auffällig);* he was ∾ by his absence *er glänzte durch Abwesenheit*

constable n.: to outrun the ∾ *Schulden machen, über seine Verhältnisse leben;* who pays the ∾? *wer bezahlt?*

constitutional n.: a daily ∾ *ein täglicher Verdauungsspaziergang*

construction n.: the house is under (in course of) ∾ *das Haus ist im Bau;* they put a good (a bad) ∾ upon his refusal *sie legten seine Weigerung gut (schlecht) aus*

constructive a.: it was a ∾ proposal, idea *es war ein positiver Vorschlag, eine konstruktive Idee;* it was a ∾ denial *es war indirekt eine Verneinung, so gut wie eine Verneinung*

consult v.tr.: to ∾ one's pillow *eine Nacht über etwas schlafen, etwas beschlafen;* a ∾ing physician *ein vom Hausarzt als Spezialist hinzugezogener Arzt;* I must ∾ her convenience *ich muß Rücksicht auf sie nehmen*

contact I. n.: useful social ∾s *gesellschaftlich vorteilhafte (nützliche) Bekanntschaften.* — **II.** v.tr.: I must ∾ Mr. X. *ich muß mich mit Herrn X. in Verbindung setzen*

contain v.tr.: ∾ your anger *mäßige dich! nicht so zornig!*

contempt n.: to be beneath ∾ *ganz verächtlich sein;* to bring into ∾ *verächtlich machen;* to fail into ∾ *in Schande geraten;* to have (to hold) in ∾ *verachten, geringschätzen;* to hold a person, a thing up to ∾ *j.en, eine Sache verächtlich machen;* he was fined for ∾ of court *er erhielt wegen ungebührlichen Benehmens vor Gericht eine Geldstrafe;* familiarity breeds ∾ (prov.) *allzu große Vertraulichkeit erzeugt Verachtung*

content n.: to one's heart's ∾ *nach Herzenslust*

contract v.tr.: to ∾ heavy debts *große Schulden machen;* to ∾ a bad habit *sich* *(dat.) etwas Schlechtes angewöhnen;* to ∾ a serious illness *ernstlich erkranken;* to ∾ a friendship *eine Freundschaft anknüpfen*

contradiction n.: a ∾ in terms *ein sprachlicher Widerspruch, contradictio in adjecto (z. B.* a brave coward *ein tapferer Feigling)*

contrary I. n.: on the ∾ *im Gegenteil;* I have heard nothing to the ∾ *ich habe nichts Gegenteiliges gehört.* — **II.** adv.: ∾ to nature, ∾ to expectation *wider die Natur, naturwidrig; wider Erwarten*

control n.: the ∾s *das Armaturenbrett eines Flugzeugs;* to be beyond ∾ *außer Rand und Band sein;* to get the situation under ∾ *Herr der Lage werden;* keep your temper under ∾! *beherrsche dich!;* to lose ∾ of *die Gewalt über etwas verlieren;* not subject to ∾ *nicht kontrollpflichtig;* under ∾ of the police *unter Aufsicht der Polizei;* a ∾-experiment *ein Kontrollversuch*

convenience n.: at your earliest ∾ *baldmöglichst;* a marriage of ∾ *eine Geldheirat;* a public ∾ *eine Bedürfnisanstalt;* to make a ∾ of a person *j.en über Gebühr ausnutzen;* suit your own ∾ *tun Sie ganz nach Ihrem Belieben, halten Sie es damit ganz, wie Sie wollen*

cook n. & v.tr.: too many ∾s spoil the broth (prov.) *viele Köche verderben den Brei;* to ∾ accounts (colloq.) *Berichte (Akten) frisieren (fälschen);* to ∾ a person's goose *j.en erledigen, ihm den Garaus machen;* the runner was ∾ed (sl.) *der Läufer war erschöpft (erschossen);* to ∾ up a story *eine Geschichte aushecken;* what's ∾ing? (sl.) *was ist los?*

cool I. a.: as ∾ as a cucumber *kaltblütig, gelassen, die Ruhe selber;* keep ∾ *reg' dich nicht auf!;* he is a ∾ customer *er ist ein frecher Patron, ein unverschämter Kunde;* it cost me a ∾ thousand *es hat mich einen glatten Tausender gekostet.* — **II.** v.i.: he has ∾ed down by now *er hat sich inzwischen beruhigt.* — **III.** v.tr.: to ∾ one's coppers, see 'copper'; to let a person ∾ his heels *j.en lange warten lassen; j.en sich (dat.) die Beine in den Bauch stehen lassen*

coon n.: (U.S. colloq.) he is a gone ∾ (rare) *er ist in einer hoffnungslosen Lage*

coot n.: as bald as a ∾ (colloq.) *ratzekahl*

cop I. v.tr. (sl.): the thief was ∾ped *der Dieb wurde geschnappt;* you'll ∾ it when you get home *du kriegst es, wenn du nach Hause kommst.* — **II.** n. (sl.): he is a ∾, ∾per *er ist Polizist, ein Schupo;* it was a fair ∾ *auf frischer Tat ertappt*

copper n.: hot ∾s *vom Zechen ausgedörrter Mund und Schlund;* to cool one's ∾s *seinen Durst (Brand) löschen;* a ∾-beech *eine Blut-, Rotbuche;* a ∾-captain (Fletcher: Rule a Wife and Have a Wife) *ein falscher Kapitän;* to write like ∾plate *wie gestochen schreiben*

copy n.: clean (fair) ∾ *Reinschrift;* rough (foul) ∾ *Entwurf, Konzept;* this incident will make good ∾ *dieser Vorfall wird gutes Material für die Zeitung abgeben;* that's a mere ∾ of your countenance *Sie wollen, daß ich das glaube, es ist aber nicht Ihre wahre Meinung;* ∾-book maxims *landläufige Grundsätze;* to blot one's ∾-book *einen Schnitzer machen, ins Fettnäpfchen treten;* you're a ∾-cat! *Affen machen alles nach! (Schule)*

core n.: rotten at (to) the ∾ *faul bis aufs Mark*

corn[1] n.: to tread on a person's ∾s *j.em auf die Hühneraugen treten*

corn[2] n.: ∾ in Egypt! *jetzt sind wir fein heraus! jetzt ist uns geholfen!*

corner n.: to be in a desperate (tight) ∾ *in einer verzwickten Lage sein;* to cut off a ∾ *eine Ecke, den Weg abschneiden;* to drive into a ∾ *in die Enge treiben;* to make a ∾ in leather (= to ∾ the market in leather) *die Ledervorräte aufkaufen, um die Preise in die Höhe zu treiben;* he has turned the ∾ *er ist über den Berg (bei einer Krankheit usw.);* the cotton ∾ *der Baumwollring (an der Börse);* hole-and-∾ transactions *dunkle Machenschaften*

corny a. (sl.): ∾ talk *triviales, altes Geschwätz*

corporation n.: he has a big ∾ (colloq.) *er hat einen Schmerbauch*

correct v.tr.: I stand ∾ed *ich gestehe meinen Fehler ein*

correction n.: I speak under ∾ *ich mag (kann) mich irren; dies ist meine unmaßgebliche Meinung*

cost I. n.: at any (all) ∾s *um jeden Preis;* at the ∾ of *auf Kosten von;* to a person's ∾ *j.em zum Schaden;* the prime ∾, ∾ price *der Gestehungs-, Einkaufs-, Selbstkostenpreis;* you must count the ∾ of your action *Sie müssen die Folge(n) Ihrer Tat (Ihres Tuns) einkalkulieren.* — **II.** v.i.: it ∾ him dear(ly) *es kam ihn teuer zu stehen*

cotton I. n.: to keep in ∾ wool *in Watte wickeln, verhätscheln.* — **II.** (colloq.) v.i.: I didn't ∾ on *ich hab's nicht mitgekriegt; ich habe nicht angebissen;* he doesn't ∾ on to people of that sort *mit solchen Leuten gibt er sich nicht ab;* they don't ∾ together (with each other) *sie harmonieren nicht miteinander;* he tried to ∾ up to her *er versuchte, sich an sie heranzumachen*

cough v.tr.: ∾ it up (sl.) *heraus mit der Sprache!;* I had to ∾ up five pounds (sl.) *ich mußte fünf Pfund herausrücken (blechen)*

counsel n.: to keep one's own ∾ *etwas für sich behalten, verschweigen;* to take ∾ with a person *sich (dat.) bei j.em Rat holen;* to take ∾ of one's pillow *eine Nacht darüber schlafen*

count I. n.: to be guilty on all ∾s *in allen Punkten schuldig sein;* to keep ∾ of *zählen;* to lose ∾ of *die Übersicht über etwas verlieren;* to take the ∾ *sterben;* take no ∾ of what he says *achte nicht auf das, was er sagt.* — **II.** v.tr.: to ∾ one's chickens before they are hatched, see 'chicken'; to ∾ noses (colloq.) *die Anwesenden zählen;* to ∾ out *(Boxkampf) auszählen;* to ∾ out the house *eine Vertagung der Unterhaussitzung durchsetzen, weil weniger als 40% der Abgeordneten anwesend sind;* to ∾ up *addieren;* to ∾ in *einschließen;* to ∾ the cost, see 'cost'. — **III.** v.i.: that does not ∾ for much *das hat nicht viel auf sich, das bedeutet nicht viel;* to ∾ upon a thing *auf etwas rechnen*

countenance n.: to change ∾ *die Farbe wechseln;* this gives ∾ to the report *dies bestärkt das Gerücht;* I could scarcely keep my ∾ *ich konnte kaum ernst bleiben, das Lachen verbeißen;* to keep a person in ∾ *j.en aufmuntern, bei Laune halten;* to put out of ∾ *außer Fassung bringen*

counter n.: a ∾-jumper (sl.) *ein Ladenschwengel*

country I. n.: to appeal (to go) to the ∾ *an die Wählerschaft des Landes appellieren.* — **II.** a.: a ∾-cousin *ein Vetter (eine Base, Unschuld) vom Lande;* a ∾-dance *Volkstanz, ländlicher Reihentanz;* a ∾ gentleman *ein Gutsbesitzer;* a ∾-house, a ∾-seat *ein Landsitz (Landhaus, Gut)*

courage n.: to have Dutch ∾ *sich (dat.) Mut angetrunken haben;* he has the ∾ of his opinions (convictions) *er hat die Zivilcourage (den Mut), nach seiner Überzeugung zu handeln;* to pluck up (to take) ∾ *Mut fassen;* to screw up one's ∾ to the sticking-place (Macbeth, I, 7) *Mut fassen;* to take one's ∾ in both hands (Gallicism) *sich (dat.) ein Herz fassen*

course n.: of ∾ *natürlich, selbstverständlich;* in the ∾ of *im Verlaufe von, während;* in the ∾ of construction *im Bau, in der Einrichtung begriffen;* in due ∾ *zur rechten (gehörigen) Zeit;* that is a matter of ∾ *das liegt in der Natur der Sache, das ist eine Selbstverständlichkeit;* things must run (take) their ∾ *man muß den Dingen ihren Lauf lassen;* to stay the ∾ *bis zum Ende aushalten*

court I. n.: to pay ∾ to a person *j.em den Hof machen;* to put a thing out of ∾ *etwas als indiskutabel erklären;* to settle out of ∾ *einen Vergleich schließen.* — **II.** v.tr.: to ∾ disaster *ein Unglück heraufbeschwören;* to ∾ a person's favour *um j.es Gunst werben*

cousin n.: to call ∾s with a person *sich auf die Verwandtschaft mit j.em berufen*

Coventry n.pr.: to send a person to ∾ *jeden Verkehr mit j.em abbrechen*

cover I. v.tr.: to ∾ a person with a gun *ein Gewehr auf j.en richten, ihn mit einem Gewehr in Schach halten;* they ∾ed twenty miles *sie legten zwanzig Meilen zurück;* he was ∾ing the trial for a newspaper *er war als Sonderberichterstatter über den Prozeß für eine Zeitung tätig;* a ∾ing letter *ein Begleitbrief;* to ∾ up a thing *etwas zu-, verdecken.* — **II.** n.: a book in paper ∾s *ein broschiertes Buch;* under this ∾ *einliegend, beigeschlossen;* under ∾ of *unter dem Schutze von; per Adresse;* under (the) ∾ of humility *unter dem Deckmantel der Bescheidenheit;* to break ∾ *aus dem Lager (Versteck) hervorbrechen (vom Wild);* to lay ∾s for four *vier Gedecke auflegen;* I read the book from ∾ to ∾ *ich las das Buch von Anfang bis zu Ende;* to take ∾ *Deckung nehmen*

cow n.: the ∾ with the iron tail *die Wasserpumpe, die benutzt wird, um die Milch zu verwässern;* till the ∾s come home *für unbestimmte Zeit, für immer*

crab I. n.: to catch (to land) a ∾ *durch einen falschen Schlag mit dem Ruder im Wasser stecken bleiben.* — **II.** v.tr.: to ∾ something *etwas herabsetzen, über etwas nörgeln (meckern)*

crack I. n.: in a ∾ *im Nu;* the ∾ of doom *der Jüngste Tag, das Jüngste Gericht;* I gave him a ∾ on the head *ich schlug ihn heftig gegen den Kopf.* — **II.** a.: he is a ∾ player *er ist ein Spitzenspieler, eine große Kanone;* ∾-brained *wunderlich, exzentrisch.* — **III.** v.tr.: he is ∾ed, ∾ers (sl.) *er ist verrückt, er hat einen Hau (mit der Wichsbürste);* his voice is ∾ing (breaking) *er ist im Stimmbruch;* get ∾ing (sl.) *nun mal los! fang' an!;* to ∾ a bottle *einer Flasche den Hals brechen;* to ∾ a crib (sl.) *in ein Haus einbrechen;* to ∾ a joke *einen Witz reißen;* to ∾ up a thing (colloq.) *etwas übermäßig loben, herausstreichen;* to ∾ a whip *mit der Peitsche knallen;* that word is a regular ∾-jaw *bei diesem Wort zerbricht man sich (dat.) die Zunge.* — **IV.** v.i.: to ∾ up (colloq.) *zusammenbrechen, einstürzen, einfallen*

craft n.: the gentle ∾ *das Angeln;* he is one of the ∾ *er ist ein Mann vom Fach, einer der unsrigen*

cram I. v.tr.: to ∾ a child *ein Kind überfüttern;* to ∾ a thing down a person's throat *j.em etwas immer wieder sagen, unter die Nase reiben, aufs Butterbrot schmieren;* the room was ∾med *das Zimmer war gedrängt voll.* — **II.** v.i.: he is ∾ming for his examination *er büffelt (ochst) für seine Prüfung.* — **III.** n.: there was a terrible ∾ *es gab ein schreckliches Gedränge*

crash I. v.i.: the aeroplane ∾ed *das Flugzeug stürzte ab;* to go (to fall) ∾ *in Stücke zerfallen.* — **II.** v.tr.: to ∾ a thing *etwas in Stücke zerschlagen.* — **III.** n.: to come a ∾ *stürzen, abstürzen*

craven a.: to cry ∾ *sich ergeben, sich als besiegt erklären*

crawl I. v.i.: my flesh ∾s to think of it *bei dem Gedanken überläuft mich eine Gänsehaut;* the town was ∾ing with tourists (sl.) *die Stadt wimmelte von Touristen;* I ∾ed home on my eyebrows *ich kam todmüde nach Hause.* — **II.** n.: a pub-∾ *eine Bierreise (Kneipenrunde)*

craze n.: it's the latest ∾ *es ist die letzte Mode(torheit), der letzte Schrei*

crazy a.: a ∾ building *ein baufälliges (wackliges) Gebäude;* a ∾ coach *ein alter Rumpelkasten;* a ∾ pavement *unregelmäßiges Mosaikpflaster;* a ∾ quilt *eine aus bunten Flicken zusammengesetzte Decke;* to be ∾ about (to do) a thing *auf etwas ganz versessen (verrückt) sein*

cream n.: the ∾ of the anecdote *die Pointe der Anekdote;* the ∾ of society *die feinste, höchste Gesellschaft*

create v.i.: you needn't ∾ about it (sl.) *du brauchst nicht soviel Aufhebens (Getue) davon (so einen Sums, so ein Theater darum) zu machen*

creature n.: ∾ comforts *leibliche Genüsse, die materiellen Annehmlichkeiten des Lebens*

credence n.: a letter of ∾ *ein Einführungs-, Beglaubigungsschreiben;* to give ∾ to a story *einer Geschichte Glauben schenken*

credit I. n.: he is a ∾ to the school *er gereicht der Schule zur Ehre;* that is not much to his ∾ *das gereicht ihm nicht zur besonderen Ehre;* it is based on the ∾ of a historian *es stützt sich auf die Autorität eines Historikers;* it does him ∾, it reflects ∾ upon him *es macht ihm Ehre;* to gain ∾ by a thing *mit etwas Ehre einlegen;* to gain ∾ with a person *bei j.em Gunst (Achtung) gewinnen;* to give ∾ to a story *einer Geschichte Glauben schenken;* to give a person ∾ for a thing *j.em etwas zutrauen;* he got ∾ for doing it *es wurde ihm als Verdienst angerechnet;* he must have the ∾ of it *man muß es ihm als Verdienst anrechnen;* to lose ∾ with a person *j.es Vertrauen verlieren;* to place (to put) to a person's ∾ *j.em etwas gutschreiben;* to stand in high ∾ with a person *bei j.em in hohem Ansehen stehen;* to take ∾ for a thing *sich (dat.) etwas als (zum) Verdienst anrechnen.* — **II.** v.tr.: to ∾ an amount to a person, a person with an amount *j.em einen Betrag gutschreiben;* to ∾ a person with a thing *j.em etwas zutrauen;* to ∾ a story *eine Geschichte glauben*

creeps n.pl.: it gave me the ∾ (colloq.) *es überlief mich eiskalt; mich überlief eine Gänsehaut*

crest I. n.: on the ∾ of the wave *auf dem Gipfel des Glücks.* — **II.** a.: ∾-fallen *niedergeschlagen*

crib I. n.: to crack a ∾ (sl.) *in ein Haus einbrechen;* to use a ∾ in translating *eine Eselsbrücke (einen Pons) beim Übersetzen gebrauchen.* — **II.** v.tr.: he has ∾bed that from another author *das hat er von einem anderen Schriftsteller unberechtigterweise abgeschrieben (geklaut)*

cricket n.: that's not ∾ (colloq.) *das ist nicht fair (ehrlich, anständig)*

crikey int. (sl.): ∾! *ach Herrje!*

crock I. n.: he is a ∾ (sl.) *er ist ein unbrauchbarer, unfähiger Kerl.* — **II.** v.i.: to ∾ up (sl.) *zusammenbrechen,-sacken, versagen*

crocodile n.: a ∾ (colloq.) *ein Mädchenpensionat in Zweierreihe beim Spaziergang;* to shed ∾'s tears *Krokodilstränen vergießen*

crook n.: he is a ∾ (sl.) *er ist ein Gauner, Schwindler;* he got it on the ∾ (sl.) *er bekam es auf unehrliche Weise;* by hook or by ∾, see 'hook'

crop I. n.: to get in the ∾ *die Ernte einbringen;* wheat is in (under) ∾ *Weizen ist angebaut;* she has an Eton ∾ *sie hat einen Bubikopf, Herrenschnitt;* a hunting-∾ *eine Reitpeitsche (mit Lederschlaufe statt Lasche);* neck and ∾ *Hals über Kopf;* a fine show and small ∾ (prov.) *viel Geschrei und wenig Wolle.* — **II.** v.tr.: to ∾ a field with barley *ein Feld mit Gerste bestellen;* to ∾ a person's feathers *j.em die Flügel stutzen, ihn demütigen;* the dog was ∾-eared *der Hund hatte die Ohren gestutzt.* — **III.** v.i.: to ∾ out (forth) *hervorbrechen, zum Vorschein kommen;* the question ∾ped up *die Frage tauchte auf*

cropper n. (sl.): to come a ∾ *einen schweren Sturz tun, hinschlagen; Mißerfolg haben*

cross I. v.tr.: a ∾ed cheque *ein Verrechnungsscheck;* ∾ your fingers (keep your fingers crossed) for me *halt' mir den Daumen, drück' mir ein Däumchen;* to ∾ a fortune-teller's hand *einer Wahrsagerin ein Geldstück geben;* to ∾ a letter *quer über die Zeilen eines Briefes schreiben;* it ∾ed my mind *es kam mir in den Sinn;* you must ∾ that out *das mußt du durchstreichen;* to ∾ one's t's and dot one's i's *sich sehr in acht nehmen, sich vorsichtig benehmen;* to ∾ swords *die Klingen kreuzen, sich messen.* — **II.** v.i.: our letters must have ∾ed *unsere Briefe müssen sich gekreuzt haben.* — **III.** a.: as ∾ as two sticks *höchst verdrießlich, äußerst ärgerlich;* don't be ∾ if I can't come *sei nicht böse, wenn ich nicht kommen kann;* he is a ∾-patch *er ist ein mürrischer Geselle;* to be at ∾ purposes *sich gegenseitig mißverstehen, sich (dat.) unabsichtlich entgegenarbeiten;* to talk at ∾ purposes *aneinander vorbeireden*

crow I. n.: as the ∾ flies, in a ∾ line *in gerader Linie, in der Luftlinie;* a white ∾ *ein weißer Rabe, eine Seltenheit;* a ∾'s nest *ein Mastkorb zum Ausguck auf Schiffen, ein Krähennest;* to eat ∾ (U.S.) *sich demütigen, zu Kreuze kriechen;* I have a ∾ to pluck with you *ich habe ein Hühnchen mit dir zu rupfen.* — **II.** v.i.: don't ∾ too soon *frohlocke nicht zu früh! man soll den Tag nicht vor dem Abend loben;* to ∾ over someone *über j.en triumphieren*

crowd n.: that would pass in a ∾ *das ginge noch eben an;* what a queer ∾! (colloq.) *welch komische Gesellschaft!*

crucial a.: this is the ∾ moment *dies ist der entscheidende Augenblick; jetzt geht's um die Wurst!*

crumb n.: all crust and no ∾, see 'crust'

crumpet n. (sl.): he is barmy on the ∾ *er hat einen Vogel, er hat sie nicht alle beieinander (zusammen)*

crush I. v.tr.: to ∾ a cup of wine (rare) *ein Glas Wein trinken;* to ∾ (out) a rebellion *einen Aufruhr unterdrücken;* to ∾ up *zerstampfen, zerknittern;* to suffer a ∾ing defeat *eine vernichtende Niederlage erleiden.* — **II.** n.: there was a great ∾ *es gab ein dichtes Gedränge;* to have a ∾ on a person (sl.) *in j.en verliebt sein, für j.en schwärmen;* a ∾ hat *ein Klapphut*

crust n.: all ∾ and no crumb *saure Arbeit und wenig Lohn;* the ∾ of the earth *die Erdrinde;* the ∾ of wine *der Niederschlag in Weinflaschen*

crusty a.: to turn ∾ *ärgerlich, mürrisch werden*

cry I. n.: a far ∾ *eine weite Entfernung;* in full ∾ *laut bellend, in hitziger Verfolgung;* to raise a hue and ∾ *ein Zetergeschrei erheben;* much ∾ and little wool *viel Geschrei und wenig Wolle;* within ∾ *in Rufweite;* to follow in the ∾ *Mitläufer sein;* to give a ∾ *einen Schrei ausstoßen;* to have a good ∾ *sich ordentlich ausweinen;* a ∾-baby *ein kleiner Schreihals, ein Heulfritze, eine Heulsuse.* — **II.** v.tr.: see 'blue, craven, cupboard, quits, shame, stink, wolf'. — with adv.: to ∾ down a thing *etwas verunglimpfen;* to ∾ off an engagement *eine Verpflichtung rückgängig machen, abblasen;* to ∾ one's heart out *sich (dat.) die Augen ausweinen;* to ∾ a thing up to the skies *etwas in den Himmel erheben.* — **III.** v.i.: to ∾ against a thing *sich laut über etwas beklagen;* to ∾ for the moon *etwas Unmögliches wünschen, Unerreichbares erstreben;* to ∾ off from a thing *sich von etwas lossagen, von etwas zurücktreten;* to ∾ out against a thing *etwas öffentlich mißbilligen;* to ∾ out for help *um Hilfe schreien;* it's no use ∾ing over spilt milk (prov.) *es hat keinen Zweck, Geschehenes zu beklagen*

cucumber n.: as cool as a ∾ *kaltblütig, gelassen, die Ruhe selber*

cud n.: to chew the ∾ *wiederkäuen; über etwas nachsinnen*

cudgel I. n.: to take up the ∾s for a person *kräftig für j.en eintreten.* — **II.** v.tr.: to ∾ one's brains *sich (dat.) den Kopf über etwas zerbrechen*

cue n.: to give a person his ∾ *j.em die Worte in den Mund legen;* to take the ∾ *einen Wink verstehen (befolgen);* to take one's ∾ from a person *sich nach j.em richten*

cup I. n.: a bitter ∾ *ein bitterer Kelch, ein bitteres Los;* his ∾ was full *sein Glück, Elend war vollkommen;* the ∾s that cheer but not inebriate (Cowper, Task, IV, 39) *der Tee;* to be in one's ∾s *zechen, betrunken sein;* a ∾ too low (rare) *mißgestimmt;* that's not my ∾ of tea *das ist nicht nach meinem Geschmack, daraus mache ich mir nichts;* there's many a slip 'twixt ∾ and lip *zwischen Lipp' und Kelchesrand schwebt der dunklen Mächte Hand; es ist noch nicht aller Tage Abend.* — **II.** v.tr.: to ∾ one's hands round a thing *die Hände um etwas wölben*

cupboard n.: ∾ love *eigennützige, berechnende Liebe;* a skeleton in the ∾ *ein peinliches Familiengeheimnis;* to cry ∾ *hungrig sein*

curdle v.i.: it made his blood ∾ with horror *das Blut erstarrte ihm vor Schrecken in den Adern*

curl I. n.: a ∾ of the lip *ein verächtliches Schürzen (Aufwerfen) der Lippen.* — **II.** v.i.: he simply ∾ed up (sl.) *er sackte einfach zusammen*

current a.: to go (to pass, to run) ∾ *allgemein als wahr (echt) angenommen werden*

curry v.tr.: to ∾ favour with a person *sich bei j.em einschmeicheln, lieb Kind machen*

curse n. & v.tr.: ∾s come home to roost *wer anderen eine Grube gräbt, fällt selbst hinein;* to be ∾d with a disease *mit einer Krankheit gestraft sein*

curtain n.: ∾ lectures *Gardinenpredigten;* behind the ∾ *hinter den Kulissen;* to draw the ∾ over a thing *etwas begraben, zudecken;* to lift the ∾ *den Schleier lüften;* to take a ∾ (theatre) *applaudiert werden;* to take one's last ∾ *zum letzten Male auftreten;* a ∾-raiser *ein Einakter*

cushy a. (sl.): he has a ∾ job *er hat eine angenehme, bequeme Stelle*

cuss n.: I don't care a tinker's ∾ *ich mache mir einen Dreck daraus*

custody n.: to give (to take) into ∾ *verhaften lassen, verhaften*

custom n.: it is the ∾ *es herrscht der Brauch, es ist üblich, es ist gang und gäbe;* to break a ∾ *sich (dat.) etwas abgewöhnen;* it has passed the ∾s *es ist verzollt worden;* I shall withdraw my ∾ from that shop *ich werde in diesem (jenem) Geschäft nicht mehr einkaufen*

customer n.: he is an awkward ∾ to deal with *er ist ein schwieriger Kunde; mit ihm ist nicht gut Kirschen essen;* a regular ∾ *ein Stammkunde*

cut I. n.: that's a ∾ above me *so weit reichen meine Kräfte nicht; das ist mir zu hoch;* the ∾ of his jib *seine äußere Erscheinung, sein Aussehen;* a ∾ in prices (in pay) *eine Preissenkung, ein Lohnabzug;* a suit of the latest ∾ *ein Anzug nach dem* *neuesten Schnitt;* it is your ∾ *du hebst ab (Kartenspiel);* to draw ∾s *Hälmchen, Lose ziehen;* to give a person the ∾ direct *j.en auffällig schneiden;* I must make a ∾ somewhere *ich muß mich irgendwie einschränken;* to take a short ∾ *einen Weg abschneiden,-kürzen.* — **II.** v.tr.: see 'caper, card, coat, concern, dash, dead, figure, fine, ice, etc.'; there was ∾-and-come-again *es war alles im Überfluß (in Hülle und Fülle) vorhanden;* he has ∾-and-dry (dried) opinions on the matter *er hat die übliche (alltägliche, landläufige) Meinung von der Sache.* — with adv.: to ∾ down expenses *die Ausgaben einschränken;* to ∾ a person off *die Telefonverbindung trennen;* to ∾ a person off with a shilling *j.en enterben;* he has ∾ me out with her *er hat mich bei ihr ausgestochen;* he is ∾ out for this work *er ist für diese Arbeit wie geschaffen;* he has his work ∾ out for him *er hat ein tüchtiges Stück Arbeit vor sich;* the book was ∾ up *das Buch wurde von der Kritik heruntergerissen;* to be ∾ up at a thing *über etwas tief traurig sein.* — **III.** v.i.: now ∾ (sl.) *nun fort mit dir! hau ab! verdufte!;* I ∾ across the field *ich nahm den kürzeren Weg durchs Feld;* to ∾ loose *sich befreien, entfliehen;* to ∾ and run (sl.) *sich aus dem Staube machen (Reißaus nehmen).* — with adv.: to ∾ away to the right *nach rechts abschwenken;* to ∾ in *ins Wort fallen;* the car ∾ in upon me *das Auto überholte mich, obwohl ein dritter Wagen entgegenkam;* to ∾ off (sl.) *sich eiligst entfernen (abhauen, verduften);* to ∾ up rough *aufgebracht sein, rauhbeinig werden;* to ∾ up well (fat) *reich sterben, ein großes Vermögen hinterlassen*

D

dab n. (colloq.): I was never a ∾ at it (at doing it) *ich war nie besonders tüchtig darin;* I'd like to have a ∾ at journalism *ich würde es gern als Journalist versuchen*

dabster n. (colloq.): she's a ∾ at cooking *sie ist eine erstklassige (prima) Köchin*

dagger n.: to be at ∾s drawn with a person *mit j.em auf sehr gespanntem Fuße stehen, sein Todfeind sein;* to look ∾s at a person *j.en mit Blicken durchbohren;* to speak ∾s to a person (Hamlet, III, 2) *j.es Herz mit grausamen Worten zerfleischen; Dolche reden (Schlegel)*

dahlia n.: a blue ∾ *etwas Unmögliches, Seltenes, Unerhörtes; ein blaues Wunder*

daily n. & a.: a ∾ *eine Wochentagszeitung;* a ∾ (maid) *eine Tageshilfe;* I did my ∾ dozens (colloq.) *ich habe meine Morgengymnastik gemacht*

daisy n.: as fresh as a ∾ *quicklebendig, quietschfidel;* he is pushing up the daisies (sl.) *er liegt im Grabe, er ist tot*

dally v.tr. & i.: to ∾ away *vertrödeln;* to ∾ with a person *mit j.em tändeln, schäkern*

damage n.: what's the ∾? (sl.) *was muß ich blechen?;* to get (to recover) ∾s *Schadenersatz erhalten*

damn I. v.tr.: O ∾, ∾ed! *ei verflucht!;* ∾ your eyes *zum Teufel (Henker) mit dir!;* to ∾ with faint praise *so zurückhaltend loben, daß es einem Tadel gleichkommt.* — **II.** n.: I don't care a ∾ *ich mache mir nicht die Bohne (mir einen Dreck) daraus;* you know a ∾ sight too much *du weißt verflucht (verflixt) zuviel;* as near as ∾-it (colloq.) *sehr nahe daran;* ∾ all (colloq.) *gar nichts;* ∾ well *sicher, bestimmt*

damp I. n.: to cast a ∾ over a person *j.en entmutigen.* — **II.** a.: a ∾ squib *ein Scherz, der nicht gelingt.* — **III.** to ∾ down a fire *ein Feuer zudecken (dämpfen)*

dance I. v.i.: he ∾s to my tune (pipe) *er tanzt nach meiner Pfeife;* to ∾ upon nothing *gehängt werden.* — **II.** v.tr.: to ∾ attendance upon a person *um j.en herumscharwenzeln.* — **III.** n.: to lead a person a ∾ *j.em Scherereien verursachen, ihm übel mitspielen, ihm das Leben schwermachen*

dander n. (colloq. esp. U.S.): to get one's ∾ up *in Zorn (Wut) geraten*

dandy a. (U.S. colloq.): that's ∾! *das ist großartig! Prima!*

danger n.: he was in ∾ of his life, his life was in ∾ *er schwebte in Lebensgefahr;* to run the ∾ of losing *Gefahr laufen zu verlieren*

dangle I. v.i.: to ∾ from *herabhängen, -baumeln von;* to ∾ about (after, round) a person *j.em nachlaufen, ihm nicht von der Seite weichen.* — **II.** v.tr.: to ∾ a thing before a person, in a person's sight *etwas verführerisch (verlockend) vor j.em baumeln lassen*

darbies n.: to clap on the ∾ (colloq.) *Handschellen anlegen*

Darby n.pr.: ∾ and Joan *ein älteres, glückliches Ehepaar*

dare I. v.i.: I ∾ say he'll come *er wird sehr wahrscheinlich kommen;* I ∾ say! *ja, Kuchen!* — **II.** v.tr.: to ∾ someone's anger *j.es Zorn Trotz bieten;* he is a ∾-devil *er ist ein Teufelskerl, Wagehals;* a ∾-devil attempt *ein tollkühner (wagehalsiger) Versuch*

dark I. a.: the ∾ ages *das Mittelalter;* the ∾ continent *Afrika;* he is a ∾ horse *er ist ein unbeschriebenes Blatt;* a ∾ lantern *eine Blendlaterne;* the ∾ side of things *die Schattenseite der Dinge;* to keep a thing ∾ *etwas geheim halten;* the ∾est hour is that before the dawn *wenn die Verhältnisse sehr schlimm sind, muß es bald besser werden;* the ∾est place is under the candlestick *derjenige, welchen die Sache am meisten angeht, weiß oft am wenigsten von ihr (davon).* — **II.** n.: to be in the ∾ about a thing *in Unkenntnis über eine Sache sein;* a leap in the ∾ *ein Sprung ins Ungewisse;* to keep a person in the ∾ *j.en im Ungewissen lassen*

darken v.tr.: never ∾ my door again *komm mir nie wieder über die Schwelle!;* to ∾ counsel (rare) *einen törichten Rat geben, die Sache verschlimmern*

dash I. v.tr.: to ∾ a person's hopes *j.es Hoffnungen zunichtemachen;* oh, ∾ it! *ei, verflucht!;* he ∾ed it off in a few minutes *er haute es in ein paar Minuten hin.* — **II.** v.i.: I must ∾ off at once *ich muß sofort weg;* he is a ∾ing appearance *er ist eine flotte Erscheinung;* a ∾ing attack *ein ungestümer Angriff.* — **III.** n.: a ∾ of brandy *ein Schuß Kognak;* a ∾ of the pen *ein Federstrich;* a ∾ of the tar-brush *eine Mischung von Negerblut;* to cut a ∾ *Aufsehen erregen, Eindruck machen (schinden);* to make a ∾ for the door *zur Tür stürzen;* to put a ∾ under a word *ein Wort unterstreichen*

date I. n.: out of ∾ *veraltet, altmodisch;* up to ∾ *modern, zeitgemäß;* to have a ∾ with a person *eine Verabredung (ein Stelldichein) mit j.em haben;* to make a ∾ with a person *sich mit j.em verabreden.* — **II.** v.tr.: to ∾ a thing from *eine Sache herleiten von;* to ∾ someone (colloq.), see 'to make a ∾'. — **III.** v.i.: the church ∾s from the 14th century *die Kirche stammt aus dem 14. Jahrhundert;* to ∾ back to a time *bis in eine Zeit zurückreichen;* the play ∾s *das Stück verrät die Zeit seiner Abfassung, ist veraltet*

davy n. (sl.): to take one's ∾ (abbr. affidavit) *beschwören*

Davy Jones's locker n.: to go to ∾ *im Meer ertrinken*

day n.: he may come any ∾ *er kann jeden Tag kommen;* I prefer that any ∾ *ich würde das immer vorziehen;* the ∾ before (after) the fair *etwas zu früh (einen Posttag zu spät) tun;* all (the) ∾ *den ganzen Tag;* ∾ by ∾, ∾ after ∾ *von Tag zu Tag;* for ever and a ∾ *auf immer und ewig;* to this ∾ (present ∾) *bis zum heutigen Tage;* these ∾s *heutzutage;* one of these (fine) ∾s *dieser Tage, demnächst;* the other ∾ *neulich, kürzlich;* every other ∾ *jeden zweiten Tag, einen Tag über den anderen;* a ∾ of grace *eine Gnadenfrist;* ∾ break *Tagesanbruch;* ∾ dream *Träumerei;* pay-∾ *Lohn-, Löhnungstag;* the Last ∾, ∾ of Judgement *das Jüngste Gericht;* this ∾ week (month) *heute über acht Tage (in einem Monat);* twice a ∾ *zweimal am Tag;* one's ∾ (at home) *Empfangstag, jour fixe für Gäste;* in the (good) old ∾s *in (den) guten alten Zeiten;* in ∾s to come *in der Zukunft;* to call it a ∾ *Feierabend, Schluß machen;* to carry (to win) the ∾ *den Sieg davon tragen;* to fall on evil ∾s *ins Unglück geraten;* to give a person the time of ∾ *j.em die Tageszeit bieten, j.en grüßen;* every dog has his ∾ (prov.) *jeder hat einmal seinen guten Tag; heute mir, morgen dir;* to know the time of ∾ *wissen, was die Glocke geschlagen hat; geistig auf der Höhe sein;* I have had my ∾ *meine besten Jahre sind vorüber;* to keep one's ∾ *pünktlich sein;* to lose the ∾ *besiegt werden (sein);* to name the ∾ *den Tag der Hochzeit festsetzen;* a red-letter ∾ *ein Freuden-, Glückstag;* men of the ∾ *Persönlichkeiten der Gegenwart;* a creature of a ∾ *eine Eintagsfliege;* to end one's ∾s *sein Lebensende verbringen;* a ∾-boy, a ∾-school *ein Externer, ein Externat;* a ∾-labourer *ein Tagelöhner;* to make a ∾ of it *sich einen vergnügten Tag machen;* sufficient for the ∾ is the evil thereof *man soll sich nicht im voraus Sorgen machen, den*

Teufel nicht an die Wand malen; palmy ∾s *Blütezeit;* (to save money) for a rainy ∾ *(Geld sparen) für die Zukunft, für den Fall, daß man es braucht*

daylight n.: in broad ∾ *am hellichten Tage;* to let ∾ into a person *j.en erstechen, erschießen;* I see ∾ *es geht mir ein Licht auf;* to throw ∾ upon a thing *etwas beleuchten, aufdecken, enthüllen;* ∾-saving (= Summer Time) *Sommerzeit in England (vom 1. April bis etwa 1. Oktober)*

dead I. a.: as ∾ as a doornail, as mutton; stone-∾ *mausetot;* a ∾-alive occupation *eine langweilige Beschäftigung;* a ∾ calm *eine Flaute;* a ∾ certainty *eine todsichere Sache;* to come to a ∾-end *in eine Sackgasse geraten;* ∾ and gone *futsch;* it was a ∾ heat *es war ein totes Rennen;* to flog a ∾ horse *Interesse für eine abgetane Sache zu erregen suchen, seine Kraft verschwenden;* a ∾ letter *ein nicht mehr geltendes Gesetz;* the ∾-letter office *das Postamt für unbestellbare Briefe;* to be on a ∾ level with *auf vollkommen gleicher Ebene sein mit;* the ∾-line (colloq.) *der äußerste Termin;* to be at a complete ∾-lock *völlig festgefahren, auf dem toten Punkt sein;* it was a ∾ loss *es war ein totaler Verlust;* to play a ∾ march *einen Trauermarsch spielen;* ∾ men, marines *leere, ausgetrunkene Flaschen;* ∾ men tell no tales (prov.) *die Toten verraten nichts;* to wait for ∾ men's shoes *auf Erbschaft lauern;* ∾ reckoning (naut.) *gegißte (geschätzte) Besteckrechnung, Koppelkurs; blinde, ungefähre Berechnung;* ∾ sea fruit *Sodomsapfel (Gallapfel);* he is a ∾ shot *er ist ein Meisterschütze;* he is the ∾ spit of his father (colloq.), see 'spit'; to come to a ∾ stop *plötzlich anhalten, vollständig stocken;* to be ∾ to the world *(durch Übermüdung) in festem Schlaf, bewußtlos sein.* — **II.** adv.: he is ∾ against it *er ist streng dagegen;* the wind is blowing ∾ against us *der Wind weht uns direkt ins Gesicht;* I am ∾ beat (or: tired) *ich bin todmüde;* he is ∾ drunk *er ist völlig betrunken;* to cut a person ∾ *j.en vollständig ignorieren;* he was ∾ on the target *er traf mitten ins Ziel.* — **III.** n.: at the ∾ of night *mitten in der Nacht;* in the ∾ of winter *im tiefsten Winter;* to rise from the ∾ *von den Toten auferstehen*

deaf a.: ∾ of an (in one) ear *auf einem Ohre taub;* as ∾ as an adder, as a post; stone-∾ *stocktaub;* none (are) so ∾ as those who won't (that will not) hear (prov.) *keiner ist so taub wie derjenige, welcher nicht hören will;* to turn a ∾ ear to a thing *taub gegen etwas sein*

deal I. n.: a good (great) ∾ of *viel, ein gut Teil, eine Menge;* it's your ∾ (cards) *du gibst (Kartenspiel);* a new ∾ *ein neuer Plan, eine neue Einrichtung;* he had a raw (square) ∾ *man hat ihn ungerecht (gerecht) behandelt.* — **II.** v.tr.: to ∾ a blow at *einen Schlag führen gegen;* to ∾ out punishment *eine Strafe (Bestrafung) austeilen (vollziehen).* — **III.** v.i.: he ∾t cruelly by it *er behandelte es grausam;* he ∾s in wine *er ist Weinhändler;* to ∾ with a person *mit j.em Geschäfte machen; sich mit j.em befassen;* it ∾s with the plot *es handelt von der Verschwörung*

dear a., adv. & interj.: for ∾ life *als wenn's ums Leben ginge;* that will cost you ∾ (or: ∾ly) *das wird dich teuer zu stehen kommen;* ∾, ∾! ∾ me!, oh, ∾! *ach Gott! Herrje!;* oh, ∾ me, no! *ausgeschlossen! auf keinen Fall! I wo!;* I would ∾ly love to go *ich möchte brennend gern gehen*

death n.: to be ∾ on a thing (sl.) *besonders gewandt sein in etwas;* to be at ∾'s door, at the point of ∾ *an der Schwelle des Todes sein, in den letzten Zügen liegen;* he will be the ∾ of me *er wird noch mein Tod sein;* it is a matter of life and ∾ *es handelt sich um Leben und Tod;* I am sick to ∾ of it *die Sache hängt mir zum Hals heraus;* to catch one's ∾ *sich (dat.) den Tod holen;* to come by one's ∾ *zu Tode kommen;* to hold on like grim ∾ *mit aller Kraft sich festhalten;* to put (to do) a person to ∾ *j.en töten, hinrichten;* to be in at the ∾ (fox-hunting) *(fig.) das Ende einer Sache (mit)erleben, den Schluß mitmachen*

debt n.: a bad ∾ *eine nicht eintreibbare Schuld;* the national ∾ *die Staatsschuld;* to be in ∾ *verschuldet sein, Schulden haben;* to be in a person's ∾ *in j.es Schuld stehen, ihm verpflichtet sein;* to contract (to incur, to run up) ∾s *Schulden machen;* to fall (to get, to run) into ∾ *in Schulden geraten;* to pay the ∾ of nature, one's ∾ to nature *sterben;* to recover a ∾ *eine Schuld eintreiben*

debunk v.tr. (colloq.): to ∾ a person, an institution *j.en (eine Einrichtung) des Nimbus berauben, in das rechte Licht rücken*

declare v.tr. & i.: have you anything to ∾? *haben Sie etwas zu verzollen?*; well, I ∾! *na, so etwas!*

decline I. v.tr. & i.: to ∾ an invitation with thanks *eine Einladung mit Dank ablehnen;* he is declining *er verfällt;* he spent his declining years in Italy *er hat seine alten Tage in Italien verbracht.* — **II.** n.: prices are on the ∾ *die Preise fallen;* to go (to fall) into a ∾ *dahinsiechen, die Schwindsucht bekommen*

deep I. a.: to go off the ∾ end *die Fassung verlieren, aufbrausen, wütend werden, aus dem Häuschen geraten;* he is a ∾ one (sl.) *er ist ein schlauer Fuchs;* between the devil and the ∾ blue sea *zwischen zwei Feuern, in großer Verlegenheit, in verzweifelter Lage;* to be in ∾ water(s) *in Not sein.* — **II.** adv.: still waters run ∾ (prov.) *stille Wasser sind tief*

default n.: in ∾ of a thing *in Ermangelung einer Sache;* a judgement by ∾ *eine Verurteilung in Abwesenheit des Beklagten, in absentia*

defiance n.: to bid ∾ to a person, to set a person at ∾ *j.em Trotz bieten;* in ∾ of his orders *seinem Befehl zum Trotz*

degree n.: by ∾s *allmählich, nach und nach;* he is lazy to a high (very large, the last) ∾ *er ist sehr (höchst, äußerst) faul;* a lady of high ∾ *eine hochstehende (hochwohlgeborene) Dame;* he is an undergraduate, he is studying for a ∾ *er ist ein junger (unexaminierter) Student, der für einen Universitätsgrad (B.A.) studiert;* when he has taken his ∾ he will be a graduate *wenn er seinen Universitätsgrad (B.A.) erlangt hat, ist er Graduierter (Examinierter);* he annoyed her to such a ∾ that she left him *er hat sie dermaßen (derartig) geärgert, daß sie ihn verließ;* to what ∾? *wie weit? in welchem Ausmaße?*

dekko n. (sl.): to take a ∾ at something *etwas ansehen*

delight n.: to take (a) ∾ in a thing *Vergnügen an etwas finden*

deliver v.tr.: he has ∾ed the goods *er hat seinen Teil der Abmachung erfüllt;* to ∾ a letter *einen Brief zustellen (austragen);* to ∾ a speech *eine Rede halten;* to be ∾ed of a child *niederkommen, entbunden werden;* to ∾ oneself of an opinion *eine Meinung äußern;* to be ∾ed of a sonnet *ein Sonett dichten*

demand I. n.: supply and ∾ *Angebot und Nachfrage;* to be in ∾ *gesucht, begehrt sein;* it was a great ∾ on my time *meine Zeit wurde sehr in Anspruch genommen;* a bill payable on ∾ *ein Sichtwechsel.* — **II.** v.tr.: to ∾ a thing of (from) a person *etwas von j.em verlangen;* ∾ his business *fragen Sie (eben), was er will!*

demon n.: he is a regular ∾ for work *er ist ein richtiges Arbeitstier*

denial n.: to meet the charge with a flat ∾ *die Beschuldigung (Anschuldigung) glatt ableugnen (abstreiten);* he won't take a ∾ *er läßt sich nicht abweisen*

deny v.tr.: there is no ∾ing, it cannot be denied *es läßt sich nicht leugnen;* to ∾ one's signature *seine Unterschrift nicht anerkennen;* to ∾ one's word *sein Wort zurücknehmen;* to ∾ oneself a thing *sich (dat.) etwas versagen;* I was denied this, this was denied me (to me) *es wurde mir verweigert (abgeschlagen)*

depend v.i.: that ∾s *das kommt darauf an; je nachdem;* ∾ upon it *verlaß dich darauf!;* she ∾s upon her needle for her living *sie verdient sich als Schneiderin ihren Lebensunterhalt*

depth n.: in the ∾ of winter *mitten im Winter;* six feet in ∾ *sechs Fuß tief;* a cry from the ∾s *ein Schrei aus innerster Seele;* to get out of (to go beyond) one's ∾ *den Boden unter den Füßen verlieren, sich vor einer zu schwierigen Aufgabe sehen;* ∾ of thought *Gedankentiefe, Tiefsinn;* ∾ of feeling *Tiefe der Empfindung;* the ∾s of despair *tiefe Verzweiflung*

desert n.: to punish (to reward) a person according to his ∾s *j.em die verdiente Strafe (den verdienten Lohn) erteilen;* he got his ∾s *er bekam seine verdiente Strafe*

design n.: he has ∾s upon you *er führt etwas gegen dich im Schilde, er will was von dir;* by ∾ *mit Absicht*

detach v.tr.: to regard things with a ∾ed mind (view) *etwas unparteiisch, objektiv ansehen;* we live in a ∾ed house *wir wohnen in einem freistehenden Hause*

detail n.: to describe in ∾, to go into ∾s *ausführlich (umständlich, in allen Einzelheiten) beschreiben, auf Einzelheiten eingehen*

deuce n.: how (what, where, who, etc.) the ∾? *wie (was, wo, wer usw.) zum Teufel?;* the ∾ he isn't! *unglaublich, daß er es nicht ist!;* the ∾ a bit *durchaus nicht, nicht das Geringste;* the ∾ is in it if I cannot *es müßte verteufelt zugehen, wenn ich das nicht könnte;* it's the ∾ to pay *es ist eine fatale Geschichte;* ∾ knows! *weiß der Teufel!;* ∾ take it! *hol's der Teufel!;* to be in a ∾ of a mess *in einer verteufelten Patsche stecken;* to have a ∾ of a temper *verteufelt jähzornig sein;* to play the ∾ with a thing *einer Sache arg mitspielen; etwas verderben, ruinieren.* — N.B. In all phrases with 'deuce' the word 'devil' may be substituted *N.B. In allen Redensarten mit 'deuce' kann auch 'devil' stehen*

device n.: a man full of ∾s *ein erfinderischer Kopf;* to be left to one's own ∾s *auf sich selbst angewiesen sein*

devil I. n.: there'll be the ∾ (and all) to pay! *da wird's etwas (Unangenehmes) geben;* the ∾ a one was there *kein Schwein war da;* he is the ∾ of a fellow *er ist ein Teufels-, Allerweltskerl;* a poor ∾ of a fellow *ein armer Schlucker;* it's the ∾ among the tailors *der Teufel ist los, es geht wüst her;* the ∾ take the hindmost! *den Letzten beißen die Hunde;* between the ∾ and the deep blue sea *zwischen zwei Feuern, in großer Verlegenheit, in verzweifelter Lage;* the ∾'s bedpost *die Kreuz- oder Treff-Vier;* the ∾'s books *Spielkarten, Teufelsblatt;* the ∾'s bones *Würfel;* a ∾-dodger (sl.) *ein Pfarrer, Pastor;* a printer's ∾ *ein Laufbursche in einer Druckerei;* ∾s on horseback *Austern in Speckscheiben gebraten;* in a ∾-may-care way *in sorgloser Weise;* to beat the ∾'s tattoo *ungeduldig mit dem Finger auf dem Tisch trommeln;* to give the ∾ his due *jedem sein Recht lassen;* to go to the ∾ *zugrunde gehen;* go to the ∾ (colloq.) *scher' dich zum Teufel!;* to hold the candle to the ∾ *dem Teufel das Pferd satteln;* to play the ∾ with *ruinieren;* talk of the ∾ and he will appear (prov.) *wenn man den Teufel nennt, kommt er gerennt; man soll den Teufel nicht an die Wand malen;* the ∾ is not so black as he is painted (prov.) *der Teufel ist nicht so schwarz, wie er gemalt wird (zur Verteidigung schlechter, angegriffener Personen gesagt);* to whip the ∾ round the post (stump) *etwas auf unehrliche Weise, auf Umwegen erreichen;* to raise the ∾ about a thing *wegen einer Sache einen Heidenlärm machen (gehörig Krach schlagen);* pull ∾, pull baker *eine Ermunterung für beide Parteien.* — **II.** v.i.: to ∾ for a lawyer (legal) *als Assistent in einer Anwaltspraxis Erfahrungen sammeln*

diamond n.: he is a rough ∾ *er ist ein grober (ungehobelter) aber wertvoller Mensch;* it was a case of ∾ cut ∾ *da stand Schelm wider (gegen) Schelm*

dick n. (sl.): I can take my ∾ to it *das kann ich beschwören;* I can take my ∾ that *ich kann beschwören, daß*

dickens n. (sl.): what (when, where, who, why, etc.) the ∾? *was (wann, wo, wer, warum usw.) zum Teufel?*

dicky a. (sl.): it's all ∾ with him *es steht sehr mau mit ihm*

die[1] n.: as straight (as true) as a ∾ *kerzengerade; grundehrlich;* it is upon the ∾ *es steht auf dem Spiele;* the ∾ is cast *die Würfel sind gefallen;* loaded dice *falsche Würfel;* the dice are loaded against the poor *die Armen ziehen den kürzeren;* to risk all on the turn of a ∾ *alles dem Glück (Zufall) überlassen*

die[2] **I.** v.i.: never say ∾ *nur Mut! gib dich nicht geschlagen!;* to ∾ game *kämpfend untergehen;* I'm dying for (to do) something *ich lechze (schmachte, sehne mich) nach etwas;* the sounds ∾d away *die Laute verschwanden (verstummten) langsam;* the excitement ∾d down *die Erregung legte sich;* he ∾d in the last ditch *er fiel in verzweifeltem Verteidigungskampf;* the rumour ∾d hard *das Gerücht war sehr hartnäckig;* to ∾ in harness *in den Sielen sterben;* the roses ∾d off one by one *die Rosen vergingen (verwelkten) eine nach der anderen;* the Red Indians have almost ∾d out *die Indianer sind fast ausgestorben;* to ∾ in one's shoes *eines gewaltsamen Todes sterben, gehängt werden;* to ∾ of cholera *an Cholera sterben;* to ∾ of laughing *sich totlachen.* — **II.** n.: a ∾-hard *einer, der bis zuletzt hartnäckig Widerstand leistet; einer, der auf dem äußersten rechten Flügel der englischen konservativen Partei steht*

differ v.i.: to ∾ from *sich unterscheiden von;* he ∾s with me in opinion *er ist ande-*

rer Meinung als ich; we agree to ∾ *wir haben den Versuch aufgegeben, uns gegenseitig zu überzeugen*

difference n.: let's split the ∾ *laßt uns den Preisunterschied teilen, uns auf halbem Wege treffen*

dig I. n.: a ∾ in the ribs *ein Rippenstoß;* that was a ∾ at you *das ging gegen Sie;* she had a quiet ∾ at him *sie machte eine versteckte Bemerkung gegen (über) ihn.* — **II.** v.i. (colloq.): to ∾ away at one's books *sich in seine Bücher vergraben, ochsen, büffeln;* to ∾ in *gut essen.* — **III.** v.tr. (colloq.): to ∾ oneself in *sich (in einer guten Stelle) festsetzen;* to ∾ someone out (up) *j.en besuchen, aufstöbern;* to ∾ up a reference (an information) *eine Referenz (Auskunft) ausfindig machen;* to ∾ one's grave with one's knife and fork *gefräßig sein, sich totfressen*

diggings, digs n.: I'm going to my ∾ *ich gehe auf meine Bude*

dilemma n.: to be on the horns of a ∾ *in einer Zwickmühle sein*

dim a.: to take a ∾ view of something (colloq.) *etwas pessimistisch betrachten*

din v.tr.: to ∾ a thing into a person (a person's ears) *j.em dauernd (bis zum Überdruß) etwas vorpredigen*

dine v.i.: to ∾ with Duke Humphrey *nichts zu essen haben, kein Mittagessen (ein)nehmen*

dint n.: by ∾ of *kraft, vermittels (gen.)*

dip I. v.tr. & i.: to ∾ one's pen in gall *bittere Worte schreiben;* to ∾ into a book *ein Buch flüchtig durchblättern;* to ∾ deep into the future *die Zukunft erforschen;* to ∾ into one's purse *tief in die Tasche greifen.* — **II.** n.: we had a ∾ in the sea *wir nahmen ein Seebad*

dirt n.: it was ∾-cheap *es war spottbillig;* to do someone ∾ (sl.) *j.em eine Gemeinheit antun;* to eat ∾ *etwas einstecken (sich demütigen) müssen;* to fling (to throw) ∾ at a person *j.en verleumden (in den Schmutz ziehen);* to treat a person like ∾ *j.en wie einen Schuhputzer behandeln*

dirty a.: they are a ∾ lot *sie sind eine gemeine Bande;* you did me a ∾ trick (the ∾) *du hast mir gemein mitgespielt, einen gemeinen Streich gespielt;* ∾ weather *Sturm und Regen;* ∾ work *unehrenhaftes (schmutziges) Handeln;* I won't always do his ∾ work for him *ich will nicht immer sein Johann sein*

disadvantage n.: to be at (to labour under) a ∾ *im Nachteil sein;* to sell to ∾ *mit Verlust verkaufen;* to take a person at a ∾ *j.es ungünstige Lage ausnutzen*

discount I. n.: to allow ∾ *Rabatt gewähren;* to be at a ∾ *unter Pari stehen; nicht beliebt sein, nicht verlangt werden;* militarism is at a ∾ *der Militarismus ist in Mißkredit geraten.* — **II.** v.tr.: you must ∾ his story *du mußt seine Erzählung mit Vorsicht aufnehmen (nur teilweise glauben)*

discretion n.: ∾ is the better part of valour (prov.) *Vorsicht ist die Mutter der Weisheit (Porzellankiste);* age (years) of ∾ *Jahre der Vernunft; das Alter, in dem man für sich selbst sorgen kann (14 Jahre nach englischem Recht);* at ∾ *nach eigenem Ermessen (Belieben);* to be settled at the ∾ of N. *nach dem Wunsche von N. zu erledigen;* to surrender at ∾ *sich bedingungslos ergeben;* to use one's own ∾ *nach Gutdünken verfahren (handeln)*

disguise I. v.tr.: to ∾ one's opinion (intention) *mit seiner Meinung (Absicht) hinter dem Berge halten;* to be ∾d in (with) drink (liquor) *betrunken sein.* — **II.** n.: it was a blessing in ∾, see 'bless'

dish v.tr.: to ∾ an opponent *einen Gegner hintergehen, erledigen (besonders politisch durch Annahme seiner Politik);* to ∾ up a meal, a story *ein Essen auftragen; eine Geschichte auftischen;* to ∾ out food (colloq.) *Essen verteilen*

dismal I. a.: the ∾ science *die Volkswirtschaftslehre.* — **II.** n.: to be in the ∾s *mutlos (niedergeschlagen) sein, Trübsal blasen*

dispose v.i.: to be well (ill) ∾d towards someone *j.em wohlgesinnt (übelgesinnt) sein;* man proposes, God ∾s (prov.) *der Mensch denkt, Gott lenkt*

dispute I. n.: it is beyond ∾ *(es ist) sicher, fraglos, unstreitig;* the matter is in ∾ *die Sache wird noch erörtert.* — **II.** v.tr.: they ∾d every inch of the ground *sie kämpften um jeden Zoll (Boden);* the will was ∾d *gegen das Testament wurde Berufung eingelegt.* — **III.** v.i.: to ∾ with (against) a person *mit j.em disputieren*

distinction n.: to draw a ∾ without a difference *einen künstlichen Unterschied machen*

ditch I. n.: to die in the last ∾ *in verzweifeltem Verteidigungskampf fallen;* as dull as ∾-water *entsetzlich langweilig (fade) sein.* — **II.** v.tr.: that's ∾ed it! (sl.) *da (so), jetzt ist es aus!;* to ∾ someone (something) (sl.) *j.en (etwas) im Stich lassen;* to ∾ a plane (sl.) *eine Notlandung auf dem Meer machen*

dither n.: to be all of (in) a ∾ *ganz verdattert (verwirrt) sein*

ditto a. & n.: a ∾ suit, a suit of ∾s (colloq.) *ein Anzug aus gleichem Stoff;* to say ∾ to *zustimmen, beipflichten*

do I. v.tr.: to ∾ battle *kämpfen;* to ∾ better *Besseres leisten;* to ∾ one's best, damnedest (sl.) *sein Möglichstes tun, sein Bestes hergeben;* to ∾ business *Geschäfte machen;* to ∾ a person's business *j.en töten, ihm den Garaus machen;* that does him credit *das macht ihm Ehre;* to ∾ a person to death *j.en töten, hinrichten;* we had done eating *wir waren mit dem Essen fertig;* to ∾ one's hair *sich frisieren;* to ∾ the handsome (thing) *j.em gegenüber (mit Geld oder Liebenswürdigkeit) großzügig sein;* to be able to ∾ it on one's head *es sehr leicht können;* to ∾ a person harm *j.em schaden;* to ∾ a person the honour of coming *j.em die Ehre antun zu kommen;* to ∾ a person justice, to ∾ justice to a thing *j.em, einer Sache gerecht werden;* to ∾ Lear (Hamlet, etc.) *die Rolle des Lear (Hamlet usw.) spielen;* this car will ∾ 100 miles an hour *dieses Auto fährt 160 km in der Stunde;* to ∾ six months *sechs Monate absitzen;* to ∾ a museum *ein Museum besichtigen;* he is a ∾-nothing *er ist ein Nichtstuer (Faulenzer);* to ∾ the polite *den Höflichen spielen;* to ∾ a room *ein Zimmer aufräumen (putzen);* he is ∾ing time *er sitzt seine Zeit ab;* to ∾ the trick *das Ziel erreichen;* to ∾ a person an ill turn *j.em einen üblen Streich spielen;* to ∾ away with a thing *etwas abschaffen, beseitigen, um die Ecke bringen;* to ∾ a person down *j.en übers Ohr hauen (reinlegen);* to ∾ a person in (sl.) *j.en töten, abmurksen;* to ∾ a person in the eye (sl.) *j.en betrügen, beschummeln, übers Ohr hauen;* to ∾ a book into English *ein Buch ins Englische übersetzen;* to ∾ a person out of a thing *j.en um etwas bringen;* to ∾ over a thing with *etwas überstreichen (überziehen) mit;* to ∾ up a thing *etwas reparieren, herrichten; etwas einpacken;* I'm done up *ich bin todmüde (erschossen);* they ∾ you well here *hier bekommst du ein gutes Essen, hier sorgt man gut für dich, hier bist du gut aufgehoben;* to ∾ one's bit *sein Teil erfüllen;* to ∾ oneself well (proud) on something *sich an etwas gütlich tun;* do you always ∾ yourself so well? *lebst du immer so gut? leistest du dir immer solche Genüsse?;* to ∾ wonders *Wunder wirken;* it is simply not done *das gibt's einfach nicht, es schickt sich einfach nicht;* it's easier said than done *es ist leichter gesagt als getan;* no sooner said than done *gesagt, getan;* well begun is half done (prov.) *frisch gewagt ist halb gewonnen;* I've been done brown (sl.) *ich bin beschwindelt worden;* you've done it now! *da hast du was Schönes angerichtet!;* the chop is done to a turn *das Kotelett ist gerade richtig;* the meat is under-(well-)done *das Fleisch ist nicht durchgebraten, ist gut durchgebraten.* — **II.** v.i.: to ∾ in Rome as the Romans ∾ *sich an die Gebräuche und Gewohnheiten seiner Umgebung anpassen;* how ∾ you ∾? how d'ye ∾? *guten Tag (Morgen usw.)!;* that will ∾ *das genügt;* that will not ∾ *das geht nicht an;* that will ∾ me nicely *das kann ich gut gebrauchen;* it will ∾ tomorrow *es hat Zeit bis morgen;* ∾ or die *friß, Vogel, oder stirb!; entweder — oder!;* to make a great to-∾ about a thing *viel Aufhebens (Getue, Sums, Theater) um etwas machen;* he is a well-to-∾ man *er ist ein wohlhabender Mann;* nothing doing! (colloq.) *nichts zu machen!;* ∾ by (to, unto) others as you would be done by them *was du nicht willst, daß man dir tu', das füg' auch keinem andern zu;* to ∾ for a person (colloq.) *j.em den Haushalt führen;* he's done for (colloq.) *er ist ruiniert, erledigt, tot;* he is doing well *es geht ihm gut, er kommt gut voran;* you must make that ∾ (make ∾ with that, ∾ with that) *damit mußt du auskommen, dich begnügen;* I could ∾ with a drink *ich könnte einen Schluck vertragen;* have you done with the dictionary? *brauchst du das Wörterbuch noch?;* to get done with a thing *etwas zu Ende führen;* done! *abgemacht!;* well done! *bravo!* — **III.** v. substitute: I chose my wife as she did her gown *ich wählte meine Frau, wie sie ihr Kleid wählte;* if you saw the truth as clearly as I ∾ *wenn du nur die Wahrheit so klar sähest wie ich;* A.: Did you see him? B.: I did. *A.: Hast du ihn gesehen? B.: Jawohl!;* A.: I paid a pound for it. B.: Did you? *A.: Ich habe ein Pfund dafür bezahlt. B.: So? Wirklich? Ach was!;* I wanted to see him, and I did so *ich wollte ihn sehen, und ich sah ihn auch;* if you want to tell him, ∾ it now *wenn du es ihm sagen willst, sag' es ihm jetzt;* you don't smoke, ∾ you? *Sie sind Nichtraucher, nicht wahr?;* you smoke, don't you? *Sie rauchen, nicht wahr?* — **IV.** v.aux.: I ∾ so wish I could *ich wünschte brennend, ich könnte es;* I did see him *ich sah ihn wirklich;* ∾ tell me *sag mir doch bitte!;* rarely does it happen *es kommt selten vor;* ∾ you recognize her? *erkennst du sie?;* I ∾ not like him *ich mag ihn nicht;* ∾ not speak so loud *sprich nicht so laut.* — **V.** n.: it was a clever ∾ (sl.) *es war ein gerissener Schwindel;* there's a big ∾ on tonight *heute Abend ist ein großes Fest*

doctor I. v.tr.: to ∾ the news, the accounts *die Nachrichten, die Rechnungen fälschen;* to ∾ a cat *einen Kater kastrieren;* to ∾ the drink (the food) *dem Getränk (Essen) etwas beimischen.* — **II.** n.: who shall decide when ∾s disagree (differ)? *wer soll entscheiden, wenn sogar die Gelehrten sich nicht einig sind?;* to put the ∾ on a man (sl.) *j.en betrügen;* to be under the ∾ *in ärztlicher Behandlung sein*

dodge n.: he is up to every ∾ *er kennt jeden Kniff (alle Schliche)*

dodger n.: he is an artful ∾ *er ist ein geriebener Kunde, ein abgefeimter Betrüger*

dodo n.: as dead as the ∾ *ausgestorben*

dog I. n.: every ∾ has his day (prov.) *jeder hat einmal seinen guten Tag; heute mir, morgen dir;* he's a gay (lucky, sad, sea-, sly) ∾ *er ist ein lustiger Geselle (ein Glückspilz, ein Schwerenöter, ein Seebär, ein schlauer Fuchs);* he's a ∾ in the manger *er ist ein Neidhammel;* the ∾s of war *die Furien des Krieges;* my ∾s are biting (sl.) *meine Füße tun mir weh;* to be ∾-tired *hundemüde sein;* to be like a ∾ with two tails *sich wahnsinnig freuen;* to come out top ∾ (sl.) *als Sieger hervorgehen;* to die a ∾'s death *in Elend oder Schande sterben;* to feel as sick as a ∾ *hundsmiserabel zu Mute sein;* give a ∾ a bad name and hang him (prov.) *wer einmal in Verruf gerät, behält seinen schlechten Leumund;* to go to the ∾s *vor die Hunde gehen, auf den Hund kommen; zum Hunderennen gehen;* he hasn't a ∾'s chance *er hat nicht die geringste Aussicht;* he hasn't a word to throw at a ∾ *er ist ein ungeselliger, hochmütig schweigsamer Mensch; er hat kein Wort für einen übrig, er ist sehr unzugänglich;* barking ∾s seldom bite (prov.) *Hunde, die bellen, beißen nicht;* a hang-∾ face *ein Galgengesicht;* a hot ∾ *ein heißes Würstchen;* to help a lame ∾ over a stile *j.em in der Not behilflich sein;* what! keep a ∾ and bark myself? *was? eine Angestellte halten und selbst die Arbeit tun!?;* to lead a ∾'s life *ein Hundeleben führen;* let sleeping ∾s lie (prov.) *rühre nicht an vergessene(n), vergangene(n) Dinge(n)! man soll den schlafenden Löwen nicht wecken!;* love me, love my ∾ (prov.) *wer mich liebt, muß alles lieben, was mein ist;* to make ∾('s)-ears in a book, to ∾('s)-ear a book *Eselsohren in ein Buch machen;* to put on ∾ (colloq.) *wichtig tun, angeben;* it's raining cats and ∾s *es gießt in Strömen, es regnet Bindfäden;* to set the ∾s on a person *die Hunde auf j.en hetzen;* to side with the under ∾ (sl.) *es mit dem Unterlegenen (Schwächeren) halten;* to slink off like a whipped ∾ *wie ein begossener Pudel davonschleichen; sich drücken;* any stick to beat a ∾ *ein Vorwand ist schnell gefunden;* to take a hair of the ∾ that bit you *weitertrinken, um den Kater zu vertreiben; den Teufel mit Beelzebub austreiben;* to be in the ∾house (colloq.) *bei j.em in Ungnade sein (stehen);* you can't teach an old ∾ new tricks (prov.), an old ∾ will learn no tricks (prov.) *einem alten, ungeschickten Menschen kann man nichts mehr beibringen; was Hänschen nicht lernt, lernt Hans nimmermehr;* to throw to the ∾s *zum Fenster hinauswerfen, verprassen;* to watch a ∾-fight in the sky *einen Kampf zwischen Jagdflugzeugen beobachten;* ∾-cheap *spottbillig;* to wear a ∾-collar *als Geistlicher einen hinten geschlossenen Kragen tragen;* to write ∾ Latin *Küchenlatein schreiben;* a ∾watch *eine zweistündige Wache am Schiff.* — **II.** v.tr.: to ∾ a person's steps *j.em auf Schritt und Tritt folgen;* to be ∾ged by misfortune *vom Unglück verfolgt sein*

dogged a.: it's ∾ does it *Beharrlichkeit führt zum Ziele*

doggo adv. (sl.): to lie ∾ *bewegungslos liegen, sich versteckt halten*

doing n.: it's all your ∾ *es ist alles deine Schuld;* fine ∾s these! *das sind mir schöne Geschichten!*

doldrums n.: to be in the ∾ *übelgelaunt sein*

dole I. n.: he's on the ∾ *er bezieht Arbeitslosenunterstützung, er geht stempeln.* — **II.** v.tr.: to ∾ out alms *Almosen spenden*

donkey n.: he would talk a ∾'s hind leg off *er redet dem Teufel ein Bein aus, er redet einen tot und lebendig (dusselig);* for ∾'s years (sl.) *seit x Jahren, seit Ewigkeiten;* ∾-work *untergeordnete (mühselige) Arbeit*

doodle v.i.: to ∾ *bedeutungslose Zeichen oder Wörter hinkritzeln, während man an etwas anderes denkt*

doodle bug n. (sl.): the factory was destroyed by a ∾ *die Fabrik wurde von einer V 1 Bombe zerstört*

door n.: as dead as a ∾nail *mausetot;* to be at death's ∾ *an der Schwelle des Todes (am Rande des Grabes) stehen;* to be next ∾ to something *einer Sache sehr nahekommen, an etwas grenzen;* to be packed to the ∾s *voll besetzt sein;* to be on the wrong side of the ∾ *ausgesperrt sein;* never darken my ∾ again *komm mir nie wieder über die Schwelle!;* to enter by (through) the front ∾ *durch die Haustür eintreten;* to lay at the ∾ of a person *j.em etwas in die Schuhe schieben (zur Last legen);* to live next ∾ (three ∾s off) *nebenan (drei Häuser weiter) wohnen;* to open a ∾ to a thing; to bang (to close) the ∾ upon a thing *etwas möglich machen; etwas unmöglich machen;* to remain within ∾s *im (zu) Hause bleiben;* to show a person the ∾ *j.em die Tür weisen;* to turn a person out of ∾s *j.en aus dem Hause werfen;* out-of-∾s *im Freien;* an out-of-∾ job *eine Beschäftigung im Freien*

dope n. (U.S. sl.): hand out the ∾ *heraus mit den neuesten Nachrichten!;* a ∾ fiend *ein Rauschgiftsüchtiger*

dormouse n.: to sleep like a ∾ *wie ein Murmeltier (Ratz) schlafen*

dot I. n.: a little ∾ *ein kleines Kind, ein Knirps;* to be off one's ∾ (sl.) *verrückt sein.* — **II.** v.tr.: a ∾ and go one gait *ein humpelnder (hinkender) Gang;* ∾ and carry one *eins hin und eins im Sinn (beim Rechnen);* my pulse went ∾ and carry one *mein Puls schlug wie wild;* to ∾ the i's and cross the t's *alle Einzelheiten klarmachen;* I ∾ted him one in the eye (sl.) *ich haute ihm eins aufs Auge*

dotty a. (colloq.): to be ∾ *schwachsinnig sein;* to be ∾ on one's legs *wackelig auf den Beinen sein;* to be ∾ on a person *in j.en verschossen (verknallt) sein*

double I. a. & adv.: he is ∾ her age *er ist doppelt so alt wie sie;* it is ∾ the size of that *es ist doppelt (zweimal) so groß wie das;* book-keeping by ∾ entry *doppelte Buchführung;* a ∾-barrelled compliment, gun, name, see 'barrelled'; a ∾-breasted coat *ein zweireihiger Rock;* that is ∾-dealing *das ist Betrug;* ∾ quick *sehr schnell;* he is a ∾-dyed scoundrel *er ist ein Erzschurke;* that is a ∾-edged argument *das ist ein zweischneidiges Argument;* she is a ∾-faced person *sie ist eine unaufrichtige (heuchlerische, falsche) Person;* to ∾-cross a person *ein doppeltes Spiel mit j.em treiben;* to ride ∾ *zu zweit auf einem Pferde reiten;* to sleep ∾ *zu zweien in einem Bett schlafen.* — **II.** n.: at the ∾ *im Laufschritt;* ∾ or quits *eine Verabredung im Glücksspiel, daß man bei Gewinn das schon Verlorene zurückerhält, bei Verlust aber doppelt bezahlt;* to have a ∾ *einen Doppelgänger haben;* mixed ∾s (Tennis, etc.) *Gemischtes Doppel (je ein Herr und eine Dame).* — **III.** v.tr.: to ∾ blow on blow *Schlag auf Schlag versetzen;* to ∾ over a leaf *ein Blatt (um)kniffen;* to ∾ a part *zwei Rollen in demselben Stück spielen.* — **IV.** v.i.: to ∾ back *schnell kehrtmachen;* to ∾ up *zusammenbrechen,-klappen*

doubt I. n.: no (without) ∾, ∾less *ohne Zweifel (unzweifelhaft, zweifellos, zweifelsohne);* past (beyond) ∾ *über allen Zweifel erhaben;* to give a person the benefit of the ∾ *im Zweifelsfalle die günstigere Auslegung annehmen* (lat. in dubio pro reo); to make no ∾ of *sich vergewissern.* — **II.** v.tr.: to ∾ a person's words *an j.es Worten zweifeln.* — **III.** v.i.: I do not ∾ that (but, but that) *ich zweifle nicht, daß;* I never ∾ed of success *ich zweifelte nie am Erfolg*

dough n.: he has the ∾ (sl.) *er hat die Moneten (den Zaster);* to raise the ∾ *den*

Teig gehen lassen; a ∾boy (sl.) *ein U.S. Infanterist;* a ∾nut *ein Berliner Pfannkuchen*

douse, dowse v.tr.: to ∾ the glim (sl.) *das Licht auslöschen*

dovecot(e) n.: to flutter the ∾s *ruhige Leute in Aufregung versetzen, aus der Ruhe aufscheuchen; Aufsehen erregen*

down I. adv.: see 'account, boil, business, come, do, dumps, foot, luck, etc.'; ∾ among the dead men *unter dem Tisch bei den leeren Flaschen;* are we ∾-hearted? *wir lassen den Kopf nicht hängen! wir lassen uns nicht unterkriegen!;* ∾ and out *vollkommen erledigt; auf den Hund gekommen;* ∾ to the ground *vollständig;* from king ∾ to the cobbler *vom König herunter bis zum Schuster;* ∾ under *bei den Antipoden, in Australien;* bread is ∾ *(das) Brot ist billiger geworden;* to be ∾ on a person *voreingenommen gegen j.en sein;* to be ∾ on a thing *etwas nicht leiden können;* the Bill is ∾ for the second reading today *die zweite Lesung der Gesetzesvorlage ist für heute angesetzt;* to be ∾ with fever *mit Fieber daniederliegen;* to get ∾ to something *sich in etwas (eine Arbeit) hineinknien;* to go ∾ *die Universität verlassen;* the book goes ∾ well *das Buch findet Anklang;* food goes ∾ *Speisen werden geschluckt;* that won't go ∾ with him *das kannst du ihm nicht weismachen, darauf fällt er nicht herein;* to grind ∾ *feinmahlen;* to hit a man who is ∾ *j.en, der schon am Boden liegt, schlagen; niederträchtig behandeln;* to let a person ∾ *j.en im Stich lassen, enttäuschen;* to put a person ∾ for (or: as) a fool *j.en für einen Narren halten;* he was sent ∾ *er wurde relegiert;* to shout someone ∾ *durch Rufe (Zurufe) j.en nicht zu Wort kommen lassen;* to write (to set, to put, to take, to copy) ∾ *niederschreiben;* ∾ with the tyrants! *nieder mit den Tyrannen!* — **II.** prep.: a cheer ran ∾ the line *ein Hurra pflanzte sich durch die Reihe fort;* to glance ∾ a page *eine Seite im Buch überfliegen;* it is situated ∾ the river *es liegt weiter flußabwärts;* to let go ∾ the wind *aufgeben, im Stich lassen.* — **III.** a.: a ∾ train *ein Zug, der von London abfährt oder kommt;* the ∾ platform *der Bahnsteig, von dem ein solcher Zug abfährt.* — **IV.** v.tr.: to ∾ an aeroplane *ein Flugzeug landen;* to ∾ tools *die Arbeit einstellen, streiken.* — **V.** n.: the ups and ∾s of life *die Wechselfälle des Lebens;* to have a ∾ on a person *j.en nicht leiden können*

downright a. & adv.: he is a ∾ man *er ist offenherzig, bieder;* he was ∾ insolent *er war geradezu unverschämt;* it's a ∾ lie *es ist eine glatte Lüge (glatt gelogen);* it's ∾ nonsense *es ist völliger Unsinn;* he is a ∾ scoundrel *er ist ein Erzschurke*

dozen n.: a baker's (devil's long, printer's) ∾ *13 Stück;* he does his daily ∾s (colloq.) *er treibt täglich Frühgymnastik;* a round ∾ *ein volles Dutzend;* he talks (his tongue goes) nineteen to the ∾ *er schwatzt unaufhörlich (das Blaue vom Himmel herunter);* it is six of one and half-a-∾ of the other *es ist ganz einerlei (gehüpft wie gesprungen, Jacke wie Hose)*

draft I. n.: to make a ∾ on an account *von einem Konto etwas abheben;* to make a ∾ on a person's friendship *j.es Freundschaft in Anspruch nehmen.* — **II.** a.: a ∾ letter, a ∾ list *ein Brief, eine Liste im Konzept (Entwurf).* — **III.** v.tr.: to be ∾ed abroad, to another company (milit.) *ins Ausland, zu einer anderen Kompanie abkommandiert sein*

drag I. v.tr.: the ship ∾s her anchor, the anchor ∾s *das Schiff schleppt den Anker, treibt vor Anker;* to ∾ one's feet (colloq.) *mit Absicht langsam arbeiten;* to ∾ a lake for a drowned person *in einem See mit Grundnetz nach einem Ertrunkenen suchen;* to ∾ a subject by the head and shoulders into the debate *einen Gegenstand ohne Notwendigkeit in die Debatte hineinziehen;* to ∾ out an argument *eine Beweisführung ausdehnen (hinschleppen);* to ∾ up a child (colloq.) *ein Kind roh erziehen.* — **II.** v.i.: the accompanying pianist ∾ged behind *die Klavierbegleitung klappte nach;* the conversation ∾ged on *die Unterhaltung schleppte sich hin.* — **III.** n.: it is a ∾ on progress *es hindert den Fortschritt*

drain I. v.tr.: to ∾ a swamp *einen Sumpf trockenlegen;* to ∾ the wealth of England *den Reichtum Englands verzehren;* to ∾ away (off) the water *das Wasser ableiten;* to ∾ a country of its resources *ein Land seiner Hilfsquellen berauben;* to ∾ a vessel to the dregs *ein Gefäß bis zur Neige leeren.* — **II.** v.i.: the water ∾ed away (off, through) *das Wasser floß ab, sickerte* *durch.* — **III.** n.: it is a great ∾ on my purse *es nimmt meinen Geldbeutel sehr in Anspruch;* a ∾ of ale *ein Schluck Bier;* down the ∾ (sl.) *verlorengegangen, verschwendet*

drake n.: to play ducks and ∾s, see 'duck'; to play ducks and ∾s with one's money, to make ducks and ∾s of one's money, see 'duck'

draught n.: there is a ∾ *es zieht;* a beast of ∾ *ein Zugtier;* beer on ∾ *Bier vom Faß;* to drink at a ∾ *auf einen Zug austrinken;* to feel the ∾ (sl.) *unter mißlichen Verhältnissen leiden*

draw I. v.tr.: to ∾ attention to a thing *die Aufmerksamkeit auf etwas lenken;* to ∾ a bead on a thing *auf etwas zielen;* to ∾ beer *Bier zapfen;* to ∾ the bit (bridle, rein) *die Zügel anziehen;* to ∾ the long bow *aufschneiden (übertreiben, flunkern);* to ∾ blood *Blut fließen lassen, blutig schlagen;* to ∾ a deep breath (sigh) *tief Atem holen, aufseufzen;* to ∾ a cheque *Geld mit Scheck abheben;* to ∾ the cloth *den Tisch abräumen;* to ∾ a cow *eine Kuh ausmelken;* to ∾ customers *Kunden anziehen;* to ∾ a deed *eine Urkunde ausfertigen;* to ∾ 20 feet of water *einen Tiefgang von 20 Fuß haben;* to ∾ one's finger over the line *mit dem Finger über die Zeile fahren;* to ∾ fowl *Geflügel ausnehmen;* to ∾ a fox (a badger) *einen Fuchs (einen Dachs) aus dem Bau locken;* to ∾ a game *unentschieden spielen;* to ∾ the line at a thing *sich weigern, so weit (oder: weiter) zu gehen, nicht mehr mitmachen;* ∾ it mild! *mach' es gnädig! übertreib' nicht so!;* to ∾ money from the bank *Geld von der Bank abheben;* to ∾ a salary *ein Gehalt beziehen;* to ∾ straws *Hälmchen ziehen, losen;* to ∾ tears *Tränen entlocken;* to ∾ the wool over a person's eyes *j.em Sand in die Augen streuen, ihn hinters Licht führen.* — with adv.: to ∾ a person along, aside, away, back *j.en mit fortschleppen, beiseitenehmen, fort-, zurückziehen;* to ∾ down a curse upon oneself *einen Fluch auf sich herabziehen;* to ∾ forth a smile *ein Lächeln hervorlocken;* to ∾ in one's horns *die Hörner einziehen, sich mäßigen;* to ∾ off the attention *die Aufmerksamkeit ablenken;* to ∾ on one's coat *den Rock anziehen;* to ∾ on a discussion *eine Diskussion herbeiführen;* to ∾ a person out *j.en zum Reden bringen;* to ∾ up a document *eine Urkunde aufsetzen;* to ∾ oneself up *sich emporrichten.* — **II.** v.i.: the chimney ∾s well *der Kamin zieht gut;* tea must ∾ *Tee muß ziehen;* to ∾ level with a person *j.en einholen;* to ∾ near *näher kommen, sich nähern;* the days are ∾ing in, out *die Tage nehmen ab (zu);* to ∾ on an account *auf ein Konto ziehen, trassieren;* to ∾ round a table *einen Kreis um einen Tisch bilden;* to ∾ to an end, a close, see 'end, close'; a carriage ∾s up *ein Wagen fährt vor;* to ∾ up with a person *j.en einholen;* England drew with Scotland *das Spiel England gegen Schottland verlief unentschieden.* — **III.** n.: the match ended in a ∾ *das Wettspiel endigte (endete) unentschieden;* the play is a box-office ∾ *das Stück ist ein Kassenerfolg;* he is quick on the ∾ *er ist schnell mit dem Revolver bei der Hand*

drawing n.: to be out of ∾ *verzeichnet sein*

dreadful a.: it is a penny ∾ *es ist ein billiger Schauerroman*

dregs n.: to drain (to drink) a vessel to the ∾ *ein Gefäß bis zur Neige leeren*

dress I. n.: ∾-circle *erster Rang (Theater);* ∾-clothes *Gesellschaftsanzug, -kleidung;* ∾-coat *Frack;* full ∾ *Gala(uniform);* ∾-rehearsal *Generalprobe.* — **II.** v.i.: to ∾ for dinner *zum Abendessen einen Gesellschaftsanzug anziehen;* she ∾es well *sie ist immer gut angezogen;* he was ∾ed (up) to the nines *er war aufs feinste (äußerst elegant, pikfein) angezogen (aufgeputzt).* — **III.** v.tr.: to ∾ a chicken *ein Huhn säubern (ausnehmen) und für den Topf fertig machen;* to ∾ (one's) hair *(sich) frisieren;* to ∾ down a horse *ein Pferd striegeln;* to ∾ leather, iron *Leder, Eisen zurichten;* to ∾ a ship *ein Schiff beflaggen;* to ∾ a shop-window *ein Schaufenster dekorieren;* to ∾ a stone *einen Stein behauen;* to ∾ a soldier's wounds *einem Soldaten die Wunden verbinden;* to ∾ a person down, to give a person a good ∾ing down *j.en abkanzeln (anschnauzen, herunterputzen);* to ∾ a person up *j.en herausputzen, verkleiden*

drift n.: the ∾ of a discourse *der Gedankengang;* the policy of ∾ *die Politik des Gehen-, Sichtreibenlassens*

drink I. v.i.: to ∾ like a fish *saufen wie ein Loch.* — **II.** v.tr.: to ∾ oneself **drunk**

sich betrinken; to ∾ oneself out of a job *eine Stelle durch Trunksucht verlieren;* to ∾ one's fill *sich satt trinken;* to ∾ (to) a person's health *auf j.es Wohl trinken;* to ∾ a person down, under the table *j.en unter den Tisch trinken;* to ∾ in a person's words *j.em begeistert zuhören, seine Worte verschlingen:* to ∾ off (or: up) a glass of wine *ein Glas Wein austrinken.* — **III.** n.: to be in ∾ *betrunken sein;* to be on the ∾ *dem Trunke frönen;* to stand ∾s round *eine Runde ausgeben;* to take (to have) a ∾ *etwas trinken;* to take to ∾ *sich dem Trunke ergeben*

drive I. v.tr.: to ∾ a good bargain *ein gutes Geschäft abschließen;* to ∾ it to the last minute *es bis zur letzten Minute verschieben;* to ∾ a person mad (out of his senses) *j.en verrückt machen, um den Verstand bringen;* to ∾ pigs to market *schnarchen, ‚sägen';* to ∾ a quill (a pen) *schreiben;* to ∾ a roaring trade *glänzende Geschäfte machen;* to ∾ the nail home *eine Angelegenheit zum Abschluß bringen;* to ∾ a thing home to a person *j.em etwas klarmachen;* to ∾ a thing into a person *j.em etwas einbleuen;* to ∾ up prices *Preise in die Höhe treiben;* he is hard driven *er muß schwer arbeiten.* — **II.** v.i.: in driving rain *in Wind und Regen (Wetter);* what is he driving at? *was hat er im Sinn? worauf will er hinaus?;* to let ∾ at a thing *auf etwas losschlagen;* to ∾ up to a house *vor einem Hause vorfahren.* — **III.** n.: to take (to go for) a ∾ *eine Spazierfahrt machen*

drop I. v.tr.: to ∾ across someone *j.en zufällig treffen;* to ∾ anchor *Anker werfen;* to ∾ a brick (sl.) *ins Fettnäpfchen treten;* to ∾ a curtsy *einen Knicks machen;* to ∾ one's h's *kein h im Anlaut sprechen;* to ∾ a hint *einen Wink geben;* to ∾ a line *ein paar Zeilen zukommen lassen;* to ∾ a person (acquaintance with a person) *nichts mehr mit j.em zu tun haben wollen;* I must ∾ you here *ich muß Sie hier absetzen, aussteigen lassen;* he was ∾ped behind the enemy's lines *er wurde hinter den feindlichen Linien mit Fallschirm abgesetzt;* to ∾ a remark *eine Bemerkung fallen lassen;* we'll ∾ the subject *wir wollen den Gegenstand fallen lassen, von etwas anderem reden;* ∾ it! *laß das! genug davon!;* to ∾ a thing like a hot potato *etwas eiligst aus der Hand werfen;* to ∾ one's voice *die Stimme senken.* — **II.** v.i.: to be ready to ∾ *zum Umfallen müde sein;* to ∾ behind, to the rear *zurückbleiben;* to ∾ in *einen kurzen Besuch, eine Stippvisite machen;* to ∾ in and out *ständig herein- und hinaushuschen;* to ∾ into a fortune (a good thing) *eine Erbschaft (einen guten Treffer) machen;* to ∾ into a chair *sich in einen Stuhl fallen lassen;* to ∾ into a habit *sich (dat.) etwas angewöhnen;* to ∾ off (or: asleep) *einschlafen;* to ∾ on (upon) a thing *zufällig auf etwas stoßen;* to ∾ through *durchfallen, zu Wasser werden.* — **III.** n.: a ∾ in the bucket (ocean) *ein Tropfen auf einen heißen Stein;* to have a ∾ in one's eye *Anzeichen von Trunkenheit aufweisen;* to take a ∾ too much *einen über den Durst trinken;* a ∾ in prices *ein Sinken der Preise;* the last ∾ makes the cup run over (prov.) *noch ein Tropfen, und das Glas (Faß) fließt (läuft) über; eine Vollbelastung kann keine weitere kleine Belastung mehr ertragen*

dropping n.: constant ∾ wears away the stone (prov.) *steter Tropfen höhlt den Stein*

drown I. v.tr.: ∾ed in tears *in Tränen gebadet;* like a ∾ed rat *durch und durch naß, naß wie eine Katze.* — **II.** v.i.: a ∾ing men (will) catch at a straw (prov.) *der Ertrinkende klammert sich an einen Strohhalm*

drub v.tr.: to ∾ a thing into a person *j.em etwas einhämmern (einbleuen, eintrichtern);* to give a person a ∾bing *j.en verprügeln*

drug n.: he has acquired the ∾ habit *er hat sich daran gewöhnt, Rauschgifte zu nehmen;* it is a ∾ in the market *es besteht keine Nachfrage danach, es ist unverkäufliche Ware, ein Ladenhüter*

drum I. v.i.: to ∾ at the door *an die Tür klopfen;* to ∾ on the piano *auf dem Klavier klimpern;* a ∾ming in the ears *Ohrensausen.* — **II.** v.tr.: to ∾ a thing into a person *j.em etwas einbleuen (einhämmern, eintrichtern);* to ∾ a soldier out of the army *einen Soldaten schimpflich aus dem Heere ausstoßen;* to ∾ up *zusammentrommeln, werben*

drunk pred.a.: blind ∾ *sinnlos betrunken;* as ∾ as a fiddler (as a lord, as a boiled owl) *so voll wie eine Kanone (Strandhaubitze), sternhagelvoll, blau wie ein Märzveilchen;* ∾ with joy *freudetrunken*

dry I. a.: as ∾ as a bone (as a stick) *knochen-, rappeltrocken;* as ∾ as dust *äußerst (höchst) langweilig;* to ∾-clean clothes *Kleider chemisch reinigen;* to die a ∾ death *den Tod anders als durch Ertrinken oder Blutvergießen finden;* to go ∾ *das Alkoholverbot einführen;* to run ∾ *trocken werden;* he sells ∾-goods *er verkauft Kurz-, Schnittwaren.* — **II.** v.tr.: ∾ up your tears *trockne deine Tränen!* — **III.** v.i.: to ∾ up *ein-, vertrocknen, verdorren;* ∾ up (colloq.) *halt's Maul!*

duck[1] n.: she is a ∾ of a girl *sie ist ein reizendes (süßes) Mädel;* he is a lame ∾ *er ist ein lahmes, krankes Huhn; er ist ein Mann, der seine Schulden an der Börse nicht bezahlen kann;* like a ∾ in a thunderstorm *vollkommen bestürzt;* it's a fine day for young ∾s *es ist Regenwetter;* to play ∾s and drakes *flache Steine über die Wasseroberfläche hüpfen lassen; Wasserjungfern werfen;* to play ∾s and drakes with (to make ∾s and drakes of) one's money *sein Geld verprassen (zum Fenster hinauswerfen, verpulvern, verwichsen);* it runs off him like water off a ∾'s back *es beeindruckt ihn nicht;* he scored a ∾'s egg (cricket) *er machte keinen einzigen Lauf (Eiform = O);* in two shakes of a ∾'s tail *im Nu;* to take to a thing like a ∾ to water *von etwas sehr angezogen werden (wie die Ente vom Wasser)*

duck[2] I. v.i.: to ∾ to a blow *sich vor einem Schlage ducken;* to ∾ doing something *unterlassen, etwas zu tun.* — **II.** v.tr.: to ∾ one's head *den Kopf ducken;* to get a good ∾ing *tüchtig naß werden*

dud (sl.) **I.** n.: it was a ∾ *es war ein Blindgänger;* he is a ∾ *er ist ein Versager (eine Niete);* my ∾s *meine Kleider (Brokken, Klamotten).* — **II.** a.: it was a ∾ show *es war eine klägliche Vorstellung*

due I. a.: after ∾ consideration *nach gehöriger (reiflicher) Überlegung;* in ∾ course (or: time) *zur rechten Zeit;* a ∾ east course *ein genau östlicher Kurs;* I am ∾ at his house at 9 o'clock *ich muß um 9 Uhr bei ihm sein;* the train is ∾ at 7.30 *der Zug soll um halb acht ankommen;* the train is over-∾ *der Zug hat Verspätung;* he is ∾ to speak tonight *er soll (ist angesetzt) heute abend (zu) sprechen;* the interest falls ∾ next month *die Zinsen sind nächsten Monat fällig;* the bad harvest was ∾ to the heavy rain *die schlechte Ernte war die Folge des vielen Regens.* — **II.** n.: to give the devil his ∾ *j.em sein Recht lassen;* to pay one's ∾s to a person *j.em das geben, was man ihm schuldet;* the harbour ∾s *die Hafengebühren;* for a full ∾ *gründlich, vollständig*

dull I. a.: as ∾ as ditch-water *entsetzlich langweilig (fade) sein.* — **II.** v.tr.: to ∾ the edge of a thing *etwas abstumpfen, weniger empfindlich, weniger interessant, weniger wirksam machen*

dumb a.: Nature is ∾ on the point *die Natur schweigt sich darüber aus;* the ∾ millions *die Millionen, die keinen Einfluß auf die Regierung haben;* a ∾ show *ein Gebärdenspiel, eine Pantomime;* to strike ∾ *sprachlos machen;* ∾-bells *Hanteln;* a ∾ waiter *ein Stummer Diener (als kleiner Tisch)*

dumps n.pl.: to be down in the ∾ *in schlechter Stimmung, mißmutig, niedergeschlagen sein, Trübsal blasen*

dunghill n.: he is a cock on his own ∾ *er ist ein Tyrann im Hause (zu Hause)*

dust I. n.: as dry as ∾ *äußerst (höchst) langweilig;* to bite the ∾ *ins Gras beißen, sterben;* to make (to raise, to kick up) a ∾ about *Staub aufwirbeln, Lärm (Krach) schlagen, Spektakel machen wegen (über);* to shake off the ∾ from one's feet *den Staub von den Füßen schütteln, entrüstet fortgehen;* to throw ∾ in a person's eyes *j.em Sand in die Augen streuen;* to turn to ∾ and ashes *zu Staub und Asche werden.* — **II.** v.tr.: to ∾ one's hands of a person *mit j.em nichts mehr zu tun haben wollen;* to ∾ a person's jacket *j.em die Jacke voll hauen*

dusty a.: that's not so ∾ (sl.) *das ist ziemlich gut*

Dutch a.: ∾ auction *eine Versteigerung, bei der die Preise fallen (anstatt zu steigen);* to offer someone ∾ comfort *j.en mit den Worten trösten: „Es könnte noch viel schlimmer kommen";* to have ∾ courage *sich (dat.) Mut angetrunken haben;* to talk double ∾ *Kauderwelsch reden;* a ∾ treat *ein Fest, bei dem jeder für sich bezahlt;* to talk to a person like a ∾ uncle *j.en väterlich zurechtweisen;* I'm a ∾man if *ich will Meier heißen, wenn*

duty n.: a ∾ call *ein Pflichtbesuch;* breach of ∾ *Pflichtverletzung;* in ∾ to *aus Ehrerbietung gegen;* on ∾ *im Dienst;* off ∾ *außer Dienst;* ∾-free *zoll-, abgabenfrei;* to do ∾ for (or: as) a thing *benutzt werden, dienen als, als Ersatz für etwas dienen;* in ∾ bound *pflichtschuldig;* I am in ∾ bound to say *ich muß pflichtgemäß sagen;* to do one's ∾ by a person *an j.em seine Pflicht tun*

dwell v.i.: to ∾ (up)on a subject *in Wort oder Schrift bei einem Gegenstand verweilen;* to ∾ upon a note *einen Ton anhalten*

dye I. n.: a scoundrel of the blackest (deepest) ∾ *ein Erzschurke.* — **II.** v.tr.: ∾d-in-the-wool *durchtrieben, ausgekocht*

E

eager a.: an ∾ beaver (sl.) *eine übereifrige Person*

ear n.: a box on the ∾ *eine Ohrfeige;* ∾-phones *(Haartracht) Schnecken;* over head and ∾s (up to the ∾s) in work, in love *bis über die Ohren in Arbeit, verliebt;* an ∾-splitting yell *ein ohrenbetäubender Schrei;* a word in your ∾ *ein Wort im Vertrauen;* were your ∾s burning last night? *klangen dir die Ohren gestern abend?;* to be all ∾s *ganz Ohr sein;* to bring a hornet's nest about one's ∾s *in ein Wespennest stechen;* to fall (up)on a person's ∾ *an j.es Ohr dringen;* to give ∾ to, to lend an (one's) ∾ to *Gehör schenken;* I would give my ∾s for a thing (to do a thing) *ich gäbe alles drum, um etwas zu haben (um etwas tun zu können);* it goes in at one ∾ and out at the other *es geht zu einem Ohr hinein und zum anderen hinaus;* to have a person's ∾ *j.es Vertrauen genießen;* to make dog('s)-∾s in a book, to dog-∾ a book *Eselsohren in ein Buch machen;* a dog-∾ed book *ein Buch mit Eselsohren;* to play by ∾ *nach Gehör spielen;* she has an ∾ for music, no ∾ *sie hat eine natürliche Liebe für Musik, sie ist musikalisch begabt; sie hat kein musikalisches Ohr (ist unmusikalisch);* it has come to my ∾s *es ist mir zu Ohren gekommen;* he has his ∾s to the ground *er ist sehr hellhörig;* to prick up one's ∾s *die Ohren spitzen;* I sent him away with a flea in his ∾ *ich habe ihm gehörig die Wahrheit gesagt (heimgeleuchtet);* to set persons by the ∾s *Leute gegeneinander aufhetzen;* to stop one's ∾s *sich (dat.) die Ohren zuhalten;* you'll get thrown out on your ∾ (sl.) *du wirst in Ungnaden entlassen werden;* to turn a deaf ∾ to *taub sein gegen;* to be within ∾-shot *in Hörweite sein;* little pitchers have long (big) ∾s (prov.) *kleine Kessel haben große Ohren; Kinder schnappen manches auf*

early a. & adv.: as ∾ as the 16th century *schon im 16. Jahrhundert;* he is an ∾ bird *er ist ein Frühaufsteher;* the ∾ bird gets the worm (prov.) *Morgenstunde hat Gold im Munde;* it is ∾ days to do that *es ist noch zu früh, das zu tun;* the ∾ part of the century *der Anfang des Jahrhunderts;* to rise ∾ *früh aufstehen;* to keep ∾ hours *früh aufstehen und früh zu Bett gehen;* at the earliest *frühestens;* at your earliest convenience *baldmöglichst*

earmark v.tr.: to ∾ something for a definite purpose *etwas für einen bestimmten Zweck bestimmen, vormerken*

earnest n.: are you in ∾? *ist das dein Ernst?;* to be in ∾ about something *etwas sehr ernst nehmen*

earth n.: why on ∾ did you do that? *warum in aller Welt hast du das getan?;* to come back to ∾ *wieder nüchtern denken;* to run a person (thing) to ∾ *j.en (etwas) ausfindig machen;* to run a fox to ∾ *einen Fuchs in den Bau treiben;* to take ∾ *sich in sein Loch verkriechen;* it will cost the ∾ (colloq.) *es wird schrecklich (höllisch) teuer sein, die Welt kosten*

earthly a.: it's no ∾ use to me (colloq.) *es hat für mich nicht den geringsten Wert;* I have not an ∾, no ∾ (sl.) *ich habe nicht die geringste Chance*

ease I. n.: to be (to feel) at one's ∾ *sich ungezwungen (behaglich) fühlen;* to do a thing with ∾ *etwas mit Leichtigkeit tun;* to put (to set) a person at ∾ *j.em die Schüchternheit, die innere Unruhe nehmen;* to be ill at ∾ *sich genieren, sich unbehaglich fühlen, ängstlich sein;* to take one's ∾ *sich ausruhen, es sich bequem machen;* a Chapel of ∾ *eine Kapelle für diejenigen, welche zuweit von der Pfarrkirche entfernt wohnen;* stand at ∾! *rührt euch!* — **II.** v.tr.: to ∾ an engine *die Geschwindigkeit eines (Schiffs-)Motors herabsetzen;* to ∾ a person of his purse *j.em die Geldbörse* *stehlen;* to ∾ away (down, off) a rope *ein Seil lockern;* to ∾ a screw *eine Schraube lösen.* — **III.** v.i.: to ∾ off *leichter werden, nachlassen;* ∾ up! *nur langsam!*

easy I. a.: it is as ∾ as ABC, as shelling peas, as falling off a log *es ist kinderleicht;* ∾ does it! *nimm dir Zeit!;* it is ∾ of access *es ist leicht zugängig;* free and ∾ manners *ungezwungenes Benehmen;* ∾ money *leicht verdientes Geld; j., von dem man leicht Geld bekommen kann;* a woman (lady) of ∾ virtue *eine Dirne;* he's in Easy Street (in ∾ circumstances) *es geht ihm wirtschaftlich gut.* — **II.** adv.: ∾ come, ∾ go (prov.) *wie gewonnen, so zerronnen;* he's an ∾-going chap *er ist ein gutmütiger, bequemer Kerl;* I'm going to take it ∾ *ich werde mich nicht überanstrengen, werde mir die Sache bequem machen;* take it ∾! *nur ruhig (langsam)!*

eat I. v.tr.: see 'crow, hat, head, humble'; the horse is ∾ing his head off *das Pferd frißt mehr als seine Arbeit wert ist;* to ∾ one's heart out *sich abhärmen, sich vor Gram verzehren;* well, don't ∾ me! *nun, friß mich nicht gleich auf!;* to ∾ a person out of house and home *j.en arm essen;* to ∾ one's terms (dinners) *an einer der Londoner Rechtsschulen* (Inns of Court) *studieren;* to ∾ one's words *seine Worte zurücknehmen (widerrufen) müssen, zu Kreuze kriechen;* he is ∾en up with pride *er platzt vor Stolz;* to ∾ away, into *auf-, verzehren (vom Meer oder als Säurewirkung);* you can't ∾ your cake and have it (prov.) *du kannst es entweder so oder so haben (aber nicht beides; man kann es nur einmal genießen).* — **II.** v.i.: the cakes ∾ crisp *die Kuchen sind knusprig.* — **III.** n.: ∾s (colloq.) *Speisen, eine Mahlzeit*

eating n.: the proof of the pudding is in the ∾ (prov.) *Probieren geht über Studieren*

ebb n.: to be at a low ∾ *sehr heruntergekommen sein, ohne Geld sein, Ebbe in der Kasse haben*

echo n.: to cheer (to applaud) a person to the ∾ *j.em tosenden Beifall spenden;* to ∾ someone's opinions *j.es Meinungen mechanisch wiederholen (nachkäuen)*

edge I. n.: on the ∾ of *kurz vor, im Begriff;* over the ∾ *übertrieben, unvernünftig;* his words have an ∾ to them *seine Worte sind scharfsinnig, schneidig;* to have plenty of ∾ (sl.) *eingebildet sein;* to be on ∾ *nervös sein;* to add (to give) an ∾ to a thing *etwas verschärfen, stärken, anspornen;* the knife has no ∾ *das Messer ist stumpf;* to have an ∾ on a person (sl.) *Groll gegen j.en hegen; j.em gegenüber im Vorteil sein;* to meet on ∾ *Kante auf Kante zutreffen;* to play with ∾d tools *mit gefährlichen Dingen spielen;* to put a person on ∾, to set his nerves (or teeth) on ∾ *j.en reizen, nervös machen;* to take the ∾ off *etwas abstumpfen, etwas der Wirkung berauben;* to turn the ∾ of a remark *eine Bemerkung abschwächen;* that will take the ∾ off your appetite *das wird deinen ersten Hunger stillen;* not to put too fine an ∾ on it *das Kind beim Namen nennen;* that is the outside ∾ (colloq.) *das ist aber die Höhe;* to sit on the thin ∾ of nothing *im Gedränge wenig Platz haben.* — **II.** v.tr. & i.: to ∾ (egg) someone on *j.en anfeuern;* to ∾ one's way through the crowd *sich einen Weg durch die Menge bahnen;* to ∾ away from something *sich allmählich entfernen (von einem Plan)*

edgeways, -wise adv.: to get a word in ∾ *ein Wort anbringen, zu Wort kommen*

eel n.: as slippery as an ∾ *aalglatt*

effect I. n.: cause and ∾ *Ursache und Wirkung;* my personal ∾s *mein persönliches Eigentum;* to be of ∾ on *wirken (wirksam sein) auf;* to be of (to) no ∾, without ∾ *umsonst, vergeblich sein;* to be in ∾ the same *im wesentlichen (Effekt) dasselbe sein;* to be calculated for ∾ *auf Wirkung (Eindruck) berechnet sein;* to carry into (to bring to) ∾ *ausführen;* he did it to good ∾ *er tat es mit guter Wirkung;* to give ∾ to a thing *einer Sache Wirkung (Kraft) verleihen;* he replied to the same ∾ *er antwortete in gleichem Sinne;* the law takes ∾ next month *das Gesetz tritt nächsten Monat in Kraft;* he wrote a letter to the ∾ that *er schrieb einen Brief des Inhalts, daß;* in ∾ *in der Tat; im wesentlichen.* — **II.** v.tr.: to ∾ a policy *eine Versicherung abschließen*

egg[1] n.: as full as an ∾ is of meat *gedrängt voll, vollgepfropft;* as sure as ∾s is ∾s (colloq.) *so sicher, wie zweimal zwei vier ist;* he's (it's) a bad ∾ (sl.) *er ist ein übler Kunde; es ist eine faule Sache;* well, old ∾! (sl.) *nun, altes Haus!;* to crush in the ∾ *im Keime ersticken;* to have (to put) all one's ∾s in one basket *alles auf eine Karte setzen;* to put by a nice little nest-∾ *einen netten Sparpfennig zurücklegen;* to teach one's grandmother to suck ∾s *einer erfahreneren Person Rat erteilen, das Ei will klüger sein als die Henne*

egg[2] v.tr.: to ∾ a person on to an act (to do a thing) *j.en zu einer Tat ermuntern, ihn antreiben, etwas zu tun*

eight n.: to have one over the ∾ *ein Glas zuviel, eins über den Durst trinken*

eke v.tr.: to ∾ out a scanty livelihood *sich kümmerlich durchschlagen*

elbow I. n.: at one's ∾ *bei der Hand, in der Nähe;* to be out at ∾s *abgetragen (von einem Rock), heruntergekommen, arm (von Personen) sein;* to be up to the ∾s in work *bis über die Ohren in Arbeit stekken;* to lift (to raise) one's ∾ (sl.) *einen trinken (heben, schmettern);* it meant a lot of ∾-grease *es erforderte viel Knochenschmalz,-schmiere, es war harte Arbeit;* I must have ∾-room *ich muß Ellbogenfreiheit haben.* — **II.** v.tr.: to ∾ a person out of the room *j.en aus dem Zimmer verdrängen;* to ∾ oneself (one's way) into a room *sich in ein Zimmer hineindrängen*

elephant n.: a white ∾ *ein kostspieliger, lästiger Besitz;* to see the ∾ *sich in der Welt umsehen; welterfahren, lebensklug werden*

eleven n.: to have (to take) one's ∾ses (colloq.) *sein zweites Frühstück (ein)nehmen*

ell n.: give him an inch and he'll take an ∾ *reich' ihm den kleinen Finger, und er nimmt (gleich) die ganze Hand*

embargo n.: to lay an ∾ on something *durch ein Verbot untersagen, verhindern*

embrace v.tr.: to ∾ a course of action, a profession *eine Handlungsweise einschlagen; einen Beruf ergreifen;* to ∾ an offer *ein Anerbieten annehmen;* the course ∾s dancing and gymnastics *der Kursus umfaßt Tanzen und Turnen*

emergency n.: the ∾ brake *die Notbremse;* the ∾ door, exit *der Notausgang;* an ∾ fund *ein Reservefonds*

end I. n.: at the ∾s of the earth *am Ende der Welt;* candle-∾s *wertlose Brokken;* all sorts of odds and ∾s *allerlei Brocken, Krimskrams;* to what ∾? *zu welchem Zwecke?;* world without ∾ *in Ewigkeit;* to be at a loose ∾ *ohne Beschäftigung sein;* to be at the ∾ of one's tether *am Ende seiner Kraft sein, nicht mehr ein noch aus wissen;* to be at one's wits' ∾ *mit seinem Verstand zu Ende sein, sich (dat.) nicht zu raten noch zu helfen wissen;* to be of no ∾ *vergebens sein;* to come to a bad ∾ *ein schlechtes Ende nehmen;* to draw to an ∾ *zu Ende gehen;* to gain one's ∾ *seinen Zweck erreichen;* the fag-∾ *der allerletzte Rest;* to get the thin ∾ of the stick *bei etwas schlecht wegkommen;* to get in the thin ∾ of the wedge *den ersten Anfang machen; erst mal in Gang kommen;* to go off the deep ∾ *die Fassung verlieren, aufbrausen, wütend werden, aus dem Häuschen geraten;* to have at one's fingers' ∾s *am Schnürchen haben;* to have no ∾ of fun *sich köstlich amüsieren;* to keep one's ∾ up *sich gut (tapfer) halten;* to lay ∾ on *mit dem Ende nach vorn legen;* to lay from ∾ to ∾ *von einem Ende zum anderen, der Länge nach hinlegen;* to make both ∾s meet *mit seinen Einkünften gerade auskommen, sich nach der Decke strecken;* to place a thing on ∾ *etwas aufrecht hinstellen;* three weeks on ∾ *drei Wochen hintereinander;* to place ∾ to ∾ *mit den Enden aneinanderlegen;* to put an ∾ to a thing *einer Sache ein Ende bereiten;* his hair stood on ∾ *die Haare standen ihm zu Berge;* to turn a thing ∾ for ∾ *eine Sache ganz umdrehen;* the ∾ justifies the means *der Zweck heiligt die Mittel.* — **II.** v.tr.: he ∾ed (up, off) his speech with the words *er schloß seine Rede mit den Worten;* ∾ it or mend it! *mach' Schluß oder mach's besser!* — **III.** v.i.: to ∾ by doing something *schließlich (letzten Endes) etwas tun;* it ∾ed in his giving up *es endete damit, daß er es aufgab;* to ∾ in smoke *in Rauch aufgehen;* All's well that ∾s well! (Shakespeare; prov.) *Ende gut, alles gut!*

enemy n.: how goes the ∾? (colloq.) *wieviel Uhr ist es?;* to make an ∾ of a person *sich (dat.) j.en zum Feinde machen*

engage v.tr. & i.: to ∾ seats *Plätze bestellen;* to ∾ (oneself) to do a thing *sich verpflichten, etwas zu tun;* to ∾ a person in a conversation *j.en in ein Gespräch verwickeln;* to ∾ for *die Gewähr bieten, ver-*

sprechen; to ∾ (with) the enemy *in Kampf mit dem Feinde geraten;* to be ∾d in (or: on) a task *mit einer Aufgabe beschäftigt sein;* to be ∾d for the evening *für den Abend eingeladen (versagt) sein;* to get ∾d to *sich verloben mit;* he has engaging manners *er hat gewinnende Manieren*

engagement n.: to be under an ∾ to a person *j.em vertraglich verpflichtet sein;* to break off an ∾ *ein Verlöbnis lösen;* it came to a sharp ∾ *es kam zu einem hitzigen Gefecht;* to enter into an ∾ *eine Verpflichtung eingehen;* I have an ∾ for tonight *ich bin heute abend eingeladen (versagt);* to meet one's ∾s *seinen Verpflichtungen nachkommen;* to put off an ∾ *eine Verabredung verschieben*

English n.: in plain ∾ *mit offenen Worten;* King's (Queen's) ∾ *Standard-Englisch*

enlighten v.tr.: to ∾ a person on (or: as to) a thing *j.en über etwas aufklären;* the Age of Enlightenment *das Zeitalter der Aufklärung*

enough I. n.: ∾ is as good as a feast (prov.) *allzuviel ist ungesund;* to have ∾ and to spare *übergenug haben.* — **II.** adv.: will you be good ∾ to do it? *willst du so gut sein, es zu tun?;* oddly ∾, he had lost his purse *seltsamerweise hatte er seine Geldbörse verloren;* sure ∾, there it was *und richtig, da war es auch!;* you know well ∾ *du weißt ganz gut (sehr wohl);* let well ∾ alone *misch' dich nicht unnötig ein! laß es gut sein!* — **III.** a.: give him ∾ rope *laß ihm Freiheit genug, um sich entwickeln zu können;* give a man rope ∾ and he will hang himself (prov.) *etwa: laß ihn ruhig so weiter machen, er wird sich schon selbst den Strick drehen*

enter I. v.tr.: to ∾ the Army (the Church) *Soldat (Priester) werden;* to ∾ an appearance at a meeting *zu einer Versammlung erscheinen;* a thought ∾ed my head *mir kam der Gedanke;* to ∾ one's name in a book *seinen Namen in ein Buch eintragen;* to ∾ a protest *einen Protest einbringen, Verwahrung einlegen.* — **II.** v.i.: to ∾ for an examination *sich zu einer Prüfung melden;* to ∾ into an agreement *ein Übereinkommen treffen;* to ∾ into conversation *eine Unterhaltung beginnen;* to ∾ into details *auf Einzelheiten eingehen;* to ∾ into an engagement *eine Verpflichtung eingehen;* to ∾ the lists *den Kampf aufnehmen;* to ∾ into one's mind *einem in den Sinn kommen;* to ∾ into relations *Beziehungen anknüpfen;* to ∾ (up)on a career *eine Laufbahn beginnen (antreten);* to ∾ (up)on a subject *ein Thema anschneiden*

entertain v.tr.: to ∾ an angel unawares, see 'angel'; they ∾ a great deal *sie geben oft Gesellschaften;* to ∾ an idea (a thought) *sich mit einem Gedanken tragen, einen Gedanken hegen;* to ∾ high hopes of something *große Hoffnungen auf etwas setzen*

equal I. a.: I am ∾ to a cup of tea (colloq.) *ich tränke ganz gern eine Tasse Tee;* to be ∾ to doing a thing *imstande (fähig) sein, etwas zu tun;* to be ∾ to the occasion *der Lage gewachsen sein;* other things being ∾ *bei sonst gleichen Umständen;* to keep an ∾ mind *ruhig, besonnen bleiben.* — **II.** n.: he has no ∾ *er hat nicht seinesgleichen;* to mix with one's ∾s *mit seinesgleichen verkehren*

err v.i.: to ∾ on the side of generosity *etwas zu freigebig sein;* it is best to ∾ on the safe side *besser zuviel Vorsicht als zu wenig*

errand n.: to go (to run) (on) an ∾ *einen Gang tun;* a fool's ∾ *ein Metzgersgang, ein nutzloses Unternehmen*

error n.: ∾s excepted *Irrtümer vorbehalten;* a clerical ∾ *ein Schreibfehler;* a printer's ∾ *ein Druckfehler;* to make (to commit) an ∾ *einen Fehler begehen;* to lead someone into ∾ *j.en verderben, verführen*

escape I. n.: to make good one's ∾ *entkommen;* he had a narrow (lucky, hairbreadth) ∾ *er ist mit knapper Not entkommen, ums Haar hätte es ihn erwischt;* there must be an ∾ of gas somewhere *irgendwo muß Gas ausströmen.* — **II.** v.tr.: the words ∾d his lips *die Worte entfuhren ihm;* his name has ∾d me *sein Name ist mir entfallen;* it has ∾d my memory *es ist meinem Gedächtnis entschwunden.* — **III.** v.i.: to ∾ from prison *aus dem Gefängnis entkommen*

even I. a.: ∾ odds *eine fifty-fifty Chance;* odd or ∾ *gerade oder ungerade;* of ∾ date (vulg.; *schlechter Stil) gleichen Datums;* to be (to get) ∾ with a person *sich an j.em rächen, mit j.em abrechnen;* ∾-handed justice *unparteiische Gerechtigkeit.* — **II.** adv.: he disputes ∾ the date *er bestreitet sogar das Datum;* I never ∾ read it *ich habe es* *nicht einmal gelesen;* ∾ if he is right *selbst wenn er recht hat;* this applies ∾ more to Music *dies bezieht sich sogar mehr auf die Musik;* ∾ so *selbst dann*

evening n.: in the ∾ *am Abend;* of an ∾, one ∾ *eines Abends;* on the ∾ of Jan. 3 *am Abend des 3. Januar;* on winter ∾s *an Winterabenden;* to make an ∾ of it *sich einen schönen Abend machen*

event n.: it is quite an ∾ *es ist ein wirkliches Ereignis;* in the ∾ of his coming *falls er kommt;* in any (either) ∾, at all ∾s *auf jeden Fall;* coming ∾s cast their shadows before (prov.) *kommende Ereignisse werfen ihre Schatten voraus;* to prophesy after the ∾ *nachher alles besser wissen;* in the natural course of ∾s *im natürlichen Verlauf der Dinge*

ever adv.: ∾ and anon *dann und wann, immer wieder;* for ∾ and ∾, ∾ and a day *in alle Ewigkeit, auf ewig und drei Tage;* I have known him ∾ since he was at school *ich kenne ihn seit seiner Schulzeit;* have you ∾ heard such nonsense? *hast du je so einen Unsinn gehört?;* be as quick as ∾ you can *mach so schnell, wie du nur irgend kannst;* what∾ does he want? *was will er denn nur?;* who∾ can it be? *wer mag es bloß sein?;* as if ∾ such a thing would happen! *als ob je so etwas passieren könnte!;* hardly (scarcely) ∾ *sehr selten;* he is ∾ so fat (∾ such a fat man) (colloq.) *er ist sehr dick;* the best (worst) ∾ (colloq.) *das allerbeste (allerschlimmste);* when(wher, how) ∾ did I drop it? *wann (wo, wie) habe ich es bloß fallen lassen?;* why ∾ didn't you say so? *warum hast du es denn nicht gesagt?;* it is ∾ so much easier now *es ist jetzt bedeutend leichter;* I waited for ∾ so long *ich habe wer weiß wie lange gewartet;* thank you ∾ so much *recht herzlichen Dank;* let him be ∾ so rich *mag er auch noch so reich sein;* did you ∾! *na, so etwas!*

every a.: ∾ bit as much the same *ganz und gar dasselbe;* ∾body else *alle anderen;* an ∾day occurrence *ein alltägliches Ereignis;* ∾ now and then, now and again *von Zeit zu Zeit, dann und wann, ab und zu;* ∾one of them is wrong *jeder einzelne von ihnen hat unrecht;* ∾one likes to have his way *jeder(mann) bekommt (hat) gern seinen Willen;* he comes ∾ other day, ∾ second day, ∾ two days *er kommt einen um den anderen Tag, jeden zweiten Tag, alle zwei Tage;* ∾thing depends on that *davon hängt alles ab;* ∾thing in the garden is lovely (colloq.) *es geht alles gut;* ∾thing's under control *alles verläuft planmäßig;* pace is ∾thing *Geschwindigkeit ist die Hauptsache;* it engaged his ∾ thought *es beschäftigte alle seine Gedanken;* I searched for it ∾where *ich suchte überall danach*

evidence n.: to give ∾ *Zeugnis ablegen;* to give (to bear) ∾ of *ein Beweis sein für;* circumstantial ∾ *Indizienbeweis;* conflicting ∾ *widersprechende Aussage;* hearsay ∾ *Beweismaterial vom Hörensagen;* it is very much in ∾ *es ist deutlich zu sehen, es fällt sehr auf;* to call a person in ∾ *j.en als Zeugen aufrufen;* to turn King's (Queen's) ∾ *als Kronzeuge auftreten, gegen Mitschuldige aussagen, um straffrei auszugehen*

evil I. a.: the Evil One *der Teufel;* the ∾ eye *der böse Blick;* to be of ∾ repute *einen schlechten Ruf haben;* to have an ∾ tongue *eine böse Zunge haben.* — **II.** n.: the king's ∾ *die Skrofulose (früher durch Handauflegen des Königs für heilbar gehalten);* of two ∾s choose the less (prov.) *wähle von zwei Übeln das geringere.* — **III.** adv.: to speak ∾ of a person *schlecht von j.em sprechen*

ewe n.: it was his ∾-lamb *(2 Samuel XII) es war sein kostbarster Besitz*

exactly adv.: ∾! *ganz recht! wie Sie sagen!*

example n.: beyond (without) ∾ *beispiellos;* by way of ∾ *um ein Beispiel zu geben;* for ∾ (abbr.e.g.) *zum Beispiel;* to give (to set) a good ∾ *mit gutem Beispiel vorangehen;* to hold up as an ∾ *als Beispiel hinstellen;* to make an ∾ of a person *an j.em ein Exempel statuieren;* to take ∾ by a person *sich (dat.) an j.em ein Beispiel nehmen*

except I. v.tr.: to ∾ a person from a thing *j.en von etwas ausnehmen, -schließen;* present company ∾ed *Anwesende ausgeschlossen.* — **II.** v.i.: to ∾ against a person *gegen j.en Einspruch erheben.* — **III.** prep.: we were all wrong ∾ him *wir hatten alle Unrecht außer (mit Ausnahme von) ihm;* he is everywhere ∾ in the right place *er ist überall, nur nicht auf dem richtigen Platz;* ∾ for the omission of accents *nur daß die Akzente fehlen*

excepting prep.: always ∾ the poorer classes *die ärmeren Klassen immer ausgenommen;* not (or: without) ∾ England *England nicht ausgenommen*

exception n.: there is no rule without an ∾ (prov.) *keine Regel ohne Ausnahme;* the ∾ proves the rule (prov.) *die Ausnahme bestätigt die Regel;* beyond ∾ *unanfechtbar;* to admit of no ∾ *keine Ausnahme zulassen;* to make an ∾ of someone *bei (mit) j.em eine Ausnahme machen, j.en als Ausnahme betrachten;* to take ∾ to a thing *an etwas Anstoß nehmen, Einwendungen gegen etwas machen*

excess n.: ∾ postage *Strafporto;* ∾ profits duty *Kriegsgewinnsteuer;* to be in ∾ of a thing *etwas übersteigen,-schreiten, über etwas hinausgehen;* to carry to ∾ *übertreiben;* to eat to ∾ *im Übermaß (übermäßig viel) essen*

exchange I. n.: ∾ is no robbery (prov.) *Tausch ist nicht Diebstahl (scherzhafte Rechtfertigung einer Übervorteilung beim Tausch);* a bill of ∾ *ein Wechsel;* the rate of ∾ *der Wechselkurs;* the Stock ∾ *die Börse;* the Labour ∾ *Arbeitsamt;* Telephone ∾ *Telefonamt;* in ∾ for *als Ersatz für, anstatt, gegen;* to lose by the ∾ *beim Tausch schlecht wegkommen;* to make an ∾ *tauschen.* — **II.** v.tr.: to ∾ one thing for another *eine Sache gegen eine andere aus-, umtauschen;* to ∾ words with a person *mit j.em Worte wechseln.* — **III.** v.i.: to ∾ from one regiment into another *durch Stellentausch sich von einem Regiment zum anderen versetzen lassen*

excuse I. v.tr.: to ∾ a person a fee *j.em eine Gebühr erlassen;* to ∾ a person from a duty *j.en von einer Pflicht entbinden.* — **II.** n.: a lame ∾ *eine faule Ausrede;* in ∾ of *als (zur) Entschuldigung*

execution n.: to carry (to put) into ∾ *zur Ausführung bringen;* to do ∾ *Wirkung haben*

exercise n.: to take ∾ *sich (dat.) Bewegung machen*

exhibition n.: to make an ∾ of oneself *sich lächerlich machen*

expect v.tr.: I shall not ∾ you till I see you *kommen Sie, wann Sie wollen; wenn Sie da sind, sind Sie da;* I ∾ to go to London *ich denke, ich werde nach London fahren;* I ∾ you to work hard *ich erwarte von Ihnen, daß Sie tüchtig arbeiten (werden);* will he come? I ∾ not *ob er kommt? ich denke, nein!*

expectation n.: according to ∾ *erwartungsgemäß, nach Erwarten;* against (contrary) to ∾ *wider (gegen) Erwarten;* to answer (to meet, to come up to) one's ∾ *j.es Erwartung erfüllen (entsprechen);* beyond ∾ *über Erwarten, über die Erwartung hinaus;* to fall short of (not to come up to) ∾ *die Erwartung enttäuschen;* to have great ∾s *Hoffnung auf eine große Erbschaft haben;* we have great ∾ of him *wir erwarten (erhoffen) viel von ihm;* in ∾ of *in Erwartung von;* the ∾ of life *die mutmaßliche Lebensdauer*

expedient n.: to be full of ∾s *sich immer zu helfen wissen;* to hit upon an ∾ *auf einen Ausweg verfallen;* he thought it ∾ to pay her a compliment *er fand es für dienlich (nützlich), ihr ein Kompliment zu machen (zu sagen)*

expense n.: at the ∾ of *auf Kosten von;* there was a laugh at his ∾ *man machte sich über ihn lustig;* I went to the ∾ of buying it *ich habe mir die Kosten gemacht, es zu kaufen;* to go to great ∾ *es sich (dat.) viel kosten lassen;* to put a person to great ∾ *j.em große Kosten verursachen, ihn in Kosten stürzen;* to bear (to cover) the ∾s *die Kosten (Auslagen) tragen (dekken)*

extent n.: to a certain (or: considerable) ∾ *bis zu einem gewissen (beträchtlichen) Grade;* to a great ∾ *in hohem Grade;* to the full (the utmost) ∾ *in vollem (äußerstem) Maße;* to some ∾ *einigermaßen;* to what ∾? *wie weit?*

extol v.tr.: to ∾ a person to the skies *j.en in den Himmel heben, (bis) über den grünen Klee loben*

extreme I. a.: to administer the ∾ unction *die letzte Ölung geben, mit ihr versehen.* — **II.** n.: ∾s meet *die Extreme (Gegensätze) berühren sich;* to go (to run) to ∾s, to rush into ∾s *in Extreme verfallen, zum Äußersten schreiten;* in the ∾ *äußerst*

extremity n.: to drive to ∾ *auf die Spitze treiben;* to go (to proceed) to extremities *die äußersten Maßnahmen ergreifen;* to be reduced to extremities *in äußerster Not sein*

eye I. n.: with an ∾ to *in der Absicht; mit Rücksicht auf;* the ∾ of day *die Sonne;* in the ∾ of the law *vom Standpunkte des Gesetzes aus;* the ∾ of a needle *das Nadelöhr;* with one auspicious and one dropping ∾ (Hamlet, I, 2) *mit einem heitern, einem nassen Aug'; mit gemischten Gefühlen;* the evil ∾ *der böse Blick;* hook and ∾ *Haken und Öse;* the mote in thy brother's ∾, the beam in thine own ∾ (Matt. VII, 3) *der Splitter in deines Bruders Auge, der Balken in deinem Auge;* my ∾(s)! *du meine (liebe) Güte!;* that's all my ∾ and Betty Martin *das ist Unsinn, dummes Zeug, Quatsch;* with the naked ∾ *mit bloßem Auge;* an ∾-opener (colloq.) *ein ernüchterndes Erlebnis;* in the twinkling of an ∾ *im Nu;* in the wind's ∾ *in der Richtung des Windes;* to be all ∾s *große Augen machen;* to be in my mind's ∾ *vor meinem geistigen Auge stehen;* to be up to the ∾s in work *bis über die Ohren in der Arbeit stecken;* to be wise in one's own ∾s *sich weise dünken;* to be in ∾shot; beyond (out of) ∾shot *in Sichtweite sein; außer Sichtweite sein;* to be a sight for sore ∾s *eine Augenweide sein;* to be an ∾sore *einen häßlichen Anblick bieten;* that is ∾-wash (sl.) *das ist Unsinn, bloßes Gerede;* to cast an ∾ on a thing *ein Auge auf etwas werfen;* to cast sheep's ∾s at a person *j.en verliebt anblicken;* to catch the Speaker's ∾ *im Unterhaus das Wort erhalten;* to clap (to set) ∾s on a person *j.en zu Gesicht bekommen;* to cry one's ∾s out *sich (dat.) die Augen ausweinen;* to draw someone's ∾-teeth *eine eingebildete Person heruntermachen;* to get a black ∾ *ein blaues Auge bekommen;* to get one's ∾ in *sich an die Entfernung gewöhnen, daher: etwas Erfahrung in einer Sache bekommen;* to hang on by the ∾lids (colloq.) *einen nur losen Halt haben, an einem Faden hängen;* to have an ∾ for a thing *für etwas ein Auge, für etwas Sinn haben;* to have an ∾ to a thing *auf etwas ein Auge haben, es auf etwas abgesehen haben;* to have an ∾ to the main chance (colloq.) *ein Auge auf (für) das Nützliche haben;* to have ∾s like saucers *Glotzaugen haben;* to have one's ∾ in a sling (colloq.) *geschlagen, bedrückt sein;* he has a cast in the ∾ *er schielt etwas;* to keep an ∾ on (to) a thing *etwas im Auge behalten, ein wachsames Auge auf etwas haben;* to keep one's ∾s skinned (colloq.) *höllisch aufpassen;* to make ∾s at a person *j.em verliebte Blicke zuwerfen;* mind your ∾! *Achtung! Sieh dich vor!;* to open a person's ∾s to a thing *j.em die Augen für etwas öffnen;* that made him open his ∾s *das ließ ihn erstaunt starren;* to pipe (to put) one's finger in one's ∾s *plärren, weinen;* to raise one's ∾brows *hochmütig auf j.en herabsehen;* to run one's ∾s along (down, over) a thing *etwas mit den Augen überfliegen;* to score a bull's ∾ *ins Schwarze treffen, eine Zwölf schießen;* to see ∾ to ∾ with a person on a thing *über etwas mit j.em derselben Meinung sein;* to see with half an ∾ *auf den ersten Blick sehen;* if you had half an ∾ *wenn du nicht ganz blind wärest;* to shut one's ∾s to a thing *sich (dat.) die Augen vor etwas verschließen;* to strike the ∾ *ins Auge fallen;* to take an ∾ful (colloq.) *gründlich betrachten;* to wipe a person's ∾ (sl.) *j.em zuvorkommen, ihn übervorteilen (beschummeln, beschwindeln, übers Ohr hauen);* argus ∾d *luchsäugig, mit Argusaugen behaftet.* — **II.** v.tr.: to ∾ (a person) askance *j.en scheel ansehen; mit Mißtrauen, Verachtung betrachten;* to ∾ a person jealously *j.en eifersüchtig beobachten*

F

face I. n.: her ∾ is her fortune *ihre Schönheit ist ihre einzige Mitgift;* a ∾ card *ein Bild (Kartenspiel);* the ∾ of a clock (watch) *das Zifferblatt einer Uhr;* the ∾ value of a note *der Nennwert einer Banknote;* in the very ∾ of day *am hellichten Tage;* on the ∾ of it *auf den ersten Blick, oberflächlich betrachtet;* to attempt a thing in the ∾ of danger *etwas trotz (angesichts) drohender Gefahr versuchen;* to be full in the ∾ *ein rundes (volles) Gesicht haben;* to bring ∾ to ∾ *gegenüberstellen;* to disappear from the ∾ of the earth *vom Erdboden verschwinden;* to flatter a person to his ∾ *j.em offen schmeicheln;* to fly in the ∾ of a person *j.em den Gehorsam verweigern, ihm offen Trotz bieten;* to fly in the ∾ of Providence *die Vorsehung herausfordern;* to fly in the ∾ of a thing *sich in schreienden Widerspruch zu etwas stellen;* a hang-dog ∾ *ein Galgengesicht;* to have the ∾ to do a thing *die Stirn haben, etwas zu tun;* to keep a straight ∾ *sich (dat.) das Lachen verbeißen;* to lie in ∾ of *gegenüberliegen;* to lose ∾ *Ansehen verlieren;* to make ∾s *Gesichter (Fratzen) schneiden;* to pull (to wear) a long ∾ *ein langes, verdrießliches Gesicht ziehen;* to put a good ∾ on a matter *gute Miene zum bösen Spiel machen;* to put a bold ∾ on a matter *gegenüber einer Sache Mut zeigen;* to put a new ∾ on a matter *einer Sache ein neues Gesicht verleihen;* to save (one's) ∾ *sein Ansehen wahren;* to say to a person's ∾ *j.em ins Gesicht sagen;* to set one's ∾ (like a flint) against a thing *sich gegen etwas stemmen, wenden; etwas mißbilligen, nicht leiden können;* to show one's ∾ *sich zeigen;* to shut the door in a person's ∾ *j.em die Tür vor der Nase zuschlagen.* — **II.** v.tr.: to ∾ a card *eine Karte aufdecken (offen hinlegen);* to ∾ a coat *einen Rock mit Aufschlägen besetzen;* to ∾ the consequences *sich auf die Folgen gefaßt machen;* to ∾ death *dem Tode ins Angesicht schauen;* to ∾ the enemy *dem Feinde die Stirn bieten;* to sit facing the engine *in der Fahrtrichtung sitzen;* to ∾ the facts *den Tatsachen Rechnung tragen;* to ∾ the knocker *betteln gehen;* to ∾ a matter out *eine Sache keck durchsetzen;* to ∾ the men about *die Leute kehrtmachen lassen;* to ∾ the music *die Folgen (Vorwürfe, Kritik) mutig auf sich nehmen;* to ∾ an opponent down *einen Gegner verblüffen, einschüchtern;* the picture ∾s page 20 *das Bild ist gegenüber Seite 20;* to be ∾d with ruin *vor dem Ruin stehen;* to ∾ the surface *die Oberfläche glätten;* to ∾ tea *Tee färben, fälschen;* to ∾ up to a situation (to the facts) *einen (unangenehmen) Zustand (unangenehme Tatsachen) hinnehmen;* the problem that ∾s us *das Problem, dem wir gegenüberstehen;* to ∾ a wall *eine Wand verkleiden;* a double-∾d person *eine doppelzüngige Person;* to be unable to ∾ someone *j.en nicht anblicken können, sich vor ihm schämen.* — **III.** v.i.: to ∾ about *sich umdrehen, kehrtmachen;* the room ∾s (on, to, the) North *das Zimmer liegt nach Norden*

facer n.: it was a ∾ *es war ein Schlag ins Gesicht; eine große und plötzliche Schwierigkeit*

facing n.: to put a person through his ∾s *j.en auf seine Fähigkeiten (hin) prüfen*

fact n.: I know it for a ∾ *ich weiß, daß es wahr ist;* the story is founded on ∾ *die Geschichte ist auf Tatsachen begründet;* to distinguish ∾ from fiction *Wahrheit von Dichtung unterscheiden;* a stubborn ∾ *eine Tatsache, die sich nicht wegleugnen läßt;* in (in point of, as a matter of) ∾ *in der Tat, in Wirklichkeit, tatsächlich;* he spoke in a matter-of-∾ way about it *er sprach in einer nüchternen (trockenen) Art und Weise darüber*

fag I. n.: it was a terrible ∾ *es war eine schreckliche Plackerei;* to suffer from a brain-∾ *an nervöser Erschöpfung leiden;* may I offer you a ∾? (sl.) *darf ich Ihnen eine Zigarette anbieten?;* the ∾-end of a thing *der wertlose Rest einer Sache; der Stummel einer Zigarette;* to act as a ∾ (school) *als Fuchs (jüngerer Schüler) für ältere Kameraden Jungschülerdienste tun.* — **II.** v.i.: to ∾ away at something (colloq.) *über etwas büffeln, ochsen, arbeiten;* to be ∾ged out *todmüde, erschöpft sein*

fail I. n.: you must do that without ∾ *das mußt du unbedingt, sofort tun.* — **II.** v.i.: I ∾ to see what you mean *ich verstehe nicht, was Sie meinen;* don't ∾ to let me know *lassen Sie mich es ja wissen!;* if everything else ∾s *wenn alle Stricke reißen;* he ∾ed to appear *er erschien nicht;* he ∾ed in the attempt *der Versuch mißlang ihm;* he ∾ed in his examination *er fiel im Examen durch;* his courage ∾ed him *sein Mut verließ ihn;* the firm has ∾ed *die Firma ist bankrott gegangen;* his voice ∾ed *seine Stimme versagte;* my memory is ∾ing *mein Gedächtnis läßt nach;* the patient is ∾ing *mit dem Patienten geht es zu Ende;* a never ∾ing source *ein nie versiegender Quell;* the play ∾s in unity *dem Stück mangelt es an Einheit;* the prophecy ∾ed *die Prophezeiung traf nicht ein;* time would ∾ me to tell *es würde mir an Zeit mangeln zu sagen;* water ∾s *es fehlt (mangelt) an Wasser.* — **III.** v.tr.: I shall never ∾ you *ich werde dich nie im Stich lassen*

failing prep.: ∾ this *in Ermangelung dessen;* ∾ him, his deputy will act *im Falle seiner Abwesenheit wird sein Stellvertreter handeln*

failure n.: he is a complete ∾ *er ist ein völliger Versager, eine verkrachte Existenz;* he died of heart-∾ *er starb an einem Herzschlag*

fain adv. (archaic): I would ∾ do so *ich möchte es gern tun*

faint I. a.: ∾ but pursuing *müde, aber noch durchhaltend;* he put up a ∾ show of resistance *er hat sich nur schwach verteidigt;* ∾ heart never won fair lady (prov.) *wer nicht wagt, der nicht gewinnt; dem Mutigen gehört die Welt.* — **II.** v.i.: the noise ∾ed away in the distance *der Lärm verklang in der Ferne;* she ∾ed (away) *sie fiel in Ohnmacht.* — **III.** n.: in a dead ∾ *in tiefer Ohnmacht, vollkommen bewußtlos*

fair[1] n.: you are a day after the ∾ *du kommst zu spät*

fair[2] **I.** a.: all's ∾ in love and war (prov.) *in der Liebe und im Kriege ist alles erlaubt;* a ∾ name *ein guter Ruf;* ∾ words butter no parsnips (prov.) *Redensarten sind billig, schöne Worte machen den Kohl nicht fett;* to stand a ∾ chance to win *gute Aussichten haben zu gewinnen;* to write a ∾ copy *eine Reinschrift machen;* to gain ∾ fame *angemessenen Ruhm ernten;* to demand ∾ field and no favour *gleiche Bedingungen beim Wettkampf verlangen;* to be ∾ game *berechtigtem Angriff (Spott, berechtigter Kritik) unterliegen;* to have ∾ hair *blondes Haar haben;* to come in for a ∾ heritage *eine reiche Erbschaft machen;* to be a ∾ judge of a thing *ein ziemlich gutes Urteil über etwas haben;* to achieve by ∾ means *auf anständige (ehrliche) Weise erreichen;* to demand ∾ play *gerechte Behandlung, ehrliches Vorgehen verlangen;* to belong to the ∾ sex *dem schönen Geschlecht angehören;* to deliver ∾ speeches *gefällige Reden führen;* to be all ∾ and square *rechtmäßig, offen und ehrlich zugehen;* to give a person a ∾ warning *j.en zeitig und ernstlich warnen;* to be in ∾ water *in reinem, klarem Wasser sein;* to be in a ∾ way to succeed *auf dem besten Wege zum Erfolg sein;* to have ∾-weather friends *unzuverlässige Freunde haben;* his work is ∾ *seine Leistung ist mäßig (könnte besser sein).* — **II.** adv.: he bids ∾ to become a great man *er verspricht, ein großer Mann zu werden;* to speak a person ∾ *j.en höflich anreden, ihm gute Worte geben, ihm gut zureden;* to fight ∾ *ehrlich kämpfen;* to strike a person ∾ in the face *j.em direkt ins Gesicht schlagen;* to write out ∾ *ins reine schreiben*

fairly adv.: it is ∾ good *es ist ziemlich gut;* he is ∾ beside himself *er ist ganz außer sich*

faith n.: in bad ∾ *in böser Absicht;* in good ∾ *in gutem Glauben;* on the ∾ of *im Vertrauen auf;* to break (to violate) one's ∾ *sein Wort brechen;* to give (to pledge, to plight) one's ∾ *sein Wort verpfänden, sich verpflichten, feierlich geloben;* to keep one's ∾ *sein Wort (Versprechen) halten;* to place (to put, to have) ∾ in a person *in j.en Vertrauen setzen;* to pin one's ∾ to (upon) a person *j.em blind (unbedingt) vertrauen*

faithfully adv.: to deal ∾ with a person *j.em gehörig die Wahrheit sagen;* to promise ∾ *fest versprechen;* yours ∾ (in letters) *Ihr ergebener, ergebenst Ihr*

fall I. v.i.: the ∾ing sickness *die Fallsucht;* a ∾ing star *eine Sternschnuppe;* her eyes fell *ihre Augen senkten sich;* his face fell *sein Gesicht wurde länger;* lambs ∾ *Lämmer werden geboren;* it now ∾s to be described *es muß jetzt beschrieben werden.* — with pred.a. or n.: to ∾ calm *windstill werden;* to ∾ due *fällig werden;* to ∾ flat (prostrate) *der Länge nach auf den Boden fallen;* the measure fell flat *die Maßnahme hatte keinen Erfolg, keine Wirkung;* to ∾ foul of a person (thing) *mit einer Person (Sache) zusammenstoßen;* to ∾ ill *krank werden;* to ∾ a prey (victim, sacrifice) to a thing *einer Sache zum Opfer fallen;* flour is ∾ing short *das Mehl wird knapp;* it ∾s short of my expectations *es bleibt hinter meinen Erwartungen zurück;* this ∾s short of a miracle *dies grenzt an ein Wunder.* — with prep.: to ∾ a-crying *anfangen zu weinen;* to ∾ asleep *einschlafen;* to ∾ among(st) thieves *unter die Räuber geraten;* to ∾ behind a person *hinter j.em zurückbleiben;* to ∾ between two stools *sich zwischen zwei Stühle setzen;* to ∾ by the ears *sich in die Haare geraten;* to ∾ for a person (thing) (sl.) *von j.em eingenommen sein, sich in j.en vergaffen (verlieben); auf etwas hereinfallen;* to ∾ from grace *in Sünde fallen;* to ∾ from a height *von einer Höhe hinabstürzen;* to ∾ in love with *sich verlieben in;* to ∾ in my way *in mein Fach schlagen;* to ∾ in two *entzweigehen;* to ∾ in line with *sich decken mit;* to ∾ into conversation *eine Unterhaltung beginnen;* to ∾ into disuse *außer Gebrauch kommen;* to ∾ into error (or: the fallacy) of *in Irrtum verfallen;* to ∾ into a habit *sich etwas angewöhnen;* to ∾ into line with *sich einreihen,* *anpassen; übereinstimmen mit;* to ∾ into three parts *in drei Teile zerfallen;* to ∾ into a rage *in Wut geraten;* to ∾ into a person's plans *sich j.es Plänen fügen;* to ∾ into a way of doing *sich eine Handlungsweise angewöhnen;* to ∾ into the work *sich einarbeiten;* to ∾ (up)on a person's ear *an j.es Ohr dringen;* to ∾ on bad times (evil days) *Unglück, schlechte Zeiten haben;* to ∾ on one's feet *auf die Füße fallen, immer Glück (Glück im Unglück) haben;* the lot fell upon me, it fell to my lot *mich traf das Los;* to ∾ (up)on a person's neck *j.em um den Hals fallen;* to ∾ (up)on a person *zu Lasten j.es fallen; über j.en herfallen;* to ∾ (up)on a thing *auf etwas stoßen, verfallen;* to ∾ out of cultivation *nicht mehr bebaut werden;* to ∾ to doing something *etwas zu tun beginnen;* plans ∾ to the ground *Pläne scheitern;* to ∾ to pieces *in Stücke fallen, zerfallen;* to ∾ to work *sich an die Arbeit machen;* the costs ∾ to you *die Kosten fallen dir zu Lasten;* to ∾ under a certain class *unter eine bestimmte Klasse fallen;* to ∾ under observation *einer Beobachtung unterworfen werden;* to ∾ within the terms *in den Bedingungen eingeschlossen sein.* — with adv.: the ship ∾s astern *das Schiff bleibt zurück;* his followers fell away from him *seine Anhänger fielen von ihm ab;* to ∾ back, back upon, see 'back'; to ∾ behind *zurückbleiben;* to ∾ down *niederfallen;* to ∾ down on something (colloq.) *einen groben Fehler machen;* to ∾ in *einstürzen;* ∾ in! *angetreten!;* the debt ∾s in *die Schuld wird fällig;* the lease ∾s in *die Pacht läuft ab;* to ∾ in with a thing *auf etwas stoßen (treffen);* he fell in with my views *er pflichtete meiner Ansicht bei;* to ∾ off *abfallen, abnehmen, geringer werden, nachlassen;* to ∾ out (mil.) *wegtreten, austreten;* it so fell out that *es ereignete (ergab) sich, daß;* to ∾ out of a habit *sich etwas abgewöhnen;* it fell out well *es hatte guten Erfolg;* to ∾ out with a person *sich mit j.em überwerfen;* to ∾ through *durchfallen, ins Wasser fallen;* to ∾ to *zulangen, zu essen beginnen; zu kämpfen beginnen.* — **II.** n.: the Fall of man *der Sündenfall;* to break a person's ∾ *j.en im Fallen auffangen, seinen Sturz mildern;* to try a ∾ *sich im Ringen messen, es aufnehmen mit*

false I. a.: ∾ pretences *Vorspiegelung falscher Tatsachen;* to sail under ∾ colours *seine Absichten verschleiern, tarnen.* — **II.** adv.: to play a person ∾ *(ein) falsches Spiel mit j.em treiben*

familiar a.: a ∾ spirit *ein Schutzgeist;* that is ∾ to me *das ist mir wohlbekannt, nichts Neues;* to be on ∾ terms with a person *mit j.em auf vertrautem Fuße stehen;* to make oneself ∾ with a subject *sich mit einem Gegenstand vertraut machen;* to behave in a ∾ way *etwas zudringlich sein*

familiarity n.: ∾ breeds contempt (prov.) *allzugroße Vertrautheit erzeugt Verachtung*

family n.: a happy ∾ *Tiere verschiedener Art in einem Käfig;* in a ∾ way *ungezwungen;* she's in the ∾ way *sie ist schwanger (in Hoffnung, in anderen Umständen);* the ∾ doctor *der Hausarzt;* a ∾ man *ein guter Hausvater;* a ∾ skeleton *ein peinliches Familiengeheimnis;* the ∾ tree *der Stammbaum*

fan[1] I. v.tr.: to ∾ the flame *die Flamme anfachen.* — **II.** v.i.: to ∾ out *sich fächerförmig ausbreiten*

fan[2] n.: he is a film ∾ *er ist ein Filmnarr;* the ∾-mail *die Post, die Film- und andere Größen von ihren Bewunderern erhalten*

fancier n.: he is a dog-∾ *er ist ein Hundeliebhaber,-kenner,-züchter*

fancy I. n.: to catch (to strike, to take, to tickle) the ∾ of a person *j.em gefallen;* to have a ∾ that *eine Ahnung haben, daß;* to take a ∾ to (for) a thing (person) *an etwas (an j.em) Gefallen finden;* a flight of ∾ *ein Phantasiegebilde.* — **II.** a.: ∾-articles *Modeartikel;* a ∾-dress ball *ein Maskenball;* a ∾ man *ein Liebhaber; ein Zuhälter;* a ∾-price *ein Liebhaber-, Phantasiepreis;* a ∾-work *eine Stickerei, feine weibliche Handarbeit.* — **III.** v.tr.: just ∾! only ∾! *denk' dir bloß! stell' dir nur vor!;* ∾ his believing it! *wie konnte er es bloß glauben!;* to ∾ a blue dahlia *sich etwas Unmögliches vorstellen;* to ∾ oneself dead *sich vorstellen, man wäre tot;* I ∾ him to be here, (that) he is here *ich nehme an, er ist hier;* I don't ∾ doing that *das tue ich nicht gerne;* he fancies himself, his game *er hat eine gute Meinung von sich, von seinem Spiel;* to ∾ a thing *an etwas Gefallen finden;* to ∾ dogs, roses *Hunde, Rosen züchten*

far I. adv.: he is ∾ (and away) the best *er ist bei weitem der Beste;* ∾ from it!

weit entfernt! keineswegs!; he is ∾ from well *es geht ihm gar nicht gut;* ∾ be it from me *es sei ferne von mir;* as ∾ as in me lies *soweit ich dazu fähig (befähigt) bin;* so ∾, I haven't seen him *bis jetzt habe ich ihn nicht gesehen;* as ∾ as that goes *was das anlangt, betrifft;* I shall go as ∾ as London *ich fahre bis London;* he will go ∾ *er wird es weit bringen;* this went ∾ to convince us *dieses trug wesentlich dazu bei, uns zu überzeugen;* a ∾-away look *ein verträumter (träumerischer) Blick;* few and ∾ between *vereinzelt, dünn gesät;* a ∾-fetched simile *ein gesuchter, an den Haaren herbeigezogener Vergleich;* so ∾ forth as *insoweit als;* ∾ gone *weit fortgeschritten; sehr krank oder verrückt; stark betrunken oder verschuldet;* the day was ∾ spent *es war spät am Tage;* ∾ and wide *weit und breit.* — **II.** n.: do you come from ∾? *kommen Sie von weit her?;* in so ∾ as *insofern als;* he is by ∾ the worst *er ist bei weitem der Schlechteste.* — **III.** a.: a ∾ cry *eine weite Entfernung;* on the ∾ side *auf der anderen Seite*

fare I. n.: the bill of ∾ *die Speisekarte;* it was coarse ∾ *es war grobe Kost;* the cabby had a ∾ *der Droschkenkutscher hatte einen Fahrgast;* what is the return ∾? *was kostet die Rückfahrtkarte?* — **II.** v.i.: how did you ∾? *wie erging es dir?;* to ∾ alike *in derselben Lage sein;* to ∾ well, ill, worse *es gut, schlecht, schlechter (schlimmer) haben;* ∾ thee well! (poet.) *fahr wohl!;* you might go farther and ∾ worse *du könntest weiter gehen und dabei schlechter fahren; sei zufrieden mit dem, was du hast*

farewell I. int.: ∾ to all that! *nichts mehr davon!* — **II.** n.: to bid a person ∾ *j.em Lebewohl sagen;* to make one's ∾s *sich verabschieden*

farther adv.: I'll see you ∾ first *ich werde dir was husten (pfeifen)*

fashion n.: to be all the ∾ *sehr populär, große Mode sein;* to bring into (to set the, to launch a, to lead the) ∾ *eine Mode aufbringen, einführen, den Ton angeben;* to repair a thing in (after) a ∾ *etwas einigermaßen (halb-und-halb) in Ordnung bringen;* to walk crab-∾ *rückwärts wie ein Krebs gehen*

fast I. a.: a ∾ colour *eine nicht verschießende, waschechte Farbe;* a ∾ friend *ein treuer Freund;* a ∾ girl *ein lockeres Mädchen;* the door is ∾ *die Tür ist fest verschlossen;* my watch is ∾ *meine Uhr geht vor;* to take ∾ hold of a thing *etwas fest ergreifen;* to pull a ∾ one over a person (colloq.) *j.em unerwartet einen Streich spielen; ihm eine kitzlige (schwierige) Frage stellen.* — **II.** adv.: ∾ bind, ∾ find (prov.) *sicher verwahrt, schnell gefunden;* to lay a person ∾ *j.en ins Gefängnis werfen, ihn einsperren, kaltstellen;* to play ∾ and loose *ein unredliches Spiel treiben;* to live ∾ *ein flottes, ausschweifendes Leben führen;* to stick ∾ *feststecken, nicht weiterkönnen*

fasten I. v.tr.: to ∾ a crime (up)on a person *j.en eines Verbrechens beschuldigen;* to ∾ one's eyes on *die Augen auf etwas heften;* to ∾ one's hopes on *auf etwas bauen;* to ∾ a nickname (up)on a person *j.em einen Spitznamen geben;* to ∾ a quarrel (up)on a person *mit j.em Streit anfangen.* — **II.** v.i.: the door will not ∾ *die Tür schließt nicht;* to ∾ (up)on a pretext, an idea *sich an einen Vorwand, eine Idee klammern*

fat I. a.: as ∾ as a porpoise *so fett wie ein Schwein;* he is a ∾-guts (sl.) *er ist ein Dickwanst;* he is a ∾-head *er ist ein Dummkopf;* he has a ∾ job *er hat einen fetten Posten;* a ∾ lot I care about it! (sl.) *da mache ich mir schon was draus!;* to cut it ∾ (sl.) *aufschneiden, sich aufspielen, angeben;* to cut up ∾ (colloq.) *reich sterben, viel Geld hinterlassen.* — **II.** n.: a bit of ∾ (colloq.) *ein unerwartetes Glück;* the ∾ is in the fire *der Teufel ist los;* to live on the ∾ of the land *ein üppiges Leben führen;* to run to ∾ *Fett ansetzen.* — **III.** v.tr.: to kill the ∾ted calf (Luke, IV, 23) *einen Festschmaus geben*

fate I. n.: to decide (to fix, to seal) a person's ∾ *j.es Schicksal besiegeln;* to meet one's ∾ *vom Tod ereilt werden;* as sure as ∾ *ganz sicher, todsicher.* — **II.** v.tr.: he was ∾d to do so; it was ∾d that he should do so *es war ihm vom Schicksal bestimmt, so zu handeln*

father I. n.: Father Christmas *der Weihnachtsmann;* the child is ∾ to (of) the man (prov.) *aus Kindern werden Leute;* the wish is ∾ to the thought (prov.) *der Wunsch ist (der) Vater des Gedankens;* he was gathered to his ∾s *er wurde zu seinen Vätern versammelt.* — **II.** v.tr.: to ∾ a thing *etwas* *väterlich betreuen;* to ∾ a thing upon a person *j.em etwas zuschreiben*

fault n.: whose ∾ is it? who is in (at) ∾? *wessen Schuld ist es? wen trifft die Schuld?;* to be at ∾ (hunt.) *die Fährte verloren haben;* to be at ∾ *in Verlegenheit sein; nicht wissen, was man tun soll;* to be generous to a ∾ *allzu freigebig sein;* to find ∾ with a person (thing) *j.en (etwas) tadeln; an j.em (an einer Sache) etwas auszusetzen haben*

favour I. n.: by ∾ of Mr. N. (written on letter) *überreicht durch Herrn N.;* she bestows her ∾s on her lover *sie schenkt ihrem Geliebten ihre Liebe;* to curry ∾ with a person *sich bei j.em einschmeicheln, lieb Kind machen;* to demand fair field and no ∾ *gleiche Bedingungen beim Wettkampf verlangen;* to do a person a ∾ *j.em einen Gefallen tun;* to be in ∾ of Free Trade *für den Freihandel sein;* to draw a cheque in ∾ of a person *einen Scheck auf j.en ausstellen;* to esteem it a ∾ *es als besondere Gunst empfinden;* to find ∾ in the eyes of a person *bei j.em Gnade finden;* to look with ∾ on a thing *etwas günstig beurteilen, billigen;* I have received your ∾ of yesterday *ich habe Ihren gestrigen Brief erhalten;* to request the ∾ of an early answer *um gefällige baldige Antwort bitten;* by your ∾ *mit Ihrer (gütigen) Erlaubnis;* under ∾ of night *unter dem Schutze der Nacht;* without fear or ∾ *unparteiisch.* — **II.** v.tr.: fortune ∾s the brave (prov.) *dem Mutigen gehört die Welt;* he ∾s his father *er gleicht seinem Vater;* will you ∾ us with a song? *wollen Sie uns mit einem Lied erfreuen?;* to ∾ doing a thing *geneigt sein, etwas zu tun;* to ∾ a person with a letter *j.en mit einem Briefe beehren;* a most ∾ed nation clause *eine Meistbegünstigungsklausel (im Handelsvertrag)*

fear I. n.: for ∾ of (that, lest) *aus Furcht, daß (vor);* no ∾! (sl.) *keine Angst!;* without ∾ or favour *unparteiisch;* to be in ∾ of (that, lest) *fürchten, daß;* to go in ∾ of one's life *in ständiger Todesangst leben;* there is no ∾ of the rope breaking *es besteht gar keine Gefahr, daß das Seil reißt.* — **II.** v.i. & tr.: never ∾! *seien Sie unbesorgt!;* to ∾ to do (doing) a thing *fürchten, etwas zu tun;* to ∾ for a person *um j.en besorgt sein;* to ∾ the worst *das Schlimmste befürchten*

fearful a.: it was a ∾ mess *es war eine furchtbare Schweinerei*

feast I. n.: enough is as good as a ∾ (prov.) *allzuviel ist ungesund;* a ∾ of reason *eine geistige Unterhaltung.* — **II.** v.tr.: to ∾ one's eyes on a thing *seine Augen an etwas weiden*

feather I. n.: birds of a ∾ flock together (prov.) *gleich und gleich gesellt sich gern;* fine ∾s make fine birds (prov.) *Kleider machen Leute;* fur and ∾ *Wild und Federwild;* in high (or: full) ∾ *in gehobener (guter) Stimmung;* that is a ∾ in his cap *darauf kann er stolz sein;* to crop a person's ∾s *j.en demütigen;* you could have knocked me down with a ∾ *man hätte mich umpusten können;* to show (to fly) the white ∾ *sich feige zeigen;* ∾-headed, ∾-brained, ∾-pated *dumm, töricht, unbesonnen;* to smooth one's ruffled ∾s *sich nach einem Streit (einer Beleidigung) beruhigen.* — **II.** v.tr.: to ∾ one's nest *sein Schäfchen ins trockene bringen;* to ∾ the oars (sport) *die Riemen plattwerfen*

feather-bed v.tr. (colloq.): to ∾ someone *j.em den Weg erleichtern, ihn verwöhnen*

feature I. n.: his ∾s *seine Gesichtszüge;* a characteristic ∾ *ein charakteristisches Merkmal, -r Zug;* a redeeming ∾ *ein versöhnender Zug, ein mildernder Umstand;* to make ∾ of doing a thing *es sich (dat.) angelegen sein lassen, etwas zu tun.* — **II.** v.tr.: that ∾s him *das charakterisiert (kennzeichnet) ihn;* a film featuring a certain actor (U.S.) *ein Film mit einem gewissen Schauspieler in der Hauptrolle*

feed I. v.tr.: to ∾ a cold *tüchtig essen, wenn man erkältet ist;* to ∾ the fishes *seekrank sein;* I'm fed up with it (sl.) *ich habe es satt, ich bin es leid, ich habe die Nase voll, es hängt mir zum Halse heraus.* — **II.** n.: to be off one's ∾ *keinen Appetit haben;* the cows are out at ∾ *die Kühe sind draußen auf der Weide*

feel I. v.tr.: to ∾ one's age *merken, daß man alt wird;* to ∾ the draught (colloq.) *die unangenehme Seite (der Lage, der Sache) zu spüren bekommen;* to ∾ it one's duty *es für seine Pflicht halten;* to ∾ one's feet (legs) *festen Boden unter sich haben, sich sicher fühlen;* to ∾ a person's pulse *j.em den Puls fühlen; auf den Busch klop-*

fen; to ∾ one's way *sich durch Tasten zurechtfinden, vorsichtig vorgehen.* — **II.** v.i.: to ∾ in one's bones *etwas ganz sicher wissen;* I ∾ like going for a walk *ich hätte Lust, spazieren zu gehen;* it ∾s like velvet *es fühlt sich an wie Samt;* I ∾ like nothing on earth (colloq.) *ich fühle mich hundeelend;* I don't ∾ up to much (quite myself) today *ich bin heute nicht ganz auf der Höhe, auf dem Damm;* I don't ∾ up to work *ich kann mich nicht zur Arbeit aufschwingen;* to ∾ sure of a thing *von einer Sache überzeugt sein;* we ∾ for them *sie dauern uns, sie tun uns leid;* to ∾ for a thing *nach etwas tasten.* — **III.** n.: it is firm to the ∾ *es fühlt sich fest an*

feeling n.: there is bad ∾ between them *sie können sich nicht vertragen, es herrscht Streit zwischen ihnen;* the ∾ went high *die Erregung ging hoch;* to hurt a person's ∾s *j.es Gefühle verletzen, brüskieren*

feign v.i. & tr.: to ∾ that one is mad, to ∾ oneself mad, to ∾ madness *sich verrückt stellen, Verrücktheit vortäuschen*

feint n.: to make a ∾ of doing so *so tun als ob*

fell a.: at one ∾ swoop *auf einmal, mit einem einzigen grimmigen Stoß*

fellow n.: the ∾ actually believed it *der dumme Kerl hat es tatsächlich geglaubt;* he became a ∾ of Christ Church *er wurde Mitglied des Christ Church College in Oxford;* my dear ∾! *mein lieber Freund!;* my good ∾! *mein lieber Mann!;* well, old ∾? (colloq.) *nun, altes Haus?;* poor ∾! *armer Kerl!;* a ∾ must eat *ich armer Kerl muß auch essen;* I shall never find his ∾ *ich werde niemals seinesgleichen finden;* shoes that are not ∾s *Schuhe, die nicht zusammengehören;* he is hail-∾-well-met with everybody *er ist gleich mit jedermann gut Freund;* stone dead hath no ∾ (prov.) *die Toten plaudern nichts mehr aus;* a ∾-citizen, ∾-passenger, etc. *ein Mitbürger, -reisender, usw.;* a ∾ traveller *ein politischer Mitläufer;* the ∾-feeling *die Sympathie eines Leidensgefährten*

fence I. n.: he is a ∾ *er ist ein Hehler;* to come down on the right side of the ∾ *sich der gewinnenden Partei anschließen;* to sit on the ∾ *neutral bleiben, eine abwartende Haltung einnehmen.* — **II.** v.i.: to ∾ with a question, a questioner *einer Frage ausweichen, Ausflüchte machen.* — **III.** v.tr.: to ∾ in *einzäunen;* to ∾ off *abwehren*

fend v.tr.: to ∾ off a blow *einen Schlag abwehren;* to ∾ for oneself *für sich selbst aufkommen, sich selber ernähren*

ferret I. v.i.: to ∾ about for a thing *nach etwas herumstöbern;* to go ∾ing *mit Frettchen jagen gehen.* — **II.** v.tr.: to ∾ out a secret *ein Geheimnis auskundschaften.* — **III.** n.: to be a ∾ *ein Detektiv sein*

fetch I. v.tr.: this song will ∾ the audience *dieses Lied wird die Zuhörer entzücken;* to ∾ a breath *Atem holen;* to ∾ a person a blow (colloq.) *j.em einen Schlag versetzen;* to ∾ a compass *einen Umweg machen;* go and ∾ a doctor *holen Sie einen Arzt;* a far-∾ed simile *ein gesuchter, an den Haaren herbeigezogener Vergleich;* the picture will ∾ a high price *das Bild wird einen hohen Preis erzielen;* to ∾ a sigh *tief aufseufzen.* — **II.** v.i.: to ∾ and carry (for someone) *niedrige Arbeiten für j.en verrichten;* he had to ∾ up (low colloq.) *er mußte sich übergeben;* he ∾ed up against the window *er stieß gegen das Fenster (an)*

fettle n.: to be in good ∾ *in guter Verfassung, Form sein*

few I. a.: every ∾ days *alle paar Tage;* ∾ words *wenige Worte;* a ∾ words *einige, ein paar Worte;* ∾ and far between *vereinzelt, dünn gesät;* no ∾er than ten newspapers *nicht weniger als zehn Zeitungen.* — **II.** n.: ∾ know the truth *nur wenige kennen die Wahrheit;* a ∾, some ∾ *einige wenige, ein paar;* that will cost him a ∾ (sl.) *das wird ihn viel kosten;* the ∾ *die wenigen, die Minderheit, die Elite;* a good ∾, quite a ∾, not a ∾ *eine ziemliche Anzahl*

fib n.: to tell a ∾ (colloq.) *lügen, flunkern, kohlen*

fiddle I. n.: a face as long as a ∾ *ein langes, betrübtes Gesicht;* as fit as a ∾ *so gesund (so wohl) wie ein Fisch im Wasser;* to hang up one's ∾ when one comes home *draußen witzig und zu Hause langweilig sein;* to play the first (the second) ∾ *die erste (zweite) Geige spielen;* ∾dedee! ∾sticks! *Papperlapapp! Unsinn! Dummes Zeug! Quatsch!;* a ∾-faddle *eine Kleinigkeit (Lappalie).* — **II.** v.i.: don't ∾ about with that *spiel' (fummele) nicht damit herum!* —

III. v.tr.: to ∾ away *vertändeln;* to ∾ something (sl.) *eine Sache drehen*

fiddler n.: ∾'s green *ein Seemannsparadies;* that is ∾'s news *das hat so einen Bart; sind olle Kamellen*

fidelity n.: to translate with ∾ *wortgetreu übersetzen*

fidget I. n.: to have the ∾s *nicht still sitzen können, herumzappeln.* — **II.** v.i.: don't ∾ (about) *zappele nicht so!*

fie int.: ∾ upon you! *pfui, schäme dich!*

field I. n.: the whole ∾ of history *das ganze Gebiet der Geschichte;* to be supreme in one's own ∾ *Meister auf seinem Gebiet (in seinem Fach) sein;* to be in the ∾ *an einem Wettbewerb teilnehmen;* to bring into the ∾ *ins Gefecht bringen;* to demand fair ∾ and no favour *gleiche Bedingungen beim Wettkampf verlangen;* to hold the ∾ *das Feld behaupten;* to keep the ∾ *den Kampf fortsetzen;* to leave one's rival in possession of the ∾ *vor seinem Nebenbuhler das Feld räumen;* to take the ∾ *ins Feld ziehen.* — **II.** v.tr.: to ∾ a ball *einen Ball auffangen und zurückwerfen.* — **III.** v.i.: to ∾ at cricket *beim Kricketspiel im Feld spielen, nicht der schlagenden Partei angehören*

fiend n.: he is a morphia-∾ *er ist Morphinist*

fiendish a.: a ∾ test (joc.) *eine schauderhafte Prüfung (scherzhaft)*

fifth a.: to be the ∾ wheel of a coach *das fünfte Rad am Wagen sein;* to smite a person under the ∾ rib *j.en töten*

fifty I. a.: to go ∾-∾ *halbpart machen.* — **II.** n.: in the fifties of the last century *in den fünfziger Jahren des vergangenen Jahrhunderts*

fig[1] n.: I don't care a ∾ for it *ich frage nicht die Bohne danach;* to dwell under one's vine and ∾-tree (I Kings IV, 25) *die Freuden eines eigenen Heims genießen*

fig[2] n.: in full ∾ *in vollem Wichs;* in good ∾ *in gutem Zustand, in guter Form*

fight I. n.: he has ∾ in him yet *er ist noch nicht abgekämpft;* to put up a good ∾ *sich tapfer schlagen;* to show ∾ *sich kampfbereit zeigen, nicht nachgeben;* a stand-up ∾ *ein regelrechter Kampf.* — **II.** v.i.: to ∾ like Kilkenny cats *bis zur Vernichtung kämpfen;* that cock won't ∾ *das geht nicht an, der Einwand zieht nicht;* to ∾ shy of a person (thing) *j.em (einer Sache) aus dem Wege gehen;* they live like ∾ing cocks *sie haben alles im Überfluß, sie leben wie Gott in Frankreich;* that beats cock-∾ing *das übertrifft alles, das ist großartig, das schießt den Vogel ab;* he stands a ∾ing chance *er hat noch Aussicht auf Erfolg, wenn er sich gehörig anstrengt.* — **III.** v.tr.: to ∾ a duel *sich duellieren;* to ∾ one's way *sich durchschlagen;* to ∾ it out *es ausfechten;* to ∾ to a standstill *bis zur beiderseitigen Erschöpfung kämpfen*

figure I. n.: double ∾s *zweistellige Zahlen;* to be a person of ∾ *eine hohe Persönlichkeit sein;* a ∾ of speech *eine Redewendung;* to be a ∾-head *Aushängeschild, Strohmann sein;* to make (to cut) a brilliant (poor, sorry) ∾ *eine glänzende (erbärmliche, traurige) Rolle spielen;* a ∾ of fun *eine komische Erscheinung (Figur).* — **II.** v.i.: it runs into six ∾s *es geht in die Hunderttausende;* to ∾ as *figurieren, eine Rolle spielen als;* I often ∾ to myself *ich stelle mir oft vor;* to ∾ on doing something (Amer.) *etwas ins Auge fassen.* — **III.** v.tr.: I must ∾ it out *ich muß es mir ausrechnen, klarmachen;* I must ∾ it up *ich muß es zusammenzählen*

file[1] n.: he is an old (deep, sly) ∾ (sl.) *er ist ein schlauer Fuchs;* to bite (to gnaw) a ∾ *sich die Zähne ausbeißen, etwas Zweckloses versuchen*

file[2] **I.** v.tr.: to ∾ a letter *einen Brief ablegen.* — **II.** n.: to look through the ∾s *die Akten durchsehen*

file[3] **I.** n.: the rank and ∾ *die Unteroffiziere und Gemeinen;* to march in single (Indian) ∾ *im Gänsemarsch gehen (marschieren).* — **II.** v.i.: to ∾ off (or: away) *in einer Reihe abmarschieren;* to ∾ past *in Reihen vorbeimarschieren*

fill I. v.tr.: to ∾ the bill *besonders hervortreten, allen Anforderungen genügen;* to ∾ out *dicker werden;* to ∾ up *voll-, ausfüllen.* — **II.** n.: to eat (to have, to drink) one's ∾ *sich satt essen (trinken);* let me have a ∾ of tobacco *laß mich mal stopfen;* to have one's ∾ of trouble *Sorgen genug haben*

fillip I. n.: it's not worth a ∾ *es ist keinen Pfifferling wert.* — **II.** v.tr.: to ∾ one's memory (wits) *sein Gedächtnis (seinen Geist) anregen*

fin n.: tip us your ∾ (sl.) *gib mir deine Hand, reich' mir deine Flosse*

find v.tr.: fast bind, fast ∾ (prov.) *sicher verwahrt, schnell gefunden;* to ∾ one's account in a thing *durch eine Sache profitieren, aus ihr Nutzen ziehen;* to ∾ (to meet) one's match *j.en treffen, dem man nicht gewachsen ist;* to ∾ fault with someone *j.en tadeln;* to ∾ one's feet *stehen (gehen) lernen; seine Fähigkeiten entwikkeln;* to ∾ one's place in the book *die Buchstelle finden, an der man zu lesen aufgehört hat;* to ∾ oneself *seine Eignung (Kräfte) entdecken; sich selbst beköstigen (versorgen);* I could not ∾ it in my heart *ich konnte es nicht übers Herz bringen;* to make someone ∾ his voice *j.em die Zunge lösen;* to ∾ a person out *j.en ertappen, j.em auf die Sprünge kommen;* to ∾ a person in clothes *j.em die Kleidung stellen;* the hotel does not ∾ tea *im Hotel gibt es nachmittags keinen Tee;* £ 2 a week and all found *zwei Pfund die Woche und freie Station;* the jury found the prisoner guilty (found a verdict of guilty) *die Geschworenen sprachen den Angeklagten schuldig;* they found for the prisoner *sie sprachen den Angeklagten frei;* they found a true bill *sie erklärten die Anklagegründe für gültig*

fine[1] I. a.: that's all very ∾, but *das ist alles gut und schön, aber;* the ∾ arts *die schönen Künste;* one of these ∾ days *eines schönen Tages;* these are ∾ doings! *das sind mir nette Geschichten!;* ∾ feathers make ∾ birds (prov.) *Kleider machen Leute;* a ∾ teacher you have been! *du bist mir ein netter Lehrer gewesen!;* ∾ (fair) words butter no parsnips (prov.) *Redensarten sind billig, schöne Worte machen den Kohl nicht fett;* a ∾ day for the ducks *Regenwettertag.* — **II.** adv.: to cut it ∾ *es haarscharf darauf ankommen lassen, noch gerade zur rechten Zeit kommen, etwas erwischen;* to run it ∾ *mit der Zeit in die Enge (in Bedrängnis) kommen.* — **III.** n.: in rain or ∾ *bei Regen oder schönem Wetter.* — **IV.** v.tr. & i.: to ∾ away (down, off) *dünn machen; abschleifen, hinschwinden*

fine[2] I. n.: in ∾ *um die Sache zusammenzufassen, schließlich, kurz (gesagt);* to come (to get, to be let) off with a ∾ *mit einer Geldstrafe davonkommen;* without the option of a ∾, see 'option'. — **II.** v.tr.: he was ∾d £ 5 *er wurde zu einer Geldstrafe von fünf Pfund verurteilt.* — **III.** v.i.: he was ∾d for the privilege *er bezahlte eine Summe Geldes für das Vorrecht*

finger I. n.: the index ∾ *der Zeigefinger;* my ∾s itch to do it *es juckt mir (mich) in den Fingern (ich brenne vor Ungeduld), es zu tun;* his ∾s are all thumbs *er ist sehr ungeschickt, er hat zwei linke Hände;* to the ∾-nails *vollständig;* to burn one's ∾s *sich die Finger verbrennen;* to catch one's ∾ in the door *sich (dat.) den Finger in der Tür klemmen;* to count (to number) on one's ∾s *an den Fingern abzählen;* to do something with a wet ∾ *etwas mit Leichtigkeit tun;* to have a ∾ in the pie *die Hand (die Finger) im Spiele haben;* to have at one's ∾-tips, ∾-ends *am Schnürchen haben, etwas an den Fingern hersagen können;* to have light ∾s *lange Finger machen, stehlen;* to lay (to put) a ∾ upon a thing *etwas leicht berühren;* to lay (to put) one's ∾ upon a thing *den Finger auf etwas legen, etwas deutlich kennzeichnen;* to look through one's ∾s *so tun, als sehe man nicht;* to let slip through one's ∾s *aus der Hand gleiten lassen, einen Vorteil durch Unvorsichtigkeit verlieren; eine Gelegenheit nicht wahrnehmen;* to snap one's ∾s at something *etwas verächtlich (als unwichtig) behandeln;* to stir a ∾ *den Finger rühren;* to turn (to twist, to wind) a person round one's little ∾ *j.en um den (kleinen) Finger wickeln.* — **II.** v.tr.: to ∾ a bribe *sich bestechen lassen;* to ∾ music *Noten mit Fingersatz versehen.* — **III.** v.i.: to ∾ at (with) a thing *an etwas herumfingern*

finish I. v.tr.: to ∾ doing a thing *aufhören, etwas zu tun;* to ∾ off *vervollkommnen; ganz aufessen.* — **II.** v.i.: to ∾ in (by, doing) *enden in, aufhören zu tun;* to ∾ up with *zu(m) Schluß dieses oder jenes tun;* I'm ∾ed *ich bin am Ende;* the ∾ing stroke (blow) *der letzte Streich, Stoß, Schlag;* to put the ∾ing touches to a picture *die letzte Hand an ein Bild (Gemälde) legen;* to ∾ up *beendigen, ein Ende machen.* — **III.** n.: to be in at the ∾ *in den Schlußkampf kommen, bei der Entscheidung dabei sein;* to fight to the ∾ *bis zur Entscheidung kämpfen;* his work lacks ∾ *seiner Arbeit fehlt der letzte Schliff*

fire I. n.: between two ∾s *zwischen zwei Feuern;* ∾ is a good servant but a bad master (prov.) *Feuer ist ein guter Diener, aber ein schlechter Herr;* the fat is in the ∾ *der Teufel ist los;* (there is) no smoke without ∾ (prov.) *kein Rauch ohne Feuer; an einem Gerücht ist oft etwas Wahres;* out of the frying-pan into the ∾ *vom Regen in die Traufe;* to be on ∾ *brennen, in Brand stehen;* to catch (to take) ∾ *Feuer fangen;* to go through ∾ and water for a person *für j.en durchs Feuer gehen;* a burnt child dreads the ∾ (prov.) *gebranntes Kind scheut das Feuer;* to hang ∾ *sich verzögern, versagen;* to heap coals of ∾ on a person's head *feurige Kohlen auf j.es Haupt sammeln;* to keep up a ∾ *ein Feuer unterhalten;* to lay the ∾ *den Ofen (Herd) anlegen;* to make up the ∾ *das Feuer schüren;* to miss ∾ *versagen;* to pour oil on (to add fuel to) the ∾ *Öl ins Feuer gießen;* to set on ∾, to set ∾ to *in Brand stecken;* he will never set the Thames on ∾ *er hat das Pulver nicht erfunden;* to succeed like a house on ∾ *ein Bombenerfolg sein.* — **II.** v.tr.: to ∾ an employee (U.S.) *einen Angestellten Knall und Fall entlassen;* to ∾ off a postcard *eine Postkarte abschicken.* — **III.** v.i.: ∾ away! *fang an! schieß los!;* to ∾ up *plötzlich aufbrausen, rot werden;* a firing squad *ein Erschießungskommando*

firm I. a.: a ∾ bid (offer) *ein festes Angebot;* ∾ friends *enge (dicke) Freunde;* to take ∾ measures *strenge Maßnahmen treffen.* — **II.** adv.: to hold ∾ to a thing *an etwas festhalten;* to stand ∾ *fest stehen, nicht nachgeben*

first I. a.: ∾-hand information *Information aus erster Hand, aus direkter Quelle;* in the ∾ place *erstens, an erster Stelle;* ∾-rate *erstklassig;* at ∾ sight (view, blush) *auf den ersten Blick;* of the ∾ water *vom reinsten Wasser, erstklassig sein;* head (feet) ∾ *mit dem Kopf (den Füßen) voran;* to come in ∾ *als erster durchs Ziel gehen, gewinnen;* I shall do it ∾ *ich werde es als erster tun;* to render ∾ aid *erste Hilfe leisten;* ∾-aid outfit *Notverbandskasten;* ∾ thing tomorrow *morgen ganz früh, als erstes morgen früh.* — **II.** n.: at ∾ *anfangs, am Anfang, zuerst;* from the ∾ *von Anfang an;* from ∾ to last *durchaus, immerfort.* — **III.** adv.: ∾ of all, ∾ and foremost *zu allererst, in erster Linie;* ∾ come, ∾ served (prov.) *wer zuerst kommt, mahlt zuerst;* ∾ and last *alles in allem, im ganzen;* ∾ or last *über kurz oder lang, früher oder später;* I will see him damned ∾ *er soll mir eher verrecken;* I'll see you farther ∾ *ich werde dir was husten (pfeifen)*

fish I. n.: as dull (mute) as a ∾ *so stumm wie ein Fisch;* all is ∾ that comes to his net *er nimmt alles, was er kriegen kann;* there's as good ∾ in the sea as ever came out of it *es gibt noch mehr auf der Welt; keine Angst, daß ein Mangel eintreten könnte;* he's neither ∾, flesh, nor good red herring *er ist weder Fisch noch Fleisch;* I have other ∾ to fry *ich habe andere, wichtigere Dinge zu tun;* that's a pretty kettle of ∾! *das ist eine nette Bescherung (eine schöne Geschichte)!;* he's an odd (a queer) ∾ (colloq.) *er ist ein komischer Kauz, ein wunderlicher Heiliger;* to cry stinking ∾ *seine eigene Ware schlechtmachen;* he drinks like a ∾ *er säuft wie ein Loch;* to feed the ∾es *seekrank sein;* I feel (I am) like a ∾ out of water *ich fühle mich nicht in meinem Element, ich komme mir ganz verlassen (komisch) vor.* — **II.** v.i.: to ∾ in troubled waters *im trüben fischen;* it is good ∾ing in troubled waters (prov.) *im trüben ist gut fischen;* to ∾ for compliments *nach Komplimenten haschen.* — **III.** v.tr.: to ∾ the anchor *den Anker kippen*

fishy a.: a ∾ affair (sl.) *ein fauler Zauber;* that looks ∾ (sl.) *das sieht verdächtig aus*

fist n.: to clench one's ∾ *die Faust ballen;* give us your ∾ (joc.) *gib mir doch die Hand!;* I know his ∾ (colloq.) *ich kenne seine Handschrift (Klaue);* to shake one's ∾ at a person *j.em mit der Faust drohen*

fit¹ n.: a ∾ of coughing *ein Hustenanfall;* in a ∾ of energy *in einer Anwandlung von Energie;* by ∾s and starts *stoßweise, dann und wann;* to beat (to knock, to lick) a person into ∾s (colloq.) *j.en gründlich und leicht besiegen (schlagen);* that will give him a ∾ (colloq.) *das wird ihn überraschen, da wird er hochgehen;* to throw (to get) a ∾ *einen Anfall bekommen;* he only works when the ∾ is on him *er arbeitet nur, wenn er Lust hat (nach Laune)*

fit² I. a.: as ∾ as a fiddle *so gesund (so wohl) wie ein Fisch im Wasser;* he is not ∾ to hold a candle to him *er kann ihm das Wasser nicht reichen;* a dinner ∾ for a king *ein Essen, das eines Königs würdig wäre;*

it is ∾ that *es schickt sich, daß;* to be ∾ for (to do, to be) *taugen zu, bereit (geeignet) sein für;* to be ∾ to sink, to drop (colloq.) *zum Umfallen müde;* to cry ∾ to burst oneself (vulg.) *ganz jämmerlich heulen;* to see (to think) ∾ to do *es für richtig halten zu tun;* the survival of the ∾test *das Überleben der Anpassungsfähigsten.* — **II.** v.tr.: your description ∾s him to a T. *deine Beschreibung paßt ganz genau auf ihn;* to ∾ a person for (to do) *j.en befähigen zu;* to ∾ on a suit *einen Anzug anprobieren;* to ∾ out (up) a fleet *eine Flotte ausrüsten;* to ∾ a ship with provisions *ein Schiff mit Vorräten versehen.* — **III.** v.i.: if the cap ∾s, put it on (wear it) (prov.) *wen's juckt, der kratze sich; wem der Schuh paßt, der ziehe ihn an; wenn eine auf andere gemünzte Kritik auch auf dich paßt, so richte dich nach ihr;* to ∾ like a glove *wie angegossen passen (sitzen);* to ∾ in (into, in with) a person's plan *in j.es Plan passen.* — **IV.** n.: it is an excellent ∾ *es sitzt wie angegossen;* it is a tight ∾ *es ist fast zu eng*

fix I. v.tr.: to ∾ a place (a time) *einen Ort (eine Zeit) festsetzen;* to ∾ a thing in (on, to) *eine Sache befestigen in, heften an;* to ∾ one's eyes (up)on a person (thing); to ∾ a person with one's eyes *j.en (eine Sache) fixieren;* I'll ∾ that (up) (colloq.) *das werde ich schon machen, einrichten, erledigen, organisieren, reparieren.* — **II.** v.i.: I have ∾ed (up)on that *ich habe mich dafür entschieden.* — **III.** n.: I'm in a ∾ (colloq.) *ich bin in der Klemme, in einer Zwickmühle*

fixture n.: he seems to be a ∾ *er scheint, zum Inventar zu gehören, nicht mehr weggehen zu wollen;* the club has many ∾s for the season *der Verein hat viele Wettkämpfe für die Spielzeit angesetzt*

fizz n.: a glass of ∾ (colloq.) *ein Glas Sekt*

fizzle I. v.i.: the whole affair ∾d out *die ganze Sache verlief im Sande, flaute ab, verpuffte.* — **II.** n.: it was a complete ∾ (colloq.) *es war ein völliger Mißerfolg (ein völliges Fiasko, eine völlige Pleite)*

flag[1] **I.** n.: a ∾-day *ein Tag, an dem durch Verkauf von Fähnchen für eine gute Sache gesammelt wird;* ∾-wagging (sl.) *Signalisieren;* the black ∾ *die schwarze Seeräuberfahne;* the red ∾ *die rote Fahne, Blutfahne der Revolution;* the yellow ∾ *die Quarantäneflagge;* the white ∾, the ∾ of truce *die weiße Parlamentärfahne;* to dip the ∾ *die Flagge als Gruß niederholen (senken) und wieder hissen;* to drop the ∾ *(bei Wettrennen) das Zeichen zum Start geben;* trade follows the ∾ *der Handel folgt der Flagge;* to keep the ∾ flying *die Fahne hochhalten;* the admiral hoists his ∾ (strikes his ∾) *der Admiral übernimmt den Befehl, gibt den Befehl auf;* to lower (to strike) one's ∾ *die Flagge streichen.* — **II.** v.tr.: the ship ∾ged that *das Schiff signalisierte durch Flaggen, daß*

flag[2] v.i.: the interest is ∾ging *das Interesse erlahmt, läßt nach*

flair n.: to have a ∾ for a thing (for doing a thing) *eine natürliche Begabung (eine feine Nase) für etwas haben*

flak n.: come down to ∾ height! (sl.) *spiel' dich nicht so auf! gib nicht so an!*

flame I. n.: she is an old ∾ of mine *sie ist eine alte Flamme von mir;* to burst into ∾(s) *in Flammen ausbrechen;* to fan the ∾ *die Glut (Leidenschaft) anfachen.* — **II.** v.i.: to ∾ out (up) *in Zorn geraten, glühend rot werden*

flank I. n.: to take the enemy in the ∾ *dem Feinde in die Flanke fallen;* to turn the ∾ of an army *ein Heer umgehen;* to turn a person's ∾ *j.en überlisten, im Wortgefecht besiegen.* — **II.** v.tr.: to ∾ a position *die Flanke einer Stellung decken oder bedrohen;* high mountains ∾ed us *hohe Berge lagen zu unserer Seite;* to ∾ a thing *seitlich um etwas herumgehen*

flap I. n.: there was an awful ∾ on (sl.) *es herrschte Hochbetrieb;* to be in (to get into) a ∾ *aufgeregt sein (werden).* — **II.** v.tr.: to ∾ one's ears *die Ohren spitzen*

flapdoodle n.: that's all ∾ *das ist ja alles Unsinn (Mumpitz, Quatsch)*

flapper n. (sl.): she is a ∾ *sie ist ein Backfisch;* the ∾-bracket *der Soziussitz am (auf dem) Motorrad*

flare I. v.tr.: to ∾ a candle at a person *j.en mit einer Kerze beleuchten;* to ∾ one's skill *mit seiner Geschicklichkeit blenden.* — **II.** v.i.: to ∾ up *aufflammen, aufbrausen.* — **III.** n.: to drop ∾s from an aeroplane

Leuchtkugeln, -zeichen vom Flugzeug abwerfen; a ∾-up *ein plötzliches Aufflammen, Aufbrausen, ein Mordsulk*

flash I. v.tr.: his eyes ∾ed fire *seine Augen sprühten Blitze;* to ∾ in the pan *abblitzen, nach auffälligem Anfangserfolg scheitern;* I had a lamp ∾ed in my face *ich wurde plötzlich durch eine Lampe geblendet;* the news was ∾ed over England *die Nachricht wurde über ganz England durch Telegramm (Rundfunk) verbreitet.* — **II.** v.i.: to ∾ round upon a person *sich plötzlich nach j.em umwenden;* it ∾ed upon me, across my mind *es fuhr mir plötzlich durch den Kopf;* to ∾ up *aufbrausen.* — **III.** n.: in a ∾ *im Nu;* a ∾ of hope *ein Hoffnungsstrahl;* it was a ∾ in the pan *es war ein mißlungener Versuch;* ∾-light *Blitz-, Blinklicht.* — **IV.** a.: it was a ∾ note *es war eine gefälschte Banknote;* in ∾ lingo it is called *in der Gaunersprache heißt es*

flat I. a.: that's ∾! *das ist klar! daran läßt sich nicht deuteln;* as ∾ as a pancake *so flach wie ein Brett;* a ∾ refusal *eine glatte Absage (Weigerung);* the beer is ∾ *das Bier ist abgestanden (schal);* the market is ∾ *der Markt ist flau;* a symphony in E ∾ major *eine Symphonie in Es-Dur;* to go into a ∾ spin (sl.) *in Aufregung geraten.* — **II.** adv.: the measure fell ∾ *die Maßnahme hatte keinen Erfolg (keine Wirkung);* to sing ∾ *unrein, falsch singen;* to go out ∾ for something (colloq.) *mit Höchstgeschwindigkeit auf etwas losbrausen.* — **III.** n.: the ∾ of the hand *die Handfläche;* he is a ∾ (sl.) *er ist ein Narr, ein Simpel, (in der Gaunersprache) ein Grüner;* the sharps and ∾s *die Kreuze und B's, die schwarzen Tasten des Klaviers*

flatly adv.: he denied it ∾ *er leugnete es rundweg (glatt) ab*

flatter v.tr.: to ∾ oneself with the belief that *sich in dem Gedanken gefallen, daß; sich (dat.) einbilden, daß;* lay not that ∾ing unction to your soul (Hamlet, III, iv, 145) *legt nicht die Schmeichelsalb' auf eure Seele (Schlegel)*

flea n.: I sent him away with a ∾ in his ear *ich habe ihm gehörig die Wahrheit gesagt, ihm ordentlich (gehörig) heimgeleuchtet;* a ∾-bite *eine geringe Unannehmlichkeit*

fleece v.tr.: to ∾ a person *j.en ausplündern (rupfen)*

flesh n.: to meet in the ∾ *sich von Angesicht zu Angesicht treffen;* he's the devil in the ∾ *er ist der leibhaftige Teufel;* proud ∾ *wildes Fleisch;* he devoured it ∾ and fell *er verschlang es mit Haut und Haaren;* to lose ∾ *abmagern;* it made my ∾ creep *ich bekam eine Gänsehaut;* to put on ∾; to run to ∾ *dick werden;* to wear the ∾ off one's bones *sich abarbeiten (-rackern, -schinden);* to have (to demand) one's pound of flesh *unerbittlich das Letzte verlangen, was einem zusteht;* the ∾-pots *die Fleischtöpfe (gutes Essen und Komfort)*

flicks n.: *Kino*

flight[1] n.: a ∾ of arrows *ein Pfeilregen, -hagel;* a ∾ of stairs *eine Treppenflucht;* a ∾ of wit *ein witziger (geistreicher) Einfall;* in the first ∾ *an führender Stelle;* a bird takes its (a) ∾, wings its ∾ *ein Vogel fliegt*

flight[2] n.: to put the enemy to ∾ *den Feind in die Flucht schlagen;* to take (to take to, to betake oneself to) ∾ *fliehen, sich aus dem Staube machen*

fling I. v.i.: to ∾ out *wüst zu schimpfen beginnen;* to ∾ out of the house *wütend, polternd aus dem Hause stürzen.* — **II.** v.tr.: to ∾ a thing in a person's teeth *j.em etwas ins Gesicht schleudern, vorwerfen.* — **III.** n.: to have a ∾ at a person *auf j.en sticheln;* to have a ∾ at a thing *sein Heil an etwas versuchen;* to have one's ∾ *sich amüsieren (sich austoben)*

flint n.: to set one's face like a ∾ *fest entschlossen sein;* to skin a ∾, to be a skin∾ *geizig (knickerig, ein Geizkragen, -hals) sein;* to wring water from a ∾ *ein Wunder vollbringen*

flit v.i. & n.: to ∾, to do a midnight ∾ *bei Nacht und Nebel ausziehen (verschwinden, ohne die Miete bezahlt zu haben)*

float I. v.i.: to ∾ with the current *mit dem Strome schwimmen.* — **II.** v.tr.: to ∾ a company *eine Handelsgesellschaft gründen;* to ∾ a loan *eine Anleihe auflegen;* ∾ing vote *schwankende (schwebende) Anzahl der Wähler;* ∾ing population *der nicht seßhafte Bevölkerungsteil*

flock I. n.: a ∾ of sheep *eine Schafherde;* a clergyman's ∾ *die Gemeinde eines Geistlichen;* ∾s and herds *Schafe und Rind-*

vieh; to come in ∾s *in Scharen kommen.* — **II.** v.i.: to ∾ to a person *j.em zuströmen;* birds of a feather ∾ together (prov.) *gleich und gleich gesellt sich gern*

flog v.tr.: to ∾ a watch (colloq.) *eine Uhr verkaufen, versetzen, verkloppen;* to ∾ a thing into a person *j.em etwas einbleuen;* to ∾ a thing out of a person *j.em etwas austreiben;* to ∾ a dead (a willing) horse see 'horse'; to give a boy a ∾ging *einem Jungen eine Tracht Prügel geben (verabfolgen)*

floor I. n.: to have the ∾ *das Wort haben;* to take the ∾ *das Wort in einer Debatte ergreifen;* to wipe the ∾ with a person *j.em eine demütigende Niederlage beibringen.* — **II.** v.tr.: to ∾ a person *j.en zu Boden schlagen;* I was completely ∾ed (colloq.) *ich war völlig sprachlos (vollkommen platt);* to ∾ the paper *alle schriftlichen Prüfungsfragen beantworten*

flop n.: the play was a ∾ (sl.) *das Stück fiel durch (war ein völliger Mißerfolg)*

fluke n.: by a ∾ *durch (einen) glücklichen Zufall*

flush a.: he is ∾ of cash *er ist gut bei Kasse;* the door is ∾ with the pavement *die Tür ist auf gleicher Höhe mit dem Bürgersteig*

flutter I. v.i.: to ∾ about (around) *herumflattern;* to ∾ with excitement *vor Aufregung beben (zittern).* — **II.** v.tr.: to ∾ the dovecotes, see 'dovecote'. — **III.** n.: to be (to put) in a ∾ *in Aufregung sein (versetzen);* to have a ∾ on the Stock Exchange *an der Börse spekulieren;* to make a ∾ *eine Sensation verursachen*

fly¹ n.: a ∾ on the wheel *j., der seinen Einfluß überschätzt;* there are no flies on him (sl.) *an ihm ist alles dran;* to break a ∾ on the wheel *offene Türen einrennen;* to catch flies *Maulaffen feilhalten;* to find a ∾ in the ointment (cf. Eccles. X, 1) *ein Haar in der Suppe finden;* ∾-blown *besudelt*

fly² I. v.i.: the bird is flown *der Vogel (der Gefangene) ist fort (entflogen);* as the crow flies *in gerader Linie, in der Luftlinie;* to ∾ at higher game *höher hinauswollen;* to ∾ at (upon) a person *über j.en herfallen;* to ∾ high *ehrgeizig sein;* to ∾ in the face of a person *j.em zu Leibe gehen, ihm offen Trotz bieten;* to ∾ into a passion (a rage) *in Wut geraten;* to ∾ off the handle (sl.) *aufbrausen, in Wut geraten;* to ∾ out at (against) a person *gegen j.en ausfallend werden;* to let ∾ at *losschlagen auf;* to make the money ∾ *das Geld schnell ausgeben;* to make the feathers (the dust) ∾ *einen Streit oder eine Aufregung verursachen;* with ∾ing colours *mit fliegenden Fahnen, mit großem Erfolg.* — **II.** v.tr.: to ∾ a kite *einen Drachen (Versuchsballon) steigen lassen.* — **III.** n.: to be on the ∾ *in Bewegung sein*

fly³ a. (sl.): they are ∾ to the dodges *sie kennen die Kniffe (Schliche)*

fob v.tr.: to ∾ a thing off upon a person *j.em etwas aufhängen, andrehen;* to ∾ a person off with a thing *j.en mit etwas abspeisen, abfertigen*

focus n.: to be in ∾ *im Brennpunkt, richtig eingestellt sein;* to be out of ∾ *nicht im Brennpunkt, nicht scharf eingestellt sein;* to bring into ∾ *in den Brennpunkt rücken*

fog n.: I am still in a ∾ about it *ich bin mir immer noch nicht klar darüber;* ∾bound *durch Nebel zurückgehalten (Flugzeug)*

foggy a.: I haven't the foggiest (idea) *ich habe nicht die leiseste Ahnung (den geringsten Schimmer)*

fogy, fogey n.: he is an old ∾ *er ist ein alter Knopp, ein altmodischer Kauz*

foist v.tr.: to ∾ in a thing *etwas heimlich hineinbringen;* to ∾ a thing upon a person *j.em etwas aufhängen (andrehen)*

folk n.: my ∾s at home *meine Angehörigen zu Hause;* the old ∾s *die alten Leute*

follow I. v.tr.: to ∾ one's bent *seiner Neigung nachgehen;* to ∾ one's own devices *sich nach seiner Art amüsieren;* to ∾ a person close *j.em auf dem Fuße folgen;* to ∾ the fashion *die Mode mitmachen;* trade ∾s the flag *der Handel folgt der Flagge;* to ∾ the hounds *auf die Hetzjagd reiten;* to ∾ one's nose *der Nase nachgehen;* to ∾ an occupation *einem Beruf nachgehen;* to ∾ the plough, the sea *Landmann sein, Seemann sein;* to ∾ someone, a lecture *j.em, einem Vortrag folgen, ihn verstehen;* to ∾ suit *Farbe bekennen (beim Kartenspiel); j.es Beispiel folgen;* to ∾ out an order *einen*

Befehl durchführen (befolgen); to ∾ up an advantage *einen Vorteil ausnutzen;* ∾ing a thing *als Folge einer Sache, im Anschluß an eine Sache.* — **II.** v.i.: to ∾ in the steps (in the wake) of a person *j.em nachfolgen;* to ∾ on *zeitlich folgen auf.* — **III.** n.: a ∾ *ein Nachläufer (beim Billardspiel); die Nachbestellung einer halben Portion*

fond a.: a ∾ father *ein närrisch (abgöttisch) liebender Vater;* to be ∾ of a person *j.en gern haben (lieben);* to be ∾ of doing a thing *etwas gern tun;* he ∾ly imagined *in seiner Unwissenheit bildete er sich ein; er war töricht genug zu glauben*

food n.: to be ∾ for fishes *ertrunken sein;* to be ∾ for powder *Kanonenfutter sein;* ∾ for thought (meditation) *Stoff zum Nachdenken;* to be ∾ for worms *tot sein, im Grabe liegen;* a ∾-card *eine Lebensmittelkarte*

fool I. n.: a ∾'s bolt is soon shot (prov.) *Narrenwitz ist bald zu Ende;* All Fools' day *der erste April;* a man is a ∾ or physician at forty *ein vernünftiger Mann braucht keinen Arzt;* no ∾ like an old ∾ (prov.) *Alter schützt vor Torheit nicht; alte Scheunen brennen lichterloh;* one ∾ makes many *ein Narr macht zehn;* to be a ∾ for one's pains *sich (dat.) vergeblich Mühe machen;* to be a ∾ to a person *j.em gegenüber ein Waisenknabe sein;* he is no ∾ *er ist nicht auf den Kopf gefallen;* to go on a ∾'s errand *in den April geschickt werden;* the more (the greater) ∾ you *das hättest du besser wissen müssen;* to live in a ∾'s paradise *in Illusionen leben, sich (dat.) goldene Berge versprechen;* to make a ∾ of oneself (of a person) *sich lächerlich machen; j.en zum Narren halten;* to make an April ∾ of a person *j.en in den April schicken;* to play the ∾ *Unsinn machen, Possen treiben;* to take a person for a ∾ *j.en für einen Narren halten;* to write on ∾scap *auf Aktenpapier schreiben;* ∾-proof *idiotensicher.* — **II.** v.tr.: to ∾ a person *j.en zum Narren halten;* to ∾ a person into doing a thing *j.en zu etwas verleiten;* to ∾ away the time *die Zeit vertrödeln (vergeuden, verplempern);* to ∾ a person out of money *j.en um Geld betrügen.* — **III.** v.i.: to ∾ about (around) *sich herumtreiben; herumlungern*

foot I. n.: to be on one's own feet *auf eigenen Beinen (Füßen) stehen;* to be carried feet foremost *mit den Füßen voran aus dem Hause (auf den Friedhof) getragen werden;* to catch one's ∾ in a trap *mit dem Fuße in einer Falle hängen bleiben;* she was carried (swept) off her feet *sie ließ sich hinreißen;* to be swift of ∾ *schnellfüßig sein;* to fall on one's feet *auf die Füße fallen (immer Glück, Glück im Unglück haben);* to find one's feet *stehen (gehen) lernen; seine Fähigkeiten entwikkeln;* to find (to know) the length of a person's ∾ *j.es Schwächen kennen lernen (kennen); j.en zu lenken wissen;* to go on ∾ *zu Fuß gehen;* to have the ball at one's feet *Herr der Lage sein;* to have cold feet (sl.) *eine Heidenangst (kalte Füße) haben;* to have feet of clay *tönerne Füße haben;* to have one ∾ in the grave *mit einem Fuße im Grabe stehen;* to keep one's feet *nicht fallen;* to measure another person's ∾ by one's own last *von sich auf andere schließen;* to put one's ∾ down *energisch auftreten, fest bei einer Absage bleiben; einen festen Standpunkt einnehmen;* to put one's ∾ in it *ins Fettnäpfchen treten;* to put one's best ∾ foremost *sich sehr beeilen, die Beine in die Hand nehmen;* to run a person off his feet *j.en bis zur Erschöpfung arbeiten lassen, ihn abhetzen;* to serve a person hand and ∾ *j.em unverdrossen (unterwürfig) dienen;* to set (to put, to have) one's ∾ on the neck of a person *j.em den Fuß auf den Nacken setzen, ihn unterdrücken;* to set a movement on ∾ *eine Bewegung in Gang bringen;* to set a person on his feet again *j.em wieder auf die Beine helfen;* to set ∾ on shore *ans Land gehen;* to trample (to tread) under ∾ *mit Füßen treten;* ∾ and horse *Infanterie und Kavallerie;* a ∾boy; a ∾man *ein Laufbursche, Page; ein Lakai, Diener;* the ∾hills *das Vorgebirge;* the ∾lights *das Rampenlicht;* to leave ∾marks, ∾prints *Fußspuren hinterlassen;* a ∾-slogger (sl.) *ein Fußgänger, Infanterist;* to be ∾sore *fußkrank sein;* to tread in a person's ∾steps *j.es Beispiel folgen, in seine Fußtapfen treten;* my ∾! (colloq.) *Unsinn, keineswegs!;* at the ∾ of the page (the steps, the hill) *am Ende der Seite (am Anfang der Treppe, am Fuße des Hügels).* — **II.** v.tr.: to ∾ it *zu Fuß gehen, tanzen;* to ∾ the bill *die Rechnung (Zeche) bezahlen;* to ∾ a stocking *einen Fuß anstricken;* to ∾ up accounts *Rechnungen (Posten) zusam-*

menzählen. — **III.** v.i.: their expenses ∾ed up to *ihre Kosten beliefen sich auf*

footer n. (sl.): to play ∾ *Fußball spielen*

footing n.: on a friendly ∾ *in freundlichem Verhältnis;* on a peace (war) ∾ *auf Friedens-, Kriegsstand;* on the same (on one, a) ∾ with *auf gleichem Fuße, ebenbürtig mit;* to gain (to get) a firm ∾ *festen Fuß fassen;* to lose one's ∾ *ausgleiten;* to pay one's (for one's) ∾ *Aufnahme-, Eintrittsgeld bezahlen*

for prep.: (expressing time) ∾ ages *eine Ewigkeit;* ∾ good, ever (and ever) *für immer;* ∾ life *lebenslänglich;* ∾ the present *für den Augenblick, augenblicklich;* he stayed with me ∾ months *er blieb monatelang bei mir;* I haven't been there ∾ months *ich bin seit Monaten nicht mehr dort gewesen;* it will stay fine ∾ the next three days *die nächsten drei Tage bleibt das Wetter schön;* it is getting on ∾ two o'clock *es geht auf zwei Uhr zu;* (cause or reason) ∾ all I care *meinetwegen, mir liegt nichts daran;* ∾ all (aught) I know *soviel ich weiß;* ∾ all (that) he says *trotz allem, was er sagt;* to be ∾ all the world like a thing *einer Sache sehr ähnlich sein;* you will be all the better (worse) ∾ it *das wird dir gut (schlecht) bekommen;* he was rewarded ∾ bravery *er wurde belohnt für seine Tapferkeit;* it is too beautiful ∾ words *es ist unsagbar schön;* ∾ fear of (that) *aus Furcht vor;* to be hard up ∾ money *knapp an Geld sein;* but ∾ his help, we would not have found the house *ohne seine Hilfe hätten wir das Haus nicht gefunden;* he is famous ∾ his kindness *er ist wegen seiner Gutmütigkeit berühmt;* ∾ want (lack) of *aus Mangel an;* his coat was the worse ∾ wear *sein Rock war sehr abgetragen;* to be out ∾ trouble *einen Streit suchen;* (purpose, intention) a cure ∾ rheumatism *ein Mittel gegen Rheuma;* to fight ∾ one's life *um sein Leben kämpfen;* to get ready ∾ the theatre *sich fertig machen für's Theater;* to go in ∾ an examination *in eine Prüfung gehen;* to go ∾ a walk *spazieren gehen;* to send ∾ a newspaper *eine Zeitung holen lassen;* the house is ∾ sale *das Haus ist zu verkaufen;* it is usual ∾ hats to be worn *es ist üblich, daß Hüte getragen werden;* what do you want the book ∾? *wofür willst du das Buch haben?;* it is ∾ you to begin *es ist an dir zu beginnen;* (wish, expectation) oh, ∾ a horse *wenn ich nur ein Pferd hätte;* to hope ∾, to ask ∾, to hunger ∾, to be eager ∾, to be anxious ∾, to have a desire ∾, to have an appetite ∾ (something) *hoffen auf, fragen nach, hungern nach, begierig sein nach, besorgt sein um, sich sehnen nach, Appetit haben auf (etwas);* to want ∾ nothing *an nichts mangeln (Mangel haben);* (destination, place, object, state) now ∾ it *nun los! jetzt aber 'ran;* to be in ∾ it *einer Bestrafung entgegensehen;* the train ∾ Paris *der Zug nach Paris;* to leave ∾ London *nach London abfahren;* to go ∾ a soldier *Soldat werden;* to make ∾ the door *zur Tür stürzen;* to take something ∾ granted *etwas als selbstverständlich annehmen;* (exchange) word ∾ word *wortwörtlich;* a change ∾ the better (worse) *Eintreten einer Besserung (Verschlimmerung);* to give (to pay) a pound ∾ something *ein Pfund für etwas geben, bezahlen;* (substitution) once ∾ all *ein für allemal;* he was mistaken ∾ another person *er wurde mit einer anderen Person verwechselt;* do you take me ∾ a fool? *hältst du mich für einen Narren?;* (favour or advantage) to be ∾ her good *ihr zum Wohle gereichen;* he has furnished an office ∾ himself *er hat (für seinen eigenen Zweck) ein Büro eingerichtet;* she doesn't care ∾ him *sie mag ihn nicht;* I cannot do it ∾ the life of me *ich kann es beim besten Willen nicht (nicht um die Welt) tun;* I must see it ∾ myself *ich muß es selbst sehen;* liking ∾, respect ∾ someone *Zuneigung zu, Achtung vor j.em;* (suitability) he is not fit ∾ this work *er ist nicht geeignet für diese Arbeit;* swimming is good ∾ you *Schwimmen ist gesund für dich;* there was nothing ∾ it but to say yes *es blieb nichts anders übrig als ja zu sagen;* as ∾ me *was mich betrifft;* I ∾ one do not believe it *ich für meine Person glaube es nicht;* ∾ that matter *was das anbetrifft;* were it not (but, except) ∾ one thing, I might be happy *wäre nicht das eine, so könnte ich glücklich sein;* ∾ certain *bestimmt, sicherlich;* ∾ shame *pfui! schäme dich!*

forbid v.tr.: God ∾! *Gott bewahre!;* a ∾ding look *ein finsterer Blick;* a ∾den fruit *eine verbotene Frucht*

force I. n.: the Armed Forces, the Forces *die Wehrmacht;* storms, earthquakes etc. are

∾s of Nature *Stürme, Erdbeben usw. sind Naturgewalten;* there is ∾ in what you say *was du sagst, hat Hand und Fuß;* by ∾; by main ∾ *gewaltsam; mit aller Gewalt;* by ∾ of *vermittels;* to attack in ∾ *in großer Stärke angreifen;* to be in ∾ *in Kraft (gültig) sein;* to come into ∾ *in Kraft treten;* to join ∾s with someone *die Kräfte vereinigen;* to put in ∾ *in Kraft treten lassen;* to say with much ∾ *mit großem Nachdruck sagen;* I can't see the ∾ of doing that *ich sehe nicht ein, weshalb ich das tun soll;* to be a ∾ for good *einen guten Einfluß haben.* — **II.** v.tr.: to ∾ an analogy (a simile) *eine Analogie (einen Vergleich) zu Tode hetzen;* to ∾ the bidding *(bei einer Auktion) das Gebot in die Höhe treiben;* to ∾ a card *bei Kartenkunststücken j.en dazu bringen, eine bestimmte Karte zu ziehen;* to ∾ a door open *eine Tür aufbrechen;* to ∾ the growth *das Wachstum künstlich beschleunigen;* to ∾ a person's hand *j.en zwingen, vorzeitig zu handeln;* to ∾ the pace (the running) *ein schnelles Tempo vorlegen, um den Gegner zu ermüden;* to ∾ the sense *dem Sinn Gewalt antun;* to ∾ a smile *sich zu einem Lächeln zwingen;* to ∾ one's voice *die Stimme zu ungewöhnlicher Höhenlage steigern;* to ∾ one's way *sich einen Weg erzwingen (bahnen);* to ∾ along *vorwärtstreiben;* to ∾ back *zurücktreiben, -schlagen;* the pilot was ∾d down *der Pilot mußte notlanden;* to ∾ tears from a person's eyes *j.en zu Tränen rühren;* to ∾ a person into an action (into doing, to do a thing) *j.en zu einer Handlung zwingen;* to ∾ the facts out of a person *j.en zur Angabe der Tatsachen zwingen;* to ∾ up the lid *den Deckel aufzwängen;* to ∾ oneself (a thing) upon a person *sich (eine Sache) j.em aufzwingen (aufdrängen)*

fore I. n.: to come to the ∾ *in den Vordergrund treten, in Führung gehen.* — **II.** adv.: ∾ and aft *Bug und Heck, vorn und hinten*

forefront n.: in the ∾ of the battle *in vorderster Schlachtlinie*

forego v.i.: the ∾ing articles *die oben erwähnten Gegenstände;* it was a foregone conclusion *es war von vornherein schon klar, es stand von vornherein fest*

foreign a.: the Foreign Office, ∾ Secretary, ∾ Affairs, ∾ Trade *das Außenministerium, der Außenminister, die Außenpolitik, der Außenhandel;* to be ∾ from (to) a thing *einer Sache fremd sein, nicht zu einer Sache gehören oder passen*

forelock n.: to take the time (occasion, etc.) by the ∾ *die Gelegenheit beim Schopfe fassen*

foremost I. a.: head (tail) ∾ *mit dem Kopf (dem Schwanz) zuerst.* — **II.** adv.: first and ∾ *zu allererst*

forfeit I. n. & a.: his life was the ∾, was ∾ *sein Leben war verwirkt;* to pay a ∾ *ein Pfand geben;* to play ∾s *Pfänderspiele machen.* — **II.** v.tr.: to ∾ a thing *etwas verwirken, einbüßen, verscherzen*

forge[1] I. v.i.: to ∾ ahead *die Führung übernehmen, an die Spitze drängen.* — **II.** v.tr.: to ∾ one's way *seinen Weg bahnen*

forge[2] v.tr.: to ∾ a coin *falschmünzen;* to ∾ a signature *eine Unterschrift fälschen;* to ∾ a tale *eine Geschichte erfinden (erdichten)*

forget v.tr.: to ∾ oneself *sich vergessen, sich vorbei benehmen;* to forgive and ∾ (past injuries) *allen Groll vergessen;* ∾ it! (colloq.) *hör mal endlich auf, davon zu reden!*

fork v.tr.: I had to ∾ out (over) the money (sl.) *ich mußte das Geld herausrücken (berappen, blechen);* a ∾ed road *eine Straße, die sich gabelt;* ∾ed lightning *Zickzackblitz*

forlorn a.: a ∾ hope (Dutch hoop = heap) *ein Sturmtrupp, ein verlorener Posten, ein verzweifeltes Unternehmen*

form I. n.: in ∾; out of ∾ *in Form, in guter Verfassung; in schlechter Form (Verfassung);* that is bad ∾ *das schickt sich nicht;* that is common ∾ *das ist nicht von besonderer Bedeutung;* in due ∾ *gehörig, vorschriftsmäßig;* he was in great ∾ *er war in bester Verfassung, sehr gut aufgelegt;* a matter of ∾ *eine Formsache;* to do something for ∾'s sake *etwas tun, weil es sich schickt;* to observe the ancient ∾s *die alten Gebräuche ehren;* what's the ∾? (colloq.) *was ist los? wie ist die Sache?* — **II.** v.tr.: to ∾ a habit *sich (dat.) etwas angewöhnen;* to ∾ an opinion *sich (dat.) eine Meinung bilden*

former I. a.: in ∾ times *in früheren Zeiten.* — **II.** pron.: the ∾, the latter *ersterer,-e,-es; letzterer,-e,-es*

forth adv.: back and ∾ *hin und her;* from this time ∾ *von nun an;* and so ∾ *und so weiter, und so fort;* so far ∾ as *insoweit wie;* to bring (to come) ∾ *hervorbringen, -kommen;* to give ∾ *von sich geben; aussprechen, veröffentlichen*

forthcoming a.: the ∾ event *das bevorstehende Ereignis;* as the money was not ∾ *da das Geld nicht bezahlt wurde*

fortnight n.: today (Monday) ∾ *heute (Montag) in vierzehn Tagen;* a ∾ ago *heute vor vierzehn Tagen;* I would rather keep him a week than a ∾ *er ist ein großer Esser*

fortune n.: ∾ favours the brave (prov.) *dem Mutigen gehört die Welt;* a soldier of ∾ *ein Glücksritter;* to come into a ∾ *ein Vermögen erben;* to make a ∾ *ein Vermögen machen;* to make one's ∾ *sein Glück machen;* to marry a ∾ *eine reiche Partie machen;* to tell a person his ∾ *j.em wahrsagen*

forty I. a.: to take ∾ winks *ein Schläfchen halten.* — **II.** n.: the roaring forties *stürmische Striche des Ozeans zwischen dem 39. und 50. südlichen Breitengrad;* in the forties of the last century *in den 40er Jahren des vergangenen Jahrhunderts*

forward I. a.: a ∾ child *ein vorlautes, frühreifes Kind;* the plants are very ∾ *die Pflanzen sind gut entwickelt.* — **II.** adv.: to bring (to carry) ∾ *auf die nächste Seite übertragen;* to look ∾ to a thing *sich auf etwas freuen;* to put ∾ a claim for a thing *auf etwas Anspruch erheben;* I can't get any ∾er (colloq. forrader) *ich komme nicht weiter.* — **III.** v.tr.: please ∾ *bitte nachsenden!* — **IV.** n.: the centre ∾ *der Mittelstürmer*

foul I. a.: ∾ linen *schmutzige Wäsche;* by ∾ means *auf unredliche Weise;* ∾ play *Verrat;* to fall (to run) ∾ of a person (thing) *mit einer Person (Sache) zusammenstoßen.* — **II.** n.: through ∾ and fair *durch dick und dünn.* — **III.** adv.: to hit ∾ *einen regelwidrigen Schlag führen;* to play a person ∾ *j.en unredlich behandeln*

fountain n.: a ∾-pen *ein Füllfederhalter;* the ∾-head *der Urquell, die Ursache*

four I. a.: a ∾flusher *ein Schwindler (Aufschneider);* a ∾-poster *ein Himmelbett;* ∾score *achtzig;* a ∾some *ein Golfspiel zu vier Personen;* the ∾ corners of the earth *die entferntesten Winkel der Erde;* within the ∾ seas *in Großbritannien;* a ∾-in-hand *ein Vierspänner, ein Viererzug;* to meet the world ∾square *bestimmt, ehrlich und furchtlos auftreten.* — **II.** n.: to be on all ∾s with a thing *einer Sache vollkommen entsprechen;* to go on all ∾s *auf allen vieren kriechen*

fox v.tr.: (colloq.) to ∾ someone *j.en (z. B. mit schwierigen Fragen) verwirren*

frailty n.: ∾, thy name is woman (Hamlet I, 2) *Schwachheit, dein Nam' ist Weib*

frame I. n.: a man of gigantic ∾ *ein Riese von Gestalt;* in a good ∾ of mind *in guter Stimmung;* a ∾-up *ein Komplott, böswilliger Anschlag.* — **II.** v.tr.: to ∾ a charge against a person *j.en grundlos anschuldigen*

fraud n.: a pious ∾ *ein frommer Schwindel*

frazzle n.: worn to a ∾ *sehr nervös*

freak n.: to play a ∾ *einen (kindischen) Streich spielen;* to escape by a ∾ *durch einen unerklärlichen Zufall entkommen;* an animal with two heads is a ∾ of Nature *ein zweiköpfiges Tier ist eine Mißgeburt (eine Laune der Natur)*

free a.: a ∾(-)booter *ein Freibeuter, Pirat;* carriage ∾ *Fracht bezahlt;* ∾ from care *sorgenfrei;* ∾ of charge *gebührenfrei, kostenlos;* the ∾ Churches *(engl.) Freikirchen;* ∾ of duty *zollfrei;* ∾ and easy *frei und ungezwungen, ungeniert;* a ∾ fight (a ∾-for-all) *eine allgemeine Schlägerei;* ∾, gratis and for nothing (colloq.) *kostenlos;* a ∾-hand drawing *eine Freihandzeichnung;* to be ∾-handed *freigebig;* ∾hold property *freier Grundbesitz;* a ∾lance journalist *ein freier Journalist;* ∾ of his money *freigebig;* ∾-spoken *freimütig (Rede);* to get off scot (= tax) ∾ *ohne Bestrafung davonkommen;* it is ∾ for (to) him to do so *es steht ihm frei, es zu tun;* to be ∾ to confess *bereit sein zu gestehen;* I did it of my own ∾ will *ich tat es freiwillig;* to make (to be) ∾ with a person *sich (dat.) j.em gegenüber zuviel herausnehmen;* to make ∾ of a thing *mit einer Sache frei schalten, wie mit seinem Eigentum mit ihr verfahren;* to set a person ∾ *j.en befreien*

freedom n.: to confer the ∾ of the city on a person *j.em das Ehrenbürgerrecht verleihen;* he has the ∾ of the library *er darf die Bibliothek uneingeschränkt benutzen;* to take ∾s with a person *sich (dat.) j.em gegenüber Vertraulichkeiten herausnehmen*

freeze I. v.i.: to ∾ on to a thing (colloq.) *etwas krampfhaft festhalten, eine starke Neigung zu etwas fassen.* — **II.** v.tr.: to ∾ a person's blood *j.em das Blut in den Adern erstarren lassen;* to ∾ a person out *j.en ausschließen;* to ∾ credits *Kredite sperren;* the frozen limit (colloq.) *das Abscheuliche (Gräßliche, Unausstehliche)*

French a.: to take ∾ leave *ohne Abschied weggehen, sich drücken, sich (auf) französisch empfehlen;* a ∾ window *ein bis zum Fußboden reichendes Flügelfenster*

frenzied a.: in a ∾ rage *in wahnsinniger Wut*

fresh I. a.: ∾ paint! *frisch gestrichen!;* as ∾ as paint, as a daisy *quicklebendig, quietschfidel;* to break ∾ ground *ein neues Gebiet erschließen;* a ∾water fish *ein Süßwasserfisch.* — **II.** n.: in the ∾ of the morning *in der Morgenfrische;* a ∾er *ein Student im ersten Jahr (Fuchs)*

fret I. v.i.: to ∾ at *sich grämen (sich Sorgen machen) um;* to ∾ and fume *vor Wut schäumen.* — **II.** v.tr.: to ∾ away (out) one's life *sein Leben verhärmen.* — **III.** n.: to be in a ∾, on the ∾ *aufgeregt, ärgerlich sein*

Friday n.: on ∾; on ∾s *am Freitag; freitags;* Good ∾ *Karfreitag*

friend n.: a ∾ in need is a ∾ indeed (prov.) *in der Not erkennt man seine Freunde; Freunde in der Not gehen tausend auf ein Lot;* a ∾ at court *ein einflußreicher Gönner;* my shyness was here my best ∾ *meine Schüchternheit tat mir hierbei die besten Dienste;* my honourable ∾ *mein ehrenwerter Freund (übliche Anrede bei Mitgliedern des englischen Unterhauses);* my learned ∾ *mein Kollege (ein Jurist in der Gerichtssitzung zum anderen);* to be ∾s with *befreundet sein mit;* to keep ∾s with *befreundet bleiben mit;* to make a ∾ *sich (dat.) einen Freund gewinnen;* to make ∾s with *Freundschaft schließen mit, sich wieder versöhnen mit;* to stand a person's ∾ *j.em als Freund zur Seite stehen;* the Society of Friends *die Quäker*

friendly a.: to be on ∾ terms with a person *mit j.em auf freundschaftlichem Fuße stehen;* to play a ∾ match *ein Freundschaftsspiel austragen;* a Friendly Society *eine gemeinnützige Kranken- oder Altersversicherung*

fright n.: to take ∾ *sich erschrecken;* you gave me a ∾ *du hast mich erschrocken;* she is a perfect ∾ *sie sieht verboten aus, sie ist eine richtige Vogelscheuche*

frighten v.tr.: to ∾ a person into (out of) doing a thing *j.en durch Schreck dahinbringen (davon abbringen), etwas zu tun;* to ∾ a person away (off, out of a place) *j.en verscheuchen;* to be ∾ed at *erschreckt sein über;* to be ∾ed of *sich fürchten vor*

frill n.: ∾s *unnötige (überflüssige) Verschönerungen oder Leistungen;* to put on ∾s *vornehm tun (sich affektiert, geziert benehmen)*

fritter v.tr.: to ∾ away one's time (money, energy, etc.) *seine Zeit (sein Geld, seine Energie usw.) vergeuden (vertrödeln, verplempern)*

frock I. n.: she had a pretty ∾ on *sie trug ein hübsches Kleid;* a ∾-coat *ein Gehrock.* — **II.** v.tr.: to ∾ a person *j.en mit einem geistlichen Amt bekleiden*

frog n.: a ∾-eater, a Froggy *ein Froschesser (Spottname für Franzosen);* leap-∾ *Bockspringen*

from prep. (starting place): ∾ a child *von Kindheit an;* ∾ before the war *aus der Zeit vor dem Krieg;* ∾ between the leaves *zwischen den Blättern hervor;* ∾ out the cave *aus der Höhle heraus;* ∾ over the hills *von jenseits der Berge her;* ∾ under her spectacles *unter ihrer Brille hervor;* to release ∾ prison *aus dem Gefängnis entlassen;* (source or origin): to judge ∾ appearances *nach dem Schein zu urteilen;* to paint ∾ nature *nach der Natur malen;* to speak ∾ experience *aus (der) Erfahrung sprechen;* ten miles ∾ Rome *zehn Meilen von Rom entfernt;* (removal, separation, prevention, protection) to be absent (to stay away) ∾ the meeting *bei der Versammlung nicht anwesend sein;* to defend (to protect, to save) someone ∾ danger *j. verteidigen gegen, schützen gegen (vor), retten aus Gefahr;* to dissuade ∾ *abraten von;* to hide, to conceal ∾ *verstecken (verbergen) vor;* to be ∾ home *nicht zu Hause sein;* to refrain ∾ doing *unterlassen zu tun;* to stop (to prevent, to keep) him ∾ talking *verhindern, daß er redet;* I am far ∾ saying *es liegt mir fern zu sagen;* to take a thing ∾ a person *j.em etwas wegnehmen;* (cause, reason): ∾ his point of view *von seinem Standpunkt aus;* to die ∾ fatigue *vor Ermüdung sterben;* to suffer ∾ an illness *an einer Krankheit leiden;* ∾ what you say *nach dem, was Sie sagen;* (showing a difference): apart ∾ *abgesehen von;* to know black ∾ white *schwarz von weiß unterscheiden;* to be different ∾ *anders sein als;* (material which loses its original form or composition in the making of something): cheese is made ∾ milk *Käse wird aus Milch gemacht;* steel is made ∾ iron *Stahl wird aus Eisen gemacht (aber:* the box is made of wood *die Schachtel ist aus Holz);* to make ∾ a thing *aus einer Sache anfertigen;* (repeated action or movement): ∾ day to day *von Tag zu Tag;* ∾ morning till night *von Morgens bis Abends;* ∾ place to place *von Ort zu Ort;* ∾ time to time *von Zeit zu Zeit;* news travels ∾ mouth to mouth *die Nachricht wird mündlich verbreitet*

front I. n.: the head and ∾ *die Hauptsache;* in ∾ *an der (die) Spitze;* in ∾ of the house *vor dem Hause;* to the ∾ *nach vorne, voraus, voran;* to be at the ∾ *an der Front sein (stehen);* to come to the ∾ *in den Vordergrund treten;* to go to the ∾ *an die Front gehen;* to have the ∾ to do a thing *die Stirn (Frechheit) haben, etwas zu tun;* to present (to show) a bold ∾ *dreist auftreten;* to stand ∾ to ∾ with *unmittelbar gegenüberstehen.* — **II.** a.: the ∾ bench *die vorderste, für Minister und ehemalige Minister reservierte Bank im englischen Unterhaus;* the ∾ door *die Haustür;* a three-pair ∾ room *ein Vorderzimmer im dritten Stock.* — **III.** v.tr.: to ∾ a person *j.em gegenübertreten, Trotz bieten;* the house ∾s the park *das Haus liegt nach dem Park;* the building is ∾ed with stone *das Gebäude hat eine Steinfront.* — **IV.** v.i.: to ∾ to (towards, [up]on) the lake *mit der Front nach dem See liegen.* — **V.** adv.: eyes ∾! *Augen geradeaus!*

froth n.: a ∾-blower (joc.) *(scherzhaft für) Biertrinker*

fruit n.: ∾ salad *(scherzhaft für) bunte Ordensschnalle;* forbidden (stolen) ∾ is sweetest (prov.) *verbotene Frucht schmeckt am besten*

fry[1] v.tr.: I have other fish to ∾ *ich habe wichtigere Dinge zu tun;* out of the ∾ing-pan into the fire *vom Regen in die Traufe*

fry[2] n.: small ∾ *kleine Kinder, unbedeutende Wesen; Grobzeug*

full I. a.: my ∾ brother *mein leiblicher Bruder;* to be ∾ of beans (colloq.) *wohlauf, strotzend vor Gesundheit sein;* in ∾ dress *im Gesellschaftsanzug, in Galauniform;* a ∾-dress debate *eine im voraus angesetzte, nicht zufällig entstehende, wichtige Parlamentsdebatte;* a ∾-dress rehearsal *eine Kostüm-, Generalprobe;* at ∾ length *in ganzer Länge, ausführlich;* a ∾-portrait *eine Ganzaufnahme;* at ∾ speed *mit höchster Geschwindigkeit;* to be in ∾ swing *auf höchsten Touren laufen;* the bus is ∾ up *der Omnibus ist voll besetzt.* — **II.** adv.: ∾ many a *so mancher,-e,-es;* I know it ∾ well *ich weiß es sehr wohl;* to look a person ∾ in the face *j.em gerade ins Gesicht sehen;* ∾-grown (-blown) *ausgewachsen;* he is a ∾-blown architect *er ist ein ausgebildeter Architekt;* to fall ∾-length *der Länge nach hinfallen;* payment in ∾ *volle Bezahlung;* he repeated it in ∾ *er gab es ungekürzt wieder;* please write your name in ∾ *bitte schreiben Sie Ihren Namen voll aus (ungekürzt hin);* I enjoyed myself to the ∾ *ich habe mich köstlich amüsiert*

fun n.: for the ∾ of the thing *des Spaßes halber;* he is good (great) ∾ *er ist ein Spaßvogel, sehr amüsant;* it was great ∾ *es war ein Hauptspaß;* there is no ∾ like work *es geht nichts über die Arbeit;* to have capital (good) ∾ *sich ausgezeichnet amüsieren;* to make ∾ of (to poke ∾ at) a person (thing) *sich über j.en (eine Sache) lustig machen;* I only said it for (in) ∾ *ich habe es nur zum Spaß gesagt*

fund n.: to be in ∾s *gut bei Kasse sein*

funeral n.: that's your ∾ (colloq.) *das ist deine Sache, das mußt du ausbaden*

funk n. (colloq.): he is in a blue (mortal) ∾ *er hat eine Mordsangst (einen Mordsbammel)*

funny a.: it's too ∾ for words *es ist unsagbar komisch (urkomisch);* the ∾-bone *der Musikantenknochen*

fur n.: ∾ and feather *Wild und Federwild*

furniture n.: the ∾ of one's mind *das geistige Rüstzeug;* the ∾ of his pocket *sein Geld;* the ∾ of my shelves *meine Bücher*

further I. adv.: I'll see you ∾ first *ich werde dir was husten (pfeifen).* — II. a.: till ∾ notice *bis auf weiteres;* ∾ particulars *weitere Einzelheiten, Näheres;* on the ∾ side *auf der entfernt liegenden Seite*

fury n.: to be in a ∾ *wütend sein;* to work like ∾ *wie toll arbeiten*

fuss n.: don't make (kick up) such a ∾ about it *mach' nicht soviel Aufhebens (Wesens, Getue) davon, mach' nicht so einen Sums (so ein Theater) darum*

fussy a.: he is a ∾ person, a fusspot *er ist ein Umstandskrämer*

future n.: there's no ∾ in it (sl.) *es ist eine undankbare Sache, es führt zu nichts*

G

gab n.: he has the gift of the ∾ *er hat ein gutes Mundwerk;* stop your ∾! (vulg.) *halte deinen Mund (Rand, Schnabel)!*

gad (colloq.) I. v.i.: she is always ∾ding about *sie ist ständig unterwegs.* — II. n.: to be on the ∾ *ständig unterwegs sein*

gadget n.: a ∾ *eine kleine Vorrichtung zu einem bestimmten Zweck*

gaff n. (sl.): to blow the ∾ (on a thing) *eine Sache verraten (verpetzen);* to stand the ∾ *etwas ruhig hinnehmen, ertragen*

gain I. v.tr.: to ∾ the day *den Sieg davontragen;* to ∾ the ear of a person *bei j.em Gehör finden;* to ∾ 5 pounds *fünf Pfund zunehmen;* to ∾ ground *(an) Boden gewinnen, vorrücken;* to ∾ the upper hand *die Oberhand gewinnen;* my watch ∾s 5 minutes a day *meine Uhr geht täglich fünf Minuten vor;* to ∾ a person over to a cause *j.en für eine Sache gewinnen.* — II. v.i.: to ∾ (up)on a person (thing) *bei der Verfolgung einer Person (Sache) näherkommen.* — III. n.: a clear ∾ *ein Reingewinn*

gall I. n.: it is ∾ and wormwood to him *es kränkt (wurmt) ihn;* to dip one's pen in ∾ *mit Erbitterung (boshaft) schreiben;* ∾ (sl.) *Frechheit.* — II. v.tr.: it ∾s him *es kränkt (wurmt) ihn*

gallery n.: to play to the ∾ *nach Effekt haschen*

gallows n.: to have a ∾ look (the ∾ in one's face) *ein Galgengesicht haben;* a ∾-bird *ein Galgenvogel*

galore I. adv.: there was meat and ale ∾ *es gab Fleisch und Bier in Hülle und Fülle.* — II. n.: in ∾ *in Hülle und Fülle*

game[1] I. n.: the ∾ is in your hand *du hast alle Karten (Trümpfe) in der Hand;* the ∾ is up *das Spiel ist aus, die Sache ist verloren;* so that's your little ∾! *das hast du also vor! darauf willst du also hinaus!;* the ∾ is not worth the candle *die Sache lohnt nicht;* to be fair ∾ *berechtigtem Angriff (Spott, berechtigter Kritik) unterliegen;* to be on (off) one's ∾ *in guter (schlechter) Form sein;* to beat a person at his own ∾ *j.en mit seinen eigenen Waffen schlagen;* to fly at higher ∾ *nach Höherem streben;* to give the ∾ away *das Geheimnis verraten;* to make ∾ of a thing *etwas zum besten halten, ins Lächerliche ziehen;* to play the ∾ *die Spielregeln beachten, mit ehrlichen Mitteln kämpfen;* to play a losing ∾ *ein verlorenes Spiel betreiben;* you are playing his ∾ *du förderst unabsichtlich (unbeabsichtigt) seine Pläne;* you can't try that ∾ on me *damit kommst du bei mir nicht durch;* big ∾ *Großwild;* a ∾-cock *ein Draufgänger, Kampfhahn;* ∾ laws *Jagdgesetze;* a ∾ licence *ein Jagdschein;* a ∾ keeper *ein Jagdhüter.* — II. v.tr.: to ∾ away money *Geld verspielen.* — III. v.i.: to ∾ for money *um Geld spielen*

game[2] a.: I am ∾ for a walk *ich bin bereit, spazieren zu gehen;* to die ∾ *kämpfend untergehen*

game[3] a.: he has a ∾ (gammy) leg *er hat ein lahmes Bein*

gander n.: what is sauce for the goose is sauce for the ∾ (prov.) *was dem einen recht ist, ist dem anderen billig*

gang up (sl.) v.i.: to ∾ with someone *sich mit j.em (zu einem bösen Zweck) verbinden*

gangway n.: members above (below) the ∾ *Parlamentsmitglieder, die mit der offiziellen Politik ihrer Partei einverstanden (nicht einverstanden) sind*

gaol n.: he is a ∾-bird *er ist ein Gewohnheitsverbrecher*

gap n.: to stop (to fill, to supply) a ∾ *eine Lücke ausfüllen;* to be a stop∾ *Lückenbüßer sein*

garden n.: a nursery ∾ *eine Baumschule;* to lead up the ∾ (path) (sl.) *irreführen*

garret n.: to be wrong in the ∾, to have one's ∾ unfurnished (sl.) *nicht richtig im Oberstübchen sein*

gas n.: (colloq.) he is a ∾-bag *er ist ein Schwätzer;* he lies like a ∾-meter *er lügt wie gedruckt;* to step on the ∾ (orig. U.S.) *Gas geben, sich beeilen*

gasp I. n.: to be at one's last ∾ *in den letzten Zügen liegen.* — II. v.i.: to ∾ for breath *nach Luft schnappen.* — III. v.tr.: to ∾ one's life away (out) *sein Leben aushauchen;* to ∾ out a word *ein Wort hervorkeuchen*

gate I. n.: between you and me and the ∾-post *im Vertrauen, unter uns gesagt;* the ∾ of horn, of ivory, see 'horn, ivory'; ∾-money *Eintrittsgeld (zum Fußballspiel).* — II. v.tr.: the undergraduate was ∾d *der Student erhielt Hausarrest*

gatecrash v.tr.: to ∾ a party *in eine Gesellschaft ohne Einladung eindringen;* to ∾ the South American market *den Südamerikanischen Markt erobern*

gather I. v.tr.: to ∾ one's breath *zu Atem kommen;* the complexion ∾s colour *die Haut gewinnt an Farbe;* he was ∾ed to his fathers *er wurde zu seinen Vätern versammelt, er starb;* to ∾ (up) from the ground *vom Boden aufheben;* to ∾ (in) the harvest *die Ernte einbringen;* to ∾ head *Kraft gewinnen, anschwellen;* to ∾ information *Erkundigungen einziehen;* a rolling stone ∾s no moss (prov.) *wälzender (rollender) Stein wird nicht moosig; ein unsteter Mensch kommt (bringt es) zu nichts;* to ∾ up a skirt *einen Rock aufraffen;* the invalid ∾s strength *der Kranke kommt zu Kräften;* to ∾ (up) strength for *Kräfte sammeln für;* to ∾ (up) one's thoughts *die Gedanken zusammennehmen;* the ship ∾s way *das Schiff kommt in Fahrt.* — II. v.i.: clouds are ∾ing *es ziehen Wolken auf;* the rumour ∾ed like a snowball *das Gerücht wuchs wie ein Schneeball;* to ∾ in a hall *sich in einem Saale versammeln;* to ∾ to a head *eitrig anschwellen;* to ∾ from the news *den Nachrichten entnehmen*

gathering n.: at a ∾ *auf einer Versammlung;* a ∾ on a finger *ein Geschwür am Finger*

gauntlet[1] n.: to fling (to throw) down the ∾ *den Fehdehandschuh hinwerfen;* to pick (to take) up the ∾ *die Herausforderung annehmen*

gauntlet[2] n.: to run the ∾ *Spießruten laufen*

gear n.: in, out of ∾ *im Gange; außer Betrieb, in Unordnung;* high (top) ∾ *höchster Gang;* low (bottom) ∾ *erster Gang;* to throw out of ∾ *in Unordnung bringen*

gen (sl.) I. n.: to give a person the ∾ *j.en über den Sachverhalt aufklären;* duff ∾ (phoney ∾; pukka ∾) *falsche (unzuverläßige; richtige) Auskunft.* — II. v.tr.: to be ∾ned up *gut informiert sein*

general I. a.: in ∾ *im allgemeinen;* in a ∾ way *in üblicher (gewöhnlicher) Weise;* the General Post Office *das Hauptpostamt;* the Post Master General *der Postminister;* a ∾ practitioner *ein praktischer Arzt;* a ∾ servant *ein Mädchen für alles.* — II. n.: 'twas caviare to the ∾ (Hamlet II, 2) *es war Kaviar für das Volk*

genial a.: it is a ∾ climate *es ist ein mildes Klima;* he is a ∾ man *er ist ein freundlicher, heiterer, geselliger Mensch*

gentle a.: the ∾ craft *das Angeln;* a ∾ heat *eine mäßige Hitze;* the ∾ reader *der geneigte Leser;* the ∾ sex *das zarte Geschlecht*

gentleman n.: the old ∾ (joc.) *der Teufel (scherzhaft);* a ∾'s agreement *ein Vertrag auf Treu und Glauben;* a ∾'s ∾ *ein Kammerdiener;* a ∾ at large *ein reicher Mann ohne Beruf*

get I. v.tr.: to ∾ the better of a person *j.en besiegen, übertreffen;* to ∾ the boot (sl.) *entlassen werden;* to ∾ with child *schwängern;* to ∾ a person to do a thing *j.en dazu bringen (kriegen), etwas zu tun;* to ∾ a thing done *etwas machen lassen, fertigmachen;* that ∾s my goat (colloq.) *das ärgert mich, da geht mir der Hut hoch;* to ∾ the hang of a thing *etwas begreifen, verstehen, wie eine Sache gemacht wird, den Dreh herauskriegen;* what has got him? *was ist mit ihm los?;* you will ∾ it! *du wirst etwas abbekommen, bestraft werden;* to ∾ it in the neck *hart mitgenommen, bestraft werden;* do you ∾ it? *hast du es verstanden, kapiert?;* we can ∾ it for you *wir können es Ihnen besorgen, beschaffen;* to ∾ knowledge (wind) of a thing *von etwas Kenntnis erhalten, Wind bekommen (krie-*

gen); to ∾ a living *den Lebensunterhalt verdienen;* that got me (colloq.) *das setzte mich in Verlegenheit;* to ∾ the mitten *einen Korb bekommen, abgewiesen werden;* to ∾ more than one bargained for *(nachteilig) mehr erhalten als erwartet oder erbeten wurde;* I haven't got a penny *ich besitze keinen Pfennig;* to ∾ a person a place *j.em eine Stelle besorgen;* to ∾ a parcel ready *ein Paket fertigmachen;* to ∾ religion (vulg. or facet.) *fromm werden, sich bekehren;* to ∾ the sack *fristlos entlassen werden;* to ∾ one's way *seinen Willen bekommen;* to ∾ no change out of a person *von j.em die erwünschte Auskunft nicht erhalten;* to ∾ the worst of it *besiegt werden, den kürzeren ziehen, am schlimmsten dabei wegkommen (fahren);* I got my wrist dislocated *ich verstauchte mir das Handgelenk.* — with adv.: he got his jokes across (over) *er hatte Erfolg mit seinen Witzen;* to ∾ one's own (some of one's own) back *sich rächen;* to ∾ one's second wind *wieder zu Atem kommen, neue Kraft gewinnen;* to ∾ a thing down *etwas herunterholen;* to ∾ one's hand in *mit etwas vertraut werden, sich einarbeiten;* to ∾ one's teeth into a thing *eine Sache (Unternehmung) feste anpacken;* to ∾ a word in edgeways *ein Wort anbringen, zu Wort kommen;* to ∾ a thing off by heart *etwas auswendig lernen;* to ∾ one's daughters off *seine Töchter an den Mann bringen;* I can't ∾ the lid off *ich kann den Deckel nicht los-, aufkriegen;* ∾ a move on! (sl.) *los! dalli!;* to ∾ a thing out *etwas herausbekommen, -kriegen;* to ∾ a thing over *etwas hinüberbringen, -heben, -kriegen, etwas hinter sich bringen;* to ∾ a bill through *einen Gesetzesantrag durchbringen;* to ∾ things together *Sachen zusammenbringen, -kriegen;* to ∾ a fire under *eine Feuersbrunst bezwingen, unterkriegen;* it is well got up *es ist gut aufgemacht;* to ∾ a person's back (monkey) up *j.en erbosen, aufregen, reizen;* to ∾ up a part *eine Rolle studieren;* to ∾ up steam *in Fahrt kommen, sich ins Zeug legen;* to ∾ the wind up (sl.) *Angst (Dampf) bekommen;* to ∾ a person wrong *j.en falsch verstehen.* — **II.** v.i.: to ∾ cracking (weaving) (sl.) *mit einer Arbeit anfangen;* to ∾ done with a thing *etwas zu Ende führen, etwas loswerden;* it has got to be done *es muß gemacht werden;* to ∾ engaged, married *sich verloben, sich verheiraten;* to ∾ killed, shot, wounded, etc., *getötet, erschossen, verwundet, usw. werden;* to ∾ to know a thing *etwas kennenlernen;* one ∾s to like it *man kommt dazu, es gern zu haben;* to ∾ quit (rid) of a thing *etwas loswerden;* to ∾ ready *sich fertigmachen;* to ∾ talking *ins Gespräch kommen;* to ∾ tired, wet, hungry, etc., *müde, naß, hungrig usw. werden;* to ∾ used to a thing *sich an etwas gewöhnen;* a ∾-rich-quick type *einer, der schnell reich werden will.* — with prep.: to ∾ at a person *j.en angreifen; bestechen; zum besten halten;* to ∾ at a thing *an etwas kommen, etwas erreichen; etwas heraus bekommen, erfahren;* what are you ∾ting at? *worauf willst du hinaus? worauf spielst du an?;* ∾-at-able *erreichbar, zugänglich;* to ∾ behind a thing *hinter etwas kommen, sich stellen;* to ∾ down to bedrock (to brass tacks) *auf die Hauptsache (zur Sache) kommen;* to ∾ into a car *in ein Auto steigen;* to ∾ into a habit *sich etwas angewöhnen;* to ∾ into a rage *in Wut geraten, wütend werden;* to ∾ off a horse *vom Pferde steigen;* ∾ off the grass! *herunter vom Rasen!;* to ∾ off an obligation *von einer Verpflichtung loskommen;* to tell a person where he ∾s off (sl.) *j.em gehörig, gründlich Bescheid sagen;* to ∾ on a horse *zu (aufs) Pferd steigen, ein Pferd besteigen;* to ∾ on a person's nerves *j.em auf die Nerven fallen;* to ∾ out of bed on the wrong side *mit dem falschen (linken) Bein aufstehen, übelgelaunt sein;* to ∾ out of one's depth *den Boden unter den Füßen verlieren, sich vor einer zu schwierigen Aufgabe sehen;* to ∾ out of a habit *sich (dat.) etwas abgewöhnen;* to ∾ over (round) a difficulty *eine Schwierigkeit überwinden (meistern);* to ∾ over a loss *einen Verlust verschmerzen;* to ∾ over a wall *über eine Mauer klettern;* to ∾ round a person *j.en beschwatzen, herumkriegen;* to ∾ through an examination *eine Prüfung bestehen;* to ∾ to a place, to ∾ to bed *an einen Ort gelangen, ins Bett kommen;* to ∾ up to page 20 *bis Seite 20 kommen;* to ∾ upon a subject *auf ein Thema zu sprechen kommen;* to ∾ to work *sich an die Arbeit machen;* where has it got to? *wo steckt es bloß?* — with adv.: see 'about, abroad, ahead, along, away, back'; to ∾ across with a thing *mit einer Sache Eindruck machen (Erfolg haben);* to ∾ behind *zurückbleiben, sich dahinterstellen;* to ∾ by with a thing *mit etwas durchkommen;*

to ∾ down *hinunter-, absteigen;* to ∾ down to business, brass tacks, see 'business, tack'; we must ∾ down to it *wir müssen uns darangeben, -machen;* to ∾ in *hineinkommen, gewählt werden;* to ∾ nowhere *nichts erreichen;* to ∾ off *absteigen;* to ∾ off with a fine *mit einer Geldstrafe davonkommen;* to ∾ off with a girl (colloq.) *mit einem Mädel anbändeln;* to ∾ on *Fortschritte machen, vorwärts-, weiterkommen;* how are you ∾ting on? *wie geht's dir?;* ∾ on or ∾ out! *entweder du arbeitest, oder du fliegst hinaus!;* ∾ on with you! (colloq.) *Unsinn! dummes Zeug!;* he is ∾ting on for seventy *er geht auf die siebzig;* I'm trying to ∾ on to him *ich versuche, ihn telefonisch zu erreichen;* to ∾ on with a person *mit j.em gut auskommen;* to ∾ on without a thing *ohne etwas auskommen;* ∾ out (colloq.) *fort mit dir! Unsinn!;* to ∾ out *aussteigen;* I got over safely *ich kam sicher hinüber;* the patient got round *der Patient erholte sich;* to ∾ there (sl.) *Erfolg haben;* he got through *er bestand die Prüfung, er kam durch;* I got through to him *ich erreichte ihn telefonisch;* to ∾ together *sich versammeln, zusammenkommen;* to ∾ up *aufstehen;* to make one's ∾away *fliehen, entkommen*

ghost n.: to give (to yield) up the ∾ *den Geist aufgeben;* to raise (to lay) a ∾ *einen Geist beschwören (bannen);* he hasn't the ∾ of a chance *er hat nicht die geringste Aussicht;* a ∾ writer *ein Lohnschreiber, dessen Arbeit unter dem Namen seines Auftraggebers erscheint*

G. I. n.: a ∾ (abbr. Government Issue) *ein Soldat der USA*

gift n.: he has the ∾ of the gab *er hat ein gutes Mundwerk;* the living is in the ∾ of the squire *der Gutsbesitzer verleiht die Pfründe;* I would not have it at a ∾ *ich möchte es nicht geschenkt haben;* to look a ∾-horse in the mouth *einem geschenkten Gaul ins Maul sehen*

gild v.tr.: to ∾ the pill *die (bittere) Pille versüßen*

gill n.: to look rosy about the ∾s *gesund aussehen*

gilt n.: to take the ∾ off the gingerbread *einer Sache den Glanz (die Anziehungskraft) rauben*

gimmick n. (sl.): a ∾ *eine Idee (ein Kniff), um ein Geschäft einträglicher zu machen; eine praktische Vorrichtung* (see: gadget)

gird v.tr.: to ∾ (up) one's loins (1.Kings XVIII, 46) *sich innerlich auf eine Unternehmung vorbereiten*

gist n.: the ∾ of the matter *des Pudels Kern*

give I. v.tr.: see 'air[2], back, battle, etc.'; the thermometer ∾s 80° *das Thermometer zeigt 80°;* an analysis ∾s the following figures *eine Analyse ergibt die folgenden Zahlen;* to ∾ as good as one gets *eine passende Antwort erteilen, einen Gegenschlag führen;* ∾n health, the thing can be done *Gesundheit vorausgesetzt, kann die Sache gemacht werden;* I gave it him hot *ich habe ihn gehörig verprügelt, es ihm ordentlich gesteckt;* I gave him a piece of my mind *ich habe ihm gehörig meine Meinung gesagt;* ∾ it a rest! (sl.) *hör' auf, davon zu reden!;* to ∾ something (someone) the go-by (sl.) *einer Sache (j.em) aus dem Wege gehen;* I ∾ you the ladies *ich trinke auf das Wohl der Damen;* all right, I ∾ you that *na schön, das gebe ich zu;* ∾ me the good old times *da lobe ich mir die guten alten Zeiten;* to ∾ a person what for (sl.) *es j.em gründlich stecken, ihm tüchtig den Kopf waschen, ihn gehörig verprügeln.* — with prep.: to ∾ in charge, marriage, see 'charge, marriage'; to ∾ into custody *verhaften lassen;* to ∾ a book to the world *ein Buch veröffentlichen.* — with adv.: to ∾ oneself away *sich verraten;* to ∾ away the show *das Geheimnis (die Sache) verraten;* to ∾ forth *von sich geben; aussprechen, veröffentlichen;* to ∾ in a report *einen Bericht einreichen;* to ∾ off heat *Hitze ausstrahlen;* to ∾ oneself out as (for) a benefactor *sich als Wohltäter ausgeben;* to ∾ oneself up *sich freiwillig stellen;* to ∾ oneself up to a thing *sich einer Sache hingeben;* to ∾ up a person (thing) *j.en (eine Sache) verloren geben, aufgeben.* — **II.** v.i.: a thing ∾s *ein Ding gibt nach (ist elastisch, federt).* — with prep.: the passage ∾s into the yard *der Gang führt auf den Hof;* the door ∾s (up)on (on to) the hall *die Tür führt auf die Diele;* the windows ∾ (up)on (on to) the garden *die Fenster gehen auf den Garten.* — with adv.: to ∾ in to a person *j.em nachgeben;* provisions gave out *die*

Lebensmittel gingen aus (zu Ende, wurden alle); to ~ over doing a thing *aufhören, etwas zu tun;* to ~ up *aufgeben, aufhören.* — **III.** n.: there is no ~ in a stone floor *ein Steinboden federt nicht;* a ~ and take *ein gegenseitiges Zugeständnis; ein Wortwechsel*

gizzard n.: (colloq.) to fret one's ~ *sich quälen, sich ärgern;* that sticks in my ~ *das liegt mir schwer im Magen, ist mir zuwider*

glad a.: I am ~ of it *ich freue mich darüber;* to give a person the ~ eye (sl.) *j.em einen verliebten Blick zuwerfen;* he donned his ~ rags (sl.) *er warf sich in gute Kluft;* to give someone the ~ hand *j.en willkommen heißen*

glance I. v.i.: to ~ aside, off *abgleiten;* to ~ (one's eye) at a thing *einen kurzen Blick auf etwas werfen;* to ~ (one's eye) over a page *eine Seite überfliegen, flüchtig durchlesen.* — **II.** n.: at a ~, at first ~ *auf den ersten Blick;* to take a ~ at a thing *einen kurzen Blick auf etwas werfen*

glass n.: a looking-~ *ein Spiegel;* a pair of ~es *eine Brille;* to raise one's ~ to a person *auf j.es Wohl trinken*

glimpse n.: to catch a ~ of a thing *etwas flüchtig zu sehen bekommen*

glove n.: to be hand in ~ with a person *mit j.em ein Herz und eine Seele sein;* to fit like a ~ *wie angegossen passen (sitzen);* to handle without ~s *nicht mit Glacéhandschuhen anfassen;* to take off the ~s *Ernst machen;* to throw down (to take up) the ~ *j.en zum Kampf herausfordern, den Fehdehandschuh hinwerfen; den Fehdehandschuh aufnehmen, die Herausforderung annehmen*

glow n.: to be in a (all of a) ~ *ganz erhitzt sein, vor Erregung glühen*

gnat n.: to strain at a ~ (cf. Matth. XXIII, 24) *ein Kleinigkeitskrämer sein*

go I. v.i.: see 'bad, bang, blind, cheap, etc.'; the sovereign (dollar) ~es anywhere *das Pfund (der Dollar) wird überall angenommen;* ~ as you please! *keine Einschränkungen, keine Regeln (Vorschriften)!;* ~ like this with your left foot *mach' diese Bewegung mit deinem linken Fuß;* his tongue ~es nineteen to the dozen *er schwatzt unaufhörlich (das Blaue vom Himmel herunter);* I am ~ing to do it tomorrow *ich werde es morgen tun;* are any cigarettes ~ing? *sind Zigaretten zu haben?;* my sight is ~ing *meine Augen werden schlecht;* it is a ~ing concern *es ist ein gut gehendes Unternehmen;* he is ~ing fifteen *er ist im fünfzehnten Lebensjahre;* the ~ing was good *der Boden (die Bahn) war gut; es wurde flott gelaufen;* to ~ while the ~ing is good *sich davonmachen, bevor etwas schiefgeht;* the play is still ~ing strong (sl.) *das Stück zieht immer noch;* he is ~ing strong (sl.) *es geht ihm gut;* he is the greatest rascal ~ing *er ist der größte Schurke, den es gibt;* ~ing! ~ing! gone! *(bei Versteigerungen) zum ersten! zum zweiten! zum dritten!;* be gone! *geh weg! scher dich fort!;* dead and gone *tot und dahin;* a gone case *ein hoffnungs-, aussichtsloser Fall;* too far gone *zu verdorben, in hoffnungslosem Zustand;* six months gone with child *im siebenten Monat schwanger;* now you've been and gone and done it! (vulg.) *da hast du etwas Nettes angerichtet!;* he is a goner (colloq.) *er ist ruiniert, ein Kind des Todes;* here ~es! *na, dann los!;* ~ it! *los, toi, toi!;* ~ easy *nicht so eilig!* — with prep.: ~ about your business *kümmere dich um deine Angelegenheiten, scher' dich weg!;* to ~ about one's work *sich an die Arbeit machen, arbeiten;* to ~ at a person (thing) *j.en angreifen, etwas in Angriff nehmen;* let it ~ at that *laß es dabei bewenden;* to ~ back on someone, on one's word (promise) *j.en verraten, im Stich lassen; sein Wort (Versprechen) widerrufen;* to ~ behind a decision *die Gründe einer Entscheidung untersuchen; eine Entscheidung umgehen;* to let the arrangement ~ by the board *die Einrichtung (das Abkommen) fallen lassen;* to ~ by the name of N. *unter dem Namen N. bekannt sein, den Namen N. führen;* to ~ by rail *mit der Bahn fahren;* to ~ by a rule *sich an eine Regel halten;* the money has gone down the drain (colloq.) *das Geld ist vergeudet (aus dem Fenster geworfen) worden;* to ~ for a doctor *einen Arzt holen;* he could ~ for an Englishman *er könnte als Engländer gelten;* it ~es for nothing *es gilt als nichts;* to ~ for a person (sl.) *j.en angreifen;* to ~ for a ride, row, walk, see 'ride, row, walk'; to ~ from strength to strength (Psalms, LXXXIV, 7) *sich (seine Lage, seinen Ruf) mit jedem Schritt verbessern;* to ~ hat in hand *einen Bittgang machen;* to ~ into hysterics *einen* *hysterischen Anfall bekommen;* to ∾ into a matter *eine Angelegenheit untersuchen;* to ∾ into mourning *Trauer anlegen;* to ∾ into a flat spin (sl.) *durchgedreht werden;* to ∾ off one's head *verrückt werden;* to ∾ off (at) the deep end *sich über etwas aufregen;* to ∾ on an errand *einen Gang tun;* to ∾ on a journey *eine Reise machen;* to ∾ on the parish *der Gemeinde zur Last fallen;* to be gone on a person (sl.) *in j.en verliebt (vernarrt) sein;* to ∾ on the streets *Prostituierte werden, auf den Strich gehen;* to ∾ on strike *die Arbeit niederlegen, in den Ausstand treten, streiken;* to ∾ all out on something (colloq.) *fest auf etwas bauen;* to ∾ out of fashion *aus der Mode kommen;* it has gone out of my head *es ist meinem Gedächtnis entschwunden;* he has gone out of his mind *er ist verrückt geworden;* to ∾ out of the (one's) way to do a thing *sich (dat.) besondere Mühe geben, etwas zu tun;* to ∾ over the details *die Einzelheiten überprüfen;* to ∾ over the top (bags) *aus dem Schützengraben zum Angriff vorgehen;* to ∾ through a difficult time *eine schwere Zeit durchmachen;* to ∾ through the motions of being sorry *tun, als ob man traurig sei, Traurigkeit heucheln;* to ∾ to the bad (the country, dogs, stool, wall) see 'bad, etc.'; to ∾ to pieces *in Stücke gehen, auseinanderfallen, versagen;* I have nothing to ∾ upon *ich habe keine Unterlagen;* to ∾ with a person *j.en begleiten; es mit j.em halten;* to ∾ with a thing *zu etwas passen;* that ∾es without saying *das versteht sich von selbst, das ist selbstverständlich.* — with adv.: see 'about, ahead, along, back, down, far'; to ∾ between *vermitteln;* to let a day ∾ by *einen Tag vorübergehen (verstreichen) lassen;* to give a person (something) the ∾-by *j.en ignorieren, schneiden; (j.em) einer Sache aus dem Wege gehen;* to ∾ in for a thing *sich mit einer Sache befassen, sich auf etwas legen;* to ∾ off *ab-, losgehen, explodieren; bewußtlos werden; schlecht werden, verderben;* to ∾ off with a bang *mit lautem Knall explodieren;* to ∾ off well, badly *Erfolg, Mißerfolg haben;* ∾ on! (colloq.) *Unsinn! Quatsch!;* to ∾ on doing (or: with) a thing *fortfahren, etwas zu tun;* to ∾ on shamefully *sich schändlich betragen;* he is ∾ing on for sixty *er geht auf die sechzig;* strange ∾ings-on *seltsame Vorkommnisse, seltsames Benehmen;* to ∾ all out to achieve a thing *die größten Anstrengungen machen (alles hergeben), um etwas zu erreichen;* the meat won't ∾ round *das Fleisch reicht nicht für alle;* to ∾ through with a thing *etwas zu Ende führen;* these colours don't ∾ together *diese Farben passen nicht zueinander, diese Farben beißen sich;* prices are ∾ing up *die Preise steigen;* when did you ∾ up? *wann gingst du zur Universität?* — **II.** v.tr.: see 'bail, better, errand, halves, hog, length, pace, shares, way'; to ∾ places (sl.) *viel herumkommen, viel unternehmen;* to ∾ it strong (sl.) *entschlossen auftreten.* — **III.** n. (colloq.): it is all (quite) the ∾ *es ist die große Mode;* it's no ∾ *es ist nichts zu machen;* it was a near ∾ for us *wir sind mit knapper Not daran vorbeigekommen;* at one ∾ *beim ersten Versuch; in einem Strich, Zug;* what a rum ∾! *welch sonderbare Geschichte!;* to be on the ∾ *in Bewegung sein;* to be full of ∾ *voller Tatkraft, mit Energie geladen sein;* to have a ∾ at a thing *etwas versuchen;* from the word ∾! *von Anfang an;* a ∾-getter (sl.) *ein Streber*

goat n.: that gets my ∾ (sl.) *das ärgert mich; da geht mir der Hut hoch;* to play the giddy ∾ *sich albern benehmen*

God n.: ∾ bless me, my life, my soul! *du meine Güte! du lieber Himmel!;* ∾ forbid! *Gott bewahre!;* my good ∾! *du großer Gott!;* grant ∾! *Gott gebe!;* so help me ∾! *so wahr mir Gott helfe!;* thank ∾! *Gott sei dank!;* would to ∾ it were true! *wollte Gott, es wäre wahr!;* ∾'s truth *die reine Wahrheit;* ∾ willing *so Gott will;* godfather, godmother *Pate, Patin;* it was a perfect godsend *es war ein wahrer Segen;* to bid a person godspeed *j.em glückliche Reise wünschen*

gold n.: all that glitters (glisters) is not ∾ (prov.) *es ist nicht alles Gold, was glänzt;* the child is as good as ∾ *das Kind ist kreuzbrav;* he is worth his weight in ∾ *er ist nicht mit Gold zu bezahlen (aufzuwiegen);* to sell a person a ∾ brick (sl.) *j.en mit etwas anschmieren;* to set in ∾ *in Gold fassen;* a ∾-digger *eine habsüchtige Frau, eine Ramschliesel*

golden a.: a ∾ key opens every lock (prov.) *mit Gold kommt man überall durch;* the ∾ mean *der goldene Mittelweg;* to win ∾ opinions *hohe Anerkennung finden;* to miss a ∾ opportunity *eine günstige Gelegenheit verpassen;* the ∾ stick in waiting *der Oberst der königlichen Leibgarde im Dienst*

good I. a.: a ∾ deal *viel, ein gut Teil, eine Menge;* ∾ God! ∾ gracious! ∾ heavens! ∾ Lord! *du lieber Gott! du lieber Himmel! du meine Güte!;* a ∾ many *ziemlich viel(e);* that's a ∾ 'un (sl.) *das ist eine Lüge, die sich lohnt;* to be as ∾ as a play *sehr unterhaltend (amüsant) sein;* to be ∾ at a thing *tüchtig (geschickt) in etwas sein;* to be ∾ for a long walk *zu einem langen Spaziergang Lust haben;* to be ∾ for any sum *für irgendeine Summe gut sein;* he is a ∾-for-nothing *er ist ein Tunichtgut (Taugenichts);* to have ∾ luck *viel Glück haben;* to have the ∾ sense to do a thing *so klug (gescheit) sein, etwas zu tun;* to have a ∾ time *sich amüsieren;* to hold (to stand) ∾ *noch gelten, gültig sein;* he made ∾ *er bewährte sich;* he made ∾ his flight *er bewerkstelligte seine Flucht;* he made ∾ my loss *er vergütete (ersetzte) mir meinen Verlust;* he made ∾ his promise *er hielt sein Versprechen;* to say a ∾ word for a person *für j.en ein gutes Wort einlegen;* to see ∾ to do a thing *für gut befinden, etwas zu tun;* ∾ egg! (sl.) *das ist glücklich!;* ∾ for you! *das hast du fein gemacht!;* (in) ∾ form *schicklich;* a ∾ life (Insurance) *Aussichten auf eine lange Lebensdauer;* she's a ∾ looker (colloq.) *sie ist hübsch;* he's a ∾ mixer *er ist ein guter Gesellschafter;* to throw ∾ money after bad *gutes Geld faulem nachwerfen;* he's a ∾ sort *er ist ein anständiger Kerl;* all in ∾ time *alles zu seiner Zeit!* — **II.** n.: what is the ∾ of it? what ∾ is it? *was hat es für einen Zweck? was nützt es?;* it's all to the ∾ *umso besser;* to be some (any, much, no) ∾ *Zweck, viel Zweck, keinen Zweck haben;* to be ten pounds to the ∾ *zehn Pfund guthaben;* to be up to (after) no ∾ *Unfug treiben;* it came to no ∾ *es verdarb, es wurde nichts daraus;* to leave a country for ∾, for ∾ and all *ein Land für immer verlassen;* you are a nice piece of ∾s! *du bist mir eine nette Person!;* he has delivered the ∾s *er hat seinen Teil der Abmachung erfüllt;* that's the ∾s (sl.) *das ist das Richtige*

goodness n.: ∾ gracious! *du lieber Himmel!;* ∾ knows where he is! *weiß der Himmel, wo er steckt!;* for ∾' sake *um Himmels willen;* my ∾! *du meine Güte!;* thank ∾! *Gott sei Dank!;* I wish to ∾ he would go! *wenn er doch um Himmels willen ginge!*

goofy a. (sl.): to be ∾ *dumm, blöde sein*

goose n.: all his geese are swans (prov.) *jedem Narren gefällt seine Kappe; bei ihm ist immer alles besser als bei andern;* what is sauce for the ∾ is sauce for the gander (prov.) *was dem einen recht ist, ist dem anderen billig;* a tailor's ∾ *ein Bügeleisen;* to swim like a tailor's ∾ *untergehen, wie eine bleierne Ente schwimmen;* it was a wild-∾ chase *es war ein vergebliches Bemühen, ein lächerliches (fruchtloses) Unternehmen;* to cook a person's ∾ *j.en erledigen, ihm den Garaus machen;* to kill the ∾ that lays the golden eggs *das Huhn schlachten, das die goldenen Eier legt;* he can't (daren't) say Bo to a ∾ *er ist äußerst scheu und ängstlich, er tut den Mund nicht auf;* to shoe a ∾ *etwas Törichtes (Zweckloses) unternehmen;* the ∾-step *der langsame Schritt, Parademarsch;* ∾flesh *Gänsehaut*

gooseberry n.: as green as a ∾ *völlig unerfahren, ein Grünschnabel;* like old ∾ (sl.) *wie ein Donnerwetter;* to play ∾ *Anstandsdame, -wauwau spielen;* to play old ∾ with a person (sl.) *j.em gehörig mitspielen, j.en hart mitnehmen*

gorge n.: my ∾ rises at the thought *mir wird übel (mir kommt es hoch) bei dem Gedanken;* to cast the ∾ at a thing *etwas mit Ekel (Widerwillen) zurückweisen*

gospel n.: ∾ truth *reine Wahrheit;* to take a thing for ∾ *etwas für ein (für's) Evangelium, für bare Münze nehmen*

governor n.: how's your ∾? (sl.) *wie geht's deinem alten Herrn?*

gown n.: town and ∾ *Bürgerschaft und Universität*

grab n.: to have the ∾ on (sl.) *sehr im Vorteil sein*

grace n.: in the year of ∾ *im Jahre des Heils;* to be in a person's good ∾s *bei j.em in Gunst stehen, gut angeschrieben sein, einen Stein im Brett haben;* he did it with a good (bad) ∾ *er tat es willig, unwillig;* he gave him a year's ∾ *er gewährte ihm ein Jahr Aufschub;* he gave himself airs and ∾s *er tat sehr vornehm, er spielte sich auf;* will you have the ∾ to do so? *willst du so anständig sein, es zu tun?;* to say ∾ *das*

Tischgebet sprechen; to take heart of ∾ *sich ein Herz fassen, Mut fassen*

gracious int.: good ∾! my ∾! ∾ me! ∾ goodness! *gütiger Himmel! ach du meine Güte!*

grade n.: he is on the up (down) ∾ *es geht mit ihm bergauf, -ab;* to make the ∾ *Erfolg haben*

grain n.: it goes against the ∾ with me *es geht mir gegen (wider) den Strich*

grand a.: a ∾ piano *ein Flügel;* the ∾ total *die Schluß-, Endsumme;* to do the ∾ (colloq.) *sich aufspielen, den Feinen herausbeißen, angeben*

grandmother I. n.: to teach one's ∾ to suck eggs *einer erfahrenen Person Rat erteilen, das Ei will klüger sein als die Henne.* — II. v.tr.: to ∾ a person *j.en verhätscheln;* to ∾ the cups *das Ausgleiten der Tassen durch Anfeuchten der Untertassen verhindern*

grant v.tr.: God (heaven) ∾ that *gebe Gott (der Himmel), daß;* I ∾ you that *das gebe ich zu;* to take a thing for ∾ed *etwas als (für) ausgemacht (selbstverständlich, erwiesen) annehmen*

grass I. n.: to be at ∾ *auf der Weide sein; ohne Arbeit sein, feiern;* he does not let the ∾ grow under his feet *er verliert keine Zeit bei der Ausführung einer Sache;* to put (to send, to turn out) to ∾ *auf die Weide treiben;* to send (to go) to ∾ *zu Boden schlagen (geschlagen werden);* a ∾ widow *eine Strohwitwe.* — II. v.tr.: to ∾ a bird *einen Vogel abschießen;* to ∾ a fish *einen Fisch ans Land bringen;* to ∾ an opponent *einen Gegner zu Boden schlagen*

grate v.i.: a false note ∾s upon my ear *ein falscher Ton beleidigt mein Ohr*

grease [gri:s] I. n.: in ∾ (in pride, prime of ∾) *fett, schlachtreif;* to let a person stew in his own ∾ *j.en in seinem eigenen Fett schmoren lassen, ihn seinem Schicksal überlassen.* — II. [gri:z] v.tr.: to ∾ a person's palm *j.en bestechen, schmieren;* like ∾d lightning *wie ein geölter Blitz;* to ∾ the wheels *dazu beitragen, daß alles reibungslos abläuft*

Greats n.: to read ∾ *klassische Philologie in Oxford studieren*

Greek n.: when ∾ meets ∾ (then comes the tug of war) *wenn zwei, die einander gewachsen sind, sich treffen;* that is ∾ to me *das sind mir böhmische Dörfer;* on the ∾ calends *an einem Tag, der nie kommen wird, niemals, am Nimmermehrstag*

green I. a.: as ∾ as a gooseberry *völlig unerfahren, ein Grünschnabel;* the ∾-eyed monster (Othello, III, 1) *die Eifersucht;* a ∾ old age *ein blühendes Greisenalter;* the ∾-room *das Künstlerzimmer.* — II. n.: she has ∾ fingers *sie ist eine geschickte Blumengärtnerin;* do you see any ∾ in my eye? *glaubst du, ich wäre so leichtgläubig? hältst du mich für so grün?;* a ∾-horn *ein Neuling, ein unerfahrener Mensch;* ∾s *Kohlgemüse;* ∾ backs *U.S. Papiergeld.* — III. adv.: to keep someone's memory ∾ *j.en in Erinnerung behalten, nicht in Vergessenheit geraten lassen*

gremlin n.: a ∾ *ein böser Geist, der für wiederholte Unglücksfälle (z. B. in einem Hause) verantwortlich gemacht wird*

grey, gray a.: the ∾ mare is the better horse *die Frau hat die Hosen an*

grief n.: to come to ∾ *verunglücken, zu Schaden kommen*

grig n.: as merry (lively) as a ∾ *kreuzfidel, quietschvergnügt*

grim a.: to hold on like ∾ death *(sich) krampfhaft festhalten*

grin I. v.i.: to ∾ and bear it *gute Miene zum bösen Spiel machen;* to ∾ like a Cheshire cat (Alice in Wonderland) *ständig und sinnlos grinsen.* — II. n.: to be on the broad ∾ *von einem Ohr zum andern grinsen*

grind I. v.tr.: to have an axe to ∾ *Privatinteressen verfolgen;* to ∾ the faces of the poor *die Armen aussaugen;* to ∾ one's teeth *mit den Zähnen knirschen;* to ∾ down *feinmahlen;* to ∾ out an oath *zähneknirschend fluchen;* to hold (to keep) a person's nose to the ∾stone *j.en ununterbrochen arbeiten (schwer schuften) lassen.* — II. v.i.: to ∾ for an examination *für eine Prüfung ochsen (büffeln).* — III. n.: it was an awful ∾ *es war eine furchtbare Plackerei*

grip n.: to be at ∾s with *im Kampfe stehen mit, handgemein sein;* to come to ∾s with a person *handgemein werden;* to come to ∾s with a problem *sich mit einem Problem auseinandersetzen;* he has a good ∾ of his subject *er beherrscht seinen Stoff*

grist n.: all is ∾ that comes to his mill *er weiß, aus allem Vorteil zu ziehen;* that brings ∾ to his mill *das ist Wasser auf seine Mühle*

grit n.: he is a man of ∾ *er ist ein mutiger, charakterfester Mann*

grope v.tr.: to ∾ one's way *seinen Weg tastend suchen*

ground I. n.: here I am on my own ∾ *auf diesem Gebiet fühle ich mich sicher;* the inquiry covers much ∾ *die Untersuchung erstreckt sich über (umfaßt) ein weites Gebiet;* to break fresh ∾ *ein neues Gebiet erschließen;* to cut the ∾ from under a person's feet *j.em die Argumente vorwegnehmen;* the habit, the idea is gaining (losing) ∾ *die Gewohnheit, die Idee gewinnt (verliert) an Boden;* to go over the ∾ *etwas überlegen, besprechen;* to hold (to stand) one's ∾ *sich behaupten, standhalten, nicht nachgeben;* to shift one's ∾ *seinen Standpunkt ändern;* that suits me down to the ∾ *das paßt mir in jeder Hinsicht (ausgezeichnet);* to be let in (to come in) on the ∾-floor *die Möglichkeit haben, sich an einem Geschäftsunternehmen unter den gleichen Bedingungen wie die Begründer zu beteiligen.* — **II.** v.tr.: to ∾ an airplane *einem Flugzeug Startverbot erteilen;* to ∾ the aerial *die Antenne erden;* to ∾ arms *das Gewehr absetzen;* to ∾ a belief on a fact *einen Glauben auf eine Tatsache gründen;* to ∾ a person in the elements of mathematics *j.em die Anfangsgründe der Mathematik gründlich beibringen;* to ∾ a ship *ein Schiff auflaufen lassen.* — **III.** v.i.: the ship ∾ed *das Schiff lief auf*

grouse v.i.: to ∾ about a thing (sl.) *über etwas meckern*

grow I. v.i.: to ∾ old, weary, etc. *alt, müde usw. werden;* bad habits ∾ on one *schlechte Gewohnheiten werden einem zur zweiten Natur;* the picture ∾s on me *mir gefällt das Bild immer besser;* to ∾ up *aufwachsen;* the ∾n-ups *die Erwachsenen.* — **II.** v.tr.: to ∾ a beard *sich (dat.) einen Bart wachsen (stehen) lassen*

grudge I. n.: to bear (to have) a ∾ against a person; to bear (to owe) a person a ∾ *einen Groll auf j.en haben, j.em etwas nachtragen; j.en auf dem Strich haben.* — **II.** v.tr.: to ∾ no pains *sich durch keine Mühe verdrießen lassen;* not to ∾ doing something *etwas recht gern tun*

gruel n.: to get (to have, to take) one's ∾ (a ∾ling) *eine schwere Strafe oder Niederlage erleiden*

Grundy n.pr.: what will Mrs. ∾ say? *was werden die prüden Leute (die Spießer) dazu sagen?;* she doesn't care for Mrs. ∾ *sie fragt nicht nach dem Gerede der Leute*

guard I. n.: to be on (to keep) ∾ *auf Wache sein, Wache halten (stehen);* to be on (off) one's ∾ *auf der (nicht auf der) Hut sein;* to go on (to mount) ∾ *auf Wache ziehen;* to put a person on his ∾ *j.en warnen;* to put (to throw) a person off his ∾ *j.en überraschen, -rumpeln.* — **II.** v.tr.: to ∾ a person from (against) a thing *j.en vor etwas schützen;* he spoke in ∾ed terms *er drückte sich vorsichtig aus.* — **III.** v.i.: to ∾ against infection *sich vor Ansteckung schützen*

guinea-pig n.: a ∾ *ein Versuchskaninchen (auch von einem Menschen gesagt)*

gum n.: to be up a ∾-tree (sl.) *in der Klemme sein, weder ein noch aus wissen*

gun n.: he is a great ∾ *er ist eine große Kanone;* as sure as a ∾ *todsicher;* to blow great ∾s *gewaltig stürmen;* to stand (to stick) to one's ∾s *festbleiben; durch-, aushalten;* ∾-running *Waffenschmuggel*

gut I. n.: it has no ∾s in it *es steckt nichts dahinter, es ist wertlos;* he has no ∾s (sl.) *er hat keinen Mut (Schneid).* — **II.** v.tr.: the warehouse was ∾ted *das Lagerhaus war völlig ausgebrannt*

guy n. (U.S. sl.): to do a ∾ *sich aus dem Staube machen;* to give the ∾ to a person *j.em ausreißen;* he's a great ∾ *er ist ein anständiger Kerl*

H

habit n.: a ∾ of mind *eine Geistesverfassung;* a man of corpulent (spare) ∾ *ein beleibter (magerer) Mann;* he is in (has fallen [got, grown] into, has taken to), the (a) ∾, he has caught (formed, made) a ∾ of doing it *er hat es sich (dat.) angewöhnt, er pflegt, es zu tun;* to break a person of a ∾ *j.em etwas abgewöhnen;* to get out of a ∾ *sich (dat.) etwas abgewöhnen*

hackle n.: a cock (a dog, a man) with his ∾s up *ein kampflustiger Hahn (Hund, Mensch)*

haemorrhage n.: he has the ∾ (sl.) *er hat die Stinkwut*

hag n.: she is an old ∾ *sie ist ein häßliches altes Weib, eine alte Hexe;* to be ∾-ridden *an Alpdrücken leiden*

hail I. int.: he is ∾-fellow-well-met with everybody *er ist gleich mit jedermann gut Freund.* — **II.** v.tr.: they ∾ed him (as) king *sie begrüßten ihn als König;* they ∾ed a taxi *sie winkten eine Taxe herbei.* — **III.** v.i.: to ∾ from a place *aus (von) einem Orte stammen.* — **IV.** n.: within ∾ *in Rufweite*

hair n.: against the ∾ *gegen den Strich;* to a ∾ *auf ein Haar, ganz genau;* his ∾ stood on end *seine Haare standen ihm zu Berge;* to comb a person's ∾ for him *j.em gehörig den Kopf waschen;* to get a person by the short ∾s *j.en vollkommen in der Gewalt haben;* to have a ∾breadth escape *mit knapper Not entkommen;* to a ∾'s breadth *haarscharf;* within a ∾'s breadth *ums Haar, um ein Haar;* keep your ∾ on! (sl.) *reg' dich nicht auf! nur keine Aufregung!;* she has put up her ∾ *sie hat sich das Haar aufgesteckt;* to split ∾s *Haarspalterei(en) treiben;* to take a ∾ of the dog that bit you *weiter trinken, um den Kater zu vertreiben; den Teufel mit Beelzebub austreiben;* he tore his ∾ *er raufte sich die Haare;* he did not turn a ∾ *er hat nicht mit der Wimper gezuckt;* she gets in my ∾ *sie irritiert mich, geht mir auf die Nerven;* to have a ∾-do *sich frisieren lassen*

hairy a.: to be ∾ about (at) the fetlocks (heels), ∾-heeled (sl.) *schlecht erzogen sein, schlechte Manieren haben*

half I. n.: to see with ∾ an eye (colloq.) *scharfsinnig sein;* ∾ of it is (∾ of them are) rotten *die Hälfte davon ist faul;* two pounds and a ∾, two and a ∾ pounds *zweieinhalb Pfund;* he is too clever by ∾ *er ist sehr gerieben, ein Schlauberger;* to do a thing by halves *etwas nur halb (unvollkommen) tun;* to cry halves *den gleichen Anteil beanspruchen;* to cut in ∾, into halves *in zwei Hälften schneiden, halbieren;* to go halves with a person in a thing *mit j.em etwas teilen, halbpart machen.* — **II.** a.: ∾-baked *simpel, albern, unreif;* that is ∾ the battle *damit hätten wir schon halb gewonnen;* a ∾-caste *ein Mischling;* ∾-hearted *lau, gleichgültig;* I have ∾ a mind to do so *ich hätte beinahe Lust, es zu tun;* ∾ a pound *ein halbes Pfund;* to be ∾-seas-over *betrunken (beschwipst) sein, Schlagseite haben.* — **III.** adv.: ∾ as much (as many) again *anderthalbmal soviel;* not ∾! (sl.) *und ob! und wie!;* he is not ∾ a bad fellow (colloq.) *er ist durchaus kein übler Kerl;* it is not ∾ long enough *es ist nicht annähernd lang genug;* he didn't ∾ swear! (sl.) *er hat vielleicht geflucht!*

halfpenny n.: to turn up again like a bad ∾ *wie ein schlechter Groschen immer wieder auftauchen;* a ∾ lick (sl.) *eine Portion Eis vom Straßenverkäufer;* three halfpence *anderthalb Penny*

halloo v.i.: don't ∾ until (till) you are out of the wood (prov.) *triumphiere (frohlocke) nicht zu früh; man soll den Tag nicht vor dem Abend loben*

hammer I. n.: a knight of the ∾ *ein Grob-, Hufschmied;* to be at ∾ and tongs with a person *mit j.em auf sehr gespanntem Fuße (auf Kriegsfuß) stehen;* to be between the ∾ and the anvil *zwischen Hammer und Amboß (in großer Bedrängnis) sein;* to bring to (to sell under) the ∾ *versteigern lassen, versteigern;* they went at him ∾ and tongs *sie gingen mit aller Macht auf ihn los.* — **II.** v.tr.: to ∾ an idea into a person's head *j.em etwas einhämmern (-bleuen, -trichtern);* to ∾ out a plan *einen Plan ausarbeiten, ersinnen.* — **III.** v.i.: to ∾ away at a task *drauflosarbeiten*

hand I. n.: ∾s off! ∾s up! *Hände weg! Hände hoch!;* all ∾s on deck! *alle Mann an Deck!;* my ∾s are full *ich habe alle Hände voll zu tun;* he is a cool ∾ *er ist ein frecher Patron, ein unverschämter Bursche (Kunde);* a factory ∾ *ein Fabrikarbeiter;* from ∾ to mouth *aus der Hand in den Mund;* a good ∾ (at cards) *ein gutes Blatt;* with a high ∾, high-∾ed *gewaltsam, anmaßend, hochfahrend;* a legible (running) ∾ *eine lesbare (flüssige) Handschrift;* the long (the short) ∾ of a watch *der große (der kleine) Zeiger einer Uhr;* an old ∾ *ein alter Praktikus;* sleight-of-∾ *Taschenspielerkunst;* to be ∾ in (and) glove with a person *mit j.em ein Herz und eine Seele sein;* to be at ∾ *nahe, bei der Hand (zur Hand) sein;* the matter in ∾ *die vorliegende Sache;* to be on ∾ *vorrätig, auf Lager sein;* to be on a person's ∾ *j.em zur Last fallen;* it is admitted on all ∾s *es wird überall zugegeben;* on the one ∾, on the other ∾ *einerseits, andererseits;* to be a good (a bad, a poor) ∾ at a thing *in einer*

Sache geschickt (ungeschickt) sein; to bear a ∾ in a thing *an etwas teilnehmen, mithelfen;* to bring a child up by ∾ *ein Kind mit der Flasche großziehen;* to buy a book (at) second ∾ *ein Buch antiquarisch kaufen;* to change ∾s *den Besitzer wechseln;* your letter has come to ∾ *ich habe Ihren Brief erhalten;* he will not do a ∾'s turn *er rührt keine Hand, er tut keinen (Hand-) Schlag;* to do a thing off ∾ *etwas unvorbereitet, auf der Stelle tun;* to do a thing for one's own ∾ *etwas auf eigene Rechnung tun;* to dust one's ∾s of a person *mit j.em nichts mehr zu tun haben wollen;* to force a person's ∾ *j.en zwingen, vorzeitig zu handeln;* to gain (to get) the upper ∾ *die Oberhand gewinnen;* to get one's ∾ in *mit etwas vertraut werden, sich einarbeiten;* to get out of ∾ *außer Rand und Band geraten;* to give a person a big ∾ (colloq.) *j.em starken Beifall spenden (klatschen);* to go ∾ in ∾ with a person *mit j.em einer Meinung sein;* to have a ∾ to ∾ fight *Mann gegen Mann kämpfen;* to have a ∾ for a thing *zu etwas Geschick haben, etwas gut können;* to have (to keep) one's ∾ in *in Übung sein (bleiben);* his ∾ is out *er ist aus der Übung;* to have information at first ∾, first-∾ information *Nachricht aus erster Hand haben;* to have the situation well in ∾ *vollkommen Herr der Lage sein;* the situation is out of ∾ *die Lage ist nicht zu meistern;* to have a person (thing) (up)on one's ∾s *für j.en (für eine Sache) die Verantwortung tragen; j.en auf dem Halse, eine Sache am Halse haben;* I have him on my ∾s *er liegt mir auf der Tasche;* to have time on one's ∾s *viel Zeit haben;* to hold one's ∾s from doing it *sich enthalten (davon absehen), es zu tun;* to join ∾s *sich verbünden;* to keep a strict ∾ upon a person *j.en in strenger Zucht halten;* to lay ∾s on a thing *einer Sache habhaft werden;* to lay ∾s on oneself *Hand an sich legen, Selbstmord begehen;* to lend a helping ∾ *behilflich sein;* I can make no ∾ of it *ich kann es mir nicht erklären;* to make a poor ∾ at a thing *sich ungeschickt anstellen, geringe Fortschritte machen;* to overplay one's ∾ (at cards) *sich übernehmen;* to overtake ∾ over fist *schnell ein-, überholen;* to pass through many ∾s *durch viele Hände gehen;* to put one's ∾ to the plough (Luke IX, 62) *Hand an den Pflug legen, eine Arbeit beginnen;* let us put our ∾s together (colloq.) *wir wollen mal ordentlich klatschen;* to run one's ∾ along (down, over) a thing *mit der Hand an etwas entlang-, herunterfahren, über etwas fahren;* to rush in on all ∾s *von allen Seiten herbeistürzen;* to serve a person ∾ and foot *j.em unverdrossen (unterwürfig) dienen;* to set one's ∾ to a document *die Unterschrift unter eine Urkunde setzen;* to set one's ∾ to a task *eine Aufgabe anfangen (anpacken);* to shake ∾s with a person, to shake a person's ∾ *j.em die Hand schütteln (geben);* to show one's ∾ *seine Karten (Pläne) aufdecken;* by show of ∾s *durch Aufheben der Hände;* to take a ∾ at bridge *eine Partie Bridge mitspielen;* to take a thing in ∾ *etwas in die Hand nehmen, etwas unter-, übernehmen;* I must take you in ∾ *ich muß dich mal vornehmen;* to take a thing off a person's ∾ *j.em etwas abnehmen;* to treat a person with a heavy ∾ *j.en grausam behandeln;* to try one's ∾ at a thing *etwas versuchen;* to turn one's ∾ to a thing *etwas in Angriff nehmen;* he can turn his ∾ to anything *er ist ein Tausendkünstler;* to wash one's ∾s of a thing *seine Hände in Unschuld waschen, mit einer Sache nichts mehr zu tun haben wollen;* to win ∾s down *mit Leichtigkeit (spielend) gewinnen;* ∾-me-downs (colloq.) *Kleider aus zweiter Hand, gebrauchte Kleidungsstücke.* — **II.** v.tr.: to ∾ down to succeeding generations (to ∾ on the torch) *(eine Tradition) kommenden Geschlechtern überliefern;* you must ∾ it to him as regards cooking (colloq.) *was das Kochen angeht, mußt du sein Können zugeben;* to ∾ in one's resignation *sein Entlassungsgesuch einreichen;* to ∾ a person into (out of) a carriage *j.em in einen (aus einem) Wagen helfen;* to ∾ on a thing *etwas weitergeben, -reichen;* to ∾ out a thing *etwas ausgeben, -teilen;* to ∾ over a thing to a person *etwas j.em überlassen, es an j.en abtreten;* to ∾ a dish round *eine Schüssel herumreichen*

handful n.: that child is a ∾ (colloq.) *dieses Kind macht einem viel zu schaffen, es ist ein Racker*

handle I. n.: the ∾ of the face (facet.) *(scherzhafte Bezeichnung für) die Nase;* to fly off the ∾ (sl.) *aufbrausen, wütend werden;* to give a ∾ to a thing *einen Vorwand für eine Sache bieten;* to go off the ∾ (sl.) *sterben, abkratzen;* to have a ∾ to one's name (colloq.) *einen Titel vor dem Namen haben;* a ∾-bar *eine Lenkstange; ein langer, geschweifter Schnurrbart.* — **II.** v.tr.: this material is difficult to ∾ *mit diesem Stoff ist schwer umzugehen;* he was roughly ∾d in prison *im Gefängnis wurde er schlecht behandelt;* the teacher understood how to ∾ the difficult boy *der Lehrer verstand, den schwierigen Jungen richtig anzufassen;* the firm ∾s cotton and jute *die Firma handelt mit Baumwolle und Jute*

handsome a.: ∾ is as ∾ does (prov.) *an ihren Früchten sollt ihr sie erkennen;* a ∾ fortune *ein beträchtliches Vermögen;* a ∾ treatment *eine edelmütige Behandlung;* to do the ∾ thing by a person *sich j.em gegenüber großzügig erweisen*

handy a.: to be ∾ at a thing *geschickt bei einer Sache sein;* that will come in ∾ *das werde ich gut gebrauchen können, das kommt mir sehr gelegen*

hang I. v.tr.: O ∾! ∾ it all! (sl.) *zum Henker! zum Kuckuck noch einmal!;* I'll be ∾ed if I do so *ich denke nicht daran, das zu tun;* to ∾ fire *sich verzögern, versagen;* to ∾ one's head *den Kopf hängen lassen;* one must not ∾ a man for his looks (prov.) *man muß einen Menschen nicht nach seinem Äußeren beurteilen;* to ∾ out a flag *eine Fahne heraushängen;* to ∾ up a matter *eine Sache vorläufig ruhen lassen, an den Nagel hängen;* a ∾-dog face *ein Galgenvogelgesicht;* a ∾-dog look *eine Arm(e)-sündermiene.* — **II.** v.i.: time ∾s heavy on my hands *die Zeit wird mir lang;* to ∾ about, around *herumlungern;* to ∾ back, off *zögern, sich sträuben;* to ∾ by a thread *an einem Faden hängen;* to ∾ on by the skin of one's teeth (colloq.) *hartnäckig durchhalten;* to ∾ on by the eyelids *einen nur losen Halt haben, an einem Faden hängen;* to ∾ on a person's mouth (lips) *an j.es Mund (Lippen) hängen;* ∾ on to that (sl.) *halte das gut fest;* where do you ∾ out? (sl.) *wo wohnst du?;* to let something go ∾ *etwas auf den Hund kommen lassen.* — **III.** n.: I don't care a ∾ (colloq.) *ich kümmere mich den Teufel darum, ich mache mir nicht die Bohne daraus;* to get the ∾ of a thing (colloq.) *hinter etwas kommen, den Zusammenhang (den Dreh) herausbekommen;* he has a ∾-over (sl.) *er hat einen Kater (Katzenjammer);* a ∾er-on *ein Schmarotzer*

haphazard n.: at (by) ∾ *aufs Geratewohl, durch Zufall*

happen v.i.: do you ∾ to know? *wissen Sie zufällig?;* it ∾ed that *es traf sich, daß;* nothing ∾ed *nichts geschah (passierte);* he ∾ed to do it *er tat es zufällig;* to ∾ (up)on a person (thing) *zufällig auf j.en (etwas) stoßen*

happy a.: I shall be ∾ to assist *ich helfe gern;* a ∾ dispatch *ein Selbstmord, wie ihn die Japaner verüben;* a ∾ family *Tiere verschiedener Art in einem Käfig;* a ∾-go-lucky chap *ein unbekümmerter (sorgloser) Bursche;* many ∾ returns of the day! *herzliche Glückwünsche (ich gratuliere) zum Geburtstag!;* as ∾ as the day is long *vollkommen glücklich;* a ∾ hunting ground *günstige Bedingungen*

harbour v.tr.: to ∾ a criminal *einen Verbrecher beherbergen;* to ∾ evil thoughts *böse Gedanken hegen*

hard I. a.: to drive ∾ bargains *aufs äußerste feilschen;* ∾ cash *Metallgeld;* ∾ facts *feste, unleugbare Tatsachen;* ∾ of hearing *schwerhörig;* ∾ labour *Zwangsarbeit, Zuchthausstrafe;* ∾ lines! ∾ cheese! (sl.) *Unglück, Pech;* as ∾ as nails *gut durchtrainiert, stahlhart;* as ∾ as the nether mill-stone *hartherzig, unerbittlich;* it is a ∾ row to hoe *eine schwierige, mühselige Arbeit;* ∾ and fast rules *starre, unabänderliche Regeln;* as ∾ as a stone *steinhart;* ∾ tack *Schiffszwieback;* ∾ware *Eisenwaren.* — **II.** n.: he got two years ∾ *er bekam zwei Jahre Zuchthaus.* — **III.** adv.: ∾ after *dicht hinter;* ∾ at hand, ∾ by *nahe (dicht) dabei;* ∾-bitten *hartnäckig, zäh;* ∾-boiled *hartgesotten, gefühllos, nüchtern;* ∾-fisted *geizig (knickerig, knauserig);* ∾-headed *praktisch, nüchtern;* a ∾-set look *ein starrer Blick;* to be ∾ at it *vollauf beschäftigt, gehörig dahinter (hinterher) sein;* to be ∾ hit *einen schweren Verlust erleiden;* to be ∾ pressed (pushed) for time *knapp Zeit haben;* I was ∾ put to it *es wurde mir schwer, es fiel mir sauer;* to be ∾ up for an excuse *um eine Entschuldigung verlegen sein;* to be ∾ up (for money) *in Geldverlegenheit, knapp bei Kasse sein;* to be ∾ upon 7 o'clock *nahezu 7 Uhr sein;* to be ∾ (up)on a person *gegen j.en streng (grausam) sein;* to die ∾ *hartnäckig sein, Widerstand leisten;* to drink ∾ *übermäßig (schwer) trinken;* it shall go

∾ but I will find them (old fash.) *ich werde sie schon finden;* it will go ∾ with him *es wird ihm zum Nachteil gereichen;* to hit ∾ *wuchtig (fest) zuschlagen;* to look ∾ at a person *j.en fest (bestimmt) ansehen;* it is raining ∾ *es regnet heftig, es gießt in Strömen;* to try ∾ *sein Bestes versuchen;* to work ∾ *schwer (tüchtig, fleißig) arbeiten*

hardly adv.: ∾-earned *schwer verdient;* ∾ had I done so *kaum hatte ich es getan*

hardy a.: a ∾ annual *eine winterharte Pflanze; ein Gegenstand, der immer wieder zur Debatte steht*

hare n.: as mad as a March ∾ *so verrückt (geil) wie ein Märzhase;* first catch your ∾ then cook him (prov.) *man soll das Fell nicht verkaufen, ehe man den Bären (erlegt) hat;* to hold (to run) with the ∾ and run (hold, hunt) with the hounds *es mit beiden Parteien halten; es mit niemandem verderben wollen;* to start another ∾ *j.en auf eine neue Fährte bringen, ein neues Thema anschneiden;* ∾ and hounds *eine Schnitzeljagd;* a ∾-brained fellow *ein zerfahrener, unbesonnener Kerl;* a ∾-lip *eine Hasenscharte*

hark v.i.: to ∾ back to a subject *auf einen Gegenstand zurückgreifen, -kommen*

harm n.: there's no ∾ in asking *Fragen schadet nichts, man darf doch mal fragen;* no ∾ done *das hat nichts zu sagen;* to be out of ∾'s way *in Sicherheit, fern vom Schuß sein;* to come to ∾ *zu Schaden kommen;* I meant no ∾ *es war nicht böse gemeint;* I see no ∾ in it *ich finde nichts dabei*

harness I. n.: to work in double ∾ *mit einem Partner arbeiten;* to die in ∾ *in den Sielen sterben.* — **II.** v.tr.: to ∾ a waterfall *Elektrizität erzeugen*

harp v.i.: he is always ∾ing on the same subject (string) *er reitet immer auf demselben Thema herum; er bleibt immer bei der alten Leier*

harrow n.: under the ∾ *in großer Not*

harum-scarum a.: a ∾ lad *ein gedankenloser, fahriger Bursche*

harvest n.: ∾ home *Erntefest*

hash n.: to make a ∾ of a thing *eine Sache verderben (verpfuschen, vermasseln, verkorksen);* to settle a person's ∾ (colloq.) *j.en erledigen, abtun, töten, ihm den Garaus machen*

haste n.: to make ∾ *sich beeilen;* more ∾, less speed (prov.) *Eile mit Weile*

hat n.: a bad ∾ (sl.) *ein übler Kunde;* as black as my ∾ *kohlrabenschwarz;* a high ∾ (sl.) *eine hochmütige (anmaßende) Person;* his ∾ covers his family *er steht allein in der Welt;* I'll eat my ∾ if (sl.) *ich fresse einen Besen, wenn;* to hang up one's ∾ *sich häuslich niederlassen;* to knock into a cocked ∾ *etwas zu Brei schlagen;* to pass (to send round) the ∾ *Geld einsammeln;* to raise (to touch) one's ∾ *den Hut ziehen, grüßen;* to talk through one's ∾ (colloq.) *übertreiben, prahlen, angeben; Unsinn reden;* keep it under your ∾ (colloq.) *behalte es für dich!*

hatch n.: to be under the ∾es *tot sein*

hatchet n.: to bury the ∾ *das Kriegsbeil begraben;* to throw the ∾ *übertreiben, flunkern;* to throw the helve after the ∾ *einen weiteren unnützen Schritt unternehmen, das Kind mit dem Bade ausschütten; gutes Geld schlechtem (faulem) nachwerfen*

hatter n.: as mad as a ∾ *total verrückt*

haul v.tr.: to ∾ a person over the coals *j.em einen scharfen Verweis (Rüffel) erteilen, ihn zur Rechenschaft ziehen, ihn abkanzeln*

have I. v.tr.: you ∾ been had (sl.) *du bist angeführt worden;* to ∾ a baby *ein Kind bekommen;* to ∾ a care *aufpassen, sich vorsehen;* to ∾ a coat made *einen Rock machen lassen;* I ∾ to do it *ich muß es tun;* he has no Greek *er versteht (kann) kein Griechisch;* ∾ a heart! (sl.) *hab' ein Herz! sei nicht so hart!;* to ∾ by heart *auswendig können;* you know where to ∾ him *man weiß, wo man bei ihm dran ist;* you ∾ had it (sl.) *das hast du mal gehabt, die Chance ist vorbei;* as Plato has it *wie Plato es ausdrückt;* to ∾ breakfast, a bath, a dance *frühstücken, ein Bad nehmen, tanzen;* what would you ∾ me do? I won't ∾ you coming home so late *was möchtest du, daß ich tue? Ich dulde nicht, daß du so spät nach Hause kommst;* ∾ it your own way! *mach', was du willst! meinetwegen! du sollst recht haben!;* to let a person ∾ it (colloq.) *es j.em gehörig geben;* he will ∾ it that *er besteht auf seiner Behauptung, daß;* to ∾ a look at a thing *sich (dat.) etwas an-*

sehen; he has nothing on me (U.S.) *er ist mir in nichts voraus;* to ~ it out with a person *sich mit j.em auseinandersetzen;* to ~ a tooth out *sich (dat.) einen Zahn ziehen lassen;* to ~ a try, a crack (sl.) at *einen Versuch machen (mit);* to be had up before a magistrate *vor den Richter gebracht werden; belangt werden;* to ~ and to hold *besitzen und erhalten.* — **II.** v.i.: to ~ at a person *j.en angreifen;* I had better (rather) go *ich täte besser, lieber gehen.* — **III.** aux.: ~ done! *hör auf!* — **IV.** n.: it was a ~ (sl.) *es war ein Schwindel (Reinfall);* the ~s and ~-nots *die Reichen und Armen (Habenichtse)*

havoc n.: to make ~ of, to play ~ among, with *verwüsten, verheeren*

hay n.: to look for a needle in a bottle (bundle) of ~, in a ~stack *sich mit nutzlosem Suchen abmühen;* to make ~ of a thing *etwas verwirren, durcheinanderwerfen;* to make ~ while the sun shines *das Eisen schmieden, solange es (noch) heiß ist;* to hit the ~ (sl.) *ins Bett gehen;* the ~box *die Kochkiste;* to go ~wire (U.S.) *aufgeregt, verwirrt werden*

he n.: a ~ must have done it *eine männliche Person muß es getan haben;* a ~-goat *ein Ziegenbock;* a ~-man *ein Kraftmensch*

head I. n.: a ~-on collision *ein Zusammenprall Kopf mit Kopf;* ~ over heels *Hals über Kopf;* the ~lines *die Schlagzeilen;* ~s or tails *Kopf oder Wappen;* ~s I win, tails you lose *ich gewinne auf jeden Fall;* over ~ and ears in work *bis über die Ohren in Arbeit;* to be at the ~ of *an der Spitze stehen;* to be taller by a ~ *einen Kopf größer sein;* to beat a person's ~ off *j.en bei weitem übertreffen;* to come into a person's ~ *j.em in den Sinn kommen;* to come to a ~ *zu einer Entscheidung, Krisis kommen; eitern;* I could do it on my ~ (sl.) *das könnte ich im Schlaf tun;* he did it out of his own ~ *er tat es aus sich heraus, nach eigener Idee;* to drag a story in by the ~ and ears (~ and shoulders) *eine Geschichte an den Haaren herbeiziehen;* the horse eats his ~ off *das Pferd kostet mehr zu unterhalten, als es wert ist;* to give a horse his ~ *einem Pferd die Zügel schießen lassen;* to go off one's ~ *verrückt werden;* to have a ~ (colloq.) *Kopfschmerzen (einen Brummschädel) haben;* to have a good ~ for business *Köpfchen für's Geschäft haben;* he has an old ~ on young shoulders *er ist trotz seiner Jugend weise;* you cannot put an old ~ (you must not expect old ~s) on young shoulders (prov.) *Jugend hat keine Tugend;* to keep one's ~ *die Ruhe (Fassung) bewahren;* to keep one's ~ above water *sich über Wasser halten;* to keep a level ~ *den Kopf nicht verlieren;* we laid (put) our ~s together *wir steckten die Köpfe zusammen, wir berieten;* to lead by a ~ *um eine Kopflänge führen;* to lose one's ~ *den Kopf verlieren;* to make ~ against a thing *einer Sache erfolgreich Widerstand leisten;* I cannot make ~ or tail of it *ich werde aus der Sache nicht klug;* to put a thing into a person's ~ *j.em etwas in den Kopf (einen Floh ins Ohr) setzen;* to put a thing out of one's ~ *sich (dat.) etwas aus dem Kopf schlagen;* to puzzle one's ~ about a thing *sich (dat.) den Kopf über etwas zerbrechen;* to run one's ~ against a stone wall *mit dem Kopf gegen die Wand rennen;* to stand ~ and shoulders above a person *j.en turmhoch überragen;* to take the ~ *die Führung übernehmen;* to take a thing into one's ~ *sich (dat.) etwas in den Kopf setzen;* to talk a person's ~ off *j.en durch vieles Reden ermüden; j.en dumm und albern (dämlich) reden; (rheinisch) j.em de Plät jeck maache;* to trouble one's ~ about a thing *sich über etwas den Kopf zerbrechen;* to turn a person's ~ *j.em den Kopf verdrehen;* my ~ turns *mir wird schwindlig;* to win by a ~ *um Kopflänge gewinnen;* the news in ~lines *die Nachrichten in Schlagzeilen;* the ~master, -mistress *der Direktor, die Direktorin.* — **II.** v.tr.: to ~ a chapter *ein Kapitel mit Kopf (Titel) versehen;* to ~ a list *an der Spitze einer Liste stehen;* to ~ (down) a plant (tree, etc.) *einer Pflanze (einem Baum usw.) die Spitze abschneiden, (sie, ihn) kappen;* to ~ in a ball *einen Ball ins Tor köpfen;* to ~ off, back *etwas ablenken, zurücktreiben.* — **III.** v.i.: the house ~s east *das Haus liegt mit der Front nach Osten;* the ship is ~ing (for) N. *das Schiff nimmt Kurs auf N.*

heap I. n.: a ~ of people (colloq.) *eine Menge Leute;* he is ~s (adv.) better (colloq.) *es geht ihm bedeutend (wesentlich) besser;* you have ~s of time (colloq.) *du hast reichlich Zeit;* I have done it ~s of times (colloq.) *ich habe es x-mal gemacht;*

I was struck all of a ∾ (colloq.) *ich war ganz platt; mir blieb die Spucke weg, mich rührte der Schlag.* — **II.** v.tr.: to ∾ coals of fire on a person *feurige Kohlen auf j.es Haupt sammeln*

hear I. v.tr.: to ∾ a case *einen Fall gerichtlich untersuchen;* to ∾ a pupil his lesson *einem Schüler die Aufgabe ab-, überhören;* to ∾ a witness *einen Zeugen verhören;* to ∾ a person out *j.en bis zu Ende anhören, ihn ausreden lassen.* — **II.** v.i.: he will not ∾ of it *er will nichts davon hören (wissen);* you will ∾ of this *man wird dich deswegen zur Rede stellen, du wirst die Folgen zu tragen haben*

heart n.: a ∾ of oak *ein mutiger Mann;* in his ∾ of ∾s *in seiner innersten Seele;* his ∾ is in it *er ist mit dem Herzen dabei;* with ∾ and soul *mit Leib und Seele;* bless my ∾! *ach, du lieber Himmel!;* bless your ∾! *(als Anerkennung) etwa: das ist aber lieb von Ihnen!;* from the bottom of one's ∾ *aus Herzensgrund, aus tiefstem Herzen;* are we down-∾ed? *wir lassen den Kopf nicht hängen, wir lassen uns nicht unterkriegen;* faint ∾ never won fair lady (prov.) *wer nicht wagt, der nicht gewinnt; dem Mutigen gehört die Welt;* half-∾ed *lau, gleichgültig;* with a heavy ∾ *schweren (blutenden) Herzens;* to be after one's ∾ *nach Wunsch gehen;* to be in (out of) ∾ *bei guter (schlechter) Laune sein;* the land is out of ∾ *der Boden ist in schlechtem Zustande;* to be in the very ∾ of a thing *inmitten einer Sache sein;* to cry one's ∾ out *sich (dat.) die Augen ausweinen;* to do a thing ∾ and hand *etwas begeistert tun;* to do a thing to one's ∾ content *etwas nach Herzenslust tun;* to eat one's ∾ out *sich abhärmen, sich vor Gram verzehren;* I cannot find it in my ∾ to do so *ich bringe es nicht übers Herz, es zu tun;* to go (to get) to the (very) ∾ of a thing *einer Sache auf den Grund gehen (kommen);* to get (to learn) a poem by ∾ *ein Gedicht auswendig lernen;* to have a ∾ to ∾ talk *sich offen aussprechen;* to have one's ∾ in one's boots *große Angst haben;* to have one's ∾ in one's mouth *zu Tode erschrocken sein;* to have one's ∾ in the right place *das Herz auf dem rechten Fleck haben;* to have at ∾ *auf dem Herzen haben;* to lay (to take) a thing to ∾ *etwas ernstlich überlegen, zu Herzen nehmen;* to lose ∾ *den Mut verlieren;* to lose one's ∾ to a person *sein Herz an j.en verlieren;* to open one's ∾ to a person *j.em sein Herz ausschütten;* to pluck up (to take) ∾, to take ∾ of grace *sich (dat.) ein Herz fassen, Mut fassen;* to set one's ∾ on a thing *sein Herz an etwas hängen, unbedingt etwas haben wollen;* to set a person's ∾ at rest *j.en beruhigen (beschwichtigen);* to speak from one's ∾ *frei (frisch) von der Leber weg sprechen;* it warms the cockles of my ∾ *es erfreut mich sehr;* to wear one's ∾ upon one's sleeve *das Herz auf der Zunge haben;* to wear a person (principle) in one's ∾ *j.en (einen Grundsatz) im Herzen tragen;* to wish with all one's ∾ *von ganzem Herzen wünschen;* ∾burn Sodbrennen; a ∾-felt, ∾whole emotion *ein herzliches, aufrichtiges Gefühl;* to pull at a person's ∾-strings *j.em das Herz zerreißen, j.en rühren;* my sweet∾, my ∾-throb (sl.) *mein Schatz*

heat n.: a dead ∾ *ein totes Rennen;* the final ∾ of a race *der Endlauf, die Ausscheidungsrunde;* the trial ∾s *die Vorrunden;* at a white ∾ *weißglühend, in höchster Erregung;* in the ∾ of the moment *in der Hitze des Gefechtes;* the bitch is on ∾ *die Hündin ist läufig*

heave I. v.tr.: to ∾ a sigh *einen Seufzer ausstoßen (aufseufzen);* to ∾ a ship down *kielholen;* ∾ ho! *Hau ruck!* — **II.** v.i.: to ∾ at a rope *an einem Tau ziehen;* to ∾ in sight *sichtbar werden;* to ∾ to *beidrehen, stoppen*

heaven n.: ∾ forbid! *Gott bewahre!;* ∾ knows! *weiß der Himmel!;* by ∾! good ∾s! *du lieber Himmel!;* thank ∾! *Gott sei Dank!;* would to ∾! *wollte Gott!;* to move ∾ and earth *Himmel und Erde in Bewegung setzen*

heavenly a.: the ∾ bodies *die Himmelskörper;* what ∾ figs! *welch köstliche Feigen!*

heavy I. a.: to be ∾ in (on) hand *langweilig, ein schlechter Gesellschafter sein;* with a ∾ heart *schweren (blutenden) Herzens;* it was ∾ news *es waren betrübliche Nachrichten;* to be ∾-handed *ungeschickt sein.* — **II.** adv.: time hangs ∾ on my hands *die Zeit wird mir lang, ich langweile mich;* it lies ∾ upon me *es bedrückt mich*

hedge I. n.: it doesn't grow on every ∾ *es ist rar, nicht hinter jedem Zaun zu fin-*

den. — **II.** v.i.: to ∾ *keine direkte Antwort oder kein Versprechen geben wollen.* — **III.** v.tr.: to ∾ someone round with rules *j.en durch Vorschriften einschränken, umzingeln*

heebie-jeebies n. (U.S. sl.): to give a person the ∾ *j.en schockieren, deprimieren*

heed n.: to give (to pay, to take) ∾ to *achten auf, beachten*

heel I. n.: a ∾ (U.S. sl.) *ein Lump;* to ∾! *bei Fuß (Befehl an einen Hund);* head over ∾s *Hals über Kopf;* to be (to come, to follow) at a person's ∾, to be (up)on a person's ∾ *j.em dicht auf den Fersen sein;* to come to ∾ *gehorsam, demütig sein;* to be down at ∾ *niedergetretene Absätze haben, schlampig, heruntergekommen sein;* to be carried with the ∾s foremost (cf. 'foot') *auf den Kirchhof getragen werden;* to be hairy about (at) the ∾s, hairy ∾ed (sl.) *schlecht erzogen sein, schlechte Manieren haben;* to be out at ∾s *Löcher im Strumpfe haben, in erbärmlichen Umständen sein;* to bring to ∾ *unterkriegen;* to clap (to lay) by the ∾s *ins Gefängnis werfen; zu Boden werfen;* to let a person cool his ∾s *j.en lange warten lassen, j.en sich (dat.) die Beine in den Bauch stehen lassen;* to have (to get) the ∾s of a person *schneller als j. laufen;* to kick one's ∾s *ungeduldig, müßig warten;* to kick up the ∾s *sterben;* to show a clean pair of ∾s, to take to one's ∾s *weglaufen, ausreißen, Fersengeld geben;* to tread on a person's ∾s *j.em auf die Hacken treten;* to turn on one's ∾ *sich rasch (kurz) umdrehen;* no ∾-taps! *ausgetrunken! Rest weg!;* under the ∾ of *unterdrückt, bedrängt.* — **II.** v.tr.: he is well ∾ed *er ist reich, (rheinisch) er hät jet an de Föß*

height n.: the fever is at its ∾ *das Fieber hat den Höhepunkt erreicht;* it is the ∾ of fashion *es ist hoch modern;* it is the ∾ of folly *es ist der Gipfel der Torheit;* six feet in ∾ *sechs Fuß hoch*

hell n. (colloq.): what the ∾ do you want? *was willst du denn zum Teufel?;* to give a person ∾ *j.em die Hölle heiß machen;* to make a ∾ of a noise *einen höllischen Lärm (einen Heidenlärm) machen;* he ran like ∾ *er lief wie der Teufel;* to raise ∾ (∾'s delight) about a thing *wegen einer Sache einen Heidenlärm machen, gehörig Krach schlagen;* to ride ∾ for leather *in rasendem Galopp reiten;* a ∾-cat *eine Xanthippe*

help I. v.tr.: so ∾ me God! *so wahr mir Gott helfe!;* I cannot ∾ hoping *ich kann nicht umhin, zu hoffen;* it can't be ∾ed; I can't ∾ that *es läßt sich nicht ändern; ich kann es nicht ändern;* don't be longer than you can ∾ *bleib nicht länger als nötig;* to ∾ a lame dog over a stile *j.em in der Not behilflich sein;* to ∾ a person on (off) with his coat *j.em beim Anziehen (Ausziehen) des Mantels behilflich sein;* may I ∾ you to some meat? *darf ich Ihnen etwas Fleisch reichen?;* please ∾ yourself *bedienen Sie sich bitte!;* God ∾s those who ∾ themselves (prov.) *hilf dir selbst, so hilft dir Gott.* — **II.** n.: there is no ∾ for it *es läßt sich nicht ändern;* a lady-∾ *eine Stütze der Hausfrau;* a mother's ∾ *eine Haustochter*

helter-skelter adv.: they ran ∾ down the hill *sie liefen holterdiepolter den Berg hinunter*

helve n.: to put the axe in the ∾ *eine Schwierigkeit lösen;* to send the axe after the ∾, to throw the ∾ after the hatchet *einen weiteren unnützen Schritt unternehmen, das Kind mit dem Bade ausschütten; gutes Geld schlechtem, faulem nachwerfen*

hen n.: like a ∾ on a hot girdle *wie auf glühenden Kohlen;* like a ∾ with one chick *wie eine aufgeregte Glucke;* to sell one's ∾s on a rainy day *töricht handeln;* a ∾-party *ein Kaffeeklatsch;* a ∾-pecked husband *ein Pantoffelheld*

hence adv.: ∾ it appears that *daraus erhellt, daß;* five years ∾ *heute in fünf Jahren;* to go ∾ *von hinnen fahren, sterben*

here adv.: ∾ below *hienieden, auf dieser Welt;* ∾ goes! *also los! ich wage es!;* ∾'s how! (colloq.) *Prost! Auf Ihr Wohl! Zum Wohlsein!;* ∾'s to the ladies! *auf das Wohl der Damen!;* ∾, there, and everywhere *überall;* that's neither ∾ nor there *das gehört nicht hierher, hat wenig Bedeutung, hat nichts mit der Sache zu tun*

Herod n.pr.: to out-∾ ∾ (Hamlet III, 2) *den Tyrannen übertyrannen (Schlegel); alles übertreffen*

herring n.: he's neither fish, flesh, nor good red ∾ *er ist weder Fisch noch Fleisch;* to draw a red ∾ across the track *ein Ablenkungsmanöver betreiben;* to throw a sprat to catch a ∾ *mit der Wurst nach der Speckseite werfen;* the ∾-pond (facet.) *Atlantischer Ozean (scherzhaft)*

herself pron.: she is not quite ∾ *sie fühlt sich nicht ganz wohl, sie ist nicht ganz auf dem Damm;* she did it all by ∾ *sie hat es ganz allein gemacht*

hide[1] n.: to save one's own ∾ *seine eigene Haut retten;* to give a person a hiding *j.en verprügeln.* — N.B. ∾-bound a.: *engherzig, sich streng an Regeln klammernd*

hide[2] v.tr.: & i.: to ∾ one's light (candle) under a bushel *sein Licht unter einen Scheffel stellen;* to play (at) ∾-and-seek *Verstecken spielen*

high I. a.: how is that for ∾? (sl.) *was sagst du dazu? famos! wie?;* a ∾ball (U.S.) *ein Whisky mit Soda in hohem Glase gereicht;* a ∾-brow (orig. U.S. sl.) *ein Intellektueller;* ∾ and dry *gestrandet, auf dem trockenen sitzend;* ∾ and mighty *hochfahrend;* with a ∾ hand *gewaltsam, anmaßend, hochfahrend;* a ∾ hat (sl.) *eine hochmütige (anmaßende) Person;* to mount (to ride) the ∾ horse *sich aufs hohe Pferd (Roß) setzen;* ∾ jinks *ausgelassene Lustigkeit, übermütige Streiche;* in ∾ life *im Leben der vornehmen Welt;* the ∾ lights of a matter *die Glanzpunkte einer Sache;* to be on the ∾ ropes *gewaltig erregt sein (vor Freude oder Wut);* to be in ∾ spirits, in ∾ feather *bei guter Laune, in gehobener Stimmung sein;* to dine at ∾ table *am Dozententisch im englischen College essen;* to have ∾ tea *eine Abendmahlzeit mit Tee und Fleischgerichten einnehmen;* it is ∾ time for you to go *es ist höchste Zeit, daß du gehst;* we had a ∾ (old) time *wir waren sehr vergnügt, wir haben uns glänzend amüsiert;* to come to (to have) ∾ words *sich zanken;* ∾ treason *Hochverrat.* — **II.** adv.: ∾falutin(g), ∾-flown *bombastisch, schwülstig, hochtrabend;* ∾-handed *gewaltsam, anmaßend, hochfahrend;* ∾-minded *hochherzig, edelgesinnt;* ∾-strung *empfindlich, reizbar;* feelings ran ∾ *es herrschte eine erregte Stimmung;* prices ran ∾ *hohe Preise wurden erzielt;* to search ∾ and low for a thing *überall nach etwas suchen;* to smell (to taste) ∾ *stark schmecken, riechen; Hautgout haben.* — **III.** n.: from on ∾ *von oben, vom Himmel;* prices reached a new ∾ *die Preise erreichten einen neuen Rekord;* he shifted into ∾ *er schaltete in den dritten Gang um*

highly adv.: to think ∾ of a person *von j.em viel halten, eine hohe Meinung haben;* to speak ∾ of a person *von j.em lobend sprechen*

hill n.: as old as the ∾s *uralt*

hilt n.: war to the ∾ *Krieg bis aufs Messer;* to prove up to the ∾ *aufs schlagendste beweisen*

himself pron.: cf. 'herself'

hinge n.: to be off the ∾s *aus den Angeln (Fugen, in Unordnung) sein*

hint n.: to drop a broad ∾ *einen Wink mit dem Zaunpfahl geben;* to take a ∾ *einen Wink verstehen*

hip[1] n.: to catch (to have) a person on the ∾ *j.en in eine ungünstige Lage bringen, Gewalt über ihn haben;* to smite ∾ and thigh (Judges, XV, 8) *j.en vollständig besiegen*

hip[2] v.tr.: he looks ∾ped (sl.) *er sieht mißmutig (niedergeschlagen) aus*

hire n.: to be on ∾ *zu vermieten sein;* to take on ∾-purchase *auf Ratenzahlung kaufen, etwas abstottern*

historic a.: it was a ∾ event *es war ein geschichtlich bemerkenswertes Ereignis*

historical a.: the ∾ method of investigation *die geschichtliche Forschungsmethode;* it is of purely ∾ interest *es hat nur geschichtliches Interesse*

hit I. v.tr.: to ∾ a person below the belt *j.em beim Boxen einen Tiefschlag versetzen; unehrlich kämpfen;* to ∾ someone's fancy *j.es Geschmack treffen;* to ∾ the hay (colloq.) *schlafen gehen;* you've ∾ it *du hast's getroffen, erraten;* to ∾ the (right) nail on the head *den Nagel auf den Kopf treffen;* to ∾ a target *ein Ziel erreichen;* to ∾ off well *treffend nachahmen;* they don't ∾ it off together (with each other) *sie vertragen sich nicht gut, sie kommen nicht gut miteinander aus;* to ∾ the roof (colloq.) *aufgeregt werden.* — **II.** v.i.: to ∾ against difficulties *auf Schwierigkeiten stoßen;* to ∾ out *kräftig um sich schlagen;* to ∾ upon an idea, a solution *auf einen Gedanken, eine Lösung verfallen.* — **III.** n.: the latest ∾ *der letzte (neueste) Schlager*

hitch I. v.tr.: to ∾ one's wag(g)on to a star *höhere Ziele haben;* to ∾ up one's trousers *die Hosen hochziehen;* to ∾-hike (orig. U.S.) *sich von einem Auto streckenweise mitnehmen lassen, trampen, „per Anhalter" fahren.* — **II.** n.: there is a ∾ somewhere *irgendwo ist ein Haken;* it went without a ∾ *es ging glatt, ohne Stockung*

hobby n.: to ride one's ∾ *sein Steckenpferd reiten*

Hobson n.pr.: ∾'s choice *das nehmen müssen, was übrig bleibt*

hock n. (sl.): to ∾ *verpfänden;* to be in ∾ *verschuldet, verpfändet sein*

hog n.: he is a road-∾ *er ist ein gefährlicher (rücksichtsloser) Autofahrer, ein Straßenschreck, ein Kilometerfresser;* to go the whole ∾ *eine Sache vollständig durchführen, nicht auf halbem Wege stehen bleiben, aufs Ganze gehen*

hoist p.p.: ∾ with his own petard (Hamlet, III, 2) *in die Grube gefallen, die man einem andern gegraben hat. „Der Spaß ist, wenn mit seinem eignen Pulver der Feuerwerker auffliegt" (Schlegel-Tieck)*

hoity-toity I. a.: with a ∾ air *mit hochmütiger Miene.* — **II.** int.: ∾! *potztausend! Donnerwetter!*

hold I. v.tr.: the court held that *das Gericht entschied, daß;* a ∾-all *ein Behälter, eine Reisetasche;* to ∾ (the attention of) an audience *die Zuhörer fesseln;* to ∾ to bail *eine Bürgschaft zulassen;* to ∾ at bay *hinhalten, in Schach halten;* to ∾ one's breath *den Atem anhalten;* to ∾ no brief for someone *weit davon entfernt sein, jemanden zu unterstützen oder zu billigen;* to ∾ in check *in Schach, im Zaume halten;* to ∾ by (to) a choice *bei einer getroffenen Wahl bleiben;* to ∾ up to derision (ridicule) *dem Gespött aussetzen, der Lächerlichkeit preisgeben;* to ∾ one's ground, one's own, see 'ground, own'; to ∾ one's hand from doing a thing *sich enthalten, etwas zu tun;* there is no ∾ing him *er läßt sich nicht halten;* to ∾ forth (out) hopes *Hoffnungen machen;* to ∾ office *ein Amt bekleiden;* to ∾ one's peace, tongue, jaw, noise, see 'peace, tongue, jaw, noise'; to ∾ a person off *j.en fernhalten, abwehren;* to ∾ a person to his word *j.en beim Worte nehmen;* to ∾ a person responsible *j.en verantwortlich machen;* to ∾ the stage *im Mittelpunkt der Vorstellung stehen;* to ∾ a thing over a person *j.en ständig mit etwas bedrohen;* to ∾ a thing over *etwas aufschieben;* to ∾ up *aufhalten; j.en auf der Straße anhalten und berauben;* to ∾ a view *eine Ansicht vertreten;* to ∾ water *wasserdicht sein; stichhaltig sein;* to be left ∾ing the baby (colloq.) *die unangenehmen Folgen tragen müssen (, nachdem sich die anderen davongemacht haben).* — **II.** v.i.: to ∾ aloof *sich fern (abseits) halten;* to ∾ forth *öffentlich reden;* to ∾ good (true) *gelten, sich bestätigen;* ∾ hard, on! *hör' auf! wart' mal!;* to ∾ on to a thing *sich an etwas halten, etwas festhalten;* to ∾ on one's way *auf dem Wege bleiben, seinen Weg fortsetzen;* to ∾ out against a thing *sich gegen etwas behaupten;* to ∾ with a person (thing) *es mit j.em halten, etwas billigen.* — **III.** n.: to catch (to get, to keep, to lay, to take) ∾ of a thing *etwas fassen, greifen;* to have a ∾ on a person *j.en beherrschen, Einfluß auf ihn haben;* to leave ∾ of a thing *etwas loslassen*

hole n.: I am in rather (a devil of) a ∾ *ich bin in einer ziemlichen (verteufelten) Klemme;* a round (square) peg in a square (round) ∾ *j. (etwas), der (das) nicht am geeigneten Platze ist;* to make a ∾ in a thing *ein Loch in eine Sache reißen, viel von ihr gebrauchen;* to pick a ∾ in a person's coat *j.em etwas am Zeuge flicken;* to pick ∾s in a thing *etwas bekritteln, bemängeln;* a ∾-and-corner meeting *eine heimliche Versammlung;* ∾-and-corner transactions *dunkle Machenschaften*

holiday n.: a blindman's ∾ *Zwielicht, Abenddämmerung;* to take a busman's ∾ *seine Ferien bei der gewohnten Tätigkeit verbringen;* to go on (to make, to take) a ∾ *in die Ferien gehen*

hollow adv.: he was beaten ∾ *er wurde vollständig, mit Leichtigkeit geschlagen*

home I. n.: to be at ∾ *zu Hause sein;* to be at ∾ in (on, with) a subject *mit einem Stoffe wohl vertraut sein;* she has her at-∾ every Wednesday *sie hat jeden Mittwoch ihren Empfangstag;* to make oneself at ∾ *es sich (dat.) gemütlich machen;* the long (last) ∾ *das Grab, die letzte Ruhestätte;* lies (faults), like crows, come ∾ to roost (prov.) *Lügen haben kurze Beine (Sprichw.).* — **II.** a.: Home Affairs *Innenpolitik;* the ∾ counties *die Grafschaf-*

ten um London (Essex, Kent, Middlesex, Surrey, manchmal auch Hertford und Sussex); ∾-made bread, clothes *zu Hause gebackenes Brot, geschneiderte Kleider;* the ∾ market, trade *der Inlandsmarkt, Binnenhandel;* to tell a person some ∾ truths *j.em einige derbe, treffende Wahrheiten (gehörig die Wahrheit, Meinung) sagen;* the Home Office, Secretary *das Ministerium, der Minister des Innern.* — **III.** adv.: to be ∾-sick *Heimweh haben;* to bring a crime ∾ to a person *j.en eines Verbrechens überführen;* to bring (to drive) a thing ∾ to a person *j.em etwas klarmachen;* to come (to go) ∾ *nach Hause kommen (gehen);* to come ∾ to a person *j.en nahe berühren;* to see a person ∾ *j.en nach Hause begleiten;* the blow struck (thrust) ∾ *der Hieb saß;* to take ∾ to oneself *verstehen, begreifen;* that's nothing to write ∾ about (colloq.) *dessen brauchst du dich nicht zu rühmen, darauf brauchst du nicht so stolz zu sein.* — **IV.** v.i.: a homing pigeon *eine Brieftaube*

honest a.: ∾ Injun (= Indian)! ∾ Injun? (School) *auf mein Wort! auf dein Wort?;* to earn (to make, to turn) an ∾ penny *ehrlich sein Brot verdienen;* to make an ∾ woman of a girl *ein verführtes Mädchen (eine Mätresse) ehelichen, heiraten;* to be quite ∾ about it ... *ehrlich gesagt ...*

honesty n.: ∾ is the best policy (prov.) *ehrlich währt am längsten*

honour n.: a point of ∾ *eine Ehrensache;* the ∾s are easy *die Honneurs (im Bridgespiel die 4-5 höchsten Karten) sind gleich verteilt; (fig.) die Vorteile sind auf beiden Seiten;* a prophet has no (has little) ∾ in his own country (prov.) *ein Prophet gilt nichts in seinem Vaterland;* to be on one's ∾ (to be bound in ∾) to do a thing *moralisch verpflichtet sein, etwas zu tun;* upon my ∾! ∾ bright! *auf mein Ehrenwort!;* to do the ∾s *die Honneurs machen, Gäste empfangen*

hoof n.: to pad the ∾ *auf Schusters Rappen reiten;* to show the cloven ∾ *den Pferdefuß, sein wahres Gesicht zeigen;* to sell cattle on the ∾ *Vieh lebend verkaufen*

hook I. n.: by ∾ or by crook *auf irgendeine Weise; so oder so; es mag biegen oder brechen;* to do a thing on one's own ∾ (sl.) *etwas auf eigene Faust, aus eigenem Antrieb machen;* to drop off the ∾s (sl.) *sterben, um die Ecke gehen;* to go off the ∾s (sl.) *verrückt werden;* to take (to sling) one's ∾ (sl.) *Reißaus nehmen, durchbrennen.* — **II.** v.tr.: to swallow something ∾, line and sinker *leichtgläubig sein (wie ein hungriger Fisch);* to ∾ it (sl.) *Reißaus nehmen, durchbrennen*

hookey n.: to play ∾ (sl.) *die Schule usw. schwänzen*

hoot n.: I don't care two ∾s (sl.) *das ist mir Wurst (ganz schnuppe), ich mache mir nicht die Bohne (einen Dreck) daraus;* it is not worth a ∾ (U.S. sl.) *es ist keinen Pfifferling wert*

hop I. v.i.: a ∾-o'-my-thumb *ein Däumling, Knirps, Dreikäsehoch;* an aeroplane ∾s off (colloq.) *ein Flugzeug startet.* — **II.** v.tr.: ∾ it! (sl.) *hau' ab! verdufte!;* to ∾ it, to ∾ the twig (stick) *verschwinden; sterben, abkratzen;* cloud-∾ping *das Fliegen von Wolke zu Wolke, um Deckung zu suchen;* hedge (wave)-∾ping *der Tiefflug über Land, Wasser.* — **III.** n.: the ∾, skip (step) and jump (gym.) *der Dreisprung;* to be on the ∾ *geschäftig hin und her rennen;* to catch on the ∾ *ertappen, erwischen;* to fly in ∾s *in Etappen fliegen;* to go to a ∾ (colloq.) *zum Tanz gehen*

hope I. n.: to hold out (forth) ∾s *Hoffnungen machen;* to ∾ against ∾ *weiterhoffen, wo nichts mehr zu hoffen ist;* to lay (to set) one's ∾s on a thing *seine Hoffnungen auf etwas setzen;* past ∾ *hoffnungslos;* some ∾s, what a ∾! (colloq.) *kein Schimmer von Hoffnung!* — **II.** v.i.: let us ∾ for the best *wir wollen das beste hoffen*

hopeful n.: a young ∾ *ein hoffnungsvoller Sprößling*

horn I. n.: to be (to find oneself) on the ∾s of a dilemma *vor einer schwierigen Wahl stehen;* the ∾ of plenty *das Füllhorn;* dreams that come by a gate of ∾ *Träume, die wahr werden;* to blow one's own ∾ *sein eigenes Lob singen;* to draw (to pull) in one's ∾s *die Hörner einziehen, sich mäßigen;* to lower one's ∾ *sich erniedrigen, sich herablassen;* to make a spoon and spoil a ∾ *etwas auf alle Fälle versuchen;* to take the bull by the ∾s *den Stier bei den Hörnern fassen (packen).* — **II.** v.i.: excuse my ∾ing in (colloq.) *entschuldige, daß ich mich einmische*

hornet n.: to bring a ∾'s nest about one's ears *in ein Wespennest stechen*

hornswoggle (sl.) **I.** n.: ∾ *Quatsch.* — **II.** v.tr. & i.: to ∾ *beschwindeln, hereinlegen*

horror n.: to have the ∾s *das Grauen haben, an Säuferwahnsinn leiden;* ∾-struck, ∾-stricken *von Entsetzen ergriffen (gepackt)*

horse n.: that's a ∾ of another colour *das ist eine ganz andere Sache;* to back the wrong ∾ *aufs falsche Pferd setzen;* to take ∾ *aufsitzen, reiten;* you may take (one may lead) a ∾ to the water, but you (twenty) can't make him drink (prov.) *man kann ein Pferd zur Tränke führen, aber nicht zum Saufen zwingen;* to put the cart before the ∾ *das Pferd am Schwanze aufzäumen, etwas verkehrt anfangen;* to win the ∾ and lose the saddle *alles oder nichts gewinnen;* the grey mare is the better ∾ *die Frau hat dic Hosen an;* a clothes-∾ *ein Wäschetrockengestell;* a towel-∾ *ein Handtuchständer;* ride a cock-∾ to Banbury Cross (nursery rhyme) *hoppe, hoppe, Reiter!;* he is a dark ∾ *er ist ein unbeschriebenes Blatt;* to flog a dead ∾ *Interesse für eine abgetane Sache zu erregen suchen; seine Kraft verschwenden;* foot and ∾ *Infanterie und Kavallerie;* hold your ∾s! *bleib ruhig!;* to look a gift-∾ in the mouth *einem geschenkten Gaul ins Maul sehen;* to mount (to ride) the high ∾ *sich aufs hohe Pferd (Roß) setzen;* to put the saddle on the right (wrong) ∾ *die Schuld auf den Richtigen (Falschen) schieben;* a one-∾ show *ein kleines, unbedeutendes Unternehmen;* the white ∾s *die weißen Wellenkämme;* to flog a willing ∾ *offene Türen einrennen;* to ride a willing ∾ to death *j.es Güte arg mißbrauchen;* to spur a willing ∾ *j.en unnötig drängen;* to grin through a ∾-collar *kindliche Späße treiben;* a ∾-laugh *ein lautes, wieherndes Gelächter;* a ∾-leech *ein unersättlicher Mensch, Wucherer;* tell that to the ∾-marines! *das kannst du deiner Großmutter erzählen!;* to have a thing straight from the ∾'s mouth *etwas aus erster Hand (Quelle) haben;* to be fond of ∾-play *gern derbe Späße machen;* to have a lot of ∾-sense (colloq.) *einen praktischen (gesunden) Menschenverstand haben*

hospital n.: he is walking the ∾ *er macht seine klinischen Semester*

hot a.: ∾ air (colloq.) *aufgeregtes, aufgeblasenes Gerede;* all ∾ and bothered (colloq.) *aufgeregt, nervös;* to blow ∾ and cold *häufig die Meinung, Einstellung wechseln;* to be in a ∾ spot *in einer kitzligen Lage sein;* a ∾ dog *ein heißes Würstchen;* to drop someone like a ∾ potato (colloq.) *die Beziehungen zu j.em plötzlich abbrechen;* ∾-foot *in aller Eile;* to get into ∾ water *in Schwierigkeiten, in einen Streit geraten;* give it to him ∾! (colloq.) *gib es ihm! sag ihm die Meinung!;* a ∾-gospeller *ein fanatischer Laienprediger;* a ∾-head *ein Hitzkopf;* to make it ∾ for someone, to give him a ∾ time *j.en ärgern, ihm Schwierigkeiten bereiten;* it's not so ∾! (colloq.) *es ist schlecht;* to sell like ∾ cakes *(rasch) verkaufen wie warme Semmeln;* ∾ stuff (sl.) *Ausdruck der Bewunderung (z. B. eines guten Tennisspielers) oder des Tadels (z. B. wegen eines gewagten Benehmens)*

hound I. n.: hare and ∾s *eine Schnitzeljagd;* to hold (to run) with the hare and run (hunt) with the ∾s *es mit beiden Parteien halten, es mit niemandem verderben wollen;* to ride to ∾s *auf die Parforcejagd reiten.* — **II.** v.tr.: to ∾ a person at a thing *j.en auf etwas hetzen;* to ∾ a person on *j.en antreiben*

hour n.: at the eleventh ∾ (cf. Matth. XX) *in letzter Stunde;* the small ∾s of the morning *die frühen Morgenstunden (1, 2 usw. Uhr);* to keep early (good, regular) ∾s *zeitig zu Bett gehen;* to keep bad (late) ∾s *nachts lange aufbleiben;* to be paid by the ∾ *Stundenlohn erhalten;* after ∾s *nach Ladenschluß*

house n.: an Englishman's ∾ is his castle (prov.) *eines Engländers Haus ist seine Burg, d. h. niemand darf gewaltsam in es eindringen;* the House of Commons, of Lords *das englische Unterhaus; Oberhaus;* a ∾breaker *ein Einbrecher;* a ∾ of call *ein Absteigequartier;* a ∾ of ill fame *ein Bordell;* like a ∾ on fire *wie toll;* as safe as a ∾ *ein sicheres Geleit;* as sure as ∾s *ganz bestimmt, todsicher;* a ∾-warming *ein Fest beim Einzug in ein neues Haus;* a public ∾ *eine Gastwirtschaft;* to bow down in the ∾ of Rimmon *seine Grundsätze aus politischen oder anderen Motiven aufgeben;* I would not give it ∾-room *ich nähme es nicht geschenkt;* to keep ∾ *den Haushalt führen;* she is ∾-proud *sie legt überaus großen Wert auf die Pflege ihres Hauses;* to keep the ∾ *das Haus hüten, nicht ausgehen;* to keep (an) open ∾ *ein gastfreies*

Haus führen; to proclaim from the ∾-tops *öffentlich verkünden, an die große Glocke hängen*

household n.: the ∾ troops *die königliche Garde;* a ∾ word *ein allgemein bekannter Ausspruch, ein Alltagswort*

howler n.: a ∾ *ein grober Schnitzer;* to come a ∾ (sl.) *zu Fall, zu Schaden kommen*

howling a.: it's a ∾ shame (sl.) *es ist eine Sünde und Schande;* a ∾ success (sl.) *ein Bombenerfolg*

hub n.: the ∾ of the universe *der Mittelpunkt der Welt*

hub-hub n.: a ∾ *Lärm (von vielen Stimmen), Tumult*

huddle n. (U.S. sl.): to go into a ∾ *die Köpfe zusammenstecken*

hue n.: to raise a ∾ and cry *ein Zetergeschrei erheben*

huff n.: to be in a ∾ *aufgebracht, in übler Laune sein;* to take ∾ at a thing *etwas übelnehmen, sich beleidigt fühlen*

hug v.tr.: to ∾ the coast (shore) *sich dicht an der Küste halten;* to ∾ oneself on (for) a thing *sich zu etwas beglückwünschen;* a ∾-me-tight *ein wollenes Umschlagetuch*

hum I. v.tr.: to ∾ a tune *eine Melodie summen.* — **II.** v.i.: to ∾ (sl.) *übel riechen;* to ∾ and haw *im Reden stocken, stottern, zögern;* to make things ∾ *Betrieb machen, eine Sache in Schwung bringen, Dampf dahinter machen;* a ∾ming bird *ein Kolibri;* a ∾ming blow on the head *ein gewaltiger Schlag auf den Kopf*

humble a.: to eat ∾ pie *Abbitte leisten, sich demütigen, zu Kreuze kriechen*

humour I. n.: I'm not in the ∾ for talking *ich bin nicht aufgelegt zu reden;* to be out of ∾ *schlecht gelaunt sein.* — **II.** v.tr.: to ∾ a person *auf j.es Wünsche eingehen, ihm den Willen tun*

hump n.: it gives me the ∾ (sl.) *es macht mich ganz verdrießlich*

hunch n.: I have a ∾ that (U.S. sl.) *ich habe so das Gefühl (so eine Ahnung), daß*

hung p.p. *von* hang: he was ∾ last year *eines seiner Bilder wurde im vorigen Jahr für die Ausstellung der Royal Academy angenommen;* to be ∾ up *aufgehalten werden*

hunger n.: ∾ is the best sauce (prov.) *Hunger ist der beste Koch*

hungry a.: as ∾ as a hunter (a hawk) *so hungrig wie ein Wolf, Bär;* a ∾ look *ein gieriger Blick;* to go ∾ *Hunger leiden*

hurry I. n.: I'm in a ∾ *ich habe es eilig;* I shall not ask again in a ∾ *ich werde so bald nicht wieder darum bitten;* you will not beat that in a ∾ *das wirst du so leicht nicht übertreffen.* — **II.** v.tr.: the patient was hurried away to hospital *der Patient wurde eilig ins Krankenhaus gebracht.* — **III.** v.i.: ∾ up! *mach' schnell! beeile dich!*

husband I. n.: ∾'s tea *dünner und kalter Tee.* — **II.** v.tr.: to ∾ one's strength, resources *mit seinen Kräften, Mitteln haushalten*

hush I. n.: a ∾-∾ affair *eine streng geheime Angelegenheit;* to pay ∾-money *Schweigegeld bezahlen.* — **II.** v.tr.: to ∾ up a matter *eine Sache vertuschen.* — **III.** v.i.: ∾! *ruhig! still! pst!*

hussy, huzzy n.: she is a pert ∾ *sie ist ein freches Frauenzimmer (Weibsbild)*

I

ice I. n.: to break the ∾ *die anfängliche Schüchternheit (Zurückhaltung) überwinden;* that cuts no ∾ with me (sl.) *das zieht bei mir nicht, das läßt mich kalt;* to skate over thin ∾ *ein heikles Thema berühren;* the harbour (the ship) is ∾-bound *der Hafen (das Schiff) ist vereist (zugefroren).* — **II.** v.tr.: to ∾ a cake (to cover it with icing, [amer.] frosting) *einen Kuchen mit Zuckerguß überziehen*

idea n.: the ∾ of it! *na, so was! stell' sich (dat.) das einer vor!;* what is the (big) ∾? (colloq.) *was soll das bedeuten?;* to form an ∾ of a thing *sich (dat.) eine Vorstellung von etwas machen;* to get ∾s into one's head *falsche Vorstellungen bekommen;* to put ∾s into someone's head *falsche Vorstellungen erwecken;* I have an ∾ that *ich habe so eine Idee (mir kommt es so vor, mir schwant es), daß (als ob);* he has no ∾ of it *er hat keine Ahnung davon;* to hit (to strike) upon an ∾ *auf einen Gedanken verfallen;* to teach the young ∾ (Thomson: Seasons, Spring 1, 1148) *den Geist des Kindes lehren*

if conj.: ∾ I haven't lost my watch! *da habe ich doch wahrhaftig meine Uhr verloren!*

ill I. a.: ∾ weeds grow apace (prov.) *Unkraut vergeht nicht;* ∾ news flies (comes) apace (prov.) *schlechte Nachrichten verbreiten sich schnell;* it's an ∾ wind that blows nobody any good (prov.) *kein Unglück ist so groß, es trägt ein Glück im Schoß;* to be (to fall, to be taken) ∾ of (with) a disease *krank sein, werden; an einem Leiden erkranken;* to do an ∾ turn to a person *j.em einen üblen Streich spielen.* — **II.** n.: to return ∾ for good *Gutes mit Bösem vergelten;* to speak ∾ of a person *von j.em schlecht sprechen.* — **III.** adv.: to be ∾ at ease *sich unbehaglich fühlen, befangen sein;* it ∾ became him to speak *es stand ihm schlecht an zu sprechen;* it would have gone ∾ with him *es wäre ihm schlecht ergangen;* my friend met some ∾-bred people *mein Freund traf einige schlecht erzogene Leute;* he was ∾-treated, and took it ∾ *er wurde schlecht behandelt und hat es übelgenommen;* he was ∾-pleased *er war unzufrieden;* he was ∾-disposed towards them *er war ihnen übelgesinnt;* he bore them ∾-will *er hegte einen Groll gegen sie;* you were ∾-advised *Sie waren schlecht beraten;* this action was ∾-judged, and was therefore ∾-fated *diese Handlung war unangebracht und war deshalb vom Glück verlassen;* Richard III was ∾-favoured and ∾-natured *Richard III. war häßlich und bösartig;* he possessed many ∾-gotten gains *er hatte viele unrechtmäßig erworbene Gewinne*

image n.: he is the very ∾ of his father *er ist das Ebenbild seines Vaters, ihm wie aus dem Gesicht geschnitten*

immemorial a.: from time ∾ *seit undenklichen Zeiten*

impose I. v.tr.: to ∾ a tax upon a thing *eine Steuer auf etwas legen;* to ∾ a thing upon a person *j.em etwas andrehen.* — **II.** v.i.: to ∾ upon a person *auf j.en einen Eindruck machen; j.en täuschen, betrügen, hintergehen;* to ∾ upon a person's kindness *j.es Güte mißbrauchen*

improve I. v.tr.: to ∾ the occasion (opportunity) *die Gelegenheit aus-, benutzen;* to ∾ away (rare) *durch Verbesserungen beseitigen.* — **II.** v.i.: he ∾s on acquaintance *er gewinnt bei näherer Bekanntschaft;* to ∾ upon a thing *etwas verbessern, überbieten*

in I. prep.: ∾ crossing the river *bei (während) der Überquerung des Flusses;* ∾ my defence *zu meiner Verteidigung;* ∾ dozens *zu Dutzenden, dutzendweise;* the latest ∾ hats *der letzte Schrei (die neucste Mode), was Hüte (an)betrifft;* ∾ honour of, ∾ remembrance of *zu Ehren von; zum Andenken an;* ∾ itself *an sich;* he is a doctor ∾ name, but is no longer ∾ practice *dem Namen nach ist er Arzt, aber er praktiziert nicht mehr;* seven ∾ number *sieben an der Zahl;* ∾ my opinion *nach meiner Meinung;* ∾ order to *um zu;* ∾ all probability *aller Wahrscheinlichkeit nach, höchstwahrscheinlich;* ∾ quest (search) of *auf der Suche nach;* they spend their time ∾ reading *sie verbringen die Zeit mit Lesen;* ∾ reply to *als Antwort auf, in Beantwortung von;* to be wanting ∾ courage *es an Mut fehlen lassen;* there is little (not much, nothing) ∾ it *es steckt wenig (nichts) darin; es lohnt sich nicht;* he is not ∾ it *er kommt nicht in Frage, er hat keine Chance;* he had it ∾ him *er hatte das Zeug dazu;* it is not ∾ him *es liegt nicht in seiner Art.* — **II.** adv.: to be ∾ *zu Hause sein;* the fire is ∾ *das Feuer brennt noch;* ∾ for a penny, ∾ for a pound (prov.) *wer A sagt, muß auch B sagen;* Labour is ∾ *die Arbeiterpartei ist an der Regierung;* the train is ∾ *der Zug ist angekommen (eingelaufen);* to be all ∾ (sl.) *völlig erschöpft (erledigt) sein;* to be ∾ for a thing *etwas zu gewärtigen haben;* you are ∾ for it *du wirst etwas abbekommen, du sitzt schön in der Tinte;* to be (to keep) ∾ with a person *mit j.em auf freundschaftlichem Fuße stehen (sich halten);* to be ∾ on a good thing (colloq.) *Aussichten haben, einen Anteil an einer guten Sache zu bekommen.* — **III.** n.: the ∾s and outs of a procedure *die Einzelheiten eines Verfahrens*

inch I. n.: an ∾ of cold iron *ein Dolchstoß;* by ∾es *Stück für Stück, nach und nach, allmählich;* a man of your ∾es *ein Mann von deiner Statur;* to flog a person within an ∾ of his life *j.en fast zu Tode prügeln;* give him an ∾ and he will take an ell (a yard) *reich' ihm (nur) den kleinen Finger, und er nimmt (gleich) die ganze Hand.* — **II.** v.i.: to ∾ along *langsam vorwärtskommen*

incline I. v.tr.: to ∾ one's ear to a person *j.em sein Ohr leihen.* — **II.** v.i.: he ∾s to corpulence *er hat Anlage zur Korpulenz;* to ∾ (to be [to feel] ∾d) to do a thing *geneigt sein (dazu neigen, die Neigung haben), etwas zu tun;* an ∾d plane *eine schiefe Ebene*

inconvenience n.: to put a person to ∾ *j.em Ungelegenheiten (Unannehmlichkeiten) bereiten*

increase n.: to be on the ∾ *im Wachsen sein, zunehmen*

incumbent a.: it is ∾ on you to help them *es liegt dir ob (es ist deine Pflicht), ihnen zu helfen*

indeed adv.: he is, ∾, a remarkable man *er ist in der Tat (tatsächlich, wirklich) ein bemerkenswerter Mann,* that was quick work ∾ *das war wirklich flott gearbeitet;* thank you very much ∾ *vielen herzlichen Dank!;* yes, ∾! *ja, wahrhaftig!;* who is this Mr. Smith? (answer) who is he, ∾! *wer ist dieser Herr Schmidt? (Antwort) das mögen Sie wohl fragen!;* there are ∾ exceptions *es gibt allerdings (freilich, indessen, zwar) Ausnahmen;* ∾ I did! *gewiß habe ich es getan!;* ∾? *so? wirklich?;* o ∾! *nicht möglich!*

indelible a.: an ∾ pencil *ein Tintenstift;* an ∾ disgrace *eine unauslöschbare Schande*

Indian a.: ∾ corn *Mais;* to march in ∾ file *im Gänsemarsch gehen (marschieren);* an ∾ summer *ein Spät-, Nachsommer*

indifferent a.: ∾ to danger, to cold *gleichgültig gegen Gefahr, Kälte;* to remain ∾ in a matter *keine Partei ergreifen;* it is quite ∾ to me what happens *es ist mir gleichgültig, was passiert;* his French is ∾, very ∾ *sein Französisch ist mittelmäßig, ziemlich schlecht*

indulge I. v.tr.: to ∾ one's children *seine Kinder verwöhnen, nachsichtig gegen sie sein;* to ∾ one's appetites *seinen Gelüsten willfahren.* — **II.** v.i.: to ∾ in a holiday *sich Ferien erlauben*

indulgent a.: ∾ (towards others) *nachsichtig (gegen andere);* self-∾ *sich gehen lassend*

inform v.tr. & i.: a well-∾ed person *eine gut unterrichtete Person;* to ∾ against someone *j.en anzeigen, denunzieren*

infra dig pred. a.: to be ∾ (abbr. lat. infra dignitatem) *unter seiner Würde, unpassend sein*

inner a.: one's ∾ man (joc.) *(scherzhaft für) Magen*

innocent a.: windows ∾ of glass *Fenster ohne Glas*

inquire I. v.tr.: to ∾ his name *nach seinem Namen fragen;* to ∾ at the station *sich am Bahnhof erkundigen.* — **II.** v.i.: to ∾ into a matter *eine Sache untersuchen, erforschen;* to ∾ after someone *sich nach j.em erkundigen;* to ∾ for someone *nach j.em fragen*

inquiring a.: he has an ∾ mind *er hat einen neugierigen, wißbegierigen Sinn;* an ∾ look *ein forschender Blick*

inside I. n.: the ∾ of a week *die Mitte der Woche;* to turn ∾ out *das Innere nach außen kehren, umkrempeln, umstülpen.* — **II.** a.: he has ∾ information *er hat geheime Nachricht (Auskunft);* to get the ∾ track of a thing *verstehen, wie etwas arbeitet (funktioniert).* — **III.** adv.: ∾ of a week (colloq.) *in weniger als einer Woche (in nahezu, fast einer Woche).* — **IV.** prep.: ∾ the house *innerhalb des Hauses*

instalment n.: to pay by (in) ∾s *in Raten, ratenweise bezahlen, abstottern;* an ∾ story *ein Fortsetzungsroman*

instance n.: at the ∾ of a person *auf j.es Bitten, Ansuchen;* for ∾ *zum Beispiel;* in the first ∾ *an erster Stelle;* in this (your) ∾ *in diesem (deinem) Falle*

instant I. a.: the letter is dated the 6th ∾ (abbr. inst.) *der Brief datiert vom 6. dieses Monats.* — **II.** n.: come here this ∾, on the ∾ *komm' sofort hierher!;* in an ∾ *im Augenblick, im Nu;* I told you the ∾ I knew *sobald ich es wußte, habe ich es dir gesagt*

insult n.: to add ∾ to injury *die Sache noch schlimmer machen*

intend v.tr.: we ∾ to go tomorrow *wir wollen morgen gehen;* we ∾ no harm *wir haben nichts Böses vor;* this is ∾ed as a stop-gap *dies ist als Notstopfen gedacht;* what do you ∾ by the word? *was willst du mit dem Worte sagen?;* we ∾ our son for the Bar *unser Sohn soll Rechtsanwalt werden;* this daub is ∾ed for me *diese Kleckserei (dieses Geschmiere) soll mich darstellen*

intended n.: her ∾ (colloq.) *ihr Zukünftiger*

intent I. n.: to all ∾s and purposes *praktisch genommen, im Grunde, in jeder Hinsicht;* with ∾ to defraud *in der Absicht zu betrügen;* with good (malicious) ∾ *in guter (böser) Absicht.* — **II.** a.: to be ∾ on doing something *eifrig darauf bedacht sein, etwas zu tun;* an ∾ look *ein gespannter, aufmerksamer Blick*

interest I. n.: to attend to a person's ∾ *über j.es Interessen wachen;* it is no ∾ of mine *es geht mich nichts an;* it is (to) your ∾ *es liegt in deinem Interesse;* he has an ∾ at court *er hat Einfluß (Freunde) bei Hofe;* to have an ∾ in an undertaking *finanziell an einem Unternehmen beteiligt sein;* to lend (to put) money out at ∾ *Geld auf Zinsen ausleihen;* to make ∾ for a person with a person *sich für j.en bei j.em verwenden;* to return a blow with ∾ *einen Schlag mit Zinsen heimzahlen;* to take ∾ in a thing *sich für etwas interessieren;* to use one's ∾ *seinen Einfluß geltend machen;* important to the landed ∾ *wichtig für die Großgrundbesitzer;* compound ∾ *Zinseszins;* vested ∾s *althergebrachte, festbegründete Rechte.* — **II.** v.tr.: to ∾ a person in an undertaking *j.en zur Beteiligung an einem Unternehmen veranlassen, gewinnen;* I am ∾ed in the subject *ich interessiere mich für das Thema;* she is in an ∾ing condition *sie ist schwanger (in Hoffnung, Umständen)*

invert v.tr.: ∾ed commas *Anführungsstriche, Gänsefüßchen*

I.O.U. n.: to give an ∾ (I owe you) *einen Schuldschein geben*

iron n.: an inch of cold ∾ *ein Dolchstoß;* to be in ∾s *gefesselt sein;* the ∾ has entered into his soul *er ist verbittert, stark verärgert;* to have many ∾s in the fire *viele Eisen im Feuer haben;* to rule with a rod of ∾ *tyrannisch herrschen (über);* strike while the ∾ is hot (prov.) *schmiede das Eisen, solange es heiß ist*

issue n.: in the ∾ *in der Folge, am Ende, schließlich;* the question at ∾ *die strittige Frage;* without male ∾ *ohne männliche Nachkommen;* to be at ∾ about a thing *über etwas streiten;* to bring to an ∾ *zum Austrag bringen;* to join ∾s *eine Sache der Entscheidung eines Gerichts überlassen;* to join ∾ with a person upon a matter *einen Streit über eine Frage mit j.em anfangen;* to make the question a live ∾ *der Frage besondere Bedeutung beilegen;* to pool ∾s *sich zu gegenseitigem Vorteil vereinigen*

it pron.: confound ∾! *hol's der Teufel (Henker)!;* you have done ∾ now! *da hast du was Schönes angerichtet!;* to foot, go, hook, hop, leg, lord, skip, ∾, see 'foot, go, etc.'; there is nothing for ∾ but to *es bleibt nichts anderes übrig als zu;* you really are ∾ (colloq.) *du bist wirklich unübertroffen, du schießt den Vogel ab*

itch I. n.: to have an ∾ for (to do) a thing *ein brennendes Verlangen nach etwas haben, darauf brennen, etwas zu tun.* — **II.** v.i.: I was ∾ing for (to do) it *ich hatte ein brennendes Verlangen danach (ich brannte darauf, es juckte mich an den Händen), es zu tun;* he has an ∾ing palm *er ist geldgierig*

ivory n.: black ∾ *Negersklaven als Ware;* dreams that come by the gate of ∾ *trügerische Träume;* to flash one's ivories (sl.) *lächeln, grinsen;* to tickle the ivories (sl.) *Klavier spielen;* to wash (to rinse, to sluice) one's ivories (sl.) *trinken, durch die Gurgel jagen, hinter die Binde gießen;* an ∾-snatcher (colloq.) *ein Zahnarzt*

J

jack n.: a ∾ass *ein männlicher Esel; ein Dummkopf;* a pair of ∾-boots *ein Paar Kanonen-, Wasserstiefel;* a ∾-in-the-box *ein Schachtelmännchen, Kastenteufel;* Jack Frost *der Frost;* Jack and Jill *Hans und Grete;* Jack Ketch *der Henker;* a ∾-knife *ein Klappmesser;* the Jack of Hearts *der Herzbube;* a ∾-o'-lantern *ein Irrlicht;* a Jack in office *ein sich wichtigtuender Beamter;* before you could say Jack Robinson *ehe man sich versah (bevor man bis drei zählen konnte), im Nu;* a Jack Tar *ein Matrose, eine Teerjacke;* a ∾-towel *ein Rollhandtuch;* Jack of all trades *Hans Dampf in allen Gassen;* Jack of all trades, master of none (prov.) *wer vieles betreibt, lernt nichts ordentlich;* a boot-∾ *ein Stiefelknecht;* a carriage-∾ *ein Wagenheber;* Cheap Jack *der Billige Jakob, Hausierer;* every man ∾ *jeder einzelne;* a steeple-∾ *ein Kirchturmarbeiter;* the Union Jack *die britische Nationalflagge;* yellow Jack *das gelbe Fieber*

jacket n.: potatoes boiled in their ∾s *Pellkartoffeln;* to dust (to warm) a person's ∾ *j.em die Jacke vollhauen;* a dinner-∾ *ein Smoking*

jam I. n.: to be in a ∾ (colloq.) *in der Klemme sein;* a traffic-∾ *eine Verkehrsstockung.* — **II.** v.tr.: to ∾ one's fingers *sich (dat.) die Finger quetschen;* to ∾ the wireless *eine Radioübertragung stören.* — **III.** v.i.: the brakes ∾med *die Bremsen klemmten*

jar v.i.: to ∾ upon a person's ears, nerves *j.es Ohr beleidigen; j.em auf die Nerven gehen;* his words ∾ with the facts *seine Worte stehen in schreiendem Gegensatz zu den Tatsachen*

jaw I. v.i.: he kept on ∾ing (colloq.) *er redete in einem fort.* — **II.** n.: hold your ∾! (low colloq.) *halte deinen Mund (Rand, deine Klappe)!;* a ∾-breaker (colloq.) *ein zungenbrecherisches Wort*

jaywalker n.: a ∾ *ein Fußgänger, der unachtsam die Straße überquert*

Jericho n.pr.: go to ∾! *scher' dich zum Teufel (Henker)!*

jerry I. n.: a ∾ (low sl.) *ein Nacht-, Pinkeltöpfchen;* a ∾-builder *j., der billige Häuser aus schlechtem Material baut, ein Bauschwindler.* — **II.** a.: ∾-built *unsolide gebaut, Bruch-*

jib[1] n.: the cut of his ∾ (sl.) *seine äußere Erscheinung, sein Aussehen*

jib[2] v.i.: they are ∾bing at the prices *sie scheuen die Preise*

jiffy n. (colloq.): in a ∾ *im Nu;* (wait) half a ∾! *einen Augenblick!*

jigger v.tr.: I'm ∾ed if I do so (sl.) *ich lasse mich hängen, ehe ich das tue*

Jim Crow n.pr.: he is a ∾ (U.S.) *er ist ein Neger;* a ∾-car *ein für Neger bestimmter Eisenbahnwagen*

jinks n.: high ∾ *ausgelassene Lustigkeit, übermütige Streiche*

jinx n. (sl.): *Person oder Sache, die Unglück bringt*

jitters n.: to be all ∾, jittery; to have the ∾ (sl.) *ganz nervös, aufgeregt sein, eine Mordsangst haben*

job n.: that's a good (bad) ∾ (colloq.) *das ist gut (schlecht);* that's the ∾! (sl.) *das ist die Masche!;* to be on the ∾ (sl.) *in Tätigkeit sein;* to be out of a ∾ (colloq.) *arbeitslos sein;* to do a person's ∾ (sl.) *j.en ruinieren, erledigen;* a ∾ber *ein Makler, Zwischenhändler;* a ∾master *ein Pferdevermieter;* a ∾-lot *eine Ramschware;* ∾-work *Stück-, Akkordarbeit*

jockey v.tr.: to ∾ a person into (out of) doing a thing *j.en in betrügerischer Weise veranlassen, etwas zu tun (zu unterlassen)*

jog I. v.i.: we must be ∾ging (colloq.) *wir müssen uns forttrollen;* matters ∾ along *es geht alles seinen alten Trott weiter;* we must ∾ along (on) somehow *wir müssen irgendwie weitermachen.* — **II.** v.tr.: to ∾ the memory *dem Gedächtnis nachhelfen.* — **III.** n.: in ∾-trot *in leichtem Trab*

join I. v.tr.: see 'battle, issue, majority'; to ∾ a club *Mitglied eines Klubs werden;* to ∾ hands in action *sich zu einer Tat vereinigen.* — **II.** v.i.: to ∾ up *Soldat werden*

joint I. n.: out of ∾ *verrenkt, aus den Fugen;* to put a person's nose out of ∾ *j.en aus dem Sattel heben, ausstechen;* to set a ∾ *ein Gelenk einrenken;* a ∾ (low colloq.) *eine Kneipe.* — **II.** a.: a ∾ action *eine gemeinsame Handlung;* during their ∾ lives *solange sie alle am Leben sind;* to be ∾ owners *gemeinsam etwas besitzen;* a ∾-stock company *eine Aktiengesellschaft*

joke n.: it is no ∾ *es ist kein Spaß, nicht zum Lachen;* to crack (to cut) a ∾ *einen Witz reißen;* to play a practical ∾ upon a person *j.em einen Schabernack spielen;* to see a (the) ∾ *einen (den) Witz verstehen*

jolly I. a.: as ∾ as a sandboy *kreuzfidel, quietschvergnügt;* he must be a ∾ fool to do so *er müßte ein rechter Narr sein (er wäre verrückt), wenn er es täte;* the ∾ Roger *die Piratenflagge.* — **II.** adv.: that serves you ∾ well right *das geschieht dir ganz recht.* — **III.** v.tr.: to ∾ someone (along) *j.em schmeicheln, j.en beschwatzen*

Jonathan n.pr.: Brother ∾ *der typische Bürger der U.S.A.*

jot I. n.: not one ∾ or tittle *nicht das kleinste bißchen.* — **II.** v.tr.: to ∾ a thing down *etwas kurz, schnell notieren*

jowl n.: cheek by ∾ *dicht aneinander, in traulicher Gemeinschaft*

joy n.: ∾-bells *Freuden-, Hochzeitsglocken;* a ∾-ride *eine Schwarz-, Vergnügungsfahrt, Spritztour im Auto;* the ∾stick *der Steuerknüppel im Flugzeug;* I wish you ∾ of it (colloq.) *viel Spaß dabei! besser du als ich*

judge n.: I am no ∾ of wine *ich bin kein Weinkenner*

jug n.: he is in ∾ (sl.) *er ist (sitzt) im Gefängnis (im Kittchen, im Loch, hinter schwedischen Gardinen)*

juice n.: to let a person stew in his own ∾ *j.en in seinem eigenen Fett schmoren lassen, ihn seinem Schicksal überlassen*

jump I. v.tr.: to ∾ a claim *ein Stück Land in Besitz nehmen, auf das ein anderer Anspruch hat;* to ∾ the gun *vor dem Pistolenschuß starten; j.em zuvorkommen;* to ∾ the queue *sich beim Schlangestehen vordrängen;* to ∾ the rails *entgleisen.* — **II.** v.i.: to wait for the cat to ∾ *sehen, wie der Hase läuft;* to ∾ at conclusions *voreilige Schlüsse ziehen;* to ∾ at an offer *ein Anerbieten freudig annehmen, mit beiden Händen zugreifen;* to ∾ down a person's throat *j.em über den Mund fahren (ihm das Maul stopfen), ihn anfahren;* to ∾ for joy *vor Freude hüpfen;* to ∾ (up)on a person *über j.en herfallen;* to ∾ out of one's skin *überrascht, freudig auffahren; aus der Haut fahren;* to ∾ over the broomstick *in wilder Ehe leben;* ∾ to it! (colloq.) *los! los!* — **III.** n.: to be on the ∾ *in Erregung, nervös sein;* to give a ∾ *auffahren, emporschnellen;* to have the ∾s *an Säuferwahnsinn leiden*

junk n.: *Krimskrams;* a ∾-shop *ein Kramladen*

just adv.: ∾ about enough *fast genug;* ∾ as I opened the door *im selben Moment, als ich die Tür aufmachte;* ∾ as you please *genau wie du willst;* I am ∾ coming *ich komme sofort;* ∾ look at this *siehe das mal eben an;* that is ∾ it *das ist es ja gerade, eben;* ∾ a moment please *einen Augenblick, bitte;* ∾ now *im Augenblick;* to take ∾ one *nur einen (eine, eins) nehmen;* ∾ so *so ist es, ganz recht;* it is ∾ splendid *es ist einfach herrlich;* ∾ then *in dem Moment;* not ∾ yet *noch nicht;* did you enjoy it? didn't I ∾ (sl.) *hat es dir gefallen? Und ob es mir gefiel!;* that's ∾ what the doctor ordered, that's ∾ the job (colloq.) *das ist genau richtig!*

justice n.: he did ∾ to the food *er sprach den Speisen tüchtig zu, er aß mit Appetit;* to do oneself ∾ *seine Fähigkeiten voll entfalten;* to do ∾ to someone *j.em gegenüber gerecht sein, ihm Gerechtigkeit widerfahren lassen*

K

keen a.: to be ∾ on a thing (on doing a thing) *erpicht (scharf) sein auf etwas, erpicht (scharf) darauf sein, etwas zu tun;* he is as ∾ as mustard on it *er ist ganz versessen (wild, toll) darauf*

keep I. v.tr.: to ∾ one's temper *sich beherrschen;* to ∾ a thing going *etwas in Gang halten;* to ∾ track of a thing *dem Lauf (der Entwicklung) einer Sache folgen;* what kept him? *was hat ihn abgehalten?;* God ∾ you! *Gott schütze dich!;* to ∾ someone waiting *j.en warten lassen;* to ∾ early (late) hours *früh (spät) zu Bett gehen;* ∾ it dark! ∾ it under your hat! (colloq.) *behalte es für dich;* to ∾ open house *sehr gastfreundlich sein;* ∾ your eyes skinned (colloq.) *paß' scharf auf!;* ∾ your nose clean, ∾ out of the rain (sl.) *halte dich heraus, misch' dich nicht (hin)ein;* ∾ your breath to cool your porridge *kümmere dich um deine eigenen Sachen.* — with prep. & adv.: to ∾ down expenses *die Ausgaben einschränken;* to ∾ down one's anger *seinen Zorn unterdrücken;* to ∾ a thing from a person *j.em etwas vorenthalten, verheimlichen;* to ∾ a person from a thing, from doing a thing *j.en an etwas hindern, j.en hindern (abhalten), etwas zu tun;* to ∾ one's hand in *in Übung bleiben;* to ∾ a pupil in *einen Schüler nachsitzen lassen;* to ∾ an assailant off *einen Angreifer fernhalten (abwehren);* ∾ your hair on! (sl.) *reg' dich nicht auf! nur keine Aufregung!;* to ∾ one's hat on *den Hut aufbehalten;* to ∾ a person out *j.en ausschließen, nicht hereinlassen;* to ∾ a person out of danger *j.en vor Gefahr bewahren;* to ∾ oneself to oneself *die Gesellschaft meiden, für sich bleiben;* to ∾ a thing to oneself *etwas für sich behalten;* to ∾ body and soul together *Leib und Seele zusammenhalten;* to ∾ up appearances *den Schein wahren;* to ∾ up a correspondence *eine Korrespondenz (einen Briefwechsel) unterhalten;* to ∾ up one's courage *den Mut nicht sinken lassen;* to ∾ one's end up *sich gut (tapfer) halten;* I must ∾ up my English *ich darf mein Englisch nicht vernachlässigen;* to ∾ up old customs *alte Gewohnheiten pflegen;* to ∾ up a quarrel *einen Zank (Streit) nicht zur Ruhe kommen lassen;* to ∾ it up *nicht nachlassen;* how long did you ∾ it up last night? *wie lange habt Ihr gestern Abend noch ausgehalten?;* to ∾ up prices *Preise auf der Höhe halten;* to ∾ up one's spirits *den Mut nicht sinken lassen.* — **II.** v.i.: where do you ∾? (rare) *wo wohnst du?;* how are you ∾ing? *wie geht es dir?;* that will ∾ *das hält sich; das hat Zeit, damit können wir noch warten;* the meat will not ∾ *das Fleisch hält sich nicht;* ∾ cool! *reg' dich nicht auf!;* to ∾ clear of a thing *sich fern-, freihalten von etwas;* to ∾ friends *Freunde bleiben;* to ∾ giggling *in einem fort kichern;* to ∾ quiet *ruhig bleiben.* — with prep. & adv.: to ∾ at someone for permission *j.en um Erlaubnis drängen;* to ∾ at work *ständig arbeiten;* to ∾ from doing a thing *sich enthalten, etwas zu tun;* to ∾ in good health *bei guter Gesundheit bleiben;* to ∾ in (to) one's bed *im Bett bleiben;* to ∾ in touch with a person *mit j.em in Fühlung bleiben;* to ∾ in with a person *sich mit j.em gut halten;* ∾ off the grass *Betreten des Rasens verboten!;* to ∾ on doing a thing *fortfahren (sich dranhalten), etwas zu tun;* to ∾ on at someone *an j.em herumnörgeln;* to ∾ straight on *geradeaus weitergehen, -fahren;* to ∾ to a promise *sein Versprechen halten;* to ∾ to oneself *für sich bleiben;* to ∾ up with a person *mit j.em Schritt halten;* to ∾ up with the Joneses *(scherzhafte Bezeichnung für das) Bestreben, immer mit dem Lebensstandard und den Anschaffungen der Nachbarn Schritt zu halten.* — **III.** n.: you don't earn your ∾ *du verdienst nicht deinen Unterhalt;* may I have it for ∾s? (colloq.) *darf ich es für immer behalten?*

keeping n.: to be in (out of) ∾ with *in Einklang (nicht in Einklang) stehen, übereinstimmen (nicht übereinstimmen) mit;* to be in safe ∾ *in sicherem Gewahrsam sein*

ken n.: that is beyond (out of) my ∾ *das entzieht sich meiner Kenntnis*

Kentish a.: ∾ fire *anhaltender Beifallssturm oder Sturm der Entrüstung*

kettle n.: the ∾ calls the pot black (prov.) *ein Esel schimpft den anderen Langohr;* that's a pretty ∾ of fish! *das ist eine nette Bescherung, eine schöne Geschichte!*

key I. n.: a master-∾ *ein Hauptschlüssel;* a skeleton-∾ *ein Dietrich;* to get (to have) the ∾ of the street *keinen Hausschlüssel haben, nachts ausgeschlossen bleiben, nicht ins Haus können, ohne Behausung sein;* to keep under lock and ∾ *unter Schloß und Riegel halten;* to turn the ∾ in the lock *den Schlüssel im Schloß umdrehen, zuschließen;* ∾ money *verlorener Zuschuß.* — **II.** v.tr.: to ∾ a person up *j.en anspornen, anfeuern;* I am all ∾ed up about it *ich bin riesig gespannt darauf*

kibe n.: to tread on a person's ∾s *j.em auf die Füße treten, ihn verletzen* (kibe = *Frostbeule)*

kibosh n.: to put the ∾ on a person (sl.) *j.em den Garaus machen, ihn erledigen*

kick I. n.: he got more ∾s than halfpence *er bekam mehr Prügel als freundliche Worte;* he has no ∾ left *er hat keinen Schwung (keine Spannkraft) mehr;* I got a great ∾ out of it *die Sache hat mir mächtig Spaß gemacht;* the ∾ of a gun *der Rückschlag eines Gewehres;* to get the ∾ (sl.) *entlassen werden;* a ∾ in the pants (sl.) *eine Enttäuschung, ein Schlag ins Gesicht.* — **II.** v.tr.: see 'bucket, heel'; to ∾ a person upstairs *j.en in eine höhere Stellung befördern, um ihn unschädlich zu machen;* to ∾ up, see 'dust, fuss, heel, noise, row, shindy, shine'. — **III.** v.i.: to ∾ against the pricks *wider den Stachel lecken (löcken);* to ∾ over the traces *über die Stränge schlagen*

kid[1] (sl.), **kiddy** (colloq.) n.: where are the ∾s, kiddies? (sl.) *wo sind die Kinder?*

kid[2] v.tr. (sl.): he's only ∾ding you *er hält dich nur zum besten, zum Narren*

kidney n.: he is a man of the right ∾ *er ist ein Mann vom richtigen Schlage*

Kilkenny n.pr.: to fight like ∾ cats *bis zur Vernichtung kämpfen*

kill I. v.tr.: to ∾ time *die Zeit totschlagen;* to ∾ two birds with one stone *zwei Fliegen mit e i n e r Klappe schlagen;* she was got up to ∾ *sie war faszinierend gekleidet (aufgemacht);* to ∾ someone with kindness *j.em aus Güte schaden;* to ∾ off *abschlachten, ausrotten, vertilgen;* a ∾-joy *ein Störenfried, Spielverderber.* — **II.** v.i.:

pigs do not ∾ well at that age *Schweine sind in dem Alter nicht schlachtreif;* she looked ∾ing (colloq.) *sie sah bezaubernd aus*

kin I. n.: kith and ∾ *Bekannte und Verwandte;* the next of ∾ *der, die nächste(n) Verwandte(n);* he comes of good ∾ *er stammt aus guter Familie.* — **II.** pred.a.: we are ∾, he is ∾ to me *wir sind verwandt, er ist mit mir verwandt*

kind[1] n.: something, nothing of the ∾ *etwas, nichts Derartiges, dergleichen;* this is the ∾ of thing I meant *so etwas meinte ich;* we had a meal of a ∾ *wir bekamen etwas, das sich eine Mahlzeit nannte;* I ∾ of expected it (colloq.) *ich erwartete es gewissermaßen, fast;* I felt a ∾ of compunction *ich spürte so etwas wie Gewissensbisse;* to differ in ∾ *der Natur, dem Wesen nach verschieden sein;* to pay in ∾ *in Waren, Naturalien bezahlen;* I repaid his rudeness in ∾ *ich zahlte ihm seine Unverschämtheit mit gleicher Münze heim*

kind[2] a.: to be so ∾ as to (to be ∾ enough to) do something *die Güte haben (so freundlich sein), etwas zu tun;* give my ∾ regards to your father *grüßen Sie Ihren Vater freundlich von mir!;* a ∾-hearted man *ein gutherziger, gütiger Mann*

kindly adv.: ∾ give me the paper *(sei so gut und) gib mir die Zeitung, bitte;* I take it ∾ of you *ich bin Ihnen sehr verbunden;* he did not take ∾ to life in England *er war nicht gern in England, er hat das englische Leben nicht lieb gewonnen*

king n.: à cat may look at a ∾ (prov.) *sieht doch die Katze den Kaiser an!;* to turn ∾'s (queen's) evidence *als Kronzeuge auftreten, gegen Mitschuldige aussagen, um straffrei auszugehen;* the ∾'s evil *die Skrofulose (früher durch Handauflegen des Königs für heilbar gehalten);* it is King Charles's head with him (David Copperfield, Mr Dick) *es ist eine fixe Idee von ihm*

kingdom n.: ∾ come (sl.) *das Jenseits*

kiss I. v.tr.: ∾ and be friends *gebt euch den Versöhnungskuß;* to ∾ the book *beim Eid die Bibel küssen;* to ∾ the dust *ins Gras beißen;* to ∾ the rod *eine Strafe unterwürfig hinnehmen.* — **II.** n.: to throw a ∾ *eine Kußhand zuwerfen*

kite n.: to fly a ∾ *einen Drachen, Versuchsballon steigen lassen;* to fly a ∾ (sl.) *ohne genügende Sicherheit borgen*

kith n.: ∾ and kin *Bekannte und Verwandte*

kitten n.: to have ∾s (sl.) *äußerst erzürnt (erregt) sein*

kittle a.: she is a ∾ cattle to shoe *sie ist eine schwer zu behandelnde Person*

knee n.: that is on the ∾s of the gods *das ruht noch im Schoße der Götter;* to bring a person to his ∾s *j.en auf die Knie zwingen*

knife n.: before you can say ∾ *im Nu, urplötzlich;* to get one's ∾ into a person *bösartig (rachsüchtig) mit j.em verfahren;* to have a horror of the ∾ *sich vor einer Operation fürchten;* to play a good ∾ and fork *beim Essen tüchtig einhauen*

knob n.: with ∾s on! (sl.) *aber feste! und wie!*

knock I. v.tr.: to ∾ back a glass of beer (sl.) *ein Glas Bier hinter die Binde gießen;* that ∾ed me back ten pounds (sl.) *das hat mich 10 Pfund gekostet;* to ∾ the bottom (the stuffing) out of an argument *eine Beweisführung vollkommen entkräften;* to ∾ one's head against a thing *sich den Schädel an etwas einrennen;* to ∾ into a cocked hat *etwas zu Brei schlagen;* to ∾ a thing on the head *eine Sache vereiteln, hintertreiben;* to ∾ a person into the middle of next week *j.en in hohem Bogen hinauswerfen;* what ∾s me are the prices (sl.) *ich bin einfach baff über die Preise;* to ∾ down a thing to a person at an auction *bei einer Versteigerung j.em etwas zuschlagen;* to ∾ a person's head off (colloq.) *j.em über sein;* to ∾ a person for a song (colloq.) *j.en auffordern, ein Lied zu singen;* to ∾ off a poem (colloq.) *ein Gedicht hinhauen;* to ∾ a pound off the bill *ein Pfund von der Rechnung absetzen;* to ∾ off work *aufhören zu arbeiten, Feierabend machen;* to ∾ together *etwas schnell zusammenstückeln;* I am quite ∾ed up, out *ich bin ganz erschöpft.* — **II.** v.i.: he has ∾ed about the world *er ist in der Welt herumgekommen;* a ∾-about suit *ein Strapazieranzug;* when do you ∾ off? *wann hörst du auf zu arbeiten, machst du Feierabend?;* to ∾ under *klein beigeben;* to ∾ up against a person *j.en treffen;* he is ∾-kneed, he has ∾-knees *er ist x-beinig, er hat x-Beine.* — **III.** n.: to give a ∾ *anklopfen;* to take the ∾ (sl.) *einen finanziellen Verlust erleiden*

knotty a.: it is a ∾ question *es ist eine schwierige Frage*

know I. v.tr.: to ∾ all the answers *ein Besserwisser sein;* I don't ∾ him from Adam *ich habe keine Ahnung, wer er ist;* not to ∾ chalk from cheese *einfältig, weltfremd sein;* to ∾ one from another *von einander unterscheiden können;* to ∾ one's own mind *wissen, was man will;* to ∾ the ropes *sich auskennen, den Rummel kennen;* to ∾ something for a fact *wissen, daß etwas wahr ist;* to ∾ what's what *nicht auf den Kopf gefallen (im Bilde) sein; wissen, was los ist (wo Barthel den Most holt);* to come to ∾ something *etwas erfahren;* to come to be ∾n *bekannt werden;* to get to ∾ something (someone) *etwas (j.en) kennen lernen;* will you go? not if I ∾ it! (colloq.) *gehst du hin? ich denke nicht daran!* — **II.** v.i.: there is no ∾ing *man kann nicht wissen;* not that I ∾ of *nicht, daß ich wüßte;* to ∾ on which side one's bread is buttered *wissen, wie man die Leute nehmen soll, um Vorteile zu gewinnen;* before you ∾ where you are *ehe man sich's versieht, im Handumdrehen;* to ∾ where the shoe pinches *Geldknappheit kennen; wissen, wo der Schuh drückt;* not to ∾ whether one is standing on one's head or one's heels *völlig durcheinander, durchgedreht sein;* to let a person ∾ *j.en wissen lassen*

know-how (sl.) n.: the manufacturing ∾ *die Spezialkenntnisse einer Herstellungsmethode*

knowledge n.: ∾ is power (prov.) *Wissen ist Macht;* it is common (public) ∾ *es ist allgemein bekannt;* to have carnal ∾ of a woman *geschlechtlichen Umgang mit einer Frau haben;* he is grown out of (all) ∾ *er ist so gewachsen, man kennt ihn nicht mehr;* to come to a person's ∾ *j.em zur Kenntnis (zu Ohren) kommen;* not to my ∾ *nicht, daß ich wüßte;* to the best of my ∾ and power (leg.) *nach bestem Wissen und Gewissen*

knuckle I. n.: near the ∾ (colloq.) *an der Grenze des Schicklichen, ziemlich gewagt;* a rap on the ∾s *ein Verweis.* — **II.** v.i.: I must ∾ down to it *ich muß mich ernsthaft darangeben (-machen);* to ∾ down (under) to a person *sich j.em beugen, unterwerfen*

L

labour I. n.: the ∾ exchange *das Arbeitsamt, der Arbeitsnachweis;* ∾ of love *Arbeit, die man gerne, unentgeltlich tut;* the Labour Party *die Arbeiterpartei;* hard ∾ *Zwangsarbeit, Zuchthausstrafe;* Love's ∾'s Lost (Shakespeare) *Verlorene Liebesmüh;* to be in ∾ *in Kind(e)snöten sein;* the constituency has gone ∾ *der Wahlkreis hat die Arbeiterpartei gewählt;* ∾-saving devices *arbeitersparende Einrichtungen.* — **II.** v.i.: the wheels ∾ in the sand *die Räder mahlen im Sand;* to ∾ under difficulties *mit Schwierigkeiten zu kämpfen haben;* to ∾ under a mistake (delusion) *sich im Irrtum befinden;* to ∾ with child *in den Geburtswehen liegen.* — **III.** v.tr.: I will not ∾ the point *ich will nicht im einzelnen auf den Punkt eingehen, ihn nicht ausführlich behandeln*

lace v.tr. & i.: tea ∾d with rum *Tee mit Rum versetzt;* strait-∾d *gestreng, engherzig, prüde*

lack I. n.: for ∾ of *aus Mangel an;* there is no ∾ of bread *Brot ist reichlich vorhanden;* ∾-lustre eyes *glanzlose, matte Augen.* — **II.** v.tr. & i.: he ∾s courage, he is ∾ing in courage *es fehlt ihm an Mut*

ladder I. n.: to get one's foot on the ∾ *einen Anfang machen mit;* she has a ∾ in her stocking *ihr läuft eine Masche im Strumpf;* to begin at the bottom (foot) of the ∾ *von der Pike auf dienen;* to knock down the ∾ *die Stellung oder die Freunde aufgeben, mit deren Hilfe man hochgekommen ist.* — **II.** v.i.: these stockings will not ∾, (are ∾-proof) *an diesen Strümpfen laufen garantiert keine Maschen*

lady n.: a ∾-bird *ein Marienkäfer;* a ∾-help *eine Stütze der Hausfrau;* a ∾-killer *ein Herzensbrecher;* my ∾-love *meine Geliebte;* a ∾ of easy virtue *eine Dirne;* a ∾-in-waiting *eine Hofdame;* your good ∾ *deine Frau;* the leading ∾ *die erste Liebhaberin;* a ∾'s man *ein Salonheld*

lag¹ I. v.i.: to ∾ behind, behind a person *zurückbleiben, hinter j.em zurückbleiben.* — **II.** n.: there is a time-∾ between higher wages and increased prices, see 'time'

lag[2] (sl.) **I.** v.tr.: to ∾ a person *j.en ins Zuchthaus bringen, verhaften.* — **II.** n.: he is an old ∾ *er ist ein alter Zuchthäusler*

lam v.tr. & i. (sl.): to ∾ (into) a person *j.en vermöbeln, verdreschen*

lamb n.: I may as well be hanged for a sheep as a ∾ *wenn schon, denn schon;* a wolf (a fox) in a ∾'s skin *ein Wolf im Schafpelz, ein Heuchler;* he did it like a ∾ *er tat es, ohne Widerstand zu leisten;* as meek as a ∾ *lammfromm*

lame a.: he is a ∾ duck *er ist ein lahmes, krankes Huhn; er ist ein Mann, der seine Schulden an der Börse nicht bezahlen kann;* that is a ∾ excuse *das ist eine faule Ausrede;* to be ∾ of (in) a leg *auf einem Bein lahm sein (lahmen), mit (auf) einem Bein hinken;* to help a ∾ dog over a stile *j.em in der Not behilflich sein*

lamp n.: to smell of the ∾ *nach der Studierlampe riechen, nächtliche Arbeit verraten; schwerfällig, geschraubt im Ausdruck sein;* to pass (to hand) on the ∾ *die Fackel weiterreichen; die Fahne der Wissenschaft hochhalten*

lance n.: he is a free ∾ *er gehört keiner Partei (Organisation) an, er ist ein Wilder; er ist ein freier Journalist;* a ∾-corporal *ein Gefreiter*

land I. n.: the ∾ of cakes *Schottland;* the ∾ o' the leal *die Gefilde der Seligen, der Himmel;* he is still in the ∾ of the living *er lebt noch;* to go to the ∾ of nod *einschlafen, einnicken, in Morpheus Arme sinken;* a ship makes the ∾ *ein Schiff kommt in Sicht des Landes;* to see how the ∾ lies *sehen, wie die Sache liegt (wie der Hase läuft);* a ∾-loper *Landstreicher;* ∾-lubber *Landratte.* — **II.** v.tr.: he ∾ed him a blow in the eye (colloq.) *er schlug ihm eins aufs Auge;* we were ∾ed in a great difficulty *wir gerieten in große Verlegenheit.* — **III.** v.i.: to ∾ first *als erster durchs Ziel gehen;* to ∾ on one's head *auf den Kopf fallen*

landed a.: ∾ gentry *Landadel;* ∾ property *Grundbesitz*

lane n.: it is a long ∾ (road) that has no turning (prov.) *es hat alles einmal sein Ende;* the red ∾ *die Kehle, die Gurgel (Kindersprache);* to form a ∾ *Spalier, eine Gasse bilden*

lantern n.: ∾-jawed *hohlwangig*

large n.: to be at ∾ *in Freiheit, auf freiem Fuße sein;* he is a gentleman at ∾ *er ist sein eigener Herr, er hat nicht nötig zu arbeiten;* he is popular with the people at ∾ *er ist bei allen Leuten beliebt;* to describe at ∾ *ausführlich beschreiben;* by and ∾ *im großen und ganzen*

lark[1] n.: if the sky fall, we shall catch ∾s (arch.) *wenn der Himmel einstürzt (herunterfällt), sind alle Spatzen tot;* to rise with the ∾ *beim ersten Hahnenschrei (in aller Herrgottsfrühe) aufstehen*

lark[2] **I.** n. (colloq.): what a ∾ it would be if *das wäre ein Jux, wenn.* — **II.** v.i.: to ∾ about *herumtollen*

lash I. v.i.: to ∾ at a person *einen heftigen Schlag gegen j.en führen;* rain ∾es down *Regen prasselt nieder;* a horse ∾es out *ein Pferd schlägt hinten aus;* he ∾ed out into strong language *er brach in ein Geschimpfe aus.* — **II.** v.tr.: he ∾ed the boy *er peitschte (verprügelte) den Jungen;* the waves ∾ed the shore *die Wellen schlugen ans Ufer;* he ∾ed him in scornful words *er geisselte (verspottete) ihn mit höhnischen Worten;* he ∾ed himself into a fury *er steigerte sich in eine Wut hinein;* to ∾ down (on) *festbinden, -machen;* to ∾ together *zusammenbinden.* — **III.** n.: the ∾ of the whip *die Peitschenschnur;* to get the ∾ *eine Tracht Prügel bekommen*

lashing n.: to get a ∾ *eine Tracht Prügel bekommen;* to have ∾s of a thing (sl.) *etwas in Hülle und Fülle haben*

last[1] n.: the cobbler must stick to his ∾ *Schuster, bleib bei deinen Leisten!;* to put on the ∾ *über den Leisten schlagen*

last[2] **I.** a.: ∾ Christmas *vorige Weihnachten;* of the ∾ importance *von der größten Wichtigkeit;* ∾ night *gestern Abend;* ∾ Tuesday, Tuesday ∾ *vorigen (vergangenen) Dienstag;* as I said in my ∾ *wie ich in meinem letzten Brief sagte;* to be on one's ∾ legs *auf dem letzten Loch pfeifen;* the ∾ thing in umbrellas *das Neueste in Regenschirmen;* ∾ thing at night *spät am Abend, als Letztes am Abend.* — **II.** n.: at ∾, at long ∾ *endlich, schließlich;* to breathe one's ∾ *den letzten Atemzug tun;*

I shall never hear the ∾ of it *das werde ich immer zu hören bekommen;* we have not seen the ∾ of it yet *die Sache ist noch nicht zu Ende; es ist noch nicht aller Tage Abend.* — **III.** adv.: ∾ not least *nicht zuletzt*

last³ v.i.: that will ∾ me eight months *damit komme ich acht Monate aus*

latch n.: the door is on the ∾ *die Tür ist nur eingeklinkt;* the ∾-key *der Hausschlüssel*

late I. a.: the ∾ prime minister *der verstorbene (frühere, zurückgetretene) Premierminister;* of ∾ years *in den letzten paar Jahren;* I haven't seen him of ∾ (∾ly) *ich habe ihn in der letzten Zeit nicht gesehen;* to keep ∾ hours *spät aufbleiben.* — **II.** adv.: ∾ of *ehemals wohnhaft in, gehörig zu;* as ∾ as the 15th century *noch im 15. Jahrhundert;* that comes rather ∾ in the day *das kommt etwas reichlich spät*

laugh I. v.i.: he ∾s best who ∾s last (prov.) *wer zuletzt lacht, lacht am besten;* to ∾ at a thing *über etwas lachen (etwas belachen);* to ∾ in (up) one's sleeve *sich ins Fäustchen lachen;* you will ∾ on the wrong side of your mouth (on the other side of your face) *dir wird das Lachen noch vergehen;* it is no ∾ing matter *es ist nicht zum Lachen.* — **II.** v.tr.: to ∾ off a thing *sich lachend über etwas hinwegsetzen;* to ∾ a person out of a thing *j.en durch Lachen von etwas abbringen;* to ∾ a thing to scorn *etwas lächerlich machen.* — **III.** n.: the ∾ is always against the loser *wer den Schaden hat, braucht für den Spott nicht zu sorgen;* to have (to get) the ∾ of a person *den Spieß umdrehen, über j.en triumphieren;* to have a good ∾ at a person (thing) *sich über j.en (eine Sache) recht lustig machen;* I had the ∾ of my life *ich habe nie im Leben so gelacht, ich habe gelacht wie noch nie;* to have the ∾ on one's side *die Lacher auf seiner Seite haben;* to join in the ∾ *mitlachen;* to raise a ∾ *ein Gelächter hervorrufen*

launch I. v.tr.: to ∾ a person, an enterprise *eine Person, ein Unternehmen lancieren;* to ∾ a person into eternity *j.en ins Jenseits befördern.* — **II.** v.i.: to ∾ forth (out) on an enterprise *ein Unternehmen beginnen;* to ∾ out into expense *sich in Unkosten stürzen*

lavender n.: to lay up in ∾ *sorgfältig aufbewahren; kaltstellen*

law n.: the ∾ of the Medes and Persians (cf. Dan. VI, 12) *ein unabänderliches Gesetz;* the ∾ of nations *das Völkerrecht;* a ∾-abiding citizen *ein friedlicher Bürger;* by ∾ *von Rechts wegen;* under the ∾ *auf Grund des Gesetzes;* father (mother, son, daughter)-in-∾ *Schwiegervater, -mutter, -sohn, -tochter;* his (her) in-∾s (colloq.) *seine (ihre) Schwiegereltern;* to be a ∾ unto oneself *seinen eigenen Standpunkt vertreten, sich nicht nach dem Herkommen richten;* to give the ∾ to a person *j.em seinen Willen aufdrängen;* to give a hare good ∾ *einem Hasen einen Vorsprung gewähren;* to go to ∾ about a matter *eine Sache vor Gericht bringen;* to have (to take) the ∾ of a person *j.en verklagen, gerichtlich gegen j.en vorgehen;* to be at ∾ *einen Prozeß führen, prozessieren;* necessity knows no ∾ (prov.) *Not kennt kein Gebot;* to lay down the ∾ *Vorschriften machen, das große Wort führen, selbstherrlich verfahren;* to read (to study) ∾, to go in for ∾ *Jura studieren;* to take the ∾ into one's own hands *sich selbst Recht verschaffen*

lay I. v.tr.: see 'account, bet, claim, cloth, fire etc.'. — with prep. & adv.: to ∾ money aside (by, up) *Geld beiseite-, zurücklegen;* to ∾ a thing at (to) a person's door (to a person's charge) *j.em etwas zur Last legen, vorwerfen;* to ∾ a person by the heels (or: fast) *j.en ins Gefängnis werfen, einsperren; kaltstellen;* to ∾ down the law, see 'law'; to ∾ down one's life for a cause *sein Leben für eine Sache hingeben;* to ∾ in provisions *sich mit Lebensmitteln eindecken;* to ∾ a person low *j.en zu Fall bringen, demütigen;* to ∾ off workmen *Arbeiter vorübergehend entlassen;* to ∾ off work (colloq.) *eine Arbeitspause machen;* ∾ off! (sl.) *hör' auf!;* to ∾ it on thick, with a trowel (colloq.) *es dick auftragen, übertreiben;* to ∾ out a garden *einen Garten anlegen;* to ∾ out goods *Sachen ausstellen;* to ∾ out money *Geld anlegen;* to ∾ oneself out for a thing *sich auf etwas rüsten, einrichten;* to ∾ a person out *j.en zu Boden schlagen;* to ∾ a thing to heart *etwas ernstlich überlegen, zu Herzen nehmen;* to ∾ heads together *die Köpfe zusammenstecken, beraten;* to ∾ a person under an obligation *j.em eine Verpflichtung auferlegen;* to ∾ up a ship (for repair) *ein Schiff (zwecks Reparatur) auf Stapel legen;* to ∾ up stores *Vorräte sammeln, für Vorrat sorgen;* to ∾ up in lavender, see 'lavender'; to be laid up with a cold *wegen einer Erkältung das Bett hüten müssen.* — **II.** v.i.: to ∾ about one *um sich schlagen;* to ∾ into a person (sl.) *j.en verprügeln, vermöbeln.* — **III.** n.: to spy out the ∾ of the land *die Lage peilen;* a ∾-by *ein Parkstreifen neben einer Hauptstraße*

lazy a.: he is a ∾-bones (colloq.) *er ist ein Faulenzer*

lead[1] n.: to cast (to heave) the ∾ *das Lot werfen, loten;* to swing the ∾ (sl.) *sich vom Dienst drücken*

lead[2] **I.** v.tr.: to ∾ apes in hell *als alte Jungfer sterben;* to ∾ astray *irreführen, verleiten;* to be led away *sich fortreißen lassen;* a led captain *ein Schmeichler, Schmarotzer;* to ∾ a person a dance *j.em Scherereien verursachen, ihm übel mitspielen (das Leben schwer machen);* a led horse *ein Handpferd;* to ∾ the king of hearts *den Herzkönig ausspielen;* to ∾ a person a life *j.em das Leben schwer (sauer) machen;* to ∾ a person by the nose *sich (dat.) j.en gefügig (hörig) machen;* to ∾ a person on to do a thing *j.en zu einer Handlung verlocken, verleiten;* to ∾ a person to suppose *j.en vermuten lassen;* to ∾ a person up the garden (path) (sl.) *j.en irreführen, täuschen;* to ∾ the way *vorangehen.* — **II.** v.i.: to ∾ off *anfangen;* to ∾ up to a subject *zu einem Thema allmählich überleiten (übergehen).* — **III.** n.: to follow the ∾ of a person *j.es Beispiel folgen;* he returned my ∾ *er brachte meine angespielte Farbe nach (Kartenspiel);* it is your ∾ *du spielst aus;* to take the ∾ *die Führung übernehmen;* the dog is on the ∾ *der Hund ist an der Leine*

leading I. a.: the ∾ article in a paper *der Leitartikel einer Zeitung;* to be a ∾ light *eine führende Rolle spielen;* the ∾ man (lady) *der (die) erste Liebhaber(in), Held(in);* a ∾ question *eine Suggestivfrage.* — **II.** n.: men of light and ∾ *verdienstvolle und einflußreiche Männer;* the ∾-business *die Hauptrollen (Theater);* in ∾ strings *am Gängelband*

leaf n.: the fall of leaves *der Herbst;* the trees are putting forth leaves (are bursting, coming into ∾) *die Bäume schlagen aus;* to take a ∾ out of a person's book *j.en nachahmen, ihn zum Muster nehmen;* to turn over a new ∾ *sich bessern, einen neuen Menschen anziehen*

leak I. n.: to spring a ∾ *ein Leck bekommen, leckwerden.* — **II.** v.i.: the news ∾ed out *die Nachricht sickerte durch*

leal n.: the land of the ∾ *das Gefilde der Seligen, der Himmel*

lean v.i.: he ∾ed over backwards to agree *er stimmte übereifrig zu*

leap I. v.i.: look before you ∾ (prov.) *erst wäge(n), dann wage(n);* to play at ∾-frog *bockspringen;* to ∾ into fame *berühmt werden;* to ∾ to the conclusion *voreilig schließen;* to ∾ to the eye *ins Auge springen.* — **II.** n.: a ∾ in the dark *ein Sprung ins Ungewisse;* to advance by ∾s and bounds *sprunghaft steigen;* a ∾-year *ein Schaltjahr*

learn I. v.tr.: he has ∾t his lesson *er hat einen Denkzettel bekommen;* to ∾ a poem by heart *ein Gedicht auswendig lernen.* — **II.** v.i.: I ∾ed that it was impossible *ich erfuhr, daß es unmöglich sei;* I am (I have) yet to ∾ how it happened *ich weiß immer noch nicht, wie es kam (ich glaube nicht daran);* to ∾ (how) to swim *schwimmen lernen*

learned a.: he is a ∾ man *er ist ein gelehrter Mann*

learning n.: the new ∾ *der Humanismus*

lease n.: to put out to ∾, to let by (out on) ∾ *verpachten;* to take a new ∾ of life *neuen Lebensmut schöpfen, neu aufleben*

leash n.: to hold in ∾ *im Zügel halten;* the dog is on the ∾ *der Hund ist an der Leine;* to strain at the ∾ *ungeduldig auf eine Erlaubnis warten*

least I. a.: the ∾ common multiple (L.C.M.) *das kleinste gemeinschaftliche Vielfache;* to take the line of ∾ resistance *den bequemsten Weg einschlagen, die leichteste Methode anwenden.* — **II.** n.: at ∾ *wenigstens, zum wenigsten;* to say the ∾ of it *gelinde gesagt;* ∾ said, soonest mended (prov.) *je weniger Worte darüber, desto besser; Reden ist Silber, Schweigen ist Gold;* (not) in the very ∾ *(nicht) im geringsten.* — **III.** adv.: last not ∾ *nicht zuletzt*

leather I. n.: ∾ and prunella (Pope, Essay, IV, 204) *ganz gleichgültige Dinge, reine Äußerlichkeiten;* nothing like ∾ *es geht nichts über Leder; die eigene Ware genügt allen Anforderungen;* patent ∾ shoes *Lackschuhe;* to lose ∾ (sl.) *sich einen Wolf reiten, sich wund reiben;* to ride hell for ∾ *in rasendem Galopp reiten.* — **II.** v.tr.: to ∾ a person *j.en (mit einem Riemen) verprügeln*

leave[1] n.: by (with) your ∾ *mit Ihrer Erlaubnis;* to be on ∾ (of absence) *auf Urlaub sein;* to take (one's) ∾ of a person *sich von j.em verabschieden;* to take ∾ of one's senses *den Verstand verlieren;* to take French ∾ *ohne Abschied weggehen, sich drücken; sich (auf) Französisch empfehlen;* without a with your ∾ or by your ∾ *ohne um Erlaubnis zu bitten*

leave[2] v.tr.: to ∾ alone *in Ruhe lassen, allein lassen;* to ∾ a bitter feeling behind *ein Gefühl der Bitterkeit zurück-, hinterlassen;* to ∾ one's card on a person *bei j.em seine Visitenkarte abgeben;* to ∾ the station on the left *den Bahnhof links liegen lassen;* that ∾s me cool *das läßt mich kalt;* ∾ go (vulg.) *laß los!;* where have I left my hat? *wo habe ich meinen Hut liegen lassen?;* ∾ him to himself *überlaß ihn sich selber, laß ihn allein damit fertig werden;* to ∾ hold of a thing *etwas loslassen;* to ∾ an impression *einen Eindruck hinterlassen;* let us ∾ it at that *lassen wir es dabei bewenden!;* I ∾ it to you *ich überlasse es Ihnen, das steht in Ihrem Belieben;* to ∾ a person in the lurch *j.en im Stich lassen;* we ∾ on Monday *wir reisen Montag ab;* it ∾s much to be desired *es läßt viel zu wünschen übrig;* to ∾ nothing undone (to ∾ no stone unturned) *nichts unterlassen, nichts unversucht lassen;* to ∾ off a garment *ein Kleidungsstück nicht mehr anziehen;* to ∾ off work *aufhören zu arbeiten, Feierabend machen;* we shall ∾ that over *das stellen wir vorläufig zurück;* that was left over *das blieb übrig;* to ∾ someone severely alone *j.en vollkommen ignorieren;* he ∾s a wife and three sons *er hinterläßt eine Frau und drei Söhne;* he left me wondering what he was going to do *er ließ mich im Unklaren, was er tun wollte;* to ∾ word *Bescheid hinterlassen*

lecture n.: to cut a ∾ *eine Vorlesung schwänzen;* to read a person a ∾ *j.em eine Strafpredigt halten, die Leviten lesen*

leek n.: to eat the ∾ (Shakespeare, Henry V, V, 1) *zu Kreuze kriechen, eine Beleidigung einstecken*

lees n.pl.: to drink (to drain) to the ∾ *bis zur Neige leeren*

leeway n.: I have much ∾ to make up *ich habe noch manches nachzuholen*

left a.: a ∾-handed compliment *ein Kompliment mit Spitze (mit einem leisen Vorwurf);* married with the ∾ hand *zur linken Hand getraut;* over the ∾ (shoulder)! (rare, sl.) *wer's glaubt! (gesagt, um anzudeuten, daß das Gegenteil einer Behauptung zu verstehen ist)*

leg I. n.: the boot is on the other ∾ *die Sache ist gerade umgekehrt;* to be all ∾s *übergroß sein;* to be off one's ∾s *schlecht zu Fuß, ganz ermüdet sein;* to be on one's ∾s again *wieder auf den Beinen sein;* to be on one's (hind) ∾s *stehen (besonders, um eine Rede zu halten);* to be on one's last ∾s *auf dem letzten Loch pfeifen;* to feel (to find) one's ∾s *eben anfangen zu laufen (bei Kindern und Erwachsenen nach Krankheiten);* to give ∾ bail *Fersengeld geben;* to give a person a ∾-up *j.em in den Sattel helfen; j.em auf die Sprünge helfen;* he has not yet got his sea-∾s *er ist noch nicht seefest;* to have the ∾s of a person *schneller laufen können als ein anderer;* he hasn't a ∾ to stand on *er kann seine Behauptungen durch nichts erhärten; er kriegt kein Bein auf die Erde;* to have a bone in one's ∾ (colloq.) *zu bequem (zu faul) sein zu gehen (etwas zu tun);* I kept my ∾s *ich bin nicht hingefallen;* to pull a person's ∾ *j.en zum besten (zum Narren) halten, ihn auf den Arm nehmen;* to put one's best ∾ foremost *sich sehr beeilen, die Beine in die Hand nehmen;* to recover one's ∾s after a fall *nach einem Sturz wieder auf die Beine kommen;* to set a person on his ∾s *j.em wieder auf die Beine helfen;* to shake a ∾ *das Tanzbein schwingen;* to show a ∾ *vom (aus dem) Bett aufstehen;* to stand on one's own ∾s *auf eigenen Füßen (Beinen) stehen, sein eigener Herr sein;* to stretch one's ∾s *sich (dat.) die Beine vertreten;* to take to one's ∾s *davonlaufen, die Beine in die Hand nehmen;* to walk a person off his ∾s *j.en tod-*

müde machen. — **II.** v.i.: to ∾ it (colloq.) *sich auf die Beine machen, schnell gehen (laufen)*

legion n.: their name is ∾ (Mark, V, 9) *es sind unzählige;* the ∾ of Honour *die Ehrenlegion;* the foreign ∾ *die Fremdenlegion*

leisure n.: to be at ∾ *Muße haben, unbeschäftigt sein;* do it at your ∾ *tun Sie es, wenn Sie Zeit haben (wann es Ihnen beliebt, bei passender Gelegenheit);* to wait a person's ∾ *warten, bis j. Zeit hat*

lend v.tr.: to ∾ ear (an ear, one's ears) to *Gehör schenken;* to ∾ a hand (a helping hand) *behilflich sein;* to ∾ life to the scene *die Szene beleben;* to ∾ point to an argument *einem Argument Nachdruck verleihen (ein A. bekräftigen);* to ∾ oneself to a scheme *sich zu einem Unternehmen hergeben;* it ∾s itself to a thing *es eignet sich (paßt) für eine Sache*

length n.: at ∾ *endlich, schließlich;* to describe at (at full, great, some) ∾ *ausführlich (sehr ausführlich, ziemlich ausführlich) beschreiben;* I will not go the ∾ of asserting *ich will nicht soweit gehen zu behaupten;* he is prepared to go all ∾s *er ist bereit, zum Äußersten zu schreiten;* he went to great ∾s to explain everything *er gab sich große Mühe, alles zu erklären;* I cannot go that ∾ with you *darin kann ich Ihnen nicht beistimmen;* to keep someone at arm's ∾ *j.en möglichst weit entfernt halten*

less I. a.: to be of ∾ importance *von geringerer Bedeutung sein;* may your shadow never grow ∾! *möge es dir immer gutgehen!;* of two evils choose the ∾ (prov.) *von zwei Übeln wähle das kleinere.* — **II.** n.: in ∾ than no time *im Nu;* we expected nothing ∾ than an attack *wir erwarteten zum mindesten einen Angriff.* — **III.** adv.: we expected nothing ∾ than an attack *wir erwarteten alles andere als einen Angriff*

lesson n.: let this be a ∾ to you *lassen Sie sich das zur Warnung dienen (eine Lehre sein)!;* he has learnt his ∾ *er hat einen Denkzettel bekommen*

let I. v.tr.: see 'alone, bag, be, down, drive etc.'; ∾ him down gently *fasse ihn sanft an, behandele ihn glimpflich;* to ∾ a person in for a thing *j.en hineinlegen;* I was ∾ in for it *ich fiel darauf herein;* you have ∾ yourself in for something *du hast dir etwas Schönes eingebrockt;* to ∾ a person into (in on) a thing *j.en in etwas einweihen;* to ∾ off a gun *ein Geschütz abfeuern;* he was ∾ off lightly *er kam glimpflich davon;* to ∾ something pass *etwas übersehen, nicht beachten;* to ∾ things slide *die Dinge gehenlassen.* — **II.** v.i.: the rooms ∾ well *die Zimmer lassen sich gut vermieten;* to ∾ into a person *über j.en herfallen;* don't ∾ on that you know anything about it (sl.) *laß dir nichts anmerken; verrate nicht, daß du etwas davon weißt;* to ∾ out at a person *j.en angreifen; beschimpfen;* to ∾ up (sl.) *aufhören.* — **III.** v. aux.: ∾ there be light *es werde Licht!;* ∾ us pray *lasset uns beten;* ∾ me see, when was that? *warte mal, wann war das doch?* — **IV.** n.: I cannot get a ∾ for the rooms *ich kann die Zimmer nicht vermieten*

letter n.: in ∾ and in spirit *dem Buchstaben und Inhalt nach;* to the ∾ *buchstäblich, bis ins einzelne;* a man of ∾s *ein Gelehrter, Literat;* the commonwealth (republic) of ∾s *die literarische Welt, die Gelehrtenwelt*

level I. n.: the ∾ of the sea *der Meeresspiegel;* on a ∾ with *auf gleicher Ebene (Höhe) mit;* on the ∾ (colloq.) *ehrlich, offen, ohne Hinterlist;* he is not up to the ∾ of the form *er steht nicht auf dem Niveau (auf der Höhe) der Klasse;* to find one's ∾ *seinen richtigen Platz im Verhältnis zu anderen finden, an die richtige Stelle kommen.* — **II.** a.: to do one's ∾ best *sein Bestmögliches tun;* to draw ∾ with a person *mit j.em gleichziehen;* to keep a ∾ head, to be ∾-headed *den Kopf nicht verlieren, nüchtern sein.* — **III.** v.tr.: that was ∾led at (against) you *das richtete sich gegen dich, das galt dir;* to ∾ to (with) the ground *dem Erdboden gleichmachen*

liable a.: to be ∾ to colds *sich leicht erkälten;* to be ∾ to duty *zollpflichtig sein;* to be ∾ to be overlooked *in Gefahr sein, übersehen zu werden;* difficulties are ∾ to occur *Schwierigkeiten ergeben sich immer wieder;* to be ∾ to a penalty *einer Strafe unterliegen;* you are ∾ to prosecution *du machst dich strafbar*

liberty n.: to be (to set) at ∾ *in Freiheit sein (setzen);* you are at ∾ to do so *es steht dir frei, es zu tun;* I take the ∾

to do (of doing) so *ich bin so frei, es zu tun;* he takes great liberties *er erlaubt sich viel, er nimmt sich viel heraus*

lick I. v.tr.: to ∾ one's chops (lips) *sich (dat.) die Finger (Lippen) lecken;* that ∾s creation (sl.) *das übertrifft alles;* to ∾ the dust *fallen, besiegt werden;* that ∾s me (sl.) *das geht über meinen Verstand;* to ∾ a person; to give a person a good ∾ing (sl.) *j.en schlagen, übertreffen; tüchtig verprügeln (durchwichsen);* the team got a good ∾ing (sl.) *die Mannschaft verlor haushoch;* to ∾ into shape *j.em Schliff (Benehmen) beibringen.* — **II.** v.i.: as hard as he could ∾ (sl.) *so schnell er nur laufen konnte.* — **III.** n.: a ∾ and a promise *eine Katzenwäsche;* at a great ∾; full (at full) ∾ (sl.) *in schnellstem Tempo*

lid n.: that was tyranny with the ∾ off *das war offene Tyrannei;* that puts the ∾ on! (sl.) *das ist aber die Höhe! das schlägt dem Faß den Boden aus! das setzt der Sache die Krone auf!*

lie[1] I. v.i.: he ∾s like a gas-meter (sl.) *er lügt wie gedruckt;* to ∾ in one's teeth (throat) (archaic or jocular) *das Blaue vom Himmel herunterlügen; lügen, daß sich die Balken biegen.* — **II.** v.tr.: to ∾ away a person's reputation *j.en durch Lügen um seinen guten Ruf bringen;* to ∾ oneself out of an accusation *sich aus einer Anschuldigung herauslügen.* — **III.** n.: a white ∾ *eine Notlüge;* to act a ∾ *j.en durch eine Handlungsweise betrügen;* to catch a person in a ∾ *j.en bei einer Lüge ertappen;* to give the ∾ to a statement *die Unwahrheit einer Aussage behaupten, beweisen;* to give a person the ∾ *j.en Lügen strafen, ihn als Lügner hinstellen;* to tell a ∾ *lügen*

lie[2] I. v.: see 'bed, close, dog, doggo, low, state, wait'; to find out how the land ∾s *herausbekommen, wie die Sachen stehen;* as far as in me ∾s *soweit es in meiner Macht liegt (steht);* it ∾s heavy on my stomach (my conscience) *es liegt mir schwer im Magen; es lastet auf meinem Gewissen;* to ∾ out of one's money *sein Geld nicht bekommen;* it ∾s with you to do so *es liegt bei dir (es ist an dir), es zu tun.* — with adv.: to ∾ by *unbenutzt liegen; sich zurückhalten, ruhig bleiben;* they took it lying down *sie nahmen es ohne Widerstand (ruhig, ergeben) hin;* to ∾ in *niederkommen, in die Wochen kommen;* that must ∾ over *das müssen wir zurückstellen;* to ∾ up *sich zurückziehen, zurückgezogen leben;* he is a ∾-abed *er ist ein Langschläfer.* — **II.** n.: the ∾ of the land *der Stand (die Lage) der Dinge*

life n.: all my ∾ *mein ganzes Leben lang;* I cannot for the ∾ of me understand *ich kann um alles in der Welt (beim besten Willen, absolut) nicht verstehen;* it is the breath of ∾ to him *er hat es unbedingt notwendig;* in high ∾ *im Leben der vornehmen Welt;* as large as ∾ *in Lebensgröße;* here he is as large as ∾ *hier ist er in eigener Person;* upon my ∾! *so wahr ich lebe!;* to be a matter of ∾ and death *eine Sache auf Leben und Tod sein;* he was the ∾ and soul of the party *er brachte Leben in die Gesellschaft;* to bring to ∾ *ins Leben rufen;* to come to ∾ *ein Lebenszeichen geben;* to escape with ∾ and limb *mit heiler Haut davonkommen;* to go in fear of one's ∾ *in ständiger Todesangst leben;* I had the time of my ∾ (colloq.) *ich habe mich amüsiert wie noch nie;* a cat has nine lives (prov.) *die Katze hat ein zähes Leben;* to lay down one's ∾ for a cause *sein Leben für eine Sache hingeben;* to lead a person a ∾ *j.em das Leben schwer (sauer) machen;* to portray to the ∾ *sprechend ähnlich (naturgetreu) zeichnen;* to receive (to get) a ∾ sentence *zu lebenslänglichem Zuchthaus verurteilt werden;* to run for one's (for dear) ∾ *ums liebe Leben laufen;* to see ∾ *das Leben kennenlernen, Erfahrungen sammeln;* to seek a person's ∾ *j.em nach dem Leben trachten;* to set one's ∾ on a chance *das Leben aufs Spiel setzen;* to take a new lease of ∾ *neuen Lebensmut schöpfen, neu aufleben;* a ∾-belt *ein Rettungsgürtel;* a ∾-boat *ein Rettungsboot;* his ∾-strings are broken (cut) *er stirbt;* he is a good (bad) ∾, his expectation of ∾ is good (bad) (insurance) *seine mutmaßliche Lebensdauer ist günstig (ungünstig);* anything for a quiet ∾ *alles um des lieben Friedens willen;* while there's ∾ there's hope *man darf die Hoffnung nie aufgeben;* he is in the prime of ∾ *er ist im besten Lebensalter;* a ∾-preserver *ein Rettungsgürtel, ein Totschläger;* not on your ∾ (sl.) *keine Bange!*

lift I. v.tr.: to ∾ cattle *Vieh stehlen;* to ∾ one's elbow (sl.) *einen trinken (heben, schmettern);* he did not ∾ a hand to do so *er machte nicht die geringste Anstrengung, es zu tun;* to ∾ one's hand *die Hand zum Schwur erheben;* to ∾ potatoes *Kartoffeln ausmachen;* the church ∾s its spire *der Kirchturm ragt in die Höhe;* to ∾ up a cry *ein Geschrei erheben;* to ∾ up one's heart *beten;* to ∾ up one's heel *einen Fußtritt geben;* to ∾ up one's horn *sein eigenes Lob singen, sich rühmen;* to ∾ up one's voice *seine Stimme erheben.* — **II.** v.i.: the fog is ∾ing *der Nebel steigt auf, lichtet sich.* — **III.** n.: to give a person a ∾ *j.en mitfahren lassen; j.em hilfreich zur Seite stehen;* to take the ∾ *den Aufzug benutzen;* shop ∾ing *Ladendiebstahl*

light¹ I. n.: in the ∾ of these facts *angesichts dieser Tatsachen;* according to one's ∾s *seinen geistigen Fähigkeiten entsprechend;* men of ∾ and leading *verdienstvolle und einflußreiche Männer;* to be a shining ∾ of science *eine Leuchte der Wissenschaft sein;* she is the ∾ of my eyes *sie ist meine Herzallerliebste;* to bring (to come) to ∾ *ans Licht bringen, kommen;* to gain the ∾ of a person's countenance *j.es Gunst gewinnen;* can you give me a ∾? *können Sie mir ein Streichholz, Feuer geben?;* to put a ∾ to a thing *etwas anzünden;* to see the ∾ *das Licht der Welt erblicken; ans Tageslicht kommen, offenbar werden;* to shed (to throw, to cast) ∾ upon a thing *Licht auf etwas werfen;* to stand in a person's ∾ *j.em im Lichte stehen;* to strike a ∾ *ein Streichholz anzünden.* — **II.** a.: a ∾-blue ribbon *ein hellblaues Band;* the ∾ blues *die Vertreter (Anhänger) der Universität Cambridge bei Sportveranstaltungen.* — **III.** v.tr.: to ∾ the fire *das Feuer anzünden (anstecken, anmachen);* to ∾ up the room *das Zimmer erleuchten;* he is lit up (sl.) *er ist beschwipst, er hat einen in der Krone.* — **IV.** v.i.: the fuel will not ∾ *der Brennstoff zündet nicht;* may I ∾ up? *darf ich meine Pfeife (Zigarre, Zigarette) anstecken?;* her face ∾ed (lit) up with delight *ihr Gesicht verklärte sich vor Entzücken*

light² I. a.: he has ∾ fingers *er macht lange Finger, er stiehlt;* to make ∾ of a thing *sich nichts aus einer Sache machen, etwas als bedeutungslos hinstellen;* ∾ gains make a heavy purse *kleine Gewinne füllen den Säckel.* — **II.** adv.: ∾ly come, ∾ly go *wie gewonnen, so zerronnen.* — **III.** v.i.: to ∾ (up)on a thing *zufällig auf etwas stoßen*

lightning n.: like greased ∾ *blitzartig, wie geschmiert, wie ein geölter Blitz*

like¹ I. a.: as ∾ as two peas *ähnlich wie ein Ei dem anderen;* ∾ father ∾ son *der Apfel fällt nicht weit vom Stamm;* ∾ master ∾ man *wie der Herr, so's Gescherr (so der Knecht);* I feel ∾ stopping work *ich hätte Lust, mit der Arbeit aufzuhören;* what is he (she, it) ∾? *wie ist er (sie, es)?;* he is ∾ that *er ist nun mal so;* that's just ∾ him *das sieht ihm ähnlich;* what does he (she, it) look ∾? *wie sieht er (sie, es) aus?;* what does it taste ∾? *wie schmeckt es?;* do you think it will rain? It looks ∾ it *glaubst du, es wird regnen? Es sieht so aus;* the weather looks ∾ lasting *es sieht aus, als ob das Wetter sich hielte;* it looks ∾ moths *es sieht nach Motten aus;* there is nothing ∾ a glass of beer *es geht nichts über ein Glas Bier;* it is nothing ∾ as good *es ist nicht annähernd so gut;* I paid something ∾ £ 10 *ich bezahlte etwa zehn Pfund;* at last something l i k e a day *endlich mal ein schöner Tag;* that is something ∾ (colloq.) *das lasse ich mir gefallen, das läßt sich hören.* — **II.** prep.: he did it ∾ a shot *er tat es sofort (blitzschnell);* he ran ∾ anything (blazes [sl.], mad) *er rannte (lief) wie besessen (wie toll, wie der Teufel, was das Zeug hielt);* do not talk ∾ that *rede nicht so.* — **III.** adv.: ∾ enough *sehr wahrscheinlich;* as ∾ as not *höchst wahrscheinlich.* — **IV.** conj.: I cannot do it ∾ he does *ich kann es nicht so machen wie er;* snow is falling ∾ in winter *es fällt Schnee wie im Winter.* — **V.** n.: mix with your ∾s *verkehre mit deinesgleichen;* I shall not see his ∾ again *ich sehe seinesgleichen nicht wieder;* did you ever see the ∾ of it? *hast du je etwas Ähnliches (so etwas) gesehen?;* the ∾s of me (colloq.) *meinesgleichen, unsereiner (d. h. in so bescheidener Stellung wie ich);* the ∾s of you (colloq.) *deinesgleichen (d. h. so vornehm wie du);* music, painting, and the ∾, or the ∾ *Musik, Malerei und so weiter, oder dergleichen*

like² I. v.tr.: to ∾ a person (thing) *eine Person (Sache) gern haben;* I should much ∾ to come *ich käme sehr gern;* how do you ∾ it? *wie gefällt es dir?;* I ∾ (iron.) your impudence! *du bist aber unverschämt!;* I ∾ beer but it doesn't ∾ me *ich trinke gern Bier, aber es bekommt mir nicht.* — **II.** v.i.: just as you ∾ *wie du willst, ganz* *nach Belieben;* I am shy if you ∾, but not misanthropic *menschenscheu mag ich schon sein, ich bin aber kein Menschenhasser;* I am shy if you ∾, but he is not *i c h mag menschenscheu sein, e r ist es aber nicht.* — **III.** n.: my ∾s and dis∾s *meine Neigungen und Abneigungen*

likelihood n.: there is every ∾ that, in all ∾ *aller Wahrscheinlichkeit nach*

likely I. a.: it is a ∾ story *(meist ironisch) es ist eine (un)glaubhafte Geschichte;* it is not ∾ he will come, he is not ∾ to come *er wird wahrscheinlich nicht (wohl schwerlich) kommen;* we are ∾ to have rain *wir bekommen wahrscheinlich Regen;* we called at every ∾ house *wir suchten jedes Haus auf, das in Frage kam;* six ∾ young fellows *sechs tüchtig aussehende junge Burschen.* — **II.** adv.: he has most (very) ∾ gone home *er ist sehr wahrscheinlich nach Hause gegangen*

likeness n.: to take a person's ∾ *j.en malen, photographieren;* in the ∾ of a bull *in der Gestalt eines Stiers;* a family ∾ *eine Familienähnlichkeit*

liking n.: is it to your ∾? *ist es nach deinem Geschmack?;* he has a ∾ for precise statement *er drückt sich gern genau aus;* to take a ∾ to a thing *an etwas Gefallen finden*

lily n.: the ∾ of the valley *das Maiglöckchen;* to paint the ∾ (Shakespeare, King John, IV, 2) *etwas Überflüssiges tun, zu sehr ausschmücken*

limb n.: we have put ourselves (gone) out on a ∾ *wir haben uns zu weit vorgewagt, wir können nicht mehr zurück;* that child is a ∾ of Satan (of the devil) *dieses Kind ist ein Teufelsbraten*

limelight n.: to be in the ∾ *im Lichte der Öffentlichkeit stehen; allgemeine Beachtung finden;* to steal the ∾ *die allgemeine Aufmerksamkeit auf sich lenken;* to be fond of the ∾ *gern im Vordergrund stehen*

limit n.: there is a ∾ to everything *alles hat seine Grenzen;* he's the ∾! (colloq.) *er ist einfach unmöglich!;* that is the (frozen) ∾! (colloq.) *das ist die Höhe! da hört (sich) doch alles auf! das schlägt dem Faß den Boden aus!;* to set ∾s to a thing *einer Sache Grenzen setzen;* within ∾s *maßvoll, in Grenzen;* the sky's his ∾ *er ist sehr ehrgeizig*

line[1] I. n.: all along the ∾ *durchweg, überall;* hard ∾s *Unglück, Pech;* just a ∾ to tell you *nur ein paar Zeilen, um dir zu sagen;* the marriage ∾s *der Trauschein;* a ship of the ∾, a ∾-of-battle ship *ein Linienschiff;* to act along (on) the same ∾s *nach denselben Grundsätzen (Richtlinien) verfahren;* to be in ∾ with a person (thing) *mit j.em (einer Sache) übereinstimmen;* it is in the ∾ of *es ist nach Art von, es folgt der Methode von;* to be in the banking ∾ *im Bankfach sein;* to be on the ∾ *auf der Grenze sein;* it is out of (not in) my ∾ *es schlägt nicht in mein Fach;* to bring into ∾ with *in Einklang bringen mit;* to cross the ∾ *den Äquator überschreiten;* to do a thing by rule and ∾ *etwas mit großer Genauigkeit machen;* to draw the ∾ at a thing *sich weigern, so weit (oder: weiter) zu gehen, nicht mehr mitmachen;* to drop a ∾ *ein paar Zeilen zukommen lassen;* to fall (to come) into ∾ with *sich anpassen, übereinstimmen mit;* to fall in ∾ with a thing *sich mit etwas dekken;* a schoolboy gets 100 ∾s *ein Schüler muß (als Strafarbeit) 100 Zeilen abschreiben;* to get a ∾ on a thing (colloq.) *über etwas Aufklärung (einen Anhaltspunkt) erhalten; sich über etwas orientieren;* to get (to run) off the ∾s *entgleisen;* to give a person ∾ enough *j.em vorläufig Bewegungsfreiheit (Spielraum) lassen, um ihn später einzufangen oder zu überführen;* to go as straight as a ∾ *schnurgerade gehen (verlaufen);* hold the ∾! the ∾ is engaged *bleiben Sie am Apparat! die Leitung ist besetzt;* to keep in ∾ *in Reih und Glied bleiben; bei der Stange bleiben;* to read between the ∾s *zwischen den Zeilen lesen;* to shoot a ∾ (sl.) *prahlen, wichtig tun, angeben;* to study one's ∾s *seine Rolle einstudieren;* to take the ∾ of least resistance *den bequemsten Weg einschlagen, die leichteste Methode anwenden;* he takes the ∾ that *er vertritt die Ansicht (den Standpunkt), daß;* to take (to keep to) one's own ∾ *nach eigener Methode verfahren, seinen eigenen Standpunkt vertreten;* to take a strong ∾ *energisch vorgehen;* to toe the ∾ *sich zum Wettlauf am Start aufstellen; sich einfügen;* to win all along the ∾ *auf der ganzen Linie siegen;* it is written on the ∾s of *es ist geschrieben nach Muster von.* — **II.** v.tr.: a face ∾d with pain *ein gramdurchfurchtes Gesicht;* to ∾ through a word *ein Wort durchstreichen.* — **III.** v.i.: to ∾ up *sich in e i n e r Reihe aufstellen;* to ∾ up against a thing *sich gegen etwas zusammenschließen*

line² v.tr.: to ∾ one's pockets *sich (dat.) die Taschen füllen;* the lining of my coat *mein Rockfutter;* every cloud has a silver lining (prov.) *alles hat seine gute Seite; auch das Schlimmste hat ein Ende; vgl. den Ausspruch von Stresemann vom „Silberstreifen an dem sonst düsteren Horizont"*

linen n.: I must change my ∾, I must put on clean ∾ *ich muß reine Wäsche anziehen;* to shoot one's ∾ (sl.) *die Manschetten durch Schütteln des Arms hervortreten lassen;* to wash one's dirty ∾ in public *seine schmutzige Wäsche in der Öffentlichkeit waschen*

liner n.: to sail by ∾ *mit dem (einem) Überseedampfer fahren;* an air-∾ *ein Verkehrsflugzeug;* a penny-a-∾ *ein Zeilenschreiber*

lion n.: a ∾ in the way (path) *ein (meist eingebildetes) Hindernis;* to beard the ∾ in his den *sich in die Höhle des Löwen begeben;* to make a ∾ of a person *j.en zum Helden des Tages machen;* a ∾-hunter *ein Gastgeber, der darauf erpicht ist, Berühmtheiten zu sich einzuladen;* to see (to show) the ∾s *die Sehenswürdigkeiten besichtigen (zeigen);* to take the ∾'s share *den Löwenanteil nehmen;* to twist the Lion's tail *den britischen Löwen reizen*

lip n.: there's many a slip 'twixt cup and the ∾ (prov.) *zwischen Lipp' und Kelchesrand schwebt der dunklen Mächte Hand; es ist noch nicht aller Tage Abend;* to bite one's ∾s *sich (dat.) auf die Lippen beißen;* to curl one's ∾ *verächtlich die Lippe aufwerfen;* the words escaped his ∾s *die Worte entfuhren ihm;* to hang one's ∾ *beschämt die Lippe hängen lassen;* to hang on a person's ∾s *an j.es Lippen (Mund) hängen;* to keep a stiff upper ∾ *sich nicht unterkriegen lassen, die Ohren steifhalten;* to lick one's ∾s *sich (dat.) die Lippen lecken;* none of your ∾! (sl.) *keine frechen Bemerkungen!;* ∾-homage *unechte Huldigung;* ∾-service *unechter Dienst*

liquor I. n.: to be in (to be the worse for) ∾ *mehr oder weniger betrunken sein.* — **II.** v.i.: to ∾ up (sl.) *einen trinken*

list n.: to be on the waiting-∾ *vorgemerkt sein;* to enter the ∾s against *in die Schranken treten gegen;* to make (out) a ∾ *eine Liste aufstellen*

listen v.i.: to ∾ in *Radio (Rundfunk) hören; belauschen, horchen;* to ∾ to a person *j.em zuhören, auf ihn hören;* to ∾ to reason *Vernunft annehmen, sich belehren lassen*

lit (p.p. *von* light): ∾ up (sl.) *blau, betrunken*

little I. a.: so that is your ∾ game! *das hast du also vor! darauf willst du also hinaus!;* ∾-go (Univ. Camb.) *die Vorprüfung;* my ∾ Mary (colloq.) *mein Magen;* the ∾ people *die Feen, Heinzelmännchen;* a ∾ something (colloq.) *ein Schuß Alkohol (in Getränk);* he's going a ∾ thin on top *er fängt an, eine Glatze zu kriegen;* I know his ∾ ways *ich kenne seine Schliche, so seine Art.* — **II.** n.: ∾ by ∾, by ∾ and ∾ *nach und nach, allmählich;* he came to after a ∾ *er kam nach kurzer Zeit wieder zu sich;* he has read a ∾ of everything *er hat von allem etwas gelesen;* to make (to think) ∾ of a thing *etwas gering achten, sich (dat.) wenig aus etwas machen.* — **III.** adv.: he ∾ knows (dreams) that *er weiß (ahnt) gar nicht, daß*

live¹ a.: ∾ embers *glühende Asche;* to make the question a ∾ issue *der Frage besondere Bedeutung beilegen;* a ∾ shell *eine scharfe Granate;* a ∾-stock dealer *ein Viehhändler;* a ∾ wire *ein elektrisch geladener Draht; eine äußerst energische (ungestüme) Person*

live² I. v.i.: see 'clover, fast, wit'; to ∾ a double life *ein Doppelleben führen;* to ∾ from hand to mouth *von der Hand in den Mund leben;* the servants ∾ in (out) *die Dienerschaft wohnt im Hause (auswärts);* ∾ and learn! (prov.) *man lernt nie aus! durch Schaden wird man klug;* he seems to ∾ on air *er scheint von der Luft zu leben;* he ∾s on his name *er zehrt von seinem Rufe;* he ∾s on his family *er lebt auf Kosten seiner Familie;* to ∾ in a small way *billig und bescheiden leben;* to ∾ to a great age *ein hohes Alter erreichen;* to ∾ to oneself *für sich leben;* to ∾ to see *er-*

leben; to ∾ up to one's income *sein ganzes Einkommen ausgeben;* to ∾ up to one's principles *seinen Grundsätzen gemäß leben;* he has enough to ∾ upon *er hat zu leben (genug zum Leben).* — **II.** v.tr.: to ∾ a lie *ein Leben der Lüge führen;* the room does not seem to be ∾d in *das Zimmer scheint nicht bewohnt zu sein;* he ∾d down the scandalous accusations *er hat die Verleumdungen durch sein Leben widerlegt;* to ∾ out the night *die Nacht überleben*

livelong a.: the ∾ day *den lieben langen Tag*

lively a.: to make it (to make things) ∾ for a person *j.en auf den (in) Trab bringen*

liver n.: the white (lily) ∾; white (lily)-∾ed *die Feigheit; feige;* to have a ∾ (colloq.) *gereizt, schlechter Laune sein*

living I. a.: no man ∾ could do better *kein Sterblicher könnte es besser machen;* within ∾ memory *seit Menschengedenken;* to be in the land of the ∾ *am Leben sein.* — **II.** n.: a ∾-room *ein Wohnzimmer;* a ∾ wage *ein Existenzminimum;* to be accustomed to good ∾ *an eine üppige Lebensweise gewöhnt sein;* to earn (to get, to make) one's ∾ *seinen Lebensunterhalt verdienen;* to be given a ∾ *eine Pfründe bekommen;* plain ∾ and high thinking *ein schlichter aber geistreicher Lebensstil*

lo int.: ∾ and behold! *und siehe da!*

load I. n.: that takes a ∾ off my mind *da fällt mir ein Stein vom Herzen;* peak ∾ *Höchstbelastung des elektrischen Netzes;* ∾s of money (colloq.) *eine Menge Geld.* — **II.** v.tr.: to ∾ dice *die Würfel fälschen*

loaf[1] n.: half a ∾ is better than no bread (prov.) *ein Sperling in der Hand ist besser als eine Taube auf dem Dache;* the loaves and the fishes *der materielle Besitz;* use your ∾ (sl.) *denk' nach! gebrauche deinen Verstand!*

loaf[2] **I.** v.i.: to ∾ around *herumbummeln, -lungern.* — **II.** v.tr.: to ∾ away the time *die Zeit vertrödeln (verplempern).* — **III.** n.: to be on the ∾ *bummeln;* I'm going to have a ∾ *ich werde einen Bummel machen*

loan n.: to have a thing on ∾ *etwas leihweise (geliehen) haben;* may I have the ∾ of your knife? *leih' mir bitte dein Messer; kann ich dein Messer haben?*

lo(a)th a.: nothing ∾ *nicht abgeneigt;* to be ∾ to do a thing *keine Lust haben, etwas zu tun*

lock I. n.: ∾, stock, and barrel *alles in allem; die ganze Geschichte;* under ∾ and key *unter Verschluß;* to be at a complete dead-∾ *festgefahren, auf dem toten Punkt sein;* ∾-up (school) *Torschluß (abends), Karzer;* a ∾-up garage *eine abschließbare Garage.* — **II.** v.tr.: to ∾ the stable door after the horse has been stolen *den Brunnen zudecken, wenn das Kind ertrunken ist;* ∾ed in sleep *in Schlaf versunken;* capital ∾ed up in land *in Landbesitz festgelegtes Kapital;* the employer ordered a ∾-out of his workmen *der Arbeitgeber ordnete eine Aussperrung seiner Arbeiter an;* to get ∾-jaw *Tetanus, Kinnbackenkrampf bekommen*

locker n.: not a shot in the ∾ *kein Geld in der Tasche;* I have still a shot in my ∾ *ich habe noch einen Pfeil im Köcher, einen Trumpf in der Hand;* to be in Davy Jones's ∾ *ertrunken sein;* to keep one's ∾ closed *seinen Schrank (Spind) verschlossen halten*

locomotive n.: use your ∾s (sl.) *nimm' die Beine in die Hand!*

lodge I. v.tr.: to be well (ill) ∾d *gut (schlecht) untergebracht sein;* to ∾ a complaint *eine Beschwerde vorbringen (führen);* to ∾ information against a person *j.en angeben, anzeigen, denunzieren;* to ∾ one's valuables in a bank *seine Wertsachen zur Bank bringen.* — **II.** v.i.: the bullet ∾d in his brain *die Kugel blieb ihm im Gehirn stecken;* to ∾ with a person *bei j.em zur Miete wohnen*

log n.: roll my ∾ and I'll roll yours *eine Hand wäscht die andere; Kuhhandel treiben;* to sleep like a ∾ *wie ein Klotz schlafen*

loggerhead n.: to be at ∾s with a person *sich mit j.em in den Haaren liegen;* to set persons at ∾s *Leute entzweien (uneinig machen)*

logic n.: to chop ∾ *pedantisch disputieren*

long I. a.: it is as broad as it is ∾ *es ist gehuppt (gehüpft) wie gesprungen, Jacke wie Hose;* a ∾ dozen *13 Stück;* in the ∾ run *auf die Dauer, am Ende, schließlich;* to draw the ∾ bow *aufschneiden (über-*

treiben, flunkern); to make a ∾ arm *über den Tisch nach etwas langen;* the ∾ arm of the law *(scherzhaft) die Polizei;* ∾-dated (bill) *langsichtig (Wechsel);* a ∾-distance call *ein Ferngespräch;* a ∾ drink (colloq.) *ein kühlendes Getränk, das Alkohol mit Wasser verdünnt;* a ∾ head *ein Schlaukopf;* to take the ∾ jump (colloq.) *gehängt werden;* at ∾ range *aus der Ferne;* ∾-sighted *weitblickend, scharfsinnig;* not by a ∾ sight! (colloq.) *bei weitem nicht!;* a sense of humour is his ∾ suit *Sinn für Humor ist seine stärkste Seite;* ∾ in the tooth (colloq.) *alt;* the ∾ vacation *die großen Ferien;* a ∾ way round *ein großer Umweg;* for a ∾ while *seit langem.* — **II.** n.: the ∾ and short of it *das Endergebnis, der langen Rede kurzer Sinn;* before ∾ *bald;* I shall not be away for ∾ *ich bleibe nicht lange weg;* it won't take ∾ *es dauert nicht lange.* — **III.** adv.: don't be ∾ *mach' schnell!;* all day ∾ *den ganzen Tag (lang);* he no ∾er lives here *er wohnt nicht mehr hier;* I shall not wait any ∾er *ich warte nicht länger;* not ∾ ago *vor kurzem, kürzlich;* so ∾! (colloq.) *auf Wiedersehen!*

look I. v.i.: he ∾s his age *man sieht ihm sein Alter an;* ∾ alive (sharp) *mach' schnell! beeile dich!;* ∾ before you leap (prov.) *erst wäge(n), dann wage(n);* to ∾ blue *mißvergnügt, niedergeschlagen aussehen;* things ∾ blue *die Aussichten sind trübe;* to ∾ grave *ernst aussehen;* ∾ here *sieh mal! hör' mal!;* she ∾s herself again *sie hat sich erholt;* it ∾s like rain *es sieht nach Regen aus;* he ∾ed small *er sah verlegen (beschämt, klein und häßlich) aus.* — with prep.: to ∾ about one *um sich sehen, vorsichtig, achtsam sein;* to ∾ after a person (thing) *auf j.en (eine Sache) achten, aufpassen;* to ∾ after No. 1 (colloq.) *für sich selbst zuerst sorgen;* to ∾ at a person (thing) *j.en (eine Sache) ansehen, betrachten;* to ∾ at him you might think *nach seinem Äußeren zu urteilen, könnte man denken;* he will not ∾ at it *er weist es verächtlich zurück, er will nichts davon wissen;* what I ∾ at is comfort *ich sehe (lege Wert) auf Bequemlichkeit;* to ∾ down one's nose *die Nase rümpfen;* to ∾ for a person (thing) *nach j.em (einer Sache) suchen;* you are ∾ing for trouble *du forderst das Unglück heraus;* to ∾ into a matter *eine Angelegenheit prüfen (untersuchen);* I ∾ (up)on him as my friend *ich betrachte ihn als meinen Freund;* to ∾ on the wine when it is red *(übermäßig) viel Wein trinken;* to ∾ over the accounts *die Rechnungen durchsehen (prüfen);* his greed ∾s through his eyes *die Gier schaut ihm aus den Augen;* ∾ to your manners *benimm dich!;* ∾ to it that you come early *sieh zu, daß du früh kommst.* — with adv.: to ∾ about for a thing *sich nach etwas umsehen;* for ten years he has never ∾ed back *er hat zehn Jahre lang stets Erfolg gehabt;* to ∾ forward to a thing *sich auf etwas freuen;* to ∾ in *einen kurzen Besuch machen, vorsprechen; fernsehen;* to ∾ on *zusehen, Zuschauer sein;* ∾ out! *sieh dich vor! paß auf! Achtung!;* that is your ∾-out *da mußt du selbst zusehen, das ist deine Sache;* he is on the ∾-out for a job *er sieht sich nach einer Stellung um;* to ∾ up to a person *zu j.m aufblicken;* things are ∾ing up *die Lage bessert sich, die Sache macht sich.* — **II.** v.tr.: to ∾ compassion *mitleidig blicken;* to ∾ daggers at a person *j.en mit Blicken durchbohren;* to ∾ death (a person) in the face *dem Tod (j.em) ins Gesicht (Auge) sehen;* to ∾ one's last at a person *j.en zum letzten Male ansehen.* — with adv.: to ∾ a person over, up and down *j.en mit den Augen mustern;* to ∾ a task over *eine Aufgabe durchsehen;* to ∾ a thing out *etwas heraussuchen;* to ∾ a person through *j.en mit den Blicken durchbohren;* to ∾ a person up *j.en aufsuchen (besuchen);* to ∾ a word up *ein Wort im Lexikon nachschlagen.* — **III.** n.: her good ∾s *ihre Schönheit;* she gave me a kind ∾ *sie warf mir einen freundlichen Blick zu;* to give a ∾ in *vorsprechen;* I didn't get a ∾ in (colloq.) *ich hatte überhaupt keine Chance;* the place has a Southern ∾ *der Ort sieht südländisch aus;* to have (to take) a ∾ at a thing *sich (dat.) etwas ansehen;* I don't like the ∾ of it *die Sache gefällt mir nicht;* to take on a ∾ *ein Aussehen annehmen;* to wear a ∾ of indifference *eine gleichgültige Miene zur Schau tragen;* I must have a ∾ round, a ∾-see (sl.) *ich muß mich mal umsehen;* she's a good ∾er (colloq.) *sie ist ein hübsches Mädchen*

loose I. a.: of a ∾ build (make) *von schlaksiger Gestalt;* to be at a ∾ end *beschäftigungslos sein;* a ∾ fish *ein lockerer Zeisig;* to shake a ∾ leg *ein liederliches Leben führen, bummeln, herumsumpfen;* with a ∾ rein *mit lockerem Zügel,* *nachsichtig;* a ∾ statement *eine vage (unklare) Angabe, Behauptung;* a ∾ thinker *ein unklarer (wirrer) Denker (Kopf);* a ∾ translation *eine freie Übersetzung (Wiedergabe);* to break ∾ *ausbrechen, sich losreißen;* to come (to get) ∾ *sich lockern, lösen, losgehen;* to have a screw (a tile) ∾ (sl.) *eine Schraube los (locker), einen Sparren haben;* to let (to set, to turn) ∾ *loslassen, freilassen; in Freiheit setzen.* — **II.** adv.: to play fast and ∾ *ein unredliches Spiel treiben;* to sit ∾ to a thing *gleichgültig gegen etwas sein, sich nicht an etwas binden.* — **III.** v.tr.: to ∾ one's hold of a thing *etwas loslassen;* the wine ∾d his tongue *der Wein löste ihm die Zunge.* — **IV.** n.: he is on the ∾ *er macht sich einen vergnügten Tag, er ist auf dem Bummel, er sumpft herum;* to give ∾ (a ∾) to one's feelings *seinen Gefühlen freien Lauf lassen*

lord I. n.: Lord knows how (who, etc.) *Gott weiß wie (wer, usw.);* the Lord's Prayer *das Vaterunser;* the Lord's Supper (Table) *das heilige Abendmahl;* in the year of our Lord *im Jahre des Herrn;* the ∾s of creation *die Herren der Schöpfung;* as drunk as a ∾ *vollkommen betrunken;* to live like a ∾ *leben wie Gott in Frankreich;* to swear like a ∾ *fluchen wie ein Landsknecht.* — **II.** v.tr.: he ∾s it over his household *er ist ein Haustyrann*

lose I. v.tr.: see 'caste, day, heart, temper, way'; to ∾ one's cold *seine Erkältung loswerden;* to ∾ ground *allmählich an Ansehen einbüßen, an Kraft verlieren;* my watch ∾s five minutes a day *meine Uhr geht täglich fünf Minuten nach;* to ∾ sight of a person (thing) *j.en (eine Sache) aus den Augen verlieren, nicht mehr in Rechnung stellen;* that will ∾ you your place *das wird dich deine Stellung kosten;* to ∾ one's train *den Zug verpassen (versäumen);* there is no love lost between them *sie können sich nicht leiden, sie haben nichts für einander übrig;* he is lost to a sense of duty *er ist ohne jegliches Pflichtgefühl;* all good words were lost upon him *alle guten Worte nutzten bei ihm nichts.* — **II.** v.i.: the matter ∾s in interest *die Sache verliert an Interesse;* the army lost heavily *das Heer hatte schwere Verluste;* the publisher lost by the book *der Verleger setzte bei dem Buch zu*

loser n.: to come off a ∾ *den kürzeren ziehen*

loss n.: a dead ∾ *ein vollständiger Verlust;* I am at a ∾ what to do *ich weiß nicht, was ich tun soll;* I am at a ∾ to understand *ich kann nicht verstehen;* to be at a ∾ for money *in Geldverlegenheit sein;* to meet with a ∾ *einen Verlust erleiden;* to recover one's ∾es *seine Verluste ersetzt bekommen;* to sell at a ∾ *mit Verlust verkaufen*

lost a.: Lost Property Office *Fundbüro;* to give up for ∾ *verloren geben;* he was ∾ to view (sight) *er verschwand*

lot n.: the (whole) ∾ *das Ganze, alles, alle;* he is a bad ∾ *er ist ein übler Bursche (Kerl);* to cast (to throw) in one's ∾ with *das Schicksal teilen, gemeinsame Sache machen mit;* to cast ∾s for *um etwas losen;* the ∾ falls to me; it falls to my ∾; it falls to me as my ∾ *mich trifft das Los; es fällt mir zu;* it takes a ∾ of doing (colloq.) *es ist eine schwierige Aufgabe;* he has a ∾ of money (colloq.) *er hat viel Geld;* he has ∾s of friends (colloq.) *er hat viele Freunde*

lounge n.: he is a ∾-lizard (colloq.) *er ist berufsmäßiger Eintänzer, Gigolo; ein Salonlöwe;* he wears a ∾-suit *er trägt einen Sakkoanzug*

lousy a. (sl.): it was a ∾ affair *es war eine ekelhafte Angelegenheit;* to be ∾ with brass (sl.) *stinkreich sein*

love I. n.: ∾ is blind (prov.) *Liebe macht blind;* calf-∾ *erste Liebe, Jugendliebe;* ∾ in a cottage *eine Ehe, die wirtschaftlich nicht genügend fundiert ist;* all's fair in ∾ and war (prov.) *In der Liebe und im Krieg ist alles erlaubt;* for the ∾ of God *um Gottes willen;* there is no ∾ lost between them, see 'lose'; what ∾s of hats; (colloq.) *welch entzückende (allerliebste) Hüte!;* the score is ∾ fifteen *das Spiel steht Null zu fünfzehn;* to be in ∾ with a person *in j.en verliebt sein;* to fall in ∾ with a person *sich in j.en verlieben;* I cannot get it for ∾ or money *ich kann es für Geld oder gute Worte nicht bekommen;* give my ∾ to your mother *grüß' deine Mutter von mir!;* to make ∾ to a person *j.em den Hof machen;* to play for ∾ *nicht um Geld spielen.* — **II.** a.: a ∾-child *ein uneheliches Kind;* a ∾-lock *eine Schmacht-*

locke. — **III.** v.tr. & i.: ∾ me, ∾ my dog (prov.) *wer mich liebt, muß alles lieben, was mein ist;* Lord ∾ you! *du lieber Gott! wahrhaftig!;* I should ∾ to come (colloq.) *ich käme liebend gern*

low I. a.: to have a ∾ opinion of someone *eine geringe Meinung von j.em haben;* to be in ∾ water *knapp bei Kasse sein;* to lay a person ∾ *j.en zu Fall bringen, demütigen;* to lie ∾ *sich ruhig verhalten, seine Zeit abwarten;* my funds are running ∾ *das Geld geht mir aus, mein Geld geht auf die Neige;* the sands are running ∾ *es geht zu Ende;* ∾-born *niedrig geboren;* ∾-bred *schlecht erzogen;* ∾-brow *geistig anspruchslos, tiefstehend;* his strength is at a ∾-ebb *seine Kräfte sind fast verbraucht.* — **II.** adv.: I must live ∾ for a time *ich muß eine zeitlang einfach essen;* I am ∾ in pocket *in meiner Börse ist Ebbe;* I have got the ∾-down on it (on the matter) (sl.) *ich kenne die wahren Tatsachen; ich habe es aus bester Quelle;* to play it ∾ down (∾) upon a person *j.en gemein (niederträchtig) behandeln*

luck n.: as ∾ would have it *wie es das Schicksal wollte; glücklicherweise, unglücklicherweise;* to have bad ∾ *Unglück (Pech) haben;* just my ∾ *mein gewöhnliches Pech!;* worse ∾ *unglücklicherweise, leider, so ein Pech!;* to be down on one's ∾ *in mißlicher Lage sein, Unglück haben, vom Pech verfolgt sein;* to be in (out of) ∾ *Glück (Schwein), Unglück (Pech) haben;* he has the ∾ of the Devil (Devil's own ∾) *ihm glückt alles;* will you take pot-∾ with us? *wollen Sie mit dem vorlieb nehmen, was es bei uns zu essen gibt?*

lucky I. a.: you're a ∾ dog (beggar, bargee, rascal) *du bist ein Glückspilz;* you may thank your ∾ star *du kannst deinem Glücksstern danken (von Glück sagen).* — **II.** n.: to cut (to make) one's ∾ (sl.) *sich aus dem Staube machen, abhauen;* to strike one's ∾, to touch ∾ (sl.) *einen glücklichen Griff tun*

lump[1] I. n.: in the ∾ *als Ganzes, in Bausch und Bogen;* he is a ∾ of selfishness *er ist die Selbstsucht in Person;* a bit of ∾ sugar *ein Stück Würfelzucker;* a ∾ sum *eine runde Summe;* I had a ∾ in my throat *meine Kehle war vor Rührung wie zugeschnürt.* — **II.** v.tr.: to ∾ together (with, in with) *zusammenwerfen, in e i n e n Topf werfen.* — **III.** v.i.: to ∾ along *schwerfällig dahintroddeln;* to ∾ down into a chair *in einen Stuhl plumpsen*

lump[2] v.tr.: if you don't like it you may ∾ it *wenn dir's nicht paßt, kannst du's ja bleiben lassen*

lurch n.: to leave a person in the ∾ *j.en im Stich lassen*

lurk n.: to be on the ∾ *auf der Lauer liegen*

lustre n.: to add ∾ to (to throw [shed] ∾ on) a thing *einer Sache Glanz verleihen*

M

M n.: to carry (to have) an ∾ under the girdle (M = Mr., Mrs., Miss, Madam) *immer höflich „Herr, Frau usw.“ bei der Anrede oder Erwähnung einer Person sagen*

mad a.: as ∾ as a March hare *so verrückt (geil) wie ein Märzhase;* as ∾ as a hatter *total verrückt;* to be ∾ after (for, on) a thing *toll (versessen, wild, verrückt) auf etwas sein;* I was rather ∾ at missing my train (colloq.) *es hat mich gefuchst, daß ich meinen Zug versäumte;* the dog ran ∾ *der Hund bekam die Tollwut;* to run like ∾ *wie toll (verrückt) laufen;* she is a ∾cap *sie ist ein Wildfang (Tollkopf)*

made a.: a ∾ man *ein gemachter Mann;* a well-(powerfully-)∾ man *ein gut, kräftig gebauter Mann*

magnitude n.: a matter of the first ∾ *eine hochwichtige Sache;* a star of the first ∾ *ein Stern erster Größe*

mahogany n.: to have one's knees under a person's ∾ *bei j.em zu Tisch sein*

mail I. n.: to look through one's ∾ *die Post durchsehen;* the letter came by air-∾ *der Brief kam per Luftpost;* by return of ∾ *postwendend;* the fan-∾ *die Post, die Film- oder andere Größen von ihren Bewunderern erhalten.* — **II.** v.tr.: to ∾ a letter *einen Brief zur Post geben;* to ∾ a person a thing *j.em etwas mit der Post schicken*

main a. & n.: by ∾ force, with might and ∾ (n.) *mit voller Kraft;* in the ∾ *in der Hauptsache;* to have an eye to the ∾ chance *auf seine eigenen Interessen bedacht sein;* to splice the ∾ brace (Navy) *Getränke an die Mannschaften austeilen; saufen*

maintain v.tr.: to ∾ an attitude *eine Haltung bewahren;* to ∾ a good cause *eine* *gute Sache unterstützen;* to ∾ a correspondence *einen Briefwechsel unterhalten;* to ∾ one's family *seine Familie unterhalten (ernähren);* to ∾ a road *eine Straße in Stand halten;* to ∾ a thing, to ∾ that *etwas behaupten; behaupten, daß*

majority n.: to attain one's ∾ *großjährig, mündig werden;* to join the ∾ *sterben*

make I. v.tr.: see 'amends, bag, best, bone, brick, card etc.'; can you ∾ anything of it? *wirst du daraus klug?;* to ∾ believe to do *vorgeben, etwas zu tun;* to ∾ oneself believe *sich (dat.) einreden;* what bird do you ∾ that to be? *was ist das nach deiner Ansicht für ein Vogel?;* to ∾ a good breakfast *gut frühstücken;* to ∾ hay of a thing *etwas verwirren;* to ∾ hay while the sun shines *das Eisen schmieden, solange es heiß ist;* the author ∾s him die in the last chapter *der Verfasser läßt ihn im letzten Kapitel sterben;* they made him king *sie machten ihn zum König;* will it ∾ it or mar it? *wird es der Sache Glück oder Unglück bringen?;* the ship ∾s the land *das Schiff kommt in Sicht des Landes;* I ∾ it five miles *ich schätze die Entfernung auf 5 Meilen;* to ∾ a port *einen Hafen anlaufen;* it ∾s pleasant reading *es liest sich gut;* I made him repeat it *ich ließ ihn es wiederholen;* to ∾ rings round a person *j.em eine vernichtende Niederlage beibringen;* it's nothing to ∾ a song about (colloq.) *es ist nichts Besonderes, keine aufregende Sache;* he will ∾ a good teacher *er wird einen guten Lehrer abgeben;* what do you ∾ the time? what (time) do you ∾ it? *wieviel ist es auf deiner Uhr?;* he is as greedy as they ∾ 'em (colloq.) *er ist so gierig, wie nur möglich;* shall we ∾ the train in time? *ob wir (recht)zeitig den Zug bekommen?* — with adv.: to ∾ out a cheque *einen Scheck ausstellen;* I made out a figure in the distance *in der Ferne konnte ich eine Gestalt erkennen;* I can't ∾ him out *ich werde nicht klug aus ihm;* to ∾ out a list *eine Liste aufstellen;* you ∾ me out (to be) a hypocrite *du stellst mich als Heuchler hin;* how do you ∾ that out? *wie kommst du zu dem Ergebnis?;* I can't ∾ this writing out *ich kann diese Schrift nicht entziffern;* the management was made over to him *die Leitung wurde ihm übertragen;* to ∾ it up *sich wieder versöhnen;* we must ∾ it up to him somehow *wir müssen es ihm irgendwie ersetzen;* to be made up of *bestehen aus;* to ∾ up an account *eine Rechnung auf-, zusammenstellen;* to ∾ up a coat *einen Rock zusammennähen;* I must ∾ up my face *ich muß mich schminken;* the ∾-up of an actor *die Maske (Verkleidung) eines Schauspielers;* to ∾ up goods into parcels *die Ware in Pakete pakken;* to ∾ up lost ground *verlorenen Boden wiedergewinnen;* I have much leeway to ∾ up *ich habe noch manches nachzuholen;* to ∾ up one's mind to do a thing *sich entscheiden, etwas zu tun;* to ∾ up a party *eine Gesellschaft zusammenbringen, auf die Beine bringen:* to ∾ up a story *eine Geschichte erfinden;* to ∾ up a certain sum *eine bestimmte Summe vollmachen.* — **II.** v.i.: see 'bold, do, free, light[1], merry, sure'; to ∾ as if *sich stellen (so tun) als ob;* I made to do it *ich schickte mich an, es zu tun.* — with prep. & adv.: to ∾ after a person *j.en verfolgen;* that ∾s against peace *das ist ungünstig für den Frieden;* to ∾ away *forteilen, sich fortmachen;* to ∾ away with a person *j.en beseitigen, töten;* to ∾ for the door *zur Tür stürzen;* that ∾s for peace *das trägt zum Frieden bei;* the thieves could ∾ off with the money *die Diebe konnten mit dem Gelde entkommen;* to ∾ towards a place *sich in die Richtung eines Ortes begeben;* to ∾ up for a thing *etwas ersetzen;* to ∾ up for lost time *verlorene Zeit ein-, nachholen;* to ∾ up to a person *sich um j.es Gunst bemühen, sich an j.en heranmachen.* — **III.** n.: that is American ∾ *das ist amerikanisches Erzeugnis;* of a loose ∾ *von schlaksiger Gestalt;* it is your ∾ *Sie müssen die Karten mischen;* is this your own ∾? *ist dies Ihr eigenes Fabrikat?;* he is on the ∾ (sl.) *er ist auf Geld aus*

making n.: that will be the ∾ of him *das wird sein Glück sein;* he has the ∾s of a scholar *er hat das Zeug zu einem Gelehrten*

malice n.: with ∾ aforethought, prepense *mit bösem Vorbedacht;* to bear ∾ *Groll hegen*

man I. n.: (all) to a ∾, to the last ∾, every ∾-jack (colloq.) *alle ohne Ausnahmen, geschlossen, bis auf den letzten Mann;* I'm your ∾ *ich mache mit, ich nehme dein Angebot an;* he is my ∾ of business *er ist mein Geschäftsberater, mein Anwalt;* I've done it ∾ and boy *ich habe es von Jugend auf getan;* if you want noise he is your ∾ *wenn du Lärm wünschst, kann er dir dienen;* her young ∾ *ihr Schatz;* the best ∾ *der Brautführer;* the ∾ in the street *der einfache Mann;* a ∾ of honour *ein Ehrenmann;* to reach ∾'s estate *volljährig werden;* a ∾ of letters *ein Gelehrter, Literat;* a ∾ about town *ein Lebemann;* a ∾-of-war *ein Kriegsschiff;* to ∾handle a person *j.en rauh anpacken.* — **II.** v.tr.: to ∾ a ship *ein Schiff bemannen;* to ∾ oneself to a deed *sich zu einer Tat ermannen*

manage v.tr. & i.: to ∾ an undertaking *ein Unternehmen führen (leiten);* can you ∾ it all right? *kommst du damit zurecht?;* can you ∾ another slice? *kannst du noch eine Schnitte vertragen, bewältigen?;* he ∾d to inform her *er brachte es fertig, sie zu benachrichtigen*

manger n.: he is a dog in the ∾ *er ist ein Neidhammel;* to live at rack and ∾ *sorglos in den Tag hineinleben*

manner n.: she rode as if to the ∾ born *sie ritt, als ob sie es von klein auf getan hätte;* in a ∾ of speaking *sozusagen;* I don't like his ∾ *ich mag seine Art und Weise nicht;* he has no ∾s *er hat kein Benehmen;* all ∾ of *alle Arten von;* by no ∾ of means *unter keinen Umständen;* in a ∾ *in gewisser Hinsicht;* what ∾ of man is he? *welche Art (von) Mensch ist er?*

many I. a.: ∾'s the tale he has told us *er hat uns so manche Geschichte erzählt;* ∾ times, ∾ a time, ∾ and ∾ a time *viele Male, so manches liebe Mal, oftmals;* to be one too ∾ *überzählig, unerwünscht sein; stören;* he was (one) too ∾ for us *er war uns über; er hat uns übertölpelt.* — **II.** n.: a good (great) ∾ *ziemlich (sehr) viele*

map I. n.: off the ∾ *aus der Erinnerung, bedeutungslos, erledigt;* on the ∾ *noch von Bedeutung, noch mitzählend.* — **II.** v.tr.: to ∾ out the details *die Einzelheiten aufzeichnen, darstellen, ausarbeiten*

march I. n.: the ∾ of events *der Gang der Ereignisse;* to steal a ∾ (up)on a person *j.em zuvorkommen.* — **II.** v.i.: to ∾ past *im Paradeschritt vorbeimarschieren.* — **III.** v.tr.: to ∾ a person off *j.en abführen*

mare n.: the grey ∾ is the better horse *die Frau hat die Hosen an;* money makes the ∾ to go (prov.) *wer gut schmeert (schmiert), der gut fährt; Geld regiert die Welt;* on Shanks's ∾ *auf Schusters Rappen;* to find a ∾'s-nest *sich (dat.) einbilden, eine wichtige Entdeckung gemacht zu haben, die sich jedoch als nichtig erweist*

marine n.: tell that to the horse-∾s! *das kannst du deiner Großmutter erzählen!*

mark I. n.: that is below the ∾ of the class *das ist unter dem Stand (Niveau) der Klasse;* that is beside (wide of) the ∾ *das hat nichts mit der Sache zu tun, ist weitgefehlt;* I'm not feeling quite up to the ∾ *ich fühle mich nicht ganz auf der Höhe;* to get a good (bad) ∾ *eine gute (schlechte) Note bekommen;* to get off the ∾ *starten;* to hit the ∾ *ins Schwarze treffen;* to make one's ∾ *sich (dat.) einen Namen machen;* to miss the ∾ *fehl-, vorbeischießen;* to overshoot the ∾ *über das Ziel hinausschießen;* (God) save (bless) the ∾! *Gott steh' uns bei! du lieber Himmel! daß Gott erbarm!* — **II.** v.tr.: a ∾ed difference *ein deutlicher (auffallender) Unterschied;* to ∾ off *abgrenzen;* the boundaries were ∾ed out *die Grenzen waren gezogen;* these men are ∾ed out for advancement *diese Männer sind zur Beförderung bestimmt;* to ∾ with a hot iron *brandmarken;* to ∾ time *auf der Stelle treten, abwarten;* ∾ my words *denk' an meine Worte!*

market n.: to bring one's eggs (hogs) to a bad ∾ *mit seinen Plänen Schiffbruch erleiden, schlechte Geschäfte machen*

marriage n.: to ask in ∾ *anhalten um;* to give (to take) in ∾ *zur Frau geben, nehmen;* a cousin by ∾ *ein angeheirateter Vetter;* the ∾ lines *der Trauschein;* ∾ articles *Ehevertrag;* ∾ portion *Mitgift;* the ∾ was made in Heaven *sie waren für einander vorbestimmt*

marry I. v.tr.: the clergyman married them (off) *der Geistliche traute sie;* he is going to ∾ an heiress *er heiratet eine reiche Erbin;* she married her daughter to a rich man *sie verheiratete (vermählte) ihre Tochter an einen reichen Mann;* to be married to a person *mit j.em verheiratet sein;* to get married to a person *sich mit j.em verheiraten;* to be married with the left hand *zur linken Hand getraut sein.* — **II.** v.i.: to ∾ for love (money) *aus Liebe (des Geldes wegen) heiraten;* he has married beneath (below) him *er hat unter seinem Stande* *geheiratet;* ∾ in haste (and) repent at leisure (prov.) *schnell gefreit, lange bereut*

martyr n.: he is a ∾ to gout *er leidet beständig an Gicht;* to make a ∾ of oneself *sich für etwas opfern*

Mary n.pr.: my little ∾ (colloq.) *mein Magen*

mash v.tr.: to be ∾ed on a person (sl.) *in j.en verschossen (verknallt) sein;* ∾ed potatoes *Kartoffelbrei, -püree*

mast n.: to nail one's colours to the ∾ *standhaft bleiben;* to sail (to serve) before the ∾ *einfacher Matrose sein*

master n.: like ∾ like man (prov.) *wie der Herr, so's Gescherr (so der Knecht);* to make oneself ∾ of a subject *eine Sache meistern;* we will see which of us is ∾ *wir wollen mal sehen, wer von uns zu sagen hat;* a ∾-stroke *ein Meisterstreich;* a ∾-key *ein Hauptschlüssel*

mat n.: to be on the ∾ (i.e. the mat of the orderly room before the Commanding Officer) (sl.) *in der Tinte sitzen*

match I. n.: he is more than a ∾ for you *er ist dir überlegen;* to find (to meet) one's ∾ *seinen Mann finden;* we shall never see his ∾ *wir werden nie seinesgleichen finden;* to make a ∾ *eine Heirat stiften;* she is an excellent ∾ *sie ist eine ausgezeichnete Partie;* to shoot a ∾ *an einem Wettschießen teilnehmen;* to take part in a ∾ *an einem Wettkampf, -spiel teilnehmen;* a ∾-maker *ein(e) Heiratsvermittler(in).* — **II.** v.tr.: to ∾ a person against another *j.en zum Kampfe gegen einen anderen aufstellen;* to ∾ a person with another *j.en vermählen mit;* they are well ∾ed *sie passen gut zu einander, sie sind einander ebenbürtig;* can you ∾ me this silk? *können Sie mir etwas geben, das zu dieser Seide paßt?;* the carpets ∾ the wall-paper *die Teppiche passen zu der Tapete.* — **III.** v.i.: these ribbons do not ∾ *diese Bänder passen nicht zusammen;* the feathers do not ∾ with your hat *die Federn passen nicht zu deinem Hut;* it was trimmed with velvet to ∾ *es war mit passendem Samt besetzt*

match[2] n.: to strike a ∾ *ein Zünd-, Streichholz anstecken;* to make ∾-wood of a thing *etwas zu Kleinholz, kurz und klein schlagen*

matchless a.: ∾ *unvergleichlich, unübertreffbar*

matter I. n.: that is a hanging ∾ for him *das kann ihn an den Galgen bringen;* it is no laughing ∾ *das ist nicht zum Lachen;* to make ∾s worse *eine Sache noch schlimmer machen;* to take ∾s easy *sich an einer Sache nicht stören;* no ∾! *es macht nichts;* no ∾ when (how, what, why, etc.) *ganz gleich wann (wie, was, warum, usw.);* printed ∾ *Drucksache;* for that ∾ *was das anlangt;* what ∾? *und wenn auch! was liegt daran? was tut es?;* and what is the ∾ with this? *und was hast du hiergegen? dies wird bestimmt gehen;* in the ∾ of *hinsichtlich;* that is a ∾ of course *das versteht sich von selbst;* it was a ∾-of-course assumption *es wurde selbstverständlich angenommen;* a ∾-of-fact description *eine prosaische (nüchterne) Beschreibung;* as a ∾-of-fact I don't know anything about it *in Wirklichkeit (tatsächlich, in der Tat, um die Wahrheit zu sagen), ich weiß nichts darüber;* that is a ∾ of taste *das ist Geschmackssache.* — **IV.** v.i.: it ∾s a great deal how (when, etc.) *es macht sehr viel aus, wie (wann, usw.);* what does it ∾? *was liegt daran? was tut's?;* a wound ∾s *eine Wunde eitert*

Maundy n.: ∾ Thursday *Gründonnerstag*

may v.aux.: it ∾ be true *es mag (kann) wahr sein;* you ∾ walk miles without seeing one *du kannst meilenlange Wege machen, ohne einen zu sehen;* you might call at the baker's *geh mal eben beim Bäcker vorbei (zum Bäcker);* you might offer to help *du könntest auch mal mithelfen;* I fear he ∾ lose his way *ich fürchte, er verläuft sich;* I hope he ∾ succeed *ich hoffe, es gelingt ihm;* ∾ all go well with you *möge es dir gut gehen!;* who ∾ you be? *wer sind Sie eigentlich?;* a might-have-been *eine verkrachte Existenz*

me pron.: it's only ∾ *ich bin es nur;* dear ∾! *du meine Güte! mein Gott!*

meal n.: to have a square ∾ *eine kräftige Mahlzeit zu sich nehmen*

mealy a.: to be ∾-mouthed *im Sprechen zurückhaltend und scheinheilig sein*

mean[1] I. n.: the golden (happy) ∾ *die goldene Mittelstraße;* it was the only ∾s of keeping him quiet *es war das einzige Mittel, ihn ruhig zu halten;* by ∾s of *vermittelst, durch;* by all (manner of) ∾s *auf jede mögliche Art und Weise;* may I do so? By all ∾s! *darf ich es tun? Aber sicher!;*

have you by any ∾s found it? *hast du es etwa (vielleicht) gefunden?;* by fair ∾s or foul *im Guten oder im Bösen;* he lives beyond his ∾s *er lebt über seine Verhältnisse;* he is a man of ∾s *er ist ein wohlhabender Mann;* by no (manner of) ∾s *auf keinen Fall, keineswegs, durchaus nicht;* by this ∾s *hierdurch;* to apply the ∾s test *die Bedürfnisfrage prüfen.* — **II.** a.: the ∾ proportional *die mittlere Proportionale;* in the ∾ time *in der Zwischenzeit, mittlerweile(n);* ∾time, ∾while *mittlerweile(n), inzwischen, unterdessen*

mean² a. & adv.: a man of ∾ birth *ein Mann von niedriger Herkunft;* he is a very ∾ person *er ist eine sehr geizige Person;* he is no ∾ scholar *er ist ein bedeutender Gelehrter;* I call that ∾ *ich nenne das gemein;* he dealt ∾ly with him *er hat gemein an ihm gehandelt;* to take a ∾ advantage of a person *j.en gemein (in häßlicher Weise) übervorteilen*

mean³ v.tr.: I ∾ to do it tomorrow *ich beabsichtige (gedenke), es morgen zu tun; ich will es morgen tun;* he ∾s business *er meint es ernst;* he is meant for a sailor *er ist zum Seemann bestimmt;* it is meant for (to be used as) a stopgap *es ist als Notbehelf gedacht;* I ∾ you to go *ich will, daß du gehst;* by that I ∾ (that) he is stingy *damit will ich sagen, daß er knauserig ist;* you don't really ∾ that, do you? *das ist doch wohl nicht dein Ernst?;* to ∾ well to (by) a person *es mit j.em gut meinen;* what do you ∾ by coming in without knocking? *was soll das heißen, hereinzukommen ohne anzuklopfen?*

meaning n.: he said it with ∾ *er sagte es bedeutungsvoll, mit Nachdruck*

measure I. n.: ∾ for ∾ *Maß für Maß, Wurst wider Wurst;* in a (some) ∾ *bis zu einem gewissen Grade, gewissermaßen;* beyond all ∾ *über alle Maßen;* the greatest common ∾ *der größte gemeinschaftliche Faktor;* a liquid ∾ *ein Flüssigkeitsmaß;* a ∾ of capacity *ein Hohlmaß;* the chain's weakest link is the ∾ of its strength *das schwächste Glied einer Kette ist der Maßstab für ihre Stärke;* to set ∾s to a thing *einer Sache Grenzen auferlegen;* to take ∾s *Maßnahmen ergreifen;* to take legal ∾s *den Rechtsweg beschreiten;* to take a person's ∾, the ∾ of a person's foot *j.en abtaxieren, sich (dat.) ein Urteil über ihn bilden;* to take a person's ∾, ∾ment for a suit *j.em zu einem Anzug Maß nehmen;* a suit made to ∾ *ein Anzug nach Maß, ein Maßanzug;* to tread to ∾ *tanzen.* — **II.** v.tr.: to ∾ one's length *der Länge nach hinfallen;* to ∾ a person with one's eye *j.en von oben bis unten besehen;* to ∾ out *aus-, zuteilen*

measured a.: to speak in ∾ terms *eine gemessene, maßvolle Sprache führen;* to walk in ∾ tread *in gemessenem Schritte gehen*

meat n.: one man's ∾ is another man's poison (prov.) *was dem einen sin Uhl (Eule), ist dem andern sin Nachtigall; des einen Tod ist des andern Brot;* that was ∾ and drink to him *das war ihm ein großer Genuß, eine Wonne*

medal n.: the reverse of the ∾ *die Kehrseite der Medaille*

meddle v.i.: to ∾ in an affair *sich in eine Sache einmischen;* to ∾ with a thing *sich unberufen mit einer Sache abgeben, mit einer Sache herumspielen*

medical a.: a ∾ *eine amtsärztliche Untersuchung*

medicine n.: to take one's ∾ *eine bittere Pille schlucken*

medium I. n.: by (through) the ∾ of *vermittelst, durch;* a coin is a ∾ of circulation *eine Münze ist ein Umlaufsmittel;* to find (to hit upon) the happy ∾ *die richtige Mitte treffen.* — **II.** a.: it is of ∾ size *es ist von mittlerer Größe*

meek a.: as ∾ as a lamb, as Moses *lammfromm*

meet I. v.tr.: that ∾s the case *das paßt; das trifft die Sache;* the supply ∾s the demand *das Angebot entspricht der Nachfrage;* to ∾ the eye *ins Auge fallen;* to ∾ heavy expenses *große Ausgaben bestreiten;* he met his fate *ihn ereilte das Schicksal;* ∾ Mr. N.! (U.S.) *darf ich dir Herrn N. vorstellen?;* to ∾ a person half-way *j.em auf halbem Wege entgegenkommen;* to ∾ a person's wishes *j.es Wünsche erfüllen.* — **II.** v.i.: to make both ends ∾ *mit seinen Einkünften gerade auskommen, sich nach der Decke strecken;* my coat won't ∾ *mein Rock geht nicht zu, ist zu eng;* to ∾ with an accident *verunglücken;* to ∾ with approval *Billigung finden;* to ∾ with a loss *einen Verlust erleiden;* to ∾ with a kind reception *freundlich aufgenommen werden;* it is not to be met with anywhere else *es ist sonst nirgendwo zu finden;* well met! *gut, daß ich dich treffe; du kommst mir wie gerufen.* — **III.** a.: it is ∾ that we do so *es ist schicklich, daß wir es tun*

meeting n.: to call a ∾ *eine Versammlung einberufen;* to hold a ∾ *eine Versammlung abhalten*

melt I. v.i.: it ∾s in the mouth *es zergeht auf der Zunge;* he looks as if butter would not ∾ in his mouth *er sieht aus, als wenn er kein Wässerchen trüben könnte;* to ∾ into tears *in Tränen zerfließen.* — **II.** v.tr.: to ∾ down *einschmelzen;* to go into the ∾ing-pot *von Grund auf neugeschaffen, umgemodelt werden*

member n.: the unruly ∾ (cf. James, III, 1) *die Zunge*

memory n.: my ∾ failed me *mein Gedächtnis ließ mich im Stich;* if my ∾ serves me right *wenn mich mein Gedächtnis nicht täuscht;* to the best of my ∾ *soweit ich mich erinnere;* in ∾ of *zum Andenken an;* within thc ∾ of man *seit Menschengedenken;* it is within living ∾ *es leben noch Leute, die sich daran erinnern;* to commit to ∾ *auswendig lernen;* to escape one's ∾ *dem Gedächtnis entschwinden (entfallen)*

mend I. v.tr.: to ∾ or end *verbessern oder abschaffen;* to ∾ the fire *das Feuer schüren, Kohlen (Holz) nachlegen;* that does not ∾ matters *das macht die Sache nicht besser;* to ∾ one's pace *die Schritte beschleunigen;* to ∾ one's ways *sich bessern;* least said, soonest ∾ed (prov.) *je weniger Worte darüber, desto besser; Reden ist Silber, Schweigen ist Gold.* — **II.** v.i.: it is never too late to ∾ (prov.) *Besserung kommt nie zu spät;* he is ∾ing *er ist auf dem Wege der Besserung.* — **III.** n.: he is on the ∾ *er ist auf dem Wege der Besserung*

mental a.: ∾ arithmetic *Kopfrechnen;* a ∾ home (asylum) *eine Irrenanstalt;* a ∾ patient *ein geisteskranker Patient;* he is ∾ (colloq.) *er ist verrückt*

mention v.tr.: not to ∾ *geschweige denn, abgesehen von;* don't ∾ it *bitte sehr! hat nichts zu sagen! keine Ursache! gern geschehen! nichts zu danken!*

merchant n.: the ∾ service *die Handelsmarine;* a ∾ ship, a ∾man *ein Handelsschiff;* he is a speed-∾ *er ist ein Kilometerfresser, ein Geschwindigkeitsfex*

mercy n.: ∾! ∾ (up)on us! *barmherziger Himmel!;* it is a ∾ he didn't break his arm *er kann von Glück sagen, daß er sich den Arm nicht gebrochen hat;* to be at the ∾ of a person *völlig in j.es Gewalt sein;* to be left to the tender mercies of one's enemies *seinen Feinden auf Gnade und Ungnade ausgeliefert sein;* to beg (to cry) for ∾ *um Gnade flehen;* to have (to take) ∾ (up)on, to show ∾ to a person *sich j.es erbarmen*

merit I. n.: to judge a matter on its own ∾s *eine Sache nach ihrem inneren Wert beurteilen;* to make a ∾ of (to take ∾ to oneself for) a thing *sich (dat.) etwas zum Verdienst anrechnen, sich (dat.) etwas zugute tun auf;* to make a ∾ of necessity *aus der Not eine Tugend machen.* — **II.** v.tr.: to ∾ a reward, punishment *eine Belohnung, Strafe verdienen*

merry a.: as ∾ as a grig (a cricket) *munter wie ein Heimchen (Eichhörnchen), kreuzfidel;* they were all very ∾ *sie waren alle etwas angeheitert;* to make ∾ *sich belustigen;* to make ∾ over a thing *sich über etwas lustig machen;* the more the merrier *je mehr desto besser;* he is a ∾-andrew *er ist ein Hanswurst, Spaßmacher;* a ∾-go-round *ein Karussell; ein Verteilerkreis;* the ∾-thought *das Brustbein (bei Geflügel)*

mess I. n.: a ∾ of pottage (Gen. XXV, 29—34) *ein Linsengericht;* to get into a pretty ∾ *sich arg in die Nesseln setzen; in eine nette Patsche geraten;* things were in a terrible ∾ *es herrschte eine schreckliche Unordnung (Schweinerei);* to make a ∾ of a thing *etwas verderben (verhunzen, verkorksen, vermasseln, verpfuschen);* the officers' ∾ *das Offizierskasino.* — **II.** v.tr.: to ∾ (up) a thing *etwas beschmutzen, in Unordnung, Verwirrung bringen.* — **III.** v.i.: to ∾ with the R.A.F. *im Kasino der Luftwaffe essen;* don't keep ∾ing about here (colloq.) *lauf', kram' nicht immer hier so herum!*

metal n.: the train leaves the ∾s *der Zug entgleist;* here's ∾ more attractive (Hamlet, III, 2) *hier ist ein stärkerer Magnet*

mettle n.: a man of ∾ *ein beherzter Bursche, ein Mann von echtem Schrott und Korn;* to be on one's ∾ *bereit sein, sein Bestes herzugeben;* to put a person on his ∾ *j.en anspornen, sein Möglichstes zu tun;* to try a person's ∾ *j.en auf die Probe stellen*

middling a.: I am only ∾ *mir geht es leidlich, so la la;* ∾ good *leidlich gut*

midnight n.: to burn the ∾ oil *bis tief in die Nacht hinein arbeiten (lesen)*

midst n.: in the ∾ of *inmitten (gen.), mitten unter;* in our (your, their) ∾ *unter uns (euch, ihnen)*

midsummer n.: it would be ∾ madness *es wäre der reinste Wahnsinn*

might n.: with ∾ and main *mit voller Kraft;* with all one's ∾ *aus Leibeskräften*

mighty a.: high and ∾ *hochfahrend;* that is ∾ easy *das ist riesig leicht*

mike n. (sl.): to be on the ∾ *faulenzen, sich drücken*

mild a.: draw it ∾ *mach' es gnädig! übertreib' nicht so!;* to put it ∾ly *gelinde gesagt*

mile n.: for ∾s *meilenweit;* a nautical ∾ *eine Seemeile;* ∾s easier (colloq.) *sehr viel leichter;* ∾s better (colloq.) *weit besser*

milk I. n.: ∾ for babes *Lehren (Schriften usw.) für einfache Geister bestimmt;* the ∾ of human kindness *die Milch der frommen Denkungsart;* that's all ∾ and water *das ist kraftloses, sentimentales Zeug, ohne Kraft und Saft;* that accounts for the ∾ in the coconut *daher der Name! das erklärt alles;* it's no use crying over spilt ∾ (prov.) *es hat keinen Zweck, Geschehenes zu beklagen;* he is a ∾-sop *er ist ein Müttersöhnchen, Schlappschwanz, Waschlappen.* — **II.** v.tr.: to ∾ the bull (ram) *etwas Unmögliches versuchen, einen Mohren weißwaschen wollen;* to ∾ a person *j.en schröpfen, rupfen;* to ∾ the wire *sich (dat.) unrechtmäßig elektrischen Strom aneignen; fremde Telegramme lesen, abfangen*

mill I. n.: the ∾s of God grind slowly (but they grind exceeding small) (prov.) *Gottes Mühlen mahlen langsam (mahlen aber trefflich fein);* he has been through the ∾ *er ist durch Erfahrung klug (gewitzigt) geworden;* to go through the ∾ *eine harte Schule durchmachen;* that brings grist to his ∾ *das ist Wasser auf seine Mühle;* as hard as the nether ∾-stone *hartherzig, unerbittlich;* to see far into a ∾-stone *überschlau sein, das Gras wachsen hören.* — **II.** v.i.: to ∾ about, around (sl.) *sich ständig im Kreise bewegen*

miller n.: to drown the ∾ *ein Getränk verwässern, pantschen*

milliner n.: a man ∾ *ein Kleinigkeitskrämer*

mince I. n.: ∾ meat *Mischung aus Korinthen, Rosinen, Zucker, Äpfeln, Zitronat usw. für Pasteten;* to make ∾(-)meat of *vernichten, kurz und klein schlagen.* — **II.** v.tr.: he doesn't ∾ matters *er nimmt kein Blatt vor den Mund;* to ∾ one's words *geziert sprechen;* a mincing gait *ein gezierter Gang*

mind I. n.: absence (presence) of ∾ *Geistesabwesenheit (-gegenwart);* out of sight, out of ∾ (prov.) *aus den Augen, aus dem Sinn;* to my ∾ *meiner Meinung nach;* that is not to my ∾ *das ist nicht nach meinem Sinne; das gefällt mir nicht;* from time out of ∾ *seit undenklichen Zeiten;* to be in my ∾'s eye *vor meinem geistigen Auge stehen;* to be in an excited frame (state) of ∾ *aufgeregt sein;* to be of a (one) ∾ with a person, to be of a person's ∾ *mit j.em übereinstimmen, j.es Meinung teilen;* he has a single-track ∾ *er hat nur einen Gedanken im Kopf;* to be of sound ∾, to be in one's right ∾ *bei vollem Verstand sein;* I was in two ∾s (I was unsettled in my ∾) about it *ich war mir selbst nicht einig darüber, ich schwankte, war unentschlossen;* to be of unsound ∾, to be out of one's ∾ *verrückt sein;* it was a load (weight) off my ∾ *es fiel mir ein Stein vom Herzen;* to bear (to have, to keep) in ∾ *im Gedächtnis behalten, berücksichtigen, nicht vergessen;* to bring (to call) to ∾ *ins Gedächtnis zurückrufen;* to change one's ∾ *sich anders besinnen;* to come into (to cross, to rush upon) one's ∾ *einem plötzlich in den Sinn kommen;* to give one's ∾ to a thing *sich einer Sache ganz widmen;* to go (to pass) out of ∾ *vergessen werden;* to have it in ∾ to do a thing *beabsichtigen (sich mit dem Gedanken tragen), etwas zu tun;* to have a good (a great) ∾ to *große Lust haben zu;* I have half a ∾ to say *ich möchte beinahe sagen;*

he doesn't know his ∾ *er weiß selbst nicht, was er will;* to lose one's ∾ *den Verstand verlieren;* to make up one's ∾ to do a thing *sich entschließen, etwas zu tun;* to make up one's ∾ to a thing *sich mit etwas abfinden;* it preys on my ∾ *es nagt an mir;* that puts me in ∾ of it *das erinnert mich daran;* it runs in my ∾ that *es geht mir im Kopfe herum (es kommt mir so vor), als ob;* to set one's ∾ on a thing *etwas unbedingt haben wollen;* to speak one's ∾ *frei von der Leber reden;* to tell a person one's ∾, to give a person a piece (bit) of one's ∾ *j.em gehörig aufs Dach steigen, die Meinung sagen, den Marsch blasen.* — **II.** v.tr.: ∾ your own business *kümmere dich um deine (eigenen) Angelegenheiten!;* never ∾ your cap! *laß die Mütze nur!;* to ∾ a child *auf ein Kind achtgeben;* I shouldn't ∾ a cup of tea *ich möchte gern eine Tasse Tee haben;* never ∾ the expense *ganz gleich, was es kostet;* ∾ your eye! (sl.) *Achtung! sieh dich vor!;* never ∾ him *kümmere dich nicht um ihn; laß ihn nur reden (machen);* to ∾ one's P's and Q's *sich sehr in achtnehmen mit seinen Worten oder seinem Benehmen;* would you ∾ ringing? *würden Sie bitte klingeln?;* ∾ the step! *Achtung, Vorsicht Stufe!* — **III.** v.i.: never ∾ *es hat nichts zu sagen, es macht nichts;* I don't ∾ *ich habe nichts dagegen; meinetwegen;* ∾ you do that tomorrow *denke daran, das morgen zu tun;* but I have no objection, ∾ you *aber ich habe nichts dagegen, müssen Sie wissen;* now ∾, make no mistake! *aber bitte, kein Irrtum!*

mine n.: this book is a ∾ of information *dieses Buch ist eine Fundgrube der Belehrung;* to spring a ∾ on a person *j.en überraschen*

minister I. v.i.: to ∾ to the wants of others *für die Bedürfnisse anderer sorgen;* a ∾ing angel *ein Schutzengel; eine Krankenschwester.* — **II.** v.tr.: to ∾ the sacraments *die Sakramente spenden*

minnow n.: a Triton among the ∾s *ein Riese unter Zwergen; als Einäugiger unter den Blinden König (sein)*

minor I. a.: ∾ details *unbedeutende Einzelheiten;* a ∾ key *eine Molltonart.* — **II.** n.: he is a ∾ *er ist minderjährig*

mint n.: a ∾ of money *eine Stange Geld*

minute[1] ['minit] **I.** n.: the very ∾ I said it *sobald ich es sagte;* to keep the ∾s *Protokoll führen;* to make a ∾ of a thing *etwas kurz aufschreiben (vermerken).* — **II.** v.tr.: to ∾ down a thing *etwas kurz aufschreiben (vermerken)*

minute[2] [mai'nju:t] a.: a ∾ description *eine genaue Beschreibung;* ∾ details *die kleinsten Einzelheiten*

miracle n.: he did it to a ∾ *er tat es überraschend gut*

mire n.: to drag into the ∾ *in den Kot ziehen;* to stick (to find oneself) in the ∾ *in Verlegenheit, in der Klemme (Patsche) sein*

mischief n.: the ∾ of it is that *das Ärgerliche dabei ist, daß;* where the ∾ have you been? *wo zum Teufel bist du gewesen?;* he is bent on (he means) ∾ *er führt Böses im Schilde;* the storm has done a great deal of ∾ *der Sturm hat großen Schaden angerichtet;* to be up to ∾ *Unfug treiben;* don't get into (keep out of) ∾! *treibt keinen Unfug!;* to make ∾ between *Unheil stiften zwischen;* to raise the ∾ about a thing *wegen einer Sache einen Heidenlärm machen, gehörig Krach schlagen*

misgive v.tr.: my mind ∾s me *mir ahnt Böses*

miss I. n.: a ∾ is as good as a mile (prov.) *verfehlt ist verspielt;* I shall give the party a ∾ *ich werde nicht zu der Gesellschaft gehen.* — **II.** v.tr.: to ∾ the bus (colloq.) *eine günstige Gelegenheit verpassen;* to ∾ fire *versagen, erfolglos sein;* to ∾ the mark *fehlschießen;* to ∾ an opportunity *eine Gelegenheit versäumen;* to ∾ a person (a thing) *j.en (eine Sache) vermissen;* to ∾ a remark *eine Bemerkung überhören, nicht verstehen;* to ∾ the train *den Zug verpassen;* to ∾ (out) a word *ein Wort auslassen*

mistake I. n.: he did it by ∾, in ∾ *er tat es irrtümlicherweise, aus Versehen;* and (make) no ∾, he will come *er wird zweifellos kommen.* — **II.** v.tr.: there is no mistaking the fact *die Tatsache läßt sich nicht verkennen;* to ∾ a person for another *j.en mit einem anderen verwechseln;* to ∾ a person's words *j.en falsch verstehen;* unless I am very much ∾n *wenn ich mich nicht sehr irre*

mite n.: not a ∾ of use *völlig nutzlos;* he is a tiny ∾ of a child *er ist ein winziges Kerlchen, ein kleines Würmchen;* may I offer my ∾? *darf ich mein Scherflein dazu beitragen?;* the widow's ∾ (Mark XII, 42) *das Scherflein der Witwe*

mitten n.: to get (to give) the ∾ (the frozen mitt) *einen Korb bekommen, geben;* to handle without ∾s *nicht mit Glacéhandschuhen anfassen*

mix I. v.tr.: ∾ it up well *vermische (verrühre) es gut!;* to ∾ up in one's mind *etwas gedanklich verwechseln;* he is ∾ed up in (with) it *er ist darin verwickelt, er hat seine Hand dabei im Spiel;* I got completely ∾ed up *ich wurde vollständig verwirrt, ich geriet ganz durcheinander;* a ∾ed school *eine Schule für Jungen und Mädchen.* — **II.** v.i.: they do not ∾ well *sie kommen nicht gut miteinander aus;* to ∾ with persons *mit Leuten verkehren;* to ∾ in good society *in der guten Gesellschaft verkehren;* oil does not ∾ with water *Öl läßt sich nicht mit Wasser vermischen;* ∾ed bathing *Familienbad*

mock a.: a ∾ marriage *eine Scheinehe;* he said it with ∾ gravity *er sagte es mit scheinbarem, erheucheltem Ernst;* a ∾-heroic style *ein burlesk-heroischer Stil;* ∾-turtle soup *falsche Schildkrötensuppe*

moil v.i.: to toil and ∾ *sich abquälen, sich abrackern*

mole n.: as blind as a ∾ *stockblind;* to make mountains out of ∾-hills *aus einer Mücke einen Elefanten machen*

molly-coddle I. n.: he is a ∾ *er ist ein Muttersöhnchen.* — **II.** v.tr.: to ∾ a child *ein Kind verzärteln (verhätscheln)*

moment n.: I was busy at the ∾ *ich war gerade beschäftigt;* one ∾, half a ∾, half a mo! *einen Augenblick!;* I came the very ∾ I heard it *ich kam, sobald ich es hörte;* come here this ∾ *komm sofort hierhin!;* timed to the ∾ *auf die Minute genau;* it is a matter of ∾ *es ist eine gewichtige Sache;* an unguarded ∾ *ein Augenblick geistiger Abwesenheit*

money n.: ∾ makes the mare to go (prov.) *wer gut schmeert (schmiert), der gut fährt; Geld regiert die Welt;* time is ∾ (prov.) *Zeit ist Geld;* ∾ is the root of all evil (prov.) *Geld ist die Wurzel alles Übels;* ∾ for jam, for old rope (sl.) *gefundenes, leicht verdientes Geld;* I cannot get it for love or ∾ *ich kann es für Geld oder gute Worte nicht bekommen;* that's not my ∾ (colloq.) *das ist nichts für mich;* to be out of (short of) ∾ *kein Geld haben, knapp bei Kasse sein;* he is coining ∾ *er verdient Geld wie Heu;* to keep a person in ∾ *j.en mit Geld versehen;* to make ∾ *Geld verdienen;* to save (to set by) ∾ *Geld zurücklegen, sparen;* to throw good ∾ after bad *gutes Geld faulem nachwerfen;* he is a ∾-grubber *er ist ein Geizhals;* a ∾-order *eine Postanweisung;* ready ∾,∾ down *bares Geld;* hush ∾ *Schweigegeld;* pin ∾ *Taschengeld*

monger n.: he is a news-∾ *er ist ein Neuigkeitskrämer;* he is a scandal-∾ *er ist ein Lästermaul;* he is a war-∾ *er ist ein Kriegshetzer*

monkey n.: a ∾ (sl.) *500 Pfund Sterling;* he is a mischievous young ∾ *er ist ein kleiner Nichtsnutz;* to get one's ∾ up (sl.) *wütend werden, hochgehen;* none of your ∾-tricks with me! *komm mir nicht mit deinen dummen Streichen!;* a ∾ puzzle *eine Araukarie (einziger Baum, den ein Affe nicht erklettern kann)*

month n.: it took a ∾ of Sundays *es dauerte eine Ewigkeit;* this day ∾ *heute in vier Wochen;* the ∾'s mind *das Seelenamt nach vier Wochen;* to pay by the ∾ *monatlich bezahlen;* for ∾s *monatelang, seit Monaten*

mooch, mouch v.i. (sl.): to ∾ about *herumlungern;* to ∾ along *daherlatschen*

mood n.: to be in the ∾ (in no ∾) for a thing (to do a thing) *zu etwas aufgelegt (nicht aufgelegt) sein;* when the ∾ was on him *wenn er in (der) Stimmung war*

moon I. n.: once in a blue ∾ *alle Jubeljahre (einmal);* a waxing (waning) ∾ *ein zunehmender (abnehmender) Mond;* to cry for the ∾ *etwas Unmögliches wünschen, Unerreichbares erstreben;* to shoot the ∾, to go between the ∾ and the milkman *bei Nacht und Nebel ausrücken, ohne (die) Miete zu bezahlen;* to think the ∾ is made of green cheese *glauben, der Mond sei ein Eierkuchen;* ∾calf *Mondkalb, Tölpel;* ∾light flitting *heimliches Ausziehen bei Nacht unter Mitnahme der Möbel;* that's all ∾shine (sl.) *das ist alles gefaselt, Unsinn;* a ∾shiner (U.S. sl.) *ein heimlicher Schnapsbrenner (Schnapsschmuggler);* ∾struck *mondsüchtig.* — **II.** v.i.: to ∾ about (around) *herumlungern.* — **III.** v.tr.: to ∾ away the time *die Zeit vertrödeln (verplempern)*

moot a.: it is a ∾ point *es ist ein strittiger, zweifelhafter Punkt*

mop[1] **I.** v.tr.: he simply ∾ped the floor with him (sl.) *er war ihm haushoch überlegen;* ∾ping operations are going on *Säuberungsaktionen sind im Gange.* — **II.** n.: Mrs ∾ *eine (die) Putzfrau*

mop[2] v.i.: to ∾ and mow *Gesichter (Grimassen) schneiden*

more I. a.: would you like some ∾ coffee? *möchten Sie noch etwas Kaffee?;* bring some ∾ (two ∾) plates *bringen Sie noch einige Teller, zwei weitere (noch zwei) Teller.* — **II.** n.: any ∾ for any ∾ (colloq.)? *möchte noch jemand?;* have you any ∾ of this material? *haben Sie noch mehr von diesem Stoff?;* I hope to see ∾ of you now *ich hoffe, Sie jetzt häufiger zu sehen.* — **III.** adv.: ∾ and ∾ *immer mehr;* once ∾ *noch einmal;* the ∾ so as (because) *um so mehr, als (weil);* you must attend ∾ to details *du mußt mehr auf Einzelheiten achten;* it is much ∾ comfortable *es ist viel bequemer;* he was ∾ frightened than hurt *er erschrak mehr, als daß er sich verletzte;* I can do it ∾ easily now *ich kann es jetzt leichter tun*

morning n.: in the ∾ *am Morgen, des Morgens;* on Sunday ∾ *am Sonntagmorgen;* this ∾ *heute morgen, heute früh;* the ∾ after the night before *der Katzenjammer (Kater)*

morrow n.: on the ∾ of a long war *in der Zeit unmittelbar nach einem langen Kriege*

mortal I. a.: a ∾ enemy *ein Todfeind;* a ∾ injury *eine tödliche Verletzung;* to be in a ∾ funk (sl.) *eine Mordsangst (einen Mordsbammel) haben;* I waited for two ∾ hours (sl.) *ich wartete zwei geschlagene Stunden.* — **II.** n.: he is a thirsty ∾ *er ist eine durstige Seele*

moss n.: a rolling stone gathers no ∾ (prov.) *wälzender Stein wird nicht moosig*

most I. a.: you have made ∾ mistakes *du hast die meisten Fehler gemacht;* for the ∾ part *meisten-, größtenteils;* ∾ people think so *die meisten Leute denken so.* — **II.** n.: to make the ∾ of a thing *etwas aufs beste ausnutzen;* he made the ∾ of his abilities *er nutzte seine Fähigkeiten gut aus; er stellte seine Fähigkeiten im besten Lichte dar;* he made the ∾ of his misfortune *er stellte sein Unglück im schlimmsten Lichte dar.* — **III.** adv.: what ∾ annoys me, what annoys me ∾ *was mich am meisten ärgert;* ∾ certainly *ganz gewiß;* the ∾ comfortable chair *der bequemste Stuhl;* it was ∾ unpleasant *es war äußerst unangenehm;* ten at ∾ *höchstens zehn;* that is at ∾ a makeshift *das ist bestenfalls ein Notbehelf*

mother n.: necessity is the ∾ of invention (prov.) *Not macht erfinderisch;* every ∾'s son of you *jeder einzelne von euch;* the ∾ tongue *die Muttersprache;* ∾ wit *gesunder Menschenverstand*

motion I. n.: to bring in a ∾ for *einen Antrag einbringen auf;* to carry a ∾ *einen Antrag annehmen;* to make a ∾ of the hand *eine Handbewegung machen;* to put (to set) in ∾ *in Bewegung setzen, in Gang bringen.* — **II.** v.tr.: to ∾ a person to a seat *j.en durch Handbewegung auffordern, Platz zu nehmen.* — **III.** v.i.: he ∾ed them to be taken away *er gab einen Wink, sie abzuführen*

mould n.: to be cast in the same ∾ *aus demselben Holz geschnitten sein;* cast in a heroic ∾ *heroischen Charakters*

mount I. v.i.: the blood ∾ed to his head *das Blut stieg ihm in den Kopf (zu Kopf);* prices are ∾ing up *die Preise steigen.* — **II.** v.tr.: to ∾ guard *auf Wache ziehen;* to ∾ a horse *zu Pferde steigen, aufsitzen;* to ∾ a machine *eine Maschine aufmontieren;* to ∾ a person *j.em aufsitzen helfen; j.em ein Pferd leihen;* to ∾ a picture *ein Bild einrahmen;* to ∾ a precious stone *einen Edelstein einfassen;* the ∾ed police *die berittene Polizei*

mountain n.: to make ∾s out of molehills *aus einer Mücke einen Elefanten machen*

mourn v.i. & tr.: to ∾ for (over) a person (thing) *um j.en (um etwas) trauern;* to ∾ the loss of a person (thing) *den Verlust einer Person (eines Dinges) beklagen (betrauern)*

mourning n.: to go into ∾ *Trauer anlegen*

mouse n.: as poor as a church ∾ *so arm wie eine Kirchenmaus;* as quiet as a ∾ *mäuschenstill;* to give a person a ∾ *j.em ein blaues Auge schlagen;* when the cat is away the mice will play (prov.) *wenn die Katze nicht im Hause ist, tanzen die Mäuse über Tische und Bänke*

mouth n.: to be down in the ∾ *in schlechter Stimmung (mißmutig, niedergeschlagen) sein;* one more useless ∾ *noch ein unnützer Esser (mehr);* by word of ∾ *mündlich;* the dog gives ∾ *der Hund gibt Laut (schlägt an);* you will laugh on the wrong side of your ∾ *dir wird das Lachen noch vergehen;* that makes my ∾ water (my ∾ waters at it, it brings the water to my ∾) *da läuft mir das Wasser im Munde zusammen;* to make a wry ∾ *ein schiefes Gesicht ziehen;* to put words into a person's ∾ *j.em Worte in den Mund legen;* to stop a person's ∾ *j.em den Mund stopfen*

move I. n.: whose ∾ is it? (chess) *wer ist am Zuge? (Schachspiel);* to be on the ∾ *in Bewegung sein;* to be up to every ∾ (to a ∾ or two); to know every ∾ (a ∾ or two) *mit allen Hunden gehetzt sein;* get a ∾ on (sl.) *mach' dich auf die Socken! beeile (rühre, tummele) dich! mal los! fang' schon an!;* shall we make a ∾? *sollen wir aufbrechen, weitergehen?;* he has made a new ∾ *er hat einen neuen Schritt unternommen;* three ∾s are as bad as a fire *dreimal umgezogen ist so gut wie einmal abgebrannt.* — **II.** v.tr.: to ∾ heaven and earth *Himmel und Erde in Bewegung setzen;* the spirit ∾s me to do so *es treibt mich der Geist, es zu tun;* to ∾ a resolution *eine Entscheidung einbringen;* he was ∾d at your kindness *er war von Ihrer Freundlichkeit ergriffen.* — **III.** v.i.: we are moving tomorrow *wir ziehen morgen um;* we are moving in (out) tomorrow *wir ziehen morgen ein (aus);* ∾ on, please! *bitte weitergehen, nicht stehen bleiben!;* the work ∾s slowly *die Arbeit schreitet langsam fort*

much I. a.: to give ∾ trouble *viel Mühe machen;* to make too ∾ noise *zuviel Lärm machen.* — **II.** n.: too ∾ of a good thing *des Guten zuviel;* he was too ∾ for him *er war ihm überlegen;* it is not ∾ of a play *an dem Stück ist nicht viel dran;* he is not ∾ of a scholar *er ist kein sonderlicher Gelehrter;* to make ∾ of a person *viel Wesens um j.en machen;* to set ∾ by a thing *viel Wert auf etwas legen;* I thought as ∾ *das habe ich mir gedacht.* — **III.** adv.: it is ∾ the same thing *es ist so ziemlich dasselbe;* it is ∾ of a size *es ist ungefähr dieselbe Größe;* as ∾ as to say *als wenn er sagen wollte;* he did not as ∾ as offer us a dinner *er bot uns nicht einmal ein Essen an;* he left without so ∾ as a word of thanks *er ging ohne auch nur ein Wort des Dankes weg (fort);* so ∾ the better, the worse *um so besser, so schlimmer;* so ∾ for that matter *damit wäre die Angelegenheit erledigt;* so ∾ nonsense *lauter Unsinn;* so ∾ for his promises *da sieht man, was seine Versprechungen wert sind*

muchness n.: it is much of a ∾ (colloq.) *es ist so ziemlich gleich, vom selben Kaliber, von derselben Art*

muck I. n.: to make a ∾ of a job (sl.) *eine Arbeit verpfuschen (verhunzen, vermasseln, verkorksen).* — **II.** v.tr.: to ∾ a job (sl.) *eine Arbeit verhunzen (verkorksen, vermasseln, verpfuschen).* — **III.** v.i.: to ∾ about (sl.) *herumlungern*

mucker n. (sl.): to come a ∾ *einen schweren Sturz tun;* to go a ∾ on (over) a purchase *sich in Unkosten stürzen*

mud n.: here's ∾ in your eye! (sl.) *Prost! Auf Ihr Wohl! Zum Wohlsein!;* to drag in the ∾ *in den Schmutz (Kot) ziehen;* to fling (to throw) ∾ at a person *j.en mit Schmutz bewerfen, verleumden;* to stick in the ∾ *sich festfahren, nicht weiter können;* he is a stick-in-the-∾ *er ist ein schwerfälliger Mensch, ein langweiliger Peter;* his name is ∾ (sl.) *er ist in Ungnade gefallen*

muddle I. n.: to be in a ∾ *in Verwirrung sein;* to make a ∾ of a thing *etwas vermasseln (verpfuschen);* he is a ∾-headed chap *er ist ein Wirr-, Dummkopf.* — **II.** v.tr. & i.: to ∾ things up (together) *Sachen durcheinander bringen (werfen);* this country ∾s through *dieses Land wurstelt (wurschtelt) sich durch*

muff n.: he is a ∾ *er ist ein Stümper;* to make a ∾ of a thing *etwas vermasseln (verkorksen)*

mufti n.: in ∾ *in Zivil*

mug[1] n. (sl.): to make a ∾, to pull a long ∾ *Grimassen schneiden*

mug[2] n. (sl.): he is an awful ∾ *er ist ein Einfaltspinsel*

mug³ v.tr. (sl.): to ∾ up a subject *sich (dat.) einen Stoff einpauken*

mull n.: to make a ∾ of a thing *etwas verpfuschen*

multiplication n.: the ∾ table *das Einmaleins*

mum int. & a.: ∾'s the word! *schweig! nichts gesagt!*; to keep ∾ *Schweigen bewahren*

mummy n.: to beat a person to a ∾ *j.en windelweich hauen*

murder n.: ∾ will out (prov.) *es ist nichts so fein gesponnen, es kommt doch endlich an die Sonnen; die Sonne bringt es an den Tag;* the ∾ is out *nun ist das Geheimnis offenbart, die Wahrheit heraus;* to cry blue ∾ *Zeter und Mordio schreien*

muscle I. n.: without moving a ∾ *ohne mit der Wimper zu zucken.* — **II.** v.i.: to ∾ in on something (sl.) *aus dem Vorteil eines anderen Nutzen ziehen*

music n.: to face the ∾ *die Folgen (Vorwürfe, Kritik) mutig auf sich nehmen;* to play from ∾ *vom Blatt spielen;* to set to ∾ *in Musik setzen, vertonen;* rough ∾ *Katzenmusik*

musical a.: ∾ chairs *die Reise nach Jerusalem (Gesellschaftsspiel)*

muslin n.: a bit of ∾ (colloq.) *eine Frau, ein Mädchen; ein Weibsbild*

must I. v.aux.: needs ∾ when the devil drives (prov.) *das Unvermeidliche muß man hinnehmen, Not kennt kein Gebot.* — **II.** n.: it is a ∾ (colloq.) *es ist unbedingt notwendig, ein Muß*

mustard n.: as keen as ∾ on something *auf etwas ganz erpicht*

muster I. n.: it will pass ∾ *es wird als genügend erachtet werden, es wird noch hingehen.* — **II.** v.tr.: to ∾ (up) courage *den Mut finden (aufbringen)*

mutton n.: to eat one's ∾ with a person *mit j.em speisen;* as dead as ∾ *mausetot;* to get back to one's ∾s *zum Thema, auf besagten Hammel zurückkommen;* a ∾-head *ein Schafskopf*

myrmidon n.: a ∾ of the law *ein Schutzmann, Gerichtsvollzieher*

mystery n.: to make a ∾ of a thing *etwas als Geheimnis behandeln, verheimlichen, geheimhalten;* wrapt in ∾ *in ein geheimnisvolles Dunkel gehüllt*

N

Naboth n.pr.: ∾'s vineyard (1 Kings, XXI) *eine von einem reichen Mann begehrte Besitzung eines armen Nachbarn*

nail I. n.: one ∾ drives out another (prov.) *ein Keil treibt den andern;* to the (a) ∾ (Horace, Sat. I, V, 32) *aufs genaueste, bis aufs Haar;* a ∾'s breadth (cf. lat. transversum unguem) *die kleinste Menge;* a ∾ in my coffin *ein Nagel zu meinem Sarg;* as hard as ∾s *gut durchtrainiert, stahlhart;* as right as ∾s *ganz richtig;* from the tender ∾ (Horace, Odes III, VI, 24) *von der frühesten Jugend an;* to bite one's ∾s *sich (dat.) an den Nägeln kauen;* he bites his ∾s for poverty *er nagt am Hungertuche;* to cut (to pare, to trim) one's ∾s *sich (dat.) die Nägel beschneiden;* to drive the ∾ home *eine Angelegenheit zum Abschluß bringen;* to fight (to struggle) tooth and ∾ *mit aller Kraft kämpfen;* to hit the (right) ∾ on the head *den Nagel auf den Kopf treffen;* to pare a person's ∾s *j.em die Nägel schneiden;* to pay on the ∾ *sofort bar bezahlen;* to stud with ∾s *mit Nägeln beschlagen.* — **II.** v.tr.: to ∾ one's colours to the mast *standhaft bleiben;* to ∾ to the counter (barndoor) *etwas als unecht (falsch) festnageln;* to ∾ a person down to a thing *j.en auf etwas festnageln;* a ∾ed-up drama *ein schlecht aufgebautes Drama, das auf glänzende Ausstattung angewiesen ist*

nailer n.: to be a ∾ at something (sl.) *etwas glänzend verstehen*

naked a.: with the ∾ eye *mit bloßem Auge;* the ∾ facts *die nackten Tatsachen;* the ∾ sword *das blanke Schwert;* the ∾ truth *die nackte (unverhüllte, reine) Wahrheit;* stark ∾ *splitternackt;* to realize a thing in its ∾ absurdity *etwas als völlig ungereimt erkennen;* to strip ∾ *sich nackt ausziehen*

name I. n.: a ∾ to conjure with *ein berühmter Name (der Wunder wirkt);* I know him by ∾ *ich kenne ihn dem Namen nach;* to mention a person by ∾ *j.en namentlich erwähnen;* somebody of (by) the ∾ of N. *j. namens N.;* Tom by ∾, by ∾ Tom *namens Tom;* Christian ∾ *Vor-, Rufname;* her maiden ∾ is N. *sie ist eine geborene N., mit ihrem Mädchennamen hieß sie N.;* proper ∾ *Eigenname;* to call a person ∾s *j.en beschimpfen;* he hasn't a penny to his ∾ *er besitzt keinen einzigen Pfennig;* give it a ∾ (colloq.) *was wollen Sie trinken?;* to keep one's ∾ on the books, to take one's ∾ off the books *Mitglied eines Vereins usw. bleiben; die Mitgliedschaft aufgeben;* to put down one's ∾ for a post *sich auf eine Stelle melden;* to take a person's ∾ in vain *j.es Namen mißbrauchen, ihn unnütz im Munde führen;* give a dog a bad ∾ and hang him *wer einen Fehltritt tut, ist ein für alle Male abgetan.* — **II.** v.tr.: to ∾ the day *den Hochzeitstag festsetzen;* that is not to be ∾d on (in) the same day with *das ist nicht in einem Atem zu nennen mit*

nap[1] I. n.: to take a ∾ *ein Schläfchen (Nickerchen) machen.* — **II.** v.i.: he was caught ∾ping *man überraschte (ertappte) ihn bei einer Nachlässigkeit, einem Fehler*

nap[2] n.: to go ∾ *alles aufs Spiel setzen*

nark n. (sl.): a copper's ∾ *ein Polizeispitzel*

narrow a.: he had a ∾ escape (squeak) *er ist mit knapper Not entkommen;* he lives in ∾ circumstances *er lebt in ärmlichen Verhältnissen;* a ∾ majority *eine knappe Mehrheit*

natter v.i. (colloq.): to ∾ *plaudern, murren*

natural I. a.: a ∾ child *ein außereheliches Kind.* — **II.** n.: a ∾ *ein Schwachsinniger*

nature n.: the debt of ∾ *der Tod;* in a state of ∾ *nackt, unbekleidet;* he is timid by ∾ *er ist von Natur ängstlich;* to draw from ∾ *nach der Natur zeichnen;* it is in (of) the ∾ of a command *es ist so gut wie ein Befehl;* he is good-∾d *er ist gutmütig*

naught, nought n.: to bring to ∾ *zerstören, durchkreuzen, vereiteln;* to come to ∾ *fehlschlagen, sich in Wohlgefallen auflösen;* to set at ∾ *für nichts achten, in den Wind schlagen*

nay I. adv.: (old fash. and lit.) he was angry, ∾ furious *er war böse, ja sogar wütend;* ∾ more, he tried to deceive me *ja noch mehr (ja was noch schlimmer ist), er versuchte, mich zu täuschen.* — **II.** n.: I cannot say him ∾ *ich kann es ihm nicht verweigern, ich kann ihm nicht widersprechen;* he will not take a ∾ *er läßt sich nicht abweisen;* a yea and ∾ *eine unentschlossene Person*

near I. adv.: far and ∾ *überall, weit und breit;* ∾ at hand (∾ by) *in der Nähe;* ∾ upon midnight *kurz vor Mitternacht;* he was ∾ (∾ly) dead with fright *er war fast zu Tode erschrocken;* not ∾ (∾ly) so numerous *nicht annähernd so zahlreich;* to go ∾ to do (to come, to go ∾ doing) a thing *etwas beinahe tun;* he lives ∾ *er lebt sparsam.* — **II.** prep.: time draws ∾ Christmas *es geht auf Weihnachten zu;* my hopes are ∾ fulfilment *meine Hoffnungen sind der Erfüllung nahe;* it lies ∾ his heart *es geht ihm zu Herzen;* the sun is ∾ setting *die Sonne geht bald unter;* who comes ∾ him in wit? *wer kommt ihm an Geist gleich?* — **III.** a.: a ∾ escape *ein knappes Entkommen;* a ∾ friend *ein vertrauter Freund;* to make a ∾ guess *etwas beinahe erraten;* a ∾ miss *ein Mißerfolg, der beinahe ein Erfolg war; etwas, das nicht geschah, aber beinahe geschehen wäre (vergl.* ∾ shave, ∾ thing); a ∾ relation *ein naher Verwandter;* a ∾ resemblance *eine große Ähnlichkeit;* a ∾ (close) shave *ein knappes Entkommen (von etwas Unangenehmen, das beinahe passiert wäre);* the ∾ side *(Fahrzeuge) links;* he is ∾-sighted *er ist kurzsichtig;* a ∾ (close) thing *ein Erfolg, der beinahe ein Mißerfolg war (um ein Haar!);* a ∾ translation *eine genaue Übersetzung*

neat a.: as ∾ as a new pin (as a bandbox) *wie aus dem Ei gepellt;* it was a ∾ way of saying it *es war eine geschickte Art, es zu sagen;* to drink brandy ∾ *Branntwein ohne Wasser (unverdünnt) trinken*

necessary n.: you must find (provide) the ∾ *du mußt das nötige Geld stellen;* the necessaries of life *die Lebensbedürfnisse*

necessity n.: ∾ knows no law (prov.) *Not kennt kein Gebot;* ∾ is the mother of invention (prov.) *(die) Not macht erfinderisch;* of ∾ *notwendigerweise;* to be under the ∾ of doing a thing *sich gezwungen sehen, etwas zu tun;* to make a virtue of ∾ *aus der Not eine Tugend machen*

neck n.: ∾ and crop, ∾ and heels *mit Sack und Pack, gänzlich;* it is ∾ or nothing *es gilt alles oder nichts; blindlings, auf jede Gefahr hin;* to break the ∾ of a task *das Schwerste einer Aufgabe hinter sich bringen;* they came in ∾ and ∾ *sie kamen Kopf an Kopf durchs Ziel;* to crane one's ∾ to see something *den Hals ausstrecken (ausrecken), um etwas zu sehen;* to get it in the ∾ (sl.) *einen Schlag ins Genick, es gehörig zu spüren bekommen; ordentlich abgekanzelt werden;* he gives me a pain in the ∾ (sl.) *er ist mir ein Greuel;* he is always sticking out his ∾ (sl.) *er mischt sich in alles ein, er ist zudringlich;* stiff-∾ed *halsstarrig, unnachgiebig;* to be up to one's ∾ in work *bis über die Ohren beschäftigt sein (in Arbeit stecken)*

need I. n.: if ∾ arise *im Notfalle;* if ∾ be *nötigenfalls;* a friend in ∾ is a friend indeed (prov.) *in der Not erkennt man seine Freunde; Freunde in der Not gehen tausend auf ein Lot;* to be in (to stand in) ∾ of (to have ∾ of) a thing *etwas nötig haben, brauchen;* there is no ∾ to worry *es besteht kein Grund zur Sorge;* he had ∾ remember *er sollte sich erinnern.* — **II.** v.tr.: he ∾s money *er braucht Geld (hat Geld nötig);* he ∾ed all his skill *es erforderte seine ganze Geschicklichkeit.* — **III.** v.aux.: he ∾ not trouble himself *er braucht sich nicht zu bemühen;* he ∾ not have done so *er hätte es nicht zu tun brauchen;* it scarcely ∾s adding *es braucht kaum hinzugefügt zu werden;* it ∾s saying *es muß einmal gesagt werden*

needful n.: the ∾ (sl.) *das (nötige) Geld*

needle n.: to get the ∾ (sl.) *ärgerlich, nervös werden;* to look for a ∾ in a bottle of hay (in a haystack) *etwas vergeblich suchen;* to ∾ one's way through *sich winden*

needs adv.: ∾ must (go) when the devil drives (prov.) *Not kennt kein Gebot (bricht Eisen); man muß einer überlegenen Macht nachgeben;* she ∾ must come today *(ironisch) ausgerechnet heute muß sie kommen;* he ∾ must answer *er muß notwendigerweise antworten*

nerve I. n.: to get on one's ∾s *einem auf die Nerven fallen;* he hasn't got the ∾ to do it *er hat nicht den Mut (die Unverschämtheit), es zu tun;* you have a ∾! (colloq.) *du hast aber Nerven! du bist aber dreist!;* he lost his ∾ *er wurde ängstlich, unentschlossen;* to strain every ∾ *alle erdenkliche Anstrengungen machen.* — **II.** v.tr.: to ∾ oneself to (do) something *sich zu etwas aufraffen*

nest n.: to feather one's ∾ *sein Schäfchen ins Trockene bringen;* to foul one's own ∾ *sein eigenes Nest beschmutzen;* he has put by a nice little ∾-egg *er hat einen netten Sparpfennig zurückgelegt*

nether a.: (archaic or jocular) the ∾ lip *die Unterlippe;* ∾ garments *Unterhosen;* the ∾ man *die Beine;* a ∾ millstone *ein hartes Herz;* the ∾ world, regions *die Hölle*

nettle n.: to be on ∾s *unruhig, aufgeregt, gespannt sein;* to grasp the ∾ *eine Schwierigkeit mutig (beherzt) anpacken.* — **II.** v.tr.: that ∾s me *das verdrießt (wurmt) mich;* to be ∾d at a thing *über etwas verdrießlich sein, sich ärgern*

never adv.: well, I ∾! I ∾ did! *nein, so was!; aber hören Sie mal!;* ∾ fear! *nur keine Angst!;* you ∾ went all that way, did you? *du bist doch nicht etwa so weit gegangen?;* ∾ mind *es hat nichts zu sagen, es macht nichts;* ∾ say die *nur Mut! gib dich nicht geschlagen!;* he ∾ so much as thanked me *er dankte mir nicht einmal;* ∾ a one *auch nicht einer; keiner;* were he ∾ so rich *wäre er noch so reich;* it is ∾ too late to mend (prov.) *Reue kommt niemals zu spät;* it ∾ rains but it pours (prov.) *ein Unglück kommt selten allein;* a ∾ (ne'er)-do-well *ein Tunichtgut, ein Taugenichts;* the ∾ ∾ system *das Ratenzahlen, das Abstottern*

Newcastle n.pr.: to carry coals to ∾ *Eulen nach Athen tragen, Überflüssiges, Unnützes tun*

news n.pl.: ill ∾ flies (comes) apace (prov.) *schlechte Nachrichten verbreiten sich schnell;* no ∾ is good ∾ (prov.) *keine Nachricht, gute Nachricht;* that is no ∾ *das ist nichts Neues;* a piece of ∾ *eine Nachricht;* to be in the ∾ *viel von sich reden machen;* to break the ∾ to a person *j.em etwas schonend beibringen;* to listen in to the ∾ *die Rundfunknachrichten hören*

next I. a.: he lives ∾ door *er wohnt nebenan;* it is ∾-door to treason *es grenzt an Verrat;* ∾ to nothing *fast nichts;* the ∾ but one *der Übernächste;* within the ∾ few days *in den nächsten Tagen;* to be ∾ best *der Zweitbeste sein;* to be ∾ best thing to *gleich kommen nach, fast so gut sein wie;* ∾ to impossible *beinahe unmöglich.* — **II.** adv.: when I saw him ∾ *als ich ihn das nächste Mal sah;* what ∾? *was noch? was jetzt?;* in the week ∾ ensuing *in der darauf folgenden Woche;* Manchester is the largest city ∾ London *Manchester ist nach London die größte Stadt.* — **III.** prep.: I was standing ∾ him *ich stand neben ihm;* I can't bear flannel ∾ my skin *ich kann kein Flanell auf der Haut vertragen.* — **IV.** n.: the ∾ of kin *der, die nächste(n) Verwandte(n);* to be continued in our ∾ *Fortsetzung in unserer nächsten Nummer;* her ∾ was a girl *ihr nächstes Kind war ein Mädchen;* ∾, please! *der nächste, bitte!*

Niagara n.pr.: to shoot ∾ *eine waghalsige Sache unternehmen*

nice I. a.: you must not be so ∾ about it *du darfst es nicht so genau nehmen;* a ∾ distinction *ein feiner Unterschied;* here is a ∾ mess! (iron.) *das ist eine schöne Schweinerei!;* it is a ∾ point *es ist ein heikler Punkt.* — **II.** adv.: the car is going ∾ and fast *der Wagen fährt schön schnell;* the house stands ∾ and high *das Haus liegt schön hoch*

nicety n.: to a ∾ *aufs genaueste, bis aufs Haar;* a point of great ∾ *ein sehr heikler Punkt;* to stand upon niceties *es allzu genau nehmen*

Nick n.pr.: old ∾ *der Teufel*

nick I. n.: in the ∾ of time *gerade zur rechten Zeit;* a ∾name *ein Spitzname.* — **II.** v.tr.: to ∾ a criminal *einen Verbrecher zu fassen kriegen;* to ∾ it, to ∾ the truth *es erraten, die Wahrheit erraten;* to ∾ a train *einen Zug noch eben erwischen*

nigger n.: a ∾ in the woodpile (fence) (U.S. sl.) *ein verdächtiger Umstand;* he works like a ∾ *er arbeitet wie ein Pferd*

night n.: all ∾, all ∾ long *die ganze Nacht;* late at ∾ *spät abends;* by ∾, during the (in the) ∾ *bei Nacht, nachts;* in (at) the dead of ∾ *mitten in der Nacht;* a first ∾ *eine Uraufführung, Premiere;* to make a ∾ of it *die ganze Nacht durchmachen (um die Ohren schlagen);* to stay the ∾ at an hotel *in einem Hotel übernachten;* it is her ∾ out *sie hat heute Ausgang;* a ∾-cap *ein Schlummerpunsch;* a ∾mare *ein Alpdrücken*

nine I. a.: it was a ∾ days' wonder *es war eine Sensation;* ∾ times out of ten *im allgemeinen.* — **II.** n.: to be dressed up to the ∾s *pikfein angezogen sein, aufgeputzt, aufgedonnert*

nineteen n.: he talks ∾ to the dozen *er schwatzt unaufhörlich (das Blaue vom Himmel herunter)*

ninety n.: in the nineties of the last century *in den neunziger Jahren des vergangenen Jahrhunderts*

nip[1] I. v.tr.: to ∾ in the bud *im Keime ersticken.* — **II.** v.i.: to ∾ in *sich hineindrängen (sich hineinschieben);* to ∾ out, off *sich eiligst, unbemerkt davonmachen*

nip[2] n.: to take a ∾ of brandy *ein Schlückchen Branntwein trinken*

nod I. v.i.: he is a ∾ding acquaintance *er ist eine flüchtige Bekanntschaft;* to ∾ off *einnicken.* — **II.** v.tr.: to ∾ assent *zustimmend nicken;* to ∾ one's head *mit dem Kopf nicken.* — **III.** n.: a ∾ is as good as a wink to a blind horse (prov.) *ein Dummer kann keinen Wink verstehen;* to be at a person's ∾ *in j.es Gewalt stehen;* to go to the land of ∾ *einschlafen, einnicken, in Morpheus Arme sinken*

noise I. n.: he is a big ∾ *er ist eine gewichtige Person, ein hohes Tier;* to kick up a ∾ *Lärm, Krach schlagen;* that makes a dickens (a hell) of a ∾ *das macht einen Heiden-, Höllenlärm;* he made a ∾ about it *er beschwerte sich heftig darüber, er machte viel Aufhebens davon;* stop that ∾ *hör' auf mit dem Lärm! sorge dafür, daß der Lärm aufhört!* — **II.** v.tr.: it was ∾d abroad *das Gerücht wurde verbreitet*

nonce n.: for the ∾ *für diesen Sonderfall, für das eine Mal;* a ∾-word *ein für einen Sonderfall geprägtes Wort*

none I. pron.: the transmission was ∾ of the clearest *die Übertragung war keineswegs klar;* ∾ but fools have ever believed it *nur Narren haben es je geglaubt;* ∾ of your lip! (sl.) *keine frechen Bemerkungen!;* ∾ other than *kein anderer als;* ∾ of this concerns me *nichts davon betrifft mich.* — **II.** adv.: I am ∾ the better for it *ich bin um nichts besser daran;* the pay is ∾ too high *die Bezahlung ist keineswegs zu hoch (sie ist ziemlich gering);* ∾ the less *nichtsdestoweniger;* I am ∾ the wiser *ich bin so klug wie zuvor*

nonplus I. n.: he was at a ∾ *er war verblüfft (verwirrt);* to reduce to a ∾ *in Verlegenheit (Verwirrung) bringen.* — **II.** v.tr.: to ∾ a person *j.en verblüffen, in Verlegenheit setzen*

nonsense n.: ∾! *Unsinn! dummes Zeug! Mumpitz!;* to stand no ∾ *sich nichts gefallen lassen, nicht mit sich spaßen lassen;*

stop that ∾! *laß den Unsinn; sorge dafür, daß der Unsinn aufhört!;* to take the ∾ out of a person *j.em den Fimmel austreiben*

nose I. n.: to be as plain as the ∾ in your face *sonnenklar sein;* to bite (to snap) a person's ∾ off *j.en scharf anfahren;* to blow one's ∾ *sich (dat.) die Nase putzen;* to count (to tell) ∾s *abzählen;* to cut off one's ∾ to spite one's face *sich (dat.) ins eigene Fleisch schneiden;* to follow one's ∾ *immer der Nase nach gehen;* to hold (to keep) a person's ∾ to the grindstone *j.en ununterbrochen arbeiten (schwer schuften) lassen;* to lead a person by the ∾ *sich (dat.) j.en gefügig (hörig) machen;* it lies under your very ∾ *es liegt dir gerade vor der Nase;* to look down one's ∾ *die Nase rümpfen;* to pay through the ∾ *übermäßig bezahlen, tüchtig bluten müssen;* to pick one's ∾ *sich (dat.) in der Nase bohren;* to poke (to thrust) one's ∾ into a thing *die Nase in etwas stecken;* the pope's (parson's) ∾ *der Bürzel (beim gebratenen Geflügel);* to put a person's ∾ out of joint *j.en aus dem Sattel heben, ihn ausstechen;* he doesn't see beyond his ∾ *er hat einen begrenzten Gesichtskreis (einen beschränkten Horizont);* to turn (to screw) up one's ∾ at a thing *über etwas die Nase rümpfen;* the aeroplane made a ∾-dive *das Flugzeug ging im Sturzflug herunter;* use your ∾-rag (low sl.) *gebrauche dein Taschentuch!* — **II.** v.tr.: he ∾s a job in everything *er wittert in allem Arbeit.* — **III.** v.i.: to ∾ about *herumschnüffeln*

nostril n.: it stinks in my ∾s *es ist mir widerwärtig (eklig)*

nosy a.: he is a ∾ Parker (sl.) *er ist ein neugieriger Patron*

note I. n.: a ∾ of exclamation *ein Ausrufungszeichen;* I'll make a ∾ of it *ich will mir's aufschreiben (merken);* he changed his ∾ *er schlug einen sanfteren Ton an;* to take ∾s of a thing *sich (dat.) über etwas Notizen machen;* to speak without ∾s *frei sprechen;* a ∾ of hand *ein Schuldschein.* — **II.** v.tr.: to ∾ down a thing *etwas aufnotieren;* he is ∾d for his skill *er ist wegen seiner Geschicklichkeit bekannt*

nothing I. n.: ∾ at all *überhaupt (gar) nichts;* ∾ but *nichts als; nur;* ∾ doing! *nicht zu machen! hat sich was!;* there is ∾ for it but to *es bleibt nichts anderes übrig als zu;* there's ∾ in the rumour *das Gerücht hat nichts auf sich;* ∾ venture ∾ have (prov.) *wer nicht wagt, der nicht gewinnt;* it is neck or ∾ *es gilt alles oder nichts; blindlings, auf jede Gefahr hin;* it came to ∾ *es wurde nichts daraus;* I got it for ∾ *ich bekam es umsonst;* to make ∾ of a thing *sich (dat.) nichts aus einer Sache machen;* I can make ∾ of it *ich kann nicht daraus klug werden, ich weiß nichts damit anzufangen;* it is ∾ less than (short of) blackmail *es ist nichts anderes als Erpressung;* there is ∾ to chose between them *der eine ist so schlimm wie der andere;* the food was shocking, like ∾ on earth (sl.) *das Essen war unbeschreiblich schlecht;* it was ∾ to write home about (sl.) *es war nichts Außergewöhnliches;* to say ∾ of *ganz zu schweigen von, geschweige denn;* he is a good-for-∾ *er ist ein Tunichtgut (ein Taugenichts).* — **II.** adv.: that differs ∾ from *das unterscheidet sich in nichts von;* that is ∾ like as (so) good *das ist nicht annähernd, keineswegs so gut*

notice I. n.: a fortnight's ∾ *eine vierzehntägige Kündigung;* till further ∾ *bis auf weiteres;* to attract (to come into) ∾ *Aufmerksamkeit erregen;* it was brought to his ∾ *es wurde ihm zur Kenntnis gebracht;* to come under a person's ∾ *zu j.es Kenntnis kommen;* I had to do it at short ∾ *ich mußte es in kürzester Frist tun;* to give a person ∾ of a thing *j.en etwas wissen lassen, j.em etwas anzeigen;* to give a person ∾ *j.em kündigen;* to have ∾ of a thing *von etwas Kenntnis haben;* to serve ∾ upon a person *j.en vor Gericht vorladen;* to take no ∾ of a thing *keine Notiz von etwas nehmen, etwas nicht beachten.* — **II.** v.tr.: to ∾ a thing to a person *j.em gegenüber etwas erwähnen (bemerken);* to ∾ a person do (doing) a thing *j.en etwas tun sehen;* he was ∾d to quit *ihm wurde gekündigt*

notion n.: the ∾ of my doing it is absurd *es ist lächerlich zu denken, ich würde es tun;* I have a ∾ that *ich habe so eine Idee, daß;* I have not the haziest ∾ *ich habe nicht die leiseste Ahnung;* he has no ∾ of obeying *er denkt nicht daran zu gehorchen;* to fall into the ∾ *auf den Gedanken kommen*

nought, see 'naught'

now adv.: ∾ and again, (every) ∾ and then *dann und wann, hin und wieder, von Zeit zu Zeit;* Oh, come ∾! *ach, hören Sie auf!*

nuisance n.: it was a terrible ∾ *es war schrecklich lästig;* commit no ∾ *Verunreinigung verboten!*

null a.: ∾ and void *null und nichtig*

number n.: a person's ∾ goes up *j. stirbt;* to lose the ∾ of one's mess *sterben;* to take care of ∾ one *auf sein eigenes Wohl bedacht sein;* he is a back ∾ (sl.) *er ist rückständig (hinter dem Mond zurück);* I have done it ∾s of times, times without ∾ *ich habe es so und so oft (-zig mal) getan*

nurse I. n.: a wet-∾ *eine Amme;* to put a child to (out to) ∾ *ein Kind in Pflege geben.* — **II.** v.tr.: he is nursing the constituency *er wirbt um den Wahlkreis (hält sich den Wahlkreis warm);* to ∾ a grievance *einen Groll hegen;* a nursing home *eine Privatklinik*

nursery n.: a ∾-garden *eine Baumschule, Schonung;* a ∾man *ein Pflanzenzüchter, Handelsgärtner;* a ∾-rhyme *ein Kinderlied*

nut n.: he is a young ∾ (sl.) *er ist ein junger Stutzer;* she is dead ∾s on him (sl.) *sie ist rein verknallt in ihn;* it is ∾s to him (sl.) *es macht ihm Mordsspaß;* to be off one's ∾ (sl.), to be ∾s *verrückt sein;* he can't shoot for ∾s (sl.) *beim Schießen ist er eine Niete (ein völliger Versager);* that is the whole matter in a ∾shell *das ist in aller Kürze die ganze Sache*

O

oak n.: a heart of ∾ *ein mutiger Mann;* to sport one's ∾ (Univ. sl.) *die äußere Doppeltür seines Zimmers schließen, um anzudeuten, daß man keinen Besuch wünscht*

oar n.: to be chained to the ∾s *hart und lang arbeiten müssen (Galeerensklave!);* to have an ∾ in every man's boat *überall seine Finger drin haben;* he pulls a good ∾ *er ist ein guter Ruderer;* to put in one's ∾ *sich einmischen;* to rest on one's ∾s *feiern, sich auf seinen Lorbeeren ausruhen*

oat n.: he feels his ∾s *ihn sticht der Hafer;* he knows his ∾s *er ist helle, er hat Köpfchen;* to sow one's wild ∾s *sich (dat.) die Hörner ablaufen*

oath n.: an ∾ of allegiance *ein Treu-, Huldigungs-, Lehnseid;* an ∾ of office *ein Dienst-, Amtseid;* the ∾ of supremacy *der Eid, der den König als Haupt in Kirchensachen in England anerkennt;* a volley of ∾s *eine Flut von Verwünschungen;* on ∾ *unter Eid;* to put a person on his ∾ *j.en vereidigen;* to take (to make, to swear) an ∾ *einen Eid leisten*

object [ˈɔbdʒikt] **I.** n.: direct, indirect ∾ *Akkusativ-, Dativobjekt;* ∾ lesson, ∾ teaching *Anschauungsunterricht;* money (time, distance, etc.) no ∾ *auf Geld (Zeit, Entfernung usw.) wird nicht gesehen;* there is no ∾ in doing that *das hat keinen Zweck;* what is your ∾? *worauf zielen Sie? worauf wollen Sie hinaus?;* to attain one's ∾ *seinen Zweck, sein Ziel erreichen;* to be an ∾ of (for) ridicule *ein Gegenstand des Gespötts sein;* the Bible was the ∾ of his study *die Bibel war der Gegenstand seines Studiums;* he looked a curious ∾ *er sah sonderbar aus;* to make it one's ∾ *es sich (dat.) angelegen sein lassen.* — **II.** [əbˈʒekt] v.tr.: against that it was ∾ed that *dem gegenüber wurde eingewandt, daß.* — **III.** v.i.: do you ∾ to my opening the window? *hast du etwas dagegen, daß ich das Fenster öffne?;* I ∾ to being treated like this *ich verwahre mich gegen eine solche Behandlung*

objection n.: I have no ∾ to him *ich habe nichts gegen ihn einzuwenden;* to lodge an ∾ against a thing *gegen etwas Einspruch erheben;* with a person *bei j.em Einspruch erheben;* to raise an ∾ *einen Einwand erheben;* to take ∾ to a thing *sich gegen etwas wenden, gegen etwas protestieren*

objector n.: a conscientious ∾ *ein Kriegsdienstverweigerer aus Gewissensbedenken*

obligation n.: to be of ∾ *obligatorisch (verpflichtend, bindend) sein;* to be under an ∾ to a person *j.em verpflichtet (verbunden) sein;* to incur an ∾ *eine Verbindlichkeit eingehen;* to put a person under an ∾ *j.en verpflichten;* to repay (to discharge) an ∾ *eine Gefälligkeit erwidern, eine Schuld begleichen;* to satisfy an ∾ *einer Verpflichtung nachkommen*

oblige v.tr.: I was ∾d to do so *ich mußte es tun;* you would ∾ me by doing so *du würdest mir damit einen Gefallen tun (mich dadurch zu Dank verpflichten);* I should be much ∾d *ich würde sehr dankbar (sehr ver-*

bunden) sein; would you ∾ us with a song? *würden Sie so freundlich sein, uns ein Lied zu singen?;* he is very obliging *er ist sehr gefällig, zuvorkommend;* an early reply will ∾ *für baldige Antwort sind wir sehr verbunden*

oblique a.: an ∾ angle *ein schiefer Winkel;* an ∾ case *ein abhängiger Fall (Grammatik);* ∾ narration (speech) *indirekte Rede*

oblivion n.: to fall (to sink) into ∾ *in Vergessenheit geraten*

oblivious a.: to be ∾ of a thing *etwas vergessen haben;* to be ∾ to (misuse, colloq.) *blind sein gegen, nicht beachten*

observation n.: an ∾ car *ein Aussichtswagen;* ∾ balloon *Fesselballon;* a matter of common ∾ *eine oft bestätigte Beobachtung;* to fall under a person's ∾ *bemerkt (wahrgenommen) werden;* to keep a person under ∾ *j.en beobachten lassen, überwachen*

observe I. v.tr.: they ∾ an old custom *sie folgen einem alten Brauch;* to ∾ the feasts of the church *die kirchlichen Feiertage halten, feiern;* to ∾ the Sabbath *die Sonntagsruhe halten;* I ∾d his design *ich durchschaute seinen Plan;* I always ∾ the rules *ich halte mich immer an die Regeln;* to ∾ silence *Stillschweigen bewahren;* this is worth observing *dies verdient, bemerkt zu werden.* — **II.** v.i.: I was going to ∾ *ich wollte gerade bemerken*

obstacle n.: to meet ∾s *Hindernissen begegnen, auf Hindernisse stoßen;* to overcome (to surmount) ∾s *Hindernisse überwinden;* to put (to throw) ∾s in the way of a person *j.em Hindernisse in den Weg legen*

obtuse a.: an ∾ angle *ein stumpfer Winkel;* an ∾ pain *ein dumpfer Schmerz;* a blow with an ∾ weapon *ein Schlag mit einer stumpfen Waffe;* to be of ∾ understanding *schwer von Begriff sein*

occasion n.: (up)on ∾ *wenn nötig, bei Gelegenheit, gelegentlich;* on the ∾ of his birthday *anläßlich seines Geburtstages;* this is a great ∾ *es ist ein großes Ereignis;* for the ∾ *eigens zu diesem Zweck;* there is no ∾ to be angry *es ist kein Grund vorhanden, böse zu sein;* to be the ∾ of *etwas veranlassen;* to give ∾ to *Anlaß geben zu;* to go about one's lawful ∾s *seinen friedlichen Beschäftigungen nachgehen;* I had no ∾ to speak English *ich hatte es nicht nötig, Englisch zu sprechen;* to improve the ∾ *die Gelegenheit ergreifen;* to rise (to be equal) to the ∾ *sich der Situation gewachsen zeigen;* to take the ∾ by the forelock *die Gelegenheit beim Schopfe fassen (packen);* to take ∾ to do a thing *die Gelegenheit wahrnehmen, etwas zu tun*

occur v.i.: silver often ∾s native *Silber kommt oft gediegen vor;* an accident ∾red *es ereignete sich ein Unglücksfall;* it ∾red to me that *es fiel mir ein, daß*

occurrence n.: it is of frequent ∾ *es kommt oft vor*

ocean n.: the German ∾ *die Nordsee;* a mere drop in the ∾ *ein Tropfen auf den heißen Stein;* he has ∾s of money *er hat Berge von Geld, Geld wie Heu;* an ∾ greyhound *ein schneller Ozeandampfer;* an ∾ tramp *ein Frachtdampfer ohne regelmäßige Route*

odd a.: how ∾! *wie sonderbar!;* twelve pounds ∾ *etwas über zwölf Pfund;* sixty ∾ *einige sechzig;* sixty thousand ∾ *etwas über sechzigtausend;* sixty ∾ thousand *zwischen sechzig- und siebzigtausend;* I have put it in some ∾ corner *ich habe es irgendwo hingelegt;* ∾ and even *gerade und ungerade, paar und unpaar;* he is an ∾ fish *er ist ein komischer Kauz, ein wunderlicher Heiliger;* I found an ∾ glove *ich fand einen einzelnen Handschuh;* he picks up ∾ jobs *er macht gelegentlich kleine Arbeiten;* the ∾ man of a team *der Ersatzmann;* do it at ∾ moments *tu es gelegentlich, in einer freien Minute;* to be ∾ man out *das fünfte Rad am Wagen, überzählig sein;* keep the ∾ money *behalte das übrigbleibende Geld;* an ∾ number *eine ungerade Zahl;* ∾ numbers (volumes) of a work *vereinzelte Nummern (Bände) eines Werks;* the ∾ six *die überzähligen sechs;* the ∾ trick *der Stich über sechs (Whist);* an ∾-come-short *ein Überrest, eines Tages;* one of these ∾-come-shortlies *eines Tages, in der nächsten Zeit*

odds n.pl.: ∾ and ends *Überreste, allerhand Krimskrams;* the ∾ are in our favour *die Chancen sind auf unserer Seite;* it is ∾ that (or but, the ∾ are that) he will do so *es besteht die Chance (Möglichkeit), daß er es tun wird;* no ∾! *macht nichts! es hat nichts zu sagen!;* what's the ∾? *was tut's? was macht es aus?;* to be at ∾ with a person *sich mit j.em zanken, Händel haben;*

they are at ∾ with fate *sie hadern mit dem Schicksal;* to fight against overwhelming ∾ *gegen eine überwältigende Mehrheit kämpfen;* to give a person ∾ *j.em beim Spiel etwas vorgeben;* I lay (I give) ∾ of three to one *ich wette drei gegen eins;* to make ∾ even *Ungleichheiten beseitigen;* to receive ∾ *eine Vorgabe bekommen;* to be by long ∾ the ablest *bei weitem, entschieden der fähigste sein;* to set at ∾ *uneinig machen, aufeinanderhetzen*

odour n.: no ∾ of intolerance *keine Spur von Unduldsamkeit;* to be in the ∾ of sanctity *im Geruche der Heiligkeit stehen;* to be in good (bad, ill) ∾ *in gutem (schlechtem) Rufe stehen*

of prep.: he ∾ all men *ausgerechnet er;* he comes in ∾ an evening *er kommt gelegentlich abends herein;* ∾ late *in letzter Zeit;* ∾ old *von alters her, aus alten Zeiten;* the city ∾ Rome *die Stadt Rom;* the name ∾ Smith *der Name Schmidt;* further examples of idiomatic usage in connection with adjectives etc. are given under the words in question *weitere Beispiele von idiomatischer Anwendung in Verbindung mit Adjektiven usw. werden unter den betreffenden Wörtern gebracht*

off I. adv.: ∾ and on *hin und wieder, ab und zu;* ∾ with his head! *Kopf ab!;* ∾ with you! *fort, weg mit dir!;* I'm ∾ *ich gehe jetzt, ich bin weg;* we are ∾ now *jetzt fahren wir los;* asparagus is ∾ *Spargel ist nicht mehr zu haben;* the engagement is ∾ *die Verlobung ist gelöst;* the butter is (has gone) ∾ *die Butter ist schlecht (ranzig) geworden;* far ∾ *weit weg;* three miles ∾ *drei Meilen entfernt;* a great way ∾ *sehr weit von hier;* to be ∾ with one's old love *mit seiner alten Liebe gebrochen haben;* to be well (badly, comfortably) ∾ *in guten (schlechten, behaglichen) Verhältnissen leben;* to declare a thing ∾ *etwas rückgängig machen;* to have a day ∾ *einen freien Tag haben;* further examples of idiomatic usage in connection with verbs etc. are given under the words in question *weitere Beispiele von idiomatischer Anwendung in Verbindung mit Verben usw. werden unter den betreffenden Wörtern gebracht.* — **II.** prep.: the ship anchored ∾ the cape *das Schiff ankerte auf der Höhe des Kaps;* to be ∾ one's chump (colloq.) *von Sinnen (furchtbar aufgeregt) sein;* to be ∾ colour *unpäßlich sein; anrüchig, verrufen sein;* to take the cover ∾ a dish *den Deckel von einer Schüssel nehmen;* to be ∾ duty (work) *dienst-, arbeitsfrei sein;* to be ∾ one's feed *keinen Appetit haben;* I can't say it ∾-hand *ich kann es nicht auf der Stelle (aus dem Stegreif) sagen;* he was very ∾-hand *er benahm sich sehr freimütig, etwas ungezogen;* to take a matter ∾ a person's hands *j.em etwas abnehmen;* he fell ∾ the ladder *er fiel von der Leiter;* to be ∾ one's legs *schlecht zu Fuß, ganz ermüdet sein;* it is ∾ the map *es ist verschwunden, es besteht nicht mehr;* it was only a short distance ∾ me *es war nur eine kurze Strecke von mir entfernt;* he eats ∾ a silver plate *er ißt vom silbernen Teller;* that is ∾ the point *das gehört nicht zur Sache, hat nichts mit der Sache zu tun;* to take something ∾ the price *den Preis herabsetzen;* he drove them ∾ the seas *er vertrieb sie von den Meeren;* he is ∾side *er steht abseits (Fußball);* in a street ∾ the market *in einer Nebenstraße vom Markt.* — **III.** a.: there is an ∾ chance that *es besteht eine schwache Möglichkeit, daß;* I'll do it on my next ∾ day *ich mache es an meinem nächsten freien Tag;* the ∾ hind leg of a horse *das rechte Hinterbein eines Pferdes;* to have an ∾-licence *eine Lizenz haben, Alkohol über die Straße zu verkaufen;* on the ∾ side of the wall *an der Rückseite der Mauer*

offence n.: the most effective defence is ∾ *der Angriff ist die beste Verteidigung;* to commit an ∾ against *sich gegen etwas vergehen, gegen etwas verstoßen;* no ∾ was meant! *nichts für ungut!;* to put up with (to pocket, to swallow) an ∾ *eine Beleidigung einstecken;* to take ∾ at a thing *an etwas Anstoß nehmen, etwas übelnehmen, sich durch etwas beleidigt fühlen*

offend I. v.i.: to ∾ against the law *gegen das Gesetz verstoßen.* — **II.** v.tr.: to ∾ a person *j.en verletzen, beleidigen;* that ∾s my sense of justice *das geht gegen mein Rechtsempfinden;* to be ∾ed at (by) a thing, with (by) a person *durch etwas, von einer Person sich verletzt (beleidigt) fühlen*

offensive I. a.: an ∾ and defensive alliance *ein Schutz- und Trutzbündnis;* he used ∾ language *er redete eine beleidigende Sprache;* an ∾ movement *eine Angriffsbewegung;* it was an ∾ smell *es war ein widerlicher (ekelhafter) Geruch.* — **II.** n.: to abandon the ∾ *die Offensive aufgeben;* to act on the ∾ *angriffsweise vorgehen;* to assume (to take) the ∾ *die Offensive ergreifen*

offer I. v.tr.: he ∾ed no apology *er entschuldigte sich nicht;* to ∾ battle *sich zum Kampf stellen;* to ∾ an opinion *eine Meinung äußern;* to ∾ prayers to God *Gebete an Gott richten, zu Gott beten;* to ∾ a few remarks *ein paar Bemerkungen machen;* to ∾ resistance *Widerstand leisten;* each age ∾s its characteristic riddles *jedes Alter bietet seine eigenen Rätsel;* to ∾ (up) a sacrifice *ein Opfer darbringen;* he ∾ed to strike me *er wollte mich schlagen (er versuchte, mich zu schlagen);* to ∾ a thing to a person *j.em etwas anbieten;* a thanks-∾ing *ein Dankopfer.* — **II.** v.i.: as opportunity (occasion) ∾s *wie sich die Gelegenheit bietet;* the first path that ∾ed *der erste Weg, der sich darbot.* — **III.** n.: these goods are on ∾ *diese Waren stehen zum Verkauf;* an ∾ of marriage *ein Heiratsantrag;* to embrace an (to jump at an) ∾ *ein Anerbieten annehmen*

office n.: the ∾s of a house *die Neben-, Wirtschaftsgebäude, Stallungen;* the booking ∾ *der Fahrkartenschalter;* the Foreign Office *das Auswärtige Amt;* the Holy Office *die Inquisition;* the inquiry-∾ *die Auskunft;* the lost-property-∾ *das Fundbüro;* the War Office *das Kriegsministerium;* it is the ∾ of the arteries *es ist die Funktion der Arterien;* it is my ∾ to do so *es ist meine Pflicht (Aufgabe), es zu tun;* a Jack in ∾ *ein sich wichtig tuender Beamter;* owing to (by) the good ∾s of *dank den freundlichen Bemühungen von;* to give (to tip) a person the ∾ *j.em einen Wink geben;* to hold ∾ *ein Amt bekleiden;* to leave (to resign, to retire from, to throw up) ∾ *ein Amt niederlegen;* to perform the last ∾s to a person *j.em die letzten Dienste erweisen, ihn begraben;* to say (divine) ∾ for the dead *ein Totenamt feiern;* to take ∾ *ein Amt antreten*

oil I. n.: it is like ∾ and vinegar *es ist ein Unterschied wie Tag und Nacht;* to burn the midnight ∾ *bis tief in die Nacht hinein arbeiten, lesen;* to pour ∾ on the flame *Öl ins Feuer gießen, die Leidenschaft schüren;* to pour ∾ on troubled waters *Öl auf die Wogen gießen, die Gemüter beruhigen;* to smell of ∾, cf. 'lamp' *nächtliche Arbeit verraten, vgl.* 'lamp'; to strike ∾ *Petroleum mittels Bohrens entdecken; auf etwas Vorteilhaftes stoßen, Glück haben;* a strap-∾ *eine Tracht Prügel (mit einem Riemen);* she's no ∾-painting (colloq.) *sie ist häßlich.* — **II.** v.tr.: to ∾ a person (a person's hand, palm) *j.en bestechen, schmieren;* to ∾ one's tongue *glatte Worte machen, schmeicheln;* to ∾ the wheels *die Räder schmieren, durch Höflichkeit oder Bestechung etwas erreichen;* to ∾ a person's wig (sl.) *j.en betrunken machen.* — **III.** v.i.: to ∾ up to a person (sl.) *sich bei j.em einschmeicheln;* to be well ∾ed (colloq.) *blau sein*

ointment n.: to find a fly in the ∾ *ein Haar in der Suppe finden*

O.K. I. int.: ∾! *in Ordnung! wird gemacht!* — **II.** a.: it's ∾ with me *mir schon recht, ich habe nichts dagegen*

old a.: any ∾ thing *irgend etwas, etwas x-beliebiges;* as ∾ as the hills *uralt;* of ∾ *von alters her, aus alten Zeiten;* the ∾ gentleman, ∾ Harry (Nick, Scratch) *der Teufel;* that's ∾ hat *das hat sooo'nen Bart;* the Old Lady of Threadneedle Street *die Bank von England;* the ∾ man of the sea *Meergreis, ein zudringlicher, nicht abzuschüttelnder Mensch;* ∾ school tie *(Kravatte mit den Farben der ehemaligen* Public School) *Einflüsse, Gebräuche, Erinnerungen, die an dieser Schule haften; herkömmlich, klassenbewußt, konservativ;* to have a fine (good, high) ∾ time *sich glänzend amüsieren;* an ∾ timer *eine altmodische Person;* an ∾ time dance *ein Tanz aus alten Zeiten;* one is never too ∾ to learn *man lernt nie aus*

olive n.: to hold out the ∾-branch *den Ölzweig hinhalten, eine Versöhnung anbieten*

Oliver n.pr.: to give a Roland for an ∾ *die passende Antwort geben, mit gleicher Münze bezahlen; wie du mir, so ich dir; Wurst wider Wurst*

omelet(te) n.: one (you) cannot make an ∾ without breaking eggs (prov.) *wo gehobelt wird, fallen Späne*

omnibus a.: an ∾ bill *ein Mantelgesetz;* an ∾ book *ein Sammelband;* an ∾ train *ein Bummelzug*

omnium gatherum n.: an ∾ (colloq.) *ein Sammelsurium, Mischmasch*

on I. prep.: the ring is ∾ his finger *der Ring ist an seinem Finger;* the picture is ∾ the wall *das Bild hängt an der Wand;* the dish is ∾ the table *die Schüssel steht auf dem Tisch;* it dropped ∾ the floor *es fiel auf den Boden;* ∾ the next day *an dem (am) nächsten Tage;* ∾ Sundays *Sonntags;* ∾ the minute *auf die Minute;* ∾ time *pünktlich, zur festgesetzten Zeit;* ∾ one's journey *auf der Reise;* ∾ arriving (∾ my arrival) *bei meiner Ankunft;* a book (a lecture) ∾ Goethe *ein Buch (ein Vortrag) über Goethe;* he is keen ∾ the work *er ist erpicht auf die Arbeit;* he is determined ∾ doing it *er hat beschlossen, es zu tun;* to think ∾ *nachdenken über;* they marched ∾ London *sie marschierten auf London los (zu);* they made an attack ∾ the position *sie machten einen Angriff auf die Stellung;* he drew his knife ∾ me *er zog sein Messer gegen mich;* he went ∾ board *er ging an Bord;* a house ∾ the river *ein Haus am Flusse;* have you a match ∾ you? *haben Sie ein Streichholz bei sich?;* the station is ∾ your right *der Bahnhof liegt rechts von Ihnen;* I got it ∾ the cheap *ich bekam es zu billigem Preis, billig;* I got it ∾ good terms *ich bekam es zu guten Bedingungen;* he did it ∾ purpose *er tat es mit Absicht, absichtlich;* to work ∾ an empty stomach *mit leerem Magen arbeiten;* he came ∾ foot *er kam zu Fuß;* she bought it ∾ the sly *sie kaufte es heimlich;* ∾ all fours *auf allen vieren;* to be ∾ one's best behaviour *sehr auf sein Benehmen achten;* ∾ business *geschäftlich;* the house is ∾ fire *das Haus brennt;* to be ∾ guard *auf Wache sein;* he was put ∾ half-pay *er wurde auf Halbsold gesetzt;* ∾ the look-out for *auf der Ausschau nach;* the moon is ∾ the wane *der Mond nimmt ab;* ∾ sale *zu verkaufen;* ∾ trial *zur Probe, versuchsweise;* ∾ an average *im Durchschnitt;* ∾ account of the weather *wegen des Wetters;* ∾ condition *unter der Bedingung;* ∾ the contrary *im Gegenteil;* ∾ further consideration *bei reiflicher Überlegung;* ∾ good authority *aus guter Quelle;* ∾ my honour *bei meiner Ehre;* ∾ the one hand, ∾ the other *einerseits, andererseits;* ∾ that ground *aus diesem Grunde;* ∾ the whole *im ganzen;* he is ∾ the committee *er sitzt im Ausschuß;* he is ∾ the Staff *er gehört zum Stab;* ∾ my part *meinerseits;* an increase of 20% ∾ last year *eine zwanzigprozentige Zunahme gegen letztes Jahr;* to put money ∾ a horse *Geld auf ein Pferd setzen;* the cat died ∾ me *die Katze ist mir gestorben;* to have nothing ∾ a person (colloq.) *nichts vor j.em voraushaben;* this is ∾ me (colloq.) *dies geht auf meine Rechnung.* — **II.** adv.: and so ∾ *und so weiter, und so fort;* off and ∾ *hin und wieder, ab und zu;* ∾ and ∾ *immer weiter;* are you ∾? (colloq.) *machst du mit? bist du dafür?;* come ∾! *vorwärts! los!;* he drew his boots ∾ *er zog seine Stiefel an;* it is getting ∾ for 2 o'clock *es geht auf zwei Uhr;* to go (to keep) ∾ *fortfahren;* later ∾ *später;* to look ∾ *zuschauen;* Macbeth is ∾ *Macbeth wird gerade gegeben;* put your coat ∾ *zieh' deinen Rock an;* he is rather ∾ *er hat einen Schwips;* to send ∾ *weiterbefördern;* to speak (to work) ∾ *weitersprechen, -arbeiten;* the water is ∾ *das Wasser läuft;* to be ∾ to a good thing (colloq.) *Kenntnis haben von einer nützlichen Sache.* — **III.** a.: an ∾-licence *eine Lizenz, Alkohol innerhalb der Gaststätte zu verkaufen*

once I. adv.: I shall do it for ∾, ∾ in a way *ich werde es diesmal, ausnahmsweise, zur Abwechslung tun;* ∾ bit, twice shy (prov.) *(ein) gebranntes Kind scheut das Feuer;* ∾ in a blue moon *(einmal) alle Jubeljahre;* he was ∾ a famous man *er war einst ein berühmter Mann;* a ∾-famous doctrine *eine einst berühmte Lehre;* ∾ for all *ein für allemal;* ∾ more (again) *noch einmal;* ∾ nought is nought *einmal Null ist Null;* ∾ or twice, ∾ and again *ein paarmal, einige Male;* ∾ upon a time there was a king *es war einmal ein König;* ∾ in a while (way) *zuweilen, gelegentlich, dann und wann;* he did it at ∾ *er tat es sofort, auf der Stelle;* all at ∾ *plötzlich;* don't speak all at ∾ *sprecht nicht alle zu gleicher Zeit, auf einmal;* he was at ∾ a painter and a poet *er war zugleich Maler und Dichter;* for this (that) ∾ *für diesmal, dieses eine Mal;* she gave him the ∾-over (sl.) *sie musterte ihn von oben bis unten.* — **II.** conj.: ∾ he hesitates, we have him *sobald er zaudert, haben wir ihn.* — **III.** n.: ∾ is enough for me *einmal genügt mir*

one I. a.: ∾ day (evening, morning, night) *eines Tages (Abends, Morgens, Nachts);* ∾ good turn deserves another (prov.) *ich werde auch ein Steinchen in deinen Garten werfen;* a ∾ horse town, show (colloq.) *eine kleine Stadt, eine dürftige Angelegenheit;* ∾ hundred *(ein)hundert;* ∾ sided *voreingenommen;* he has a ∾ track mind *er ist von einer Idee besessen;* to do something like ∾ o'clock *etwas flott (schnell) machen;* no ∾ man can do it *einer allein kann es nicht schaffen;* some ∾ man must direct *nur einer darf die Leitung haben;* for ∾ thing, he drinks *erstens einmal, er trinkt;* ∾ or two people *ein paar Leute;* the ∾ way to do it *der einzige Weg, es zu tun;* it is ∾

and undivided *es ist unteilbar eins;* they were made into ∾ *sie heirateten;* it remains for ever ∾ *es bleibt immer das gleiche;* a ∾ way street *eine Einbahnstraße.* — **II.** n.: ∾ of these days *dieser Tage, bald, in Kürze;* ∾ and all *samt und sonders;* ∾ another *einander, gegenseitig;* ∾ by ∾, ∾ after another *einzeln, einer nach dem anderen;* by ∾s and twos *einzeln und zu zweien;* all in ∾ *alles in einem;* I for ∾ do not believe it *ich für meine Person glaube es nicht;* never a ∾ *keiner, kein einziger;* that ∾ (the ∾ in the window) will do *das eine (das eine im Schaufenster) genügt;* which (what) kind of ∾ (∾s) do you want? *welches, was für welche willst du haben?;* you are ∾ too many for me *du bist mir zu stark (zu überlegen);* to be ∾ up on someone (colloq.) *j.em etwas voraus haben;* it is all ∾ to me *es ist mir alles eins (egal, gleich);* to be at ∾ with *einig, im Einklang sein mit;* he gave him ∾ in the eye *er schlug ihm eins aufs Auge;* to get ∾ in the eye (colloq.) *eine Enttäuschung, einen Rückschlag erleben;* to go ∾ better *eins mehr bieten, überbieten;* to have ∾ over the eight (sl.) *blau sein;* have ∾ for the road *trink' noch ein Gläschen für den Heimweg;* pick me out a good ∾ (some good ∾s) *such' mir ein gutes (einige gute) heraus;* to know ∾ from another *unterscheiden können;* they sell hundreds where they sold ∾s *sie verkaufen Hunderte, wo sie früher nur einzelne verkauften;* to take care of number ∾ *auf sein eigenes Wohl bedacht sein;* taken ∾ with another *im Durchschnitt genommen;* write down a ∾ (three ∾s) *schreib' eine Eins (drei Einsen) hin.* — **III.** pron.: ∾ can say *man kann sagen;* he behaves like ∾ frenzied *er gebärdet sich wie ein Besessener;* I bought it from ∾ Arnold *ich kaufte es von einem gewissen Arnold;* the Evil ∾ *der Teufel;* the Holy ∾, the ∾ above *Gott;* what a ∾ he is to make excuses! *der kommt aber auch ewig mit Entschuldigungen!;* it offends ∾ to be told that ∾ is not wanted *es verletzt einen zu hören, daß man nicht erwünscht ist*

oner n. (sl.): that was a ∾ *das war eine faustdicke Lüge;* to be a ∾ at a thing *etwas aus dem ff. verstehen;* he gave him a ∾ *er versetzte ihm eins*

onion n.: to be off one's ∾ (sl.) *verrückt sein;* to know one's ∾s (sl.) *gut unterrichtet, auf der Höhe sein*

only I. a.: the ∾ child of his parents *das einzige Kind seiner Eltern;* my one and ∾ hope *meine einzige Hoffnung.* — **II.** adv.: I ∾ but succeeded *es gelang mir beinahe (fast);* he has ∾ just come *er ist gerade erst gekommen;* if ∾ some one would come! *wenn doch nur j. käme!;* I ∾ thought I would do it *ich nahm mir nur vor, es zu tun;* I was ∾ too glad *ich war nur zu froh, heilsfroh;* it was ∾ yesterday that I heard *ich hörte erst gestern;* ∾ you (you ∾) can guess *du allein (nur du) kannst erraten;* I not ∾ heard it, but saw it *ich hörte es nicht nur, ich sah es auch.* — **III.** conj.: he buys good hats, ∾ he always loses them *er kauft gute Hüte, nur verliert er sie immer;* ∾ that you are busy, I should stay *wenn du nicht beschäftigt wärest, würde ich bleiben*

oof n. (sl.): to have ∾ *Geld (Moneten, Zaster) haben;* he is an ∾-bird *er ist ein reicher Kerl, er hat Moneten (Zaster)*

open I. a.: ∾ and above board *aufrichtig;* in the ∾ air *in der frischen Luft, im Freien, unter freiem Himmel;* an ∾ scholarship *ein Universitäts-, Schulstipendium, das allen Bewerbern offensteht;* an ∾ verdict *ein unentschiedener Urteilsspruch;* ∾ weather, ∾ winter *frostfreies Wetter, frostfreier Winter;* I am ∾ to conviction *ich lasse mich gern überzeugen;* to be ∾ to criticism *nicht frei von Schuld sein;* his bowels are ∾ *er leidet nicht an Verstopfung;* the river (harbour) is ∾ *der Fluß (Hafen) ist eisfrei;* to force an ∾ door *eine offene Tür einrennen, dem Gebefreudigen nachhelfen;* to keep ∾ doors, an ∾ house *ein gastfreies Haus führen;* to lay oneself ∾ to attack *sich einem Angriff aussetzen.* — **II.** n.: in the ∾ *im Freien, vor allen Augen;* to come into the ∾ *klaren Wein einschenken; die Karten auf den Tisch legen.* — **III.** v.tr.: a medicine to ∾ the bowels *ein Abführmittel;* to ∾ one's designs *seine Pläne enthüllen;* to ∾ the ground *den Boden pflügen;* that ∾s up new prospects *das eröffnet neue Aussichten;* an ∾ Sesame *eine einfache Lösung zu einem Problem.* — **IV.** v.i.: the harbour light ∾ed *der Leuchtturm des Hafens kam in volle Sicht;* the door ∾s into the passage *die Tür führt (geht) auf den Gang hinaus;* the room ∾s on to the lawn *das Zimmer geht auf den Rasen hinaus;* he quite ∾ed out *er wurde ganz gesprächig;* to ∾ upon a subject *über einen Gegenstand zu reden anfangen;* the wonders of astronomy were ∾ing to him *die Wunder der Astronomie erschlossen sich ihm*

opening n.: he could find no ∾ *er konnte keine Stelle, keinen Wirkungskreis finden;* that would be a good ∾ for a young man *das wäre eine gute Anfangsstelle für einen jungen Mann*

opera n.: an ∾-cloak *ein Abendmantel (Umhang) für Damen;* an ∾-hat *ein Klapphut*

operate I. v.i.: the tax ∾s to our disadvantage *die Steuer wirkt sich zu unseren Ungunsten aus;* he tried to ∾ (up)on my fears *er versuchte, meine Angst auszunutzen;* he was ∾d (up)on *er wurde operiert;* the operating-table (-theatre) *der Operationstisch (-saal).* — **II.** v.tr.: energy ∾s changes *Energie bewirkt Änderungen*

operation n.: the ∾ of breathing *die Atemtätigkeit;* its ∾ is easily explained *es ist leicht zu erklären, wie es wirkt;* the order comes into ∾ *die Verordnung tritt in Kraft;* the telegraph-line is in ∾ *die Telegraphenlinie ist im Betrieb;* to undergo an ∾, to submit to an ∾ *sich einer Operation unterziehen, sich operieren lassen*

opinion n.: in my ∾ *meiner Ansicht (Meinung) nach;* expert ∾ *fachmännisches Gutachten;* to pass an ∾ *seine Ansicht kundtun;* I am of ∾ that *ich bin der Ansicht, daß;* it is a matter of ∾ *es ist Ansichtssache;* to have the courage of (to act up to) one's ∾s *den Mut haben, nach seiner Überzeugung zu handeln;* I have no ∾ of him *ich halte nicht viel von ihm;* to win golden ∾s *Hochachtung, Bewunderung erregen*

opportunity n.: to find (to get, give, make, seize, take, afford) an ∾ *eine Gelegenheit finden (bekommen, geben, schaffen, ergreifen, bieten)*

oppose v.tr.: it is the duty of an opposition to ∾ *es ist die Pflicht einer Opposition zu opponieren;* characters strongly ∾d *stark widersprechende Charaktere;* to Plato I ∾ Aristotle *Plato stelle ich Aristoteles entgegen;* he ∾d himself to it with all his power *er stemmte sich mit seiner ganzen Kraft dagegen;* you are opposing things that are practically identical *du stellst Dinge einander gegenüber, die praktisch identisch sind;* black is ∾d to white *Schwarz ist das Gegenteil von Weiß*

opposite I. a.: they went in ∾ directions *sie gingen in entgegengesetzter Richtung davon;* my ∾ number *mein Gegenspieler (Partner, Gegenstück);* he is much liked by the ∾ sex *er wird von dem anderen Geschlecht gern gesehen;* on the ∾ side of the square *auf der gegenüberliegenden Seite des Platzes;* the tree ∾ to the house *der Baum gegenüber dem Hause.* — **II.** n.: I thought quite the ∾ *ich habe genau das Gegenteil geglaubt;* you are calm, she is the ∾ *du bist ruhig, sie ist das Gegenteil;* the most extreme ∾s have some qualities in common *auch gänzlich entgegengesetzte Dinge haben einige gemeinsame Eigenschaften.* — **III.** adv.: there was an explosion ∾ *es gab eine Explosion gegenüber;* to play ∾ *als Gegenspieler auftreten (Theater, Film).* — **IV.** prep.: that happened ∾ the museum *das fand gegenüber dem Museum statt*

option n.: he was sentenced to imprisonment without the ∾ of a fine *er wurde zu Gefängnis verurteilt ohne die Möglichkeit, dafür eine Geldstrafe zu wählen;* it is at your ∾ *es steht Ihnen frei;* I have no ∾ but to *ich habe keine andere Wahl, es bleibt mir nichts anderes übrig als*

oracle n.: to work the ∾ in one's favour *zu seinem Vorteil hinter den Kulissen arbeiten*

orange n.: to squeeze the ∾ *etwas (j.en) wie eine Zitrone auspressen;* a squeezed (sucked) ∾ *eine ausgepreßte Zitrone, ein völlig erschöpfter Mensch*

order I. n.: the ∾ of the Garter *der Hosenbandorden;* in alphabetical ∾ *in alphabetischer Reihenfolge;* considerations of quite another ∾ *Erwägungen ganz anderer Art;* by ∾ *auf Befehl, im Auftrage;* the classical ∾s *die klassischen Säulenordnungen;* of the first (highest) ∾ *von erstem (höchstem) Range;* an equation of the first ∾ *eine Gleichung ersten Grades;* the higher (lower) ∾s *die höheren (niederen) Klassen;* in ∾ that *damit;* in ∾ to *um zu;* a money (postal) ∾ *eine Postanweisung;* that is a tall ∾ (sl.) *das ist sehr viel verlangt;* to be in (holy) ∾s *dem geistlichen Stande angehören;* to be in working ∾ *betriebsfähig sein;* to be on ∾ *bestellt sein;* to be out of ∾ *in Unordnung sein;* to call to ∾ *zur Ordnung rufen;* he gave ∾s (an ∾, the ∾) for a thing to be done (that it should be done) *er gab Befehl, etwas zu machen, er befahl, daß etwas gemacht würde;* my suit was made to ∾ *mein Anzug ist nach Maß gemacht;* to place an ∾ *eine Bestellung aufgeben;* he rises to (to a point of) ∾ *er* *spricht zur Geschäftsordnung;* to set in ∾ *in Ordnung bringen;* to take (holy) ∾s *die heiligen Weihen empfangen;* take them in ∾ *nimm sie der Reihe nach.* — **II.** v.tr.: to ∾ a person to do (that a person should do) a thing *j.em befehlen, etwas zu tun;* to ∾ a thing to be done (that a thing should be done) *befehlen (anordnen), daß etwas gemacht wird;* I won't be ∾ed about *ich lasse mich nicht hin und her schicken;* to ∾ one's affairs *seine Angelegenheiten in Ordnung bringen;* to ∾ a car *einen Wagen bestellen;* he was ∾ed to Egypt *er wurde nach Ägypten kommandiert;* the doctor ∾ed him a mustard plaster *der Arzt verordnete ihm ein Senfpflaster;* fate ∾ed it otherwise *das Schicksal bestimmte es anders*

ordinary I. a.: an ∾ seaman *ein Leichtmatrose;* in an ∾ way (in the ∾ run of things) I should refuse *unter gewöhnlichen Umständen würde ich mich weigern.* — **II.** n.: an ∾ *ein Speisehaus, eine Wirtstafel;* the physician in ∾ to the king *der Leibarzt des Königs;* a ship in ∾ *ein abgetakeltes, außer Dienst gestelltes Schiff;* something out of the ∾ *etwas Außergewöhnliches*

other I. a.: the ∾ day *neulich, kürzlich, dieser Tage, vor einigen Tagen;* it happens every ∾ day *es kommt jeden zweiten Tag vor;* a few ∾ examples would be useful *ein paar weitere Beispiele wären nützlich;* a world far ∾ from ours *eine ganz andere Welt als die unsrige;* on the ∾ hand *andererseits;* give me some ∾ ones *gib mir einige andere;* ∾ people think ∾wise *andere Leute denken anders;* you will go to the ∾ place *du kommst in die Hölle;* I do not wish him ∾ than he is *ich will ihn nicht anders haben;* any person ∾ than yourself *irgend j. außer dir;* it was no (none) ∾ than Z. *es war niemand anderes als Z.;* ∾ things being equal, I should prefer you to him *bei sonst gleichen Umständen würde ich dich ihm vorziehen;* the ∾ two *die beiden anderen;* some one or ∾ *irgend j., irgend ein Unbekannter;* some workmen or ∾ have taken it away *irgendwelche Handwerker haben es abgeholt;* I shall do it some time or ∾ *ich werde es irgendwann mal tun.* — **II.** n., pron.: one or ∾ of us will be there *der eine oder andere von uns wird dort sein;* I cannot tell one from the ∾ *ich kann die beiden nicht auseinander halten;* the ∾ six, the six ∾s *die anderen sechs;* let ∾s talk, I act *laßt andere reden, ich handle;* give me some ∾s *gib mir einige andere, noch welche;* do good to ∾s *tut anderen Gutes;* they neutralize each ∾ *sie heben sich gegenseitig auf;* I can do no ∾ than agree *ich kann nichts anderes tun als ja sagen.* — **III.** adv.: you must read it ∾ than cursorily *du mußt es anders als nur flüchtig lesen;* somehow or ∾ *auf die eine oder andere Weise, irgendwie*

otherwise adv.: I could not have acted ∾ *ich hätte nicht anders handeln können;* I should not wish it ∾ *ich wünschte es mir nicht anders;* he is lazy, but not ∾ blameworthy *er ist faul (bequem), aber sonst (in anderer Beziehung) nicht zu tadeln;* Elizabeth, ∾ called Lizzy *Elisabeth, sonst Lieschen genannt;* his ∾ dullness *seine sonstige Dummheit;* seize the chance, ∾ you will regret it *ergreife die Gelegenheit, sonst wirst du es bedauern;* ∾-minded *gegenteiliger, anderer Meinung*

ought v.aux.: you ∾ not to allow that *das solltest du nicht gestatten;* you ∾ not to have allowed that *das hättest du nicht gestatten sollen;* it ∾ to be done at once *es sollte sofort gemacht werden;* it ∾ to have been done yesterday *es hätte gestern gemacht werden sollen*

out I. adv.: ∾ and ∾ *durch und durch, ganz und gar;* ∾ with him! *hinaus mit ihm!;* my arm is ∾ *ich habe mir den Arm verrenkt;* beards are ∾ *Bärte sind aus der Mode gekommen;* the book is ∾ *das Buch ist erschienen;* the chicken is ∾ *das Küken ist ausgeschlüpft;* to cross ∾ *durchstreichen;* she had her cry ∾ *sie weinte sich aus;* the Conservatives are ∾ *die Konservativen sind nicht an der Regierung;* the girl is ∾ *das Mädchen ist in die Gesellschaft eingeführt worden;* the miners are ∾ *die Bergarbeiter streiken;* Mrs. N. is ∾ *Frau N. ist nicht zu Hause;* murder will ∾ (prov.) *die Sonne bringt es an den Tag;* tell him right ∾ *sage es ihm geradeheraus;* the rose is ∾ *die Rose ist aufgeblüht;* the secret is ∾ *das Geheimnis ist verraten;* speak ∾! *heraus damit!;* she has her Sunday ∾ *sie hat ihren freien Sonntag;* I am tired ∾ *ich bin hundemüde;* on the voyage ∾ *auf der Ausreise, auf der Reise ins Ausland;* before the week is ∾ *bevor die Woche zu Ende ist;* he is ∾ and about again *er läuft schon wieder herum, ist wieder auf den Beinen (nach einer Krankheit);* an ∾-patient *ein Patient in ambulanter Behandlung;* to be ∾ at elbows *abgetragen (von einem Rock), heruntergekommen, arm (von Personen) sein;* to be ∾

and away the best *bei weitem der (die, das) beste sein;* I am ∾ of cigarettes, my supply has given ∾ *ich habe keine Zigaretten mehr, mein Vorrat ist zu Ende;* to be ∾ for (or: to do) a thing *darauf aus sein, etwas zu tun, trachten nach;* I was ∾ in my calculations *ich habe mich bei meinen Berechnungen geirrt;* to fall ∾ with a person *sich mit j.em überwerfen;* to go ∾ for a walk *einen Spaziergang machen, spazieren gehen;* he went all ∾ for it *er setzte seine ganze Kraft dafür ein;* to have it ∾ with a person *sich mit j.em auseinandersetzen;* keep him ∾! *halte ihn draußen!;* I'll see it ∾ *ich mache bis zu Ende mit.* — **II.** prep.: ∾ of doors *im Freien;* an ∾-of-door job *eine Beschäftigung im Freien;* it is ∾ of doubt *es ist unzweifelhaft, zweifellos;* it is ∾ of drawing *es ist falsch gezeichnet;* I am ∾ of training (of condition) *ich bin außer Übung;* from ∾ the dungeon came a groan *aus dem Verließ ertönte ein Stöhnen;* ∾ of harm's way *in Sicherheit;* come ∾ of the house! *komm heraus aus dem Haus!;* it took place ∾ of the house *es fand außerhalb des Hauses statt;* his remark was ∾ of place, ∾ of keeping *seine Bemerkung war unpassend, deplaciert;* he is ∾ of a place *er ist arbeitslos;* to be ∾ of sorts, ∾ of temper *unpäßlich, verdrießlich sein;* ∾ of the way *abgelegen, ungewöhnlich;* I am now completely ∾ of it *ich bin nun ganz heraus, ich weiß nicht, wo ich dran bin;* I feel ∾ of it *ich fühle mich ausgeschlossen, abseits;* he was swindled ∾ of his money *er wurde um sein Geld betrogen;* times ∾ of number *unzählige Male;* I must choose ∾ of these *ich muß hierunter wählen;* a child ∾ of wedlock *ein uneheliches Kind;* what did you make it ∾ of? *woraus hast du es gemacht?;* further examples in connection with nouns are given under the nouns in question *weitere Beispiele in Verbindung mit Substantiven sind unter den betreffenden Wörtern zu finden.* — **III.** n.: the ins and ∾s of a procedure *die Einzelheiten eines Verfahrens;* an ∾-and-∾er (sl.) *ein Prachtmensch.* — **IV.** a.: the ∾ match *das Rückspiel;* an ∾ size *eine Übergröße*

outright I. a.: it is an ∾ shame *es ist eine Sünde und Schande.* — **II.** adv.: I bought it ∾ *ich habe es ohne Vorbehalt gekauft;* he was killed ∾ *er wurde auf der Stelle getötet;* he laughed ∾ *er lachte aus vollem Halse*

outrun v.tr.: to ∾ the constable *Schulden machen, über seine Verhältnisse leben*

outside I. n.: the ∾ looked all right *die Außenseite sah ganz gut aus;* impressions from the ∾ *Eindrücke von der Außenwelt;* he knows only the ∾s of books *er schlägt nie ein Buch auf;* to open the door from the ∾ *die Tür von außen öffnen;* to ride on the ∾ of an omnibus *auf dem Verdeck eines Omnibusses fahren;* there were a hundred at the (very) ∾ *es waren (aller)höchstens hundert da.* — **II.** a.: an ∾ seat *ein Außensitz;* an ∾ porter *ein Gepäckträger, der Gepäck vom Bahnhof zum Wagen oder nach Hause trägt;* it's the ∾ edge (sl.) *das ist aber die Höhe;* ∾ work *Arbeit außerhalb des Hauses.* — **III.** adv.: it is black ∾ *es ist außen schwarz;* what is it like ∾? *wie sieht es draußen aus?;* ∾ of his own family no one will speak to him *außer seiner eigenen Familie spricht keiner mit ihm;* to be ∾ of a horse *zu Pferde sitzen;* come ∾! *komm heraus!;* to get ∾ of a meal (sl.) *eine Mahlzeit vertilgen.* — **IV.** prep.: one cannot go ∾ the evidence *man kann nicht über das Beweismaterial hinausgehen;* natural forces are ∾ morality *Naturgewalten stehen außerhalb von Moral*

outstay v.tr.: to ∾ one's welcome *länger bleiben, als man gern gesehen wird*

over I. adv.: ∾ and ∾, ∾ again, ∾ and ∾ again *immer wieder, immer und immer wieder;* ∾ and above *noch dazu, überdies, obendrein;* ∾ against that, I must say *dem gegenüber muß ich sagen;* he is ∾ in America *er ist drüben in Amerika;* he is not ∾ particular *er nimmt es nicht allzu genau;* the struggle is ∾ *der Kampf ist vorbei (zu Ende);* I asked him ∾ *ich lud ihn ein herüberzukommen;* don't let the milk boil ∾ *laß die Milch nicht überkochen;* you must brush (paint) it ∾ *du mußt es überstreichen, übermalen;* to fall (to knock) ∾ *umfallen, umstoßen;* to roll ∾ and ∾ *immer weiterrollen;* take this ∾ to the post-office *trag dies hinüber zur Post!;* talk the matter ∾ with your father *besprich die Sache mit deinem Vater!;* think the matter ∾! *überleg dir die Sache mal!;* turn it ∾! *dreh es um!;* I did it twice ∾ *ich tat es zweimal hintereinander.* — **II.** prep.: all the world ∾ *in der ganzen Welt;* ∾ and above the fact that *von der Tatsache ganz zu schweigen, daß;* ∾ head and ears in work *bis über die Ohren in Arbeit;* he did it ∾ our heads *er tat es, ohne uns zu fragen (ohne unser Wissen, über unsern Kopf hinweg);* it was hanging ∾ the table *es hing über dem Tisch;* he laughed ∾ the absurdity of it *er lachte über diesen Unsinn;* he will not live ∾ today *er überlebt den heutigen Tag nicht;* to sit ∾ the fire *am Feuer sitzen;* he spoke ∾ the heads of the children *er sprach zu gelehrt (über die Köpfe der Kinder hinweg);* a fog spread ∾ the land *ein Nebel breitete sich über das Land aus;* ∾ the left (shoulder) (rare, sl.) *wer's glaubt (gesagt, um anzudeuten, daß das Gegenteil einer Behauptung zu verstehen ist);* can you stay till ∾ Wednesday? *kannst du den Mittwoch über noch bleiben?;* you'll get ∾ it *du wirst es überstehen*

overbearing a.: in an ∾ manner *in einer anmaßenden (herrischen, hochfahrenden) Art und Weise*

overcast a.: the sky is ∾ *der Himmel ist bedeckt (bewölkt)*

overdo v.tr.: to ∾ it *die Sache übertreiben, zu weit gehen;* the meat is overdone *das Fleisch ist zu sehr (stark) gebraten (gekocht)*

overdue a.: the aeroplane (the ship) is ∾ *das Flugzeug (Schiff) ist überfällig*

overgrow I. v.tr.: he has ∾n his strength *er ist zu schnell gewachsen.* — **II.** v.i.: he is ∾n *er ist zu sehr gewachsen, zu groß geworden*

overhead a.: the ∾ expenses *die Spesen, laufenden Unkosten*

overreach v.tr.: to ∾ a person *j.en übervorteilen (anführen, prellen);* to ∾ oneself *sich überanstrengen*

overshoot v.tr.: to ∾ the mark *übers Ziel schießen;* to ∾ oneself *zu weit gehen, des Guten zuviel tun*

oversight n.: by an ∾ *aus Versehen*

oversleep v.tr.: I overslept myself (the time) *ich habe mich (die Zeit) verschlafen*

overstay v.tr.: to ∾ one's time *über seine Zeit hinaus bleiben;* to ∾ one's welcome *länger bleiben als erwünscht ist*

overtake v.tr.: to ∾ arrears of work *Rückstände aufarbeiten;* to ∾ a car *einen Wagen überholen;* I was ∾n by the storm *ich wurde vom Sturm überrascht;* he is ∾n in drink *er ist betrunken*

overtime adv.: to work ∾ *Überstunden machen*

owe I. v.tr.: to ∾ a person a grudge *j.em grollen;* to ∾ a person money *j.em Geld schulden;* I ∾ him much *ich verdanke ihm viel;* we ∾ to Newton the principle of gravity *wir verdanken Newton das Gesetz der Schwerkraft.* — **II.** v.i.: to ∾ a person for a thing *in j.es Schuld für etwas sein*

owing pred. a.: he paid all that was ∾ *er bezahlte alles, was noch ausstand;* all this was ∾ merely to ill luck *es war alles nur eine Folge von unglücklichen Umständen;* ∾ to his carelessness he lost his job *infolge seiner Nachlässigkeit verlor er seine Stelle;* ∾ to the drought, crops are short *infolge der Dürre ist die Ernte knapp*

owl n.: as tight as a boiled ∾ (sl.) *sternhagelvoll, blau wie ein Märzveilchen;* to fly with the ∾ *ein Nachtschwärmer sein;* to take ∾ at a thing *etwas übelnehmen*

own I. a.: my ∾, my ∾ sweetheart! *mein süßer Schatz!;* God's ∾ country *die U.S.A.;* to call a thing one's ∾ *etwas sein eigen nennen;* to come into one's ∾ *zu seinem Rechte kommen;* he did it on his ∾, of his ∾ accord *er tat es aus sich heraus, auf eigene Verantwortung, mit eigenen Mitteln;* he has an estate of his ∾ *er hat ein eigenes Gut;* it has a value all its ∾ *es hat einen ganz besonderen Wert;* may I have it for my (very) ∾? *darf ich es für mich (als mein Eigentum) haben?;* I have nothing of my ∾ *ich nenne nichts mein eigen;* to be on one's ∾ *allein, unbegleitet sein;* to hold one's ∾ *sich behaupten, standhalten, nicht nachgeben;* I saw it with my ∾ eyes *ich sah es mit eigenen Augen.* — **II.** v.tr.: he ∾s a house *er besitzt ein Haus;* to ∾ a person as a son *j.en als seinen Sohn anerkennen.* — **III.** v.i.: he ∾s (that) he did not know *er gibt zu, daß er es nicht gewußt hat;* he ∾s to having done it *er gesteht ein, es getan zu haben;* now, ∾ up *gestehe es nur!*

ox n.: the black ∾ has trod on his foot *ihm ist ein Unglück zugestoßen; das Alter macht sich bei ihm bemerkbar*

Oxford n.: ∾ bags *sehr weite Hosen;* ∾ blue *dunkelblau;* an ∾ drawl *eine affektierte, gedehnte Aussprache;* he is an ∾ man *er hat in Oxford studiert*

P

P n.: to mind one's ∾s and Q's *sich mit seinen Worten oder seinem Benehmen sehr in acht nehmen*

p. t. n.: (physical training) *Leibesübungen*

pace I. n.: to go the ∾ *flott leben;* to keep ∾ with a person, with the times *mit j.em Schritt halten, mit der Zeit mitgehen;* to put a horse through his ∾s *hohe Schule reiten;* to put a person through his ∾s *j.en auf Herz und Nieren prüfen, ihn tüchtig heranholen;* to set the ∾ *Schrittmacher sein, das Tempo angeben;* to slacken one's ∾ *seine Schritte verlangsamen;* to walk at a great (slow) ∾ *sehr schnell (langsam) gehen.* — **II.** v.tr.: to ∾ a distance *eine Entfernung abschreiten.* — **III.** v.i.: to ∾ up and down a room *in einem Zimmer auf und ab gehen*

pack I. n.: a ∾ of cards *ein Spiel Karten;* a ∾ of hounds *eine Meute;* it is all a ∾ of lies, nonsense *es sind lauter Lügen, es ist lauter Unsinn;* a ∾ of thieves *eine Diebesbande.* — **II.** v.tr.: the room was ∾ed *das Zimmer war gedrängt voll;* to ∾ a jury *eine Geschworenenbank mit parteiischen Geschworenen besetzen;* to ∾ away (up, out) one's things *seine Sachen weg-, ein-, auspacken;* to ∾ a person off *j.en fortschicken;* to ∾ on all sail *alle Segel setzen.* — **III.** v.i.: to ∾ off *sich davonmachen;* the engine ∾ed up (sl.) *der Motor setzte aus;* to send a person ∾ing *j.en sich packen heißen, fortjagen, hinauswerfen*

packaged a.: to take a ∾ tour for two weeks *zwei Wochen mit einer Reisegesellschaft fahren*

packet n.: to buy a ∾ (sl.) *niedergeschossen werden;* to get (to catch, to cop) a ∾ (sl.) *sich in die Nesseln setzen, eins abbekommen, sich (dat.) einen Heimatschuß besorgen*

pad I. n.: a gentleman (knight, squire) of the ∾ *ein Straßenräuber.* — **II.** v.tr.: a ∾ed cell *eine Gummizelle;* to ∾ the hoof, to ∾ it *auf Schusters Rappen reiten;* to ∾ (out) a letter *einen Brief mit leeren Worten ausfüllen;* to ∾ the road *zu Fuß auf der Straße einhergehen*

paddle v.tr.: to ∾ one's own canoe *sich aus eigener Kraft durchs Leben schlagen*

pagoda n.: to shake the ∾-tree *in Indien schnell zu Geld kommen*

pain n.: forbidden on (under) ∾ of death *bei Todesstrafe verboten;* her ∾s have begun *ihre Geburtswehen haben begonnen;* no ∾s no gains *ohne Fleiß kein Preis;* to be in great ∾ *heftige Schmerzen leiden;* it gives me ∾ to say *es schmerzt mich, sagen zu müssen;* you give me a ∾ in the neck (sl.) *du langweilst, irritierst mich;* he got a thrashing for his ∾s *für seine Bemühungen erhielt er noch Prügel;* to have one's labour for one's ∾s *sich umsonst abmühen;* the law inflicts ∾s and penalties *das Gesetz verhängt Strafen;* you may save your ∾s *du kannst dir die Mühe sparen;* to take great ∾s, to be at great ∾s, to go to great ∾s *sich (dat.) große Mühe geben*

paint I. v.tr.: he is not so black as he is ∾ed *er ist nicht so schlimm wie er dargestellt wird, er ist besser als sein Ruf;* to ∾ the door green *die Tür grün anstreichen;* to ∾ **the lily (Shakespeare, King John IV, 2)** *etwas Überflüssiges tun, zu sehr ausschmükken;* to ∾ the town red *die ganze Stadt auf den Kopf stellen.* — **II.** n.: wet ∾! *frisch gestrichen!*

painter n.: to cut (to slip) the ∾ *eine Verbindung lösen, sich aus dem Staube machen*

pair I. n.: a ∾ of scissors, spectacles, tongs, trousers *eine Schere, Brille, Zange, Hose;* the ∾ of you *euch beide;* a carriage and ∾ *ein Zweispänner;* where is the ∾ to this sock? *wo ist der andere, der dazu passende Strumpf?;* that's another ∾ of shoes *das ist etwas ganz anderes, das steht auf einem anderen Blatt;* a three-∾ back (front) room *ein Hinter- (Vorder)zimmer im dritten Stock;* to show a clean ∾ of heels *sich schleunigst davon machen.* — **II.** v.tr. & i.: to ∾ off *in Paaren anordnen, paarweise fortgehen*

pale n.: within the ∾ of the church *im Schoße der Kirche;* within (beyond) the ∾ of decency *innerhalb (außerhalb) der Grenzen des Anstands;* to leap the ∾ *die Grenzen überspringen, über die Stränge schlagen*

pall v.i.: that ∾s on me *das widert mich an, das läßt mich kalt*

palm¹ n.: to bear (to carry off, to win) the ∾ *die Siegespalme erringen, den Sieg davontragen;* to yield the ∾ *das Feld räumen;* ∾-oil *Palmenöl, Handsalbe; Schmiergeld (vgl.* palm²)

palm² I. n.: to grease a person's ∾ *j.en bestechen, schmieren;* to have an itching ∾ *gierig auf Geld sein.* — **II.** v.tr.: to ∾ oneself off as *sich ausgeben für (als);* to ∾ a thing off on a person *j.en mit etwas betrügen, j.em etwas andrehen*

palmy a.: in its ∾ days *zu seiner Glanz-, Blütezeit*

pan I. n.: a flash in the ∾ *ein mißlungener Versuch;* out of the frying-∾ into the fire *vom Regen in die Traufe.* — **II.** v.i.: to ∾ out to a person *sich j.em gegenüber frei aussprechen;* this ∾s out well *das läßt sich gut an, hat Erfolg*

pancake I. n.: as flat as a ∾ *so flach wie ein Brett.* — **II.** v.i.: an aeroplane ∾s (sl.) *ein Flugzeug sackt durch*

panel n.: a doctor on the ∾ *ein zur Krankenkasse zugelassener Arzt;* a ∾-patient *ein Kassenpatient*

pant I. v.i.: to ∾ for breath *nach Luft schnappen;* to ∾ for (after, or: to do a) thing *nach etwas lechzen, sich sehnen, etwas zu tun.* — **II.** v.tr.: to ∾ out a word *ein Wort hervorkeuchen*

pants n.: to catch a person with his ∾ down (vulg.) *j.en in eine äußerst peinliche Lage versetzen*

paper I. n.: a daily ∾ *eine Tageszeitung;* on ∾ he is the better man *nach seinen Zeugnissen ist er der bessere;* they are only ∾ profits *die Gewinne stehen nur auf dem Papier;* it was a very stiff ∾ *es war eine sehr schwierige Prüfungsarbeit;* a white-∾ *ein Weißbuch;* a ∾-chase *eine Schnitzeljagd;* a ∾-hanger *ein Tapezierer;* a ∾-weight *ein Briefbeschwerer;* to commit to ∾ *zu Papier bringen, auf-, niederschreiben;* to put (to set) pen to ∾ *die Feder ansetzen (ergreifen), anfangen zu schreiben;* to read a ∾ on a subject *einen Vortrag über einen Gegenstand halten;* to send in (to receive) one's ∾s *den Abschied nehmen, verabschiedet werden.* — **II.** v.tr.: to ∾ a room *ein Zimmer tapezieren;* to ∾ a theatre *ein Theater durch Freikarten füllen*

par n.: the ∾ of exchange *der Parikurs;* at, above, below ∾ *Pari, über Pari, unter Pari;* to be on a ∾ with a person *mit j.em auf gleichem Fuße stehen; ihm ebenbürtig (gleich) sein;* I don't feel quite up to ∾ *ich fühle mich nicht ganz auf der Höhe*

parade n.: to make a ∾ of one's virtues *mit seinen Tugenden prunken*

parallel I. a.: he is good on the ∾ bars *er ist ein guter Barrenturner;* to run ∾ to *parallel laufen mit.* — **II.** n.: without ∾ *ohnegleichen;* to draw a ∾ between *einen Vergleich ziehen zwischen;* to put oneself on a ∾ with *sich j.em gleichstellen*

parcel I. n.: to be part and ∾ of a thing *einen wesentlichen Bestandteil von etwas bilden.* — **II.** v.tr.: to ∾ out in (into) *aufteilen in*

pardon n.: I beg your ∾! I beg your ∾? *ich bitte um Verzeihung; wie beliebt? wie bitte?;* a general ∾ *eine Amnestie*

pare v.tr.: to ∾ a person's nails *j.em die Flügel beschneiden, den Brotkorb höher hängen;* to ∾ to the quick *ins lebendige Fleisch schneiden*

parish n.: the ∾ register *das Kirchenbuch;* ∾ relief *Gemeindeunterstützung;* a ∾-pump politician *ein Kirchturmspolitiker;* to come (to go) on the ∾ *der Gemeinde zur Last fallen, Gemeindeunterstützung erhalten*

parley n.: to beat (to sound) a ∾ *eine Schamade schlagen, Unterhandlungen anbieten*

parsnip n.: fair (fine) words butter no ∾s *Redensarten sind billig, schöne Worte machen den Kohl nicht fett*

part I. n.: discretion is the better ∾ of valour (prov.) *Vorsicht ist die Mutter der Weisheit (Porzellankiste);* (a) ∾ of it was spoilt *ein Teil davon war verdorben;* in ∾ *teilweise;* on the ∾ of *von seiten;* for the most ∾ *meistens;* a man of (good) ∾s *ein fähiger Kopf;* the ∾s of speech *die grammatischen Wortarten (Redeteile);* it was not my ∾ to interfere *es war nicht meine Sache, mich einzumischen;* he is a stranger in these ∾s *er ist hier fremd;* to be ∾ and parcel of a thing *einen wesentlichen Bestandteil von etwas bilden;* the book will come out in ∾s *das Buch erscheint in Lieferungen;* I have done my ∾ *ich habe mein Teil getan;* to have neither ∾ nor lot in a thing *nicht das geringste mit einer Sache zu tun haben;* to make a payment in ∾ *eine Abschlagszahlung machen;* to play a ∾ *betrügerisch handeln;* to play a noble ∾ *eine edle Rolle spielen;* to sing in ∾s *mehrstimmig singen;* to take (to bear) ∾ in a thing *an etwas teilnehmen;* to take a person's ∾ *j.es Partei ergreifen, sich auf j.es Seite schlagen;* to take it in good ∾ *es gut, humorvoll aufnehmen.* — **II.** adv.: made ∾ of iron and ∾ of wood *zum Teil aus Eisen, zum Teil aus Holz gemacht;* a lie that is ∾ truth *eine Lüge, die ein Fünkchen Wahrheit enthält.* — **III.** v.tr.: to ∾ brass rags with a person (naut. sl.) *alle näheren*

Beziehungen zu j.em abbrechen; to ∾ company with a person *sich von j.em trennen;* he ∾s his hair on the left *er scheitelt sein Haar links;* an islet ∾s the stream *eine kleine Insel teilt den Strom.* — **IV.** v.i.: the cord ∾ed *die Schnur zerriß;* the crowd ∾ed and let him through *die Menge teilte sich und ließ ihn durch;* let us ∾ friends *laßt uns als Freunde scheiden;* to ∾ from a person *sich von j.em verabschieden;* I have ∾ed with my car *ich habe meinen Wagen verkauft*

partake I. v.tr.: to ∾ a person's fate *j.es Schicksal teilen.* — **II.** v.i.: he partook of our lowly fare *er aß unsere einfache Kost mit;* he ∾s in his brother's popularity *er ist ebenso beliebt wie sein Bruder;* his manner ∾s of insolence *er hat eine etwas freche Art*

Parthian a.: a ∾ shot (shaft) *eine letzte spitze Bemerkung*

partial a.: his judgement was ∾ *sein Urteil war parteiisch;* the performance was only a ∾ success *die Vorstellung war nur teilweise ein Erfolg;* he is very ∾ to wine *er trinkt sehr gern Wein*

participate I. v.tr.: to ∾ a thing with a person *mit j.em etwas teilen, gemeinsam haben.* — **II.** v.i.: he ∾s in the advantages of a thing *er genießt die Vorteile einer Sache;* he ∾s in the business *er nimmt teil an dem Geschäft;* his poems ∾ of the nature of satire *seine Gedichte haben etwas Satirisches an sich*

particle n.: he has not a ∾ of sense *er hat keinen Funken Verstand;* there is not a ∾ of truth in the rumour *an dem Gerücht ist kein Fünkchen Wahrheit*

particular I. a.: a full and ∾ account *ein ausführlicher und ins einzelne gehender Bericht;* the doctrine of ∾ election and redemption *die Lehre der Erlösung durch besondere Gnadenwahl;* he is my ∾ friend *er ist mein besonderer Freund;* for no ∾ reason *aus keinem besonderen Grunde;* this ∾ tax is no worse than others *gerade (speziell) diese Steuer ist nicht schlimmer als andere;* he took ∾ trouble *er gab sich besondere Mühe;* he is very ∾ about (as to) what he eats *er ist sehr wählerisch im Essen;* he mentioned one ∾ case (one case in ∾) *er führte besonders einen Fall an.* — **II.** n.: for further ∾s apply to Mr. N. *das Nähere (nähere Umstände) zu erfragen bei Herrn N.;* to go (to enter) into ∾s *auf Einzelheiten eingehen;* a London ∾ *ein dichter Londoner Nebel*

parting n.: his ∾ is on the left *sein Haar ist links gescheitelt;* a ∾ shot *letzte treffende Bemerkung eines Abgehenden;* the ∾ of the ways *der Scheideweg (fig.), die Trennung;* his ∾ words *seine Abschiedsworte*

party n.: a ∾ wall *eine gemeinsame Mauer (Brandmauer) zwischen zwei Häusern;* a ∾ line *eine gemeinsame Telefonleitung;* to follow the ∾ line (politics) *den Anweisungen der Partei getreu sein;* an old ∾ with spectacles *ein alter Knopp mit Brille;* the parties concerned *die Beteiligten;* I will be no ∾ to this affair *ich will mit der Sache nichts zu tun haben;* to give (to throw) a ∾ *eine Gesellschaft geben;* we have been invited to a dinner ∾ *wir sind zum Abendessen eingeladen worden;* to make one of a ∾ *sich einer Gesellschaft anschließen*

pash n.: (sl., = passion) to have a ∾ on (a ∾ for) a teacher *für einen Lehrer schwärmen*

pass[1] **I.** v.i.: kingdoms and nations ∾ *Königreiche und Völker vergehen;* his remarks ∾ed unnoticed *man nahm keine Notiz von seinen Bemerkungen;* time ∾es rapidly *die Zeit geht schnell vorüber;* I saw what was ∾ing *ich sah, was vorging;* to ∾ along, down, over, on, etc. *entlang-, hinunter-, hinüber-, weiter- usw. schreiten;* I saw the procession ∾ by *ich sah den Aufzug vorbeiziehen;* we'll let that ∾ (by) *das wollen wir übergehen (nicht berücksichtigen);* he ∾ed by the name of N. *er ging unter dem Namen N.;* she could ∾ for thirty *sie könnte noch für dreißig gelten;* he ∾ed hence (from us, away) *er verschied (starb);* to ∾ into a person's possession *in j.es Besitz übergehen;* the pain ∾ed off *der Schmerz ging vorüber;* it ∾ed off without a hitch *es verlief ohne Stockung;* to ∾ out (sl.) *ohnmächtig werden;* I ∾ed over the bridge *ich ging über die Brücke;* I ∾ed through a terrible time *ich machte eine schreckliche Zeit durch;* he will never bring that to ∾ *das wird er nie bewirken.* — **II.** v.tr.: to ∾ the baby (colloq.) *einer Verantwortung entgehen;* to ∾ a bill *einen Gesetzantrag annehmen;* he has ∾ed the chair *er ist schon Vorsitzender gewesen;* it ∾es my comprehension *es geht über meinen Verstand;* to ∾ the buck to someone else (sl.) *die Verantwortung auf einen anderen schieben;* to ∾ a compliment *ein Kompli-*

ment machen; to ∾ an examination *eine Prüfung bestehen;* to ∾ forged notes *falsche Geldscheine in Umlauf bringen;* it will ∾ muster *es wird als genügend erachtet werden, es wird noch hingehen;* to ∾ a person *an j.em vorbeigehen;* to ∾ a remark *eine Bemerkung fallen lassen;* to ∾ troops in review *eine Parade abhalten;* please ∾ me the salt *reichen Sie mir bitte das Salz!;* the judge ∾ed the death sentence upon the accused *der Richter verurteilte den Angeklagten zum Tode;* to ∾ the time *die Zeit verbringen;* to ∾ the time of day *die Tageszeit bieten, grüßen;* he ∾ed the winter in Egypt *er verbrachte den Winter in Ägypten;* he ∾ed his hand across his forehead *er strich (fuhr) mit der Hand über die Stirn;* to ∾ away the time *die Zeit vertreiben;* to ∾ in one's checks *sterben;* he ∾ed it off upon me as (for) genuine *er drehte es mir als echt an;* he ∾ed himself off as (for) a detective *er gab sich als Detektiv aus;* please read this and ∾ it on *bitte lesen und weitergeben!;* ∾ it over to me *reich' es mir herüber;* we will ∾ it over in silence *wir wollen es mit Stillschweigen übergehen;* he ∾ed his sword through him *er durchbohrte ihn mit seinem Schwert;* to ∾ a thing up *etwas hinaufreichen; auf etwas verzichten.* — **III.** n.: that is a pretty ∾! *das ist eine nette Bescherung!;* to bring to ∾ *zustande bringen;* to come to ∾ *sich ereignen;* things have come to such a strange ∾ that *die Lage der Dinge ist derart seltsam, daß;* to make a ∾ at a person *beim Fechten einen Stoß nach j.em führen; mit j.em anzubändeln suchen;* a ∾-book *ein Bankkontobuch;* a ∾-key *ein Hauptschlüssel, Drücker;* what is the ∾word? *wie lautet die Parole?;* a free ∾ *ein Freifahrtschein*

pass² n.: to hold the ∾ *die Stellung halten;* to sell the ∾ *eine Sache verraten*

passage n.: a bird of ∾ *ein Zugvogel;* a verbal ∾ of (at) arms *ein Wortgefecht;* he booked (took) a ∾ to America *er bestellte (nahm) eine Schiffskarte nach Amerika;* he had a stormy ∾ *er hatte eine stürmische Überfahrt*

passion n.: he has a ∾ for music *er hat eine Vorliebe für Musik;* to fall (to fly, to get) into a towering ∾ about a thing *wegen einer Sache mordswütend werden*

passport n.: to get (to take out) a ∾ *sich einen Paß verschaffen;* flattery is the sole ∾ to his favour *man kann seine Gunst nur durch Schmeichelei erringen*

past I. a.: his prime is ∾ *seine Blütezeit ist vorbei;* he has been ill for some time ∾ *er ist seit einiger Zeit krank;* he is a ∾ master in (of) the subject *er ist ein Altmeister des Fachs.* — **II.** n.: she is a woman with a ∾ *sie ist eine Frau mit (einer) Vergangenheit;* one cannot undo the ∾ *man kann die Vergangenheit nicht ungeschehen machen.* — **III.** prep.: it is ∾ cure *es ist unheilbar;* it is ∾ endurance *es läßt sich nicht mehr ertragen;* I put nothing ∾ her *ich traue ihr alles zu, ihr ist alles zuzutrauen;* it is ∾ hope *es ist hoffnungslos;* he ran ∾ the house *er lief an dem Hause vorbei;* he is an old man ∾ seventy *er ist ein alter Mann über siebzig;* it is half ∾ three *es ist halb vier;* he stayed till ∾ two o'clock *er blieb bis nach zwei Uhr da.* — **IV.** adv.: he hastened ∾ *er eilte vorbei*

pat¹ v.tr.: I must ∾ myself on the back *ich muß mich selbst loben*

pat² adv. & a.: it came ∾ to his purpose *es entsprach genau seinem Zwecke, es kam ihm sehr gelegen;* to stand ∾ *mit Bestehendem zufrieden sein;* he has the story ∾ *er hat (kann) die Geschichte am Schnürchen*

patch I. n.: he is not a ∾ on him *er ist nicht mit ihm zu vergleichen, er kann nicht an ihn tippen;* to strike a bad ∾ *Pech haben;* a cross-∾ (fam.) *eine mürrische Person.* — **II.** v.tr.: to ∾ up a quarrel *einen Streit beilegen*

patent a.: a ∾ fastener *ein Druckknopf;* he wears ∾ leather shoes *er trägt Lackschuhe;* a ∾ error *ein deutlicher Irrtum;* ∾ letters *Privilegsurkunde*

patience n.: I have no ∾ (I am out of ∾) with him *ich kann ihn nicht länger ertragen;* he has the ∾ of Job *er hat eine Engelsgeduld*

patient a.: he is ∾ of his sufferings *er trägt sein Leiden geduldig;* the facts are ∾ of two interpretations *die Tatsachen lassen zwei Auslegungen zu*

Paul n.pr.: to rob Peter to pay ∾ *ein Loch aufreißen, um ein anderes zuzustopfen; hier borgen, um dort zu bezahlen;* he is a ∾ **Pry** *er ist ein neugieriger Patron*

pave v.tr.: the way to hell is ∾d with good intentions (prov.) *der Weg zur Hölle ist mit guten Vorsätzen gepflastert;* to ∾ the way for a reform *einer Reform den Weg ebnen*

pawn[1] n.: he is only a ∾ *er ist nur eine Schachfigur, ein Strohmann*

pawn[2] n.: to give a thing in ∾ *etwas verpfänden, versetzen;* a ∾broker *ein Pfandverleiher;* a ∾shop *ein Pfandhaus*

pay I. v.i.: this does not ∾ *das macht sich nicht bezahlt, das lohnt sich nicht;* to ∾ on the nail *sofort bar bezahlen;* to ∾ through the nose *übermäßig bezahlen, tüchtig bluten müssen;* to ∾ up and look pleasant *mit guter Miene bezahlen.* — **II.** v.tr.: see 'address, intention, coin, regard, respect, way'; to ∾ a compliment to a person *j.em ein Kompliment machen;* to ∾ the debt of nature *sterben;* to ∾ honour to a person *j.em Ehre erweisen;* to ∾ one's way *ohne Zuschuß auskommen;* to ∾ off old scores *alte Schuldposten abtragen, sich an j.em rächen;* to ∾ out a rope *einem Tau langsam nachgeben;* there was the devil to ∾ *der Teufel war los;* to ∾ a visit (a call) *einen Besuch abstatten (machen);* the ship's crew was paid off *die Schiffsmannschaft wurde abgemustert;* I shall ∾ him out *ich werde es ihm heimzahlen;* to ∾ up the amount *den Betrag voll bezahlen;* to put paid to a thing *etwas als erledigt betrachten, den Schlußstrich unter etwas ziehen*

payment n.: to stop ∾ *die Zahlungen einstellen;* to stop ∾ of a cheque *die Auszahlung eines Schecks verhindern*

payroll n.: to be put off the ∾ *entlassen werden*

pea n.: as like as two ∾s *ähnlich wie ein Ei dem andern;* a ∾-nut *eine Erdnuß;* a ∾-shooter *ein Blasrohr;* a ∾-souper *ein dicker, gelber Nebel;* a bunch of sweet ∾s *ein Strauß Wicken*

peace n.: at ∾ *in Frieden;* a breach of the ∾ *ein Friedensbruch;* a justice of the ∾ (abbr. J.P.) *ein Friedensrichter;* to hold one's ∾ *schweigen;* to keep the ∾ *Ruhe halten;* he left me no ∾ *er ließ mir keine Ruhe;* to make ∾ *Frieden schließen;* to make one's ∾ with a person *sich mit j.em aussöhnen;* to be sworn of the ∾ *als Richter vereidigt werden*

peach[1] n.: she is a ∾ (sl.) *sie ist ein entzückendes Mädel;* he has a ∾ of a car (sl.) *er hat einen prachtvollen Wagen*

peach[2] v.i. (sl.): to ∾ against (upon) an accomplice *einen Mittäter verpfeifen*

peacock I. n.: as proud as a ∾ *(so) stolz wie ein Spanier.* — **II.** to ∾ oneself on a thing *sich mit etwas brüsten (dicke tun).* — **III.** v.i.: to ∾ about *einherstolzieren*

peak I. v.i.: to ∾ and pine *sich vor Gram verzehren, dahinsiechen.* — **II.** a.: during the ∾ hour *bei Hochbetrieb*

peal n.: a ∾ of applause *ein Beifallssturm;* a ∾ of bells *ein Glockengeläute;* a ∾ of laughter *ein schallendes Gelächter;* a ∾ of thunder *ein Donnerschlag*

pearl n.: to cast ∾s before swine *Perlen vor die Säue werfen;* the ∾ies *die Ost-Londoner Obsthändler, die ihre Trachten mit Perlmutterknöpfen schmücken*

peck[1] n.: a ∾ of dirt *ein Haufen Schmutz;* to be in a ∾ of troubles *in großer Bedrängnis sein*

peck[2] **I.** v.i.: he only ∾s at his food *er ißt wie ein Spatz;* he is always ∾ing at me *er hackt immer auf mir herum.* — **II.** n.: ∾ and booze (sl.) *Essen und Trinken*

pecker n.: to keep one's ∾ up (sl.) *den Mut nicht sinken lassen*

peckish a. (colloq.): I'm feeling rather ∾ *ich habe einen ziemlichen Hunger*

peculiar a.: he has always been a little ∾ *er ist immer ein wenig eigen (absonderlich) gewesen;* it has a ∾ flavour *es hat einen eigenartigen Geschmack;* it is a matter of ∾ importance *es ist eine besonders wichtige Sache*

peculiarly adv.: it is ∾ annoying *es ist besonders ärgerlich;* that does not affect him ∾ *das betrifft ihn nicht persönlich;* they dress ∾ *sie kleiden sich eigenartig*

pedlar n.: she is a ∾ of gossip *sie ist eine Klatschbase;* ∾'s French *die Diebessprache, das Rotwelsch*

peeled a.: keep your eyes ∾ (sl.) *paß' gut auf, halt' die Augen offen*

peep n.: at the ∾ of dawn (day) *bei Tagesanbruch;* a ∾-hole *ein Guckloch;* to take a ∾ at a thing *einen kurzen Blick auf etwas werfen*

peer n.: you will not easily find his ∾ *du wirst nicht leicht seinesgleichen finden;* the ∾s of the realm *die Pairs des Reiches, die Mitglieder des Oberhauses*

peeved a.: (colloq.) to be ∾ at something *ärgerlich über etwas sein*

peg I. n.: a round (square) ∾ in a square (round) hole *j. (etwas), der (das) nicht am* *geeigneten Platze ist;* he uses it as a ∾ to hang his discourse on *er benutzt es als einen Vorwand zu reden;* to come down a ∾ or two *einige Pflöcke zurückstecken, etwas kleinlaut werden;* to have a ∾ *ein Glas Whisky (Kognak) mit Sodawasser trinken;* to put a soldier on the ∾ (sl.) *einen Soldaten wegen eines Vergehens vor den Kommandeur zitieren;* to take a person down a ∾ or two *j.en demütigen.* — **II.** v.tr.: it was ∾ged down to this *es wurde hierauf eingeschränkt.* — **III.** v.i.: to ∾ away at a task *ständig an einer Aufgabe arbeiten (büffeln, ochsen);* to ∾ out (sl.) *sterben, abkratzen*

pell-mell adv.: *Hals über Kopf, blindlings, durcheinander, kunterbunt*

pelt I. v.tr.: to ∾ a person with questions *j.en mit Fragen bestürmen.* — **II.** v.i.: to ∾ along *dahinrasen;* it was ∾ing with rain, there was a ∾ing rain *der Regen prasselte in Strömen nieder, es war ein ordentlicher Platzregen.* — **III.** n.: at full ∾ *mit höchster Geschwindigkeit*

pen n.: a ∾-knife *ein Taschenmesser;* a ∾-name *ein Schriftstellername;* a fountain-∾ *ein Füllfederhalter;* to make a living with one's ∾ *als Schriftsteller seinen Lebensunterhalt verdienen;* to put (to set) ∾ to paper *die Feder ansetzen (ergreifen), anfangen zu schreiben;* he wields a formidable ∾ *er führt eine gewaltige Feder*

pending I. a.: a suit was then ∾ *damals schwebte noch ein Gerichtsverfahren.* — **II.** prep.: ∾ these negotiations *während dieser Unterhandlungen;* ∾ his return *bis zu seiner Rückkehr*

penny n.: a ∾ for your thoughts! *(zu einem in Gedanken Versunkenen gesagt) ich gäbe etwas darum zu wissen (ich möchte wissen), was Sie jetzt denken!;* a ∾ plain and twopence coloured *billig und geschmacklos aufgemacht;* ∾ wise and pound foolish *am unrechten Ende sparsam;* that is a pretty ∾ *das ist ein schönes Stück Geld!;* in for a ∾, in for a pound (prov.) *wer A sagt, muß auch B sagen;* take care of the pence and the pounds will take care of themselves (prov.) *wer den Pfennig nicht ehrt, ist des Talers nicht wert;* to earn (to make, to turn) an honest ∾ *Geld durch ehrliche Arbeit verdienen;* to spend a ∾ (colloq.) *der Toilettenfrau einen Groschen geben, auf die Toilette gehen;* a ∾ dreadful *ein Schundroman, Schauerblatt;* a ∾-a-liner *ein Zeilenschreiber, Scribent;* to arrive in ∾ numbers *einzeln, langsam, einer nach dem anderen ankommen;* a ∾-in-the-slot machine *ein Automat;* that was a good (bad) ∾-worth *das war ein gutes (schlechtes) Geschäft*

people n.: the English ∾; the English-speaking ∾s *das englische Volk; die englisch sprechenden Völker;* the ∾ here are furious *die Leute hier sind wütend;* ∾ say *die Leute sagen, man sagt;* his ∾ are sure to hear of it *seine Angehörigen werden sicher davon hören*

pep I. n.: he is full of ∾ *er ist voller Tatkraft, geladen mit Energie;* a ∾ talk *eine zündende Ansprache.* — **II.** v.tr.: to ∾ up *kräftigen, beleben*

pepper n.: to take ∾ in the nose *Anstoß nehmen; sich beleidigt fühlen, böse werden;* we pay a ∾corn rent *wir zahlen eine nominelle Pacht*

peppery a.: a ∾ old colonel *ein bärbeißiger alter Oberst*

perch n.: a bird takes its ∾ *ein Vogel läßt sich nieder;* to hop the ∾ *sterben, abkratzen;* to knock a person off his ∾ *j.en besiegen*

perfect a.: he is a ∾ idiot *er ist ein Vollidiot;* he has a ∾ mania for doing it *er hat eine wahre Sucht, es zu tun;* that's ∾ nonsense *das ist reiner Unsinn;* he is a ∾ nuisance *er ist ein äußerst lästiger Bursche;* he is a ∾ stranger to me *er ist mir vollkommen fremd;* to be ∾ in a thing, to have a thing ∾ *etwas gründlich verstehen;* practice makes ∾ (prov.) *Übung macht den Meister*

perfection n.: the pink of ∾ *die Vollkommenheit selbst;* she cooks to ∾ *sie ist eine perfekte Köchin;* she plays to ∾ *sie spielt meisterhaft*

perk v.i.: to ∾ up *sich erholen, den Kopf emporrecken*

perks n. (perquisites): *Nebeneinnahmen, Nebenverdienst*

personal a.: it is my ∾ opinion *meine eigene Meinung ist ...;* a ∾ interview *eine persönliche Unterredung;* ∾ remarks *anzügliche Bemerkungen;* avoid being ∾ *werde nicht anzüglich;* ∾ beauty *körperliche Schönheit;* ∾ property (legal) *bewegliches Eigentum;* the ∾ column of a newspaper *Geburts-, Heirats-, Todesanzeigen und Nachrichten*

persuasion n.: it is my private ∾ that he is mad *persönlich bin ich davon überzeugt, daß er wahnsinnig ist;* he is of the Roman Catholic ∾ *er ist römisch-katholischen Glaubens;* no one of the male ∾ was there *es war kein männliches Wesen da*

pestle n.: a knight of the ∾ *ein Apotheker*

pet[1] n.: he is in a ∾ *er ist schlecht gelaunt;* to take the ∾ at a thing *etwas übelnehmen*

pet[2] **I.** n.: her ∾ was a white cat *ihr Lieblingstier war eine weiße Katze;* that is my ∾ aversion *das ist mir ein Greuel;* he has a ∾ name for her *er hat einen Kosenamen für sie.* — **II.** v.tr.: to ∾ a child *ein Kind hätscheln*

petard n.: hoist with his own ∾ *in die Grube fallen, die man anderen gegraben hat; vgl.* 'hoist'

Peter n.pr.: to rob ∾ to pay Paul *ein Loch aufreißen, um ein anderes zuzustopfen; hier borgen, um dort zu bezahlen*

peter v.i.: the vein of ore ∾ed out *die Erzader hörte allmählich auf;* the stream ∾ed out in the sand *der Bach verlor sich im Sande;* the attack ∾ed out *der Angriff ließ nach (flaute ab, hörte auf)*

petticoat n.: I have known him since he was in ∾s *ich kenne ihn seit seiner frühesten Jugend;* she is a Cromwell in ∾s *sie ist ein weiblicher Cromwell;* he is under ∾ government *er steht unter dem Pantoffel (unter Weiber-Regiment)*

philosopher n.: the ∾'s stone *der Stein der Weisen*

phiz n. (physiognomy): (fam.) *Gesicht*

phoney a. (sl.): ∾ *falsch, unecht;* ∾ gen (sl.) *unzuverlässige Auskunft;* the ∾ war *die Kriegsjahre 1939—40*

physical a.: ∾ jerks *gymnastische Übungen*

phut adv.: to go ∾ (sl.) *zusammenbrechen, kaputt gehen*

pi a. (pious): (school sl.) *fromm, religiös;* ∾-jaw *eine fromme Rede*

pick I. v.tr.: to ∾ a bone *einen Knochen abnagen (abknabbern);* I have a bone to ∾ with you *ich habe ein Hühnchen mit dir zu rupfen;* to ∾ and choose *wählerisch sein;* to ∾ flowers *Blumen pflücken;* to ∾ holes in a thing *etwas bekritteln (bemängeln);* to ∾ a lock *ein Schloß mit Dietrich öffnen;* to ∾ one's nose *sich (dat.) in der Nase bohren;* to ∾ a thing to pieces *etwas zerpflücken, kritisieren, über etwas herziehen;* beware of ∾pockets! *vor Taschendieben wird gewarnt!;* to ∾ a quarrel with a person *mit j.em Streit anfangen;* to ∾ one's teeth *in den Zähnen stochern;* to ∾ one's way (steps) *sich vorsichtig bewegen, den reinlichsten Weg aussuchen;* to ∾ one's words *seine Worte sorgfältig wählen;* the sharpshooter ∾ed off one by one *der Scharfschütze schoß einen nach dem anderen ab;* to ∾ out the meaning of a passage *den Sinn einer Stelle herausbekommen;* he ∾ed out the tune by ear *er spielte die Melodie nach dem Gehör;* to ∾ up an acquaintance *eine Bekanntschaft machen;* I ∾ed it up cheap *ich habe es billig gekauft;* to ∾ up courage *Mut fassen;* he ∾ed up English very quickly *er lernte sehr schnell Englisch;* to ∾ up information *Nachrichten erfahren (aufschnappen);* I ∾ed up Moscow last night *gestern Abend bekam ich Moskau im Rundfunk;* to ∾ oneself up *sich nach einem Fall wieder erheben;* the train stops to ∾ up passengers *der Zug hält, um Fahrgäste aufzunehmen;* he ∾s up a few pence now and then *er verdient sich ab und zu ein paar Groschen;* to ∾ up strength *wieder zu Kräften kommen;* I shall ∾ you up on my way back *ich hole dich ab, wenn ich zurückfahre;* a ∾-me-up *ein belebender Trunk, eine Stärkung.* — **II.** v.i.: to ∾ and steal *stehlen, mausen, stibitzen;* he has ∾ed up wonderfully *er hat sich prachtvoll erholt;* to ∾ up with a person *eine Bekanntschaft mit j.em machen.* — **III.** n.: it was (he is) the ∾ of the basket (the bunch) *es war (er ist) das (der) beste von allen, das beste Stück, das beste Pferd im Stall*

pick-a-back adv.: he carried him ∾ (piggy-back) *er trug ihn huckepack*

pickle I. n.: I have a rod in ∾ for him *ich habe ein Hühnchen mit ihm zu rupfen;* he is in a sad (sorry, nice, pretty) ∾ *er sitzt schön in der Tinte;* that child is a ∾ *das Kind ist ein Wildfang.* — **II.** v.tr.: he is ∾d (sl.) *er ist betrunken*

picnic n.: it was no ∾ (colloq.) *es war keine leichte Sache*

picture I. n.: her hat is a ∾ *ihr Hut ist bildschön;* to be in the (not in the) ∾ *von Bedeutung, nicht von Bedeutung sein;* that is out of (does not come into) the ∾ *das* *gehört nicht zur Sache;* she looks the very ∾ of health *sie sieht aus wie die verkörperte Gesundheit;* let's go to the ∾s *laßt uns ins Kino gehen;* a ∾ postcard *eine Ansichtskarte.* — **II.** v.tr.: to ∾ the situation *die Lage schildern;* to ∾ a thing to oneself *sich etwas ausmalen, vorstellen*

pidgin n.a. (Chinese = business): ∾ English *Verkehrssprache zwischen Engländern und Chinesen;* that's not my ∾ (colloq.) *das ist nicht meine Sache*

pie[1] n.: to eat humble ∾ *Abbitte leisten, sich demütigen, zu Kreuze kriechen;* to have a finger in the ∾ *die Hand im Spiele haben;* an apple-∾ bed, see 'apple'; in apple-∾ order (colloq.) *in größter Ordnung*

pie[2] n.: to go to (to fall into) ∾ *(beim Drucker) zu Zwiebelfischen zusammenfallen, in Verwirrung geraten*

piece I. n.: a ∾ of advice *ein Ratschlag;* a ∾ of cake (sl.) *eine günstige Angelegenheit;* a ∾ of good luck *ein Glücksfall;* you are a nice ∾ of goods! *du bist mir eine nette Person!;* a ∾ of impudence *eine große Unverschämtheit;* to be of a ∾ with *im Einklang stehen mit;* to be paid by the ∾ *Stücklohn erhalten;* to give a person a ∾ of one's mind *j.em gehörig aufs Dach steigen, die Meinung sagen, den Marsch blasen;* to go to ∾s *in Stücke gehen, scheitern;* to pick (to tear) to ∾s *zerpflücken;* to pull a book to ∾s *ein Buch herunterreißen (-machen);* to say one's ∾ (colloq.) *das sagen, was man zu sagen hat;* to do the work ∾ meal *die Arbeit stückweise machen.* — **II.** v.tr.: to ∾ on one thing to another *zwei Dinge aneinanderstücken;* the provisions were ∾d out *die Vorräte wurden verteilt;* to ∾ out a chain of evidence *eine Beweiskette aufreihen;* to ∾ up a quarrel *einen Streit beilegen*

pig I. n.: ∾s might fly! *es könnte ein Wunder geschehen!;* ∾s in clover *Emporkömmlinge ohne gute Manieren;* a ∾'s whisper *eine ganz kurze Zeit;* please the ∾s! *scherzhaft für „Das walte Gott!";* don't be such a ∾ *sei nicht so gefräßig!;* I have brought my ∾s to a fine (pretty, the wrong) market! *da habe ich aber ein schlechtes Geschäft gemacht!;* to buy a ∾ in a poke *die Katze im Sack kaufen;* to drive ∾s (to market) *schnarchen;* a ∾-headed fellow *ein dickköpfiger, sturer Bursche;* a ∾-tail *ein Haarzopf.* — **II.** v.i.: to ∾ it, to ∾ together *eingepfercht zusammen wohnen, -schlafen*

pigeon n.: a carrier-∾, a homing ∾ *eine Brieftaube;* a ∾-breast *eine Hühnerbrust;* to ∾-hole a document *ein Schriftstück zur späteren Bearbeitung in ein Fach legen;* ∾-livered *furchtsam, schüchtern;* a ∾ pair *Zwillinge von verschiedenem Geschlecht;* to milk the ∾ *versuchen, etwas Unmögliches zu tun;* to pluck a ∾ *einen Dummen rupfen;* this is not my ∾, see 'pidgin'

pikestaff n.: as plain as a ∾ *sonnenklar, so klar wie Kloßbrühe, wie dicke Tinte*

pile I. n.: a ∾ of arms *eine Gewehrpyramide;* a funeral ∾ *ein Scheiterhaufen;* a noble ∾ of buildings *ein stattliches Gebäude;* to have ∾s of money *einen Haufen Geld, Geld wie Heu haben;* to make one's ∾ (colloq.) *ein Vermögen machen, sein Schäfchen ins Trockene bringen.* — **II.** v.tr.: ∾ arms *setzt die Gewehre zusammen!;* you need not ∾ it on *du brauchst nicht zu übertreiben;* to ∾ up (on) the agony *in Sensation machen, gruselig schildern*

pill I. n.: a ∾ to cure an earthquake *eine halbe Maßnahme;* to gild (to sugar) the ∾ *die Pille versüßen;* to swallow a bitter ∾ *eine bittere Pille schlucken;* a ∾-box *ein Maschinengewehrunterstand.* — **II.** v.tr.: he was ∾ed *er fiel bei der Ballotage (Wahl) durch*

pillar n.: he was driven from ∾ to post *er wurde von Pontius zu Pilatus geschickt;* a ∾-box *ein Briefkasten*

pillion n.: a ∾-seat *ein Soziussitz am Motorrad*

pillow n.: to take counsel of one's ∾ *eine Nacht über etwas schlafen, etwas beschlafen*

pilot n.: to drop the ∾ *einen bewährten Ratgeber entlassen, ausbooten;* the ∾-light of a geyser *die Stichflamme eines Gasbadeofens*

pin I. n.: he is on his ∾s again (colloq.) *er ist wieder auf den Beinen;* I don't care a ∾ *ich mache mir nicht die Bohne (ich mache mir einen Dreck) daraus;* I have ∾s and needles in my arm *ich habe Ameisenkribbeln im Arm;* to be on ∾s and needles *(wie) auf glühenden Kohlen sitzen;* I can no longer bear the constant ∾-pricks *ich kann die ständigen Nadelstiche nicht mehr ertragen;* ∾ money *Taschengeld;* there's not a ∾ to chose between them *es ist kein Deut Unterschied zwischen den beiden.* — **II.** v.tr.: to

∾ one's faith (up)on a person *sein ganzes Vertrauen auf j.en setzen;* I ∾ned him down to his promise *ich nagelte ihn auf sein Versprechen fest;* to ∾-point something *etwas genau bezeichnen;* a ∾-up girl *eine bekannte Schönheit, deren Bild man an die Wand heftet*

pinch I. n.: a ∾ of snuff, of salt *eine Prise Schnupftabak, Salz;* I could do it at a ∾ *ich könnte es zur Not (im Notfalle) tun;* to be in a ∾ *im Druck (in der Klemme) sein;* to come to the ∾ *zum Äußersten kommen.* — **II.** v.tr.: he was ∾ed with cold *er war starr vor Kälte;* to ∾ a person in (of, for) food *j.en im Essen knapp halten;* he ∾ed my watch (sl.) *er hat mir die Uhr geklaut (gemaust, stibitzt).* — **III.** v.i.: he knows where the shoe ∾es *er weiß, wo der Schuh drückt, was Geldknappheit bedeutet*

pine v.i.: to ∾ for (after, to do) a thing *sich nach etwas sehnen (nach etwas schmachten), sich danach sehnen (danach schmachten), etwas zu tun;* to peak and ∾ *sich vor Gram verzehren, dahinsiechen*

pink n. & a.: in the ∾ (of health) *bei bester Gesundheit;* the ∾ of perfection *die Vollkommenheit selbst;* strike me ∾ (sl.) *da schlag' aber einer lang hin!;* hunting ∾ *scharlachroter Jagdrock*

pip[1] n.: it gives me the ∾ (sl.) *es langweilt mich, widert mich an;* I've got the ∾ (sl.) *ich bin nicht ganz auf dem Damm, ich habe es satt*

pip[2] n.: the ∾s *das Greenwicher Zeitzeichen im Radio;* he has three ∾s *er hat drei Sterne, er ist Hauptmann*

pip[3] v.tr.: (colloq.) to ∾ a person *j.en besiegen; mit Schrot treffen; bei einer Ballotage durchfallen lassen*

pipe I. n.: put that in your ∾ and smoke it *das kannst du dir an den Hut (hinter den Spiegel) stecken, hinter die Ohren schreiben;* to put a person's ∾ out (sl.) *j.es Pläne durchkreuzen.* — **II.** v.tr.: to ∾ the crew up *die Mannschaft durch Pfeifensignal auf Deck rufen;* to ∾ one's eye(s) *weinen.* — **III.** v.i.: to ∾ down (sl.) *stiller, kleinlaut werden*

piper n.: to pay the ∾ and call the tune *die Kosten tragen, die Zeche bezahlen, und die Sache nach seinem Willen leiten*

piping a.: in this weak ∾ time of peace (Shakesp.) *in dieser schlaffen Friedenszeit;* it is ∾ hot *es ist kochend heiß*

pique I. v.tr.: to be ∾d at a thing *auf etwas ärgerlich sein;* to ∾ oneself on a thing *sich mit etwas brüsten.* — **II.** n.: in a fit of ∾ *in einem Anfall von Ärger;* he had a ∾ against me *er hatte einen Pik auf mich*

pistol n.: to beat the ∾ *voreilig starten, handeln*

pit I. n.: the ∾ of the stomach *die Magengrube;* the ∾ of the theatre *das Parterre;* to dig a ∾ for a person *j.em eine Grube graben, eine Falle stellen;* to go down into the ∾ (of hell) *zur Hölle fahren;* to shoot the ∾ *heimlich ausziehen, ohne die Miete zu bezahlen;* it was a ∾fall *es war eine Falle.* — **II.** v.tr.: the combatants were ∾ted against each other *die Kämpfer standen sich gegenüber;* he is ∾ted with smallpox *er ist blatternarbig*

pitch I. n.: his work is of a high ∾ *seine Arbeit steht auf hoher Stufe;* to fly a high ∾ *sich hoch aufschwingen;* the ∾ of a note *die Tonhöhe einer Note;* to queer the ∾ for a person (sl.) *j.em die Aussichten (das Geschäft, Spiel) verderben.* — **II.** v.tr.: to ∾ a ball *einen Ball werfen;* it was a ∾ed battle *es war eine regelrechte Schlacht;* he ∾es it strong (colloq.) *er übertreibt (beim Reden);* to ∾ a tent *ein Zelt aufschlagen;* to ∾ a yarn (sl.) *Garn spinnen, eine Geschichte erzählen.* — **III.** v.i.: the ship ∾es *das Schiff stampft;* to ∾ in (colloq.) *kräftig ans Werk gehen;* to ∾ into a person (colloq.) *es j.em ordentlich geben;* he ∾ed into his food (colloq.) *er fiel über das Essen her;* to ∾ on one's head *heftig auf den Kopf fallen;* to ∾ upon a thing *auf eine Sache verfallen*

pitcher n.: little ∾s have long (big) ears (prov.) *kleine Kessel haben große Ohren;* the ∾ went once too often to the well *der Krug ging so lange zu Wasser, bis (daß) er (zer)brach (Das selbe Spiel ist zu oft versucht worden)*

pith n.: the ∾ and marrow of a thing *die Quintessenz, der Kern einer Sache;* enterprises of great ∾ and moment (Shakesp. Haml. III, 1, 86) *Unternehmungen voll Mark und Nachdruck*

pity I. n.: what a ∾! the ∾ of it! *wie schade!;* more's the ∾! *um so schlimmer!;* for ∾'s sake! *um der Barmherzigkeit willen!;* it is a thousand pities *es ist jammerschade, ewig schade;* to feel ∾ for (to take ∾ on) a person *mit j.em Mitleid haben.* —

II. v.tr.: I ∾ you if you think that *du tust mir leid, wenn du das denkst*

place I. n.: in, out of ∾ *angebracht, unangebracht;* in the first, second ∾ *erstens, zweitens;* it is not my ∾ to do so *es ist nicht meine Sache, das zu tun;* there is no ∾ for doubt *es ist nicht daran zu zweifeln;* this gave ∾ to a heated discussion *hierauf folgte eine hitzige Aussprache;* we hope to go ∾s (colloq.) *wir wollen die Sehenswürdigkeiten besuchen, etwas unternehmen;* he has also a nice ∾ in the country *er hat auch einen schönen Landsitz;* he has a sore ∾ on his wrist *er hat eine wunde Stelle am Handgelenk;* to keep a person in his ∾ *j.en in seine Schranken zurückweisen;* servants must know their ∾ *Diener müssen wissen, wohin sie gehören;* to put oneself in a person's ∾ *sich in j.es Lage versetzen;* to take ∾ *stattfinden;* Mr. B is taking Mr. A's ∾ this afternoon *Herr B kommt an Stelle von Herrn A heute nachmittag.* — **II.** v.tr.: to ∾ confidence in a friend *Vertrauen auf einen Freund setzen;* he ∾d a contract with the firm *er schloß ein Geschäft mit der Firma ab;* I know his face but I can't ∾ him *sein Gesicht kommt mir bekannt vor, aber ich weiß nicht, wo ich ihn unterbringen soll;* I have ∾d an order for wood *ich habe Holz bestellt;* he wants to ∾ his son in the firm *er will seinen Sohn bei der Firma unterbringen*

plain I. a.: as ∾ as a pikestaff, see 'pikestaff'; it is ∾ *es ist klar, selbstverständlich;* a ∾ cloth *ein ungemusterter Stoff;* in ∾ clothes *in Zivil;* ∾ food *einfache, nicht fette, gewürzte Kost;* I am a ∾ man *ich bin ein schlichter Mann;* a pity the girl is so ∾ *schade, daß das Mädchen so unansehnlich ist;* to be ∾ with a person *j.em die Wahrheit sagen;* say it in ∾ words *sag' es in einfachen, klaren Worten;* when we have done that it will all be ∾-sailing (correctly: plane sailing — nautical) *wenn wir das hinter uns haben, wird die ganze Sache einfach sein, glatt vonstattengehen.* — **II.** adv.: ∾-spoken *offen, ehrlich*

plan n.: that would be a good ∾ *das wäre ein guter Gedanke;* to hit (to strike) upon a ∾ *auf einen Plan verfallen*

plank I. n.: the pirates made them walk the ∾ *die Seeräuber ließen sie über die Schiffsplanke gehen, sie ertränkten sie;* that is a new ∾ in the platform *das ist ein neuer Punkt im Parteiprogramm.* — **II.** v.tr.: I had to ∾ down five pounds (sl.) *ich mußte auf der Stelle fünf Pfund berappen (blechen, herausrücken)*

plant I. n.: the ∾ of a factory *die Maschinen einer Fabrik;* that is a regular ∾ *das ist ein grober Schwindel;* to be in ∾ *im Wachstum stehen;* to lose ∾ *absterben;* to miss ∾ *(von Samen) nicht aufgehen.* — **II.** v.tr.: to ∾ a blow *einen Schlag führen;* to ∾ a colony *eine Kolonie gründen;* to ∾ an idea in a person's mind *j.em einen Gedanken eingeben;* to ∾ oneself *sich hinpflanzen (hinstellen);* to ∾ a fraudulent scheme (sl.) *einen betrügerischen Plan aushecken;* there I was, fairly ∾ed *ich stand nun vollkommen verlassen da*

plate n.: to have too much on one's ∾ *zu viel zu tun haben, überbeansprucht sein*

play I. v.tr.: see 'devil, duck, fool, foul, joke, part, etc.'; they won't ∾ ball (colloq.) *sie wollen nicht mitmachen (mitwirken);* to ∾ one's cards well *alle Möglichkeiten geschickt ausnützen;* to ∾ the game *sich an die Spielregeln, an den allgemeinen Ehrenkodex halten;* to ∾ a good knife and fork *beim Essen tüchtig einhauen;* to ∾ one off against another *einen gegen den anderen ausspielen;* our horses were ∾ed out *unsere Pferde waren völlig erschöpft;* he decided to ∾ possum *er entschloß sich zu drücken, sich verborgen zu halten.* — **II.** v.i.: see 'booty, fast, gallery, square, truant'; to ∾ it on (low on, low down on) a person *j.en in gemeiner Weise übertölpeln;* to ∾ up to a person *j.en unterstützen, ihm schmeicheln;* to ∾ upon a person's credulity *j.es Leichtgläubigkeit ausnutzen.* — **III.** n.: a ∾ on words *ein Wortspiel;* I said it only in ∾ *ich sagte es nur im Scherz;* to be as good as a ∾ *sehr unterhaltend, amüsant sein;* to bring (to call) a thing into ∾ *etwas in Gang (zur Wirkung) bringen, einsetzen;* to come into ∾ *in Gang (zur Wirkung) kommen;* to give full ∾ *freien Spielraum lassen;* to go to the ∾ *ins Theater gehen;* to hold (to keep) in ∾ *in Gang halten, beschäftigen, hinhalten*

plead I. v.i.: to ∾ guilty, not guilty *sich schuldig, nicht schuldig bekennen;* to ∾ for a person, in a person's favour *zu j.es Gunsten sprechen, ihn verteidigen;* to ∾ with a person for a thing *j.en flehentlich um etwas bitten.* — **II.** v.tr.: to ∾ a cause *eine Sache zum Beweise heranziehen, geltendmachen;* to ∾ a person's cause *j.es Sache* *vertreten;* to ∾ ignorance *sich mit Unwissenheit entschuldigen*

please v.tr.: if you ∾! bitte!; and now, if you ∾, he expects me to pay for it *und jetzt, bitte, erwartet er, daß ich es bezahle;* ring the bell, ∾ *bitte klingeln!;* take as many as you ∾ *nimm soviel du willst!;* ∾ God! *so Gott will!;* ∾ the pigs, see 'pig'; his last book will ∾ you *sein letztes Buch wird dir gefallen;* ∾ yourself *mach, wie du willst!;* he was as ∾d as Punch *er freute sich wie ein Schneekönig*

pleasure n.: a man of ∾ *ein Lebemann;* during His Majesty's ∾ *(bei einer Strafe) auf Lebenszeit;* it can be altered at ∾ *es kann nach Gutdünken (Belieben) abgeändert werden;* I shall not consult his ∾ *ich werde seine Wünsche nicht berücksichtigen;* he takes (a) ∾ in contradicting *er findet Vergnügen daran zu widersprechen*

pledge I. n.: in ∾ of good faith *als Pfand dafür (zum Zeichen), daß es ehrlich gemeint ist;* under the ∾ of secrecy *unter dem Siegel der Verschwiegenheit;* to put a thing in ∾ *etwas verpfänden, versetzen;* to take (to sign) the ∾ *sich verpflichten, dem Alkohol zu entsagen, dem Blauen Kreuz beitreten.* — **II.** v.tr.: to ∾ a person's health *auf j.es Wohl trinken, ihm zuprosten;* he ∾d himself to do so *er verpflichtete sich, es zu tun;* I have ∾d my watch *ich habe meine Uhr versetzt, ins Pfandhaus gebracht;* I ∾ my word of honour *ich gebe dir mein Ehrenwort*

plentiful a.: as ∾ as blackberries *so feil wie Brombeeren*

plenty I. n.: in ∾ *im Überfluß, reichlich;* the horn of ∾ *das Füllhorn;* we are in ∾ of time *wir haben reichlich Zeit;* to have ∾ of *reichlich versehen sein mit, in Hülle und Fülle haben.* — **II.** adv.: ∾ large enough *reichlich groß*

plight¹ v.tr.: to ∾ one's faith (troth) *sein Wort verpfänden;* they are ∾ed lovers *sie sind verlobt*

plight² n.: he is in a sorry (evil, hopeless) ∾ *er ist in einer traurigen (üblen, hoffnungslosen) Lage*

plod v.i.: to ∾ along *schwerfällig aber unverdrossen dahingehen;* to ∾ at *sich abplacken, abmühen, büffeln, ochsen*

plot n.: the ∾ thickens *die Handlung wird noch spannender*

plough I. n.: to put one's hand to the ∾ (Luke IX, 62) *Hand an den Pflug legen, eine Arbeit beginnen;* to be at the ∾-tail *Landarbeit verrichten.* — **II.** v.tr.: to ∾ a lonely furrow *arbeiten ohne Hilfe oder Unterstützung;* to ∾ the sand (sands) *den Sand pflügen, Vergebliches, Unnützes tun;* to ∾ one's way *sich einen Weg bahnen;* to ∾ with another's heifer *aus einer mit Unrecht erworbenen Auskunft Nutzen ziehen (Das Buch der Richter: „Wenn ihr nicht hättet mit meinem Kalbe gepflügt, ihr hättet mein Rätsel nicht getroffen");* he was ∾ed in the examination *er fiel in der Prüfung durch*

pluck v.tr.: I have a crow to ∾ with you *ich habe ein Hühnchen mit dir zu rupfen;* to ∾ a pigeon *einen Dummen rupfen;* he was ∾ed in his examination *er fiel in der Prüfung durch;* to ∾ up heart (spirits, courage) *sich (dat.) ein Herz fassen, Mut fassen*

plucky a.: *mutig, beherzt*

plug I. v.i.: to ∾ away at *sich abmühen, sich abrackern;* he is a ∾-ugly (U.S. sl.) *er ist ein Rowdy, übler Bursche.* — **II.** v.tr.: to ∾ someone (sl.) *j.en erschießen, mit der Faust schlagen;* to ∾ a song on the radio *ein Lied durch häufige Wiederholung im Radio bekannt machen*

plum n.: the ∾ of his collection *die Perle, das beste Stück seiner Sammlung*

plumb I. n.: out of ∾ *nicht lotrecht.* — **II.** a.: it is ∾ nonsense (U.S. sl.) *es ist der reinste Unsinn.* — **III.** adv.: he is ∾ crazy (U.S. sl.) *er ist total verrückt;* it points ∾ in the same direction *es zeigt genau in dieselbe Richtung*

plume I. n.: to adorn oneself with borrowed ∾s *sich mit fremden Federn schmükken.* — **II.** v.tr.: to ∾ oneself on a thing *sich mit etwas brüsten*

plump¹ a.: as ∾ as a partridge *so dick wie ein Mops*

plump² I. a.: my answer was a ∾ No *meine Antwort war ein glattes Nein.* — **II.** adv.: I told him ∾ *ich sagte es ihm rund heraus.* — **III.** v.i.: to ∾ down on one's seat *auf seinen Sitz hinplumpsen;* to ∾ for one candidate *einem (unter mehre-*

ren) Kandidaten seine Stimme geben. — **IV.** v.tr.: to ∾ a stone into water *einen Stein ins Wasser fallen (plumpsen) lassen*

plunge I. n.: to take the ∾ *den entscheidenden Schritt tun.* — **II.** v.tr.: to ∾ a nation into war *ein Volk in den Krieg stürzen.* — **III.** v.i.: to ∾ into difficulties *sich in Schwierigkeiten stürzen*

plus a.: to wear ∾-fours *sehr weite Kniehosen (Golfhosen) tragen*

ply[1] **I.** n.: to take a ∾ *eine Richtung annehmen;* ∾-wood *Sperrholz;* three-∾ wool *dreifädige Wolle*

ply[2] **I.** v.tr.: to ∾ one's business *sein Geschäft betreiben;* to ∾ one's oars *aus (mit) allen Kräften rudern;* to ∾ a minister with questions *einem Minister mit Anfragen zusetzen;* to ∾ someone with wine *j.em Wein aufdrängen, wiederholt anbieten.* — **II.** v.i.: the bus plies between London and Windsor (from London to Windsor) *der Autobus verkehrt regelmäßig zwischen London und Windsor (von London nach Windsor)*

poach I. v.i.: to ∾ on a person's preserves *j.em ins Gehege kommen, ins Handwerk pfuschen.* — **II.** v.tr.: ∾ed eggs *verlorene Eier*

pocket I. n.: a ∾ of resistance *ein Widerstandsnest;* I am five pounds in ∾ (out of ∾) by the transaction *an dem Geschäft habe ich fünf Pfund verdient (verloren);* out-of-∾ expenses *Auslagen, Spesen;* she has him in her ∾ *sie hat ihn völlig in ihrer Gewalt;* you must be prepared to put your hand in your ∾ *du mußt dich darauf gefaßt machen, daß es dich etwas kosten wird;* to put one's pride in one's ∾ *seinen Stolz verleugnen, sich demütigen;* he will suffer in his ∾ *das wird ihn viel kosten.* — **II.** v.tr.: to ∾ an affront (insult) *eine Beleidigung einstecken*

point I. n.: a ∾ to ∾ race *ein Querfeldeinrennen;* the ∾ of no return *der Punkt auf einer Flugreise, nach dem eine Umkehr verboten ist, weil der Benzinvorrat nicht mehr reicht; auch bildlich;* a knotty ∾ *eine verwickelte (schwierige) Frage;* a moot ∾ *ein strittiger Punkt;* possession is nine ∾s of the law (prov.) *sei im Besitz, und du bist im Recht;* that is beside (or: not to) the ∾ *das ist abwegig, trifft die Sache nicht;* a case in ∾ *ein zutreffender Fall, ein Beispiel;* four ∾ six (4·6) *vier Komma sechs (4,6);* in ∾ of fact *in der Tat, tatsächlich;* that is just the ∾ *das ist es ja gerade;* from this ∾ of view (view-∾) *von diesem Gesichtspunkte (Standpunkte) aus;* up to a certain ∾ *bis zu einem gewissen Grade;* to be a ∾ of honour *Ehrensache sein;* to be at the ∾ of death *an der Schwelle des Todes stehen, in den letzten Zügen liegen;* there is no ∾ in doing so *es hat keinen Zweck, es zu tun;* to be on (upon) the ∾ of doing it *im Begriffe sein, es zu tun;* to be to the ∾ *Hand und Fuß haben;* to carry one's ∾ *mit seiner Meinung durchdringen, seine Sache durchsetzen;* to come to a ∾ *spitz zulaufen;* to come to the ∾ *zur Hauptsache kommen;* when it came to the ∾ he declined *im entscheidenden Moment lehnte er ab;* to dine on potatoes and ∾ *nichts als Kartoffeln essen;* to give ∾s to a person *j.em etwas vorgeben (Sport), ihm überlegen sein;* to go to the ∾ of saying *soweit gehen zu behaupten;* to keep to the ∾ *bei der Sache bleiben;* his remarks lack ∾ *seine Bemerkungen treffen nicht ins Schwarze;* he made an interesting ∾ *er machte eine interessante Feststellung, stellte eine interessante Behauptung auf;* to make a ∾ of *auf etwas bestehen (dringen); sich (dat.) etwas zur Aufgabe machen; es sich (dat.) angelegen sein lassen;* not to put too fine a ∾ upon it *rund heraus, ungeschminkt reden;* put me in ∾ *(Ausruf eines Versteigerers:) was wird jetzt geboten?;* to see the ∾ of a joke *die Pointe eines Witzes sehen;* singing is not his strong ∾ *Singen ist nicht seine starke Seite;* to speak on a ∾ of order *zur Tagesordnung (Geschäftsordnung) sprechen;* to stretch (to strain) a ∾ *es nicht so genau nehmen, ein Auge zudrücken;* a constable on ∾-duty *ein Verkehrsschutzmann.* — **II.** v.tr.: to ∾ a finger at a person *mit dem Finger auf j.en zeigen;* to ∾ a pencil *einen Bleistift spitzen;* to ∾ out a fact *auf eine Tatsache hinweisen.* — **III.** v.i.: the small hand ∾s to five *der kleine Zeiger weist auf fünf*

point-blank I. a.: at ∾ distance *auf Kernschußweite.* — **II.** adv.: I told him ∾ it would not do *ich sagte ihm rund heraus, daß das nicht ginge;* I refused it ∾ *ich lehnte es entschieden (rundweg) ab*

poison n.: one man's meat is another man's ∾ (prov.) *wat dem einen sin Uhl, is dem annern sin Nachtigall; des einen*

Tod ist des anderen Brot; they hate each other like ∾ *sie hassen sich bis auf (in) den Tod;* a ∾ pen *bösartige anonyme Briefe*

poke I. n.: to buy a pig in a ∾ *die Katze im Sack kaufen.* — **II.** v.tr.: to ∾ fun at a thing (at a person) *sich über etwas (j.en) lustig machen;* to ∾ a hole *ein Loch stoßen;* to ∾ a person in the ribs *j.em einen Rippenstoß geben;* don't ∾ your nose into my affairs *steck' deine Nase nicht in meine Angelegenheiten;* to ∾ up the fire *das Feuer schüren.* — **III.** v.i.: to ∾ about, to ∾ and pry *herumstöbern; neugierig sein*

poker[1] n.: as stiff as a ∾ *so steif wie ein Stock;* by the holy ∾! (facet.) *zum Teufel! Donnerwetter!*

poker[2] n.: a ∾-face *ein undurchdringliches Gesicht*

poky a.: a ∾ little room *ein enges, dumpfes, erbärmliches Zimmerchen*

pole n.: under bare ∾s *vor Topp und Takel, ohne Segel;* to be up the ∾ *in der Klemme sein;* ∾-jumping *Stabhochsprung*

policy[1] n.: honesty is the best ∾ (prov.) *ehrlich währt am längsten*

policy[2] n.: to take out a ∾ on one's life *eine Lebensversicherung abschließen*

polish v.tr.: to ∾ it off *schnell abfertigen; schnell aufessen;* I must ∾ up my English *ich muß meine englischen Kenntnisse auffrischen*

pooh-pooh v.tr.: he ∾ed the idea *er verwarf den Gedanken, tat ihn geringschätzig ab*

pool I. n.: he plays the (football) ∾s *er spielt im Toto.* — **II.** v.tr.: we'll ∾ expenses, resources *wir werden unser Geld zusammenlegen, unsere Kräfte vereinigen*

poor a.: that is a ∾ consolation *das ist ein schwacher Trost;* he made a ∾ dinner *er aß nur wenig zu Mittag;* it will be ∾ fun *es wird nur wenig Spaß geben;* a ∾ look-out *schlechte, trübe Aussichten;* ∾ Mr. N. *der selige (verstorbene) Herr N.;* the patient has passed a ∾ night *der Patient hat eine schlechte (unruhige) Nacht gehabt*

poorly pred.a.: he is looking very ∾ *er sieht sehr krank aus;* I think ∾ of him *ich halte nicht viel von ihm*

pop I. v.tr.: to ∾ at a bird *auf einen Vogel schießen;* to ∾ corn *Mais rösten, bis die Körner puffend platzen;* a ∾-gun *eine Knallpistole;* to ∾ a letter into a pillar-box *einen Brief einwerfen;* to ∾ the question (colloq.) *einen Heiratsantrag machen;* a ∾-shop (sl.) *ein Pfandhaus;* to ∾ a watch (sl.) *eine Uhr versetzen;* to ∾ out one's tongue *die Zunge herausstrecken.* — **II.** v.i.: to ∾ along *fortgehen;* to ∾ down *plötzlich herabkommen;* to ∾ forth *plötzlich erscheinen;* to ∾ in *hereinplatzen, -schneien; vorsprechen, einen kurzen Besuch (eine Stippvisite) machen;* to ∾ into bed *ins Bett springen;* to ∾ off (the hooks) (sl.) *verschwinden, sterben;* his eyes fairly ∾ped out of his head *er machte schöne Stielaugen;* to ∾ up *wieder erscheinen, wieder auftauchen.* — **III.** n.: a glass of ∾ (colloq.) *ein Glas Sekt;* my watch is in ∾ (sl.) *meine Uhr ist im Pfandhaus;* to have (to take) a ∾ at a thing *nach etwas schießen.* — **IV.** adv.: I heard it go ∾ *ich hörte es knallen*

poppycock n.: that's all ∾ (sl.) *das ist alles Unsinn (Quatsch, Mumpitz)*

pore v.i.: to ∾ on a question *über eine Frage nachdenken, brüten;* to ∾ over one's books *über seinen Büchern sitzen (hocken)*

porridge n.: keep your breath to cool your porridge *schone deine Lunge, behalte deine Meinung für dich*

possess v.tr.: to ∾ oneself of a thing *sich einer Sache bemächtigen;* to ∾ oneself (one's soul, mind) in patience *sich in Geduld fassen;* to be ∾ed of a thing *etwas besitzen;* to be ∾ed by (with) an idea *von einer Idee besessen sein*

possession n.: ∾ is nine points (nine-tenths) of the law (prov.) *sei im Besitz, und du bist im Recht;* he showed great self-∾ *er zeigte große Selbstbeherrschung (Fassung);* to take ∾ of a thing *von einer Sache Besitz ergreifen (etwas in Besitz nehmen)*

post[1] I. n.: as deaf as a ∾ *stocktaub;* between you and me and the bed ∾ *im Vertrauen, unter uns gesagt;* he was driven from pillar to ∾, see 'pillar'; the starting-∾, the winning-∾ *der Start, das Ziel;* to be beaten on the ∾ *kurz vor dem Ziel geschlagen werden;* to be left at the ∾

zurückbleiben. — **II.** v.tr.: to ∾ up a placard *ein Plakat anschlagen*

post² **I.** n.: to answer by return of ∾ *postwendend antworten;* the ∾mark *der Post-, Briefstempel.* — **II.** adv.: to ride ∾ *als Kurier, schnell reiten;* ∾-haste *eiligst.* — **III.** v.tr.: to ∾ a letter *einen Brief zur Post bringen;* I shall keep you ∾ed *ich halte dich auf dem laufenden;* to ∾ up the ledger *das Hauptbuch vervollständigen;* to ∾ up a person *j.en mit genauen Angaben versehen*

post³ **I.** n.: an advanced ∾ *ein vorgeschobener Posten;* last ∾ *(Hornsignal zum) Zapfenstreich;* a trading-∾ *eine Handelsstation;* to be at one's ∾ *auf seinem Posten sein.* — **II.** v.tr.: he has been ∾ed to X *er ist nach X versetzt worden*

pot **I.** n.: the ∾ calls the kettle black (prov.) *ein Esel schimpft den anderen Langohr;* he is a big ∾ (sl.) *er ist ein großes (hohes) Tier;* a watched ∾ never boils (prov.) *ein Topf, auf dessen Kochen man wartet, kocht nie; man soll Geduld haben, sich nicht aufregen;* to go to ∾ (sl.) *zugrunde gehen; flöten gehen, auf den Hund kommen;* go to ∾! *scher dich zum Teufel!;* to have a ∾ in the pate (sl.) *betrunken sein, einen in der Krone haben;* to make the ∾ boil, to keep the ∾ boiling *sich (dat.) den Lebensunterhalt verdienen; die Sache in Gang halten;* a ∾-boiler *eine Brotarbeit, ein Kunstwerk, das nur des Geldes wegen geschaffen wird; ein Künstler, der das tut;* to make a ∾ (∾s) of money *einen Haufen (eine Stange) Geld verdienen;* to put the ∾ on (racing sl.) *sehr hoch wetten;* to upset the ∾ (racing sl.) *den Favoriten schlagen;* a ∾-belly *ein Schmerbauch;* a ∾-hat *ein steifer Hut, eine Melone;* a ∾-hole *ein Schlagloch;* a ∾-house *eine Kneipe;* a ∾-hunter *ein Sportler, der nur auf Preise ausgeht;* to take ∾ luck with a person *mit dem vorliebnehmen, was es bei j.em zu essen gibt;* a ∾-shot *ein nur für den Tisch abgegebener Schuß; ein leichter Schuß aus nächster Nähe, ein Zufallstreffer;* he is ∾-valiant *er hat sich (dat.) Mut angetrunken.* — **II.** v.tr.: to ∾ meat etc. *Fleisch usw. in einem Topf einmachen (einwecken).* — **III.** v.i.: to ∾ at a bird *nach einem Vogel schießen*

potato n.: to dine on ∾es and point *nichts als Kartoffeln essen;* it is not quite the ∾ (sl.) *es ist wohl nicht das Richtige, es schickt sich nicht*

pother n.: he made a ∾ about it *er schlug deswegen Krach*

potty a. (sl.): ∾ examination questions *kinderleichte Prüfungsfragen;* a ∾ little state *ein unbedeutender kleiner Staat;* to be ∾ about a person *ganz vernarrt in j.en sein*

pounce **I.** n.: to be on the ∾ to do a thing *sprungbereit sein, etwas zu tun;* to make a ∾ upon a thing *über etwas herfallen.* — **II.** v.i.: to ∾ upon a blunder *sich auf einen Fehler stürzen*

pound¹ n.: penny wise and ∾ foolish *am unrechten Ende sparsam;* in for a penny, in for a ∾ (prov.) *wer A sagt, muß auch B sagen;* to claim one's ∾ of flesh (cf. Shylock) *sein volles Recht verlangen*

pound² **I.** v.tr.: to ∾ a thing into a jelly *etwas zu Mus stampfen.* — **II.** v.i.: to ∾ along *schwerfällig gehen (laufen);* the guns ∾ed away at the fort *die Geschütze bollerten auf die Festung los*

pour **I.** v.tr.: to ∾ cold water on a plan *von einem Vorhaben abraten, abschrecken;* to ∾ oil on troubled waters *Öl auf die Wogen gießen, die Gemüter beruhigen;* please ∾ me out a cup of tea *schenken Sie mir bitte eine Tasse Tee ein.* — **II.** v.i.: it never rains but it ∾s (prov.) *ein Unglück kommt selten allein;* it is ∾ing with rain *es regnet (gießt) in Strömen*

pout **I.** v.tr.: to ∾ the lips *die Lippen spitzen.* — **II.** n.: to be in the ∾s, to have the ∾s *in übler Laune sein, schmollen, maulen*

powder n.: food for ∾ *Kanonenfutter;* it's not worth ∾ and shot *es ist keinen Schuß Pulver wert;* to keep one's ∾ dry *sein Pulver trocken halten, auf alle Fälle vorbereitet sein;* put more ∾ into it *setz' mehr Kraft dahinter!;* to smell of ∾ *kampferfahren sein*

power n.: a ∾ of attorney *eine Vollmacht;* the ∾s that be *die Obrigkeit, die Machthaber;* merciful ∾s *barmherziger Gott!;* more ∾ to your elbow! *Glück zu!;* the third ∾ of 2 is 8 *die dritte Potenz von 2 ist 8;* I saw a ∾ of people *ich sah eine Menge Leute*

practical a.: to play a ∾ joke upon a person *j.em einen Schabernack spielen;* it is ∾ly certain *es ist so gut wie sicher;* it is ∾ly impossible *es ist nahezu unmöglich*

practice n.: ∾ makes perfect (prov.) *Übung macht den Meister;* sharp ∾ *unredliches Handeln;* that has been the ∾ for years *das ist seit Jahren Brauch;* he makes a ∾ of cheating *er hat die Gewohnheit zu betrügen;* to put a plan into ∾ *einen Plan ausführen*

practise I. v.tr.: to ∾ the same method *dieselbe Methode anwenden;* ∾ what you preach! *lebe deine Lehre vor! geh mit gutem Beispiel voran!* — **II.** v.i.: he is a practising doctor *er führt eine ärztliche Tätigkeit wirklich aus (er hat sich nicht zur Ruhe gesetzt, er hat nicht nur die Qualifikation als Arzt);* to ∾ (up)on a person's credulity *j.es Leichtgläubigkeit ausnutzen*

praise I. to be loud in one's ∾s *des Lobes voll sein;* to bestow ∾ upon a person *j.em Lob spenden;* to give ∾ to a person *j.en loben;* to sound (to sing) the ∾s of a person *j.es Lob singen.* — **II.** v.tr.: to ∾ a person to the skies *j.en in den Himmel heben, bis über den grünen Klee loben*

prank n.: to play a ∾ upon a person *j.em einen Streich spielen*

prayer n.: the Lord's ∾ *das Vaterunser;* morning (evening, family) ∾s *Morgen-, Abend-, Familienandacht;* to be at (to say one's, to give) ∾s *sein Gebet verrichten;* to put up a ∾ to God for *zu Gott beten um*

precarious a.: a ∾ living *eine unsichere Existenz;* the ∾ life of a fisherman *das gefährliche Leben eines Fischers*

precaution n.: as a ∾ *der Vorsicht halber;* to take ∾s against *Vorsichtsmaßregeln treffen gegen*

precedence n.: to give a person the ∾ *j.em den Vortritt lassen;* to take (the) ∾ of a person *den Vorrang vor j.em einnehmen;* to yield ∾ to a person *j.em den Vorrang einräumen*

precedent n.: there is no ∾ for this, it is without ∾ *es ist noch nie dagewesen, es ist beispiellos;* to serve as ∾ *als Präzedenzfall dienen*

precious I. a: a ∾ stone *ein Edelstein;* you have made a ∾ mess of it (colloq.) *du hast die Sache schön verkorkst;* it cost a ∾ sight more than you think (colloq.) *es hat bedeutend mehr gekostet, als du meinst.* — **II.** adv.: (colloq.) I took ∾ good care *ich nahm mich höllisch in Acht;* ∾ little of it *verflucht wenig davon*

prejudice n.: he has a ∾ against (in favour of) mathematicians *er hat ein Vorurteil gegen (eine Vorliebe für) Mathematiker;* to the ∾ of *zum Schaden von;* without ∾ to a thing *unbeschadet einer Sache*

premium n.: that will put a ∾ on fraud *das wird Anreiz zum Betrug geben;* gold is now at a ∾ *Gold steht jetzt über pari;* these goods are now at a ∾ *diese Waren sind jetzt sehr gesucht*

presence n.: a man of (a) noble ∾ *ein Mann von edler Gestalt;* ∾ of mind *Geistesgegenwart*

present[1] I. a.: in the ∾ case *im vorliegenden Falle;* the ∾ volume *der vorliegende Band;* the ∾ writer *der Schreiber dieses;* no one else was ∾ at the proceedings *es war sonst keiner bei den Verhandlungen zugegen;* to be ∾ to the mind (imagination) of a person *j.em gegenwärtig (lebendig) sein;* all ∾ *alle Anwesenden.* — **II.** n.: I don't want any more at ∾ *ich brauche im Augenblick keine mehr;* he is at ∾ in Egypt *er ist gegenwärtig in Ägypten;* that will do for the ∾ *das genügt für jetzt, vorläufig, einstweilen*

present[2] n.: to make a person a ∾, a ∾ to a person *j.em etwas schenken;* to make a person a ∾ of a thing, to make a ∾ of a thing to a person *j.em etwas zum Geschenk machen*

present[3] v.tr.: to ∾ a ragged appearance *ein zerlumptes Aussehen darbieten;* to ∾ a clergyman to a living *einen Geistlichen zu einer Pfründe vorschlagen;* to ∾ one's compliments (respects) to a person *sich j.em empfehlen;* the case ∾s some difficulties *der Fall weist einige Schwierigkeiten auf;* to ∾ a person to another *j.en einem anderen vorstellen;* to ∾ a revolver at a person *einen Revolver gegen j.en richten;* to ∾ a thing to a person, a person with a thing *j.em etwas schenken;* to ∾ a thing in its proper light *etwas ins rechte Licht setzen (rücken)*

presently adv.: I shall do that ∾ *ich werde es gleich (bald) tun;* ∾, he began to move *bald darauf fing er an, sich zu bewegen*

press I. n.: in the ∾ of business *im Drange der Geschäfte;* under a ∾ of sail (canvas) *mit vollen Segeln;* the book is in the ∾ *das Buch ist im Druck;* to correct the ∾ *Korrektur lesen;* to send to (the) ∾ *in Druck geben.* — **II.** v.tr.: to ∾ the button *auf den Knopf drücken; den entscheidenden ersten Schritt tun;* to ∾ one's suit *seinen Antrag, seine Werbung nachdrücklich betreiben;* I am ∾ed for time *ich bin mit der Zeit im Druck.* — **III.** v.i.: time ∾es *die Zeit drängt;* to ∾ for an answer *auf eine Antwort drängen;* to ∾ on (forward) *vorwärtsdrängen, -eilen*

pressing a.: a ∾ invitation *eine dringende, herzliche Einladung;* a ∾ need *eine dringende Notwendigkeit*

pressure n.: to bring ∾ to bear on someone *auf j.en Druck ausüben;* to work under ∾, at high ∾ *unter Druck, mit Hochdruck arbeiten;* ∾ group *eine Gruppe, die in der Lage ist, zu ihrem besonderen Zweck Druck auf die Regierung usw. auszuüben*

presume I. v.tr.: I ∾ that he will come *ich nehme an, daß er kommt;* it is ∾d that you can speak French *man setzt voraus, daß Sie Französisch sprechen;* do not ∾ to invite him *erdreisten Sie sich nicht, ihn einzuladen!* — **II.** v.i.: may I ∾ upon a short acquaintance? *darf ich auf eine kurze Bekanntschaft pochen?;* to ∾ upon her generosity *ihre Freigebigkeit mißbrauchen;* a presuming person *eine anmaßende, vermessene Person*

pretence n.: devoid of all ∾ *ohne jede Schaustellung, ohne jedes Getue;* under false ∾s *unter Vorspiegelung falscher Tatsachen;* under the ∾ of *unter dem Vorwand (Schein, der Maske) von;* to make ∾ to a thing *auf etwas Anspruch erheben;* to make no ∾ at being *sich nicht den Anschein geben zu sein*

pretend I. v.tr.: to ∾ illness (to ∾ to be ill) *Krankheit vortäuschen; vorgeben, krank zu sein;* he does not ∾ to be a scholar *er gibt nicht vor, Gelehrter zu sein;* we are ∾ing to be (that we are) Red Indians *wir spielen Indianer.* — **II.** v.i.: I do not ∾ to piety *ich bilde mir nicht ein, fromm zu sein;* to ∾ to a person *um j.es Hand anhalten;* to ∾ to a title *Anspruch auf einen Titel erheben*

pretension n.: what ∾! *welche Anmaßung!;* he has no ∾s to the name *er hat keinen berechtigten Anspruch auf den Namen;* to have great (no) ∾s *anspruchsvoll, -los sein*

pretty I. a.: a ∾ kettle of fish (a ∾ pickle)! *eine nette Bescherung, eine schöne Geschichte!;* he has earned a ∾ sum *er hat eine schöne (beträchtliche) Summe verdient.* — **II.** adv.: I find it ∾ difficult *ich finde es ziemlich schwierig;* that is ∾ much the same thing *das ist so ungefähr dasselbe*

prevail v.i.: to ∾ against (or: over) *die Oberhand gewinnen über, erfolgreich sein;* I could not ∾ on myself to do so *ich konnte es nicht übers Herz bringen, es zu tun;* to ∾ (up)on a person to do it *j.en bewegen, es zu tun*

previous I. a.: you have been a little too ∾ *du bist etwas voreilig gewesen.* — **II.** adv.: ∾ to that time *vor jener Zeit*

price I. n.: ∾ is no object *der Preis spielt keine Rolle;* above (beyond, without) ∾ *unschätzbar;* how about the ∾? *wie steht's mit dem Preis?;* that must be done at any ∾ *das muß um jeden Preis getan werden;* what ∾ the Concert of Europe? *was hältst du jetzt von dem vielgepriesenen Europäischen Konzert?* — **II.** v.tr.: to ∾ oneself out of the market *unerschwingliche Preise nehmen*

pricey a.: *teuer*

prick I. n.: ∾s of conscience *Gewissensbisse;* to kick against the ∾s (Acts, IX, 5) *wider den Stachel löcken (lecken).* — **II.** v.tr.: to ∾ a (the) bladder (bubble) *eine Seifenblase zum Platzen bringen; die innere Hohlheit eines Menschen oder einer Sache aufdecken;* my conscience ∾ed me *das Gewissen schlug mir.* — **III.** v.i.: to ∾ up one's ears *die Ohren spitzen*

pride I. n.: ∾ will have (∾ goes before) a fall (prov.) *Hochmut kommt vor dem Fall;* in ∾ of grease *fett, schlachtreif;* ∾ of the morning *Frühnebel oder Regenschauer bei Sonnenaufgang;* a peacock in his ∾ (herald.) *ein Pfau, der ein Rad schlägt;* to share ∾ of place *denselben Rang einnehmen;* to take a ∾ in a thing, to make a thing one's ∾ *stolz auf etwas* *sein, seinen Stolz in etwas setzen.* — **II.** v.refl.: to ∾ oneself (up)on a thing *auf etwas stolz sein, sich mit etwas brüsten*

prime n.: in the ∾ of life, manhood *in der Blüte der Jahre, im besten Mannesalter;* he is past his ∾ *er ist überaltert, seine schönsten Jahre sind vorbei*

primrose n.: to tread the ∾ path of dalliance (Hamlet, I, 3, 50) *den Blumenpfad der Lust betreten* (Schlegel)

prince n.: Hamlet without the ∾ of Denmark *eine leere Hülle, eine taube Nuß*

principle n.: to be a man of high ∾ *ein Mann von erhabenen Grundsätzen sein;* I refuse on ∾ *ich weigere mich grundsätzlich;* it is the same in ∾ *im Grunde (im Prinzip) ist es dasselbe*

print n.: the book is out of ∾ *das Buch ist vergriffen*

private I. a.: a ∾ soldier *ein gemeiner Soldat;* this is for your ∾ ear *das ist vertraulich.* — **II.** n.: may I speak to you in ∾? *darf ich Sie unter vier Augen sprechen?*

privy I. a.: ∾ parts *Schamteile;* Lord Privy Seal *Geheimsiegelbewahrer;* he was ∾ to the secret *er wußte um das Geheimnis.* — **II.** n.: I must go to the ∾ *ich muß mal austreten, zur Toilette gehen*

pro & con n.: the pros & cons *das Für und Wider*

proceed v.i.: the case will now ∾ *der Fall nimmt nun seinen Fortgang;* "in each case", he ∾ed, "our course is clear." *„in jedem Fall", fuhr er fort, „ist es klar, wie wir handeln müssen.";* to ∾ against a person *gerichtlich gegen j.en vorgehen;* sobs were heard to ∾ from the next room *man hörte Schluchzen aus dem Nebenzimmer dringen;* to ∾ to another subject *auf ein anderes Thema übergehen;* to ∾ to business *an die Arbeit gehen, anfangen;* he ∾ed to do so *er machte sich daran, es zu tun;* to ∾ to the degree of M.A. *den Magistergrad erwerben;* to ∾ with an investigation *eine Untersuchung fortsetzen*

proceeding n.: it was a high-handed ∾ *es war ein willkürliches (gewaltsames) Verfahren;* to institute (to take) legal ∾s *gerichtliche Schritte unternehmen*

proceeds n.pl.: the ∾ will be devoted to charity *der Ertrag fließt der Wohltätigkeit zu*

prodigy n.: an infant ∾ *ein Wunderkind;* Samuel Hahnemann was called a ∾ of learning *S. H. wurde ein Wunder der Gelehrsamkeit genannt*

profess I. v.tr.: they ∾ extreme regret *sie geben vor, es tief zu bedauern;* they ∾ themselves quite content *sie erklären, sie seien sehr zufrieden.* — **II.** v.i.: he does not ∾ to be a scholar *er beansprucht nicht, ein Gelehrter zu sein;* I ∾ (that) this is news to me *ich gestehe, das ist mir neu*

professed a.: he is a ∾ woman-hater *er ist ein erklärter Weiberfeind*

profession n.: in practice if not in ∾ *praktisch, effektiv, wenn auch nicht eingestandenermaßen;* accept my sincere ∾s of condolence *seien Sie meines aufrichtigen Beileids versichert;* spare me further ∾s *ersparen Sie mir weitere Erklärungen;* he is a carpenter by ∾ *er ist von Beruf Zimmermann*

professional I. a.: the ∾ man *der Geistes-, Kopfarbeiter;* a ∾ player *ein Berufsspieler.* — **II.** n.: he is a ∾ (abbr. pro) *er ist Berufsspieler*

progress n.: to make slow ∾ *langsame Fortschritte machen;* an inquiry is in ∾ *eine Untersuchung ist im Gange*

proof I. n.: ∾ on ∾ of *immer neue Beweise für;* alcohol above ∾ *Alkohol von über Normalstärke (ca. 50%);* ∾ against temptation *gefeit gegen die Versuchung;* the ∾ of the pudding is in the eating (prov.) *Probieren geht über Studieren;* in ∾ of my assertion *zum Beweise meiner Behauptung;* it must be brought (put) to the ∾ *es muß bewiesen werden;* to challenge a ∾ *es auf den Beweis ankommen lassen;* ∾-reading *Korrekturlesen.* — **II.** a.: bomb-∾, shell-∾, bullet-∾, shot-∾ *bombensicher, kugelfest, schußsicher;* sound-∾, water-∾ *schalldicht, wasserdicht;* weather-∾ *wetterfest*

proper a.: a ∾ noun (name) *ein Eigenname;* there will be a ∾ row about it *es wird einen gehörigen Krach deswegen geben;* in the ∾ sense of the word *im eigentlichen Sinne des Wortes;* within the sphere of architecture ∾ *im Bereiche der eigentlichen Architektur;* she is so distressingly ∾ *sie sieht so peinlich auf gesellschaftliche Formen;* would it be quite ∾ to say so? *wäre es schicklich, das zu sagen?;* to choose the ∾ time *die passende Zeit wählen;* to do the ∾ thing *tun, was sich schickt;* to do a thing the ∾ way *etwas in der richtigen Weise tun;* to think ∾ *für gut halten*

properly adv.: ∾ speaking, he is not qualified for the job *richtig (streng) genommen ist er nicht für den Posten geeignet;* he very ∾ refused *er weigerte sich mit Recht;* to behave ∾ *sich anständig benehmen (betragen);* do it ∾ or not at all *mach' es ordentlich oder gar nicht;* it puzzled him ∾ *es verwirrte ihn ordentlich*

prophet n.: a ∾ has little honour in his own country (prov.) *ein Prophet gilt nichts in seinem Vaterlande*

proportion I. n.: a large ∾ of the profits *ein großer Teil des Gewinns;* his success bore no ∾ to his abilities *sein Erfolg stand in keinem Verhältnis zu seinen Fähigkeiten;* the costs were out of all ∾ to the work done *die Kosten waren unverhältnismäßig hoch für die geleistete Arbeit.* — **II.** v.tr.: we must ∾ the punishment to the crime *wir müssen die Strafe dem Verbrechen anpassen*

proposal n.: she has had a ∾ *sie hat einen Heiratsantrag erhalten*

propose I. v.tr.: we ∾ a change (that a change should be made) *wir schlagen eine Änderung vor;* the object that I ∾ to myself *das Ziel, das ich mir vornehme;* to ∾ a toast *einen Trinkspruch ausbringen.* — **II.** v.i.: man ∾s, God disposes (prov.) *der Mensch denkt, Gott lenkt;* I ∾ to do (doing) it *ich habe vor, es zu tun;* he ∾d to her *er machte ihr einen Heiratsantrag*

propriety n.: I doubt the ∾ of the term *ich zweifle an der Richtigkeit des Ausdrucks;* a breach of ∾ *ein Verstoß gegen den Anstand;* we must observe the proprieties *wir müssen den Anstand wahren*

prosecute v.tr.: to ∾ one's studies *sein Studium fortsetzen;* to ∾ a trade *einem Gewerbe nachgehen;* trespassers will be ∾d *unbefugtes Betreten bei Strafe verboten!*

prosecutor n.: the public ∾ *der Staatsanwalt*

prospect n.: a fine ∾ *eine schöne Aussicht;* I have nothing in ∾ at present *ich habe augenblicklich nichts in Aussicht;* to hold out the ∾ of a reward to someone *j.em eine Belohnung in Aussicht stellen*

proud I. a.: as ∾ as a peacock *(so) stolz wie ein Spanier;* I am ∾ of his acquaintance, of knowing him, to know him *ich bin stolz auf seine Bekanntschaft, stolz darauf, ihn zu kennen;* ∾ flesh *wildes Fleisch.* — **II.** adv.: you do me ∾ *du tust mir eine große Ehre an*

prove I. v.tr.: to ∾ one's case *seine Behauptung beweisen;* to ∾ the truth of a thing, a thing to be true, that a thing is true *die Wahrheit einer Sache beweisen.* — **II.** v.i.: he ∾d (to be) the heir *er erwies sich als Erbe;* he ∾d to know nothing about it *es erwies sich (stellte sich heraus), daß er nichts davon wußte*

provide I. v.i.: the law ∾s that *das Gesetz sieht vor, daß;* to ∾ against an attack *sich rüsten (wappnen, Vorsorge, Anstalten treffen) gegen einen Angriff;* to ∾ for entertainment *für Unterhaltung sorgen.* — **II.** v.tr.: to ∾ a person with a thing, a thing for (to) a person *j.en mit etwas versehen;* I shall ∾ the provisions *ich werde die Lebensmittel stellen;* providing (that), ∾d (that) all is safe *vorausgesetzt, daß alles sicher ist*

province n.: that is not within my ∾ *das ist nicht meines Amtes, das schlägt nicht in mein Fach*

pub n. (colloq.): to go to a ∾ *in eine Kneipe gehen;* to go on a ∾-crawl *eine Bierreise machen*

public a.: a ∾ house *eine Gastwirtschaft;* a ∾ school *eine dotierte höhere Schule mit Alumnat;* a ∾ relations department *Propaganda-, Informations-Abteilung*

pucker v.tr.: to ∾ (up) one's brow *die Stirn(e) runzeln*

pudding n.: the proof of the ∾ is in the eating (prov.) *Probieren geht über Studieren;* to get more praise than ∾ *mit bloßen Worten abgespeist werden*

puff I. v.i.: to ∾ and blow *keuchen, schnaufen;* he ∾ed away at his cigar *er paffte an seiner Zigarre.* — **II.** v.tr.: to be ∾ed with pride *vor Stolz aufgeblasen sein;* he was rather ∾ed *er war ziemlich außer Atem;* he could only ∾ out a few words *er konnte nur ein paar Worte hervorkeuchen;* to ∾ up goods *Waren marktschreierisch anpreisen; die Preise von Waren in die Höhe treiben*

pull I. v.tr.: see 'devil, face, leg, etc.'; to ∾ a person's sleeve, a person by the sleeve *j.en am Ärmel zupfen;* to ∾ a thing out of the fire *die Karre aus dem Dreck ziehen;* he looks ∾ed down *er sieht angegriffen aus;* to ∾ off the prize *den Preis gewinnen, davontragen;* to ∾ oneself together *sich zusammennehmen, -reißen;* to ∾ up a person *j.em Vorwürfe machen, j.en ins Gebet nehmen, zurechtweisen;* to ∾ up short *plötzlich (jäh) anhalten, zum Halten bringen.* — **II.** v.i.: the train ∾ed out of the station *der Zug fuhr aus dem Bahnhof heraus;* to ∾ round *sich wieder erholen;* to ∾ through an illness *eine Krankheit überstehen;* to ∾ together *einträchtig zusammenarbeiten, an demselben Strang (am gleichen Seil) ziehen;* the carriage ∾ed up at the gate *der Wagen machte an dem Tore halt.* — **III.** n.: a good ∾-up for lorry drivers *eine Fernfahrer-Raststätte;* that will be an heavy ∾ upon his purse *das wird ihn viel kosten;* to get the job you will need some ∾ *um die Stelle zu bekommen, wirst du Beziehungen (Fürsprache, Protektion) nötig haben;* to give a strong (hearty) ∾ *kräftig ziehen;* to have (to take) a ∾ at the bottle *einen Zug (Schluck) aus der Flasche nehmen;* to have the ∾ of a person *j.em etwas voraushaben, einen Vorteil vor j.em haben*

pulse n.: to feel a person's ∾ *j.em den Puls fühlen, ihn prüfend ausfragen, ihm auf den Zahn fühlen, bei ihm auf den Busch klopfen;* to stir one's ∾s *in Erregung versetzen;* to have one's finger on the ∾ of the nation *die öffentliche Meinung richtig einschätzen*

pump I. n.: a parish-∾ politician *ein Kirchturmpolitiker.* — **II.** v.tr.: to ∾ (information out of) a person *j.en gehörig ausfragen, ihm auf den Zahn fühlen, bei ihm auf den Busch klopfen;* he was completely ∾ed *er war völlig außer Atem*

pump-handle v.tr.: to ∾ a person *j.em kräftig die Hand schütteln*

Punch n.pr.: he was as pleased as ∾ *er freute sich wie ein Schneekönig*

punch I. v.tr.: I ∾ed his head *ich schlug ihm eins gegen den Kopf;* to ∾ a hole in a thing *ein Loch in etwas schlagen;* he ∾ed my ticket *er knipste meine Fahrkarte.* — **II.** n.: there is no ∾ in it *dahinter steckt keine Kraft;* I gave him a ∾ on the head *ich schlug ihm eins gegen den Kopf*

punch-drunk a.: to be ∾ from a blow *von einem Schlag benommen sein;* he was still ∾ with excitement *er war vor Aufregung noch ganz benommen*

pup n.: he is a conceited ∾ *er ist ein eingebildeter Laffe;* the bitch is in ∾ *die Hündin ist trächtig;* to have ∾s (sl.) *böse, aufgeregt, ärgerlich sein; vgl. es ist zum Jungehunde kriegen;* to sell a person a ∾ *j.en beschwindeln, über den Löffel barbieren (balbieren)*

purchase n.: his life is not worth an hour's ∾ *er lebt keine Stunde mehr*

pure a.: it was a mistake ∾ and simple *es war schlechthin ein Versehen*

purler n.: to come a ∾ *zu Fall kommen, einen schweren Sturz tun*

purple I. a.: the ∾ patches of a book *die Glanzstellen eines Buches;* to be ∾ with rage *rot vor Wut sein.* — **II.** n.: to be born in ∾ *als Prinz geboren werden;* to be raised to the ∾ *Kardinal werden*

purpose n.: infirm of ∾ *unentschlossen;* on ∾, of set ∾ *absichtlich, vorsätzlich, mit Fleiß;* to no ∾ *zwecklos, umsonst;* to be (to talk) at cross ∾s, see 'cross'; to small (little) ∾ *mit geringem Erfolg;* to all intents and ∾s, for all practical ∾s *praktisch genommen, im Grunde, in jeder Hinsicht;* this is nothing to the ∾ *das gehört nicht zur Sache, hat mit der Sache nichts zu tun;* what is the ∾ of this law? *was bezweckt dieses Gesetz?;* a novel with a ∾, a ∾-novel *ein Tendenzroman;* he is wanting in ∾ *er ist nicht zielbewußt;* this nail will serve (answer) the ∾ *dieser Nagel tut's, paßt;* to turn a thing to good ∾ *eine Sache nutzbringend anwenden*

purse I. n.: you cannot make a silk ∾ out of a sow's ear (prov.) *etwa: Bauer bleibt Bauer;* to hold the ∾-strings *über den Geldbeutel verfügen;* to make up a ∾ *Geld sammeln;* to tighten the ∾-strings *den Daumen auf dem (den) Beutel halten;* to be ∾-proud *geldstolz, protzig sein.* — **II.** v.tr.: to ∾ (up) one's brow *die Stirn(e) runzeln;* to ∾ (up) one's lips *den Mund spitzen*

push I. v.tr.: to ∾ a person for payment *j.en zur Zahlung drängen;* to ∾ a thing too far *etwas zu weit treiben;* to be ∾ed for time *nur wenig Zeit haben;* to ∾ up the daisies (sl.) *auf dem Friedhof liegen;* to ∾ up production (colloq.) *die Produktion erhöhen.* — **II.** v.i.: I must ∾ on *ich muß weitergehen;* I must ∾ off (colloq.) *ich muß abhauen.* — **III.** n.: when it comes to the ∾ *im entscheidenden Augenblick, wenn Not am Mann ist;* he has plenty of ∾ *er hat viel Ehrgeiz, Energie;* I could do it at a ∾ *ich könnte es im Notfall tun;* to give (to get) the ∾ (sl.) *den Laufpaß geben, bekommen;* to make a ∾ for home *sich auf den Heimweg machen;* to make a ∾ to get a thing done *sich anstrengen, um etwas zu erreichen;* a ∾-bike (sl.) *ein Fahrrad*

put I. v.tr.: to ∾ the cart before the horse *das Pferd beim Schwanze aufzäumen, eine Sache verkehrt anfangen;* to ∾ the case *den Fall unterbreiten;* ∾ the case it is so *gesetzt den Fall, es wäre so;* to ∾ one's finger on someone (on the trouble) *j.en (die Ursache eines Übels) identifizieren;* to ∾ a question *eine Frage stellen, richten;* to ∾ the stone (or: weight) *Steinstoßen (Leichtathletik);* what a way you have of ∾ting things *du drückst dich aber merkwürdig aus;* to ∾ paid to a thing *etwas als erledigt betrachten, den Schlußstrich unter etwas ziehen.* — with prep.: to ∾ a person at ease *j.em die Schüchternheit, die innere Unruhe nehmen;* to ∾ a horse at (to) a fence *ein Pferd über einen Zaun setzen lassen;* I should ∾ it at 2/6s *ich würde den Preis auf zweieinhalb Schilling setzen;* to ∾ the circulation at 60 000 *die Auflage auf 60 000 schätzen;* to ∾ in, see 'foot, mind, spoke, way'; to ∾ someone inside (colloq.) *j.en verhaften;* to ∾ it into Dutch *es ins Holländische übersetzen;* to ∾ a thing into a person's head *j.em etwas in den Kopf (einen Floh ins Ohr) setzen;* to ∾ a knife into a person *j.en erstechen;* to ∾ oneself (a matter) into a person's hands *sich (eine Sache) j.em anvertrauen;* the land was ∾ into turnips *das Land war mit Rüben bestellt;* to ∾ into words *in Worte fassen (kleiden);* to ∾ on, see 'blame, face, guard, lid, mettle, oath'; I ∾ my decision on the grounds stated *meine Entscheidung stützt sich auf die vorgebrachten Gründe;* who ∾ him on this wild scheme? *wer hat ihn auf den ungeheuerlichen Plan gebracht?;* to ∾ out of, see 'countenance, court, head, nose'; I ∾ nothing past her *ich traue ihr alles zu, ihr ist alles zuzutrauen;* to ∾ a person through his paces, see 'pace'; to ∾ a bullet through a person *j.em eine Kugel durch den Leib jagen;* to ∾ to, see 'blush, death, expense, flight, inconvenience, sale etc.'; surprising what he can do when he is ∾ to it *erstaunlich, was er leistet, wenn man ihm zusetzt, wenn er im Druck ist;* I was hard ∾ to it *es fiel mir schwer (es wurde mir sauer), sie fernzuhalten;* it is time he was ∾ to school *es ist Zeit, daß er in die Schule kommt;* I ∾ it to you that you were after no good *Sie müssen doch zugeben, daß Sie nichts Gutes im Sinne hatten;* to ∾ the wind up a person (sl.) *j.em Angst (Schrecken) einjagen;* I will ∾ the work in hand *ich werde die Arbeit in Angriff nehmen lassen.* — with adv.: see 'about, across, aside, away, back, behind, by'; to ∾ down to a person's account *j.es Konto belasten, auf j.es Rechnung setzen;* to ∾ one's foot down *energisch auftreten, fest bei einer Absage bleiben; einen festen Standpunkt einnehmen;* to ∾ one's best foot foremost, see 'best'; to ∾ one's name down on a list *sich in eine(r) Liste eintragen;* to ∾ a person down for (as) a fool *j.en für einen Narren halten;* to ∾ a person down for a thing *j.en für etwas vormerken;* to ∾ it down to his nervousness *es seiner Nervosität zuschreiben;* to ∾ the clock fast *die Uhr vorstellen;* to ∾ forward a claim for a thing *auf etwas Anspruch erheben;* to ∾ in, see 'appearance, care, claim, oar, word'; to ∾ in some time at a task *einige Zeit für eine Aufgabe aufwenden;* to ∾ it mildly, it is unpleasant *gelinde gesagt, ist es unangenehm;* to ∾ a person off from doing a thing *j.en davon abbringen, etwas zu tun;* to ∾ off an engagement *eine Verabredung verschieben;* to ∾ off a person with an excuse *j.en mit einer Ausrede abspeisen;* to ∾ a thing off with a jest *etwas mit einem Scherz abtun;* to ∾ off a thing upon a person *j.en mit etwas betrügen, anführen;* to ∾ on the clock *die Uhr vorstellen;* to ∾ on one's clothes *sich anziehen;* to ∾ on dog *wichtig tun, angeben;* to ∾ on flesh, weight *an Körperfülle, Gewicht zunehmen;* to ∾ on a special train *einen Sonderzug einlegen;* to ∾ it on *es übertreiben, angeben;* to ∾ money out at interest *Geld auf Zinsen ausleihen;* to ∾ a child out to nurse *ein Kind* *in Pflege geben;* to ∾ out the fire *das Feuer löschen;* to ∾ oneself out *sich ereifern, sich besondere Mühe machen;* to ∾ a person out *j.en ärgern, aus dem Konzept, außer Fassung bringen;* to ∾ out one's shoulder *sich die Schulter verrenken;* don't ∾ yourself out *keine Umstände!;* to ∾ a person through to another *j.en telephonisch mit einem anderen verbinden;* we ∾ (laid) our heads together *wir steckten die Köpfe zusammen, wir berieten;* to ∾ the parts together *die Teile zusammensetzen;* to ∾ this and that (or: two and two) together *eins zum anderen nehmen, seine Schlüsse ziehen, sich (dat.) etwas zusammenreimen;* to ∾ up, see 'affair, back, banns, fight, hair, prayer, sale'; to ∾ up a person for a night *j.en für eine Nacht aufnehmen, beherbergen, unterbringen;* to ∾ a person up to an affair *j.em von einer Sache Kenntnis geben, j.en in einer Sache unterweisen, j.en zu einer Sache anstiften;* to ∾ a person up for election *j.en als Wahlkandidaten aufstellen;* to ∾ up one's sword *sein Schwert einstecken;* to be ∾ upon *betrogen (beschwindelt) werden;* to ∾ a person wise to a thing (U.S. colloq.) *j.en über etwas unterrichten (aufklären);* ∾ a sock in it! (sl.) *hör' auf zu reden, halt's Maul.* — **II.** v.i.: the ship ∾ about *das Schiff wendete;* to ∾ back to harbour *in den Hafen zurückkehren;* to ∾ in for a post *sich um eine Stelle bewerben;* to ∾ off from shore *vom Ufer abstoßen;* to ∾ out to sea *in See stechen;* to ∾ over a river *über einen Fluß setzen;* to ∾ up at an inn *in einem Gasthof absteigen, einkehren;* to ∾ up for a club *sich zur Aufnahme in einem Klub melden;* to ∾ up with a thing *sich (dat.) etwas gefallen lassen, etwas dulden, mit etwas vorliebnehmen*

puzzle I. v.tr.: to ∾ one's brains about (over) a thing *sich (dat.) den Kopf über etwas zerbrechen;* that ∾s me *das macht mir Kopfzerbrechen;* to ∾ out a problem *die Lösung eines Problems herausbekommen, austüfteln.* — **II.** v.i.: to ∾ about (over) a thing *sich (dat.) über etwas den Kopf zerbrechen*

Q

Q n.: to mind one's P's and ∾'s *sich mit seinen Worten oder seinem Benehmen sehr in acht nehmen*

q.t. n.: on the strict ∾ (quiet) (colloq.) *ganz im Vertrauen, im geheimen*

qualify v.tr. & i.: an adjective qualifies a noun, an adverb qualifies a verb, adjective or another adverb *ein Adjektiv bestimmt näher ein Substantiv, ein Adverb bestimmt näher ein Verb, ein Adjektiv oder ein anderes Adverb;* he is ∾ing (himself) for the Church, for the Bar *er studiert, um die Reife in Theologie, in Jura zu erwerben;* I must ∾ my statement *ich muß meine Aussage modifizieren, einschränken;* you may ∾ him as intelligent *man kann ihn als intelligent bezeichnen;* she is not qualified to give an opinion *sie ist nicht befähigt zu urteilen;* they gave qualified applause *sie zollten mäßig Beifall*

quarrel I. n.: to espouse a person's ∾, to fight a person's ∾s for him *j.em im Streite beistehen, sich für j.en einsetzen;* to find a ∾ in a straw *an allem etwas auszusetzen haben;* to pick a ∾ with a person *mit j.em Streit anfangen.* — **II.** v.i.: to ∾ with a person about (for) a thing *mit j.em um etwas streiten;* to ∾ with one's bread and butter *sich (dat.) selbst im Lichte stehen, den Ast absägen, auf dem man sitzt;* a bad (an ill) workman always ∾s with (blames) his tools (prov.) *ein schlechter Handwerker schimpft (immer) auf sein Werkzeug*

quarter n.: to ask for (to cry, to crave) ∾; to give (to show) ∾; to receive ∾ *um Gnade, Pardon bitten; Pardon geben; Pardon erhalten;* a bad ∾ of an hour *ein kurzes, unangenehmes Erlebnis;* to beat up the ∾s of a person *j.en aufsuchen;* to blow from all ∾s at once *aus allen vier Himmelsrichtungen zugleich wehen;* to come to close ∾s *heftig aneinander geraten, handgemein werden;* it has gone the ∾ *es hat Viertel geschlagen;* to have the news from a good ∾ *Nachrichten aus guter Quelle haben;* the head-∾s of a general *das Hauptquartier eines Generals;* in this ∾ *in dieser Gegend, hier zu Lande;* to live in the residential ∾ of a town *im Wohnviertel einer Stadt leben;* no help to be looked for in that ∾ *von der Seite ist keine Hilfe zu erwarten;* to take up one's ∾s in a place, with a person (= to ∾ oneself upon a person) *sich irgendwo, sich bei j.em einquartieren;* what ∾ is the wind in? *aus welchem Loch pfeift der Wind? wie steht die Sache?*

queen n.: ∾ Anne is dead *die Geschichte hat so einen Bart, das sind olle Kamellen;* to turn ∾'s evidence, see 'king'

queer I. a.: he is a ∾ chap (cove, card, customer) *er ist ein sonderbarer Heiliger;* he is in Queer Street (sl.) *er ist in Not (Geldschwierigkeiten, in der Klemme);* I feel ∾ (colloq.) *ich fühle mich nicht ganz wohl.* — **II.** v.tr.: to ∾ the pitch for a person (sl.) *j.em die Aussichten, das Geschäft (Spiel) verderben, einen Strich durch die Rechnung machen*

quench v.tr.: to ∾ the smoking flax (Is. XLII, 3) *den glimmenden Docht auslöschen, eine Entwicklung hemmen, im Entstehen unterdrücken;* to ∾ one's thirst *seinen Durst löschen*

question I. n.: what is the ∾? *worum handelt es sich? wovon ist die Rede?;* to ask a person a ∾, to put a ∾ to a person *an j.en eine Frage stellen (richten);* ask no ∾s and you'll be told no lies *wer viel fragt, bekommt viel Antwort;* to beg the ∾ *der Hauptfrage ausweichen; etwas Umstrittenes als ausgemachte Tatsache hinstellen;* beyond all, beyond, out of, past, without ∾ *fraglos, ohne Frage;* to call in ∾ *in Zweifel ziehen, in Frage stellen;* to come into ∾ *in Frage kommen;* a leading ∾ *eine Suggestiv-Frage;* to make no ∾ of a fact but that it is so *eine Tatsache nicht in Frage stellen;* there is no ∾ but that *es ist fraglos, daß;* to be out of the ∾ *ausgeschlossen sein, nicht in Frage kommen;* to pop the ∾ (colloq.) *einen Heiratsantrag machen;* to put the ∾ *zur Abstimmung schreiten.* — **II.** v.tr.: to ∾ a person *j.en befragen, einem Verhör unterziehen;* it cannot be ∾ed but that, but *es läßt sich nicht bestreiten, es ist fraglos, daß;* to ∾ the honesty of a person *an j.es Ehrlichkeit zweifeln*

queue v.i.: to ∾ up *Schlange stehen, anstehen*

quick I. a.: as ∾ as thought *gedankenschnell;* a ∾ child *ein gewecktes, kluges Kind;* a ∾ ear, eye *ein feines Ohr, scharfes Auge;* be ∾, be ∾ about it *mach' schnell; beeile dich damit!;* to be ∾ at figures *ein guter Rechner sein;* to be ∾ at repartee *schlagfertig sein;* to be ∾ in the uptake *etwas schnell begreifen;* to be ∾ of resource *sich schnell zu helfen wissen;* to be ∾ of scent *eine feine Nase haben;* to be ∾ to take offence *leicht etwas übelnehmen;* to be ∾ with child *die Bewegungen des Kindes im Mutterleib spüren;* to go down ∾ into hell *lebend zur Hölle fahren;* to have a ∾ temper *leicht aufbrausend sein;* to have ∾ wits (be ∾-witted) *schnell begreifen.* — **II.** n.: the ∾ and the dead *die Lebenden und die Toten;* he is a Tory to the ∾ *er ist konservativ bis auf die Knochen;* to cut to the ∾ *ins lebendige Fleisch (bis auf den Nerv) schneiden;* the insult stung him to the ∾ *die Beleidigung kränkte ihn aufs empfindlichste (tat ihm in der Seele weh).* — **III.** adv.: I ran as ∾ as I could *ich lief so schnell ich konnte;* a ∾-firing gun *ein Schnellfeuergeschütz*

quiet I. a.: as ∾ as a mouse *mäuschenstill;* on the strict ∾, see 'q.t.'; ∾ resentment *heimlicher Groll;* she had a ∾ dig at him *sie machte eine versteckte Bemerkung gegen (über) ihn.* — **II.** v.tr.: to ∾ one's conscience *sein Gewissen beruhigen.* — **III.** v.i.: to ∾ down *sich beruhigen*

quit I. pred. a.: I am glad to be ∾ of the trouble *ich freue mich, daß ich die Mühe los (quitt) bin (vom Halse habe).* — **II.** v.tr.: to ∾ hold of a thing *etwas loslassen;* to ∾ love with hate *Liebe mit Haß vergelten;* to ∾ the neighbourhood *fortziehen;* to ∾ office *ein Amt niederlegen;* to ∾ a person in anger *im Zorn von j.em scheiden;* to ∾ the ranks *aus dem Gliede treten;* death ∾s all scores *der Tod gleicht alle Schuld aus;* to give a tenant notice to ∾ *einem Mieter kündigen*

quite adv.: that is ∾ another thing *das ist etwas ganz anderes;* it ∾ covers it *das deckt es vollkommen;* it is ∾ too delightful of you (colloq.) *es ist einfach zu reizend von Ihnen;* it is ∾ a disappointment *es ist eine große (herbe) Enttäuschung;* it is ∾ a good thing *es ist eine sehr gute Sache;* he is ∾ a hero *er ist ein wahrer Held;* I ∾ like him *ich habe ihn ganz gern;* I am ∾ by myself *ich bin ganz allein;* ∾ another than *ganz verschieden von;* it is ∾ the thing *es ist hochmodern;* it is not ∾ the thing *es ist nicht ganz schicklich;* ∾ so! ∾! *ganz recht! eben!*

quits pred. a.: to be ∾ with a person *mit j.em quitt sein, eine Sache ausgeglichen haben;* I will be ∾ with him yet *ich werde es ihm schon vergelten, heimzahlen;* double or ∾, see 'double'; to cry ∾ *seine Rechnung mit j.em für ausgeglichen erklären*

quittance n.: omittance is no ∾ *aufgeschoben ist nicht aufgehoben*

quiver n.: a full ∾ of all children *ein ganzer Stall Kinder;* to have an arrow (or: shaft) left in one's ∾ *noch ein Eisen im Feuer haben*

quod n. (sl.): to be in ∾ *im Gefängnis (hinter schwedischen Gardinen, im Loch, im Kittchen) sein*

quotation n.: it is a ∾ from Shakespeare *es ist ein Zitat aus Shakespeare;* ∾-marks *Anführungsstriche (Gänsefüßchen)*

quote v.tr.: he is always quoting the Bible *er zitiert immer die Bibel (er führt immer die B. an);* to ∾ a passage from an author *eine Stelle aus einem Schriftsteller zitieren (anführen);* the prices are ∾d at *die Preise sind notiert (angegeben) mit;* he is ∾d as having said *er soll gesagt haben*

R

R. letter: the three ∾s (reading, (w)riting, (a)rithmetic) *Lesen, Schreiben, Rechnen (als Grundlagen der Volksschulbildung);* the ∾ months *die Monate mit R im Namen (Austernsaison)*

rabbit[1] n.: to be a ∾ (colloq.) *ein schlechter Spieler, ein Stümper im Sport sein;* Welsh ∾ (rarebit) *geröstete Brotschnitte mit Käse überbacken;* ∾'s food, ∾'s meat (colloq.) *grüner Salat*

rabbit[2]: odd ∾ it (vulg.) *Gott verdamm' mich!*

rabid a.: he is a ∾ democrat *er ist ein wütender (fanatischer) Demokrat;* a ∾ dog *ein tollwütiger Hund;* to be filled with ∾ hate *von rasendem Haß erfüllt sein*

race[1] **I.** n.: to go to the ∾s (to a ∾ meeting) *die Pferderennen besuchen;* he breeds ∾ horses and has a private ∾ course *er züchtet Rennpferde und hat eine eigene Rennbahn;* the mill-∾ *das Mühlgerinne;* to run a ∾ *einen Wettlauf machen (um die Wette laufen);* ere he had run half his ∾ *bevor er die Hälfte seiner irdischen Laufbahn vollendet hatte;* the tide set with a strong ∾ *die Flut setzte mit starker Strömung ein.* — **II.** v.i.: a racing man *ein Liebhaber des Rennsports;* to ∾ with (against) a person *mit j.em um die Wette laufen.* — **III.** v.tr.: I'll ∾ you to the gate *ich laufe mit dir um die Wette bis ans Tor;* he ∾d his bicycle against a motorcar *er radelte mit einem Auto um die Wette;* the Government ∾d the bill through the House *die Regierung peitschte den Gesetzesantrag durch das Unterhaus;* he ∾d me through the exhibition *er hetzte mich durch die Ausstellung;* he ∾d me along at great speed *er raste mit mir daher*

race[2] n.: he belongs to the ∾ of dandies *er gehört zum Schlage der Stutzer;* the feathered ∾ *die Vogelwelt;* the four-footed ∾ *die Vierfüßler;* he is of noble ∾ *er ist von edlem (adligem) Geschlecht*

rack[1] n.: to go to ∾ and ruin *völlig zugrunde gehen*

rack[2] **I.** v.tr.: he had a cough that seemed to ∾ his whole body *er hatte einen Husten, der seinen ganzen Körper zu erschüttern schien;* to ∾ one's brains about (over) a thing *sich (dat.) den Kopf über etwas zerbrechen;* I have a ∾ing headache *ich habe rasende Kopfschmerzen;* to be ∾ed with pain *von Schmerzen gepeinigt (geplagt, gequält) werden;* to demand ∾-rent *eine kaum erschwingliche Pacht fordern.* — **II.** n.: to live at ∾ and manger *sorglos in den Tag hinein leben;* to put a person on the ∾ *j.en auf die Folter spannen*

racket I. n.: what's the ∾? (sl.) *was ist los?;* to be on the ∾ *ein tolles (wildes) Leben führen;* to be on (to) a person's ∾ *j.em auf der Spur sein, hinter j.es Schliche kommen;* to kick up (to make, to raise) a ∾ about a thing *einen Heidenlärm (Höllenspektakel) wegen einer Sache machen;* to stand the ∾ *erfolgreich die Probe bestehen; die Folgen tragen, die Rechnung (Zeche) bezahlen;* to work a ∾ *auf illegale oder gewaltsame Weise in den Besitz von Geld oder anderen Dingen gelangen.* — **II.** v.i.: to ∾ about *lärmen, poltern; ein tolles, wildes Leben führen*

racy a.: a ∾ flavour *ein kräftiger, würziger Geschmack, Geruch;* ∾ of the soil *bodenständig*

radiant a.: ∾ with pleasure (joy) *freudestrahlend*

radiate v.tr.: he ∾s health *er strotzt vor Gesundheit*

radical a.: the ∾ rottenness of human nature *die radikale, angeborene Verderbtheit der menschlichen Natur;* the ∾ sign (math.) *das Wurzelzeichen;* to commit a ∾ error *einen Grundfehler begehen;* to submit to a ∾ cure *sich einer Radikalkur unterziehen;* to undergo a ∾ change (reform) *eine grundlegende Änderung (eine Reform an Haupt und Gliedern) erfahren*

radically adv.: there is something ∾ wrong with (about) it *daran ist etwas grundverkehrt*

rag[1] n.: ∾tag and bobtail *Krethi und Plethi;* ∾time music *synkopierte Musik;* not a ∾ of evidence *nicht die Spur eines Beweises;* his clothes were all in ∾s (worn to ∾s) *seine Kleider waren in Fetzen (zerlumpt);* to chew the ∾ (sl.) *auf einer alten Beschwerde herumreiten, meckern;* cooked to ∾s *ganz, völlig zerkocht;* to feel like a ∾ *sich ganz elend fühlen;* not to have a ∾ to one's back *keinen Fetzen am Leibe haben;* I read it in our local ∾ (contempt.) *ich las es in unserem Käseblatt;* to take the ∾ off (the bush) (U.S. sl.) *alles übertreffen (schlagen);* to tear to ∾s *in Fetzen reißen; heruntermachen, kein gutes Haar lassen an;* a ∾-and bone-man *ein Lumpenhändler, -sammler*

rag[2] **I.** v.tr. (sl.): I gave him a good ∾ging *ich putzte (machte) ihn tüchtig herunter.* — **II.** n. (sl.): to play a ∾ upon a person *bei j.em einen Budenzauber veranstalten, j.em einen Schabernack spielen;* to get one's ∾ out (colloq.) *hochgehen, zornig werden*

rage I. n.: the open-air cure is now the (all the) ∾ *die Freiluftbehandlung ist jetzt die große Mode;* to fly (to get) into a ∾ *in Wut geraten;* he has a ∾ for (for collecting) first editions *er ist ein wütender Sammler von Erstausgaben.* — **II.** v.i.: a violent battle is raging *es tobt (wütet) eine heftige Schlacht;* cholera is raging in the land *die Cholera wütet im Lande;* to ∾ at (against) one's fate *gegen sein Schicksal wüten (toben, rasen);* to ∾ about the house *im Hause herumtoben.* — **III.** v.refl.: the storm ∾d itself out *der Sturm tobte sich aus*

raid I. n.: the police made a ∾ on (∾ed) the black market *die Polizei machte eine Razzia auf dem Schwarzen Markt;* an air ∾ *ein Luftangriff*

rail[1] **I.** n.: to go (to send) by ∾ *mit der Eisenbahn fahren (senden);* a ∾-head *eine Kopfstation, Endstation;* the train went (ran) off the ∾s *der Zug entgleiste;* to be off the ∾s *in Unordnung gebracht sein, nicht richtig funktionieren; abwegig sein.* — **II.** v.tr.: to ∾ goods *Waren mit der Bahn schicken;* to ∾ in (off) a field *ein Feld einfriedigen*

rail[2] v.i.: to ∾ at (against) a thing *auf etwas schimpfen*

rain I. n.: as right as ∾ *in schönster Ordnung, in bester Verfassung, sauwohl;* ∾ or shine *bei Regen und Sonnenschein, in guten und schlechten Tagen;* to get caught in the ∾ *vom Regen überrascht werden;* it is pouring with ∾ *es regnet (gießt) in Strömen.* — **II.** v.i.: it never ∾s but it pours (prov.) *ein Unglück kommt selten allein;* it is ∾ing in torrents *es gießt wie mit Mulden;* tears ∾ed down her cheeks *Tränen strömten ihr die Wangen hinunter;* blows ∾ed upon him *Schläge hagelten auf ihn nieder.* — **III.** v.tr.: it is ∾ing cats and dogs *es regnet Bindfäden;* it has ∾ed itself out *es hat sich ausgeregnet;* he ∾ed benefits upon me *er überschüttete mich mit Wohltaten*

rainy a.: to provide against a ∾ day *einen Notgroschen zurücklegen*

raise v.tr.: see 'blister, Cain, devil, dough, dust, elbow, etc.'; to ∾ a person from the dead *j.en von den Toten auferwecken;* to ∾ a large family *eine große Familie aufziehen;* to ∾ a monument to a person *j.em ein Denkmal errichten;* to ∾ one's own vegetables *sein eigenes Gemüse ziehen*

rake I. v.tr.: to ∾ all history for proofs *die Geschichte nach Beweisen durchstöbern;* to ∾ a ship with shot *ein Schiff mit Geschützfeuer bestreichen;* to ∾ off (together, up) the leaves *das Laub weg-, zusammenharken;* to ∾ off the profit *den Gewinn einheimsen;* a ∾-off (sl.) *ein Gewinnanteil (meist an einem unredlichen Geschäft);* to ∾ out *auskundschaften;* to ∾ out the fire *das Feuer ausharken;* to ∾ up (together) all possible charges *alle möglichen Anklagen hervorsuchen, zusammentragen;* to ∾ up an old story *eine alte Geschichte ausgraben.* — **II.** v.i.: to ∾ among (in, over, into) old records *in alten Urkunden herumstöbern;*

to be ∾d fore and aft (nautical) *hoffnungslos verliebt sein*

rally I. v.tr.: he rallied his troops for a new attack *er sammelte seine Truppen (wieder) zu einem neuen Angriff;* he rallied his party round (to) him *er scharte seine Partei um sich.* — **II.** v.i.: his troops rallied for a new attack *seine Truppen sammelten sich (wieder) zu einem neuen Angriff;* to ∾ from an illness *sich von einer Krankheit erholen;* the market rallied from the slump *der Markt erholte sich von dem Preissturz;* to ∾ (round) to a person's opinion *sich j.es Meinung anschließen;* his party rallied round (to) him *seine Partei scharte sich um ihn.* — **III.** n.: a great ∾ of the party *eine Massenversammlung der Partei, ein Parteitag;* it was a long ∾ (lawn tennis) *es war ein langer Ballwechsel;* he died after a short ∾ *er starb nach einem kurzen Wiederaufflackern der Kräfte*

ram v.tr.: he ∾med his head against the wall *er rannte mit dem Kopf gegen die Wand;* he ∾med his horse at the fence *er spornte sein Pferd an, über den Zaun zu springen;* he ∾med his hat down on his head *er stülpte sich den Hut auf den Kopf;* he tried to ∾ it down my throat *er versuchte, es mir glaubhaft zu machen;* to ∾ the argument home *der Beweisführung Nachdruck verleihen;* he ∾med his clothes into a bag *er stopfte seine Kleider in einen Sack;* the list of names was ∾med into me *die Namensliste wurde mir eingehämmert (eingetrichtert, eingebleut)*

ramp I. v.i.: the plants ∾ in the damp heat *die Pflanzen wuchern in der feuchten Hitze;* the lion ∾s *der Löwe stellt sich auf die Hinterbeine;* he will ∾ when he hears the news *er wird rasen (toben), wenn er die Nachricht hört.* — **II.** v.tr.: the front of the building is ∾ed *die Vorderseite des Gebäudes ist mit einer Rampe versehen.* — **III.** n.: the sale of tickets was a ∾ *der Kartenverkauf war ein Schwindel, ein Neppgeschäft*

rampage n.: to go (to be) on the ∾ *herumtoben, -wüten*

random I. n.: to choose at ∾ *aufs Geratewohl (auf gut Glück, blindlings) wählen;* to talk at ∾ *faseln, drauflosschwatzen.* — **II.** a.: a ∾ shot *ein zufälliger Schuß, ein Schuß ins Blaue*

range I. v.tr.: he has ∾d himself on the side of the enemy *er hat sich auf die Seite des Feindes geschlagen;* they ∾d themselves on each side of the road *sie stellten sich auf beiden Seiten der Straße in Reihen auf;* they were ∾d against (among, with) us *sie standen gegen (unter, mit) uns.* — **II.** v.i.: to ∾ along (over, through) the district *die Gegend durchstreifen;* he ∾s among (with) the great writers *er zählt zu den großen Schriftstellern;* the nightingale ∾s from the Channel to Warwickshire *die Nachtigall kommt vom Kanal bis Warwickshire vor;* the price ∾s between 1 and 5 shillings *der Preis schwankt zwischen 1 und 5 Schilling;* the prices ∾ from 1 to 5 shillings *die Preise bewegen sich zwischen 1 und 5 Schilling;* the gun ∾s over a mile *das Geschütz trägt über eine Meile;* his thoughts ∾ over past, present and future *seine Gedanken erstrecken sich über Vergangenheit, Gegenwart und Zukunft;* a 12mo does not ∾ well with a folie *ein Duodezband macht sich nicht gut neben einem Folioband;* to have a ranging fancy for a thing *eine unbeständige Neigung zu etwas haben.* — **III.** n.: a ∾ of mountains *eine Gebirgskette;* the whole ∾ of politics *der ganze Bereich der Politik;* there is a lower ∾ of prices today *die Preise stellen sich heute niedriger;* this chart gives the ∾s of all species *diese Karte verzeichnet, wo alle Gattungen vorkommen;* the ∾ of the strata is east and west *die Schichten verlaufen von Osten nach Westen;* the ∾ of her voice *der Umfang ihrer Stimme;* to find the ∾ of a target *die Entfernung eines Zieles ermitteln;* to give one's fancy (its) free ∾ *seiner Phantasie die Zügel schießen lassen;* at short (or: close) ∾ *auf kurze, aus naher Entfernung;* to keep in ∾ with a thing *sich in einer Linie (Richtung) mit etwas halten;* to come into one's ∾ of thought (vision) *in seinen Ideen-, Gesichtskreis kommen;* his knowledge is of very wide ∾ *seine Kenntnisse erstrecken sich über sehr weite Gebiete;* the target is out of ∾ *das Ziel ist außer Schußweite;* Hebrew is out of my ∾ of knowledge *Hebräisch fällt nicht in den Bereich meiner Kenntnisse, Hebräisch kann ich nicht;* a ∾-finder *ein Entfernungsmesser;* a shooting ∾ *ein Schießstand;* we have a good ∾ in our kitchen *wir haben einen guten Herd in unserer Küche*

rank[1] **I.** n.: the ∾ and file *die Unteroffiziere und Gemeinen;* in ∾ and file *in Reih und Glied;* the ∾ and file of a party *die einfachen Mitglieder einer Partei;* he is a man of ∾ and fashion *er gehört der vornehmen Gesellschaft an;* people of all ∾s and orders *Leute aller Stände und Klassen;* a person of high (or: exalted) ∾ *eine Standesperson;* to join the ∾s *ins Heer eintreten;* to keep ∾, to break ∾ *im Gliede bleiben, aus dem Gliede treten;* to reduce to the ∾s *degradieren;* to rise from the ∾s *aus dem Mannschaftstande hervorgehen, von der Pike auf dienen;* to stand in the front (rear) ∾ *im ersten (hinteren) Gliede stehen;* to take ∾ of *den Vorrang haben vor;* to take high ∾ *große Bedeutung gewinnen, hoch gewertet werden;* to take ∾ with *auf gleicher Stufe stehen mit.* — **II.** v.tr.: to ∾ a person *den Vortritt vor j.em haben;* to ∾ a person with *j.en in eine Klasse setzen mit.* — **III.** v.i.: the state ∾s among the great Powers *der Staat rechnet zu den Großmächten;* he ∾s next to the king *er rangiert (kommt gleich) hinter dem König*

rank[2] a.: the soil is too ∾ to grow corn *der Boden ist zu fett, um Korn anzubauen;* it is ∾ nonsense *es ist heller (krasser) Unsinn;* it was ∾ treason *es war reiner (offenkundiger) Verrat;* to grow ∾ *üppig (geil) wachsen;* to smell ∾ *ranzig, widerlich riechen;* he is a ∾ outsider *er ist ein Schuft (gemeiner Kerl)*

ransom n.: it is worth a king's ∾ *es ist von ungeheurem Wert;* to hold a person to ∾ *j.en bis zur Zahlung eines Lösegeldes festhalten*

rap[1] **I.** n.: to give a ∾ at the door *anklopfen;* to give a person a ∾ on the knuckles *j.em einen Klaps auf die Finger geben; j.em einen Verweis erteilen;* to take the ∾ (colloq.) *eines anderen Strafe auf sich nehmen.* — **II.** v.tr.: to ∾ out an oath *einen Fluch ausstoßen.* — **III.** v.i.: to ∾ at the door *anklopfen*

rap[2] n.: I don't care a ∾ what he says *es ist mir einerlei (egal, Wurst, schnuppe), was er sagt*

rapids n.: to shoot the ∾ *über die Stromschnellen fahren*

rapt a.: to listen with ∾ attention *mit gespannter Aufmerksamkeit zuhören*

rapture n.: to be in (to go into) ∾s over a thing *über etwas ganz entzückt sein, in Verzückung geraten*

rare a.: the ∾ atmosphere of the mountain tops *die dünne Luft der Berggipfel;* it is ∾ for a person to do so, it is only ∾ly that he does so *es kommt selten vor, daß j. das tut;* a miracle of ∾ device *ein Wunder außergewöhnlicher Art;* I had ∾ fun with him *ich hatte einen Heidenspaß mit ihm;* do you like your meat ∾? *mögen Sie das Fleisch nicht ganz durchgebraten?*

rascal I. n.: you're a little ∾ *du bist ein kleiner Strick!;* you lucky ∾! *du Glückspilz!* — **II.** a.: the ∾ rout *das gewöhnliche Volk, das Lumpenpack*

raspberry n.: to give (to get) the ∾ (sl.) *auspfeifen, abfahren lassen; ausgepfiffen werden, eine Zigarre bekommen*

rat I. n.: ∾s! (sl.) *Unsinn! Quatsch!;* like a drowned ∾ *so naß wie eine Katze, pudelnaß;* to smell a ∾ *Lunte, den Braten riechen.* — **II.** v.i.: he ∾ted on his party *er ist übergelaufen, er hat seine Partei verraten*

rate[1] **I.** n.: at any ∾ *auf jeden Fall;* at that ∾ *auf diese Weise, unter diesen Umständen; wenn du so weiter machst;* the ∾ of interest (wages) is to be regulated *der Zinsfuß (der Lohnsatz) soll geregelt werden;* the birth-∾ is rising *die Geburtenziffer steigt;* he is a first-∾ player *er ist ein erstklassiger Spieler;* the high ∾s charged by the railway *die hohen Sätze, welche die Bahn verlangt;* the low ∾ at which you value it *der geringe Wert, den Sie der Sache beimessen;* to buy at the ∾ of 1 shilling a thousand *zum Preise von 1 Schilling pro 1000 kaufen;* to dash off at a great ∾ *im Eiltempo davonsausen;* to drive at the ∾ of 50 miles an hour *mit einer Stundengeschwindigkeit von 80 km fahren;* the ∾s are high here *die Kommunalsteuern sind hier hoch.* — **II.** v.tr.: I do not ∾ his merits high *ich schätze seine Verdienste nicht hoch ein, ich bewerte sie nicht hoch;* each offence is ∾d at a fixed sum by way of penalty *für jedes Vergehen ist eine bestimmte Summe als Geldstrafe festgesetzt;* his influence is grossly over-(under-)∾d *sein Einfluß wird stark über-(unter-)schätzt;* I ∾ him among my benefactors *ich zähle ihn zu meinen Wohltätern;*

we are highly ∾d for education *wir müssen hohe Kommunalsteuern für das Erziehungswesen zahlen.* — **III.** v.i.: to ∾ high (low) *einen hohen (niedrigen) Rang (Wert) haben*

rate² v.tr.: to ∾ a person, to give a person a good rating *j.en tüchtig ausschimpfen*

rather adv.: the ∾ that *um so mehr, als;* the performance was ∾ good *die Aufführung war ziemlich gut;* it was ∾ a steep hill *es war ein ziemlich steiler Hügel;* it is ∾ good than bad *es ist eher gut als schlecht;* orderliness is not the result of law; ∾ it is the cause of it *Ordnung ist nicht das Ergebnis der Gesetze, sie ist vielmehr deren Ursache;* late last night, or ∾ early this morning *gestern Abend spät, oder vielmehr heute früh;* I ∾ think you know him *ich meine doch, du kennst ihn;* it is ∾ the worse for wear *es ist ziemlich abgetragen;* I am ∾ the worse for wear *ich bin nicht mehr so jung;* the desire to seem clever ∾ than honest *das Verlangen, lieber (eher) klug als ehrlich zu erscheinen;* I had ∾ he did not come *es wäre mir lieber, er käme nicht;* I had ∾ not say anything *ich möchte lieber nichts sagen;* would you ∾ take tea or wine? *möchten Sie lieber Tee oder Wein?;* I would much ∾ not go *ich würde (möchte) viel lieber nicht gehen;* have you been here before? ∾! *bist du schon mal hier gewesen? Das will ich meinen! Freilich! Und ob!*

ration n.: we're on short ∾s *bei uns ist Schmalhans Küchenmeister;* to keep a person on short ∾s *j.em den Brotkorb höher hängen*

rattle I. v.i.: to ∾ along (away, on) *munter drauflosschwatzen, -plappern;* the cart ∾d along (down) the street (past the house) *der Wagen ratterte die Straße entlang (hinunter, an dem Hause vorbei);* to ∾ at the door *an der Tür rappeln;* I had a rattling good dinner *ich aß ganz vorzüglich zu Mittag;* he hurried on at a rattling pace *er eilte im Sturmschritt weiter;* there was a rattling wind *es wehte ein kräftiger Wind.* — **II.** v.tr.: to ∾ a bill through the House *einen Gesetzesantrag durch das Unterhaus peitschen;* to ∾ the sabre *mit dem Säbel rasseln;* he ∾d off the whole poem *er rasselte das ganze Gedicht herunter;* to get ∾d *verwirrt, aufgeregt, ängstlich werden.* — **III.** n.: to hear the death-∾ *das Todesröcheln hören;* the child has the ∾s *das Kind hat Halsbräune (Krupp);* he is a ∾-brained (∾-headed, ∾pated) fellow *er ist ein Hohlkopf, ein zerfahrener Kerl;* it is an old ∾trap *es ist ein alter Klapperkasten*

rave I. v.i.: he ∾d at (or: against) the injustice done him *er tobte gegen das ihm zugefügte Unrecht;* in his delirium he ∾d about (of) the strangest things *in seinem Wahne faselte (phantasierte) er die seltsamsten Dinge;* to ∾ about (of) a person (or: thing) *von einer Person (Sache) mit größter Bewunderung sprechen, für eine Person (Sache) schwärmen;* he is raving mad *er ist tobsüchtig.* — **II.** v.tr.: to ∾ oneself hoarse *sich heiser schreien;* the wind ∾d itself out *der Wind tobte sich aus*

raw I. a.: a ∾-boned horse *ein hagerer (magerer) Gaul;* he is a ∾ country-lad *er ist ein ungehobelter Bauernbursche;* it was a ∾ deal *es war eine ungerechte Behandlung;* they are ∾ recruits *es sind unausgebildete Rekruten, unerfahrene Neulinge, blutige Anfänger;* he has a ∾ sore on his arm *er hat eine offene Wunde am Arm;* he drinks his whisky ∾ *er trinkt seinen Whisky unverdünnt.* — **II.** n.: to touch a person on the ∾ *j.en an seiner wunden (verwundbaren, empfindlichen) Stelle treffen*

razor n.: to be on the ∾('s) edge *auf des Messers Schneide stehen;* to set a ∾ *ein Rasiermesser schärfen (abziehen)*

razzle-dazzle n. (sl.): to be on the ∾ *herumsumpfen;* to go on the ∾ *auf den Bummel gehen*

reach I. v.tr.: to ∾ a person a thing (a thing to a person) *j.em etwas reichen;* to ∾ a person a blow *j.em einen Schlag versetzen;* this ∾es your case *das erstreckt sich auf Ihren Fall;* to ∾ a conclusion *zu einem Schluß gelangen;* he ∾ed down his hat *er nahm seinen Hut herunter;* ∾-me-downs (colloq.) *Konfektionskleidung, Kleidung von der Stange; auch: Kleider aus zweiter Hand (getragene Kleider);* to ∾ out one's hand *die Hand ausstrecken.* — **II.** v.i.: as far as eye could ∾ *so weit das Auge reichte;* to ∾ forward to an ideal *ein Ideal erstreben;* a dominion ∾ing from the Ebro to the Carpathians *ein Reich, das sich vom Ebro bis zu den Karpathen erstreckte;* to ∾ out further *weiter ausholen.* — **III.** n.: above (beyond, out of) (one's) ∾ *unerreichbar,* *außer(halb) Reichweite;* within one's ∾, within ∾ of *erreichbar, innerhalb Reichweite;* it is within easy ∾ of the railway *es ist von der Bahn aus leicht zu erreichen;* this gun has a wide ∾ *dieses Geschütz hat eine große Tragweite;* to make a ∾ for *greifen (langen) nach*

read I. v.tr.: my silence is not to be ∾ as consent *mein Schweigen ist nicht als Zustimmung zu deuten (aufzufassen);* to ∾ a child to sleep *ein Kind in den Schlaf lesen;* to ∾ a dream *einen Traum deuten;* to ∾ a person's hand *j.em aus der Hand lesen (wahrsagen);* to ∾ law *Jura studieren;* to ∾ a person a lesson *j.em eine Lektion erteilen, die Leviten lesen;* to ∾ music *vom Blatt spielen;* to ∾ a riddle *ein Rätsel raten (lösen);* the thermometer ∾s 33° *das Thermometer zeigt 33° an;* to ∾ a passage aloud (out) *eine Stelle laut vorlesen;* to ∾ off a difficult text *einen schwierigen Text so herunterlesen;* to ∾ over (or: through) a book *ein Buch durchlesen.* — **II.** v.i.: to ∾ about (of) a thing *über etwas (von etwas) lesen;* it ∾s as follows *es lautet wie folgt;* the book ∾s well *das Buch liest sich gut;* he is well-read *er ist sehr belesen;* to ∾ for a degree *sich auf eine Universitätsprüfung vorbereiten.* — **III.** n.: this afternoon I'm going to have a quiet ∾ *heute nachmittag will ich mal in aller Ruhe lesen*

reading n.: this book is dull ∾ *dieses Buch ist langweilig zu lesen, ist eine langweilige Lektüre;* the first ∾ of a bill *die erste Lesung eines Gesetzesantrages;* there is plenty of ∾ in it *es bietet einen reichlichen Lesestoff;* he is a man of vast ∾ *er ist ungeheuer belesen;* what is your ∾ of the facts? *wie deuten Sie die Tatsachen?;* his ∾ of Iago was generally condemned *seine Auffassung von Iago wurde allgemein verurteilt*

ready I. a.: to be ∾ at excuses *mit Entschuldigungen rasch bei der Hand sein;* to give a ∾ consent *bereitwillig zustimmen;* I was ∾ to drop (colloq.) *ich war fertig, erledigt;* to be ∾ to hand *griffbereit sein;* to demand ∾ money *Bargeld verlangen;* to write a ∾ pen *eine gewandte Feder führen;* to use a ∾ reckoner *eine Rechentabelle benutzen;* to meet with a ∾ sale *schnellen Absatz finden;* to constitute a ∾ source of income *eine gute Einnahmequelle bilden;* to have ∾ wit *schlagfertig sein;* to get ∾ to (for) *sich fertig machen zu (für);* to make everything ∾ for *alles fertig machen (vorbereiten) für.* — **II.** adv.: the boxes are ∾ packed *die Koffer stehen fertig gepackt;* to buy ∾-made clothes *fertige Kleider (Konfektion) kaufen;* the child that answers readiest *das Kind, das am schnellsten antwortet.* — **III.** n.: the rifles were held at the ∾ *die Gewehre wurden schußbereit gehalten;* I had to plank down the ∾ *ich mußte Bargeld zücken*

real a.: he deals in ∾ estate *er ist ein Grundstückmakler;* he paid ∾ money *er zahlte in klingender Münze;* to have a ∾ good feed (colloq.) *sich rundherum satt essen*

realize v.tr.: these details help to ∾ the scene *diese Einzelheiten tragen dazu bei, die Szene naturgetreu darzustellen;* to ∾ a thing *etwas klar erkennen, einsehen;* he ∾d that he had not succeeded *er sah ein, daß er keinen Erfolg gehabt hatte;* I cannot ∾ how that happened *ich kann mir nicht vorstellen, wie das geschah;* to ∾ a fortune *ein Vermögen erwerben;* it ∾d a high price *es erzielte einen hohen Preis;* to ∾ securities *Wertpapiere zu Geld machen*

reap I. v.i.: they that sow in tears shall ∾ in joy (Ps. 126, 5) *die mit Tränen säen, werden mit Freude ernten;* to ∾ where one has not sown *aus der Arbeit anderer Nutzen ziehen.* — **II.** v.tr.: to ∾ advantage from a thing *aus einer Sache Vorteil ziehen;* for they have sown the wind and they shall ∾ the whirlwind (Hos. VIII, 7) *denn sie säen Wind und werden Ungewitter (Sturmwind) ernten*

rear I. v.n.: to bring (to close) up the ∾ *den Nachtrab bilden, der letzte sein;* I saw them far in the ∾ *ich sah sie weit hinten;* to take the enemy in the ∾ *den Feind im Rücken angreifen, von hinten fassen.* — **II.** v.tr.: the snake ∾ed its head *die Schlange erhob ihr Haupt (ihren Kopf);* they ∾ed a monument to his memory *sie errichteten ein Denkmal zu seiner Erinnerung;* we ∾ chickens and ducks *wir züchten Hühner und Enten.* — **III.** v.i.: to ∾ (up) against injustice *sich gegen Unrecht auflehnen;* the horse ∾ed up *das Pferd bäumte sich auf*

reason I. n.: with ∾ *mit Grund, mit Recht;* against all (contrary to) ∾ *gegen* *alle Vernunft;* all the more ∾ that *ein um so triftigerer Grund, daß;* by ∾ of *auf Grund von, wegen;* there is ∾ in what he says *was er sagt, hat Hand und Fuß;* there is every ∾ to believe *alles spricht dafür;* for that very ∾ *gerade aus dem Grunde;* without rhyme or ∾ *ohne Sinn und Verstand;* to bring someone to ∾ *j.en zur Vernunft bringen;* to do things in (all) ∾ *maßvoll handeln, in vernünftigen Grenzen bleiben;* I will do anything in ∾ *ich will alles nur Erdenkliche tun;* to hear (to listen) to ∾ *Vernunft annehmen, sich belehren lassen;* to lose one's ∾ *den Verstand verlieren;* it stands to ∾ that *es ist selbstverständlich (es ist für jeden vernünftig denkenden Menschen klar), daß.* — **II.** v.i.: to ∾ about (of, upon) a subject *über ein Thema vernunftmäßig denken, debattieren;* to ∾ from premises *von Voraussetzungen aus schließen;* to ∾ with a person *j.en zu überzeugen suchen.* — **III.** v.tr.: to ∾ a person into doing a thing *j.en durch Zureden veranlassen, etwas zu tun;* theirs not to ∾ why (Tennyson) *es war nicht ihre Sache zu fragen, warum;* to ∾ out a problem *ein Problem zu Ende durchdenken;* I tried to ∾ him out of his prejudice *ich versuchte, ihm seine Voreingenommenheit auszureden*

rebound n.: to take (to catch) a person on (or: at) the ∾ *im günstigen Augenblick, durch Ausnützung einer Reaktion j.en zu einer entgegengesetzten Handlung überreden*

recall n.: beyond (past) ∾ *unwiderruflich*

receipt n.: I beg to acknowledge ∾ of your letter *ich bestätige dankend den Empfang Ihres Briefes;* on ∾ of *nach Empfang (Erhalt) von;* to give (to make out) a ∾ for *eine Quittung ausstellen über*

receive v.tr.: to ∾ as certain, as a prophecy *als sicher, als Prophezeiung ansehen;* to ∾ stolen goods *Hehler sein;* an axiom universally ∾d *ein allgemein anerkannter Grundsatz*

reckon I. v.tr.: to ∾ a person wise *j.en für klug halten;* I do not ∾ him among the great singers *ich zähle (rechne) ihn nicht zu den großen Sängern;* this was a mistake, I ∾ *das war ein Irrtum, glaube ich;* to ∾ up figures *Zahlen zusammenzählen.* — **II.** v.i.: can I ∾ (up)on you? *kann ich mich auf Sie verlassen? kann ich auf Sie zählen (rechnen)?;* I will ∾ (up) with you later *mit dir werde ich später abrechnen;* we did not ∾ with bad weather *wir haben nicht mit schlechtem Wetter gerechnet;* to ∾ without one's host *die Rechnung ohne den Wirt machen, die Lage unterschätzen*

reckoning n.: the day of ∾ *der Tag der Abrechnung (Vergeltung);* to be out in one's ∾ *sich verrechnet haben*

reclaim I. v.tr.: to ∾ land *Land urbar machen;* to ∾ someone from sin, error *j.en von einem Laster bekehren, auf den rechten Weg bringen;* to ∾ lost property *verlorenes Gut zurückfordern.* — **II.** n.: beyond ∾ *unverbesserlich*

recollection n.: to the best of my ∾ *soweit ich mich erinnere;* it is in my ∾, it happened within my ∾ *ich erinnere mich daran*

reconcile v.tr.: he is quite ∾d to his lot *er hat sich mit seinem Los abgefunden;* I cannot ∾ your statement with the facts *ich kann Ihre Behauptung nicht mit den Tatsachen in Einklang bringen*

record n.: his ∾ is against him *seine Vergangenheit spricht gegen ihn;* second-hand gramophone-∾s for sale *gebrauchte Gramophonplatten (Schallplatten) zu verkaufen;* he has an honourable ∾ of service *er blickt auf eine ehrenvolle Dienstzeit zurück;* to be on ∾ *registriert sein, eine historische Tatsache sein;* to bear ∾ of *bezeugen, Spuren aufweisen von;* that bears ∾ to what I said *das beweist, was ich sagte;* to break (to cut, to beat, to set up) a ∾ *einen Rekord brechen (schlagen, aufstellen);* to keep a ∾ of *aufzeichnen, niederschreiben, Buch führen über;* to place on ∾ *zu Protokoll geben;* this information is off the ∾ (colloq.) *diese Nachricht ist inoffiziell, vertraulich*

recourse n.: to have ∾ to *seine Zuflucht nehmen zu, greifen zu, sich verlegen auf*

recover I. v.tr.: to ∾ one's breath *wieder zu Atem kommen;* to ∾ damages *Schadenersatz erhalten;* to ∾ a debt *eine Schuld eintreiben;* to ∾ one's legs after a fall *nach einem Sturz wieder auf die Beine kommen;* to ∾ one's losses *seine Verluste ersetzt erhalten;* to ∾ one's senses *wieder* *zu(r) Besinnung kommen;* to ∾ lost time *verlorene Zeit ein-, nachholen.* — **II.** v.i.: he ∾ed after a short time *er kam nach kurzer Zeit wieder zu sich;* to ∾ from an illness *sich von einer Krankheit erholen*

recruit I. n.: they are raw ∾s *es sind unausgebildete Rekruten, unerfahrene Neulinge, blutige Anfänger.* — **II.** v.tr.: to ∾ a person for the army *j.en als Rekruten fürs Heer anwerben;* to be ∾ed from *sich rekrutieren (ergänzen) aus.* — **III.** v.i.: to go to the country to ∾ *aufs Land gehen, um sich zu erholen*

recur v.i.: the problem did not ∾ again *das Problem tauchte nicht wieder auf;* it did not ∾ to me (to my mind) at once *es fiel mir nicht gleich ein;* a ∾ring decimal *ein periodischer Dezimalbruch*

red I. a.: a ∾-brick university *eine Universität moderner Gründung (ohne Tradition);* a ∾-cap *ein Militärpolizist;* it's not worth a ∾ cent *es ist keinen roten Heller wert;* to be caught ∾-handed *auf frischer Tat ertappt werden;* a ∾ hat *ein Kardinalshut; (Spitzname für) britischen Stabsoffizier;* he's neither fish nor flesh nor good ∾ herring *er ist weder Fisch noch Fleisch;* to draw a ∾ herring across the trail *ein Ablenkungsmanöver betreiben;* ∾-hot *rotglühend;* the ∾ lane *die Kehle, Gurgel (in der Kindersprache);* a ∾-letter day *ein Freuden-, Glückstag;* to see the ∾ light *eine drohende Gefahr erkennen;* ∾ meat *Ochsen- oder Hammelfleisch;* it is a ∾ rag to him *es wirkt auf ihn wie ein rotes Tuch;* an all-∾ route *ein Reiseweg, der nur über britisches Gebiet führt (rot auf der Landkarte);* ∾ tape *Bürokratismus, Amtsschimmel;* to paint the map ∾ *das britische Empire ausdehnen;* to paint the town ∾ *die (ganze) Stadt auf den Kopf stellen.* — **II.** n.: to be in the ∾ *verschuldet, bankrott sein, in der Tinte sitzen;* to see ∾ *rot sehen, einen mörderischen Wutanfall (eine Mordswut) bekommen*

redeem v.tr.: the eyes ∾ the face from ugliness *die Augen verschönern das sonst häßliche Gesicht;* to ∾ a fault *einen Fehler wiedergutmachen (ausgleichen);* to ∾ one's honour *seine Ehre wiederherstellen;* to ∾ pledged goods *verpfändete Waren einlösen;* to ∾ a prisoner, a slave *einen Gefangenen, einen Sklaven erretten, loskaufen;* the case has one ∾ing feature *eines spricht für den Fall*

redemption n.: beyond (past, without) ∾ *nicht mehr zu retten;* in the year of our ∾ *im Jahre des Heils;* that blow was (proved) his ∾ *der Schlag erwies sich als seine Rettung;* he became a member of a livery company by ∾ *er kaufte sich in eine Zunft ein*

re-do v.tr.: to ∾ the work *die Arbeit noch einmal machen;* to ∾ the house *das Haus renovieren lassen*

redound v.i.: this procedure will ∾ to our advantage *dieses Vorgehen wird uns zum Vorteil gereichen;* the benefits that ∾ to us from it *die Wohltaten, die uns daraus erwachsen;* his praises ∾ upon himself *seine lobenden Worte fallen auf ihn selbst zurück*

redress v.tr.: to ∾ the balance *das Gleichgewicht wiederherstellen;* to ∾ grievances *Beschwerden abhelfen, Mißstände abstellen;* to ∾ injuries *Unrecht wiedergutmachen*

reduce v.tr.: to ∾ to ashes *in Asche verwandeln;* in ∾d circumstances *in bedrängten Verhältnissen;* to ∾ to despair *zur Verzweiflung bringen;* to ∾ an equation *eine Gleichung lösen;* he works at a ∾d fee *er arbeitet für ein ermäßigtes Honorar;* to ∾ a fraction *einen Bruch kürzen;* to ∾ to poverty *an den Bettelstab bringen;* to ∾ a rule to practice *eine Regel in die Praxis umsetzen;* at a ∾d price *zu herabgesetztem (ermäßigtem) Preise;* to ∾ to the ranks *degradieren;* to ∾ anomalies to rule *Abweichungen unter eine Regel bringen;* on a ∾d scale *in verkleinertem Maßstabe;* to ∾ pounds to shillings *Pfunde in Schillinge verwandeln;* to ∾ someone to silence *j.en zum Schweigen bringen;* ∾d to a skeleton *zum Skelett abgemagert;* he is in a very ∾d state *er befindet sich in sehr geschwächtem Zustand;* to ∾ someone to tears *j.en zu Tränen rühren*

reed n.: a broken ∾ *ein schwankendes Rohr;* to lean on a ∾ *auf eine schwache Sache (Person) vertrauen;* the ∾s *die Blasinstrumente im Orchester*

reef n.: to take in a ∾ *reffen; vorsichtig vorgehen*

reel[1] I. n.: off the ∾ *auf der Stelle, ununterbrochen, schnell hintereinander.* —

II. v.tr.: he ∾ed off the whole poem *er rasselte das ganze Gedicht herunter*

reel[2] **I.** v.i.: the tower ∾ed from the shock *der Turm schwankte von der Erschütterung;* to ∾ to and fro *torkeln, taumeln;* everything ∾ed before his eyes *alles drehte sich vor seinen Augen.* — **II.** n.: without a ∾ or a stagger *ohne zu taumeln oder zu schwanken;* in a ∾ of vice and folly *in einem Taumel von Laster und Torheit*

refer I. v.tr.: to ∾ (a cheque) to drawer (R.D.) *(einen Scheck) an den Aussteller zurückgeben;* I ∾red him to your address *ich verwies ihn an Ihre Adresse;* to ∾ miraculous tales to ignorance *Berichte über Wunder der Unwissenheit zuschreiben;* to ∾ a question for decision to a person *j.em eine Frage zur Entscheidung vorlegen.* — **II.** v.i.: to whom (to what) do you ∾? *auf wen (worauf) nehmen Sie Bezug?;* to ∾ to a dictionary *ein Wörterbuch nachschlagen;* to ∾ to one's watch *auf die Uhr blicken*

reference n.: in (with) without ∾ to *mit, ohne Bezug auf;* a question outside the ∾ (the terms of ∾) of the committee *eine Frage außerhalb des Untersuchungsbereiches des Ausschusses;* a book of ∾ *ein Nachschlagebuch, -werk;* a cross ∾ *ein Hinweis auf eine andere Stelle desselben Buches, Kreuzverweis;* a ∾ bible *eine Bibel mit Angabe von Parallelstellen;* a ∾ library *eine Handbibliothek;* to have good ∾s *gute Empfehlungen (Zeugnisse) haben;* to make (a)∾ to *verweisen (anspielen) auf*

reflect I. v.tr.: the laws ∾ the moral attitude of a half century earlier *die Gesetze spiegeln die moralische Haltung vor 50 Jahren wider;* his conduct ∾s great credit on him *sein Verhalten gereicht ihm zur großen Ehre;* to shine with ∾ed light *in fremdem Glanze strahlen.* — **II.** v.i.: now that I ∾ (up)on it I believe you are right *jetzt, wo ich es mir überlege, glaube ich, daß du recht hast;* I do not wish to ∾ (up)on him *ich will nichts Nachteiliges über ihn sagen*

reflection n.: that is a ∾ (up)on his character *das wirft ein schlechtes Licht auf seinen Charakter;* on ∾, I doubt whether I was right *bei näherer Überlegung zweifle ich, ob ich recht hatte;* I cast (throw) no ∾ (up)on him *ich sage nichts Nachteiliges über ihn, ich tadle ihn nicht*

refresher a.: a ∾ fee *(Anwalt) ein Extrahonorar;* a ∾ course *ein Wiederholungskursus*

refuge n.: a house of ∾ *ein Asyl für Obdachlose;* to find, to seek, to take ∾ in *Zuflucht finden, suchen (in, bei), nehmen (zu)*

refusal n.: I met with a flat ∾ *es wurde mir glatt (rundweg) abgeschlagen;* I stipulated for the ∾ of the house *ich sicherte mir das Vorkaufsrecht auf das Haus;* he will take no ∾ *er will keine abschlägige Antwort annehmen (entgegennehmen)*

regard I. v.tr.: that does not ∾ me *das geht mich nichts an (betrifft mich nicht);* he does not ∾ my advice *er beachtet meinen Rat nicht;* to ∾ a person intently *j.en scharf ansehen;* it is to be ∾ed as a wild beast *es ist als wildes Tier anzusehen;* I ∾ him as my friend *ich betrachte ihn als meinen Freund;* as ∾s (∾ing) wheat, prices are rising *was Weizen betrifft (anlangt), so steigen die Preise.* — **II.** n.: in ∾ to (of); with ∾ to *hinsichtlich (gen.), was betrifft;* to act without ∾ to (of) decency *ohne Rücksicht auf Anstand handeln;* to have (to pay) ∾ to a thing *auf etwas Rücksicht nehmen, einer Sache Rechnung tragen (Beachtung schenken);* to have a high ∾ for a thing *eine hohe Meinung von einer Sache haben;* give him my kind (or: best) ∾s *grüßen Sie ihn freundlich (bestens) von mir;* with due ∾ to *unter gebührender Rücksicht auf.* — **III.** a.: ∾ful, ∾less, of the consequences *mit Rücksicht, ohne Rücksicht auf die Folgen*

register I. v.tr.: to ∾ a fact *eine Tatsache im Geiste festhalten;* the thermometer ∾s ten degrees of frost *das Thermometer zeigt zehn Grad Kälte;* to ∾ a letter, a parcel *einen Brief, ein Paket einschreiben lassen;* to ∾ one's luggage *sein Gepäck aufgeben.* — **II.** v.i.: guests are requested to ∾ *die Gäste werden gebeten, sich einzutragen*

registry n.: a servant's ∾ (office) *ein Stellenvermittlungsbüro für Hausangestellte;* to get married at a ∾ (office) (= a registrar's office) *sich standesamtlich trauen lassen*

regret n.: to express ∾ for *Bedauern ausdrücken wegen;* to hear with ∾ of (that) *mit Bedauern hören von (oder: daß);*

to refuse with much ∾ (many ∾s) *mit großem Bedauern ablehnen*

regular a.: he belongs to the ∾ clergy *er gehört der Ordensgeistlichkeit an;* she cooks as well as a ∾ cook *sie kocht so gut wie eine gelernte Köchin;* a ∾ customer *ein Stammkunde;* to keep ∾ hours *nach der Uhr leben;* I should like to have a ∾ meal *ich möchte eine ordentliche Mahlzeit haben;* he's a ∾ rascal *er ist ein richtiger Halunke*

rehash v.tr.: to ∾ old ideas to fill a new book *alte Gedanken wieder aufwärmen, um ein neues Buch zu füllen*

rein n.: to break a horse to the ∾ *ein Pferd zureiten;* to draw ∾ *die Zügel anziehen, anhalten;* to give ∾ (the ∾s) to *die Zügel schießen lassen;* to give ∾ (the ∾s) to one's imagination *seiner Phantasie freien Lauf lassen;* to take (to assume) the ∾s *die Zügel ergreifen, die Leitung übernehmen;* to keep a tight ∾ on someone *j.en straff am Zügel halten, j.em die Zügel straff halten*

reinforce v.tr.: to ∾ a person's health with food *j.es Gesundheit mit Nahrungsmitteln kräftigen;* ∾d concrete *Eisenbeton*

rejoice I. v.tr.: the news ∾d him *die Nachricht erfreute ihn;* I am ∾d to hear it *ich freue mich, es zu hören;* I am ∾d that it should be so (at it, by it) *ich freue mich darüber.* — **II.** v.i.: to ∾ at (over) a thing *sich über etwas freuen;* he ∾s in (at) doing so *er macht sich ein Vergnügen daraus, es zu tun;* to ∾ in the possession of a thing *sich des Besitzes einer Sache erfreuen;* they were rejoicing over the victory *sie feierten gerade den Sieg;* there were great rejoicings at the wedding *bei der Hochzeit gab es ein großes Fest*

relate I. v.tr.: to ∾ a story to a person *j.em eine Geschichte erzählen;* to ∾ the phenomena with (to) each other *die Erscheinungen zu einander in Beziehung bringen;* he is ∾d to the royal family *er ist mit der königlichen Familie verwandt.* — **II.** v.i.: he notices nothing but what ∾s to himself *er beachtet nur das, was sich auf ihn selbst bezieht*

relation n.: in ∾ to *in bezug auf;* the ∾ of a story *die Erzählung einer Geschichte;* is he any ∾ of yours? *ist er irgendwie mit dir verwandt?;* to bear no (to be out of all) ∾ to *in keiner Beziehung (in keinem Verhältnis) stehen zu*

relative I. a.: he lives in ∾ comfort *er lebt verhältnismäßig behaglich;* supply is ∾ to demand *Angebot und Nachfrage decken sich.* — **II.** n.: he is a ∾ of mine *er ist ein Verwandter von mir*

relatively adv.: ∾ speaking *im Vergleich*

relax v.tr. & i.: to ∾ (to ∾ in) one's efforts *seine Anstrengungen vermindern, in seinen Anstrengungen nachlassen;* a ∾ing climate *ein erschlaffendes Klima*

release v.tr.: to ∾ a film *einen Film auf den Markt bringen, zur Aufführung freigeben;* to ∾ information *eine Nachricht für die Öffentlichkeit freigeben;* to ∾ a right *ein Recht aufgeben;* to ∾ from *befreien von*

relief[1] n.: the medicine brought ∾ *die Medizin brachte Erleichterung;* it is a ∾ to come across an optimist *es ist eine nette Abwechslung, es tut einem gut, einem Optimisten zu begegnen;* a comic scene follows by way of ∾ *zur Entspannung folgt eine komische Szene;* recipients of public ∾ are not eligible *Unterstützungsempfänger sind nicht wählbar;* the victory meant the ∾ of the fortress *der Sieg bedeutete den Entsatz der Festung;* to go to a person's ∾ *j.em zur Hilfe eilen; j.en ablösen;* a ∾ train *ein Vorzug*

relief[2] n.: to bring out in ∾, to bring (to throw) into ∾ *hervorheben, hervortreten lassen;* to stand out in ∾ *hervortreten, sich scharf abheben*

relieve v.tr.: the fortress was ∾d *die Festung wurde entsetzt (befreit);* I am much ∾d to hear it *es ist mir eine große Erleichterung, das zu hören;* he devotes himself to relieving distress *er widmet sich der Linderung der Not;* to ∾ one's feelings *seinen Gefühlen Luft machen;* to ∾ nature, oneself *sein Bedürfnis verrichten;* the white lace ∾d the black silk *die weiße Spitze hob sich von der schwarzen Seide ab;* you will be ∾d at 10.30 *du sollst um halb elf abgelöst werden;* to ∾ a person of a load *j.en von einer Last befreien;* the tramp ∾d him of his purse *der Landstreicher stahl ihm die Börse*

religion n.: to get ∾ (vulg. or facet.) *fromm werden, sich bekehren*

religious a.: to do something with ∾ care *etwas mit gewissenhafter Sorgfalt tun*

relish I. n.: to have a ∾ of *schmecken nach;* meat has no ∾ when one is ill *Fleisch schmeckt nicht, wenn man krank ist;* to eat with great ∾ *es sich gut schmecken lassen;* he has no ∾ for poetry *er findet keinen Gefallen an Gedichten;* a bottle of tasty ∾ *eine Flasche schmackhafter Sauce.* — **II.** v.tr.: he thought he could ∾ a chicken *er glaubte, ihm würde ein Hähnchen schmecken;* I do not ∾ the prospect of getting no coal *die Aussicht, keine Kohlen zu bekommen, behagt mir nicht.* — **III.** v.i.: to ∾ of *schmecken nach, einen Beigeschmack (einen Anflug) haben von;* it ∾es well, badly *es schmeckt gut, schlecht*

reluctant a.: I am very ∾ to admit *ich gebe höchst ungern zu;* he gave me ∾ assistance *er half mir widerwillig, nur ungern*

rely v.i.: I ∾ (up)on you to do it (your doing it) *ich verlasse mich darauf, daß du es tust;* I ∾ (up)on its being done today *ich verlasse mich darauf, daß es heute getan wird;* you may rely (up)on it that he will be here in time *du kannst dich darauf verlassen, daß er rechtzeitig hier sein wird*

remember v.tr.: as far as I can ∾ *soweit ich mich erinnern kann;* to ∾ a person *sich an eine Person (sich einer Person) erinnern;* if I ∾ right(ly) *wenn ich mich recht erinnere;* he ∾ed me in his will *er bedachte mich in seinem Testament;* ∾ the porter *denken Sie an das Trinkgeld für den Gepäckträger!;* ∾ me to your wife! *grüßen Sie Ihre Frau von mir!*

remembrance n.: this is a ∾ of our stay in India *das ist ein Andenken an unseren Aufenthalt in Indien;* in ∾ of *zum Andenken an;* that has happened more than once within my ∾ *das habe ich mehr als einmal erlebt;* to bear (to keep) in ∾ *im Andenken (Gedächtnis) bewahren;* to call to ∾ *ins Gedächtnis zurückrufen;* to escape one's ∾ *seinem Gedächtnis entschwinden;* to have no ∾ of it *keine Erinnerung daran haben;* I have a pleasant ∾ of him *er steht bei mir in gutem Andenken;* to put a person in ∾ of a thing *j.en an etwas erinnern;* give my kind ∾s to him *grüßen Sie ihn freundlich von mir*

remind v.tr.: to ∾ a person of a thing *j.en an etwas erinnern*

reminder n.: to give (to send) a person a ∾ *j.en mahnen*

remit I. v.tr.: you must not ∾ your efforts *du darfst in deinen Anstrengungen nicht nachlassen;* may God ∾ your sins! *möge Gott dir deine Sünden vergeben!;* I have ∾ted you the money *ich habe dir das Geld überwiesen;* it has been ∾ted (in)to the previous state *es ist in den früheren Zustand versetzt worden;* the case has been ∾ted to (till) next week *der Fall ist auf nächste Woche verschoben (vertagt) worden;* the matter was ∾ted for decision to a higher instance *die Angelegenheit ist zur Entscheidung einer höheren Stelle überwiesen worden;* his sentence was ∾ted *die Strafe wurde ihm erlassen.* — **II.** v.i.: his enthusiasm is beginning to ∾ *seine Begeisterung beginnt nachzulassen*

remonstrate v.i.: to ∾ against a course of action *gegen eine Handlungsweise protestieren (Einwendungen machen);* to ∾ with a person (up)on a matter *j.em über (wegen) etwas Vorstellungen machen*

remote a.: memorials of ∾ ages *Denkmäler aus grauer Vorzeit;* he is a ∾ kinsman *er ist ein entfernter Verwandter;* the house lies ∾ from the road *das Haus liegt fernab der Straße;* he passed remarks ∾ from the subject *er machte Bemerkungen, die nichts mit der Sache zu tun hatten;* I have not the ∾st conception what he means *ich habe nicht die geringste (leiseste) Ahnung, was er meint;* ∾ control *Fernsteuerung*

remove I. v.tr.: to ∾ the last doubts *den (die) letzten Zweifel beheben;* to ∾ one's hat *den Hut ziehen;* to ∾ mountains *Berge versetzen;* at dinner there was fish ∾d by mutton *beim Essen folgte Hammelfleisch auf den Fisch;* he is my first cousin once (twice) ∾d *er ist mein Vetter zweiten (dritten) Grades;* it is not many degrees ∾d from the brute *es ist vom Tierischen nicht weit entfernt.* — **II.** v.i.: I am removing from London to Oxford *ich ziehe von London nach Oxford um.* — **III.** n.: the pupil has not got his ∾ *der Schüler ist nicht versetzt worden;* it is but one ∾ (few ∾s) from *es ist nur um eine Stufe (wenige Stufen) entfernt von*

rend I. v.tr.: shouts ∾ the air *Schreie gellen durch die Luft;* to ∾ one's hair *sich* *die Haare raufen;* to ∾ off, away, out of, from, asunder, in two, apart, to pieces *ab-, weg-, heraus-, entzwei-, in Stücke reißen.* — **II.** v.i.: the veil ∾s *der Schleier zerreißt*

render v.tr.: to ∾ (an) account of *Rechenschaft ablegen über;* on account ∾ed *laut erhaltener Rechnung;* to ∾ assistance *Beistand (Hilfe) leisten;* to ∾ fat *Fett auslassen;* to ∾ a fortress *eine Festung übergeben;* to ∾ good for evil *Böses mit Gutem vergelten;* to ∾ homage to a person *j.em huldigen;* to ∾ impossible *unmöglich machen;* to ∾ judgement *ein Urteil fällen;* age has ∾ed him peevish *das Alter hat ihn launisch (verdrießlich) gemacht;* to ∾ good service *gute Dienste leisten;* to ∾ thanks *Dank abstatten;* the dramatist's conception was well ∾ed *die Auffassung des Dramatikers wurde gut wiedergegeben;* how can it be ∾ed in German? *wie kann man das (auf) deutsch wiedergeben?;* to ∾ Latin into English *Latein ins Englische übersetzen (übertragen);* the grave ∾s up its dead *das Grab gibt seine Toten wieder*

renounce v.tr.: to ∾ a person's authority *j.es Autorität nicht anerkennen;* to ∾ a claim (a right, a possession) *auf einen Anspruch (ein Recht, einen Besitz) verzichten;* to ∾ the world *der Welt entsagen*

repair I. v.tr.: to ∾ an error, a wrong *einen Fehler, ein Unrecht wiedergutmachen;* to ∾ a loss *einen Verlust ersetzen;* to ∾ one's strength *seine Kraft wiederherstellen.* — **II.** n.: to be in good ∾ *in gutem Zustande (gut erhalten) sein;* to be out of ∾ *in schlechtem Zustande, baufällig, abgerissen sein;* to be under ∾ *sich in Reparatur (in der Ausbesserung) befinden*

repent I. v.tr.: you shall ∾ this! *das sollst du noch bereuen!* — **II.** v.i.: I have nothing to ∾ of *ich habe nichts zu bereuen;* to ∾ in sackcloth and ashes *in Sack und Asche Buße tun*

report I. n.: the ∾ goes *es geht das Gerücht, es verlautbart;* of good (ill) ∾ *von gutem (schlechtem) Ruf;* idle ∾s *Gerüchte, Klatsch;* the term's ∾ *das (Trimester) Schulzeugnis;* faithful in good and evil ∾ *in guten und bösen Tagen treu;* to give (to hand) in a ∾ *einen Bericht einreichen;* it went off with a loud ∾ *es explodierte mit lautem Knall.* — **II.** v.tr.: it is ∾ed *man sagt, es verlautbart;* ∾ed speech *indirekte Rede.* — **III.** v.i.: to ∾ to a person (up)on a thing *j.em über etwas Bericht erstatten;* to ∾ to the police *sich bei der Polizei melden*

reproach I. v.tr.: to ∾ a person with negligence *j.em Nachlässigkeit vorwerfen.* — **II.** n.: a term of ∾ *ein Schimpfwort;* the state of the road is a ∾ to the district *der Zustand der Straße ist eine Schmach für die Gegend;* to abstain from ∾ *sich des Tadels enthalten;* to heap ∾es on a person *j.en mit Vorwürfen überhäufen*

reproof n.: a glance of ∾ *ein tadelnder Blick;* to speak in ∾ of a thing *tadelnd von etwas sprechen*

republic n.: he is well known in the ∾ of letters *er ist in der literarischen Welt (Gelehrtenwelt) wohl bekannt*

repulse n.: to meet with (to suffer) a ∾ *zurückgeschlagen werden*

request I. n.: at the ∾ of, by ∾ of *auf die Bitte, auf das Ersuchen von;* to accede to (to comply with, to grant) a ∾ *einer Bitte nachkommen, eine Bitte gewähren;* to be in great ∾ *sehr begehrt sein;* to grow out of ∾ *nicht mehr begehrt werden, aus der Mode kommen;* to make a ∾ for a thing *um etwas bitten.* — **II.** v.tr.: to ∾ a favour of a person *j.en um eine Gefälligkeit bitten;* to ∾ a person to do (that he should do) something *j.en bitten (ersuchen), etwas zu tun*

require I. v.tr.: the emergency ∾s it (∾s that it should be done) *die Notlage verlangt (erfordert) es (macht es nötig, erforderlich);* they ∾ me (of me) to appear, of me that I should appear (they ∾ my appearance) *sie verlangen, daß ich erscheine (mein Erscheinen)*

requite v.tr.: to ∾ like for like *Gleiches mit Gleichem vergelten*

resign v.tr.: the ministers have ∾ed (office) *die Minister sind zurückgetreten;* he has ∾ed himself (he is ∾ed) to his fate *er hat sich mit seinem Schicksal abgefunden, sich in sein Los ergeben*

resignation n.: the minister has given (handed in, sent in, tendered) his ∾ *der Minister hat sein Entlassungsgesuch eingereicht;* to show great ∾ *große Gelassenheit zeigen*

resistance n.: to take the line of least ∾ *den bequemsten Weg einschlagen, die leichteste Methode anwenden*

resolution n.: the ∾ of the problem was easy *die Lösung des Problems war leicht;* to adopt (to pass) a ∾ *eine Entschließung annehmen;* to come to a ∾ *einen Entschluß fassen, sich entschließen;* to form (to make) good ∾s *gute Vorsätze fassen;* to show great ∾ *große Entschlossenheit zeigen*

resolve I. v.tr.: all doubts were ∾d *alle Zweifel waren behoben;* a thing is ∾d (∾s itself) into its elements *etwas löst sich in seine Bestandteile auf;* the House ∾s itself into a committee) *das Unterhaus konstituiert sich als Ausschuß.* — **II.** v.i.: a thing ∾s into its elements *etwas löst sich in seine Bestandteile auf;* to ∾ upon an action (upon doing, to do, a thing) *sich entschließen (beschließen), etwas zu tun;* he (was) ∾d that nothing should induce him *er war entschlossen (er beschloß), daß nichts ihn dazu bewegen sollte.* — **III.** n.: to keep one's ∾ *bei seinem Beschluß bleiben, an seinem Entschluß festhalten;* of high ∾ (Shakespeare) *von großer Entschlossenheit*

resort I. v.i.: to ∾ to force *seine Zuflucht zur Gewalt nehmen;* pilgrims ∾ed to the shrine *Pilger besuchten den Schrein.* — **II.** n.: in the last ∾ *als letzte Zuflucht, als letzter Ausweg;* repetition of the experiment was the only ∾ *es blieb nichts anderes übrig, als den Versuch zu wiederholen;* it cannot be done without ∾ to compulsion *es ist nicht ohne Zwang zu erreichen;* the town is a famous health ∾ *die Stadt ist ein berühmter Kurort;* a place of public ∾ *ein allgemein besuchter Ort*

resource n.: flight was his only ∾ *es blieb ihm nur die Flucht;* reading is a pleasant ∾ *Lesen ist eine angenehme Zerstreuung;* he is full of ∾ *er weiß sich stets zu helfen;* I am at the end of my ∾s *ich bin zu Ende mit meinen Mitteln;* a man of no ∾s *ein Mann ohne geistige Fähigkeiten*

respect I. n.: in all (in many) ∾s *in jeder (mancher) Hinsicht;* in one (every, some, this) ∾ *in einer (jeder, gewisser, dieser) Hinsicht;* with all ∾ for your advice *unter voller Würdigung deines Rates;* without ∾ of persons *ohne Ansehen der Person;* with ∾ to *mit Bezug auf;* without ∾ to the result *ohne Rücksicht auf das Ergebnis;* to give (to send) one's ∾s to a person *j.en grüßen lassen;* to have ∾ for a person *Achtung vor j.em haben;* to have ∾ to a thing *sich auf etwas beziehen;* he is held in ∾ *er ist hoch geachtet;* to pay ∾ to colour *auf Farbe achten;* to pay ∾ to a person *j.em Achtung zollen;* to pay one's ∾s to a person *j.em seine Aufwartung machen.* — **II.** v.tr.: to ∾ a person *j.en achten, schätzen;* he ∾ed my silence *er achtete mein Schweigen;* legislation ∾ing property *Gesetzgebung das Eigentum betreffend;* I am at a loss ∾ing his whereabouts *ich weiß nicht, wo er sich aufhält*

respective a.: they retired to their ∾ lodgings *sie kehrten jeder in seine Wohnung zurück;* the election depends on the ∾ popularity of the candidates *die Wahl hängt von der Beliebtheit der betreffenden Kandidaten ab;* A and B contributed the ∾ sums of 4s and 3s *A und B steuerten 4 beziehungsweise 3 Schillinge bei*

rest[1] I. v.i.: to ∾ from one's labours *sich von seiner Arbeit ausruhen;* to ∾ upon one's oars *zeitweilig aufhören zu arbeiten, sich auf seinen Lorbeeren ausruhen;* I ∾ upon your promise *ich verlasse mich (ich baue) auf dein Versprechen.* — **II.** v.tr.: ∾ your men for an hour *gönne deinen Leuten eine Stunde Ruhe!;* to ∾ one's elbow on the table *den Ell(en)bogen auf den Tisch stützen.* — **III.** n.: to be at ∾ *ruhen, in Ruhe sein, die ewige Ruhe haben;* to give a person a ∾ from work *j.em eine Ruhepause gönnen;* to go (to retire) to ∾ *sich zur Ruhe begeben;* to set a person's mind (heart) at ∾ *j.en beruhigen, beschwichtigen;* to take a ∾ *sich ausruhen;* he was ordered a ∾-cure *ihm wurde eine Liegekur (Erholung) verschrieben*

rest[2] v.i.: it ∾s with you to propose terms *es liegt an dir, Bedingungen vorzuschlagen;* the affair ∾s a mystery *die Sache bleibt ein Geheimnis;* you may ∾ assured *du kannst versichert sein*

rest[3] n.: all the ∾ *der ganze Rest, alle übrigen, alles Übrige;* as for the ∾ *was den Rest, die übrigen (das Übrige) anbelangt*

restraint n.: to keep under ∾ *in Haft (Verwahrsam) halten;* to speak without ∾ *frei von der Leber reden*

retail I. n.: to sell by ∾ *im Kleinhandel verkaufen.* — **II.** v.tr.: to ∾ gossip *Klatsch verbreiten*

retreat n.: to beat a ∾ *zum Rückzug trommeln; sich aus dem Staube machen;* to sound the ∾ *zum Rückzug blasen;* to make good one's ∾ *sicher entkommen;* to go into ∾ *Exerzitien machen;* a country ∾ *ein Landhaus*

retreating a.: to have a ∾ chin *ein fliehendes Kinn haben*

return I. v.i. & tr.: gone never to ∾ *auf Nimmerwiedersehen verschwunden;* to ∾ home *nach Hause zurückkehren, -kommen;* to ∾ a ball *einen Ball zurückschlagen;* to ∾ a borrowed book *ein entliehenes Buch zurückgeben;* to ∾ a compliment *ein Kompliment erwidern;* the accused were all ∾ed guilty *die Angeklagten wurden alle (für) schuldig befunden;* to ∾ one's partner's lead *die Farbe nachspielen, die der Partner angespielt hat;* to ∾ like for like *Gleiches mit Gleichem vergelten;* his investments ∾ a profit *sein angelegtes Geld wirft einen Gewinn ab;* to ∾ one's sword to the scabbard *sein Schwert wieder in die Scheide stecken.* — **II.** n.: by ∾ of post *postwendend;* what do I get in ∾? *was bekomme ich dafür (dagegen)?;* in ∾ for *als Gegenleistung für;* on my ∾ home *bei meiner Rückkehr nach Hause;* a first-class ∾ (ticket) to L. *eine Rückfahrkarte erster Klasse nach L.;* many happy ∾s of the day! *herzliche Glückwünsche (ich gratuliere) zum Geburtstag!;* small profits and quick ∾s *kleine Gewinne und schneller Umsatz;* he secured his ∾ for C. *er sicherte sich seine Wiederwahl für C.;* to submit a nil ∾ *eine Fehlanzeige melden (erstatten)*

revenge I. v.tr.: to be ∾d on a person (to take ∾ on a person) for something *sich an j.em für etwas rächen;* I must have my ∾ (in a game) *ich muß Revanche haben*

reverse n.: ∾s of fortune *Schicksalsschläge;* the case is quite the ∾ *der Fall liegt gerade umgekehrt;* the very ∾ of what we expected *das gerade Gegenteil von dem, was wir erwarteten;* the troops met with (suffered) a ∾ *die Truppen erlitten eine Niederlage;* in the ∾ order *in umgekehrter Reihenfolge;* in ∾ gear *im Rückwärtsgang*

review I. n.: to come under ∾ *zur Besprechung kommen;* to pass in ∾ *mustern; gemustert werden.* — **II.** v.tr.: to ∾ books *Bücher besprechen, rezensieren;* to ∾ the past *Rückschau über die Vergangenheit halten;* to ∾ troops *eine Parade abhalten*

rhyme n.: without ∾ or reason *ohne Sinn und Verstand*

rib n.: to poke a person in the ∾s *j.em einen Rippenstoß geben;* to smite a person under the fifth ∾ *j.en töten*

rid v.tr.: to ∾ oneself of a thing *sich etwas vom Halse schaffen;* to get ∾ of a thing *etwas loswerden*

riddance n.: a good ∾! *gut, daß wir es (dich, euch, ihn, sie) los sind!*

ride I. v.i.: to ∾ bodkin *eingequetscht zwischen zwei anderen Personen fahren;* ∾ a-cock-horse to Banbury Cross (nursery rhyme) *Hoppe, hoppe, Reiter!;* to ∾ roughshod over a person *rücksichtslos mit j.em umgehen; ihn roh behandeln;* to ∾ at anchor *vor Anker liegen;* to ∾ off on a side issue *von dem Kernpunkte abschweifen;* the ship ∾s on the waves *das Schiff schwimmt auf den Wogen;* the bird ∾s on the wind *der Vogel schwebt in der Luft;* to ∾ to hounds *auf (die) Parforcejagd reiten.* — **II.** v.tr.: to ∾ a bicycle *radfahren;* to ∾ a ford *eine Furt durchreiten;* to ∾ hell for leather *in rasendem Galopp reiten;* to ∾ the high horse *sich aufs hohe Pferd (Roß) setzen;* to ∾ a subject to death *ein Thema zu Tode hetzen;* to ∾ a willing horse to death *j.es Güte arg mißbrauchen;* to ∾ a person on a rail *j.en auf einem Brett herumtragen (Lynchjustiz);* to ∾ Shanks's mare *auf Schusters Rappen;* nightmare ∾s a sleeper *Alpdrücken quält einen Schläfer;* to ∾ for a fall *ein gefährliches Spiel treiben, ein Unglück heraufbeschwören;* to ∾ out the storm *den Sturm überstehen;* he is ridden by fears *ihn quält die Angst;* he is ridden by prejudices *er steckt voller Vorurteile.* — **III.** n.: to go for (to take) a ∾ *ausreiten, -fahren;* to take a person for a ∾ (U.S.) *j.en verulken, auf den Arm nehmen;* the gangsters took him for a ∾ (U.S.) *die Gangster entführten ihn im Auto, um ihn zu töten;* to steal a ∾ *als blinder Passagier mitfahren*

rider n.: a ∾ *eine Zusatzklausel, ein Anhängsel*

ridicule n.: to hold up to ∾ *lächerlich machen, verspotten*

rift n.: a little ∾ within the lute (Tennyson, Merlin and Vivien, l. 388) *ein kleiner, aber verhängnisvoller Fehler; ein*

Mißverständnis; eine Verstimmung (auch von beginnendem Wahnsinn gesagt)

rig[1] **I.** n.: to run a ∾ (old-fash.) *einen Streich spielen.* — **II.** v.tr.: to ∾ the market *die Preise künstlich steigern oder senken*

rig[2] v.tr.: to ∾ out (up) a person with *j.en ausstaffieren mit;* to ∾ up a booth *eine Bretterbude hastig aufschlagen*

right **I.** a.: ∾! ∾ you are! all ∾! ∾ oh! *ganz recht! in Ordnung!;* as ∾ as rain, as a trivet *in schönster Ordnung, in bester Verfassung, sauwohl;* it is only ∾ that you should know *es ist nur recht und billig, daß du erfährst;* he is the ∾ man in the ∾ place *er ist der rechte Mann am rechten Platze;* a fault on the ∾ side *ein angenehmer, vorteilhafter Fehler;* on the ∾ side of forty *noch nicht vierzig Jahre alt;* to be in one's ∾ mind *bei vollem Verstand sein;* to get (to put, to set) things ∾ *Dinge wieder in Ordnung bringen;* to get on the ∾ side of a person *sich (dat.) j.es Gunst verschaffen;* to give a ∾ account of a matter *einen wahrheitsgetreuen Bericht von einer Sache geben;* to send a person to the ∾-about *j.en hinauswerfen, fortjagen;* to set a person ∾ *j.en eines Besseren belehren;* he sits at (on, to) my ∾ hand *er sitzt rechts von mir, mir zur rechten.* — **II.** v.tr. & refl.: to ∾ the helm *das Ruder mitschiffs legen;* to ∾ a person *j.em ein Unrecht wiedergutmachen;* the boat ∾s herself *das Boot richtet sich wieder auf.* — **III.** n.: by ∾ of a thing *kraft, vermöge einer Sache;* she is peeress in her own ∾ *sie ist von Geburt Trägerin der Pairswürde;* to assert (to stand on) one's ∾s *auf seinem Recht bestehen;* to be in the ∾ *recht haben, im Recht sein;* to be on (to) my ∾ *auf meiner rechten Seite (mir zur Rechten, rechts von mir) sein;* it belongs to him of (by) ∾ *es gehört ihm von Rechts wegen;* to do a person ∾ *j.em Gerechtigkeit widerfahren lassen;* to have the ∾ of way *das Durchgangs-, Vorfahrtsrecht haben;* to have a person dead to ∾s (U.S.) *j.en in eine ungünstige Lage gebracht haben;* keep to the ∾! *rechts halten! rechts fahren!;* to set (to put) to ∾s *in Ordnung bringen;* Mr. Right is not yet come *der rechte Freier ist noch nicht erschienen.* — **IV.** adv.: a ∾-down shame *eine regelrechte (wahre) Schande;* the ∾ reverend bishop *seine Hochwürden der Bischof;* a veranda ∾ round the house *eine Veranda ganz (rund) um das Haus herum;* he was abused ∾ and left *er wurde tüchtig ausgeschimpft;* he did it ∾ off (or: away) *er tat es sofort;* he knows ∾ well *er weiß sehr wohl (recht gut);* to put oneself ∾ with a person *sich mit j.em gutstellen;* it sank ∾ to the bottom *es sank bis auf den Grund;* that serves you ∾ *das geschieht dir recht;* he stood ∾ in the middle of the street *er stand mitten auf der Straße;* he took the gate ∾ off the hinges *er hob das Tor ganz aus den Angeln;* he turned ∾ round *er drehte sich ganz um;* he went ∾ at him *er ging gerade auf ihn los*

Rimmon n.pr.: to bow down in the house of ∾ (2 Kings V, 18) *seine Grundsätze aus politischen oder anderen Motiven aufgeben*

ring **I.** v.i.: it still ∾s in my ears *es klingt mir noch in den Ohren;* his confession ∾s false *sein Geständnis klingt unwahr;* this coin ∾s true *diese Münze klingt echt;* a shot rang out *ein Schuß ertönte (knallte);* the whole town ∾s with his fame *die ganze Stadt hallt von seinem Ruhme wider;* he was received with ∾ing cheers *er wurde mit brausenden Hochrufen empfangen;* there was a ∾ing frost *es herrschte ein klirrender Frost;* I have a ∾ing in my ears *ich habe Ohrensausen; mir klingen die Ohren.* — **II.** v.tr.: to ∾ one's own bell *sein eigenes Lob singen;* to ∾ the bell to (for) prayers *zum Gebet läuten;* does that ∾ a bell? *fällt dir dabei etwas ein? bringt dich das darauf? ist der Groschen gefallen?;* to ∾ the changes on a subject *ein Thema in der mannigfachsten Weise behandeln; dieselbe Sache in immer neuen Formen behandeln; alle Tonarten versuchen;* to ∾ the knell of something *etwas zu Grabe läuten;* to ∾ a person's praises *j.es Lob verkünden;* to ∾ up a person *j.en telephonisch anrufen, anklingeln;* to ∾ off *ein Telephongespräch beenden, den Hörer einhängen (auflegen);* to ∾ out the old year *vom alten Jahr Abschied nehmen.* — **III.** 1.n.: three ∾s for the porter! *für den Pförtner dreimal klingeln (schellen, läuten)!;* give the bell a ∾ *klingele mal eben!;* to give a person a ∾ *j.en telephonisch anrufen.* — 2.n.: to make ∾s round someone *j.em weit überlegen sein*

riot **I.** n.: to quell a ∾ *einen Aufruhr unterdrücken;* to run ∾ *(von Hunden) eine* *falsche Fährte verfolgen;* to let one's fancy run ∾ *der Phantasie freien Lauf lassen;* the flowers run ∾ in our garden *die Blumen wuchern in unserem Garten;* to read the ∾ act *j.en verwarnen.* — **II.** v.i.: to ∾ in highflown expectations *in hochfliegenden Erwartungen schwelgen;* to ∾ in wine *in Wein schwelgen.* — **III.** v.tr.: to ∾ away money *Geld verprassen (verpulvern, verwichsen);* to ∾ out one's life in dissipation *sein Leben in Ausschweifungen vergeuden*

rip¹ n.: an old ∾ *ein alter Klepper;* he is an old (a sad) ∾ *er ist ein alter Lebemann, Wüstling*

rip² **I.** v.tr.: to ∾ up old wounds *alte Wunden aufreißen.* — **II.** v.i.: let things ∾ (colloq.) *laß die Dinge laufen! (laß den Dingen ihren Lauf);* I had a ∾ ping time (sl.) *ich habe mich glänzend amüsiert*

ripe a.: soon ∾, soon rotten (prov.) *was schnell reift, fällt bald ab;* to die at a ∾ age *im hohen Alter sterben*

ripper n.: he is a ∾ (sl., old fash.) *er ist ein Prachtkerl*

rise **I.** v.i.: her colour rose *sie errötete;* the dough will not ∾ *der Teig will nicht gehen;* Parliament will ∾ next week *das Parlament vertagt sich nächste Woche;* the sun ∾s *die Sonne geht auf;* to ∾ above a thing *über etwas erhaben sein;* to ∾ again (from the dead) *von den Toten auferstehen;* my gorge ∾s at the thought *mir wird übel (mir kommt es hoch) bei dem Gedanken;* to ∾ in the world *eine höhere gesellschaftliche Stellung erreichen, vorwärtskommen, es zu etwas bringen;* to ∾ in arms *zu den Waffen greifen;* the river ∾s in the mountains *der Fluß entspringt im Gebirge;* the curtain ∾s on the scene *der Vorhang geht hoch über der Szene;* the hair rose on his head *die Haare standen ihm zu Berge;* to ∾ to the bait (to it) *anbeißen, auf den Leim gehen (kriechen), darauf hereinfallen;* to ∾ to the occasion *sich der Lage gewachsen zeigen, sich schnell in die Lage finden;* to ∾ with the lark *beim ersten Hahnenschrei (in aller Herrgottsfrühe) aufstehen.* — **II.** n.: the ∾ and fall *das Steigen und Fallen, der Aufstieg und der Sturz;* a ∾ in the road *eine Steigung der Straße;* to ask for a ∾ *um eine Lohn-, Gehaltserhöhung bitten;* prices are on the ∾ *die Preise steigen;* to get (to take) a ∾ out of a person *j.en in die Wolle bringen, reizen; j.en lächerlich machen;* to give ∾ to a thing *zu etwas Anlaß geben;* it has (takes) its ∾ in (from) *es entspringt in (aus);* he has had a ∾ in life *er hat seine gesellschaftliche Stellung gebessert (es zu etwas gebracht);* the chapel stands on a ∾ *die Kapelle steht auf einer Anhöhe*

rising **I.** n.: a ∾ *eine Anschwellung, ein Geschwür;* to suppress a ∾ *einen Aufstand niederschlagen.* — **II.** a.: the ∾ generation *die heranwachsende Generation;* on ∾ ground *auf ansteigendem Gelände;* a ∾ lawyer *ein emporkommender Rechtsanwalt;* to be ∾ twenty five *ins 25. Lebensjahr gehen*

risk **I.** n.: at the ∾ of falling *auf die Gefahr hin hinzufallen;* at the ∾ of one's life *mit (unter) eigener Lebensgefahr;* there is the ∾ of his catching cold *es besteht die Gefahr, daß er sich erkältet;* to run (to take, to incur) ∾s (a ∾, the ∾ of) *Gefahr laufen.* — **II.** v.tr.: to ∾ the jump *den Sprung riskieren (wagen);* to ∾ one's reputation *seinen Ruf aufs Spiel setzen;* to ∾ a sprained ankle *Gefahr laufen, sich den Fuß zu verstauchen*

river n.: a ∾ novel *eine Familiensaga in mehreren Bänden*

roach n.: as sound as a ∾ *kerngesund, so gesund wie ein Fisch im Wasser*

road n.: the high (or: main) ∾ *die Hauptstraße;* the high ∾ to perdition *die breite Straße, die zur Verdammnis führt;* he is on the high ∾ to success *er ist auf dem besten Wege zum Erfolg;* there is no royal ∾ to knowledge (learning) (prov.) *es gibt keinen mühelosen Weg zu Kenntnissen; ohne Fleiß kein Preis;* to be on the ∾ *unterwegs, auf der Reise sein;* get out of my ∾! *geh mir aus dem Weg!;* I'm going by ∾ *ich gehe zu Fuß, ich benutze die Landstraße;* to go on the ∾ *Geschäftsreisen machen;* to keep to the rule of the ∾ *sich nach der Verkehrsordnung richten;* to ride at anchor in the open ∾ *auf offener Reede vor Anker liegen;* to take the ∾ *eine Reise antreten;* to take the ∾ of a person *an j.em vorbeifahren, ihn überholen;* to take to the ∾ *Landstreicher werden;* he is a ∾-hog *er ist ein gefährlicher (rücksichtsloser) Autofahrer, ein Straßenschreck, ein Kilometerfresser;* trees grow by the ∾-side *Bäume wachsen am Straßenrand;* a ∾-side inn *ein Gasthaus* *an der Landstraße;* to keep to the ∾way *auf dem Fahrdamm bleiben*

roar I. n.: ∾s of laughter *ein schallendes (brüllendes) Gelächter;* his remarks set the table in a ∾ *seine Bemerkungen riefen ein schallendes Gelächter bei der Tischgesellschaft hervor;* to set up a ∾ *ein lautes Geschrei (Gebrüll) erheben.* — **II.** v.i.: to ∾ for help (mercy) *um Hilfe (Gnade) schreien;* to ∾ with laughter (pain) *vor Lachen (Schmerz) brüllen.* — **III.** v.tr.: he was ∾ed down *er wurde niedergebrüllt;* to ∾ out words *Worte herausbrüllen*

roaring a.: the ∾ forties *stürmische Striche des Südatlantischen Ozeans zwischen dem 39. und 50. Breitengrad;* he is in ∾ health *er strotzt vor Gesundheit;* we spent a ∾ night *wir verbrachten eine tolle (wilde) Nacht;* he drives a ∾ trade *er macht Bombengeschäfte*

roast n.: to rule the ∾ (roost) *herrschen, den Ton angeben, die erste Geige spielen*

rob v.tr.: to ∾ Peter to pay Paul *ein Loch aufreißen, um ein anderes zuzustopfen; hier borgen, um dort zu bezahlen*

robe n.: the long ∾ der Talar; gentlemen of the ∾ *Rechtsanwälte, Richter*

robin n.: a ∾ redbreast *ein Rotkehlchen;* a round ∾ *eine Bittschrift, bei der die Unterschriften im Kreise stehen, damit man nicht weiß, wer zuerst unterschrieben hat*

rock n.: to be on the ∾s (sl.) *in Geldverlegenheit sein, auf dem trockenen sitzen;* to run upon the ∾s *Schiffbruch erleiden;* to see ∾s ahead *Gefahren voraussehen;* ∾-bottom prices *allerniedrigste Preise*

rocker n.: to be off one's ∾ (sl.) *verrückt sein, einen Vogel (Sparren) haben*

rocket n.: to get (to stop) a ∾ (colloq.) *einen ernsten Verweis, eine Rüge erhalten*

rod n.: the divining (or: dowsing) ∾ *die Wünschelrute;* I have a ∾ in pickle for him *er hat bei mir noch etwas im Salz liegen;* to kiss the ∾ *eine Strafe unterwürfig hinnehmen, sich unter die Rute beugen;* to make a ∾ for one's own back *sich (dat.) eine Rute aufbinden, sich die Rute selber flechten;* spare the ∾ and spoil the child (prov.) *wer die Rute spart, verzieht das Kind*

Roger n.pr.: Sir ∾ de Coverley *ein englischer Volkstanz; die Melodie dazu;* the Jolly ∾ *die schwarze Seeräuberflagge*

Roland n.pr. to give a ∾ for an Oliver *die passende Antwort geben; mit gleicher Münze bezahlen; wie du mir, so ich dir; Wurst wider Wurst*

roll[1] n.: to call the ∾ *die Namen vorlesen, um festzustellen, wer fehlt;* we must be in time for ∾-call *wir müssen rechtzeitig zur Namenverlesung da sein;* his name is on the ∾ of honour *sein Name steht auf der Ehrentafel;* to strike off the ∾s *aus der Liste der Rechtsanwälte streichen;* he has ∾s of fat on him *er ist dick mit Fett gepolstert;* to have a ∾ for breakfast *ein Brötchen zum Frühstück essen*

roll[2] **I.** v.tr.: to ∾ a cigarette *sich (dat.) eine Zigarette drehen;* ∾ your hoop (U.S. sl.) *kümmere dich um deine eigenen Angelegenheiten!;* to ∾ the lawn *den Rasen walzen;* he ∾ed himself from side to side *er wälzte sich von einer Seite auf die andere;* ∾ my log and I'll ∾ yours *eine Hand wäscht die andere; Kuhhandel treiben;* saint and philosopher ∾ed into one *Heiliger und Philosoph in einem;* to ∾ a person over *j.en um-, niederwerfen;* he ∾ed himself up in the blankets *er wickelte sich in die Wolldecken ein.* — **II.** v.i.: the ship ∾s and pitches *das Schiff schlingert und stampft;* years ∾ on (by) *Jahre rollen dahin;* he ∾ed up last night *er ist gestern abend erschienen, eingetrudelt;* he is ∾ing in money *er ist steinreich, er schwimmt im Gelde;* a ∾ing plain *eine weite wellenförmige Ebene;* ∾ing stock *rollendes Material;* a ∾ing stone gathers no moss (prov.) *rollender (wälzender) Stein wird nicht moosig.* — **III.** n.: a ∾ of the drum *ein Trommelwirbel;* a ∾ of thunder *ein Donnergrollen*

Roman a.: a ∾ holiday *ein Genuß, unter dem andere zu leiden haben*

Rome n.pr.: ∾ was not built in a day (prov.) *Rom ist nicht an einem Tage erbaut worden;* to do in ∾ as ∾ does, as the Romans do, to do as they do at ∾ *mit den Wölfen heulen, sich den Landessitten anpassen*

romp I. v.i.: the horse ∾ed in (home) *das Pferd gewann das Rennen leicht.* — **II.** n.: to have a game of ∾s *sich balgen, sich austoben*

rook v.tr.: to ∾ someone (colloq.) *j.en betrügen, über's Ohr hauen*

room n.: there is ∾ and to spare *es ist reichlich Platz vorhanden;* in the ∾ of *an Stelle von;* it takes up too much ∾ *es nimmt zuviel Platz ein;* there's ∾ for improvement *es läßt zu wünschen übrig;* there's no ∾ for doubt *es läßt sich nicht bezweifeln;* there's no ∾ to swing a cat *man kann sich hier kaum umdrehen, der Raum ist sehr beengt;* there's plenty of ∾ *es ist viel Platz da;* I would rather have his ∾ than his company *ich wäre ihn gerne los;* he made the whole ∾ laugh *er brachte alle im Zimmer zum Lachen;* to be in ∾s *eine möblierte Wohnung haben*

roost n.: to be at ∾ *schlafen, im Bett sein;* to be the cock of the ∾ *Hahn im Korbe sein;* to go to ∾ *schlafen gehen, zu Bett gehen;* curses come home to ∾ *wer anderen eine Grube gräbt, fällt selbst hinein*

root I. n.: it is a ∾ fallacy to believe *es ist grundfalsch zu glauben;* to destroy ∾ and branch *mit Stumpf und Stiel ausrotten;* to go to (to get at) the ∾ of a matter *einer Sache auf den Grund gehen;* to pull up by the ∾s *mit den Wurzeln ausziehen, ausrotten;* to take (to strike) ∾ *Wurzel schlagen.* — **II.** v.tr.: her affection was deeply ∾ed *ihre Zuneigung war tief verwurzelt;* fear ∾ed him to the ground *er blieb vor Furcht wie angewurzelt stehen;* to ∾ out *ausrotten.* — **III.** v.i.: some plants ∾ freely *manche Pflanzen fassen schnell Wurzel*

rope I. n.: a ∾ of sand *ein lockeres, schwaches Band;* money for old ∾ (sl.) *gefundenes, leicht verdientes Geld;* the mountaineer is on the ∾ *der Bergsteiger ist angeseilt;* to be on the high ∾s *gewaltig erregt sein (vor Freude oder Wut), hochgestimmt sein;* to give a person ∾ *j.en gewähren (schalten und walten) lassen;* to give a person ∾ enough to hang himself *j.en gewähren lassen, in der Erwartung, daß er sich selbst schadet;* to know the ∾s *sich auskennen, den Rummel kennen;* to learn the ∾s *den Rummel kennenlernen;* to perform on the tight-∾ *als Seiltänzer auftreten;* to put a person up to the ∾s *j.en in den Betrieb (den Rummel) einweihen;* to work the ∾s *eine Sache heimlich leiten, bewerkstelligen.* — **II.** v.tr.: to ∾ a person in *j.en in eine Sache hineinziehen, -locken, ihn als Anhänger gewinnen*

ropey a.: ∾ ideas *altmodische, abgetane Gedanken*

rose n.: a ∾ without a thorn *eine Rose ohne Dorn, eine ungemischte Freude;* under the ∾ *insgeheim, im Vertrauen;* it is not all ∾s (it is no bed of ∾s) for me *ich bin nicht auf Rosen gebettet;* a path strewn with ∾s *ein Leben voller Freuden;* a thorn between two ∾s *ein Herr zwischen zwei Damen;* to gather ∾s (life's ∾s) *Vergnügungen nachgehen;* she has quite lost her ∾s *sie hat ihre blühende Farbe verloren;* he sees things through ∾-coloured spectacles, he takes ∾-coloured views *er sieht alles durch eine rosenrote Brille;* a crumpled ∾-leaf *ein kleines Ärgernis, welches das allgemeine Glück stört;* revolutions are not made with ∾-water *bei Revolutionen geht es nicht sanft her*

rot I. n.: a ∾ set in (sport, war, etc.) *eine unerklärliche Reihe von Mißerfolgen trat ein, es ging alles schief;* don't talk such (tommy) ∾ (sl.) *rede doch nicht so einen Blödsinn (so ein Blech).* — **II.** v.i.: he was left to ∾ in gaol *man ließ ihn im Gefängnis vermodern;* he is only ∾ting (sl.) *er macht nur Unsinn;* the fruit ∾ted off *das Obst fiel faul vom Baum.* — **III.** v.tr.: that has ∾ted the whole plan (sl.) *das hat den ganzen Plan über den Haufen geworfen*

rote n.: to do (to know, to learn, to say) by ∾ *etwas rein mechanisch tun; etwas auswendig wissen, lernen, hersagen*

rotten a.: something is ∾ in the state of Denmark (Hamlet) *etwas ist faul im Staate Dänemark;* it is a ∾ concern (sl.) *es ist ein fauler Kram;* he had ∾ luck (sl.) *er hatte Saupech*

rotter n. (sl.): he's a ∾ *er ist ein unbrauchbarer, übler Bursche*

rough I. a.: a ∾ copy *ein erster Entwurf (Konzept);* a ∾ diamond *ein grober (ungehobelter), aber wertvoller Mensch;* a ∾ house *ein Tumult, eine Schlägerei;* to ∾-house a person; to ∾-house *mit j.em rauh umgehen; Krach machen;* that is ∾ (∾luck) on him *das ist hart für ihn, da hat er aber Pech;* a ∾-neck *ein Rowdy;* a ∾ and ready measure *eine Notbehelfsmaßnahme;* I gave him a lick with the ∾ side of my tongue *ich habe ihn gehörig angefahren, herunter-*

geputzt; to have a ∾ time *eine schwere Zeit durchmachen;* a ∾-and-tumble fight *eine rohe (wüste) Schlägerei.* — **II.** adv.: to cut up ∾ *aufgebracht sein, rauhbeinig werden;* to ride ∾-shod over a person *rücksichtslos mit j.em umgehen, ihn roh behandeln;* ∾-spoken *grob (derb) redend.* — **III.** n.: he is a ∾ *er ist ein Grobian (Raufbold, Rowdy);* the ∾(s) and the smooth(s) of life *die rauhen und angenehmen Seiten des Lebens;* through ∾ and smooth *durch Dick und Dünn;* to shape from the ∾ *aus dem Groben formen.* — **IV.** v.tr.: to ∾ it *sich mühselig durchschlagen;* to ∾ in (or: out) the outlines *die Umrisse im groben skizzieren;* to ∾ a person up the wrong way *j.en ärgern*

roughly adv.: ∾ speaking, there were one thousand people present *es waren ungefähr (etwa) eintausend Leute da*

round I. a.: a ∾-the-clock programme *ein durchgehendes (Tag- und Nacht-)Programm;* a ∾ dozen *ein volles Dutzend;* a ∾ game *ein Gesellschaftsspiel;* a ∾ number *eine abgerundete Zahl;* a ∾ robin, see 'robin'; a ∾ unvarnished tale (Shakespeare) *die reine (ungeschminkte) Wahrheit;* he declared in ∾ terms *er erklärte offen (rund) heraus;* at a ∾ trot *in kräftigem Trab;* to bring up with a ∾ turn *mit plötzlichem Ruck anhalten.* — **II.** n.: a ∾ of beef *eine Rinderkeule;* the ∾ of a ladder *die Sprosse einer Leiter;* the daily ∾ *die gewöhnliche Tagesarbeit;* this earthly ∾ *diese Erde;* a knockout in the first ∾ *ein Niederschlag in der ersten Runde;* to go (to make) one's ∾s *die Runde machen;* to go for a good ∾ *einen langen Spaziergang machen;* a story goes the ∾(s) of the town *eine Geschichte geht in der Stadt (her)um.* — **III.** adv.: he is an all-∾ sportsman *er ist ein vielseitiger Sportsmann;* all the neighbours for a mile ∾ *alle Nachbarn eine Meile im Umkreis;* all the year ∾ *das ganze Jahr hindurch;* to ask a person ∾ *j.en zu sich bitten;* to bring (to win) a person ∾ to one's opinion *j.en zu seiner Ansicht bekehren (herumkriegen);* to come ∾ *vorbeikommen, einen Besuch machen; sich erholen, wieder zu sich kommen;* to go ∾ to a person *bei j.em vorsprechen;* the wheels go ∾ and ∾ *die Räder drehen sich in einem fort;* you must make the cake go ∾ *du mußt sehen, daß jeder ein Stück Kuchen bekommt;* to go a long way ∾ *einen langen (großen) Umweg machen;* a room hung all ∾ with pictures *ein ringsum mit Bildern behangenes Zimmer;* to order the car ∾ *den Wagen ans Haus bestellen;* to pass (to send) the hat ∾ *Geld einsammeln, den Hut herumgehen lassen;* tea was served ∾ *es wurde Tee herumgereicht;* to show a person ∾ *j.en herumführen;* to sleep the clock ∾ *12 oder 24 Stunden lang schlafen;* he turned short ∾ *er drehte sich kurz um.* — **IV.** prep.: he's ∾ the bend (sl.) *er ist verrückt;* he hawks them ∾ the cafés *er verhökert sie in den Cafés;* it turns ∾ its centre of gravity *es dreht sich um seinen Schwerpunkt;* it is just ∾ the corner *es ist gerade um die Ecke;* she has a wrapper ∾ her *sie hat sich (dat.) ein Tuch umgeschlagen;* she diffuses cheerfulness ∾ her *sie verbreitet Frohsinn um sich;* shells burst ∾ me *Granaten platzten um mich herum;* to get ∾ a person *j.en beschwatzen, herumkriegen;* to sit ∾ the table *um den Tisch herum sitzen;* to write a book ∾ a subject *ein Buch über etwas schreiben;* to argue ∾ and ∾ a subject *um eine Sache herumreden;* a tour ∾ (all ∾, right ∾) the world *eine Reise rund um die Welt.* — **V.** v.tr.: to ∾ a dog's ears *einem Hund die Ohren stutzen;* to ∾ off a thing *etwas abrunden;* to ∾ up cattle *Vieh zusammentreiben.* — **VI.** v.i.: her form is ∾ing *ihre Gestalt rundet sich;* to ∾ on a person *j.em eine unerwartete Antwort geben; j.en anzeigen, verpfeifen*

roundabout I. n.: a (traffic) ∾ *ein Verteilerkreis;* to lose on the swings what you make on the ∾s *hier verlieren, was man dort gewonnen hat, ein Geschäft ohne Gewinn betreiben.* — **II.** a.: a ∾ way *ein Umweg; ein umständliches Verfahren*

roundly adv.: he ∾ asserts that it is true *er behauptet rundweg, es sei wahr;* he was ∾ abused *er wurde tüchtig ausgeschimpft;* to go ∾ to work *sich gründlich an die Arbeit machen;* I told him ∾ *ich sagte ihm offen heraus*

rousing a.: to give a ∾ cheer *ein brausendes Hoch ausbringen*

rout I. n.: to put to ∾ *in die Flucht schlagen.* — **II.** v.tr.: to ∾ a person out of (from) bed *j.en aus dem Bette treiben*

rove n.: to be on the ∾ *herumwandern, auf der Wanderschaft sein*

row¹ n.: a hard ∾ to hoe *eine schwierige (mühselige) Arbeit*

row² n.: what's the ∾? *was ist los?; I* shall get into a ∾ *ich werde ausgeschimpft (ausgescholten) werden;* to have a ∾ with a person *heftigen Streit mit j.em haben;* to kick up (to make) a ∾ *Krach, Spektakel machen*

row³ I. v.tr.: to ∾ a race *wettrudern;* to ∾ down *im Rudern überholen.* — **II.** n.: to go for a ∾ *rudern gehen*

royal a.: there is no ∾ road to knowledge (learning) (prov.) *es gibt keinen mühelosen Weg zu Kenntnissen; ohne Fleiß kein Preis;* we had a ∾ time *wir haben uns königlich amüsiert;* they were in ∾ spirits *sie waren bei (in) bester Laune (Stimmung)*

rub I. v.tr.: to ∾ shoulders with a person *mit j.em verkehren;* to ∾ a person the wrong way *j.en reizen, ärgern;* to ∾ down a horse *ein Pferd striegeln;* you need not ∾ it in *du brauchst es mir nicht ständig unter die Nase zu reiben (aufs Butterbrot zu schmieren);* to ∾ up one's memory *sein Gedächtnis auffrischen.* — **II.** v.i.: to ∾ along (on, through) *sich durchschlagen, sich über Wasser halten.* — **III.** n.: there's the ∾! (Hamlet) *da ist der Haken! da liegt der Hase im Pfeffer!;* the ∾s and worries of life *die Sorgen und Nöte des Lebens;* to give a thing a ∾-down, ∾-up *etwas abreiben*

rubberneck(s) I. n.: ∾ (sl.) *Touristen, neugierige, schaulustige Personen.* — **II.** v.i.: to ∾ *sich den Hals verrenken, um alles zu sehen*

rubber-stamp v.tr.: we are not prepared to ∾ his actions *wir sind nicht bereit, seine Handlungen zu billigen*

rubbish n.: ∾! *Unsinn! Quatsch!;* a good riddance of (or: to) bad ∾! *ihn wären wir gut los!;* to shoot ∾ *Schutt abladen*

ruction n. (sl.): there will be ∾s *es wird großen Spektakel geben*

ruddy a.: it's a ∾ shame (sl.) *es ist eine verdammte (verfluchte) Schande*

ruin n.: to bring to ∾ *ins Verderben stürzen;* it will be the ∾ of him *es wird seinen Untergang bedeuten;* to go to rack and ∾ *völlig zugrunde gehen*

rule I. n.: as a ∾ *in der Regel;* the ∾ *of three Regeldetri;* hard and fast ∾s *unumstößliche Gesetze; starre, unabänderliche Regeln;* to do a thing by ∾ of thumb *etwas nach einfachen, praktischen Regeln erfahrungsmäßig bewerkstelligen;* to go by a ∾ *sich an eine Regel halten;* to keep to the ∾ of the road *sich nach der Verkehrsordnung richten;* to lay down a ∾ *eine Regel aufstellen;* to make it a ∾ *es sich zur Regel machen;* the exception proves the ∾ (prov.) *die Ausnahme bestätigt die Regel;* to work to ∾ *als Ersatz für offenen Streik streng nach den Vorschriften arbeiten und dadurch die Leistung mindern.* — **II.** v.tr.: to be ∾d by one's conscience *sich von seinem Gewissen leiten (raten) lassen;* to ∾ the roast (roost) *herrschen, den Ton angeben, die erste Geige spielen;* to ∾ out *ausschließen;* his objection was ∾d out *sein Einwand wurde als nicht stichhaltig erklärt;* to ∾ a person out of order (parl.) *j.em das Wort entziehen (verbieten zu sprechen);* to ∾ a sheet of paper *einen Bogen Papier linieren.* — **III.** v.i.: the king reigns but does not ∾ *der König herrscht aber regiert nicht;* to ∾ over millions *über Millionen herrschen;* prices ∾d high, low *die Preise standen hoch, niedrig;* a ruling passion *eine vorherrschende Leidenschaft*

rum a. (sl.): he is a ∾ customer *er ist ein seltsamer Kunde, ein komischer Kauz*

rummage I. v.tr.: to ∾ out (up) *auskramen, durchstöbern.* — **II.** v.i.: to ∾ about among (in) *wühlen, herumstöbern in.* — **III.** n.: a ∾-sale *ein Ramschverkauf*

run I. v.i.: see 'cold, dry, foul, high, low, mad, short, wild'; the candle ∾s *die Kerze tropft;* the colours ∾ in the wash *die Farben sind nicht waschecht;* courage ∾s in the family *Mut liegt in der Familie;* to cut and ∾ (sl.) *ausreißen;* the play ran for 100 nights *das Stück wurde hundertmal gegeben;* a heavy sea is ∾ning *es ist hoher Seegang;* the story ∾s as follows, like this *die Geschichte lautet wie folgt, folgendermaßen;* time ∾s *die Zeit vergeht;* how your tongue ∾s! *dir steht doch der Mund nie still!;* the tune ∾s in my head *die Melodie geht mir im Kopf herum;* our pears are ∾ning big *unsere Birnen werden groß.* — with prep.: to ∾ across, against, see 'across, against'; to ∾ for it, for one's life *ausreißen, fortrennen;* to ∾ into debt *in Schulden geraten;* the book ran into five editions *das Buch erlebte fünf Auflagen;* to ∾ into a person *j.en zufällig treffen;* the train ran off the lines *der Zug entgleiste;* the talk ran on the elections *man sprach von den Wahlen;* we have ∾ out of provisions *der Proviant ist uns ausgegangen;* the car ran over the child *das Auto überfuhr das Kind;* I ran over the lines *ich überflog die Zeilen;* I ran through the items *ich überprüfte die einzelnen Posten;* he has ∾ through his money *er hat sein Geld durchgebracht;* he ∾s to coarseness *er neigt zur Derbheit;* to ∾ to extremes, fat, seed, sentiment, meet one's troubles, see 'extreme, fat, seed, sentiment, trouble'; events ran to pattern *die Ereignisse verliefen wie gewöhnlich;* the bill ∾s to five pounds *die Rechnung beläuft sich auf fünf Pfund;* I couldn't ∾ to that *soviel könnte ich nicht ausgeben;* I ran upon my friend *ich traf zufällig meinen Freund;* his thoughts ran upon the subject *seine Gedanken beschäftigten sich dauernd mit dem Gegenstand.* — with adv.: to ∾ back over the past *einen kurzen Blick auf die Vergangenheit werfen;* to ∾ down (over, up) to a place for a flying visit *zu kurzem Besuch irgendwo hinfahren;* the clock has ∾ down *die Uhr ist abgelaufen;* he ran on incessantly *er sprach unaufhörlich weiter;* his sands are ∾ning out *seine Stunden sind gezählt;* our supplies have ∾ out *unsere Vorräte sind zu Ende gegangen;* the beans are ∾ ning up *die Bohnen schießen hoch;* to ∾ up to town for the day *auf einen Tag nach London, in die Stadt fahren.* — **II.** v.tr.: see 'business, course, earth, errand, eye, gauntlet[2], hand, rig, riot, risk'; to ∾ the blockade *die Blockade brechen;* to ∾ brandy *Branntwein schmuggeln;* Labour is ∾ning a candidate *die Arbeiterpartei hat einen Kandidaten aufgestellt;* he ∾s two cars *er hat zwei Wagen laufen;* to ∾ cattle *Vieh auf die Weide treiben;* to ∾ a chance of winning *(eine) Aussicht haben zu gewinnen;* the company ∾s a coach *die Gesellschaft läßt einen Autobus verkehren;* to ∾ a comb (one's fingers) through one's hair *mit einem Kamm (mit den Fingern) durch die Haare fahren;* to ∾ one's head against a thing *mit dem Kopf gegen etwas stoßen;* to ∾ a horse in the Derby *ein Pferd im Derby laufen lassen;* to ∾ a knife into a person *j.em ein Messer in den Leib rennen (jagen);* to ∾ a nail into one's foot *sich (dat.) einen Nagel in den Fuß stoßen (treten);* to ∾ a parallel (simile) too far *einen Vergleich zu weit treiben;* to ∾ one's pen through a line *eine Zeile durchstreichen;* to ∾ a person close, hard *j.em dicht auf den Fersen sein, ihm Konkurrenz machen;* to ∾ a race *einen Wettlauf machen;* to ∾ the rapids *die Stromschnellen durchfahren;* to ∾ a rope through an eyelet *ein Tau durch eine Öse laufen lassen;* to ∾ a scent *einer Spur (Fährte) folgen;* to ∾ a ship aground *ein Schiff auflaufen lassen;* to ∾ the show *die Sache schmeißen;* to ∾ the streets *ein Straßenjunge sein;* to ∾ a subject dry *einen Gegenstand erschöpfen;* to ∾ a sword through a person *j.en mit einem Schwert durchbohren;* he is ∾ning a temperature (colloq.) *er hat Fieber;* to ∾ things fine *es haarscharf darauf ankommen lassen, mit der Zeit in die Enge kommen (geraten);* the fountains ran wine *aus den Springbrunnen sprudelte Wein.* — with adv.: to ∾ a person (a thing) down *j.en (etwas) niederrennen; j.en einholen, ausfindig machen; j.en (etwas) abfällig beurteilen, heruntermachen;* I am much ∾ down *ich bin gesundheitlich sehr herunter;* to ∾ in a car *einen Wagen einfahren;* to ∾ a person in *j.en verhaften (einlochen);* to ∾ a person off his feet *j.en bis zur Erschöpfung arbeiten lassen, ihn abhetzen;* I ran it over in my mind *ich überlegte es mir;* just ∾ this list over *sehen Sie eben diese Liste durch!;* to ∾ a person through *j.en durchbohren;* to ∾ up an account *auf Kredit kaufen, anschreiben lassen;* to ∾ up a bill *eine Rechnung auflaufen (anwachsen) lassen, Schulden machen;* to ∾ up a flag *eine Fahne hissen;* to ∾ up a hut *eine Hütte schnell aufbauen.* — **III.** n.: in the long ∾ *auf die Dauer, am Ende, schließlich;* to be on the ∾ *auf der Flucht sein, auf den Beinen sein, geschäftig hin und her rennen;* to come down with a ∾ *plötzlich herunterstürzen;* to go for (to have, to take) a ∾ *einen Lauf machen;* to go for a ∾ on the Continent *einen kurzen Ausflug aufs Festland machen;* to have a ∾ for one's money *etwas für sein Geld (seine Anstrengungen) haben;* the goods have a considerable ∾ (go with a ∾) *die Waren finden reißend Absatz;* to put a person to the ∾ *j.em Beine machen;* a ∾ on the bank *ein Ansturm auf die Bank;* the ∾ of the hills is N.W. *die Hügelkette verläuft in nordwestlicher Richtung;* to have the ∾ of a person's house *freien Zutritt bei j.em haben;*

a ∾ of bad luck *eine Pechsträhne;* the ∾ of the market *die Tendenz des Marktes;* the common (or: ordinary) ∾ of men *Leute gewöhnlichen Schlages;* the ∾ of the metre *der Rhythmus des Versmäßes;* the quality of these books is the general ∾ of the mill *die Qualität dieser Bücher ist durchschnittlicher Art:* the play had a ∾ of 50 nights *das Stück erlebte 50 Aufführungen hintereinander;* a long ∾ of office *eine lange Amtsdauer;* a long ∾ of pipe *eine lange Rohrleitung;* there was a ∾ on rubber *es herrschte eine starke Nachfrage nach Gummi;* to have the ∾ of one's teeth *freie Kost haben*

runaway a.: a ∾ match, marriage *eine Heirat nach Entführung;* to give a ∾ knock, ring *Klingelmännchen machen, Mäuschen fangen*

runner n.: a Bow-Street ∾ (rare) *eine frühere Bezeichnung für einen Polizisten;* the scarlet ∾ *die türkische Feuerbohne;* the ∾-up in a competition *der zweite Sieger bei einem Wettbewerb*

running I. n.: to be in (out of) the ∾ *Aussichten (keine Aussichten) auf Erfolg haben;* to make (to take up) the ∾ *die Führung übernehmen, das Tempo angeben.* — **II.** a.: to have a ∾ account *ein laufendes Konto haben;* a ∾ commentary *eine Rundfunkreportage, ein laufender Kommentar;* a ∾ fight *ein Rückzugsgefecht;* a ∾ fire *ein Schnellfeuer;* a ∾ hand *eine Kurrentschrift;* a ∾ knot *ein Schifferknoten;* a ∾ sore *eine eiternde Wunde; ein ständiges Ärgernis;* ∾ water *fließendes Wasser*

rush[1] n.: I don't care a ∾ about it *ich frage gar nichts danach;* it's not worth a ∾ *es ist keinen Pfifferling (Heller) wert*

rush[2] I. v.tr.: I refuse to be ∾ed *ich lasse mich nicht hetzen;* to ∾ a bill through Parliament *eine Gesetzesvorlage durch das Parlament peitschen;* to ∾ an obstacle *über ein Hindernis hinwegsetzen;* they ∾ you shockingly at that hotel *in dem Hotel werden entsetzlich hohe (unverschämte) Preise verlangt, man wird dort übers Ohr gehauen.* — **II.** v.i.: to ∾ into extremes *in Extreme verfallen, zum Äußersten schreiten;* his past life ∾ed into his memory *er erinnerte sich plötzlich an seine Vergangenheit;* to ∾ into print *etwas voreilig seine Ansicht durch den Druck veröffentlichen.* — **III.** n.: a ∾ of blood to the head *ein Blutandrang zum Kopfe;* a ∾ of business *ein äußerst lebhafter Geschäftsgang;* there was a ∾ for tickets *man schlug sich förmlich um Eintrittskarten;* to carry the citadel with a ∾ *die Zitadelle im Sturm nehmen;* to make a ∾ for the door *zur Tür stürzen;* the ∾-hours *die Hauptverkehrsstunden;* a ∾ job *eine schnell (unordentlich) angefertigte Arbeit*

rusty a.: his Greek is a little ∾ *im Griechischen ist er nicht mehr auf der Höhe;* he easily turns ∾ *er wird leicht ärgerlich, mürrisch*

rut n.: everything goes on in the same old ∾ *es geht alles seinen alten Trott*

rye n.: to go from clover to ∾-grass *vom Pferd auf den Esel kommen (besonders von zweiten Ehen gesagt)*

S

Sabbath n.: to keep (to break) the ∾ *den Sonntag heiligen (entheiligen)*

sabbatical a.: a ∾ year *ein Feriensemester (Ferienjahr) für Professoren zu Studienzwecken*

sack I. n.: to give a person (to get) the ∾ *j.en fristlos entlassen; fristlos entlassen werden;* to do penitence in ∾cloth and ashes *in Sack und Asche Buße tun;* a ∾-race *Sackhüpfen.* — **II.** v.tr.: to ∾ a person *j.en fristlos entlassen;* to ∾ a town *eine Stadt plündern*

sad a.: a ∾der and (a) wiser man (Coleridge, The Ancient Mariner), *j., der durch trübe Erfahrungen klug geworden ist;* he is a ∾ coward *er ist ein erbärmlicher Feigling;* he is a ∾ dog *er ist ein Schwerenöter;* in ∾ earnest *in vollem Ernst;* you have made a ∾ mess of it *du hast die Sache gehörig verpfuscht;* ∾ to say *bedauerlicherweise;* he writes ∾ stuff *er schreibt ein elendes Zeug;* you have made ∾ work of it *du hast etwas Schönes angerichtet*

saddle I. n.: to be in the ∾ *eine leitende Stelle (inne)haben; zur Arbeit bereit sein;* to put the ∾ on the right (wrong) horse *die Schuld auf den Richtigen (Falschen) schieben;* to win the horse or lose the ∾ *alles oder nichts gewinnen.* — **II.** v.tr.: he is ∾d with a great responsibility *eine große Verantwortung lastet auf ihm;* to ∾

a burden (up)on a person *j.em etwas aufbürden*

safe I. a.: ∾ bind, ∾ find *sicher verwahrt, schnell gefunden;* as ∾ as a house *vollkommen (absolut) sicher;* a ∾ conduct *ein sicheres Geleit;* ∾ and sound *gesund und munter, wohlbehalten;* it is ∾ to say *man kann ruhig (ohne Übertreibung) sagen;* to be (to keep) on the ∾ side *sicher gehen;* the dog is not ∾ to touch *es ist gefährlich, den Hund anzufassen;* it is best to err on the ∾ side *besser zuviel Vorsicht als zu wenig*

safety n.: ∾ first! *eine Mahnung, im Straßenverkehr, vor allem an die Sicherheit zu denken;* there is ∾ in numbers (prov.) *man ist sicher, wenn man zu mehreren ist;* I cannot do it with ∾ *ich kann es nicht ohne Gefahr tun;* he is playing for ∾ *er geht auf Numero sicher;* a ∾-razor *ein Rasierapparat;* to sit on the ∾-valve *eine Politik der Unterdrückung befolgen*

sail I. n.: to carry all ∾ *mit vollen Segeln fahren;* to crowd ∾ *alle Segel beisetzen;* to hoist ∾ *die Segel hissen;* to lower (to strike) ∾ *die Segel streichen;* to make (to set) ∾ for a port *nach einem Hafen in See stechen;* to shorten ∾ *die Segel einziehen;* to take in ∾ *seine ehrgeizigen Pläne zurückschrauben;* to take the wind out of a person's ∾s *j.em den Wind aus den Segeln nehmen;* to trim one's ∾s to the wind *den Mantel nach dem Wind hängen; sich nach den Umständen richten, sich nach der Decke strecken;* it is a ten days' ∾ *das Schiff fährt zehn Tage;* to go for a ∾ *eine Segelpartie machen.* — **II.** v.i.: to ∾ close to (or: near) the wind *sich an der Grenze des Erlaubten oder des Schicklichen bewegen;* to ∾ into a person *auf j.en schimpfen, über ihn herziehen;* when we have done that it will all be plain ∾ing *wenn wir das hinter uns haben, wird die ganze Sache einfach sein (glatt vonstatten gehen).* — **III.** v.tr.: to ∾ the sea *das Meer durchsegeln*

sailor n.: I am a good (bad) ∾ *ich werde nicht seekrank, ich werde leicht seekrank*

sake n.: for God's (goodness') ∾! *um Gottes willen!;* do it for my ∾ *tu es mir zuliebe!;* for the ∾ of peace *um des lieben Friedens willen;* for old ∾'s ∾ *im Andenken an alte Zeiten*

salad n.: ∾ days (Shakesp., A. & C. I, 5, 73) *Tage jugendlicher Unerfahrenheit;* fruit ∾ *(scherzhaft für) bunte Ordensschnalle*

sale n.: a clearance ∾ *ein Ausverkauf;* to be on (or: for) ∾ *zu verkaufen sein; zum Verkauf stehen;* to meet with a ready ∾ *schnellen Absatz finden;* to put up for ∾, to put to ∾ *zum Verkauf stellen, feilbieten;* ∾s resistance *Kaufunlust des Verbrauchers*

salt I. n.: his talk is full of ∾ *sein Reden ist voller Witz;* he is an old ∾ *er ist ein alter Seebär;* to be true to one's ∾ *seinem Dienstherrn treu sein;* to eat a person's ∾ *j.es Gastfreundschaft genießen; in j.es Diensten stehen;* I am not made of ∾ *ich bin nicht von Zucker, ich kann ruhig naß werden, den Regen vertragen;* there was no ∾ in his tears *seine Tränen kamen ihm nicht von Herzen;* to sit above (below) the ∾ *an der Spitze, am unteren Ende der Tafel sitzen;* to take with a grain of ∾ *mit Vorsicht aufnehmen;* he is not worth his ∾ *er ist seines Lohnes nicht wert, er taugt nichts.* — **II.** v.tr.: to ∾ an account *eine gesalzene Rechnung aufstellen;* to ∾ the books *die Bücher fälschen;* to ∾ a mine *Erz in ein Bergwerk einführen, um reiches Vorkommen vorzutäuschen;* to ∾ down money *Geld beiseitelegen, sicher anlegen*

salvo n.: with an express ∾ of their rights *unter ausdrücklichem Vorbehalt ihrer Rechte*

Sam n.pr.: upon my ∾ *bei Gott!;* I shall stand ∾, ∾my *ich werde euch alle freihalten, die Zeche bezahlen (berappen);* a ∾ Browne *ein lederner Offiziersgürtel mit Schulterriemen;* Uncle ∾ *die Regierung der USA; ein typischer Bürger der USA*

same I. a.: the very ∾, just the ∾, one and the ∾ *genau, ganz, ein und der- (die-, das-)selbe;* at the ∾ time *gleichzeitig;* it is much the ∾, it comes to the ∾ thing *es ist so ziemlich dasselbe;* it is (all) the ∾ to me *es ist mir ganz einerlei (gleich, egal, Wurst);* the sick man is much (about) the ∾ *es geht dem Kranken nicht besser, aber auch nicht schlechter;* we are all in the ∾ boat (box) *es geht uns allen gleich.* — **II.** pr.: we must all say (do) the ∾ *wir müssen alle dasselbe sagen (tun);* the ∾ to you *danke gleichfalls.* — **III.** adv.: all the ∾ *nichtsdestoweniger,* *dennoch, trotzdem;* just the ~ *gleichwohl;* at the ~ time *nichtsdestoweniger*

sanctify v.tr.: the end sanctifies (justifies) the means (prov.) *der Zweck heiligt die Mittel*

sanctuary n.: London, the ~ of political refugees *London, die Freistatt für politische Flüchtlinge;* to take (to seek) ~ in a church *zu einer Kirche Zuflucht nehmen, in einer Kirche Schutz suchen;* to violate (to break) ~ *j.en an einem geheiligten Orte verhaften, mißhandeln*

sand n.: to build on ~ *auf Sand (ohne genügende Vorsicht) bauen;* to plough the ~, ~s *den Sand pflügen, Vergebliches, Unnützes tun;* a rope of ~ *ein lockeres, schwaches Band;* his ~s are running out *seine Stunden sind gezählt;* as jolly as a ~boy *kreuzfidel, quietschvergnügt*

sandwich I. n.: a ham ~ *ein Schinkenbrot;* a ~-man *ein Mann, der auf Rücken und Brust ein Reklameplakat herumträgt.* — **II.** v.tr.: to be ~ed between *eingepfercht sitzen zwischen;* to ~ a thing between *etwas einschieben*

Santa Claus n.pr.: ~ *der Weihnachtsmann*

sap (sl.) **I.** v.i.: to ~ away at lessons *büffeln (ochsen, pauken).* — **II.** n.: he is a ~ *er ist ein Streber, Dummkopf;* it is such a (too much) ~ *es ist eine solche (eine zu große) Plackerei, Schinderei*

sardine n.: they were packed like ~s *sie standen (saßen) wie die Heringe*

sauce n.: hunger is the best ~ (prov.) *Hunger ist der beste Koch;* what is ~ for the goose is ~ for the gander *was dem einen recht ist, ist dem anderen billig;* to serve a person with the same ~ *j.em mit gleicher Münze heimzahlen, Gleiches mit Gleichem vergelten;* a ~-boat *eine Sauciere;* none of your ~ *keine Unverschämtheit!, sei nicht so unverschämt!;* a ~-box *eine freche, schnippische Person*

saucer n.: eyes like ~s, ~-eyes *Glotzaugen*

save[1] v.tr. & i.: to ~ appearances *den Schein wahren;* to ~ one's bacon *sich in Sicherheit bringen, mit heiler Haut davonkommen;* to ~ one's breath *die Lungen schonen, schweigen;* to ~ one's face *sein Ansehen wahren;* his secretary ~s him much labour *sein Sekretär erspart ihm viel Arbeit;* (God) ~ the mark! *Gott steh' uns bei! du lieber Himmel! daß Gott erbarm'!;* God ~ me from my friends! *Gott bewahre mich vor wohlmeinenden Freunden!;* to ~ up money *Geld sparen;* a stitch in time ~s nine (prov.) *ein kleines Mittel zur rechten Zeit spart viel Mühe; Vorsicht ist besser als Nachsicht;* you may ~ your pains *du kannst dir die Mühe sparen;* to write hurriedly to ~ the post *eilig schreiben, um die Post noch zu erreichen;* to ~ one's skin *sich in Sicherheit bringen*

save[2] **I.** prep.: ~ and except *mit Ausnahme von;* all ~ him *alle außer ihm.* — **II.** conj.: I am well ~ that I have a slight cold *außer einer leichten Erkältung geht es mir gut;* I am happy ~ for one want *mir fehlt nur eins zum Glück*

saving I. a.: a ~ clause *eine Vorbehaltsklausel;* he has the ~ grace of humour *sein Humor ist seine einzige gute Eigenschaft;* to be ~ of a thing *sparsam mit einer Sache umgehen;* ~ your presence (old-fash.) *mit Verlaub zu sagen.* — **II.** n.: he has lost all his ~s *er hat seine ganzen Ersparnisse verloren;* a ~s-bank *eine Sparkasse.* — **III.** prep.: ~ my father *meinen Vater ausgenommen*

savour v.i.: to ~ of a thing *nach etwas riechen, schmecken; einen Anflug (Beigeschmack) von etwas haben*

saw[1] **I.** n.: to let the ~-dust out of a person *j.es Anmaßung, Hohlheit aufdecken (bloßstellen).* — **II.** v.tr.: a ~-bones (sl.) *ein Chirurg*

saw[2] n.: there is an old (a wise) ~ *es gibt einen alten (weisen) Spruch*

sawder n.: soft ~ *Schmeichelei, verbindliche Redensarten*

say I. v.tr.: that is ~ing a great deal *das besagt sehr viel, will viel (be)sagen;* to ~ grace *das Tischgebet sprechen;* to ~ one's lessons *seine Aufgaben auf-, hersagen;* to ~ Mass *die Messe lesen;* to ~ a person nay *j.em etwas verweigern;* to ~ the word *den Befehl geben;* to ~ a good word for a person *für j.en ein gutes Wort einlegen;* he is said to be *er soll sein;* it is said in the Bible *es heißt in der Bibel;* when all is said and done *letzten Endes;* no sooner said than done *gesagt, getan.* — **II.** v.i.: I ~, Jack, who was that? *sag mal* *(hör mal), Hans, wer war das?;* I ∾, what a beauty! *Donnerwetter, welch Prachtexemplar!;* I dare ∾ *(ironisch) ja, Kuchen!;* I dare ∾ he will come *ich glaube wohl, daß er kommen wird;* I dare ∾ you are right *ja, freilich;* that is to ∾ *das heißt, mit anderen Worten;* have you nothing to ∾ for yourself? *hast du nichts zu deiner Entschuldigung (Rechtfertigung) vorzubringen?;* you don't ∾ so! *was Sie nicht sagen!;* £ 500, ∾ five hundred pounds *£ 500, in Worten (sage und schreibe) fünfhundert Pfund;* any country, let us ∾ Sweden, might do the same *irgendein Land, sagen wir mal (zum Beispiel) Schweden, könnte dasselbe tun;* well, ∾ it were true, what then? *nun, gesetzt es wäre wahr, was dann?;* what he ∾s, goes *was er sagt, wird akzeptiert, seine Befehle werden befolgt.* — **III.** n.: ∾ your ∾ *sage, was du zu sagen hast; sprich dich aus;* let him have his ∾ *laß ihn seine Meinung sagen;* he has no ∾ in the matter *er hat nichts in der Angelegenheit zu sagen (mitzusprechen)*

saying n.: as the ∾ is (goes) *wie das Sprichwort lautet, wie man so zu sagen pflegt;* there is no ∾ *es läßt sich nicht sagen;* that goes without ∾ *das versteht sich von selbst, das ist selbstverständlich*

scabbard n.: to fling (to throw) away the ∾ *sich darauf festlegen, eine Sache bis zu Ende durchzukämpfen*

scale I. n.: a pair of ∾s *eine Waage;* to hold the ∾s (even) *unparteiisch sein;* to throw one's sword into the ∾s *sein Schwert in die Waagschale werfen, einen Anspruch mit Waffengewalt unterstützen;* to turn the ∾ *den Ausschlag geben;* he turns the ∾s at 2 cwt. *er wiegt zwei Zentner.* — **II.** v.tr.: to ∾ prices (wages) up (down) *Preise (Löhne) nach einem gewissen Maßstab erhöhen (herunterschrauben)*

scalp n.: to be out for ∾s *auf dem Kriegspfad sein; angriffs-, kampflustig sein*

scarce a.: to make oneself ∾ *sich aus dem Staube, sich dünne machen, sich drücken*

scare I. v.tr.: to ∾ a person stiff (sl.) *j.en zu Tode erschrecken;* a ∾crow *eine Vogelscheuche.* — **II.** a.: ∾ headlines *sensationelle (Zeitungs-)Überschriften*

scarlet a.: the ∾ runner *die türkische Feuerbohne;* the ∾ woman (Rev. XVII) *die römische Kirche;* to flush (to turn) ∾ *puterrot werden*

scatter-brain I. n.: he is a ∾ *er ist ein Wirrkopf, schusseliger Kerl.* — **II.** a.: a ∾ed fellow *ein Wirrkopf, schusseliger Kerl*

scent I. v.tr.: to ∾ treachery *Verrat wittern;* the roses ∾ed the whole room *das ganze Zimmer duftete nach Rosen.* — **II.** n.: to follow up a ∾ *eine Spur verfolgen;* to have a fine ∾ for a thing *eine feine Nase für etwas haben;* to put (to throw) a person off the ∾ *j.en von der Fährte (Spur) abbringen*

schedule v.tr.: he is ∾d to arrive at 10 o'clock *planmäßig kommt er um 10 Uhr an*

school I. n.: at ∾ *in der Schule;* a primary ∾ *eine Elementarschule;* a public ∾ *eine dotierte höhere Schule mit Alumnat;* a secondary ∾ *eine höhere Schule;* a ∾-fellow, ∾mate *ein Mitschüler, Schulkamerad;* the ∾master is abroad *Bildung verbreitet sich überall;* to tell tales out of ∾ *aus der Schule plaudern (schwatzen).* — **II.** v.tr.: he must ∾ his temper *er muß sich beherrschen lernen;* to ∾ oneself to patience *sich an Geduld gewöhnen, sich zur Geduld erziehen*

science n.: our ∾ master *unser Lehrer in den Naturwissenschaften;* the dismal ∾ *die Volkswirtschaftslehre;* the noble ∾ *das Boxen*

scold I. n.: she is an old ∾ *sie ist ein zänkisches (keifendes) Weib, eine Xanthippe.* — **II.** v.tr.: to ∾ a person, to give a person a good ∾ing *j.en tüchtig ausschelten*

sconce n.: a crack on the ∾ *ein Schlag auf den Schädel*

scoop n.: with a (at one) ∾ *mit éinem Schub, Griff;* a newspaper ∾ (sl.) *eine sensationelle Allein-,Erstmeldung einer Zeitung;* to make a ∾ (sl.) *einen großen Gewinn machen*

scope n.: he has ample (full, free) ∾ for his abilities *er hat freien Spielraum für seine Fähigkeiten;* it is beyond (within) his ∾ *es ist außerhalb (innerhalb) seines Bereiches*

scorch I. v.tr.: the ∾ed earth policy *die Politik der verbrannten Erde (beim Rückzug alles verbrennen oder vernichten, was dem Feinde nützen könnte).* — **II.** v.i.: to ∾ (colloq.) *schnell und rücksichtslos fahren*

scorcher n.: today has been a ∾ (sl.) *heute hatten wir eine Bullenhitze*

score I. n.: the ∾s of the whip showed on his back *die Peitschenstriemen waren auf seinem Rücken zu sehen;* on the ∾ of a thing *auf Grund von, wegen einer Sache;* rejected on the ∾ of absurdity *als lächerlich zurückgewiesen;* you may be easy on that ∾ *darüber kannst du beruhigt sein;* he is given to making cheap ∾s (sl.) *er geht auf billige Triumphe aus;* what a ∾! (sl.) *welch ein Dusel!;* the days of our years are three ∾ years and ten (Ps. 90, 10) *unser Leben währet siebenzig Jahre;* ∾s of people *eine Unmenge Leute;* to go off at ∾ *flott drauflosschwatzen;* the team made (put up, ran up) a good ∾ *die Mannschaft machte viele Läufe, schoß viele Tore, gewann viele Punkte;* what is the ∾ now? *wie steht jetzt das Spiel?;* to pay one's ∾ *seine Rechnung begleichen;* to pay (to wipe) off old ∾s *alte Rechnungen begleichen, erlittenes Unrecht heimzahlen.* — **II.** v.tr.: to ∾ a goal *ein Tor schießen;* to ∾ an offence against (to) a person *j.em eine Beleidigung ankreiden;* to ∾ a success *einen Erfolg buchen;* to ∾ out (under) words *Wörter ausstreichen, unterstreichen;* to ∾ up a debt against (to) a customer *einem Kunden eine Schuld anschreiben, ankreiden.* — **III.** v.i.: the team failed to ∾ *die Mannschaft machte keinen Lauf, schoß kein Tor, gewann keinen Punkt;* that is where he ∾s *da ist er im Vorteil;* we shall ∾ by it *das wird uns zum Vorteil gereichen;* to ∾ off a person (sl.) *über j.en triumphieren*

scorn I. n.: to be a ∾ to (the ∾ of) a person *der Gegenstand des Spottes für j.en sein;* to hold a thing in ∾, to think ∾ of a thing *etwas verachten;* to laugh a thing to ∾ *etwas lächerlich machen.* — **II.** v.tr.: he ∾s lying (a lie, to lie) *er verschmäht es zu lügen*

scot n.: to pay ∾ and lot *Gemeindeabgaben bezahlen, auf Heller und Pfennig bezahlen;* to go (to get off) ∾-free *ungestraft davonkommen*

scourge n.: the white ∾ *die Tuberkulose, Schwindsucht*

scram int. (sl.): ∾! *hau' ab!, verdufte!*

scramble v.tr.: ∾d eggs *Rührei*

scrap[1] I. n.: not a ∾ *nicht das kleinste Stückchen;* some ∾s of meat *einige Fleischbrocken;* a ∾ of paper *ein Fetzen Papier;* to consign to the ∾-heap *in die Müllgrube (zum alten Eisen) werfen;* a ∾-heap policy *der Brauch, veraltete Sachen sofort abzulegen;* I can only write you a short ∾ *ich kann dir nur ein paar Zeilen schreiben;* ∾-iron, ∾-metal *Schrott.* — **II.** v.tr.: to ∾ a thing *etwas zum alten Eisen werfen, verschrotten, ausrangieren*

scrap[2] n. (sl.): to have a bit of a ∾ with a person *eine kleine Schlägerei (Balgerei) mit j.em haben*

scrape I. v.tr.: to ∾ acquaintance with a person *sich um j.es Bekanntschaft bemühen; j.em seine Bekanntschaft aufdrängen;* to ∾ one's feet *mit den Füßen scharren;* to ∾ a speaker down *einen Redner durch Scharren zum Schweigen bringen.* — **II.** v.i.: work and ∾ as one may *man mag noch so sehr schuften und schrappen;* I must ∾ along somehow *ich muß mich irgendwie durchschlagen;* he just managed to ∾ through his exam *er hat seine Prüfung mit Ach und Krach bestanden;* we must ∾ up enough for a good meal *wir müssen genug für eine ordentliche Mahlzeit zusammenschrappen, -kratzen;* to bow and ∾ *dienern, sich mit Kratzfuß verbeugen.* — **III.** n.: to get into a ∾ *in eine Patsche (Klemme) geraten;* bread and ∾ *dünn geschmiertes Brot*

scratch[1] I. v.tr.: ∾ my back and I'll ∾ yours (prov.) *eine Hand wäscht die andere;* I have ∾ed my hands badly *ich habe mir arg die Hände zerkratzt;* to ∾ one's head *sich (dat.) über etwas den Kopf kratzen (zerbrechen);* to ∾ a horse from a race *die Meldung eines Pferdes zu einem Rennen zurückziehen;* ∾ a Russian, and you find a Tartar *in jedem Russen steckt etwas von einem Tartaren;* he only ∾ed the surface of the problem *er drang nicht tief in das Problem ein, er berührte es nur oberflächlich;* to ∾ words off (out, through) *Wörter aus-, durchstreichen;* to ∾ together (up) *zusammenkratzen.* — **II.** v.i.: to ∾ from a competition *seine Meldung zu einem Wettbewerb zurückziehen;* we shall ∾ along somehow *wir werden uns irgendwie durchschlagen.* — **III.** n.: with a ∾ of a pen *mit einem Federstrich;* to be up to ∾ *auf der Höhe sein;* to bring a person up to (the) ∾ *j.en zwingen, seiner Verpflichtung nachzukommen;* to come (up) to (the) ∾ *sich rechtzeitig einstellen, sich nicht drücken, eine Entscheidung treffen;* to get off with a ∾ or two *mit ein paar Kratzern davonkommen;* to keep someone up to ∾ *j.en bei der Stange halten;* to start from ∾ *ohne Vorgabe starten, ohne Hilfe anfangen;* she is a ∾-cat *sie ist eine Kratzbürste.* — **IV.** a.: a ∾ crew (team) *eine ungleichartige (unausgeglichene, zusammengewürfelte) Mannschaft*

Scratch[2] n.pr.: Old ∾ *der Leibhaftige, Teufel*

scream I. v.i.: to ∾ with laughter *vor Lachen schreien (brüllen);* to ∾ out *laut aufschreien.* — **II.** v.tr.: to ∾ out one's lungs *sich (dat.) die Lunge aus dem Leib (aus dem Hals) schreien.* — **III.** n.: it was a ∾ (sl.) *es war zum Schreien, zum Brüllen*

screen I. n.: a folding-∾ *eine spanische Wand;* a smoke-∾ *eine Vernebelung;* under the ∾ of night *im Schutze der Nacht (der Dunkelheit);* to put on a ∾ of indifference *Gleichgültigkeit zur Schau tragen;* I saw it on the ∾ *ich sah es im Film.* — **II.** v.tr.: he has been ∾ed *er ist durchleuchtet worden, seine politische Zuverlässigkeit ist festgestellt worden;* to ∾ a person from something *j.en vor etwas schützen, ihn decken*

screw I. n.: he is an old ∾ *er ist ein alter Geizkragen;* a ∾-driver *ein Schraubenzieher;* a ∾-wrench *ein Schraubenschlüssel (Engländer);* an endless ∾ *eine Schraube ohne Ende;* a female ∾ *eine Schraubenmutter;* a male ∾ *eine Schraubenspindel;* there is a ∾ loose somewhere *irgendwo ist etwas nicht in Ordnung;* to draw one's ∾ (sl.) *sein Gehalt beziehen;* he has a ∾ loose (colloq.) *bei ihm ist eine Schraube los (locker), er hat einen Sparren;* to put the ∾ on a ball *einem Ball Effet geben;* to put the ∾ on a person *auf j.en einen Druck ausüben, ihm (die) Daumenschrauben anlegen;* to put on the ∾ *die Schraube anziehen, sparsamer verfahren;* to put a person under the ∾ *j.en drängen, zwingen.* — **II.** v.tr.: to ∾ one's courage to the sticking-place (Macbeth, I, 7), to ∾ up one's courage *Mut fassen;* the boards are ∾ed down *die Bretter sind festgeschraubt;* to ∾ one's face into wrinkles *das Gesicht in Falten legen;* his head is ∾ed on the right way *er ist ein heller Kopf, er ist nicht auf den Kopf gefallen;* to ∾ money out of a person *j.en erpressen;* to ∾ up a door *eine Tür zuschrauben;* to ∾ up one's eyes *die Augen zusammenkneifen;* to ∾ up the prices *die Preise hochschrauben;* the matter wants ∾ing up *man muß Dampf dahinter machen;* he is regularly ∾ed *er ist regelrecht betrunken*

scribe n.: he is no great ∾ *das Schreiben fällt ihm schwer, ist nicht seine starke Seite*

scrounge v.tr. (sl.): to ∾ a thing *eine Sache klauen (mausen, stibitzen, „organisieren")*

scrub I. v.tr.: to ∾ the floor *den Boden scheuern (schrubben).* — **II.** v.i.: to ∾ hard for a living *sich schinden ums liebe Leben;* I would rather ∾ for my living *ich ginge lieber Steine klopfen;* let's ∾ round that (sl.) *lassen wir diese Sache fallen, geben wir diese Sache auf.* — **III.** n.: it needs a good ∾ *es muß tüchtig gescheuert werden*

scruff n.: to take a person by the ∾ of the neck *j.en beim Genick fassen, beim Kanthaken nehmen*

scruple n.: he is a man of no ∾s *er ist ein gewissenloser Mensch;* he did it without ∾ *er tat es ohne Bedenken;* to have ∾s about doing a thing *sich (dat.) ein Gewissen machen, etwas zu tun;* to make no ∾s to do a thing *kein Bedenken haben, etwas zu tun*

scrupulously adv.: he is ∾ honest *er ist grundehrlich;* the house was ∾ clean *das Haus war peinlich sauber*

scunner n.: to take a ∾ against (at) a thing *einen Widerwillen gegen etwas empfinden*

scurvy a.: it was a ∾ trick *es war ein gemeiner (niederträchtiger) Streich*

sea n.: a ∾ like a looking-glass, like a sheet of glass *eine spiegelglatte See;* when the ∾ gives up its dead *bei der Auferstehung der Toten;* the four ∾s *die Meere um Großbritannien;* the seven ∾s *das nördliche und südliche Eismeer, der nördliche und südliche Stille Ozean, der nördliche und südliche Atlantik, der indische Ozean;* between the devil and the deep (blue) ∾ *zwischen zwei Feuern, in großer Verlegenheit, in verzweifelter Lage;* countries beyond (over) the ∾, ∾s *überseeische Länder;* by ∾ and land *zu Wasser und zu Lande;* to be at ∾ *auf dem Meere, auf See, zur See sein;* I am quite (all) at ∾ *ich bin ganz* *ratlos, ich tappe ganz im Dunklen (Finstern);* to be half-∾s over *betrunken, beschwipst sein, Schlagseite haben (zeigen);* to follow the ∾ *Seemann sein;* to go to ∾ *Seemann werden;* praise the ∾ but keep on land (prov.) *das Wasser hat keine Balken;* to put to ∾ *in See stechen;* you son of a ∾-cook! *du Lump!;* an old ∾-dog *ein alter Seebär;* the white ∾-horses *die weißen Schaumkronen der Wellen;* he has not yet got his ∾-legs *er ist noch nicht seefest;* to go to the ∾side *an die See fahren*

seal I. n.: Lord Privy ∾ *Geheimsiegelbewahrer;* given under my hand and ∾ *unter Brief und Siegel;* he has the ∾ of death in his face *er ist vom Tode gezeichnet;* under the ∾ of silence *unter dem Siegel der Verschwiegenheit;* to set one's ∾ to a thing *etwas besiegeln, bekräftigen, bestätigen.* — **II.** v.tr.: it is a ∾ed book (a book with seven ∾s) to me *es ist mir (für mich) ein Buch mit sieben Siegeln;* to ∾ a person's lips *j.en zum Stillschweigen verpflichten;* ∾ing-wax *Siegellack*

seamy a.: the ∾ side of life *die Schattenseite des Lebens*

sear, sere a.: the ∾ and yellow leaf *das Greisenalter*

search I. v.tr.: ∾ me! (colloq.) *keine Ahnung!;* to ∾ men's hearts *die Herzen der Menschen prüfen;* to ∾ a house *eine Haussuchung veranstalten (durchführen);* they ∾ed my pockets for cigarettes *sie durchsuchten meine Taschen nach Zigaretten;* to ∾ a wound *eine Wunde sondieren.* — **II.** v.i.: to ∾ for a thing *nach etwas suchen.* — **III.** n.: the ∾ for him was in vain *die Suche nach ihm war vergebens;* to be in ∾ of a thing *auf der Suche nach etwas sein;* a ∾-light *ein Scheinwerfer*

season I. n.: in ∾ and out of ∾ *zu jeder passenden und unpassenden Zeit, immer wieder;* the close ∾ for game *die Schonzeit für Wild;* strawberries are now in ∾ *jetzt ist die Erdbeerzeit;* a word in ∾ *ein Wort zur rechten Zeit;* a ∾-ticket *eine Dauer-, Zeitkarte, ein Abonnement;* the compliments of the ∾ to you *mit den besten Weihnachtsgrüßen.* — **II.** v.tr.: when mercy ∾s justice (Merchant of Venice IV, 1) *wenn Gnade bei dem Recht steht (Schlegel-Tieck);* to ∾ oneself (to be ∾ed) to a thing *sich abhärten gegen, sich an etwas gewöhnen;* a conversation ∾ed with humour *eine mit Humor gewürzte Unterhaltung;* highly ∾ed dishes *scharf gewürzte Speisen;* well ∾ed timber *gut abgelagertes Holz*

seasonable a.: a ∾ aid *eine rechtzeitige, angebrachte Hilfe;* it is ∾ weather *das Wetter entspricht der Jahreszeit*

seat I. n.: keep your ∾ *behalten Sie Platz, bleiben Sie sitzen;* he lost his ∾ *er ist nicht zum Parlament wiedergewählt worden;* pray, take a ∾ *nehmen Sie bitte Platz, setzen Sie sich bitte;* take your ∾s, please! *bitte einsteigen!* — **II.** v.tr.: the hall ∾s (is ∾ed for) 5.000 *der Saal hat 5000 Sitzplätze;* to ∾ oneself *sich setzen;* pray be ∾ed *nehmen Sie bitte Platz, setzen Sie sich bitte;* to ∾ a candidate *einen Kandidaten zum Parlament wählen;* to ∾ a pair of trousers *einen Hosenboden einsetzen*

second I. a.: it is ∾ to none *es ist unübertroffen (unerreicht);* he is my ∾ cousin *er ist mein Vetter zweiten Grades;* it rains every ∾ day *es regnet alle zwei Tage;* I only know it at ∾-hand *ich weiß es nur von Hörensagen;* it is a ∾-hand book, I bought it ∾-hand, at a ∾-hand bookshop *das Buch ist antiquarisch, ich habe es in einem Antiquariat gekauft;* begging has become ∾ nature to him *das Betteln ist ihm zur zweiten Natur geworden;* a ∾-rate hotel *ein zweitklassiges (minderwertiges) Hotel;* ∾ sight *Hellsehen;* on ∾ thoughts *bei (nach) näherer Überlegung;* to come off ∾-best *unterliegen, den kürzeren ziehen.* — **II.** n.: to make a good ∾ to a person *j.em nicht viel nachstehen;* to run a close ∾ to a thing *einer Sache sehr nahekommen.* — **III.** v.tr.: to ∾ a motion *einen Antrag unterstützen;* to ∾ words with deeds *den Worten Taten folgen lassen*

secret n.: to be in the ∾ *in etwas eingeweiht sein;* to let a person into the ∾ *j.en in das Geheimnis einweihen*

secure a.: ∾ against assault *sicher vor einem Angriff;* ∾ from interruption *sicher vor Störungen*

security n.: to give (to stand) ∾ *Bürgschaft leisten, Kaution stellen*

sedulous a.: he played the ∾ ape to modern writers *durch fleißige Imitation moderner Schriftsteller hat er sich einen Schriftstil angeeignet*

see I. v.i.: ∾? do you ∾? *verstehst du?;* ∾ if I don't *und ob ich das tue!;* ∾ that it is done *sieh zu, daß es gemacht wird;* ∾ you don't catch your feet *gib acht, daß du nicht mit den Füßen hängen bleibst;* I ∾! *ich verstehe! ach so!;* I don't ∾ being made use of like that *ich lasse mich nicht so ausnutzen;* you ∾ *du verstehst doch, wohlgemerkt;* let me ∾ *warte mal!;* to ∾ eye to eye with a person on a thing *über etwas mit j.em derselben Meinung sein.* — with prep.: to ∾ about a thing *für etwas Sorge tragen, etwas besorgen;* to ∾ after a thing *auf etwas acht geben, für etwas sorgen;* I must ∾ into it *ich muß die Sache untersuchen;* to ∾ far into a millstone *überschlau sein, das Gras wachsen hören;* to ∾ over a house *ein Haus besichtigen;* to ∾ through a person (a thing) *j.en (etwas) durchschauen;* to ∾ through a brick wall *überschlau sein, das Gras wachsen hören;* to ∾ to one's business *auf sein Geschäft achten;* ∾ to it that it does not happen again *sorge dafür, daß es nicht nochmals vorkommt;* to ∾ with half an eye, at a glance *mit halbem Auge, auf den ersten Blick sehen.* — **II.** v.tr.: see 'back, company, farther, fun, good, green, home, joke, life etc.'; to ∾ fair play *für ehrliches Vorgehen sorgen;* to ∾ fit to do something *es für richtig halten, etwas zu tun;* to ∾ a newspaper to bed (journalism) *eine Zeitung druckfertig machen;* I must have my shoes seen to *ich muß meine Schuhe nachsehen lassen;* it remains to be seen *es bleibt abzuwarten;* what the eye does not ∾ the heart does not grieve over (prov.) *was ich nicht weiß, macht mich nicht heiß;* to ∾ a thing done, to ∾ to it *darauf achten, daß etwas gemacht wird;* go and ∾ who is at the door *sieh mal nach, wer an der Tür ist.* — with adv.: to ∾ a person off *j.en zur Bahn begleiten;* to ∾ a person out *j.en hinausbegleiten;* to ∾ a person through with a thing *j.em bei einer Sache durchhelfen;* to ∾ a thing through (out) *etwas durchhalten;* to ∾ how the land lies *sehen, wie die Sache steht*

seed n.: to go (to run) to ∾ *in Samen schießen, verblühen, verkümmern, schäbig werden;* to sow the ∾s of discord *Zwietracht säen;* to be No 1 ∾ (tennis) *als erstes As gerechnet werden*

seedy a. (colloq.): I feel a bit ∾ *ich fühle mich nicht ganz wohl;* a ∾ fellow *ein schäbig aussehender Bursche*

seeing conj. & prep.: ∾ that no other course is open to us *angesichts der Tatsache, daß (weil) uns ja kein anderer Weg offen steht;* ∾ your ignorance *in Anbetracht deiner Unwissenheit*

seem v.i.: I do not ∾ to like him *irgendwie mißfällt er mir;* as ∾s likely *wie es wahrscheinlich ist*

seesaw a. & adv.: a ∾ motion *eine wippende Bewegung;* to go ∾ *hin- und herschwanken, wechseln, wippen*

self I. n.: his better ∾ *seine wahre Natur;* one's own ∾ *das eigene Ich;* my poor ∾ *meine Wenigkeit;* one's second ∾ *sein zweites Ich, seine rechte Hand;* it is his very ∾ *das ist er, wie er leibt und lebt.* — **II.** a.: a ∾-coloured thing *eine einfarbige, naturfarbene Sache.* — **III.** pref.: ∾-absorbed *in sich selbst vertieft (versunken);* ∾-abuse *Selbstbefleckung, Onanie;* ∾-acting *selbsttätig;* ∾-assertive, ∾-assured *selbstbewußt;* ∾-centred *egozentrisch;* ∾-command, ∾-control *Selbstbeherrschung;* ∾-complacent *selbstgefällig;* ∾-conceit *Eigendünkel;* ∾-conscious *befangen;* ∾-contained *für sich allein, in sich abgeschlossen (von einer Wohnung);* in ∾-defence *in Notwehr;* a ∾-employed person *ein Einmanngeschäft;* ∾-evident *selbstverständlich;* ∾-indulgence *Genußsucht;* ∾-interest *Eigennutz;* a ∾-made man *ein Emporkömmling;* the ∾-same thing *einunddasselbe;* a ∾-starter *ein Anlasser;* a ∾-taught man *ein Autodidakt;* ∾-willed *eigenwillig;* a ∾-winder (colloq.) *ein selbständiger Arbeiter*

sell I. v.tr.: to ∾ the pass *die Sache verraten;* to ∾ a person an idea (colloq.) *j.en überreden, einen Vorschlag zu akzeptieren;* to ∾ a person a pup (sl.) *j.en beschwindeln, über den Löffel barbieren (balbieren);* sold again! (sl.) *wieder angeführt (angeschmiert)!* — **II.** v.i.: that will never ∾ *das läßt sich niemals verkaufen.* — **III.** n.: it was an awful (no end of a) ∾ (sl.) *es war ein schauderhafter Reinfall*

send I. v.tr.: to ∾ a person to the right-about *j.en kurzerhand entlassen;* God ∾ it may not be so! *Gott gebe, daß es nicht so ist!;* to ∾ a person about his business *j.em heimleuchten, die Tür weisen;* to ∾ a person to Coventry *jeden Verkehr mit j.em abbrechen;* to ∾ a person one's love *j.en herzlich grüßen;* to ∾ a person mad (crazy) *j.en verrückt (rasend) machen;* to ∾ a person packing *j.en sich schicken heißen, fortjagen, hinauswerfen;* to ∾ word to someone *j.en benachrichtigen, j.em Nachricht senden.* — with adv.: to ∾ an undergraduate down *einen Studenten relegieren;* to ∾ one's name in *sich anmelden (lassen);* to ∾ a person off *bei j.es Abreise zugegen sein;* please ∾ on (letter) *bitte nachsenden!;* to ∾ round *in Umlauf setzen;* to ∾ the hat round *eine Kollekte veranstalten;* that sent the temperature up *das trieb die Temperatur hinauf;* that sent prices up *das trieb die Preise in die Höhe.* — **II.** v.i.: I sent for him *ich ließ ihn holen.* — **III.** n.: a ∾-off *ein feierlicher Abschied;* the book got a good ∾-off *das Buch wurde günstig besprochen*

senior a.: the ∾ service *die englische Kriegsmarine*

sense I. n.: to be in one's ∾s *bei Sinnen (Verstand) sein;* are you out of (have you taken leave of) your ∾s? *bist du von Sinnen (nicht mehr ganz bei Trost)?;* he is frightened out of his ∾s *er ist halb wahnsinnig vor Schreck(en);* to bring a person to his ∾s *j.en zur Besinnung (Vernunft) bringen;* he will soon come to his ∾s *er wird bald zur Vernunft kommen;* he had the ∾ to do so *er war so gescheit, es zu tun;* to have common ∾ *gesunden Menschenverstand haben;* to have a ∾ of duty *Pflichtbewußtsein haben;* to have a keen ∾ of humour *einen feinen Sinn für Humor haben;* to have a ∾ of pain *ein Gefühl des Schmerzes haben;* this does not make ∾ *das gibt keinen Sinn;* can you make ∾ of this? *kannst du hier einen Sinn hineinbringen?;* to recover one's ∾s *wieder zur Besinnung kommen;* now you are talking ∾ *jetzt redest du vernünftig;* what you say is true in a ∾ *was du sagst, ist in gewissem Sinne (in gewisser Hinsicht) wahr;* to take the ∾ of a meeting *die Meinung einer Versammlung feststellen.* — **II.** v.tr.: to ∾ danger *Gefahr ahnen (wittern)*

senseless a.: to knock a person ∾ *j.en bewußtlos schlagen*

sensible a.: there is a ∾ difference *es besteht ein merklicher Unterschied;* he was ∾ of his peril *er war sich der Gefahr bewußt;* that is very ∾ of him *das ist sehr vernünftig von ihm*

sentence I. n.: to be under ∾ of death *zum Tode verurteilt sein;* to get a life ∾ *eine lebenslängliche Zuchthausstrafe bekommen;* to pass ∾ (up)on a person *über j.en ein Urteil fällen;* to serve a ∾ *eine Strafe abbüßen (absitzen).* — **II.** v.tr.: to ∾ a murderer to death *einen Mörder zum Tode verurteilen*

sentiment n.: these are (them's [facet.]) my ∾s *so denke ich darüber;* to conclude a speech with a ∾ *eine Rede mit einem Spruch schließen;* the book runs to ∾ *das Buch hat eine sentimentale Färbung (einen sentimentalen Anstrich)*

separate[1] a.: the ∾ members of the body *die einzelnen Körperteile (Glieder);* to live in ∾ rooms *in getrennten Zimmern leben (wohnen);* one is quite ∾ from the other *das eine ist vom anderen ganz verschieden;* to keep ∾ from *auseinanderhalten*

separate[2] **I.** v.tr.: to ∾ a married couple *Eheleute trennen;* to ∾ milk *Milch entrahmen;* to ∾ ores *Erze scheiden;* to ∾ one thing from another *eine Sache von einer anderen unterscheiden, auseinanderhalten.* — **II.** v.i.: the opponents ∾d *die Gegner trennten sich;* the Southern States ∾d from the Union *die Südstaaten sagten sich von der Union los*

sepulchre n.: a whited ∾ (Matt. XXIII, 27) *ein Heuchler, Scheinheiliger*

sere a.: see 'sear'

serene a.: all ∾! *alles in Ordnung!*

serious a.: are you ∾? *meinst du es im Ernst?*

sermon n.: the ∾ on the Mount *die Bergpredigt;* to preach (to deliver) a ∾ *eine Predigt halten*

serpent n.: the (old) ∾ (Gen. III. Rev. XX) *der Teufel*

serve I. v.i.: he ∾s well (tennis) *er hat einen guten Aufschlag;* as occasion ∾s *wie es sich fügt, bei passender Gelegenheit;* a sofa ∾s as (for) a bed *ein Sofa dient als Bett;* the tide will ∾ at 5 o'clock *die Flut wird um 5 Uhr eintreten;* to ∾ at table *bei Tisch servieren (aufwarten);* to ∾ up *auftischen.* — **II.** v.tr.: first come, first ∾d (prov.) *wer zuerst kommt, mahlt zuerst;* dinner is ∾d *das Essen ist aufgetragen;* to ∾ one's apprenticeship *seine Lehrzeit durchmachen;* a player ∾s a ball *ein Spieler schlägt einen Ball auf;* to ∾ a mare *eine Stute decken lassen;* that would ∾ me for a week *damit käme ich eine Woche aus;* it ∾s me well *es leistet mir gute Dienste;* wood ∾s the purpose of coal *Holz wird an Stelle von Kohle benutzt;* to ∾ a sentence *eine Strafe absitzen (verbüßen);* to ∾ one's time *seine Zeit dienen;* to ∾ time *eine Strafe absitzen (verbüßen);* to ∾ trick *einen Streich spielen;* to ∾ a person a turn *j.em einen Dienst erweisen;* to ∾ a warrant (a writ) on a person *j.em einen Haftbefehl zustellen;* I shall manage to ∾ him out *ich werde ihm sein Teil schon geben;* if my memory ∾s me right *wenn ich mich recht erinnere;* that ∾s you right *das geschieht dir recht;* to ∾ drinks round *Getränke herumreichen;* he ∾d me shamefully *er hat mich schändlich behandelt;* to ∾ dinner up *das Essen auftragen;* to ∾ a person with the same sauce *j.em mit gleicher Münze heimzahlen, Gleiches mit Gleichem vergelten;* to ∾ a town with water *eine Stadt mit Wasser versorgen.* — **III.** n.: whose ∾ is it? (tennis) *wer schlägt auf? wer gibt?*

service n.: the ∾ at the hotel is good *die Bedienung im Hotel ist gut;* whose ∾ is it? (tennis) *wer schlägt auf? wer gibt?;* the ∾s, the fighting ∾s *die Kriegsmarine, das Heer, die Luftwaffe;* the Civil ∾ *der Staatsdienst;* On His (Her) Majesty's Service (abbr. O.H.M.S. [on letters]) *frei durch Ablösung;* a regular railway ∾ *ein regelmäßiger Eisenbahnverkehr;* the girl is in (goes out to) (domestic) ∾ *das Mädchen ist in Stellung (ist Hausangestellte);* to attend divine ∾ *den Gottesdienst besuchen;* to do (to render) a person a ∾ *j.em einen Dienst (Gefallen) tun (erweisen);* to place a thing at a person's ∾ *j.em etwas zur Verfügung stellen;* the troops saw ∾ in Africa *die Truppen machten den Krieg in Afrika mit;* this coat has seen ∾ *dieser Rock ist viel getragen worden, sieht abgetragen aus;* to take ∾ with a person *in j.es Dienst treten;* a ∾-flat *eine Etagenwohnung mit Restaurationsbedienung*

session n.: Parliament is in ∾ *das Parlament tagt*

set I. v.tr.: see 'axe, bone, bound, cap, clock, dog, example, eye, face, fashion, fire, foot, etc.'; the play is ∾ in Greece *das Stück spielt in Griechenland;* the sky is ∾ with stars *der Himmel ist mit Sternen übersät;* to ∾ a hen *eine Glucke auf Eier setzen;* to ∾ a jewel *ein Juwel fassen;* to ∾ a machine going *eine Maschine in Gang bringen (setzen);* to ∾ oneself to do a thing *sich (dat.) angelegen sein lassen, etwas zu tun;* to ∾ a person thinking *j.em zu denken geben;* to ∾ a saw *eine Säge richten;* to ∾ a stone rolling *einen Stein ins Rollen bringen, etwas (Unvorhergesehenes) in Gang setzen;* all ∾! (colloq.) *fertig!* — with prep.: to ∾ one thing against (over against) another *eine Sache gegen eine andere abwägen;* to ∾ at, see 'bay, defiance, ease, liberty, etc.'; to ∾ persons by the ears *Leute gegen einander aufhetzen;* to ∾ in, see 'action, gold, motion, order, roar, way'; to ∾ on, see 'fire, foot'; to ∾ a person over others *j.en als Befehlshaber (Aufseher) über andere einsetzen;* to ∾ to music *in Musik setzen, vertonen.* — with adv.: to ∾ apart (aside) for future use *zur späteren Verwendung aufbewahren;* to ∾ aside an objection *einen Einwurf verwerfen;* to ∾ aside all precaution *jede Vorsicht außer Acht lassen;* to ∾ back the clock *die Uhr zurückstellen, die Geschichte zurückschrauben;* this meal will ∾ you back two dollars (U.S.) *diese Mahlzeit wird dich zwei Dollar kosten;* to ∾ by money *Geld zurücklegen, sparen;* to ∾ down to carelessness *der Nachläßigkeit zuschreiben;* to ∾ down in writing *schriftlich niederlegen;* I had to ∾ him down *ich mußte ihn zurechtweisen (ducken);* to ∾ a passenger down *einen Fahrgast absetzen;* to ∾ a person down as (for) a swindler *j.en für einen Schwindler halten;* to ∾ forth the reasons *die Gründe auseinandersetzen;* the bright colours ∾ off the dress *die hellen Farben heben das Kleid;* that ∾ him off laughing (talking) *das brachte ihn zum Lachen (Reden);* to ∾ off one thing against another *eine Sache gegen eine andere anrechnen, kompensieren;* to ∾ a person to do a thing *j.en antreiben, etwas zu tun;* to ∾ out the advantages *die Vorteile dartun;* to ∾ out to the best advantage *im besten Lichte zeigen;* to ∾ out in a row *in einer Reihe anordnen;* to ∾ out time and place *Zeit und Ort bestimmen;* this tonic will ∾ you up *dieses Kräftigungsmittel wird dich gesund machen;* I am ∾ up with books *ich bin mit Büchern versorgt;* a well ∾-up man *ein körperlich gut entwickelter, gut trainierter Mann;* to ∾ up a notice *eine Bekanntmachung anschlagen;* to ∾ up a protest *laut Protest erheben;* to ∾ up the roof of a house *ein Haus richten;* to ∾ up (a) shop *ein Geschäft eröffnen;* to ∾ up a shriek, a roar *ein Geschrei erheben;* he ∾ up his son as a tobacconist *er richtete seinem Sohn einen Tabakladen ein; er etablierte ihn als Tabakwarenhändler;* to ∾ up a theory *eine Theorie aufstellen.* — **II.** v.i.: the blossoms have ∾ well *die Blüten haben gut angesetzt;* eyes ∾ in death *die Augen brechen im Tode;* a face ∾s *ein Gesicht nimmt einen starren Ausdruck an;* plaster of Paris ∾s quickly *Gips wird rasch fest;* his star has (is) ∾ *sein Stern (Glanz) ist erloschen;* the sun (moon) ∾s *die Sonne (der Mond) geht unter.* — with prep. and adv.: to ∾ about doing (out to do) a thing *sich anschicken, etwas zu tun;* to ∾ forth (off, out) on a journey *eine Reise antreten;* rain ∾ in, it ∾ in to rain *Regen setzte ein;* to ∾ on a person *über j.en herfallen;* he must ∾ out for a time *er muß eine Zeitlang aussetzen;* he ∾ out by (with) excusing his behaviour *er begann damit, sein Verhalten zu entschuldigen;* the opponents ∾ to *die Gegner begannen zu kämpfen, gingen gegen einander los;* to ∾ to work to do a thing *sich daran machen, etwas zu tun;* I shall ∾ up as a dentist *ich werde mich als Zahnarzt niederlassen;* he ∾s up for a scholar *er spielt sich als Gelehrter auf, er gibt sich für einen Gelehrten aus;* to ∾ up to be something *sich anmaßen, etwas zu sein.* — **III.** a.: a ∾ battle *eine regelrechte Schlacht;* at a ∾ distance *in abgemessener Entfernung;* to be ∾ on doing something *darauf versessen (erpicht) sein, etwas zu tun;* with ∾ eyes *mit starren Augen;* with a ∾ face *mit starrer Miene;* ∾ fair (barometer) *beständig;* the ∾ form of oath *die vorgeschriebene Eidesformel;* of ∾ purpose *mit Fleiß, absichtlich;* a ∾ speech *eine vorbereitete, wohldurchdachte Rede;* a ∾ task *eine vorgeschriebene Aufgabe;* at the ∾ time *zur festgesetzten Zeit.* — **IV.** n.: a ∾ of billiard balls *ein Satz Billiardbälle;* a ∾ of chairs *eine Garnitur Stühle;* the ∾ of the drapery *der Faltenwurf;* the ∾ of his head *seine Kopfhaltung;* the ∾ of the hills *der Verlauf der Hügel;* a ∾ of lectures *ein Vortragszyklus;* a fine ∾ of men *eine stattliche Gruppe von Männern;* the ∾ of his mind is towards intolerance *er neigt zur Intoleranz;* it was ∾ (point; tennis) *das Spiel stand so, daß die eine Seite nur noch einen Punkt zum Satz benötigte;* the ∾ of public opinion *die Tendenz der öffentlichen Meinung;* it has got a ∾ to the right *es ist nach rechts verschoben;* a ∾ of swindlers *eine Schwindlerbande;* a ∾ of teeth *ein künstliches Gebiß;* she has a nice ∾ of teeth *sie hat hübsche Zähne;* a ∾ of tracks *ein Schienenstrang;* a railway with a single ∾ of tracks *eine eing(e)leisige Eisenbahn;* to make a dead ∾ at a person *j.en heftig angreifen;* she is making a dead ∾ at him *sie bemüht sich sehr um ihn, sie angelt nach ihm;* he has got into a fast ∾ *er ist in liederliche (leichtsinnige) Gesellschaft geraten;* the smart ∾ *die elegante Welt;* a tea ∾ *ein Teeservice;* a toilet ∾ *eine Toilettengarnitur;* a serious ∾-back *ein ernsthafter Rückschlag;* he needs a good ∾-down *er müßte gehörig geduckt werden;* she is a ∾-off to him *sie sticht gegen ihn ab;* this is a ∾-off against (to) our gross earnings *das muß von unserem Bruttogewinn in Abzug gebracht werden;* at the first ∾-out *gleich beim (zu) Anfang;* the ∾-out of the goods *die Auslage der Waren;* a girl's ∾-out *die Aussteuer eines Mädchens;* there was a fierce ∾-to *es gab eine wüste Schlägerei;* the ∾-up of a person *j.es Körperhaltung;* the ∾-up of an organisation *die Struktur (der Aufbau) einer Organisation*

settle I. v.tr.: will you ∾ for me, please? *erledige es (bezahle) bitte für mich!;* what have you ∾d? ∾d on? *was hast du abgemacht? wofür hast du dich entschieden?;* to ∾ an annuity on a person *j.em eine Jahresrente aussetzen;* to ∾ one's affairs *seine Angelegenheiten ordnen (regeln), ein Testament machen;* to ∾ a bill *eine Rechnung begleichen;* to ∾ a person's business *j.en töten, ihm den Garaus machen;* to ∾ coffee *Kaffee sich setzen lassen;* to ∾ colonists *Kolonisten ansiedeln;* a man of ∾d convictions *ein Mann von festen Grundsätzen;* to ∾ the day *den Tag bestimmen (festsetzen);* a liqueur to ∾ one's dinner *ein Schnäpschen zur Verdauung;* to ∾ a person's hash (sl.) *j.en erledigen, abtun, töten, ihm den Garaus machen;* that ∾s him *damit wäre er erledigt;* to ∾ an invalid in cushions *es einem Kranken mit Kissen bequem machen;* to ∾ the matter *die Angelegenheit regeln;* to ∾ oneself in a chair *sich in einem Stuhl niederlassen;* to ∾ a quarrel *einen Streit schlichten;* to ∾ a question *eine Frage entscheiden;* to ∾ the succession *die Nachfolge regeln;* to ∾ up accounts *die Bilanz ziehen.* — **II.** v.i.: a foundation ∾s *ein Fundament setzt sich;* the ship began to ∾ *das Schiff begann abzusacken;* the weather seems to be settling *das Wetter scheint beständig zu werden.* — with prep. and adverb: let the excitement ∾ down *laß die Aufregung sich legen;* to marry and ∾ down *heiraten und einen Hausstand gründen;* to ∾ down as a doctor *sich als Arzt niederlassen;* to ∾ down to reading *sich gemütlich zum Lesen hinsetzen, sich ernstlich ans Lesen geben (machen);* it is settling for rain *es wird Regenwetter geben;* I shall ∾ in Australia *ich werde mich in Australien ansiedeln;* things will soon ∾ into shape *die Sache wird bald Gestalt annehmen, es wird sich schon machen;* to ∾ on doing a thing *sich entschließen, etwas zu tun;* a bird ∾s on a tree *ein Vogel läßt sich auf einem Baum nieder;* he cannot ∾ to work *er kann sich an keine geregelte Arbeit gewöhnen;* to ∾ with creditors *sich mit Gläubigern abfinden (einigen)*

settlement n.: a marriage ∾ *ein Ehevertrag;* to come to a ∾ *einen Vergleich (ein Übereinkommen) treffen;* to make a ∾ on a person *j.em etwas aussetzen (vermachen)*

settler n.: that was a ∾ *das schlug durch, das gab ihm den Rest*

settling-day n.: on ∾ *am Abrechnungs-, Liefertage*

seven n.: to be at sixes and ∾s *kunterbunt (wie Kraut und Rüben) durcheinander liegen;* take them by ∾s *nimm sie in Sätzen (Gruppen) zu sieben*

seventeen n.: sweet ∾ *das liebliche Alter, ein (hübsches) Mädchen von siebzehn Jahren*

seventy n.: in the seventies of the last century *in den siebziger Jahren des vorigen Jahrhunderts;* I am turned (of) ∾ *ich bin über siebzig*

sever I. v.tr.: to ∾ a connection *eine Verbindung lösen;* to ∾ a friendship *eine Freundschaft abbrechen.* — **II.** v.i.: the rope ∾ed under the strain *das Seil riß unter dem Druck*

several I. a.: each ∾ case *jeder einzelne Fall;* each has his ∾ ideal *jeder hat sein besonderes Ideal;* all of us in our ∾ stations *wir alle in unseren verschiedenen Lebensstellungen;* I tried ∾ times *ich versuchte mehrere (verschiedene) Male.* — **II.** pron.: ∾ of you have seen him *mehrere (verschiedene) von euch haben ihn gesehen*

severely adv.: to leave (to let) a person ∾ alone *nichts mit j.em zu tun haben (wollen)*

sew v.tr.: to ∾ a person up (sl.) *j.en völlig erschöpfen;* he is ∾ed up (sl.) *er ist betrunken, er hat einen in der Krone*

sex n.: the fair (gentle, softer, weaker) ∾ *das schöne (zarte, schwächere) Geschlecht;* the sterner ∾ *das stärkere Geschlecht*

shabby a.: he played me a ∾ trick *er spielte mir einen gemeinen Streich;* a ∾-genteel man *ein verarmter Reicher*

shade I. n.: the delicate ∾s of meaning *die feinen Bedeutungsunterschiede;* the same colour in a lighter ∾ *dieselbe Farbe in einer helleren Schattierung, einen Ton heller;* the shadow of a ∾, see 'shadow'; I am a ∾ better today *heute geht es mir eine Kleinigkeit besser;* to go down to the ∾s *zur Unterwelt fahren, sterben;* to leave in the ∾ *weit hinter sich lassen;* to throw into the ∾ *in den Schatten stellen.* — **II.** v.tr.: he ∾d his eyes with his hand *er schützte mit der Hand seine Augen vor dem Licht;* a sullen look ∾d his face *ein mürrischer Ausdruck verdüsterte sein Gesicht.* — **III.** v.i.: the yellow ∾d off into green *das Gelb ging allmählich in Grün über*

shadow I. n.: may your ∾ never grow less! *möge es dir immer gut gehen!;* coming events cast their ∾s before (prov.) *kommende Ereignisse werfen ihre Schatten voraus;* without the ∾ of a doubt *ohne den leisesten Zweifel;* the ∾ of a shade *etwas Wesenloses, Unwirkliches;* to be afraid of one's own ∾ *sehr ängstlich sein;* to be reduced to a ∾ *sehr abgemagert sein.* — **II.** v.tr.: a detective ∾ed him *ein Detektiv folgte ihm unbemerkt auf Schritt und Tritt.* — **III.** a.: a ∾ factory *eine Schattenfabrik;* a ∾ cabinet *ein Kabinett, das im Notfall sofort in Tätigkeit gesetzt werden kann*

shady a.: a ∾ bargaining *ein Kuhhandel;* a ∾ business *ein fauler Zauber;* a ∾ character *eine zweifelhafte (anrüchige)*

Person; she is on the ∾ side of thirty *sie ist aus dem Schneider (heraus)*

shake I. v.tr.: that shook the witness's evidence *das entkräftete die Aussagen des Zeugen;* to ∾ one's fist in a person's face *j.em die Faust unter die Nase halten;* to ∾ hands, ∾ a person by the hand *sich die Hand geben, j.em die Hand schütteln;* to ∾ one's head *den Kopf schütteln;* to ∾ a leg *das Tanzbein schwingen; sich beeilen;* to ∾ a loose leg *ein liederliches Leben führen, herumsumpfen, bummeln;* to ∾ one's sides with laughing *sich vor Lachen schütteln, vor Lachen biegen (bersten) wollen;* I was much shaken by (with, at) the news *die Nachricht hat mich erschüttert;* to ∾ a person out of his sleep *j.en aus dem Schlaf rütteln.* — with adv.: to ∾ down fruit *Obst vom Baume schütteln;* I can give you a ∾-down *ich kann dir ein Notlager bereiten, du kannst bei mir schlafen (pennen);* to ∾ off the dust from one's feet *den Staub von den Füßen schütteln, entrüstet fortgehen;* to ∾ a person off *j.en abschütteln, loswerden;* to ∾ up a person *j.en aufrütteln;* to ∾ up a pillow *ein Kopfkissen aufschütteln.* — **II.** v.i.: to ∾ in one's shoes *vor Angst beben (zittern);* you will soon ∾ down *du wirst dich bald einleben (eingewöhnen);* to ∾ with cold *vor Kälte beben (zittern).* — **III.** n.: in two (a couple of) ∾s, in a brace of ∾s, in two ∾s of a lamb's tail *im Handumdrehen, im Nu;* to be all of a ∾ *ganz zitterig sein;* it's no great ∾s (colloq.) *es ist nichts Besonderes;* he is no great ∾s at it (colloq.) *er leistet nichts Besonderes darin;* to give a thing a good shaking *etwas gehörig schütteln;* to have the ∾ *Schüttelfrost haben;* wait a ∾ (colloq.) *einen Augenblick!*

shallow a.: a ∾ argument *ein triviales, wenig stichhaltiges Argument;* a ∾-brained (∾-pated) fellow *ein Hohlkopf, Einfaltspinsel;* to run ∾ *oberflächlich werden, verflachen*

sham I. v.tr.: to ∾ Abraham *Krankheit, Not, Unkenntnis vortäuschen, den kranken Mann spielen.* — **II.** v.i.: he is only ∾ming *er verstellt sich bloß, er stellt sich nur so.* — **III.** n.: this age of ∾s *dieses Zeitalter des Lugs und Trugs;* a pillow-∾ *ein Paradekissen.* — **IV.** a.: a ∾ fight *ein Scheingefecht, Manöver*

shame I. n.: ∾ on you! for ∾! *pfui, schäme dich!;* it is a downright ∾ *es ist eine wahre Schande (eine Affenschande)!;* more's the ∾! *um so schlimmer!;* to bring ∾ upon a person *j.em Schande bereiten;* to cry ∾ upon a person (thing) *sich über j.en (etwas) entrüsten;* to flush with ∾ *vor Scham erröten;* to put a person to ∾ *j.en beschämen;* to put a thing to ∾ *etwas in den Schatten stellen;* to think ∾ to do a thing *es für eine Schande halten, etwas zu tun;* ∾-faced *schamhaft, verschämt.* — **II.** v.tr.: a dog's fidelity ∾s us *die Treue eines Hundes beschämt uns;* to ∾ a person into (out of) doing a thing *j.en durch Beschämung antreiben (davon abhalten), etwas zu tun*

Shanks'(s) n.: on ∾'s mare *auf Schusters Rappen*

shape I. v.tr.: it is ∾d like a pear *es ist birnenförmig;* to ∾ the course for *Kurs nehmen auf.* — **II.** v.i.: it ∾s well *es entwickelt sich gut.* — **III.** n.: in any ∾ or form *gleich welcher Gestalt;* in the ∾ of *in Gestalt von;* spherical in ∾ *kugelförmig;* a monster in human ∾ *ein Ungeheuer in menschlicher Gestalt;* to get one's ideas into ∾ *seine Gedanken ordnen;* to lick into ∾ *j.em Schliff (Benehmen) beibringen;* to take ∾ *feste Form (Gestalt) annehmen*

share I. n.: ∾ and ∾ alike *zu gleichen Teilen;* a fair ∾ *ein gerechter Anteil;* preference (preferred) ∾s *Vorzugsaktien;* I bore (took) my ∾ of the burden *ich trug meinen Anteil (von) der Last;* it fell to his ∾ to do so *es fiel ihm zu, es zu tun;* to go ∾s in a thing with a person *mit j.em etwas teilen;* to hold ∾s (to be ∾holder) in a company *Aktionär einer Gesellschaft sein;* to take the lion's ∾ *den Löwenanteil nehmen.* — **II.** v.tr.: he would ∾ his last crust with you *er würde die letzte Brotkruste mit dir teilen;* to ∾ a room with another *mit einem anderen das Zimmer teilen;* to ∾ out *aus-, verteilen.* — **III.** v.i.: to ∾ in a thing *an etwas teilnehmen, -haben*

shark I. n.: he is a ∾ *er ist ein Bauernfänger (Beutelschneider, Gauner).* — **II.** v.i.: he ∾s for his living *er lebt von Betrügereien*

sharp I. a.: as ∾ as a needle *äußerst intelligent;* a ∾ child *ein schlaues Kind;* a ∾ flavour *ein herber Geschmack;* a ∾ pain *ein stechender Schmerz;* ∾ practice *unredliche Handlungsweise;* a ∾ tongue *eine böse Zunge;* a ∾ walk *ein flotter Spaziergang;* a ∾ wind *ein schneidender Wind;* ∾ words *bittere Worte;* ∾'s the word *jetzt heißt's aber voran, dalli;* that was ∾ work *das war schnelle (fixe) Arbeit;* he was too ∾ for me *er hat mich übervorteilt, er war mir über;* to keep a ∾ look-out *scharf Umschau halten, wachsam sein;* the road takes a ∾ turn to the left *die Straße biegt im spitzen Winkel nach links ab.* — **II.** n.: the ∾s and flats *die Kreuze und B's, die schwarzen Tasten des Klaviers.* — **III.** adv.: ∾-set *hungrig;* ∾ to time *genau zur Zeit;* at six o'clock ∾ *pünktlich um sechs Uhr;* to look ∾ *sich beeilen (sich sputen);* she is singing ∾ *sie singt zu hoch*

shave I. n.: by a ∾ *um ein Haar, um Haaresbreite;* to get a ∾ *sich rasieren lassen;* I must have a ∾ *ich muß mich rasieren (lassen);* I had a close (narrow) ∾ of it *ich bin mit knapper Not daran vorbeigekommen.* — **II.** v.tr.: to ∾ an egg *geizig handeln.* — **III.** v.i.: to ∾ through *gerade noch durch eine Prüfung durchkommen*

shaver n.: a young ∾ (colloq.) *ein Bürschchen, Grünschnabel, Milchgesicht*

shed v.tr.: the Prime Minister ∾s his colleagues *der Premierminister läßt seine Kollegen fallen;* a snake ∾s its skin *eine Schlange häutet sich;* a tree ∾s its leaves *ein Baum wirft seine Blätter ab;* to ∾ light on a thing *Licht auf etwas werfen, etwas aufklären;* to ∾ radiance around one *einen Glanz um sich verbreiten;* to ∾ tears *Tränen vergießen*

sheep n.: the black ∾ of the family *das schwarze (räudige) Schaf der Familie;* to cast ∾'s eyes at a person *j.en verliebt ansehen;* I may as well be hanged for a ∾ as a lamb *wenn schon, denn schon*

sheepish a.: to look ∾ *schamhaft, verlegen aussehen*

sheer[1] **I.** a.: by ∾ force *mit reiner (purer) Gewalt;* a ∾ impossibility *eine völlige (glatte) Unmöglichkeit;* a ∾ necessity *eine einfache (nackte) Notwendigkeit;* ∾ nonsense *lauter (reiner) Unsinn;* a ∾ rock *ein schroffer (steiler) Felsen;* ∾ stockings *hauchdünne Strümpfe;* a ∾ waste *eine reine Verschwendung.* — **II.** adv.: to fall 3.000 feet ∾ *3000 Fuß senkrecht abfallen;* to rise ∾ from the water *sich steil aus dem Wasser erheben;* to tear ∾ out by the roots *mit der Wurzel vollkommen ausreißen*

sheer[2] v.i.: ∾ off (colloq.) *mach', daß du fortkommst! scher' dich weg!*

sheet n.: a ∾ anchor *ein Notanker, die letzte Rettung;* a ∾ of glass *eine Glasplatte, -scheibe;* ∾ lightning *Wetterleuchten;* a ∾ of notepaper *ein Bogen Schreibpapier;* a ∾ of pins *ein Brief Stecknadeln;* a ∾ of water *eine Wasserfläche;* three ∾s in the wind (sl.) *betrunken;* a winding ∾ *ein Leichentuch;* the book is in ∾s *das Buch ist geheftet;* it is coming down in ∾s *es regnet Bindfäden;* to have a clean ∾ *eine reine Weste haben;* to stand in a white ∾ *im Büßerhemd stehen, bereuen;* to turn in between the ∾s *zu Bett gehen*

shelf n.: to be on the ∾ *ausrangiert, zum alten Eisen getan, sitzengeblieben sein;* to put on the ∾ *auf die lange Bank schieben*

shell I. n.: ∾-proof *bombensicher;* to go into (to come out of) one's ∾ *sich zurückziehen, schweigsam werden bzw. auftauen (in Gesellschaft).* — **II.** v.tr. it is as easy as ∾ing peas *es ist kinderleicht;* to ∾ a town *eine Stadt bombardieren;* to ∾ out money (sl.) *Geld herausrücken.* — **III.** v.i.: to ∾ off *sich abschälen*

shelter I. n.: an air-raid ∾ *ein Luftschutzraum, -keller, Bunker;* to find (to take) ∾ from the rain *gegen den (vor dem) Regen Schutz finden, suchen.* — **II.** v.tr.: to ∾ a person *j.en beherbergen, j.em Zuflucht gewähren;* to ∾ a person from blame *j.en vor Tadel schützen;* to ∾ oneself behind (beneath, under) a thing *sich hinter einer Sache verbergen.* — **III.** v.i.: we ∾ed till the rain stopped *wir stellten uns unter, bis der Regen aufhörte*

shelve v.tr.: the matter has been ∾d *die Angelegenheit ist aufgeschoben worden;* to ∾ a person *j.en ausrangieren, kaltstellen*

shield n.: that is the other side of the ∾ *das ist die andere Seite der Frage*

shift I. v.tr.: to ∾ the blame from one person to (on) another *die Schuld von einem auf den anderen schieben;* to ∾ one's ground *seinen Standpunkt ändern;* to ∾ one's lodging *umziehen;* to ∾ the scene *die Szene verlegen;* to ∾ one's shirt (arch.) *das Hemd wechseln;* to ∾ off the responsibility to another *einem anderen die*

Verantwortung zuschieben. — **II.** v.i.: the cargo ∾ed *die Ladung verlagerte sich;* the scene ∾s *die Szene wechselt;* the wind ∾s round to the East *der Wind springt nach Osten um;* I must ∾ as I can *ich muß irgendwie zurechtkommen (mich durchschlagen);* he must ∾ for himself *er muß für sich selbst sorgen, sich (dat.) selbst helfen.* — **III.** n.: the ∾ of crops *der Fruchtwechsel;* the day (night) ∾ *die Tages-, Nachtschicht;* to make ∾ (a ∾) to do a thing *etwas möglich machen;* I must make ∾ with it *ich muß mich damit behelfen;* I must make ∾ without it *ich muß irgendwie ohne die Sache auskommen;* to make but poor ∾ *sich kümmerlich behelfen;* a make-∾ *ein Notbehelf*

shilling n.: a ∾-shocker *ein billiger Roman;* to cut off one's son with a ∾ *seinen Sohn enterben;* to take the King's (Queen's) ∾ *sich als Soldat anwerben lassen*

shilly-shally v.i.: to ∾ *durch Unentschlossenheit Zeit vergeuden*

shin I. v.i.: to ∾ up a tree *an einem Baum hinaufklettern.* — **II.** v.refl.: to ∾ oneself against *mit dem Schienbein stoßen gegen*

shindy n.: to kick up (to raise) a ∾ *Lärm (Krach) schlagen*

shine I. v.i.: he does not ∾ in conversation *er hat keine besondere Unterhaltungsgabe;* he is a shining example *er ist ein leuchtendes Vorbild;* his face shone with gratitude *sein Gesicht leuchtete (strahlte) vor Dankbarkeit.* — **II.** v.tr.: to ∾ boots *Schuhe wichsen (putzen).* — **III.** n.: rain or ∾ *bei Regen und Sonnenschein, in guten und schlechten Tagen;* to take a ∾ to a person (colloq.) *sich in j.en verlieben;* to take the ∾ out of a thing (colloq.) *einer Sache den Glanz nehmen, sie übertreffen, in den Schatten stellen;* to kick up a ∾ (sl.) *Lärm (Krach) schlagen*

ship I. n.: the ∾ of the desert *das Wüstenschiff, das Kamel;* when my ∾ comes home *wenn das große Geldschiff ankommt, wenn ich mein Glück mache;* to take ∾ for *sich einschiffen nach;* to travel by ∾ *mit dem Schiff (per Schiff) reisen.* — **II.** v.tr.: to ∾ goods to Africa *Waren nach Afrika verfrachten;* to ∾ oars *die Riemen einlegen (einziehen);* his father ∾ped him off for (to) America *sein Vater verschiffte ihn nach Amerika;* to spoil the ∾ (rightly sheep) for a ha'porth o' tar *durch falsches Sparen einen großen Verlust haben.* — **III.** v.i.: to ∾ for *sich einschiffen nach;* to ∾ as a sailor *sich als Matrose verdingen*

shipshape I. a.: everything was ∾ (and Bristol fashion) *alles war in bester Ordnung.* — **II.** adv.: to put ∾ *in Ordnung bringen*

shirk v.tr.: to ∾ work *sich vor der Arbeit drücken*

shirker n.: a ∾ *ein Drückeberger*

shirt n.: a boiled ∾ (colloq.) *ein Frackhemd;* near is my ∾, but nearer is my skin *das Hemd ist mir näher als der Rock;* stripped to the ∾, in ∾-sleeves *in Hemdsärmeln;* to get a person's ∾ off *j.en erzürnen, böse machen, auf die Palme bringen;* to give a person a wet ∾ *j.en arbeiten lassen, bis er schwitzt;* he hasn't a ∾ to his back *er hat kein Hemd auf dem Leibe;* keep your ∾ on (sl.) *reg' dich nicht auf, tritt dir nicht ins Hemd;* to put one's ∾ upon a horse (colloq.) *alles (seinen letzten Pfennig) auf ein Pferd setzen*

shirty a.: (colloq.) *ärgerlich, verdrießlich*

shiver I. n.: he was all in (of) a ∾ *er zitterte wie Espenlaub;* it gives me the ∾s *ich kriege eine Gänsehaut.* — **II.** v.tr.: ∾ my timbers (naut.) *etwa: da soll doch der Teufel dreinschlagen!*

shock I. n.: a ∾ of an earthquake *ein Erdstoß;* an electric ∾ *ein elektrischer Schlag;* ∾ tactics *Überrumpelungsversuche;* ∾ troops *Stoßtruppen;* I nearly died of ∾ *ich wäre vor Schrecken fast gestorben;* you'll get the ∾ of your life *du wirst dein blaues Wunder erleben;* to give a person a ∾ *j.es Gefühle beleidigen.* — **II.** v.tr.: I was ∾ed at (by, to hear) the news *die Nachricht erschütterte mich*

shocking I. a.: ∾ conduct *empörendes Verhalten (Benehmen);* a ∾ state of disorder *eine fürchterliche Unordnung;* we had ∾ weather *wir hatten scheußliches Wetter.* — **II.** adv.: a ∾ bad road (colloq.) *eine entsetzlich schlechte Straße*

shoe I. n.: that's another pair of ∾s *das ist etwas ganz anderes, das steht auf einem anderen Blatt;* over ∾s over boots *wenn schon, denn schon;* to be (to stand) in a person's ∾s *an j.es Stelle sein, in j.es Haut stecken;* to die in one's ∾s *eines gewaltsamen Todes sterben, gehängt werden;*

to know where the ∾ pinches *wissen, wo der Schuh drückt; Geldknappheit kennen;* to put the ∾ on the right foot *die Schuld dem Richtigen zuschieben;* now the ∾ is on the other foot *jetzt ist die Sache umgekehrt, es paßt ihm nicht mehr in seinen Kram;* to shake in one's ∾s *vor Angst zittern, einen Bammel haben;* to step into another person's ∾s *j.es Amt (Stelle) übernehmen;* to tread the ∾ awry *vom Wege der Tugend abweichen, einen Fehltritt tun;* to tread the ∾ straight *rechtschaffen sein;* to wait for dead men's ∾s *auf Erbschaft lauern;* he ∾-horned himself into his car *er zwängte sich in seinen Wagen;* he is as honest a man as ever trod ∾-leather *er ist ein grundehrlicher Mensch.* — **II.** v.tr.: to ∾ a goose *etwas Törichtes (Zweckloses) unternehmen;* to ∾ a horse *ein Pferd beschlagen*

shoestring n.: she dresses on a ∾ *sie kleidet sich mit ganz wenig Geld;* the resolution obtained a ∾ majority *der Beschluß wurde mit knapper Mehrheit angenommen*

shoot I. v.i.: ∾! *heraus mit der Sprache, schieß los!; (Film) mach' jetzt die Aufnahme! knipse!;* the buds (trees) are ∾ing *die Knospen sprießen, die Bäume schlagen aus;* a flash ∾s across the sky *ein Feuerschein zuckt über den Himmel;* to ∾ ahead (of someone) *vorwärtseilen, j.en überholen;* to ∾ over preserves *in einem Jagdrevier schießen;* to ∾ off one's mouth (sl.) *prahlen, renommieren;* prices ∾ up *die Preise steigen plötzlich.* — **II.** v.tr.: to ∾ a bolt *einen Riegel vorschieben;* to have shot one's bolt *sein Letztes getan haben;* to ∾ a bridge *unter einer Brücke durchfahren;* to ∾ the cat (vulg.) *sich übergeben, kotzen;* to ∾ a line (sl.) *prahlen, wichtig tun, angeben;* to ∾ one's linen *die Manschetten*

8791 - Engl. Redewendg. - II. Teil - Sp. 69

durch Schütteln des Armes hervortreten lassen; to ∾ a match *an einem Wettschießen teilnehmen;* to ∾ the moon, the pit (sl.) *heimlich (bei Nacht und Nebel) ausziehen (ausrücken), ohne die Miete zu bezahlen;* to ∾ Niagara *eine waghalsige Sache unternehmen;* to ∾ the rapids *die Stromschnellen hinabschießen;* to ∾ rubbish *Schutt, Müll abladen;* to ∾ the sun *die Mittagshöhe der Sonne durch Sextanten bestimmen;* shot silk *changierendes Taft;* I'll be shot if . . . *ich lasse mich umbringen, wenn . . .* — **III.** n.: to go the whole ∾ *alles mitmachen, das Ganze mitnehmen*

shooting I. a.: a ∾ pain *ein stechender Schmerz;* a ∾ star *eine Sternschnuppe.* — **II.** n.: a ∾-box *eine Jagdhütte;* a ∾-range *ein Schießstand*

shop I. n.: all over the ∾ (sl.) *überall verstreut, in großer Unordnung;* to knock a person all over the ∾ (boxing) *j.en gehörig verprügeln;* the other ∾ (sl.) *das Konkurrenzunternehmen;* to come to the wrong ∾ *an die falsche Adresse geraten;* to set up (a) ∾ *ein Geschäft eröffnen;* to shut up ∾ *die Bude (den Laden) zumachen; aufhören, etwas zu tun;* shut your ∾ (sl.) *halt's Maul! halt den Rand!;* to sink the ∾ *nicht vom Geschäft reden, nicht fachsimpeln; seinen Beruf verheimlichen;* to smell of the ∾ *nach Fachsimpelei klingen;* to talk ∾ *fachsimpeln;* a ∾-lifter *ein Ladendieb;* a ∾-steward *ein Vertrauensmann der Arbeiter im Betrieb;* a ∾-walker *ein(e) aufsichtsführend(e) Angestellte(r) im Warenhaus, Rayonchef;* he has everything in the ∾-window *er ist sehr oberflächlich;* to put all one's goods in the ∾-window *sich mit seinen Vorzügen brüsten.* — **II.** v.i.: to ∾, to go ∾ping *einkaufen, einkaufen gehen.* — **III.** v.tr.: to ∾ a person (sl.) *j.en ins Gefängnis werfen, einsperren*

shopping n.: to do one's ∾ *Einkäufe machen, seine Einkäufe besorgen*

short I. a.: a ∾ circuit *ein Kurzschluß;* to keep on ∾ commons *bei schmaler Kost halten;* to take a ∾ cut *einen Weg abschneiden, -kürzen;* at ∾ date *auf kurze Sicht;* a drop of something ∾ (colloq.) *ein Gläschen Schnaps;* to win by a ∾ head *knapp gewinnen (bei weniger als einer Pferdekopflänge);* a ∾-list *eine Auswahlliste, engere Wahl;* at ∾ range *auf kurze, aus naher Entfernung;* a ∾ rib *eine falsche Rippe;* a ∾ sea *eine böige See;* a ∾ story *eine Novelle;* to be in ∾ supply of a thing *knapp an einer Sache sein;* he has a ∾ temper, is ∾-tempered *er braust leicht auf;* to take ∾ views *nur die Gegenwart sehen;* to give ∾ weight *etwas zu knapp wiegen;* to make ∾ work of (to give ∾ shrift to) a thing *kurzen Prozeß (nicht viel Umstände) mit etwas machen;* to be ∾ of breath *atemlos, außer Atem sein;* to be ∾ of cash *kein Geld haben, knapp bei Kasse sein;* to be ∾ of hands, ∾-handed *nicht genügend*

Arbeitskräfte haben; little ∾ of *beinahe, etwas weniger als;* to be nothing ∾ of marvellous *geradezu wunderbar, ein Wunder sein;* to come ∾ of a thing *einer Sache nicht entsprechen, hinter etwas zurückbleiben;* she falls ∾ of my expectations *ich hätte mehr von ihr erwartet;* to go ∾ of food *dürftig leben;* we ran ∾ of tea, our tea ran ∾ *unser Tee wurde knapp (ging uns aus);* he was very ∾ with me *er war sehr kurz angebunden zu mir, er fertigte mich kurz ab.* — **II.** adv.: to bring (to pull) up ∾ *plötzlich (jäh) anhalten, zum Halten bringen;* to cut it ∾ (sl.) *um es kurz zu machen, kurz und gut;* cut it ∾! (sl.) *fass' dich kurz!;* to cut (to take up) a person ∾ *j.en unterbrechen;* to sell ∾ *ohne Deckung verkaufen;* to stop ∾ *plötzlich innehalten (aufhören);* to be taken ∾ (fam.) *Durchfall bekommen;* I tried everything ∾ of force *ich versuchte alles bis auf (außer) Gewalt;* a ∾-set man *ein untersetzter Mann.* — **III.** v.tr.: to ∾-circuit official proceedings *eine umständliche Prozedur abkürzen, umgehen.* — **IV.** n.: the long and the ∾ of it *das Endergebnis, der langen Rede kurzer Sinn;* he is called Bob for ∾ *er heißt kurz Bob;* in ∾ *in Kürze, kurz*

shot[1] n.: not a ∾ in the locker *kein Geld in der Tasche;* ∾-proof *schußsicher, kugelfest;* a Parthian ∾ *eine letzte spitze Bemerkung, ein letzter wütende Blick eines Abgehenden;* a random ∾ *ein zufälliger Schuß, ein Schuß ins Blaue;* a snap∾ *eine Momentaufnahme, ein Schnappschuß;* to be a good (crack, bad, no) ∾ *ein guter (ausgezeichneter, schlechter) Schütze sein;* to be within (out of) ∾ *in (außer) Schußweite sein;* he did it like a ∾ *er tat es sofort, blitzschnell;* to have a ∾ at a thing *etwas versuchen;* you've made a bad ∾ *du hast daneben getroffen, falsch geraten;* a ∾ of morphia *eine Morphiumspritze;* a big ∾ (sl.) *ein hohes Tier*

shot[2] n.: to pay one's ∾ *seinen Anteil bezahlen*

shoulder I. n.: a ∾ of mutton sail *ein dreieckiges Segel;* with one's ∾ to the collar *fest(e) bei der Arbeit;* to drag a story in by the head and ∾s *eine Geschichte an den Haaren herbeiziehen;* to give someone the cold ∾, to turn the cold ∾ upon someone *j.em die kalte Schulter zeigen;* it was given straight from the ∾ *der Schlag, die Bemerkung saß;* he has broad ∾s *er hat einen breiten Buckel;* to lay the blame (burden) on the right ∾s *dem Richtigen die Schuld (Last) aufbürden;* to put (to set) one's ∾ to the wheel *kräftige Anstrengungen machen, sich ernstlich an die Arbeit machen;* you cannot put old heads on young ∾s (prov.) *Jugend hat kein Tugend;* to rub ∾s with a person *mit j.em verkehren;* to stand head and ∾s above someone *j.em weit voraus (überlegen) sein;* soft ∾s! (Am.) *Bankett unbefahrbar!* — **II.** v.tr.: ∾ arms! *das Gewehr über!;* to ∾ a burden *eine Last schultern, etwas Unangenehmes auf sich nehmen;* to ∾ one's way through a crowd *sich einen Weg durch die Menge bahnen.* — **III.** v.i.: to ∾ through *sich durchdrängen*

shout I. v.i.: to ∾ for joy *vor Freude jauchzen;* to ∾ with laughter *vor Lachen brüllen;* to ∾ at a person *j.en anschreien;* to ∾ for a person *nach j.em rufen.* — **II.** v.tr.: the crowd ∾ed approbation *die Menge drückte laut ihre Billigung aus;* to ∾ a person down *j.en niederschreien, -brüllen.* — **III.** n.: it's my ∾ *ich bin an der Reihe (dran), etwas zu bestellen;* to give a ∾ *einen Schrei ausstoßen;* it's all over but (bar) the ∾ing *der Erfolg ist so sicher, daß nur der Beifall noch fehlt*

shove (sl.) **I.** v.i.: ∾ along! *weitergehen!;* I'll ∾ off *ich werde verduften.* — **II.** n.: to give someone a ∾ *j.em einen Stoß geben (versetzen)*

show I. v.tr.: to ∾ cause for a thing *die Gründe (Motive) für etwas angeben;* to ∾ a clean pair of heels *sich auf und davon machen, weglaufen, ausreißen;* to ∾ the cloven hoof *das Böse (Finstere) im Charakter oder in den Absichten verraten;* to ∾ one's colours *Farbe bekennen;* to ∾ a person the door *j.em die Tür weisen;* to ∾ one's face *sich sehen lassen;* to ∾ the white feather *sich feige zeigen;* to ∾ fight *sich kampfbereit zeigen, nicht nachgeben;* to ∾ one's hand *seine Karten (Pläne) aufdecken;* to ∾ a leg *vom (aus dem) Bett aufstehen;* to ∾ a thing off to the best advantage *etwas im besten Lichte zeigen;* to ∾ a person up *j.en bloßstellen, entlarven;* ∾ him up *führe ihn hinauf.* — **II.** v.i.: the stain doesn't ∾ *der Fleck ist nicht zu sehen;* he has nothing to ∾ for it *er hat keinen*

Beweis dafür; he is fond of ∾ing off *er brüstet sich (renommiert) gern, er gibt gern an;* he did not ∾ up the next day *am nächsten Tag erschien er nicht.* — **III.** n.: a dumb ∾ *ein Gebärdenspiel, eine Pantomime;* a flower (motor, etc.) ∾ *eine Blumen-(Automobil-, usw.)ausstellung;* a peep-∾ *ein Guckkasten;* a ∾ of fashions *eine Modenschau;* under a ∾ of gratitude *unter dem Scheine der Dankbarkeit;* to vote by ∾ of hands *durch Aufheben der Hände abstimmen;* a ∾ of reason *eine Spur von Vernunft;* to be on ∾ *zu besichtigen, ausgestellt sein;* he is fond of ∾ *er ist prachtliebend, er gibt gern an;* to boss (to run) the ∾ *an der Spitze stehen, eine Sache (ein Geschäft) leiten, die Sache schmeißen;* he did it for ∾ *er tat es, um zu renommieren;* to give away the ∾ (colloq.) *das Geheimnis, die Sache verraten;* give him a fair ∾ (colloq.) *laß ihm Gerechtigkeit widerfahren, gib ihm Gelegenheit, sich zu verteidigen;* we are going to a ∾ tonight *wir gehen heute Abend ins Theater;* to make a ∾ of doing a thing *sich stellen (so tun), als täte man etwas;* to make a ∾ of oneself *sich lächerlich machen;* to make a fine ∾ *prächtig aussehen;* to force a ∾-down *eine Aufdeckung der Karten, eine Entscheidung erzwingen;* to put up a good ∾ *eine gute Leistung vollbringen;* to steal (to run away with) the ∾ (colloq.) *alle anderen Anwesenden in den Schatten stellen*

shower I. n.: a ∾-bath *ein Brausebad, eine Dusche;* a ∾ of gifts *eine Fülle (Menge) Geschenke;* letters came in ∾s *Briefe trafen in großer Zahl ein;* to be caught in a ∾ *von einem Regenschauer überrascht werden.* — **II.** v.tr.: to ∾ a person with honours, to ∾ honours upon a person *j.en mit Ehrenbezeigungen überhäufen.* — **III.** v.i.: to ∾ down *gießen, in Strömen regnen*

showing n.: on your own ∾ *nach Ihrer eigenen Aussage (Behauptung);* the ∾ of a film *die Vorführung eines Filmes*

shred n.: without a ∾ of clothing on him *ohne einen Fetzen auf dem Leib;* not a ∾ of evidence *nicht die Spur eines Beweises;* to tear in(to) ∾s *in Fetzen reißen*

shrift n.: a short ∾ *eine Galgenfrist;* to give someone short ∾ *kurzen Prozeß mit j.em machen*

shrink I. v.i.: to ∾ from doing a thing *etwas ungern (widerwillig) tun;* to ∾ back from doing a thing *davor zurückschrecken (sich scheuen), etwas zu tun;* to ∾ into oneself *sich in sich zurückziehen.* — **II.** v.tr.: his face has a shrunken look *sein Gesicht sieht eingefallen aus*

shroud n.: the crime is wrapped in a ∾ of mystery *das Verbrechen ist in Dunkel gehüllt*

shuffle I. v.i.: he ∾s along painfully *er schleppt sich mühsam fort;* to ∾ with one's feet *mit den Füßen scharren;* he is only shuffling *er macht nur Ausflüchte.* — **II.** v.tr.: to ∾ the cards *die Karten mischen; eine neue Politik versuchen;* when we have ∾d off this mortal coil (Hamlet III, 1, 67) *wenn wir den Drang des Ird'schen abgeschüttelt (Schlegel);* to ∾ off the responsibility upon others *die Verantwortung auf andere abwälzen;* to ∾ on one's clothes *in seine Kleider schlüpfen*

shut I. v.tr.: to ∾ the door upon a thing *sich weigern, etwas zu berücksichtigen; etwas unmöglich machen;* to ∾ one's eyes to a thing *die Augen vor etwas verschließen, etwas nicht sehen wollen;* he ∾ his finger into the door-hinge *er klemmte sich den Finger in der Türangel;* we are ∾ of him (vulg.) *wir sind ihn los;* to ∾ off the gas *das Gas absperren (abstellen);* to ∾ the door to *die Tür fest schließen;* to ∾ up shop *die Bude (den Laden) zumachen; aufhören, etwas zu tun.* — **II.** v.i.: the lid ∾s automatically *der Deckel schließt automatisch;* the works ∾ down next week *die Fabrik wird nächste Woche stillgelegt;* ∾ up (sl.) *halt's Maul! halt den Rand!*

shutter n.: to put up the ∾s *die Fensterläden schließen, den Laden für den Tag oder für dauernd zumachen*

shuttle n.: to start a ∾-service between two towns *einen Pendelverkehr zwischen zwei Städten einrichten*

shy¹ a.: I am ∾ three quid (sl.) *ich habe drei Pfund Sterling verloren (minus gemacht);* to fight ∾ of a person or thing *j.em (einer Sache) aus dem Wege gehen;* he is work-∾ *er ist arbeitsscheu*

shy² n.: to have a ∾ at a thing (sl.) *nach einem Gegenstand werfen; etwas versuchen*

sick a.: to be (to get) ∾ *erbrechen, sich übergeben;* he is awfully ∾ at being beaten (colloq.) *er ist sehr ärgerlich (betrübt, enttäuscht) über seine Niederlage;* to be ∾ at heart *sehr betrübt (bekümmert) sein;* to be home-∾ *Heimweh haben;* to be ∾ for a sight of *sich nach einem Anblick sehnen;* to be ∾ of a fever *an Fieber erkrankt sein;* I am ∾ and tired of it all *ich bin die Sache leid, ich habe es satt, die Sache hängt mir zum Hals heraus;* it makes me ∾ to think of it *mir wird ganz übel bei dem Gedanken, der Gedanke macht mich rasend;* to make a patient ∾ *einem Kranken ein Brechmittel eingeben*

sicken I. v.i.: to ∾ at a thing *sich vor etwas ekeln;* the child is ∾ing for something *das Kind hat irgendeine Krankheit in den Gliedern;* to ∾ of a thing (colloq.) *einer Sache überdrüssig werden.* — **II.** v.tr.: I was ∾ed of trying to make peace *ich wurde den Versuch, Frieden zu stiften, leid;* it was a ∾ing sight *es war ein ekelhafter Anblick*

sickly a.: a ∾ climate *ein ungesundes Klima;* a ∾ smell *ein widerlicher Geruch;* a ∾ smile *ein schmerzliches Lächeln*

side I. n.: he attacked me on my blind ∾ *er griff mich an meiner schwachen Seite an;* ∾ by ∾ *Seite an Seite;* the country-∾ *Land(strich), Gegend;* prices were on the high ∾ *die Preise waren ziemlich hoch;* to go to the sea∾ *an die See fahren;* Cambridge has a strong ∾ *Cambridge hat eine starke Mannschaft;* to get out of bed on the wrong ∾ *mit dem falschen (linken) Bein zuerst aus dem Bett steigen, den ganzen Tag übel gelaunt sein;* to be born on the wrong ∾ of the blanket *außerehelich geboren sein;* to be the wrong ∾ of the door *ausgesperrt sein;* on the right (wrong) ∾ of forty *unter (über) vierzig Jahre alt sein;* to hold one's ∾s with laughter *sich den Bauch vor Lachen halten;* to keep on the right ∾ of a person *es mit j.em gut halten;* he puts on too much ∾, has too much ∾ *er prahlt zu sehr, er tut zu vornehm;* to put ∾ on a ball *einem Ball Effet geben;* to shake (to split) one's ∾s (with laughing) *sich krank-, totlachen, sich vor Lachen schütteln (biegen), vor Lachen bersten wollen;* to take ∾s *sich für eine Sache, Partei entschließen;* to take ∾s with a person *sich j.em anschließen;* the ∾-car of a motorbicycle *der Beiwagen eines Motorrads;* a ∾-note *eine Randbemerkung;* a ∾-saddle *ein Damenreitsattel;* the plane (the car) began to ∾-slip *das Flugzeug begann abzurutschen, der Wagen geriet ins Schleudern;* a ∾-slip (colloq.) *ein uneheliches Kind;* to ∾-step a thing *einer Sache ausweichen;* to ∾-track a person (a thing) *j.en kaltstellen, etwas auf ein Nebengleis schieben, ablenken;* the ∾-walk (U.S.) *der Bürgersteig.* — **II.** v.i.: to ∾ with a person *es mit j.em halten, j.es Partei ergreifen*

sidelong I. adv.: to move ∾ *sich seitwärts bewegen.* — **II.** a.: a ∾ glance *ein Blick von der Seite*

sidle v.i.: to ∾ along *sich seitwärts fortbewegen;* to ∾ up to a person *sich an j.en heranschlängeln*

siege n.: a state of ∾ *ein Belagerungszustand;* to lay ∾ to a town *eine Stadt belagern;* to push the ∾ *die Belagerung kräftig fortsetzen;* to raise the ∾ *die Belagerung aufheben*

sight n.: to be a ∾ for sore eyes *eine Augenweide sein;* the roses were a ∾ to see, a ∾ *die Rosen waren herrlich anzusehen;* it is a long ∾ better *es ist bei weitem (bedeutend) besser;* to catch ∾ of a thing *etwas erblicken;* it will cost a ∾ of money (colloq.) *es wird eine Stange Geld kosten;* to get a ∾ of a thing *etwas zu Gesicht bekommen;* to look a ∾ *häßlich aussehen;* to lose ∾ of a thing *etwas aus den Augen verlieren;* to lose one's ∾ *blind werden;* to make a ∾ of oneself *sich auffällig kleiden, benehmen;* to ruin one's ∾ *sich (dat.) die Augen verderben;* to see the ∾s *die Sehenswürdigkeiten besichtigen;* to take a ∾ of (at) a person *j.em eine lange Nase machen;* to take a careful ∾ *genau zielen;* I hate the very ∾ of him *ich kann ihn nicht ausstehen;* not by a long ∾ (colloq.) *bei weitem (noch lange) nicht;* a bill payable at ∾ *ein Sichtwechsel;* love at first ∾ *Liebe auf den ersten Blick;* to play music at ∾ *vom Blatt spielen;* to know by ∾ *von Ansehen kennen;* to be in (out of) ∾ *in Sicht (außer Sicht) sein;* to find favour in a person's ∾ *bei j.em Gunst (Gnade) finden;* to heave in (to come in, into) ∾ *in Sicht kommen, sichtbar werden;* to be on ∾ *zu sehen, zu besichtigen sein;* to do something on ∾ *etwas sofort (ohne zu zögern) tun;* out of my ∾! *mir aus den*

Augen!; out of ∾, out of mind (prov.) *aus den Augen, aus dem Sinn;* to put a thing out of ∾ *etwas verstecken, etwas verschwinden lassen;* we watched the car out of ∾ *wir sahen dem Auto nach, bis es verschwand*

sign I. v.tr.: he ∾ed assent *er gab durch Zeichen seine Zustimmung;* ∾ed, sealed and delivered (legal) *unterschrieben, gesiegelt und vollzogen;* he ∾ed away his property (his liberty) *er hat sein Eigentum (seine Freiheit) durch Unterschrift aufgegeben (abgetreten).* — **II.** v.i.: he ∾ed for the goods *er hat den Empfang der Waren bestätigt (quittiert);* to ∾ off *eine Radiosendung beenden* (see „signature"); he made a ∾-off bid of twenty pounds *er machte ein endgültiges Angebot von zwanzig Pfund;* to ∾ on *anwerben, anmustern, sich verdingen;* to ∾ on the dotted line *in etwas einwilligen, sich mit etwas einverstanden erklären, keinen Widerspruch erheben*

signal a.: a ∾ success *ein außergewöhnlicher Erfolg;* a ∾ victory *ein hervorragender Sieg*

signatory a.: the ∾ powers to a treaty *die Signatarmächte eines Vertrags*

signature n.: a ∾ tune *eine besondere Melodie, die das Spielen einer bestimmten Kapelle ankündigt;* over his ∾ *von ihm unterschrieben*

silence n.: ∾ gives consent (prov.) *Schweigen ist auch eine Antwort;* to pass into ∾ *in Vergessenheit geraten;* to put to ∾ *zum Schweigen bringen*

silent a.: a ∾ partner *ein stiller Teilhaber;* history is ∾ upon it *die Geschichte schweigt sich darüber aus*

silk n.: you cannot make a ∾ purse out of a sow's ear (prov.) *etwa: Bauer bleibt Bauer;* to take ∾ *Anwalt der Krone werden*

silly I. a.: the ∾ season *die Sauregurkenzeit.* — **II.** n.: don't be a ∾ *sei nicht so albern!*

silver n.: speech is ∾, silence is golden (prov.) *Reden ist Silber, Schweigen ist Gold;* every cloud has a ∾ lining (prov.) *auch das Schlimmste hat ein Ende, alles hat seine gute Seite;* the ∾side *der beste Teil der Rindskeule;* to be born with a ∾ spoon in one's mouth *ein Glückskind, Kind reicher Eltern sein;* the ∾ streak *der (Englische) Kanal;* to have a ∾ tongue *beredt sein*

Simon Pure n.pr.: the real ∾ *die wahre (echte) Person (Sache)*

simple I. a.: it was a mistake pure and ∾ *es war schlechthin ein Versehen.* — **II.** n.: to be cut for the ∾s *sich auf Dummheit behandeln lassen*

sin I. v.i.: I am a man more ∾ned against than ∾ning (Lear, III, 2, 60) *ich bin ein Mann, an dem man mehr gesündigt, als er sündigte* (Schlegel-Tieck). — **II.** n.: ugly as ∾ *häßlich wie die Nacht (Sünde)*

since I. adv.: he has been healthy ever ∾ *er ist seitdem gesund geblieben;* I have not seen him ∾ *ich habe ihn seitdem (seither) nicht gesehen;* many years ∾ *vor vielen Jahren;* how long ∾ is it? *wie lange ist es her?* — **II.** prep.: I have been here ∾ Monday *ich bin seit Montag hier;* ∾ seeing you I have heard all *seitdem ich dich sah, habe ich alles gehört.* — **III.** conj.: what have you done ∾ we met? *was hast du gemacht, seitdem wir uns trafen?;* ∾ that is so, there is nothing more to be said *da dem so ist (da die Sache so steht), ist nichts mehr zu sagen;* a more dangerous, ∾ unknown foe *ein gefährlicherer, da unbekannter Feind*

sincerely adv.: yours ∾ N. N. *Ihr ergebener N. N.*

sinews n.: money is the ∾ of war (prov.) *Geld ist die Seele des Krieges*

sing I. v.i.: to have a ∾ing in one's ears *Ohrensausen haben;* to ∾ small *kleinlaut werden, klein beigeben;* to ∾ true *richtig singen;* to ∾ out for a person *laut nach j.em rufen.* — **II.** v.tr.: to ∾ another song (tune) *andere, sanftere Töne anschlagen, andere Saiten aufziehen;* to ∾ a child to sleep *ein Kind in den Schlaf singen;* to ∾ a person's praises *j.es Lob singen;* to ∾ out the names of the stations *die Haltestellen laut ausrufen;* to ∾ the same song *in dasselbe Horn stoßen*

singe v.tr.: to ∾ one's feathers (wings) *sich (dat.) die Finger verbrennen*

single I. a.: ∾ blessedness (facet. cf. Shakespeare M.N.D. I, 1) *scherzhaft für Junggesellen-, Ledigenstand;* a ∾breasted coat *ein einreihiger Rock;* in ∾ combat *im Zweikampf;* bookkeeping by ∾-entry *einfache Buchführung;* with a ∾ eye to duty *nur auf seine Pflicht bedacht;* to march in ∾ file *im Gänsemarsch gehen (marschie-*

ren); he did it ∾-handed (adv.) *er tat es ohne Hilfe;* a ∾ heart (mind) *ein einfacher, aufrichtiger Charakter;* ∾ life (or: state) *der ledige Stand (Ledigenstand);* not a ∾ one *kein einziger, keine einzige, kein einziges.* — **II.** n.: let's play a ∾ *laßt uns ein Einzelspiel machen;* a ∾ to N. *eine einfache Fahrkarte nach N.* — **III.** v.tr.: to ∾ out a person (thing) as (for) *j.en (etwas) auswählen (aussondern, bestimmen) als (für, zu)*

singular I. a.: all and ∾ *zusammen und getrennt genommen;* a ∾ attempt *ein ungewöhnlicher (auffallender) Versuch;* ∾ behaviour *ein eigenartiges (sonderbares) Benehmen;* a ∾ instance *ein hervorragendes Beispiel;* a ∾ opportunity *eine äußerst günstige Gelegenheit.* — **II.** n.: 'tooth' is the ∾ of 'teeth' *„Zahn ist die Einzahl von „Zähne"*

sink I. v.i.: it is ∾ or swim *hier heißt's entweder — oder; friß, Vogel, oder stirb;* my heart sank *mir schwand der Mut, ich war verzweifelt;* the patient is ∾ing fast *mit dem Kranken geht es rasch zu Ende;* the river is ∾ing *der Fluß fällt;* to ∾ into a chair *sich auf einen Stuhl fallen lassen;* the impression ∾s into the memory *der Eindruck prägt sich dem Gedächtnis ein;* to ∾ into oblivion *in Vergessenheit geraten;* a ∾ing fund *ein Tilgungsfonds;* with a ∾ing heart *mit Angstgefühl;* with a ∾ing stomach *mit Hungergefühl;* with sunken cheeks *mit eingefallenen Wangen.* — **II.** v.tr.: to ∾ a debt (fund) *eine Schuld tilgen, ein Kapital amortisieren;* to ∾ a die *einen Stempel schneiden (gravieren);* to ∾ one's differences *allen Streit beilegen, die Streitaxt begraben;* to ∾ a fact *eine Tatsache verheimlichen;* to ∾ one's own interests *selbstlos sein;* to ∾ money *Geld fest anlegen;* to ∾ one's name (title) *seinen Namen (Titel) aufgeben;* to ∾ the shop *nicht vom Geschäft reden, nicht fachsimpeln; seinen Beruf verheimlichen;* to ∾ a well *einen Brunnen bohren.* — **III.** n.: a ∾ of iniquity *ein Sündenpfuhl*

sit I. v.i.: the ∾ting tenant *der jetzige (Haus)mieter;* ∾s the wind there? *pfeift der Wind aus dém Loch?;* his principles ∾ loosely on him *er handelt nicht nach seinen Grundsätzen;* it ∾s heavy on the stomach *es liegt (drückt) schwer im (auf den) Magen;* ∾ tight *bleib fest auf deinem Platz! gib nicht nach!;* he ∾s tight *er bleibt bei seiner Meinung.* — with prep. & adv.: he ∾s at his desk all day *er sitzt den ganzen Tag am Schreibtisch;* to ∾ back *eine passive Haltung einnehmen;* to ∾ down to dinner *sich zum Essen hinsetzen;* to ∾ down to do a thing *sich anschicken, etwas zu tun;* a ∾-down strike *ein Sitzstreik;* to ∾ down under an insult, to take it ∾ting down *eine Beleidigung einstecken;* to ∾ for a constituency *einen Wahlkreis vertreten;* to ∾ for an examination *sich einer Prüfung unterziehen;* to ∾ for one's portrait *sich malen lassen;* to ∾ in judgement on a person *über j.en richten;* to ∾ in *Babysitter sein;* to ∾ on the bench *Richter sein;* to ∾ on a case *einen Fall untersuchen;* to ∾ on the fence *neutral bleiben, eine abwartende Haltung einnehmen;* to ∾ on one's hands *nicht applaudieren;* to ∾ on horseback *zu Pferde sitzen;* to ∾ on a jury *Geschworener sein;* to ∾ up late *lange aufbleiben;* to ∾ under someone *j.en als Lehrer oder Prediger anhören;* to make a person ∾ up *j.en aufrütteln, in Schrecken, Staunen versetzen;* to ∾ up for someone *auf j.es Heimkehr (am späten Abend) warten;* to ∾ up and take notice (colloq.) *ein plötzliches Interesse für eine Sache zeigen;* he wants ∾ting upon *er muß geduckt werden;* a ∾-still party *eine Gesellschaft ohne Tanz.* — **II.** v.tr.: to ∾ a horse *ein Pferd reiten;* to ∾ out a dance *einen Tanz auslassen;* to ∾ out a person *länger bleiben als j.;* to ∾ out a play *ein Stück bis zu Ende anhören*

sitter n.: that was a ∾ (colloq.) *das war eine Kleinigkeit, eine leichte Sache*

sitting n.: a ∾ room *ein Wohnzimmer*

six I. a.: a coach and ∾ *ein Sechsspänner;* it is ∾ of one and half-a-dozen of the other *es ist ganz einerlei, es ist gehupft wie gesprungen, Jacke wie Hose, Pott wie Deckel.* — **II.** n.: things were at ∾es and sevens *es lag alles kunterbunt (wie Kraut und Rüben) durcheinander*

sixty n.: in the sixties of the last century *in den sechziger Jahren des vergangenen Jahrhunderts*

size I. n.: that's about the ∾ of it (colloq.) *da hast du es gerade getroffen, darauf läuft die Sache hinaus!;* they are both of a ∾ *sie sind beide gleich groß;* what is your ∾? *welche Größe (Nummer) haben Sie?* — **II.** v.tr.: to ∾ up a person (colloq.) *j.en richtig ab-, einschätzen (beurteilen)*

skate v.i.: to ∾ on thin ice *ein heikles Thema berühren;* a skating rink *eine künstliche Eisbahn, Rollschuhbahn*

skeleton n.: a ∾ in the family cupboard *ein peinliches Familiengeheimnis;* a ∾ at the feast *eine Mahnung an Elend und Tod inmitten eines Vergnügens;* a ∾ key *ein Dietrich;* a ∾ service *ein Not-, Bereitschaftsdienst*

skew n.: on the ∾ (a∾) *schief, von der Seite;* ∾-eyed *schielend, scheel*

skim I. v.tr.: to ∾ the cream off *den Rahm abschöpfen;* to ∾ a subject *ein Thema flüchtig berühren.* — **II.** v.i.: to ∾ along *schnell dahingleiten;* to ∾ over the pages *die Seiten überfliegen.* — **III.** a.: ∾ milk *Magermilch*

skin I. n.: near is my shirt, nearer my ∾ *das Hemd ist mir näher als der Rock;* it has got under my ∾ (colloq.) *es fesselt (interessiert) mich sehr;* one cannot change one's ∾ *man kann nicht aus seiner Haut;* to escape with (by) the ∾ of one's teeth *mit knapper Not entkommen;* to get off with a whole ∾ *mit heiler Haut davonkommen;* to jump out of one's ∾ *überrascht, freudig auffahren; aus der Haut fahren;* to save one's ∾ *sich in Sicherheit bringen;* wet to the ∾ *naß bis auf die Haut, patschnaß;* beauty is but ∾-deep (prov.) *man kann nicht nach dem Äußeren urteilen;* a ∾-game *ein Schwindel.* — **II.** v.tr.: I'll ∾ you (colloq.) *ich werde dich umbringen!;* to ∾ the cat (gym.) *den Kreuzaufzug machen;* to ∾ a flea for its hide (lard) *äußerst geizig (knickerig) sein;* to ∾ a flint, to be a ∾-flint *geizig (knickerig, ein Geizkragen, -hals) sein;* keep your eyes ∾ned (colloq.) *sei auf der Hut!*

skip I. v.i.: girls ∾ *Mädchen springen Seil;* he ∾s as he reads *er läßt beim Lesen vieles aus;* to ∾ from one subject to another *von einem zum anderen Thema abschweifen, vom Hölzchen aufs Stöckchen kommen;* ∾ it! *verschwinde, hau' ab!* — **II.** v.tr.: I ∾ped (over) a few pages *ich ließ einige Seiten aus;* he ∾ped every tenth row *er überging jede zehnte Reihe*

skittle n.: ∾s! *Unsinn, Quatsch!;* life is not all beer and ∾s (prov.) *das Leben ist nicht (nur) eitel Lust und Freude;* a ∾-alley *eine Kegelbahn*

skullduggery n.: (colloq.) *Betrug, Gaunerei*

sky n.: if the ∾ fall we shall catch larks (arch.) *wenn der Himmel einstürzt (herunterfällt), sind alle Spatzen tot;* to laud (to praise) a person to the skies *j.en in den Himmel heben, (bis) über den grünen Klee loben;* a ∾-pilot (sl.) *ein Geistlicher (Himmelskutscher);* a ∾-scraper *ein Wolkenkratzer*

sky-rocket v.tr.: to ∾ prices *die Preise in die Höhe treiben*

slack I. a.: I feel very ∾ today *ich fühle mich heute sehr schlapp, abgespannt;* to keep a ∾ hand (rein) *die Zügel locker lassen;* ∾ lime *gelöschter Kalk;* a ∾ market *ein flauer Markt;* to perform on the ∾ rope (wire) *als Seiltänzer auftreten;* ∾ water *totes Wasser, Ebbe.* — **II.** adv.: ∾-baked bread *nicht ausgebackenes Brot.* — **III.** n.: to haul in the ∾ *das Tauende einholen;* I'm going to have a good ∾ this afternoon (sl.) *heute nachmittag werde ich ordentlich faulenzen;* the girl wears ∾s *das Mädchen trägt lange Hosen.* — **IV.** v.tr.: to ∾ up a train *einen Zug langsam fahren lassen.* — **V.** v.i.: to ∾ off *loslassen, vermindern, eine Anstrengung verlangsamen;* I have ∾ed shockingly this term *ich habe dieses Semester schrecklich gebummelt*

slacker n.: he is a ∾ *er ist ein Faulenzer, Drückeberger*

slam I. v.tr.: he ∾med the door in my face *er schlug mir die Tür vor der Nase zu;* to ∾ down the lid *den Deckel heftig zuschlagen.* — **II.** v.i.: the door ∾med to *die Tür fiel heftig zu*

slant n.: on the (a) ∾ *schief, schräg, von der Seite;* a ∾ of wind *eine günstige Brise;* to get a ∾ on something (colloq.) *Auskunft über eine Sache erhalten;* to get a new ∾ on something (colloq.) *eine Sache in einem neuen Licht betrachten*

slap I. v.tr.: to ∾ a person's face, a person in the face *j.en ohrfeigen;* a ∾ping dinner (colloq.) *ein vorzügliches Essen (Pfundsessen);* a ∾ping great fellow (colloq.) *ein sehr großer Bursche, ein Mordskerl;* to walk at a ∾ping pace *sehr schnell, im Geschwindschritt gehen.* — **II.** n.: a ∾ in the face *ein Schlag ins Gesicht, eine Beleidigung, eine Ab-, Zurückweisung.* — **III.** adv.: he hit me ∾ in the eye (colloq.)

er schlug mir direkt aufs Auge; ∾-bang, ∾-dash *Hals über Kopf, ungestüm, blindlings;* ∾-up (sl.) *famos, erstklassig;* a ∾-stick comedy *eine Clownskomödie*

slate I. n.: to clean the ∾ *reinen Tisch machen;* to have a clean ∾ *eine reine Weste haben;* he has a loose ∾ (sl.) *bei ihm ist eine Schraube los, er hat einen Sparren (zu viel, zu wenig).* — **II.** v.tr.: to ∾ someone (colloq.) *j.en ausschimpfen, heruntermachen*

slating n.: a ∾ (colloq.) *eine Strafpredigt*

slave n.: the white-∾ traffic *der Mädchenhandel*

sledge-hammer n.: ∾ blows (fig.) *Keulenschläge*

sleep I. n.: the beauty-∾ *der Schlaf vor Mitternacht;* I shall try to get a ∾ *ich werde versuchen zu schlafen;* to go to ∾, fall a∾ *einschlafen;* to walk in one's ∾ *nachtwandeln.* — **II.** v.i.: to ∾ in *im Hause schlafen;* to ∾ out *auswärts schlafen;* not to ∾ a wink *kein Auge zutun;* to ∾ the clock round *12 oder 24 Stunden lang schlafen;* let ∾ing dogs lie (prov.) *rühre nicht an vergessene(n), vergangene(n) Dinge(n)!;* to ∾ like a dormouse (log, top) *wie ein Murmeltier (Dachs, Ratz) schlafen;* to ∾ (up)on (over) a question *eine Frage beschlafen;* a ∾ing partner *ein stiller Teilhaber.* — **III.** v.tr.: to ∾ oneself sober *seinen Rausch ausschlafen;* to ∾ the hours away *die Stunden verschlafen;* to ∾ off a headache *Kopfschmerzen durch Schlaf vertreiben*

sleepy a.: ∾ pears, bananas *angestoßene, faule Birnen, Bananen*

sleeve n.: to have a card up one's ∾ *etwas in Reserve, noch einen Trumpf in der Hand haben; einen Plan in petto haben;* to laugh in one's ∾ *sich (dat.) ins Fäustchen lachen;* to turn (to roll up) one's ∾ *sich (dat.) die Ärmel aufkrempeln;* to wear one's heart upon one's ∾ *das Herz auf der Zunge haben (tragen); seine Gefühle offen zur Schau tragen*

sleight n.: ∾-of-hand *Taschenspielerkunst*

slender a.: a ∾ acquaintance with a subject *eine oberflächliche Kenntnis eines Gegenstandes;* ∾ diet, fare *magere Kost;* a ∾ girl *ein schlankes Mädchen;* ∾ hopes *schwache Hoffnungen;* ∾ means *geringe Mittel*

slice n.: a ∾ of bread and butter *ein Butterbrot;* a ∾ of ham *eine Scheibe Schinken;* a ∾ of good luck *ein glücklicher Zufall, eine Portion Glück;* a ∾ of the profits *ein Anteil am Gewinn;* a fish-∾ *eine Fischkelle*

slick I. a.: a ∾ performance *eine geschickte Leistung;* he did it out of ∾ perversity *er tat es aus purem Eigensinn.* — **II.** adv.: I hit him ∾ in the eye *ich schlug ihn mitten (direkt) aufs Auge*

slide I. v.i.: to let things ∾ *die Dinge laufen lassen;* to ∾ over a delicate subject *ein heikles Thema übergehen;* a sliding-rule *ein Rechenschieber;* a sliding-scale *eine bewegliche Lohn-, Preisskala.* — **II.** v.tr.: to ∾ the drawer into its place *die Schublade wieder einschieben.* — **III.** n.: (lantern-)∾s *Einschiebebilder für einen Projektionsapparat*

slight I. a.: to pay ∾ attention to a person (a thing) *j.em (einer Sache) nur geringe Aufmerksamkeit schenken;* I have a ∾ cold *ich bin leicht (etwas) erkältet;* a ∾ disturbance *eine geringfügige Störung;* not the ∾est excuse *nicht die geringste Entschuldigung;* raised on ∾ foundations *auf schwachem Fundament errichtet;* I have made a ∾ inquiry into it *ich bin der Sache etwas nachgegangen.* — **II.** v.tr.: to ∾ a person (matter) *j.en geringschätzig behandeln; eine Angelegenheit nicht beachten.* — **III.** n.: to put a ∾ upon a person *j.en geringschätzig behandeln*

slim v.tr.: proposals for ∾ming organisation of a business *Vorschläge, ein Geschäft zu rationalisieren*

slink v.i.: to ∾ off like a whipped dog *(wie ein begossener Pudel) davonschleichen*

slip I. v.i.: he ∾s now and then in his grammar *er macht hin und wieder grammatische Schnitzer;* to let a chance ∾ *sich (dat.) eine Gelegenheit entgehen lassen;* just ∾ across to the baker's *spring mal eben zum Bäcker hinüber!;* to ∾ along at a great speed *dahinsausen;* how time ∾s away (by)! *wie die Zeit doch vergeht!;* he ∾ped off without saying good-bye *er (ver)drückte sich, ohne Abschied zu nehmen;* to ∾ up(on) something (colloq.) *einen Fehler (bei etwas) machen, versagen.* —

II. v.tr.: to ∾ anchor *den Anker lichten;* the point has ∾ped my attention *der Punkt ist meiner Aufmerksamkeit entgangen;* to ∾ one's cable *sterben;* a cow ∾s its calf *eine Kuh kalbt vorzeitig;* a dog ∾s its collar *ein Hund zieht sich das Halsband über den Kopf;* to let ∾ the dogs of war (Shakesp., Jul. Caes. III, 1) *die Furien des Krieges entfesseln;* it has ∾ped my memory *es ist mir entfallen;* to ∾ a tip into the porter's hand *dem Gepäckträger ein Trinkgeld in die Hand drücken;* to ∾ in a word *ein Wort einfließen lassen;* to ∾ on an overcoat *einen Mantel anziehen (überwerfen).* — **III.** n.: there's many a ∾ 'twixt cup and lip (prov.) *„Zwischen Lipp' und Kelchesrand schwebt der dunklen Mächte Hand"; es ist noch nicht aller Tage Abend;* he is a ∾ of a boy *er ist ein schmächtiges Kerlchen;* a ∾ of paper *ein Zettel;* a ∾ of the pen *ein Flüchtigkeitsfehler, Schreibfehler;* a ∾-road *eine kleine Nebenstraße;* the ∾-stream *der Luftschraubenstrahl, Schraubenstrom (Luftfahrt);* it was a ∾ of the tongue *ich habe mich versprochen;* to give a person the ∾ *j.em ausweichen;* to make a ∾ *einen Fehltritt tun*

slippy a. (colloq.): look ∾ about it, be ∾ *mach fix!*

slipshod a.: a ∾ piece of work *eine nachlässige (liederliche) Arbeit, eine Schlamperei*

slip-slop a.: ∾ talk *sentimentales Gerede (Gewäsch)*

slog v.i.: to ∾ away at a thing *sich bei etwas abplacken*

slogan n.: a ∾ *ein Schlachtruf, Wahlspruch, Schlagwort*

slot n.: a ∾-machine *ein Verkaufsautomat*

sloth n.: ∾ is the mother of poverty (prov.) *Müßiggang ist aller Laster Anfang*

slouch n.: he is no ∾ at it (sl.) *er versteht seine Sache;* a ∾ hat *ein Schlapphut*

slough n.: the ∾ of Despond (Bunyan) *der Sumpf der Verzweiflung*

slow I. a.: ∾ and steady wins the race (prov.) *eile mit Weile; kleine, aber ständige Anstrengungen führen zum Ziel;* my watch is ten minutes ∾ *meine Uhr geht zehn Minuten nach;* to be ∾ of payment *ein schlechter Zahler sein;* to be ∾ of speech *eine schwere Zunge haben, mundfaul sein;* to be ∾ in arriving *unpünktlich ankommen;* to be ∾ on the uptake *eine lange Leitung haben;* to be ∾ to anger (wrath) *nicht leicht böse, zornig werden;* to be ∾ to do a thing *etwas ungern tun;* he was not ∾ to do so *damit war er rasch bei der Hand;* to be ∾ to take offence *nicht leicht etwas übelnehmen;* he is a ∾-coach *er ist ein langsamer, schwerfälliger Mensch, ein Trödelfritze;* a ∾-combustion stove *ein Dauerbrandofen;* a ∾-motion picture *eine Zeitlupenaufnahme;* a ∾-train *ein Personen-, Bummelzug;* a ∾worm *eine Blindschleiche.* — **II.** adv.: my watch goes ∾ *meine Uhr geht nach.* — **III.** v.i.: ∾ down *langsam fahren!* — **IV.** v.tr.: to ∾ down (up) a ship *ein Schiff langsamer fahren lassen*

slug v.i. (arch.): to ∾ in bed *faul im Bett liegen;* a ∾-a-bed *ein Langschläfer;* his ∾-a-bed habit *seine Angewohnheit, lang im Bett zu liegen*

sly a.: a ∾boots (in playful use) *(scherzhaft gemeint) ein Schlauberger;* he is a ∾ dog *er ist ein schlauer Fuchs, ein Schlauberger;* on the ∾ *im geheimen, hinter j.es Rücken*

smack[1] I. n.: there is a ∾ of the old Adam in him *in ihm steckt noch etwas von dem alten Adam.* — **II.** v.i.: his manner ∾ed of superciliousness *seine Art hatte einen Anflug von Hochmut*

smack[2] I. n.: a ∾ in the eye (colloq.) *eine Enttäuschung, eine Zurückweisung; ein Schlag ins Gesicht, ins Kontor;* to have a ∾ at a thing (colloq.) *etwas versuchen.* — **II.** v.tr.: to ∾ one's lips *mit den Lippen schmatzen, schnalzen;* to ∾ a whip *mit einer Peitsche knallen.* — **III.** adv. (colloq.): I hit him ∾ on the nose *ich schlug ihn direkt auf die Nase*

smacking n.: a good ∾ *eine tüchtige Tracht Prügel*

small I. a.: ∾-arms *Handwaffen:* ∾ beer *unbedeutende Sachen;* to think no ∾ beer of oneself *sehr von sich überzeugt sein;* to chronicle ∾ beer (Othello II, 1) *Lappalien als wichtig darstellen;* ∾ blame to them *sie haben (taten) ganz recht;* ∾ change *Kleingeld;* ∾ fry *kleine Kinder, unbedeutende Wesen; Grobzeug;* a ∾ gross *zehn Dutzend;* a ∾ holding *ein Kleinlandbesitz;* the ∾ hours of the morning *die* *frühen Morgenstunden (1, 2 usw. Uhr);* his ∾ spiteful nature *seine gemeine gehässige Natur;* ∾pox *die schwarzen Pocken, Blattern;* ∾ talk *Geplauder;* the ∾ still voice *das Gewissen;* in a ∾ way *bescheiden, unbedeutend, im kleinen;* to look (to feel) ∾ *sich schämen.* — **II.** n.: the ∾ of the back *das Kreuz.* — **III.** adv.: to sing ∾ *kleinlaut werden, klein beigeben*

smart I. a.: a ∾ Alec *ein Alleswisser, (derb) Klugscheißer;* ∾ dealing *eine gerissene Handlungsweise;* a ∾ lad *ein intelligenter Bursche;* at a ∾ pace *in flottem Schritt;* a ∾ rap *ein kräftiger Schlag;* the ∾ set *die elegante Welt;* to look ∾ *elegant aussehen.* — **II.** v.i.: you shall ∾ for this *das sollst du mir noch büßen.* — **III.** n.: ∾-money *Schmerzensgeld*

smash I. v.i.: a ∾-and-grab raid *ein Überfall, bei dem die Verbrecher nach Einschlagung eines Schaufensters eiligst mit der Beute verschwinden.* — **II.** adv.: to go ∾ (to ∾) *zertrümmert, ruiniert, bankrott werden;* the engine went ∾ into a goods train *die Lokomotive fuhr krachend auf einen Güterzug*

smattering n.: I only have a ∾ of the subject *ich habe nur eine oberflächliche Kenntnis des Faches*

smear v.tr.: a ∾ing campaign *ein Bemühen, j.es Ruf durch üble Nachrede zu schädigen*

smell I. n.: to take a ∾ at a thing *an etwas riechen, etwas beriechen.* — **II.** v.tr.: to ∾ a rat *Lunte, den Braten riechen;* to ∾ out a secret *ein Geheimnis entdecken.* — **III.** v.i.: to ∾ of the lamp *nach der Studierlampe riechen, nächtliche Arbeit verraten; schwerfällig, geschraubt im Ausdruck sein;* to ∾ of the shop *nach Fachsimpelei klingen*

smile v.i.: to come up smiling (boxing) *mutig einer neuen Schwierigkeit entgegentreten, den Kopf nicht hängen lassen;* keep smiling *Kopf hoch!*

smite v.tr.: to ∾ hip and thigh (Judges XV, 8) *j.en vollständig besiegen;* he is smitten with the girl *er ist in das Mädchen verliebt*

smithereens n.pl.: to knock (to smash) in(to) ∾ *etwas kurz und klein schlagen*

smog n. (= smoke and fog): *Londoner Nebel, mit Rauch vermischt*

smoke I. n.: no ∾ without fire (prov.) *kein Rauch ohne Feuer, an einem Gerücht ist oft etwas Wahres;* from ∾ into smother *vom Regen in die Traufe;* he did it like ∾ *er tat es ohne Schwierigkeit;* to have a ∾ *eine Zigarre, usw. rauchen;* to end in ∾ *in Rauch aufgehen.* — **II.** v.tr.: put that in your pipe and ∾ it *das kannst du dir an den Hut (hinter den Spiegel) stecken, hinter die Ohren schreiben!;* to ∾ out a wasps' nest *ein Wespennest ausräuchern.* — **III.** v.i.: he ∾s like a chimney *er raucht wie ein Schlot*

smother n.: from smoke into ∾ *vom Regen in die Traufe*

snack n.: a ∾-bar *eine Imbißstube;* to go ∾s in a thing *sich in etwas teilen;* to have (to take) a ∾ *einen Happen essen*

snag n.: there is a ∾ in it *die Sache hat einen Haken*

snail n.: at a ∾'s gallop (pace) *im Schneckentempo*

snake n.: a ∾ in the grass *eine verborgene Gefahr, ein geheimer Feind;* to raise (to wake) ∾s *in ein Wespennest stechen;* to scotch the ∾ *etwas unschädlich machen, ein Gerücht niederschlagen;* to warm (to cherish, to nourish) a ∾ in one's bosom *eine Schlange am Busen nähren*

snap I. v.tr.: to ∾ one's fingers at a person *j.en verächtlich behandeln, verhöhnen;* to ∾ a person's nose off *j.en hart anfahren;* to ∾ out an answer *kurz, ärgerlich antworten.* — **II.** v.i: to ∾ at an offer *ein Angebot gierig annehmen;* ∾ into it! (U.S. sl.) *ein bißchen Dalli!;* to ∾ out of it (U.S. sl.) *eine schlechte Laune, Gewohnheit loswerden.* — **III.** n.: a cold ∾ *eine Kältewelle;* a soft ∾ (U.S. sl.) *eine leichte Aufgabe;* to make a ∾ at a thing *nach etwas schnappen;* a ∾ division *eine plötzlich vorgenommene Abstimmung;* a ∾shot *eine Momentaufnahme, ein Schnappschuß*

snappy a. (U.S. colloq.): make it ∾ *ein bißchen Dalli!*

snatch I. v.tr.: to ∾ a kiss *einen Kuß rauben;* to ∾ an opportunity *eine Gelegenheit gierig ergreifen, beim Schopfe fassen (packen);* he was ∾ed away from us by a premature death *er wurde uns durch einen vorzeitigen Tod entrissen;* he ∾ed up his hat *er ergriff hastig seinen Hut.* — **II.** v.i.: to ∾ at an offer *nach einem Angebot schnappen;* a drowning man will ∾ (catch) at a straw (prov.) *ein Ertrinkender* *klammert sich an einen Strohhalm.* — **III.** n.: to make a ∾ at a thing *gierig nach etwas greifen, schnappen;* he only works by ∾es *er arbeitet nur ruckweise, unregelmäßig;* ∾es of sleep *kurze Augenblicke des Schlafes*

sneak v.i.: to have a ∾ing kindness for a person *eine unerklärliche, heimliche, stille Neigung zu j.em haben;* to ∾ off *sich davonschleichen, sich (ver)drücken*

sneeze v.i.: that is not to be ∾d at *das ist nicht zu verachten;* to ∾ into a basket (euphem.) *guillotiniert (enthauptet) werden*

sniff I. n.: to get a ∾ of fresh air *frische Luft schöpfen.* — **II.** v.i.: the offer is not to be ∾ed at *über das Angebot soll man nicht die Nase rümpfen*

snook n.: to cock (to cut, to make) a ∾ at *eine lange Nase machen*

snoop v.i. (colloq.): to ∾ around *herumschnüffeln*

snow I. n.: where are the ∾s of yesteryear? *Sinn: verschwunden wie der vorjährige Schnee;* the ∾s of old age *die weißen Haare des Alters.* — **II.** v.tr.: we were ∾ed under with invitations *wir wurden mit Einladungen überschüttet*

snub I. v.tr.: to ∾ someone *j.en schroff zurechtweisen.* — **II.** n.: to meet with a ∾ *kurz abgefertigt werden.* — **III.** a.: a ∾-nose *eine Stupsnase*

snuff n.: a pinch of ∾ *eine Prise Schnupftabak;* he is up to ∾ (sl.) *er ist nicht auf den Kopf gefallen, er hat es faustdick hinter den Ohren; er ist mit allen Hunden gehetzt, er läßt sich kein X für ein U vormachen;* to give a person ∾ *j.en grob (unsanft) behandeln;* to take a thing in ∾ (arch.) *etwas übelnehmen, über etwas verschnupft sein;* ∾ and butter *bräunlich gelb (von Mischlingen einer weißen und braunen Rasse gesagt)*

snug a.: as ∾ as a bug in a rug *behaglich, mollig, urgemütlich*

so I. adv. of degree: he was ∾ lucky as to escape *er hatte das Glück, davonzukommen;* he couldn't stand, he was ∾ tired (colloq.) *er war so müde, daß er nicht stehen konnte;* I'm ∾ glad (ever ∾ glad) you came (colloq.) *ich freue mich so, daß Sie gekommen sind;* she has ever ∾ many presents *sie bekam riesig (furchtbar) viele Geschenke;* ∾ far, ∾ good *so weit gut;* it is all right ∾ far *so weit ist es in Ordnung;* now that he has gone ∾ far, he will not come back *jetzt, wo er so weit gegangen ist, wird er nicht zurückkehren;* ∾ far as I know *soweit ich weiß;* ∾ far as I am concerned *was mich betrifft;* ∾ far from doing something *weit entfernt, etwas zu tun;* ∾ long! (sl.) *auf Wiedersehen!;* ∾ long as it does not rain *vorausgesetzt, daß es nicht regnet;* ∾ many *soundsoviel;* he didn't ∾ much as say thank you *er sagte nicht mal dankeschön;* ∾ much the better (the worse) *umso besser (schlimmer);* ∾ much for his promises *da sieht man, was seine Versprechungen wert sind;* ∾ much ∾ that *dermaßen;* ∾ much for that! *Schluß damit!;* ∾ much nonsense *lauter Unsinn;* ∾ there! *da hast du's! nun weißt du's!* — **II.** adv. of manner: you must not talk ∾ *du darfst nicht so reden;* ∾, and ∾ only *nur auf diese Art;* and ∾ on, and ∾ forth *und so weiter, et cetera;* you will not believe me, but it is ∾ *du wirst (es) mir nicht glauben, aber es ist so;* even ∾ *selbst dann, selbst in dem Falle;* if ∾ *wenn ja;* just ∾, quite ∾ *ganz recht, eben;* that was lucky. ∾ it was *das war ein Glück! Tatsächlich! das stimmt;* an hour or ∾ *etwa eine Stunde;* is that ∾? *wirklich? so?;* why ∾? *warum denn das?;* ∾ help me God! *so wahr mir Gott helfe!;* it ∾ happened that he arrived *er kam zufällig;* I phoned ∾ that he would know *ich rief an, damit er Bescheid wußte;* it will cost ten pounds or ∾ *es wird ungefähr 10 Pfund kosten;* ∾ and ∾ *der (Herr) Soundso;* how are you? oh, ∾-∾ (colloq.) *wie geht es Ihnen? Danke, einigermaßen;* ∾-to-say, ∾-to-speak *sozusagen.* — **III.** conj.: ∾ do I *ich auch;* it was raining, ∾ I stayed at home *es regnete, also blieb ich zu Hause;* ∾ that's that (colloq.) *Schluß damit!;* ∾ you've got married *also, du hast geheiratet!* — **IV.** pron.: I don't think ∾ *das glaube ich nicht;* I told you ∾ *ich habe es dir ja gesagt;* you don't say ∾! *was Sie nicht sagen!;* ∾ saying, he disappeared *bei diesen Worten verschwand er*

soak I. v.tr.: I am ∾ed to the skin *ich bin naß bis auf die Haut;* he is ∾ed in the subject *er hat sich in dieses Fach (diesen Gegenstand) vertieft;* to ∾ washing *Wäsche einweichen;* to ∾ peas *Trockenerbsen quellen lassen;* the rain has ∾ed through *der Regen ist durchgesickert;* the dealer ∾ed him (sl.) *der Händler hat ihn geschröpft.* — **II.** n.: an old ∾ (sl.) *ein Säufer*

soaking n.: to get a ∾ *durch und durch naß werden*

soap n.: a cake of ∾ *ein Stück Seife;* soft ∾ *Schmierseife; Schmeichelei;* a ∾-box *eine improvisierte Rednerbühne*

sob I. v.tr.: to ∾ out, to ∾ one's heart out *bitterlich weinen.* — **II.** n.: ∾-stuff (U.S.) *rührseliges (sentimentales) Zeug*

sober I. a.: as ∾ as a judge *vollkommen nüchtern;* to appeal from Philip drunk to Philip ∾ *an j.es nüchternen Verstand appellieren;* in ∾ earnest *in vollem Ernst, allen Ernstes;* in ∾ fact *in Wirklichkeit, tatsächlich;* a ∾-minded man *ein ruhiger, besonnener Mann;* a ∾sides *ein Philister, Trauerkloß.* — **II.** v.i.: to ∾ down *ernüchtern*

sock[1] n.: pull up your ∾s! (colloq.) *streng' dich mal an!;* put a ∾ in it! (sl.) *schweig'!*

sock[2] **I.** v.tr. (sl.): to ∾ a person one *j.em einen knallen, langen, latschen, verpassen;* to ∾ a stone at a person *einen Stein nach j.em werfen.* — **II.** n.: give him ∾s (sl.) *gib ihm Saures!*

soft I. a.: a ∾ answer turneth away wrath (Proverbs XV, 1) (prov.) *eine sanftmütige Antwort stillet den Zorn;* as ∾ as butter *butterweich;* a ∾ drink (U.S.) *ein nichtalkoholisches Getränk;* ∾ goods *Textilwaren;* ∾-headed, ∾-witted *schwachköpfig, schwachsinnig;* a ∾ job (sl.) *eine leichte Beschäftigung;* ∾ nothings *verliebtes Gerede, Süßholzraspelei;* ∾ sawder *Schmeichelei, verbindliche Redensarten;* ∾ soap, see ∾ sawder; to be touched on one's ∾ spot *weich werden;* to have a ∾ spot in one's heart for a person *ein weiches Herz für j.en haben;* he is ∾-spoken *er hat eine angenehme Redeweise;* ∾ tack (colloq.) *Weißbrot;* ∾ weather *regnerisches (feuchtes) Wetter, Tauwetter;* to be ∾ (up)on a person *in j.en verliebt sein;* to go ∾ *weich werden, verweichlichen.* — **II.** n.: he is a ∾y *er ist ein Schwächling, Einfaltspinsel*

sold p.p. von to sell (v.tr.): you were ∾, ∾ a pup *du bist beschwindelt worden*

soldier n.: a ∾ of fortune *ein Glücksritter;* an old ∾ *eine leere Flasche, ein Zigarrenstummel;* to come the old ∾ over a person *j.em etwas vormachen wollen;* to go (to enlist) for a ∾ (colloq.) *sich als Soldat anwerben lassen*

some I. a. (= a little, few, a small quantity): give me ∾ cake, ∾ books *gib mir etwas Kuchen, einige Bücher;* have ∾ chocolate? *möchtest du ein Stück Schokolade?;* (= certain, particular): he married ∾ Frenchwoman *er hat irgendeine Französin geheiratet;* I shall stay in ∾ hotel (or other) *ich werde in irgendeinem Hotel wohnen;* (= a fairly large number): it was ∾ years ago *es ist schon einige Jahre her;* it cost ∾ money *es hat ziemlich viel Geld gekostet;* (= about): ∾ forty people came *ungefähr 40 Personen kamen;* (= vague, uncertain): I'll do it ∾time *ich werde es irgendwann (eines Tages) tun;* it was ∾ heat (colloq.) *es war eine Affenhitze.* — **II.** pron. (= certain, not all): ∾ of the people wore hats *einige von den Leuten trugen Hüte;* ∾ came, others didn't *einige kamen, andere nicht*

somebody n.: he thinks himself a ∾ *er hält sich für ein großes Tier, für j.en;* ∾ else *j. anders;* ∾ or other *irgendjemand*

somehow adv.: he dropped behind ∾ *er blieb irgendwie zurück;* I must finish it ∾ *ich muß es auf irgendeine Weise beendigen;* ∾ or other I never liked him *aus irgendeinem Grunde mochte ich ihn nie*

somersault n.: to turn a ∾ *einen Purzelbaum schlagen, einen Salto machen*

something I. n.: I am ∾ of a joiner *ich kann etwas schreinern;* it is ∾ to be at home again *es ist eine Beruhigung, wieder zu Hause zu sein;* there is ∾ in the wind *es tut sich etwas;* there is ∾ in what you say *was Sie sagen, läßt sich hören;* I hope to see ∾ of you *ich hoffe, Sie gelegentlich zu sehen;* he thinks himself ∾ *er hält sich für eine wichtige Person.* — **II.** adv.: it was shaped ∾ like a cigar *es hatte etwa die Form einer Zigarre;* this is ∾ like a pudding *das ist doch wenigstens ein Pudding;* that's ∾ like (sl.) *das ist famos! das lasse ich mir gefallen!*

sometime I. a.: ∾ professor in London *weiland (ehemaliger) Professor in London.* — **II.** adv.: ∾ or other *irgendwann;* phone ∾! *ruf' mal an!*

somewhat I. adv.: it is ∾ difficult *es ist etwas schwierig.* — **II.** pron.: it was ∾ of a blow *es war ein ziemlicher Schlag*

somewhere adv.: I'll see him ∾ first (colloq.) *er kann mir den Buckel runter rutschen;* he lives ∾ near us *er wohnt irgendwo in unserer Nähe;* the book is ∾ about the house *das Buch ist irgendwo im Hause*

son n.: every mother's ∾ of you *jeder einzelne von euch*

song n.: I bought (sold) it for a ∾ (a mere, an old ∾) *ich habe es für ein Butterbrot (einen Apfel [Appel] und ein Ei) gekauft (verkauft);* it is nothing to make a ∾ about *es ist nichts Wichtiges;* to burst into ∾ *laut zu singen beginnen*

soon adv.: least said, ∾est mended (prov.) *je weniger Worte darüber, desto besser; Reden ist Silber, Schweigen ist Gold;* no ∾er said than done *gesagt, getan;* we had no ∾er reached the house than it began to rain *wir hatten das Haus kaum erreicht, als es anfing zu regnen;* ∾er or later *eines Tages;* I would ∾er die than do so *ich stürbe lieber, als daß ich das täte;* I would just as ∾ stay at home *ich bliebe ebenso gern zu Hause;* we arrived too ∾ *wir kamen zu früh*

sop I. n.: to throw a ∾ to Cerberus *zu beschwichtigen suchen;* he is a milk∾ *er ist ein Muttersöhnchen, Schlappschwanz, Waschlappen.* — **II.** v.tr.: to ∾ bread in broth *Brot in die Suppe eintunken;* to ∾ up water *Wasser aufsaugen.* — **III.** v.i.: I am ∾ping wet *ich bin bis auf die Haut durchnäßt, patsch-, klatschnaß*

soppy (colloq.) a.: to be ∾ on a person *in j.en verliebt (vernarrt) sein*

sore I. a.: he is very ∾ about his defeat *er ist sehr ärgerlich (gekränkt) über seine Niederlage;* to be in ∾ distress *in arger Not sein;* to be a sight for ∾ eyes *eine Augenweide sein;* like a bear with a ∾ head *wie ein alter Brummbär, mürrisch, verdrießlich;* I touched him on a ∾ place *ich berührte ihn an einer empfindlichen Stelle;* a ∾ subject *ein peinliches (heikles) Thema;* to have a ∾ throat *Halsschmerzen haben;* to be foot∾ *wund an den Füßen sein.* — **II.** n.: to have a bed∾ *sich wund gelegen haben;* to be an eye∾ *einen häßlichen Anblick bieten;* to reopen old ∾s *alte Wunden aufreißen;* to be an open, a running ∾ *ein ständiges Ärgernis sein.* — **III.** adv.: to be ∾ oppressed *arg bedrückt sein*

sorry a.: ∾! *Verzeihung!;* a ∾ excuse *eine klägliche (faule) Entschuldigung;* a ∾ fellow *ein armseliger Kerl;* I felt ∾ for him *er tat mir leid;* I am very ∾ for that *das bedauere ich sehr;* you will be ∾ for this some day *das wirst du eines Tages bereuen;* in a ∾ plight *in jämmerlicher (elender) Lage;* I am ∾ to say *leider muß ich sagen*

sort n.: we got coffee of a ∾ *wir bekamen so etwas wie Kaffee;* he is an awfully good ∾ (colloq.) *er ist ein ganz famoser Kerl;* nothing of the ∾ *nichts dergleichen, Derartiges;* to be out of ∾s *sich nicht wohl fühlen, unpäßlich sein;* he is a painter of ∾s *er ist so etwas wie ein Maler;* in some ∾, after a ∾ *bis zu einem gewissen Grade;* I ∾ of expected it (colloq.) *ich erwartete es gewissermaßen*

sound[1] I. a.: as ∾ as a bell *kerngesund, gesund wie ein Fisch im Wasser;* a ∾ argument *ein begründetes (stichhaltiges) Argument;* a ∾ firm *eine solide Firma;* a ∾ flogging *eine gehörige Tracht Prügel;* in ∾ health *bei guter Gesundheit;* safe and ∾ *gesund und munter;* a ∾ scholar *ein gründlicher (tüchtiger) Gelehrter;* a ∾ sleep *ein fester Schlaf.* — **II.** adv.: to be ∾ asleep *fest schlafen, in tiefem Schlaf liegen*

sound[2] I. n.: to the ∾ of *unter dem Klang von;* without a ∾ *lautlos;* within ∾ of *in Hörweite;* a tale ——— full of ∾ and fury, signifying nothing (Macbeth V, 5) *ein Märchen ——— voller Klang und Wut, das nichts bedeutet (Schlegel-Tieck).* — **II.** v.tr.: to ∾ a person's praises *j.es Lob singen, ausposaunen;* to ∾ the retreat *zum Rückzug blasen.* — **III.** v.i.: to ∾ hollow *hohl klingen*

sound[3] v.tr.: to ∾ a person about (on, as, to) a matter *j.en ausfragen, ihm auf den Zahn fühlen, bei ihm auf den Busch klopfen*

soup n.: to be in the ∾ *in der Patsche (Tinte) sitzen;* ∾-kitchen *Volksküche*

sourpuss n.: *ein Spaßverderber, eine mürrische Person*

southpaw n.: *ein Linkshänder*

sovereign a.: with ∾ contempt *mit tiefster Verachtung;* a ∾ remedy *ein äußerst wirksames Mittel*

sow[1] v.tr.: for they have ∾n the wind and they shall reap the whirlwind (Hos.

VIII, 7) *denn sie säen (den) Wind und werden Ungewitter (Sturm) ernten;* to ∾ one's wild oats *sich austoben, sich (dat.) die Hörner ablaufen*

sow² n.: to get the wrong ∾ by the ear *nicht den Richtigen (das Richtige) treffen;* you cannot make a silk purse out of a ∾'s ear (prov.) *etwa: Bauer bleibt Bauer*

space I. n.: in the ∾ of an hour *innerhalb einer Stunde;* let us rest for a ∾ *laßt uns eine Weile ruhen;* the ∾-bar of a typewriter *die Zwischenraumtaste einer Schreibmaschine;* a ∾-writer *ein Zeitungsschreiber, der nach dem Umfang seines Beitrages bezahlt wird;* a ∾-ship *ein Raumschiff.* — **II.** v.i.: don't forget to ∾ *vergiß nicht zu sperren, Zwischenraum zu lassen.* — **III.** v.tr.: to ∾ out words in printing *gesperrt drucken*

spade n.: to call a ∾ a ∾ *das Ding (Kind) beim rechten Namen nennen;* ∾-work *Vorarbeit, Pionierarbeit*

Spain n.pr.: to build castles in ∾ *Luftschlösser bauen*

spangle v.tr.: the Star-∾d Banner *das Sternenbanner der USA*

spanking (colloq.) **I.** a.: we had a ∾ time *wir haben es herrlich gehabt.* — **II.** adv.: she is a ∾ fine woman *sie ist eine sehr stattliche, bildschöne Frau*

spanner n.: to chuck a ∾ into the works *die Sache verderben, j.em einen Prügel (Knüppel) zwischen die Beine werfen*

spare I. a.: I have no ∾ cash *ich habe kein überflüssiges Geld;* I can't get any ∾ parts *ich kann keine Ersatzteile bekommen;* you can sleep in our ∾ room *du kannst in unserem Fremdenzimmer schlafen;* what do you do in your ∾ time? *was machst du in deiner Freizeit?* — **II.** v.tr.: enough and to ∾ *vollauf, reichlich;* if I am ∾d *wenn ich noch lebe;* you must not ∾ expense *du darfst die Kosten nicht scheuen;* you could have ∾d the explanation *du hättest dir die Erklärung sparen können;* ∾ his feelings *schone seine Gefühle;* ∾ him *verschone ihn, schenk' ihm das Leben;* to ∾ no pains *keine Mühe scheuen;* no time to ∾ *es ist keine Zeit zu verlieren, es eilt;* can you ∾ me a penny? *kannst du mir einen Groschen geben, ablassen?;* ∾ the rod and spoil the child (prov.) *wer die Rute spart, verzieht das Kind;* I cannot ∾ him just now *ich kann ihn augenblicklich nicht entbehren*

spark n.: he is a gay ∾ *er ist ein flotter Lebemann, Stutzer*

speak I. v.i.: to ∾ by the card (Hamlet V, 1) *sehr genau (pedantisch) reden;* I can ∾ to his being there *ich kann bestätigen, daß er dort war;* that ∾s well for him *das spricht zu seinen Gunsten;* generally ∾ing, roughly ∾ing *im allgemeinen;* not to ∾ of *ganz zu schweigen von;* nothing to ∾ of *nichts Nennenswertes;* plainly ∾ing *offen gesagt;* so to ∾ *sozusagen;* to ∾ highly of someone *j.en loben;* strictly ∾ing *streng genommen;* to ∾ up, out *laut, deutlich, frei heraussprechen;* to ∾ up for a person *sich für j.en verwenden;* to ∾ with one's tongue in one's cheek *ironisch, unaufrichtig sprechen;* a ∾-easy (U.S.) *ein unerlaubter Alkoholausschank.* — **II.** v.tr.: to ∾ one's mind *seine Meinung sagen;* that ∾s a little mind *das beweist (verrät) einen kleinen Geist;* to ∾ a person fair *j.en höflich anreden, ihm gute Worte geben, ihm gut zureden*

speaking I. n.: a ∾ acquaintance *eine flüchtige, oberflächliche Bekanntschaft;* I am not on ∾ terms with him *ich spreche nicht mehr mit ihm.* — **II.** a.: a ∾ likeness *eine auffallende Ähnlichkeit (Porträt)*

specimen n.: he is a queer ∾ *er ist eine komische Marke*

spectacle n.: a pair of ∾s, (colloq.) specs *eine Brille;* to make a ∾ of oneself *sich lächerlich machen;* to see things through rose-coloured ∾s *alles durch eine rosenrote Brille sehen*

speed I. n.: at full ∾, with all ∾ *mit größter Geschwindigkeit (Eile);* more haste, less ∾ (prov.) *eile mit Weile;* to gather ∾ *an Geschwindigkeit zunehmen.* — **II.** v.tr.: to ∾ the parting guest (archaic) *dem scheidenden Gast Glück auf den Weg wünschen;* God ∾ you! good ∾! *viel Glück!;* to ∾ up *beschleunigen*

spend v.tr.: a spent force (bullet) *eine verbrauchte Kraft;* to ∾ a penny (colloq.) *zur Toilette gehen;* to ∾ money like water *Geld verschwenden (vergeuden);* ∾ing money *Taschengeld*

spick a.: ∾ and span *geschniegelt und gebügelt;* ∾-and-span new *funkelnagelneu*

spike v.tr.: to ∾ a person's guns *durch eine plötzliche drastische Handlung j.es Pläne vereiteln*

spill v.tr.: to ∾ the beans (colloq.) *ein Geheimnis verraten (ausplappern); die Katze aus dem Sack lassen;* it's no use crying over spilt milk (prov.) *es hat keinen Zweck, Geschehenes zu beklagen*

spin I. v.tr.: to ∾ a yarn *eine Geschichte erzählen, ein Garn spinnen.* — **II.** v.i.: I sent him ∾ning *ich schlug ihm eins, daß er taumelte;* to ∾ out *in die Länge ziehen.* — **III.** n.: to get into a flat ∾ (colloq.) *in Aufregung geraten;* to go for a ∾ *eine kurze Fahrt machen*

spirit I. n.: in high (great) ∾s *in übermütiger (ausgelassener) Laune;* in low (poor, out of) ∾s *niedergeschlagen;* to keep up one's ∾s *den Mut nicht sinken lassen;* he touches no ∾s *er trinkt keinen Alkohol;* public ∾ *soziale Gesinnung.* — **II.** v.tr.: to ∾ away (off) *wie durch Zauber verschwinden lassen*

spit n.: he is the dead (very) ∾ of his father (colloq.) *er ist das genaue Ebenbild seines Vaters, seinem Vater wie aus dem Gesicht geschnitten (gespuckt der Vater);* ∾ and polish *das „Wienern" der Soldaten;* a ∾fire *ein Hitzkopf*

spite I. n.: in ∾, out of ∾, from pure ∾ *aus Bosheit, aus reiner Bosheit;* in ∾ of *trotz;* in ∾ of the fact that *obwohl.* — **II.** v.tr.: to cut off one's nose to ∾ one's face *sich (dat.) ins eigene Fleisch schneiden*

spiv n.: a ∾ *ein Schieber*

splash I. n.: a ∾ of soda-water *ein Schuß Mineralwasser;* to make a ∾ *Aufsehen erregen.* — **II.** a.: ∾ headlines *Schlagzeilen*

spleen n.: to vent one's ∾ on *seinem Ärger Luft machen, seinen Ärger auslassen an*

splice I. v.tr.: to ∾ the main brace (Navy) *Getränke an die Mannschaften austeilen; saufen;* to get ∾d (colloq.) *sich verheiraten.* — **II.** n.: to sit on the ∾ (cricket) *sehr vorsichtig spielen*

split I. v.tr.: let's ∾ the difference *laßt uns den Preisunterschied teilen, uns auf halbem Weg treffen;* to ∾ hairs *Haarspalterei treiben;* a ∾ infinitive *ein Infinitiv, bei dem zwischen* 'to' *und dem Verbum ein Adverb steht;* in a ∾ second *im Bruchteil einer Sekunde;* to ∾ one's sides *sich krank-, totlachen.* — **II.** v.i.: my head is ∾ting, I have a ∾ting headache *ich habe rasende Kopfschmerzen;* to ∾ on a person (colloq.) *j.en verraten (verpetzen)*

spoil I. v.tr.: spare the rod and ∾ the child (prov.) *wer die Rute spart, verzieht das Kind;* to ∾ the Egyptians (Exod. XII, 16) *durch Schlauheit von seinen Feinden etwas bekommen;* a ∾-sport *ein Spielverderber.* — **II.** v.i.: to be ∾ing for a fight *rauflustig sein*

spoke n.: to put a ∾ in a person's wheel *j.es Pläne durchkreuzen, j.em einen Knüppel zwischen die Beine werfen*

sponge I. n.: to have a ∾ *sich abwaschen;* let us pass the ∾ over it *Schwamm drüber!;* to throw (to chuck) up the ∾ (boxing) *sich für besiegt erklären, sich geschlagen (den Kampf, das Spiel verloren) geben.* — **II.** v.i.: to ∾ on a person *bei j.em schmarotzen, nassauern*

spoon[1] n.: to be born with a silver ∾ in one's mouth *ein Glückskind, ein Kind reicher Eltern sein;* he must have a long ∾ that sups with the devil (prov.) *mit dem Teufel paktieren ist gefährlich, mit hohen (großen) Herren ist nicht gut Kirschen essen;* to make a ∾ and spoil a horn (old-fash.) *etwas auf alle Fälle versuchen;* a table-∾ *ein Eßlöffel;* to be ∾-fed *wie ein Kind gefüttert, viel geholfen bekommen, sehr gefördert werden*

spoon[2] I. n.: to be ∾s on a person *in j.en närrisch verliebt sein.* — **II.** v.i.: to ∾ (colloq.) *poussieren*

sport I. n.: he is a good ∾ *er ist ein anständiger (famoser) Kerl;* to be the ∾ of Fortune *Spielball des Glücks sein;* to go in for (to indulge in) ∾ *Sport treiben;* we never had such a ∾ *wir hatten noch nie soviel Spaß;* to make ∾ of a thing *sich über etwas lustig machen.* — **II.** v.tr.: to ∾ one's oak (Oxon. & Camb.) *die äußere Doppeltür seines Zimmer schließen, um anzudeuten, daß man keinen Besuch wünscht;* to ∾ a red tie *einen roten Schlips zur Schau tragen*

spot I. n.: a tender ∾ *eine wunde Stelle;* to be in a ∾ (sl.) *in einer Notlage (in Schwierigkeiten) sein;* on the ∾ *auf der*

Stelle, sofort; to be on the ∾ *wachsam, der Lage gewachsen sein;* to have a ∾ of lunch (colloq.) *einen Happen essen;* to knock ∾s off a person (sl.) *j.en nach Strich und Faden besiegen;* to put on the ∾ (U.S. sl.) *j.es Ermordung beschließen;* ∾ cash, ∾ goods *sofortige Zahlung bei Lieferung; sofort lieferbare Ware, Lokoware.* — **II.** v.tr.: I ∾ted him at once as an American (colloq.) *ich erkannte ihn sofort als einen Amerikaner*

spout n.: his watch is up the ∾ (sl.) *seine Uhr ist im Pfandhaus, ist versetzt*

sprat n.: to throw a ∾ to catch a herring (mackerel, whale) *mit der Wurst nach der Speckseite werfen*

spread I. v.tr.: to ∾ butter on bread *Butter aufs Brot streichen;* to ∾ oneself *(sich) dicke tun; sehr gastfreundlich sein;* a ∾ eagle *ein Adler mit ausgespreizten Flügeln;* ∾-eagleism *Hurrapatriotismus;* ∾-over *Verteilung der Arbeitsstunden in der Industrie.* — **II.** v.i.: the news ∾ like wildfire *die Nachricht verbreitete sich wie ein Lauffeuer (wie der Blitz).* — **III.** n.: we had no end of a ∾ (colloq.) *wir hatten ein reichliches Essen, wir konnten uns rundum satt essen*

spree n.: to be on the ∾ *sich amüsieren;* to go on the ∾ *auf den Bummel gehen*

spring I. v.i.: where do you ∾ from? *wo kommst du so plötzlich her?* — **II.** v.tr.: to ∾ a mine (or: surprise) on a person *j.en überraschen;* to ∾ a leak *ein Leck bekommen, leck werden*

spur I. n.: on the ∾ of the moment *einer plötzlichen Eingebung folgend, ohne Überlegung;* to put (to set) ∾s to a horse *einem Pferde die Sporen geben;* to win one's ∾s *sich die Sporen verdienen.* — **II.** v.tr.: to ∾ a willing horse *j.en unnötig drängen*

squab adv.: to come down ∾ on the floor *hinplumpsen*

squad n.: an awkward ∾ *Rekruten in der Ausbildung; eine unbeholfene (ungeschickte) Gesellschaft;* a firing ∾ *ein Erschießungskommando*

squall n.: to look out for ∾s *auf der Hut sein, sich auf ein Donnerwetter gefaßt machen*

square I. n.: to act (to be) on the ∾ *ehrlich handeln;* to be on the ∾ *Freimaurer sein;* to break ∾s *von der gewohnten Ordnung abweichen;* that breaks no ∾s *das hat nichts zu bedeuten, das schadet nichts.* — **II.** a.: a ∾ dance *ein Kontertanz, eine Quadrille;* a ∾ deal *eine ehrliche Abmachung, ein ehrliches Geschäft;* a ∾head *ein Skandinavier in USA und Kanada;* a ∾ meal *eine richtige, reichliche Mahlzeit;* a ∾ peg in a round hole *j. (etwas), der (das) nicht am geeigneten Platze ist;* a ∾ refusal *eine glatte Absage, Weigerung;* he is an old ∾-toes *er ist ein Frömmler, ein alter Pedant;* to be all (fair and) ∾ *rechtmäßig, offen und ehrlich zugehen;* four-∾ *fest gegründet, unerschütterlich;* we'll call the matter ∾ *wir werden die Sache als erledigt betrachten;* to be (to get) ∾ with a person *mit j.em quitt sein (werden);* to get everything ∾ *alles aufräumen, Ordnung schaffen.* — **III.** adv.: I hit him ∾ on the jaw *ich traf ihn genau aufs Kinn;* to play ∾ *ehrlich spielen.* — **IV.** v.tr.: he has been ∾d to hold his tongue *er ist bestochen worden, reinen Mund zu halten;* to ∾ an account *eine Rechnung begleichen;* to ∾ accounts with a person *sich an j.em rächen;* to ∾ the circle *den Kreis quadrieren, etwas Unmögliches tun;* I decline to ∾ my conduct with his interests *ich lehne es ab, mein Verhalten seinen Interessen anzupassen;* to ∾ one's conscience *sein Gewissen beruhigen;* to ∾ one's elbows *Boxerstellung einnehmen, sich in die Brust werfen;* to ∾ a person *sich mit j.em abfinden, j.en befriedigen;* to ∾ up a matter *eine Sache (Rechnung) begleichen.* — **V.** v.i.: his practice does not ∾ with his principles *seine Taten stehen nicht in Einklang mit seinen Grundsätzen;* to ∾ up to a person *j.en zum Boxen herausfordern, j.em drohen;* to ∾ up to difficulties (problems) *Schwierigkeiten (Problemen) mit Mut und Entschlossenheit entgegentreten*

squeak I. v.i.: to ∾ on a person (sl.) *j.en angeben, verraten, verpetzen.* — **II.** n.: to have a narrow (tight) ∾ *mit knapper Not davonkommen;* to utter a ∾ (colloq.) *ein Geheimnis verraten*

squeal v.i.: to make a person ∾ (sl.) *Geld von j.em erpressen;* to ∾ on someone *j.en (der Polizei) verraten*

squeeze I. v.tr.: a ∾d orange *eine ausgepreßte Zitrone; ein völlig erschöpfter Mensch.* — **II.** n.: I gave him a ∾ (of the hand) *ich drückte ihm die Hand;* it was a tight ∾ *es war ein dichtes Gedränge; eine kritische Lage*

squint n.: let's have a ∾ at it (colloq.) *laß mich mal gucken!*

stable n.: to lock (to shut) the ∾ when the steed is stolen *den Brunnen zudecken, wenn das Kind ertrunken (hineingefallen) ist*

stack n.: I have ∾s (a whole ∾) of books to read *ich habe noch Stöße (noch einen ganzen Stoß) von Büchern zu lesen*

staff n.: you are the ∾ of his old age *du bist die Stütze seines Alters;* to have the better end of the ∾ *überlegen sein*

stag n.: a ∾ party (colloq.) *eine Herrengesellschaft;* to go ∾ *ohne Dame gehen*

stage n.: to go on the ∾ *zur Bühne gehen, Schauspieler(in) werden;* to hold the ∾ *im Mittelpunkt der Vorstellung stehen;* to travel by easy ∾s *in kleinen Tagesreisen, gemächlich reisen;* to tread the ∾ *Schauspieler(in) sein;* to have ∾-fever *einen unbändigen Drang zur Bühne haben;* to suffer from ∾-fright *Lampenfieber haben;* to be ∾-struck *für die Bühne schwärmen;* to say a thing in a ∾-whisper *in lautem Flüstertone sprechen;* at this ∾ *in diesem Stadium*

stager n.: he is an old ∾ *er ist ein alter Praktikus*

stagger v.tr.: that ∾s all belief *das macht allen Glauben zuschanden;* to ∾ office hours (school holidays) *Bürostunden (Schulferien) über einen Zeitraum verteilen, um den Verkehr zu entlasten*

staging a.: a ∾ post *eine Zwischenstation im Luftverkehr*

stair n.: it was discussed below ∾s *es wurde im Souterrain (Kellergeschoß), bei der Dienerschaft besprochen*

stake I. n.: to have a ∾ in the country *materiell am Wohlergehen des Landes interessiert sein;* to be at ∾ *auf dem Spiele stehen;* to be condemned to the ∾ *zum Tode auf dem Scheiterhaufen verurteilt werden.* — **II.** v.tr.: to ∾ money on a horse *Geld auf ein Pferd setzen;* to ∾ out (off) a claim *ein Landstück abstechen, abpfählen*

stalemate v.tr.: to ∾ someone *j.en Patt setzen (Schachspiel)*

stalk v.i.: a ∾ing-horse *ein Vorwand, eine Tarnung*

stall v.tr.: to ∾ cattle *Vieh im Stall füttern, mästen;* the car was ∾ed by the snow *das Auto ist im Schnee festgefahren (steckengeblieben);* he ∾ed the plane *er hat das Flugzeug überzogen;* he ∾ed the question *er vermied es, die Frage klar zu beantworten*

stand I. v.i.: he ∾s condemned of the crime *er ist des Verbrechens überführt;* I ∾ corrected *ich gebe meinen Irrtum, mein Unrecht zu;* he ∾s six foot high in his stockings *er mißt sechs Fuß ohne Schuhe;* the remark ∾s good *die Bemerkung hat ihre Richtigkeit;* to ∾ pat *mit Bestehendem zufrieden sein;* that stood me four pounds *das hat mich vier Pfund gekostet;* to ∾ security *Bürgschaft leisten;* ∾ at ease! *rührt euch!;* to ∾ by *in Bereitschaft sein;* to ∾ by one's word *zu seinem Worte stehen;* to ∾ for a constituency *für einen Wahlkreis kandidieren;* to ∾ in for someone *j.en vertreten;* to ∾ in need of a thing *etwas nötig haben;* to ∾ a person in good stead *j.em gut zustatten kommen;* to ∾ in with a person *mit j.em im Bunde stehen;* to ∾ off *sich abseits halten;* to ∾ out *auffällig sein, in die Augen fallen;* it ∾s agreed *es steht fest, es ist abgemacht;* he is very ∾-offish *er ist unnahbar, zugeknöpft, steif, unfreundlich;* to ∾ on ceremony *auf Förmlichkeiten Wert legen;* his hair stood on end *seine Haare sträubten sich;* to ∾ out for better pay *auf besserer Bezahlung bestehen;* to ∾ out against a measure *sich einer Maßnahme widersetzen;* this matter must ∾ over *die Angelegenheit muß zurückgestellt (verschoben) werden;* to ∾ to one's guns *auf seinem Standpunkt, seiner Pflicht beharren; festbleiben, durch-, aushalten;* I ∾ to it that *ich behaupte fest, daß; ich bleibe dabei, daß;* it ∾s to reason *es ist selbstverständlich (es ist für jeden vernünftig denkenden Menschen klar), daß;* whoever loses I ∾ to win *wer auch immer verliert, ich werde sicherlich gewinnen;* to ∾ up for a person (a cause) *für eine Person (Sache) eintreten;* to ∾ up to an opponent *einem Gegner mutig entgegentreten;* this material will ∾ (up to) hard wear *diesen Stoff kann man strapazieren;* to ∾ up with a person *mit j.em zum Tanz antreten;* he ∾s fair to win *er hat gute Aussichten zu gewinnen.* — **II.** v.tr.: to ∾ a good chance of getting a thing *gute Aussichten haben, etwas zu bekommen;* to ∾

comparison with a thing *einen Vergleich mit etwas aushalten;* he stood drinks all round *er hielt die ganze Gesellschaft frei;* I can't ∾ the fellow *ich kann den Menschen nicht leiden;* to ∾ one's ground *sich behaupten;* he can ∾ a lot *er kann viel vertragen, aushalten;* I shall ∾ no nonsense *ich lasse nicht mit mir spaßen, ich lasse mir nichts gefallen;* to ∾ pain *Schmerz aushalten;* to ∾ the racket (sl.) *die Folgen tragen;* to ∾ the test *die Probe bestehen;* to ∾ treat *die Zeche bezahlen;* to ∾ out a performance *eine Vorstellung bis zum Ende aushalten.* — **III.** n.: a ∾ of arms *eine vollständige Soldatenausrüstung;* the ∾ of colours *die Regimentsfahne(n);* to bring (to come) to a ∾ (∾still) *zum Stehen, Stillstand bringen (kommen);* to make a ∾ against an enemy *sich einem Feinde widersetzen;* to make a ∾ for a principle *für einen Grundsatz eintreten;* he took his ∾ near the door *er stellte sich in der Nähe der Tür auf;* I take my ∾ on the precise wording of the act *ich stütze mich auf den genauen Wortlaut des Gesetzes;* a band-∾ *ein Musikpavillon;* a cab-∾ *ein Halteplatz für Droschken*

standard n.: the gold ∾ *die Goldwährung;* ∾ English *mustergültiges Englisch;* the ∾ gauge *die Normalspurweite der Eisenbahn;* a ∾ lamp *eine Stehlampe;* the ∾ of life *die Lebenshaltung;* the ∾ size *die Normalgröße;* the ∾ work on the subject *das klassische (führende, maßgebende) Werk über das Thema;* he is not (does not come) up to the ∾ of the form *er steht nicht auf dem Stand (Niveau), er genügt nicht den Anforderungen der Klasse;* the work is of low ∾ *die Arbeit ist mittelmäßig;* to set a ∾ for a thing *den Maßstab für etwas abgeben*

standing I. n.: good ∾ *bewährter Ruf;* men of high ∾ *hochangesehene Männer;* a dispute of long ∾ *ein alter, langjähriger Streit;* he is of no ∾ *er genießt kein Ansehen.* — **II.** a.: a ∾ army *ein stehendes Heer;* a ∾ invitation *eine (bleibende) feste Einladung;* ∾ orders (parl.) *Geschäftsordnung*

star I. n.: his ∾ has (is) set *sein Stern (Glanz) ist erloschen;* the Stars and Stripes, the Star-spangled Banner *das Sternenbanner der USA;* his ∾ was in the ascendant *es ging aufwärts mit ihm;* a shooting ∾ *eine Sternschnuppe;* to be born under a lucky (an unhappy, evil) ∾ *unter einem Glücksstern (einem Unstern) geboren sein;* to hitch one's wag(g)on to a ∾ *große Ambitionen haben; sich (dat.) die Kräfte höherstehender Personen zunutze machen;* I see ∾s *mir flimmert es vor den Augen; ich sehe Sternchen;* you may thank your ∾s (your lucky ∾s) you were not there *du kannst deinem Schicksal dankbar sein (du kannst heilsfroh sein, vom Glück reden), daß du nicht dort warst.* — **II.** v.tr.: a play ∾ring N.N. *ein Theaterstück mit N. N. in der Hauptrolle;* ill-∾red *unglücklich, vom Glück verlassen*

stare I. v.i.: to ∾ at (upon) a person (a thing) *j.en (etwas) anstarren;* to make a person ∾ *j.en in Erstaunen setzen;* to go staring mad *völlig (ganz und gar) verrückt werden;* to wear a staring red tie *einen grell-, knallroten Schlips tragen.* — **II.** v.tr.: to ∾ a person in the face *j.em ins Gesicht starren;* the facts ∾ us in the face *die Tatsachen liegen sonnenklar vor Augen;* ruin ∾d him in the face *er stand unmittelbar vor dem Untergang;* to ∾ a person down (out of countenance) *j.en durch Anstarren außer Fassung bringen*

stark a. & adv.: ∾ and stiff *starr und steif;* ∾ naked *splitternackt*

starry-eyed a. (colloq.): a ∾ idea *ein unpraktisches, undurchführbares Ideal*

start I. v.i.: he ∾ed at the sound of my voice *er fuhr auf (zusammen, in die Höhe), als er meine Stimme hörte;* to ∾ in to do a thing *etwas beginnen;* to ∾ on a journey *eine Reise antreten;* to ∾ out to do a thing *Schritte unternehmen, sich (dat.) vornehmen, etwas zu tun;* many difficulties have ∾ed up *viele Schwierigkeiten sind entstanden;* the motor ∾ed up *der Motor sprang an;* you have no right to be here, to ∾ with *du hast, erstens, kein Recht, hier zu sein;* the club had only 6 members to ∾ with *der Verein hatte am Anfang (anfangs) nur 6 Mitglieder.* — **II.** v.tr.: to ∾ a business *ein Geschäft anfangen;* to ∾ an engine *eine Maschine in Gang setzen;* to ∾ game from its lair *Wild aufjagen;* that ∾ed me coughing *das reizte mich zum Husten;* to ∾ a person in life *j.em den Weg ins Leben ebnen;* to ∾ a rumour *ein Gerücht in die Welt setzen.* — **III.** n.: by fits and ∾s *stoßweise, dann und wann;* to get (to have) the ∾ of a person *j.em zuvorkommen; einen Vorsprung, Vorteil vor j.em haben;*

to give a ∾ *zusammen-, auffahren;* to give a person a ∾ *j.en erschrecken;* I will give you 60 paces ∾ *ich gebe dir einen Vorsprung von 60 Schritten*

starve I. v.i.: I'm simply starving *ich komme bald um vor Hunger;* we are starving for news *wir hungern nach Nachrichten.* — **II.** v.tr.: to ∾ a garrison into surrender *eine Garnison durch Hunger zur Übergabe zwingen;* to ∾ a fortress out *eine Festung aushungern*

state I. n.: what a ∾ you are in! *wie siehst du denn nur aus!;* he was in quite a ∾ about it *er war darüber sehr erregt (aufgebracht);* a ∾ of bad health *ein schlechter Gesundheitszustand;* to keep ∾ *seine Würde bewahren, schwer zugänglich sein;* to lie in ∾ *auf dem Paradebett liegen, aufgebahrt sein;* to live in ∾ *großen Aufwand machen.* — **II.** a.: a ∾ criminal *ein Staatsverbrecher.* — **III.** v.tr.: to ∾ one's opinion(s) *seine Meinung äußern;* he is ∾d to have done it *er soll es getan haben;* no precise time was ∾d *es wurde keine genaue Zeit angegeben (festgesetzt)*

stave v.tr.: to ∾ in *ein Loch einschlagen;* to ∾ off *aufhalten, verschieben*

stay I. v.tr.: to ∾ the course *bis zum Ende durchhalten;* to ∾ a decision *eine Entscheidung hinausschieben;* to ∾ one's hand *ein Verfahren (einen Angriff) einstellen;* to ∾ a person's hand (fig.) *j.es Hand hemmen, binden;* to ∾ one's stomach *seinen Hunger stillen;* can you ∾ to supper? *kannst du bleiben und mit uns zu Abend essen?;* he has no ∾ing power *er hat keine Ausdauer, Widerstandskraft.* — **II.** v.i.: ∾! you forgot one thing *halt! du hast eins vergessen;* this measure has come to ∾ *diese Maßnahme hat sich eingebürgert;* to ∾ put *festbleiben;* to ∾ up for the vacation *die Universität während der Ferien nicht verlassen.* — **III.** n.: to make a long ∾ *sich lange aufhalten;* the ∾ of my old age *die Stütze meines Alters;* the ∾ of execution *die Zurückstellung der Ausführung;* it was a ∾ upon his activity *seine Tätigkeit wurde dadurch gehemmt*

stead n.: in a person's ∾, in∾ of a person *an j.es Stelle;* in∾ of doing so *anstatt es zu tun;* to stand a person in good ∾ *j.em gut zustatten kommen*

steady I. a.: ∾!, ∾ now! *nun mal langsam! vorsichtig!;* as ∾ as a rock *unerschütterlich;* he is not ∾ on his legs *er steht nicht fest (nicht sicher) auf den Beinen;* he is a ∾ (∾-going) young man *er ist ein zuverläßiger, keinen Ausschweifungen ergebener junger Mann;* to keep a ship ∾ *den Kurs unverändert geradeaus halten;* to run at a ∾ pace *mit gleichmäßiger Geschwindigkeit laufen.* — **II.** v.tr.: adversity will ∾ him *das Unglück wird ihn festigen, zur Vernunft bringen.* — **III.** v.i.: he will soon ∾ down *er wird bald gesetzt (ruhig) werden, zur Vernunft kommen*

steal I. v.tr.: to ∾ a march upon a person *j.em zuvorkommen;* who ∾s my purse ∾s trash (Othello, III, 3) *wer meinen Beutel stiehlt, nimmt Tand (Schlegel-Tieck);* this announcement will ∾ their music *diese Bekanntmachung wird ihnen den Wind aus den Segeln nehmen;* a mist stole over the valley *ein Nebel legte sich übers Tal*

steam I. n.: at full ∾ *mit Volldampf;* to get up (to put on) ∾ (colloq.) *in Fahrt kommen, sich ins Zeug legen;* to let off (to work off) ∾ (colloq.) *seinen Gefühlen freien Lauf lassen, sich austoben.* — **II.** v.i.: to ∾ ahead (away) *mit aller Kraft arbeiten, große Fortschritte machen;* ∾ing hot *kochend heiß*

steel n.: cold ∾ *ein Schwert (Dolch);* a foe worthy of one's ∾ *ein beachtlicher, gefürchteter Gegner;* a grip of ∾ *ein stahlharter Griff*

steep a. (colloq.): it is a bit ∾ that we should have to do both *es ist zu viel verlangt (es ist ein starkes Stück), daß wir beides machen sollen;* to pay a ∾ price *einen übermäßig hohen (gepfefferten) Preis zahlen;* a ∾ story *eine übertriebene, unglaubhafte Erzählung*

steer v.i.: to ∾ clear of a person (a thing) *j.en (etwas) meiden, j.em (etwas) aus dem Wege gehen*

step I. v.i.: ∾ this way, please *kommen Sie bitte hier mit;* I had to ∾ in *ich mußte einschreiten;* to ∾ off on the wrong foot *einen Anfangsfehler machen;* to ∾ on the gas (colloq.) *Gas geben, das Tempo beschleunigen;* to ∾ out, to ∾ lively *sich beeilen;* to ∾ out of line *selbständig handeln; aus der Reihe tanzen;* a ∾ping stone *ein Schrittstein (im Wasser oder Schmutz); ein Sprungbrett (zum Erfolg).* — **II.** v.tr.: to ∾ it *tanzen;* to ∾ up production *die Produktion steigern.* — **III.** n.: ∾ by ∾ *Schritt* *für Schritt;* a ∾ in the right direction *ein angemessener Schritt, eine vernünftige Maßnahme;* it is but a ∾ to my house *es sind nur ein paar Schritte bis zu meinem Hause;* to be out of ∾ *aus der Reihe tanzen;* to bend (to direct, to turn) one's ∾s to a place *seine Schritte nach einem Ort lenken;* to break ∾ *ohne Tritt gehen;* to feel out of ∾ *sich befangen fühlen;* to get one's ∾ *befördert werden;* to keep ∾ with a person *mit j.em Schritt halten;* mind the ∾! *Achtung, Vorsicht Stufe!;* to take ∾s in a matter *Schritte in einer Angelegenheit unternehmen;* to tread (to walk) in a person's ∾s *in j.es Fußstapfen treten, seinem Beispiel folgen;* watch your ∾! (colloq.) *sei auf der Hut! paß auf!;* ∾-ins (colloq.) *Unterhose*

sterling a.: he is a ∾ fellow *er ist ein Mann von echtem Schrot und Korn*

stern a.: ∾ necessity *harte Notwendigkeit;* the ∾er sex *das stärkere Geschlecht*

stew I. v.i.: to let a person ∾ in his own juice (grease) *j.en in seinem eigenen Fett schmoren lassen; ihn seinem Schicksal überlassen;* he ∾s the whole day (sl.) *er büffelt (ochst) den ganzen Tag.* — **II.** v.tr.: the tea is ∾ed *der Tee hat zu lange gezogen, ist bitter.* — **III.** n.: we were in a terrible ∾ (colloq.) *wir waren sehr aufgeregt (nervös); sehr in Verlegenheit*

stick I. v.tr.: I am stuck *ich sitze fest, kann nicht weiter;* ∾ no bills *Plakate ankleben verboten!;* ∾ a few commas in *füge ein paar Kommata ein;* I can't ∾ him (colloq.) *ich kann ihn nicht ausstehen (riechen);* I can't ∾ it (it out) any longer (colloq.) *ich kann es nicht länger ertragen;* just ∾ it down anywhere (sl.) *lege es nur irgendwo hin;* to be stuck on a thing (sl.) *auf etwas versessen sein;* to ∾ up a person (sl.) *j.em die Pistole vorhalten und ihn berauben;* that will ∾ him up (sl.) *das wird ihn in Verlegenheit bringen;* he is a stuck-up ass (colloq.) *er ist ein eingebildeter Esel;* to ∾ up one's nose at a thing (colloq.) *die Nase über etwas rümpfen;* to be stuck up for a thing (colloq.) *äußerst verlegen um etwas sein.* — **II.** v.i.: see 'burr, colour, gizzard, gun, mud'; he ∾s at home (indoors) all day *er klebt (hockt) den ganzen Tag zu Hause;* he will ∾ at nothing *er schreckt vor nichts zurück;* to ∾ by a person *j.em treu bleiben;* some of the money stuck in (or: to) his fingers *von dem Geld hat er sich unrechtmäßig etwas angeeignet;* to ∾ it on (sl.) *einen übermäßigen Preis verlangen; übertreiben, angeben;* to ∾ out for better terms *auf besseren Bedingungen bestehen;* it ∾s out from the others *es ragt unter den anderen hervor;* it ∾s out a mile (colloq.) *es ist offensichtlich (nicht zu leugnen);* the name stuck to him *der Name blieb an ihm haften;* to ∾ to it, to one's guns *dabei beharren, den Versuch nicht aufgeben;* to ∾ to a person through thick and thin *mit j.em durch dick und dünn gehen;* to ∾ to the point *bei der Sache bleiben;* to ∾ to one's promise *sich an sein Versprechen halten;* to ∾ to what one finds *behalten, was man findet;* friends should ∾ together *Freunde sollten zusammenhalten;* his hair ∾s straight up *seine Haare stehen ihm zu Berge;* to ∾ up for a person (a thing) *für j.en (eine Sache) eintreten;* to ∾ up to a person *sich j.em widersetzen.* — **III.** n.: see 'cleave, cross, dry'; a ∾ of bombs *ein Bombenbündel;* any ∾ to beat a dog *ein Vorwand ist schnell gefunden;* a few ∾s of furniture *einige einfache Möbelstücke;* he is a poor ∾ *er ist ein armseliger, unbeholfener Kerl;* don't be such a ∾ at it *stell' dich nicht so ungeschickt dabei an;* to cut one's ∾ (colloq.) *sich aus dem Staube machen;* to have (to get) the right (thin, wrong) end of the ∾ *gut (schlecht) bei etwas wegkommen;* to get hold of the wrong end of the ∾ *die Sache falsch auffassen; mißverstehen;* to hop the ∾ (sl.) *sterben, abkratzen;* to play a good ∾ *ein guter Fechter sein;* to take the ∾ to a person *j.en verprügeln;* he wants the ∾ *er verdient den Stock, eine Tracht Prügel*

stickler n.: he is a ∾ for principles *er ist ein Prinzipienreiter;* she is a great ∾ for proprieties *sie hält peinlich auf äußeren Anstand*

sticky a.: he was very ∾ about giving me leave (colloq.) *er erhob allerlei Einwendungen gegen meine Beurlaubung, gab mir nur zögernd Urlaub;* he'll come to a (he'll meet) a ∾ end (colloq.) *es wird ein höchst unangenehmes Ende mit ihm nehmen*

stiff I. a.: as ∾ as a poker *so steif wie ein Stock, stocksteif;* stark and ∾ *starr und steif;* it was a ∾ climb *es war eine beschwerliche Kletterei;* a ∾ denial *ein hartnäckiges Leugnen;* a ∾ drink *ein kräf-*

tiger, alkoholreicher Trunk; a ∾ examination *eine schwierige Prüfung;* to keep a ∾ upper lip *sich nicht unterkriegen lassen, die Ohren steifhalten;* ∾-necked *halsstarrig, unnachgiebig;* a ∾ price *ein gepfefferter (gesalzener) Preis;* to bore a person ∾ (colloq.) *j.en tödlich langweilen;* to scare a person ∾ (colloq.) *j.en zu Tode erschrekken.* — **II.** n.: he is a big ∾ (sl.) *er ist ein hoffnungsloser, unbelehrbarer Mensch;* to do a bit of ∾ (sl.) *Geld auf einen Wechsel geben*

stile n.: to help a lame dog over a ∾ *j.em in der Not behilflich sein*

still I. a.: a ∾ birth, a ∾-born child *eine Totgeburt, ein totgeborenes Kind;* ∾ hock *nicht schäumender Rheinwein;* the small ∾ voice *das Gewissen;* ∾ waters run deep (prov.) *stille Wasser sind tief.* — **II.** n.: in the ∾ of night *in der Stille der Nacht.* — **III.** v.tr.: to ∾ a person's scruples *j.es Bedenken beseitigen.* — **IV.** v.i.: when the tempest ∾s *wenn der Sturm sich legt.* — **V.** adv.: ∾ greater, greater ∾ *noch größer;* we are ∾ of the same opinion *wir sind immer noch derselben Meinung;* ∾, I shouldn't say so *immerhin (trotz alledem), ich würde es nicht sagen*

stilted a.: a ∾ style *ein gespreizter (geschraubter, hochtrabender) Stil*

sting I. v.tr.: a bee stung his finger *eine Biene stach ihn in den Finger;* he was stung for a fiver (sl.) *er wurde um fünf Pfund geneppt;* pepper ∾s one's tongue *Pfeffer beißt einem auf der Zunge;* to ∾ a person into rage *j.en zur Wut (bis aufs Blut) reizen, in Wut bringen;* the insult stung him to the quick *die Beleidigung kränkte ihn aufs empfindlichste, tat ihm in der Seele weh;* my tooth ∾s *mein Zahn sticht (schmerzt);* ∾ing nettle *Brennessel.* — **II.** n.: the ∾ is in the tail *das dicke Ende kommt nach;* the air has no ∾ in it *die Luft ist erschlaffend (ermüdend);* a jest with a ∾ in it *ein Witz mit einer scharfen Pointe;* the ∾s of remorse *Gewissensbisse*

stink I. v.i.: to ∾ of money (sl.) *enorm reich sein, vor (nach) Geld stinken;* it ∾s in my nostrils *es ist mir widerwärtig (eklig); es hängt mir zum Halse heraus;* to cry ∾ing fish *seine eigene Ware schlechtmachen.* — **II.** v.tr.: you can ∾ it miles off (sl.) *man kann es meilenweit riechen.* — **III.** n.: our ∾s master (school sl.) *unser Chemielehrer*

stinker n. (sl.): I wrote him a ∾ *ich habe ihm einen gepfefferten Brief geschrieben*

stint I. v.tr.: to ∾ a person in (of) food *j.en im Essen knapp halten.* — **II.** n.: to do one's daily ∾ *sein tägliches Arbeitspensum erledigen;* he laboured without ∾ *er arbeitete unverdrossen*

stir I. v.tr.: it ∾s my bile *es ekelt mich an;* to ∾ a person's blood *j.en in Erregung versetzen;* not to ∾ an eyelid *keine Überraschung oder Aufregung zeigen; nicht reagieren;* not to ∾ a finger *keine Hilfe leisten, keinen Finger rühren;* to ∾ the fire *das Feuer schüren;* to ∾ the soup *die Suppe umrühren;* ∾ your stumps! (colloq.) *nimm' die Beine in die Hand!;* to ∾ up strife *Streit erregen (anfachen, anfangen);* he wants ∾ring up *er muß aufgerüttelt werden.* — **II.** v.i.: don't ∾ *rühre dich nicht!;* he never ∾s abroad (out of the house) *er geht nie aus;* he is up and ∾ring (is not ∾ring yet) *er ist schon auf; er liegt noch im Bett (er regt sich noch nicht);* there is no news ∾ring *es gibt nichts Neues;* to lead a ∾ring life *ein tätiges Leben führen;* to deliver a ∾ring speech *eine begeisternde Rede halten;* these are ∾ring times *es sind aufregende Zeiten.* — **III.** n.: not a ∾ *nicht die geringste Bewegung;* I can't get a ∾ out of him *ich kann ihn nicht aufrütteln, ihn nicht zu irgendeiner Handlung bewegen;* full of ∾ and movement *voller Aufregung und Bewegung;* it made a great ∾ *es erregte großes Aufsehen, hat viel Staub aufgewirbelt;* to give the fire a ∾ *das Feuer schüren*

stitch n.: a ∾ in time saves nine (prov.) *ein kleines Mittel zur rechten Zeit spart viele Mühe; Vorsicht ist besser als Nachsicht;* to drop (to take up, to pick up) a ∾ *eine Masche fallen lassen, eine Masche aufnehmen;* to have a ∾ in one's side *Seitenstechen (Seitenstiche) haben;* he hasn't a dry ∾ on him *er hat keinen trokkenen Faden am Leib;* the doctor had to put 6 ∾es *der Arzt mußte 6 Nadeln legen*

stiver n.: I don't care a ∾ *ich mache mir keinen Deut (nicht die Bohne) daraus*

stock I. n.: ∾s and stones *leblose Dinge; stumpfsinnige Leute;* to have (to keep) in

∾ *auf Lager (vorrätig) haben, halten;* lock, ∾ and barrel *alles in allem; die ganze Geschichte;* money in the ∾s *Geld in Staatspapieren;* the ship is on the ∾s *das Schiff liegt auf Stapel;* to be out of ∾ *ausverkauft, nicht mehr vorrätig sein;* a ∾-broker *ein Effektenmakler;* the Stock Exchange *die Börse;* he has a great ∾ of information *er ist sehr gut informiert;* a ∾ jobber *ein Börsenspekulant;* the ∾ market *der Effektenmarkt;* a ∾ phrase *eine stehende Redensart;* a ∾-pot *ein Suppentopf;* it was ∾(-)still *es war mäuschenstill;* his whole ∾-in-trade *sein ganzer Warenvorrat;* a politician's ∾-in-trade catchwords *die stereotypen Schlagwörter eines Politikers;* dead and live ∾ *totes und lebendes Inventar;* to come of good ∾ *von guter Herkunft (von gutem Erbgut) sein;* a laughing ∾ *ein Gegenstand, eine Zielscheibe des Spottes;* rolling ∾ *rollendes Material;* to lay great ∾ by a thing *etwas hochschätzen;* to lay in (to renew) a ∾ of goods *einen Warenvorrat (-bestand) anlegen, ergänzen;* to make ∾ of a thing *aus einer Sache Vorteil ziehen;* to take ∾ *Inventur machen;* to take ∾ of a person (a thing) *j.en (eine Sache) in Augenschein nehmen, abschätzen;* to take ∾ of one's soul *mit sich selbst zu Rate gehen;* he did not take much ∾ in it *er machte sich nicht viel daraus, er hielt nicht viel davon.* — **II.** v.tr.: to ∾ a farm *ein Gut mit Vieh versehen;* we do not ∾ the out sizes *die übergroßen Nummern führen wir nicht;* a well-∾ed larder *eine gut gefüllte Speisekammer;* a well-∾ed library *eine reichhaltige (gut ausgestattete) Bibliothek*

stomach I. n.: what a ∾ he has got! *hat der aber einen Schmerbauch!;* my ∾ is out of order *ich habe mir den Magen verdorben;* my ∾ rises (turns) *mir wird übel, mir kommt es hoch;* it goes against my ∾ *es widert mich an, davor ekelt mir;* he had no ∾ for the fight *er hatte keine Lust zum Kampfe;* it still sticks in my ∾ *es liegt mir immer noch schwer im Magen;* it turns my ∾ *es kehrt mir den Magen um, verursacht mir Übelkeit.* — **II.** v.tr.: to ∾ an affront (insult) *eine Beleidigung einstecken*

stone I. n.: as hard as a ∾ *steinhart;* ∾-blind, ∾-dead, ∾-deaf, see 'blind, dead, deaf'; at a ∾'s throw from here *in Steinwurfweite, nur ein Katzensprung von hier;* ∾-walling *äußerst vorsichtiges Schlagen beim Kricketspiel; parlamentarische Obstruktion;* the philosopher's ∾ *der Stein der Weisen;* a rolling ∾ gathers no moss (prov.) *rollender Stein wird nicht moosig; ein unsteter Mensch kommt (bringt es) zu nichts;* stocks and ∾s *leblose Dinge; stumpfsinnige Leute;* to break ∾s *Steine klopfen; in äußerster Not sein;* to harden into ∾ *versteinern, hart werden;* to kill two birds with one ∾ *zwei Fliegen mit éiner Klappe schlagen;* not to leave a ∾ standing *keinen Stein auf dem anderen lassen;* to leave no ∾ unturned *nichts unversucht lassen;* to mark with a white ∾ *als besonders glücklich (günstig) bezeichnen, rot im Kalender anstreichen;* those who live in glasshouses should not throw ∾s (prov.) *wer im Glashaus sitzt, soll(te) nicht mit Steinen werfen.* — **II.** v.tr.: to ∾ a person to death *j.en steinigen;* to ∾ plums *Pflaumen entkernen;* to ∾ a street *eine Straße beschottern (pflastern)*

stony I. a.: a ∾ stare *ein starrer Blick.* — **II.** adv.: I am ∾-broke (colloq.) *ich bin pleite*

stool n.: to fall between two ∾s *sich zwischen zwei Stühle setzen;* to go to ∾ *Stuhlgang haben;* to kick the ∾ from under a person *j.em den Boden unter den Füßen wegziehen;* a ∾-pigeon *ein Lockvogel*

stoop I. v.i.: to ∾ to some unworthy action *sich zu einer unwürdigen Tat erniedrigen.* — **II.** v.tr.: to ∾ one's head to listen *den Kopf neigen, um zu hören.* — **III.** n.: to walk with a ∾ *gebückt (krumm) gehen*

stop I. v.tr.: see 'blow[2], bullet, ear, gap, mouth, noise, nonsense, payment, thief, tooth, wages, way'; to ∾ doing a thing *aufhören, etwas zu tun;* to ∾ a person doing a thing *dafür sorgen, daß j. etwas nicht tut;* to ∾ a person short *j.en unterbrechen;* a badly ∾ped letter *ein Brief mit schlechter Zeichensetzung;* to ∾ down a lens (phot.) *eine Linse abblenden;* to ∾ up a hole *ein Loch zustopfen.* — **II.** v.i.: my watch has ∾ped *meine Uhr ist stehengeblieben;* I shall ∾ at home (in) *ich bleibe zu Hause;* the train does not ∾ at (before) N. *der Zug hält nicht in (vor) N.;* to ∾ dead (short) *plötzlich anhalten, innehalten;* shall you ∾ for dinner? *bleibst du zum Essen da?;* I shall ∾ on (out, up) *ich bleibe länger (fort, auf);* a ∾-over ticket (U.S.) *eine Fahrkarte, die Fahrtunterbrechung gestattet;* to ∾ with a person *bei j.em zu Besuch sein;* ∾-press news *nach Redaktionsschluß eingelaufene Nachrichten.* — **III.** n.: to be at a ∾ *nicht mehr weiter können;* to bring (to come) to a ∾ *zum Halten bringen; zum Halten kommen;* to make a ∾ *haltmachen;* to put a ∾ to a thing *einer Sache Einhalt gebieten, ihr einen Riegel vorschieben;* the train runs without a ∾ from N. to N. *der Zug fährt, ohne zu halten, durch von N. bis N.;* to come to a dead (full) ∾ *plötzlich anhalten, vollständig aufhören;* a full ∾ *ein Punkt (Zeichensetzung);* the glottal ∾ *der Kehlverschlußlaut;* to put on (to pull out) the pathetic ∾ *das pathetische Register ziehen;* a ∾-gap *ein Notstopfen, -behelf;* a ∾-go signal *eine Verkehrsampel*

stopper n.: I must put a ∾ on that *dem muß ich Einhalt gebieten*

store I. n.: that article is not in ∾ *dieser Artikel ist nicht auf Lager;* a surprise is in ∾ for you *dir steht eine Überraschung bevor;* to buy at a ∾ *im Laden kaufen;* ∾ clothes *Konfektionskleider;* a ∾house *ein Lagerhaus, Magazin, Speicher;* to be a ∾house of information *eine Fundgrube der Belehrung sein;* a ∾-keeper *ein Ladenbesitzer;* the ∾s, departmental ∾s *das Warenhaus;* the cooperative ∾s *der Konsumvereinsladen;* to have a ∾, good ∾, ∾s of a thing *eine Fülle (einen Reichtum, Schatz) von etwas haben;* I set (I lay) no great ∾ by it *ich lege keinen großen Wert (kein großes Gewicht) darauf, ich messe der Sache keinen Wert bei.* — **II.** v.tr.: to ∾ up a saying in one's heart *einen Ausspruch im Herzen (auf)bewahren*

storey, story n.: a house of five ∾s (stories); a five ∾ed (storied) house *ein Haus mit fünf Stockwerken, ein fünfstöckiges Haus;* he is a little wrong (he has something wrong) in the (his) upper ∾ *er ist nicht ganz richtig im Oberstübchen*

storm I. n.: a ∾ in a teacup *ein Sturm im Wasserglase;* to take by ∾ *im Sturm nehmen, erstürmen.* — **II.** v.i.: to ∾ at a thing *gegen eine Sache toben (wüten)*

story n.: the ∾ is the least part of the book *die Handlung spielt die geringste Rolle in dem Buch;* the ∾ goes that *es geht das Gerücht (es wird erzählt), daß;* as the ∾ goes *wie verlautet, wie es heißt;* but that is another ∾ *aber das ist etwas anderes (Formel, um eine Erzählung abzubrechen und durch die Anspielung den Leser auf die Folter zu spannen);* a cock-and-bull ∾ *ein Ammenmärchen;* it is always the old ∾ *es ist immer das alte Lied (die alte Leier);* according to his own ∾ *nach seiner eigenen Darstellung;* a short ∾ *eine Novelle;* a tall ∾ *eine unglaubhafte Geschichte;* I shall give you a ∾ *ich werde euch eine Geschichte zum besten geben;* to make a long ∾ short *kurz und gut;* don't tell stories *erzähle mir keine Märchen, flunkere nicht!;* oh, you ∾! (colloq.) *du Flunkerer!*

stout a.: he is a ∾ fellow *er ist ein wackerer, kräftiger Bursche;* to keep a ∾ heart *Mut zeigen;* he made a ∾ resistance *er leistete tapferen Widerstand*

stow v.tr.: ∾ that nonsense *laß den Unsinn!;* to ∾ a thing away *etwas verstauen;* a ∾away *ein blinder Passagier*

straight I. a.: as ∾ as a die *kerzengerade; grundehrlich;* to keep ∾ *ehrlich bleiben;* to put things ∾ *die Sache in Ordnung bringen;* to keep a ∾ face *ernst bleiben;* a ∾forward answer *eine offene, ehrliche Antwort;* to have ∾ hair *glattes Haar haben;* ∾ thinking *folgerichtiges, nüchternes Denken;* to vote the ∾ ticket (U.S.) *für die Kandidatenliste (das Parteiprogramm), wie sie (es) ist, stimmen;* a ∾ tip *ein richtiger, zuverlässiger Tip.* — **II.** n.: to be out of the ∾ *krumm, schief sein.* — **III.** adv.: to come ∾ to the point *ohne Umschweife eine Erklärung abgeben;* he comes ∾ from London *er kommt direkt (gerade[n]wegs) aus London;* to go ∾ home *direkt nach Hause gehen;* to hit ∾ from the shoulder *offene, ehrliche Kritik üben;* keep ∾ on *halte dich geradeaus;* put it ∾ down *lege es sofort hin;* to think ∾ *logisch denken;* I cannot tell you ∾ off *ich kann es dir nicht auf der Stelle sagen;* to work ten hours ∾ off the reel *zehn Stunden ununterbrochen arbeiten;* I told him ∾ out *ich sagte es ihm offen heraus;* to keep on the ∾ and narrow (path) (colloq.) *ein tugendhaftes Leben führen;* a tip ∾ from the horse's mouth *eine Auskunft aus erster Hand*

strain I. v.tr.: to ∾ one's authority *seine Machtbefugnisse überschreiten;* to ∾ one's ears *gespannt zuhören;* to ∾ one's eyes (voice) *die Augen (Stimme) überanstren-*

gen; to ∾ every nerve *alles aufbieten, sein Äußerstes tun;* to ∾ a liquid *eine Flüssigkeit durchsieben (filtrieren);* to ∾ a point in someone's favour *zugunsten j.es etwas zu weit gehen;* to ∾ one's wrist *sich das Handgelenk verstauchen;* the quality of mercy is not ∾ed (Merchant of Venice IV, 1) *die Art von Gnade weiß von keinem Zwang (Schlegel);* a ∾ed interpretation *eine gezwungene Auslegung;* a ∾ed laugh *ein gezwungenes (unnatürliches) Lachen;* ∾ed relations *gespannte Beziehungen.* — **II.** v.i.: let it ∾ *laß es durchsickern;* to ∾ after effect *nach Effekt haschen;* to ∾ at a gnat (cf. Matth. XXIII, 24) *ein Kleinigkeitskrämer sein;* the porter was ∾ing under his load *der Träger mühte sich unter seiner Last ab.* — **III.** n.: the ∾ of modern life *das Aufreibende des heutigen Lebens;* all his senses were on the ∾ *seine Sinne waren aufs äußerste gespannt;* he is a ∾ on my nerves *er fällt mir auf die Nerven;* it was a great ∾ on my resources *es war eine starke Belastung (Inanspruchnahme) meiner Geldmittel;* the ∾ on the rope was tremendous *das Seil war aufs straffste gespannt;* there is a ∾ of weakness in him *er hat eine Anlage (Neigung) zur Schwäche;* to come of a good ∾ *von gutem Geschlecht, guter Rasse abstammen;* to go on in the same ∾ *im alten Stil weitermachen, -reden;* to the ∾s of a harp *zu den Klängen einer Harfe*

strait I. a.: a ∾ jacket *eine Zwangsjacke;* a ∾-laced person *eine sittenstrenge, engherzige, prüde Person.* — **II.** n.: to be in (financial) ∾s *in einer schwierigen Lage (in Not, in der Klemme) sein*

straiten v.tr.: to be ∾ed for money *in Geldverlegenheit sein;* to live in ∾ed circumstances *in beschränkten Verhältnissen leben*

strand v.tr.: to be left ∾ed *auf dem trockenen sitzen; mittel-, hilflos zurückgelassen werden*

strange a.: ∾ to say *merkwürdigerweise, seltsamerweise;* how ∾ that you should not have heard anything about it *seltsam (sonderbar), daß du nichts davon gehört hast!;* I am quite ∾ here *ich bin hier ganz fremd;* to feel ∾ *sich schwindlig fühlen*

stranger n.: he is a ∾ to fear *er kennt keine Furcht;* he is no ∾ to me *ich kenne ihn gut; er ist kein Fremder für mich;* you are quite a ∾ *ich habe dich ewig nicht gesehen;* the little ∾ *der kleine Ankömmling, das neugeborene Kind;* to make a ∾ of someone *j.en wie einen Fremden behandeln;* I see (I spy) ∾s *Formel, die ein Mitglied des englischen Unterhauses anwendet, wenn er die Räumung des Hauses von Fremden beantragt*

strap I. n.: to give a boy the ∾ *den Jungen mit einem Riemen (ver)prügeln;* a ∾-hanger *ein stehender Fahrgast, der sich an dem ledernen Handgriff hält;* a ∾-oil *eine Tracht Prügel (mit einem Riemen).* — **II.** v.tr.: to ∾ a boy *einen Jungen mit einem Riemen (ver)prügeln;* to ∾ (strop) a razor *ein Rasiermesser abziehen;* to ∾ a thing up (down) *eine Sache festschnallen;* a ∾ping girl *ein strammes, dralles Mädchen*

straw n.: a man of ∾ *ein Strohmann;* a ∾ shows (will show) which way the wind blows (prov.) *eine kleine Andeutung genügt (kann viel besagen);* it is the last ∾ that breaks the camel's back (prov.) *etwa: noch ein Tropfen, und das Glas (der Krug) fließt (läuft) über;* it is not worth a ∾ *es ist keinen Pfifferling wert;* I don't care a ∾, two ∾s *ich mache mir nicht die Bohne (ich mache mir einen Dreck) daraus;* to catch at a ∾ *nach einem Strohhalm greifen;* to draw ∾s *Hälmchen ziehen, losen;* my eyes draw ∾s *mir fallen die Augen zu;* to look for a needle in a bottle of ∾ *etwas vergeblich suchen;* to make bricks without ∾ (Exod. V, 7) *ohne das nötige Material arbeiten müssen;* to split ∾s *Haarspalterei treiben, sich um Kleinigkeiten streiten;* he stumbles at a ∾ *er ist ein Kleinigkeitskrämer, er stolpert über einen Strohhalm;* to stumble at a ∾ and leap over a block *in Kleinigkeiten gewissenhaft und in wichtigen Dingen sorglos sein;* a ∾ vote (ballot) *eine Volksbefragung, Probeabstimmung*

strawberry n.: the ∾ leaves *die Herzogswürde;* a ∾-mark *ein rötliches Muttermal*

stray I. v.i.: to ∾ from the path of virtue *vom Pfade der Tugend abweichen.* — **II.** n.: that dog is a ∾ *das ist ein herrenloser (verirrter) Hund;* waifs and ∾s *Abfälle, Überreste; heimatlose, verwahrloste Kinder.* — **III.** a.: he was hit by a ∾ bullet *er wurde von einer verirrten Kugel* *getroffen;* in a few ∾ instances *in einigen vereinzelten Fällen*

streak n.: he has a ∾ of humour in him *er besitzt einen Anflug von Humor;* like a ∾ of lightning *wie der Blitz;* the silver ∾ *der (Englische) Kanal*

stream n.: to go with (against) the ∾ *mit dem (gegen den) Strom schwimmen;* the ∾ of thought is the other way *im allgemeinen denkt man anders*

streamline v.tr.: to ∾ procedure *eine Handlung (ein Vorgehen) vereinfachen (rationalisieren) und daher beschleunigen*

street n.: the man in the ∾ *der einfache Mann, der Mann auf der Straße;* to be in Queer ∾ *in Not (Geldschwierigkeiten, in der Klemme) sein;* he is not in the same ∾ with N. *er ist nicht mit N. zu vergleichen, er kann nicht an N. tippen;* it is right up my ∾ (sl.) *es ist ganz nach meinem Geschmack, es liegt mir sehr;* to go on (to walk) the ∾s *Prostituierte werden, sein; auf den Strich gehen;* a ∾-walker *eine Straßendirne (Schneppe);* to be ∾s ahead of someone *j.em weit überlegen sein*

strength n.: it was beyond (too much for) my ∾ *es ging über meine Kräfte;* I did it on the ∾ of your promise *ich tat es im Vertrauen auf dein Versprechen;* on the ∾ *in der Stammrolle eingetragen;* the invalid gathers ∾ *der Kranke kommt zu Kräften;* union is ∾ (prov.) *Einigkeit macht stark*

strengthen v.tr.: to ∾ a person's hands *j.en zu energischem Handeln ermuntern*

stress I. n.: the ∾ is on the first syllable *der Akzent liegt auf der erste Silbe;* driven by (or: under) ∾ of poverty *gezwungen durch die (unter dem Druck der) Armut;* to lay ∾ on a thing *Nachdruck (Gewicht) auf etwas legen.* — **II.** v.tr.: to ∾ a point *einen Punkt betonen (unterstreichen)*

stretch I. v.tr.: to ∾ boots *Schuhe ausweiten;* to ∾ one's credit *seinen Kredit überschreiten;* to ∾ one's legs *die Beine ausstrecken; sich (dat.) die Beine vertreten (Bewegung verschaffen);* to ∾ one's legs according to the coverlet *sich nach der Decke strecken;* to be ∾ed at full length *lang ausgestreckt liegen;* to ∾ a murderer *einen Mörder aufhängen, -knüpfen;* to ∾ oneself *sich recken, sich rekeln;* to ∾ a person on the ground *j.en zu Boden strecken (niederstrecken);* to ∾ a point *fünf gerade sein lassen, es nicht so genau nehmen, ein Auge zudrücken;* to ∾ the truth *es mit der Wahrheit nicht genau nehmen; übertreiben, aufschneiden.* — **II.** v.i.: the houses ∾ along the river *die Häuser erstrecken sich längs des Flusses;* it ∾es like elastic *es dehnt sich wie Gummi;* my memory ∾es down to the end of last century *meine Erinnerungen reichen bis ans Ende des vorigen Jahrhunderts;* he began to ∾ out *er begann, größere Schritte zu machen.* — **III.** n.: he is doing a five years' ∾ *er sitzt seine fünf Jahre ab;* a ∾ of open country *eine Strecke offenen Landes;* a ∾ of years *eine Reihe von Jahren;* he gave a ∾ and a yawn *er rekelte sich und gähnte;* he works ten hours at a ∾ *er arbeitet zehn Stunden hintereinander;* he did it by a ∾ of authority *er tat es unter Überschreitung seiner Machtbefugnisse;* with every faculty on the ∾ *mit Anspannung (unter Aufbietung) aller Kräfte;* a ∾ of the imagination *eine Anstrengung der Einbildungskraft*

strict a.: it was told me in ∾ confidence *es wurde mir streng vertraulich gesagt;* ∾ly speaking *streng (genau) genommen*

stride n.: to get into one's ∾ *richtig in Schwung kommen;* to take a thing in one's ∾ *etwas ohne Schwierigkeiten (spielend leicht) machen;* to make great ∾s *große Fortschritte machen*

strife n.: to be at ∾ *Streit haben, uneins sein*

strike I. v.tr.: see 'attitude, average, balance, bargain, blow², camp, dumb, eye, fancy, one's flag, all of a heap, iron, light, one's lucky, match, oil, track, work, etc.'; it ∾s me that *es fällt mir auf, daß; es kommt mir so vor, als ob; ich finde, daß;* ∾ me dead! I couldn't tell you (colloq.) *du kannst mich totschlagen, ich könnte es dir nicht sagen;* to ∾ terror into someone *j.em Schrecken einjagen (einflößen);* to ∾ out a line for oneself *eigene Wege einschlagen (gehen);* to ∾ up an acquaintance with a person *Bekanntschaft mit j.em machen;* to ∾ up a tune *eine Melodie anstimmen;* to be struck upon a person (colloq.) *in j.en verliebt sein;* to be struck up with a thing (U.S.) *durch etwas verwirrt, von etwas fasziniert sein;* a stricken heart *ein gequältes Herz;* stricken in years *altersschwach;* stricken with pestilence *von der Pest heimgesucht;* horror-stricken *von Entsetzen ergriffen (gepackt).* — **II.** v.i.: the miners are going to ∾ *die Bergarbeiter wollen streiken;* the match will not ∾ *das Streichholz geht nicht an;* his hour has struck *seine Stunde hat geschlagen;* to ∾ at the root of a thing *etwas an der Wurzel treffen; es zu vernichten drohen;* the blow struck home *der Hieb (Schlag) saß; es war ein sicherer Treffer;* to ∾ in *unterbrechen, in die Rede fallen;* to ∾ into another direction *eine andere Richtung einschlagen;* to ∾ into a subject *ein Thema anschlagen;* to ∾ out for oneself *sich (dat.) seinen eigenen Weg bahnen;* the band ∾s up *die Kapelle fängt an zu spielen.* — **III.** n.: the miners are on ∾ *die Bergarbeiter streiken;* to come out (to go) on ∾ *die Arbeit niederlegen, in den Ausstand treten, streiken;* to call off a ∾ *einen Streik abblasen;* a sympathetic ∾ *ein Sympathiestreik*

string I. n.: the ∾s *die Streichinstrumente;* a ∾ of pearls *eine Perlenschnur, -kette;* the first ∾ of players *die Spitzenspieler;* he is tied to his mother's apron-∾s *er ist ein Muttersöhnchen;* to file past in a long ∾ *in einer langen Reihe vorüberziehen (vorbeimarschieren);* to have a person on a ∾ *j.en vollständig in der Gewalt haben; j.en lange Zeit in Ungewißheit lassen; j.en beschwindeln (anführen);* to have two ∾s to one's bow *mehrere (zwei) Eisen im Feuer haben, mehr als éin Mittel bereit haben (halten);* to harp on one ∾ *auf einem Thema herumreiten;* to pull the ∾s *der Drahtzieher sein;* to touch a ∾ in a person's heart *eine Saite in j.es Herz anschlagen;* to touch the ∾s *die Saiten anschlagen (spielen);* there are no ∾s to the agreement *die Vereinbarung ist ohne Nebenbedingungen.* — **II.** v.tr.: to ∾ a bow *einen Bogen spannen;* a high-strung (highly-strung) person *eine zart besaitete (überempfindliche, nervöse) Person;* to ∾ up a person *j.en aufhängen (aufknüpfen)*

strip I. v.tr.: to ∾ a person to the skin *j.en bis auf die Haut entkleiden;* to ∾ a person of his titles *j.en seiner Titel berauben;* ∾ped of fine names, it is a swindle *ohne die schönen Namen ist die Sache ein Schwindel;* to ∾ (off) the wrapper from the book *den Umschlag des Buches abstreifen.* — **II.** v.i.: we had to ∾ *wir mußten uns nackt ausziehen;* a ∾-tease act *eine Varietenummer, bei der die Artistin nach und nach sich fast aller Kleider entledigt.* — **III.** n.: to tear a ∾ off (someone) (sl.) *(j.en) zurechtstauchen, anschnauzen*

stripe n.: to get one's ∾ *die Unteroffiziertressen bekommen;* to lose one's ∾ *degradiert werden*

strive v.i.: to ∾ to do (for, after) a thing *sich bemühen, etwas zu tun; nach etwas streben;* to ∾ against (with) temptation *gegen die Versuchung ankämpfen;* to ∾ together (with) each other *sich streiten, zanken*

stroke I. n.: a ∾ of business *ein gutes Geschäft;* a ∾ of genius *ein genialer Einfall;* a ∾ of luck *ein Glücksfall;* I shall come on the ∾ of nine *ich komme Schlag neun;* I was there on the ∾ *ich war auf den Schlag dort;* with a ∾ of the pen *mit einem Federstrich;* he has not done a ∾ of work *er hat keinen Strich (Schlag) gearbeitet;* to have a ∾ *einen Schlag(anfall) bekommen;* to dash off a picture with a few ∾s *ein Bild mit ein paar Strichen hinhauen;* he gave him the finishing ∾ *er gab ihm den Gnadenstoß;* to put the finishing ∾s to a thing *die letzte Hand (Feile) an etwas legen;* a master-∾ *ein Meisterstreich;* a sun-∾ *ein Hitzschlag;* to pull (row) ∾ *als Schlagmann rudern.* — **II.** v.tr.: to ∾ a person down *j.en besänftigen;* to ∾ a person (a person's hair) (up) the wrong way *j.en ärgern, reizen*

stroll I. n.: to go for (to take) a ∾ *einen Bummel machen.* — **II.** v.i.: to ∾ about *herumstreifen, -bummeln;* a ∾ing company, ∾ing players *ein Wandertheater, eine Wandertruppe*

strong a.: a ∾-box, ∾-room *ein Geldtresor;* ∾ drink *starkes (scharfes) Getränk;* ∾ meat *kräftige Kost;* ∾-minded *willensstark, energisch;* that is his ∾ point *das ist seine starke Seite;* he is as ∾ as a horse *er hat Bärenkräfte;* a ∾ candidate for the post *ein aussichtsreicher Kandidat für den Posten;* to have a ∾ hold over (upon) a person *großen Einfluß auf j.en ausüben;* to be a ∾hold of Protestantism *ein Bollwerk des Protestantismus sein;* to use ∾ language *Kraftausdrücke gebrauchen;* an army 10,000 ∾ *ein 10000 Mann starkes Heer;* how many are you ∾? *wie groß ist* *eure Gesamtstärke?;* to feel ∾(ly) about a thing *sich über etwas erregen;* he is going ∾ (sl.) *es geht ihm gut;* to come (to go) it ∾ (sl.) *es argmachen, stark auftragen*

struggle I. v.i.: to ∾ against (with) a difficulty *gegen eine Schwierigkeit ankämpfen;* to ∾ for breath *nach Atem ringen;* to ∾ to do a thing *sich ernstlich bemühen, etwas zu tun;* to ∾ to one's feet *mühsam hochkommen;* to ∾ through, up, along, in *sich seinen Weg mühsam hindurch-, hinauf-, entlang-, hineinbahnen;* a struggling artist *ein um Anerkennung ringender Künstler;* there is no struggling with necessity (prov.) *Not bricht Eisen; Not kennt kein Gebot.* — **II.** n.: the ∾ for existence *der Daseinskampf;* mental ∾ *Seelenkampf;* to carry on a ∾ *einen Kampf durchführen*

strut v.i.: to ∾ about *einherstolzieren*

stub I. n.: a ∾ of a cigarette *ein Zigarettenstummel, eine Kippe;* a ∾ of a chequebook *der Kontrollabschnitt eines Scheckheftes.* — **II.** v.tr.: to ∾ one's toe against a thing *mit der Zehe schmerzhaft an (gegen) etwas stoßen;* to ∾ out a cigarette *eine Zigarette ausmachen*

stubby a.: a ∾ man *ein untersetzter Mann*

study I. n.: to be in a brown ∾ *in Nachdenken (Gedanken) versunken sein;* to make a ∾ of a matter *eine Angelegenheit sorgfältig untersuchen.* — **II.** v.tr.: I must ∾ that up for the exam *das muß ich mir zum Examen einpauken*

stuff I. n.: we are such ∾ as dreams are made on (Tempest, IV, 1) *wir sind solcher Zeug', wie der zu Träumen (Schlegel);* that's the ∾ to give 'em (colloq.) *so mußt du's machen! immer feste drauf!;* ∾ and nonsense *Unsinn, dummes Zeug!;* the doctor's ∾ *Arznei, Medizin;* food∾s *Nahrungsmittel;* hot ∾ *hervorragende sportliche Leistung;* (sl.) *tolle Frau; äußerst gewagtes Buch, Kino-, Theaterstück.* — **II.** v.tr.: ∾ a cold and starve a fever *bei einer Erkältung soll man viel, bei Fieber wenig essen;* to ∾ a person *j.em etwas vorflunkern;* to ∾ up *zu-, ausstopfen*

stuffed-shirt n. (sl.): a ∾ *eine anmaßende, aber bedeutungslose Person*

stuffing n.: to knock the ∾ out of someone *j.en fassungslos, unschädlich machen, ihm die Einbildung austreiben*

stumble v.i.: to ∾ at a straw *ein Kleinigkeitskrämer sein, über einen Strohhalm stolpern;* to ∾ over a person *j.em gerade in den Weg laufen;* to ∾ (up)on (across, into) a thing *zufällig auf etwas stoßen, in etwas geraten;* a stumbling-block *ein Hindernis, ein Stein des Anstoßes*

stump I. n.: to go on the ∾ (colloq.) *eine politische Agitationsreise machen;* stir your ∾s (colloq.) *nimm die Beine in die Hand!* — **II.** v.tr.: I was ∾ed for an answer (colloq.) *ich war um eine Antwort verlegen.* — **III.** v.i.: I had to ∾ up (colloq.) *ich mußte das Geld herausrücken (blechen, berappen)*

subdue v.tr.: a ∾d colour *eine matte Farbe;* a ∾d light *ein gedämpftes Licht;* in a ∾d mood *in gedrückter Stimmung*

subject[1] I. a.: ∾ to your approval (consent) *vorbehaltlich Ihrer Billigung (Zustimmung);* ∾ to correction *Irrtümer vorbehalten;* it is ∾ to criticism *es ist der Kritik ausgesetzt;* ∾ to duty *zollpflichtig;* he is ∾ to fits of anger *er wird leicht zornig;* to be ∾ to rheumatism *er neigt zu Rheuma.* — **II.** n.: the grammatical ∾ *das grammatische Subjekt;* the liberty of the ∾s *die Freiheit der Untertanen;* on the ∾ of a thing *hinsichtlich einer Sache;* to dwell on a ∾ *bei einem Gegenstand (Thema) verweilen;* to change the ∾ *das Thema wechseln;* to touch upon a ∾ *einen Gegenstand (ein Thema) berühren;* the ∾-matter of a book *der Stoff (Inhalt) eines Buches*

subject[2] v.tr.: to ∾ a people *ein Volk unterwerfen (unterjochen);* to ∾ to great heat *großer Hitze aussetzen*

sublime a.: from the ∾ to the ridiculous there is but one step *vom Erhabenen zum Lächerlichen ist nur ein Schritt*

submerge v.tr.: the ∾d tenth *der Teil des Volkes, der in dauernder Not ist*

submission n.: my ∾ is that *ich gebe zu erwägen, daß;* with all due ∾ *mit allem schuldigen Respekt*

submit I. v.tr.: to ∾ a case to the court *einen Fall dem Gericht übergeben.* — **II.** v.i.: I ∾ that a material fact has been passed over *ich unterstelle (behaupte), daß eine wesentliche Tatsache übersehen worden ist;* to ∾ (oneself) to a thing *sich einer Sache unterwerfen;* to ∾ to an operation *sich einer Operation unterziehen;* I shall never ∾ to being parted from you *ich* *werde mich nie darin fügen, daß ich von dir getrennt werde*

subordinate I. a.: a ∾ clause *ein Nebensatz;* to be ∾ to a thing *einer Sache untergeordnet sein, ihr an Bedeutung nachstehen.* — **II.** n.: he leaves everything to his ∾s *er überläßt alles seinen Untergebenen*

subscribe I. v.tr.: to ∾ one's name to a document *seinen Namen unter eine Urkunde setzen;* he ∾d £ 10 *er zeichnete (stiftete) zehn Pfund.* — **II.** v.i.: to ∾ for a book *auf ein Buch subskribieren;* to ∾ to a newspaper *(auf) eine Zeitung abonnieren;* I cannot ∾ to that *ich kann das nicht unterschreiben; damit kann ich mich nicht einverstanden erklären*

subscription n.: to raise the ∾ *den Beitrag erhöhen;* to take out a ∾ for a periodical *sich auf eine Zeitschrift abonnieren*

subsequent a.: ∾ to his departure *nach seiner Abreise;* ∾ upon an illness *infolge einer Krankheit*

subside v.i.: the excitement ∾d *die Aufregung ließ nach (legte sich);* he ∾d into an armchair *er ließ sich in einen Lehnstuhl fallen*

subsist I. v.i.: the custom still ∾s there *dort herrscht noch der Brauch;* to ∾ by begging *vom Betteln leben;* to ∾ on vegetables *sich von Gemüse ernähren.* — **II.** v.tr.: to ∾ a family *eine Familie ernähren (unterhalten)*

substance n.: a man of ∾ *ein vermögender Mann;* there is no ∾ in it *es steckt kein Gehalt darin;* I agree with you in ∾ *ich stimme im wesentlichen mit dir überein;* I can give you the ∾ of his speech *ich kann dir den Hauptinhalt seiner Rede wiedergeben;* to sacrifice the ∾ for the shadow *das Wesen dem bloßen Schein opfern;* to waste one's ∾ *sein Kapital vergeuden, von der Substanz leben*

substantial a.: the ghost proved ∾ after all *das Gespenst erwies sich schließlich doch als wirklich;* a man of ∾ build *ein Mann von kräftiger Gestalt;* a ∾ point *ein wesentlicher Punkt;* to make ∾ progress *beträchtliche Fortschritte machen*

succeed I. v.tr.: day ∾s day *ein Tag folgt dem (auf den) anderen;* Elizabeth ∾ed Mary on the throne *Elisabeth folgte Maria auf dem Thron.* — **II.** v.i.: I ∾ed in doing so *es gelang mir, es zu tun;* to ∾ to an estate *ein Gut erben;* to ∾ to the throne *auf dem Thron folgen*

success n.: nothing succeeds like ∾ (prov.) *nichts hilft so gut wie der Erfolg*

such I. a.: ∾ was his ambition that *sein Ehrgeiz war so groß, daß;* he is just ∾ another *er ist geradesoeiner;* I never heard ∾ applause *einen solchen (derartigen) Beifall habe ich noch nie gehört;* ∾ grapes as you never saw *so schöne, große Trauben, wie du sie noch nie gesehen hast;* you needn't be in ∾ a hurry about it *du brauchst dich nicht so sehr damit zu beeilen;* ∾ as it is *so wie die Dinge liegen;* ∾ is life *so geht's im Leben;* ∾ master ∾ man *wie der Herr, so's Gescherr;* he is ∾ a one for football (colloq.) *er ist ganz versessen auf Fußball;* ∾-and-∾ a person *eine bestimmte, gewisse Person;* there was no ∾ thing as keeping them indoors *es war einfach unmöglich, man konnte sie schlechterdings nicht zu Hause halten;* a mistake ∾ as this one *ein derartiger Fehler; ein Fehler, wie zum Beispiel dieser.* — **II.** pron.: ∾ as sit in darkness *diejenigen, welche im Dunkeln sitzen;* ∾ was not my intention *das war nicht meine Absicht;* so perish all ∾! *mögen so alle derartigen Leute umkommen!;* theatres, cinemas, and ∾, ∾like *Theater, Kinos und dergleichen*

suck I. v.tr.: to ∾ the blood of a person *j.em das Blut aussaugen;* to ∾ a person's brains *die Ideen eines anderen verwerten.* — **II.** v.i.: to ∾ at a pipe *an einer Pfeife ziehen;* to ∾ up to a person (colloq.) *sich bei j.em einschmeicheln, sich an j.en heranmachen;* a ∾ing child *ein Säugling;* a ∾ing pig *ein Spanferkel.* — **III.** n.: a mother gives ∾ to her child *eine Mutter gibt ihrem Kind die Brust (säugt, stillt ihr Kind);* to have (to take) a ∾ at a thing *an etwas lutschen;* what a ∾!, ∾s! (sl.) *welch ein Reinfall!*

sucker n.: (U.S. sl.) he is a ∾ *er ist ein Grünschnabel*

sudden n.: (all) of a ∾, on a ∾ *(ganz) plötzlich*

sue I. v.tr.: to ∾ a person for damages *gegen j.en auf Schadenersatz klagen.* — **II.** v.i.: to ∾ for a favour *um eine Gunst werben*

suffer I. v.tr.: to ∾ defeat, a loss *eine Niederlage, einen Verlust erleiden;* not to ∾ fools gladly (2 Corinthians XI, 19) *wenig Geduld mit dummen Leuten haben;* how can you ∾ his insolence? *wie kannst du nur seine Frechheit ertragen, zulassen?;* to ∾ a person to do a thing *j.em erlauben, etwas zu tun, j.en etwas tun lassen.* — **II.** v.i.: the attackers ∾ed severely *die Angreifer erlitten schwere Verluste;* he ∾ed from (in) doing so *er erlitt dadurch Schaden;* he ∾s from rheumatism *er leidet an Rheuma*

suffice v.i.: ∾ it to say that *es mag genügen zu sagen, daß*

sugar I. n.: a ∾-daddy (sl.) *ein älterer Beschützer und Geldgeber einer Kokotte;* a ∾ plum *ein Zuckerplätzchen; etwas sehr Schönes.* — **II.** v.tr.: to ∾ (to gild) the pill *die Pille versüßen;* well, I'm ∾ed (sl.) *da bin ich aber platt!* — **III.** v.i.: to ∾ (sl.) *faulenzen, sich von (vor) der Arbeit drücken*

suggest I. v.tr.: it ∾ed itself to me *es kam mir in den Sinn;* he ∾ed a retreat (that they should retreat) *er schlug einen Rückzug vor;* I ∾ that *ich unterstelle (wage zu behaupten), daß*

suit I. n.: a ∾ at cards *eine der vier Farben beim Kartenspiel;* a ∾-case *ein Handkoffer;* a ∾ of clothes *ein Anzug;* a ∾ of dittos (colloq.) *ein Anzug aus gleichem Stoff;* a dress ∾ *ein Gesellschaftsanzug, Frack;* a law-∾, a ∾ at law *ein Prozeß;* to bring a ∾ against a person *j.em einen Prozeß machen;* to follow ∾ *Farbe bekennen (beim Kartenspiel); j.es Beispiel folgen;* to make a ∾ to a person *ein Gesuch an j.en richten;* to press (to push) one's ∾ *seinen Antrag (seine Werbung) nachdrücklich betreiben;* to prosper in one's ∾ *mit seinem Antrag (seiner Werbung) Glück haben.* — **II.** v.tr.: to be ∾ed to be (for) an artist *zum Künstler taugen;* to ∾ the action to the word *dem Wort die Tat folgen lassen;* red does not ∾ her complexion *rot steht ihrer Gesichtsfarbe nicht (paßt nicht zu ihrer Gesichtsfarbe);* mercy ∾s a king *Gnade steht einem König an;* it ∾s me (my book) to put up with him *es liegt in meinem Interesse (es paßt mir in den Kram), mit ihm vorliebzunehmen;* that ∾s me down to the ground *das paßt mir in jeder Hinsicht (ausgezeichnet);* to ∾ one's style to the audience *seinen Stil den Zuhörern anpassen;* that doesn't ∾ all tastes *das ist nicht nach jedermanns Geschmack;* ∾ yourself *tu, wie es dir beliebt (wie es dir am besten paßt).* — **III.** v.i.: that date will ∾ *das Datum wird passen (genehm sein);* to ∾ with a thing *zu etwas passen;* to be ∾ed with *etwas Passendes gefunden haben*

sulk n.: to be in the ∾s *schmollen, in schlechter Laune sein*

sum I. n.: in ∾ *kurz, in éinem Wort;* the ∾ and substance of his objections *Inhalt und Wesen seiner Einwendungen;* the ∾ total *die Gesamtsumme;* a lump ∾ *eine runde Summe;* he is good at ∾s *er kann gut rechnen;* the pupil must do his ∾s *der Schüler muß seine Rechenaufgaben machen.* — **II.** v.tr.: to ∾ up evidence *das Ergebnis der Beweisaufnahme zusammenfassen.* — **III.** v.i.: the judge ∾s up *der Richter gibt vor Schluß der Verhandlung eine Übersicht über den Fall*

summer n.: an Indian ∾ *ein Spät-, Altweibersommer*

summon v.tr.: to ∾ a conference *eine Konferenz einberufen;* to ∾ a witness *einen Zeugen vorladen;* to ∾ up one's courage to do (for) a deed *Mut fassen, sich zu einer Tat ermannen*

sun n.: his ∾ has (is) set *sein Stern (Glanz) ist erloschen;* against (with) the ∾ *gegen den (mit dem) Uhrzeiger;* to adore (to hail) the rising ∾ *sich bei einer neu aufkommenden Macht lieb Kind machen;* to have the ∾ in one's eye, to have been in the ∾shine (sl.) *betrunken (beduselt, beschwipst, angesäuselt) sein;* to hold a candle to the ∾ *etwas Überflüssiges tun;* to make hay while the ∾ shines *das Eisen schmieden, solange es (noch) heiß ist;* to see the ∾ *am Leben sein;* to take the ∾ *sich sonnen;* to take (to shoot) the ∾ *den Breitengrad nach der Höhe der Sonne bestimmen;* under the ∾ *auf Erden, unter der Sonne;* with the ∾ *mit Tagesanbruch*

Sunday n.: it took a month of ∾s *es dauerte eine Ewigkeit;* he was wearing his ∾ best *er trug seinen Sonntagsanzug*

sundry a.: all and ∾ *alle miteinander, allesamt*

sundries n.: *Verschiedenes, Diverses*

sunny a.: to be on the ∾ side of forty *noch nicht vierzig Jahre alt sein;* to look on the ∾ side of things *das Leben von der heiteren Seite nehmen*

sup I. v.i.: he must have a long spoon that ∾s with the devil (prov.) *mit dem Teufel paktieren ist gefährlich, mit hohen (großen) Herren ist nicht gut Kirschen essen;* to ∾ off cold meat *kalt(es Fleisch) zu Abend essen;* to ∾ with Pluto *sterben.* — **II.** n.: neither bit (bite) nor ∾ *weder einen Bissen noch einen Schluck*

superior I. a.: to remark with a ∾ air *mit überlegener Miene bemerken;* to be overcome by ∾ numbers *von der Übermacht überwältigt werden;* to be a very ∾ person *eine sehr herablassende (überhebliche) Person sein;* to be ∾ in speed to any other machine *jede andere Maschine an Geschwindigkeit übertreffen;* to be ∾ to bribery *über Bestechung erhaben sein;* to rise ∾ to one's sufferings *sich über seine Leiden erhaben zeigen.* — **II.** n.: he is my ∾ *er ist mein Vorgesetzter;* you are my ∾ in ability *du bist mir an Fähigkeiten überlegen, über;* he has no ∾ in courage *ihn übertrifft keiner an Mut;* the Mother (Lady) ∾ *die Oberin*

superlative n.: his talk is all ∾s *er übertreibt immer, redet immer in den höchsten Tönen*

supper n.: the Lord's Supper *das heilige Abendmahl;* to set a person his ∾ *j.em ein nicht nachahmbares (unübertreffbares) Kunststück vormachen*

supply I. v.tr.: to ∾ the loss *den Verlust ersetzen;* to ∾ the market *den Markt mit Waren beliefern;* to ∾ a long-felt want *einem lange empfundenen Bedürfnis abhelfen;* to ∾ oneself with provisions *sich verproviantieren.* — **II.** n.: to be in short ∾ of a thing *an einer Sache knapp sein;* ∾ and demand *Angebot und Nachfrage;* a ∾ teacher *ein Ersatzlehrer*

support I. v.tr.: to ∾ a family *eine Familie unterhalten (ernähren);* what ∾ed him was a good conscience *was ihn aufrecht hielt, war ein reines Gewissen;* the foundation ∾s the house *das Fundament trägt das Haus;* I cannot ∾ such insolence any longer *ich kann solche Frechheit nicht länger ertragen;* to ∾ a policy *eine Politik unterstützen.* — **II.** n.: to give ∾ to a cause (a person) *eine Sache (Person) unterstützen;* the troops kept in ∾ *die in Reserve gehaltenen Truppen;* to speak in ∾ of a resolution *zu Gunsten (zur Bekräftigung) einer Resolution sprechen*

suppose v.tr.: I ∾ so *ich nehme es an, vermutlich;* you will not be there, I ∾ *du wirst wohl nicht dort sein;* I don't ∾ he will come *ich nehme nicht an, daß er kommt; er wird wohl nicht kommen;* well, ∾ it were so *nun, angenommen, es wäre so;* ∾ we went for a walk *wie wäre es, wenn wir einen Spaziergang machten?;* that ∾s a creator *das setzt einen Schöpfer voraus;* he is ∾d to leave tomorrow *er soll morgen abreisen;* he is not ∾d to do that *es ist gar nicht seine Sache, das zu tun;* supposing black were white *angenommen, weiß wäre schwarz;* the ∾d king was a beggar *der angebliche König war ein Bettler*

sure I. a.: he is ∾ to come *er kommt sicher (bestimmt);* well I'm ∾! *da bin ich aber platt!;* I'm ∾ I didn't want to hurt you *ich wollte dir bestimmt nicht wehtun;* are you ∾? *wirklich nicht?;* to be ∾, she is not pretty *sie ist bestimmt (beileibe) keine Schönheit;* so it is, to be ∾! *wahrhaftig, es ist so!;* to be (to feel) ∾ of (about) a thing *einer Sache gewiß (sicher) sein;* be ∾ to go (and go) *vergiß ja nicht zu gehen (gehe ja);* I made ∾ of the facts *ich vergewisserte mich der Tatsachen;* I made ∾ that the door was locked *ich überzeugte (vergewisserte) mich, daß die Tür abgeschlossen war;* I made ∾ that he would come *ich erwartete bestimmt, daß er kommen würde;* ∾-footed *fest auf den Füßen.* — **II.** adv.: ∾! (U.S.) *sicher! jawohl!;* as ∾ as eggs is eggs, as ∾ as a gun, as ∾ as houses (colloq.) *so sicher, wie zweimal zwei vier ist, ganz bestimmt, todsicher, bombensicher;* I said it would be, and ∾ enough, it is *ich sagte, es würde so sein, und richtig, so kam es auch;* he will come ∾ enough *er wird schon kommen*

surely adv.: he knows full ∾ that *er weiß sehr wohl, daß;* it ∾ cannot have been he *er kann es doch nicht gewesen sein;* ∾ I have met you before *ich habe Sie doch schon mal kennen gelernt;* there is no truth in it, ∾ *daran ist doch sicher nichts Wahres*

surety n.: to stand ∾ *Sicherheit (Bürgschaft) leisten*

surface n.: on the ∾ of the matter *bei oberflächlicher Betrachtung;* his politeness is only on the ∾ *seine Höflichkeit ist nur oberflächlich*

surmount v.tr.: to ∾ a difficulty *eine Schwierigkeit überwinden;* peaks ∾ed with snow *schneebedeckte Gipfel*

surprise I. n.: what a ∾! *welche Überraschung!;* a ∾ visit *ein unangemeldeter Besuch;* to give a person a ∾, to spring a ∾ on a person *j.en überraschen;* to take a person by ∾ *j.en überraschen (überrumpeln).* — **II.** v.tr.: I shouldn't be ∾d *es sollte mich nicht wundern;* I am ∾d at your conduct *ich bin entrüstet über dein Benehmen;* I was ∾d into consent *ich wurde überrumpelt und sagte ja*

surrender I. v.tr.: to ∾ a fortress *eine Festung übergeben;* to ∾ hopes *die Hoffnungen aufgeben;* to ∾ an insurance policy *eine Versicherungspolice zurückkaufen;* to ∾ oneself to a habit *sich einer Gewohnheit hingeben.* — **II.** v.i.: to ∾ to one's bail *sich dem Gericht wieder stellen.* — **III.** n.: unconditional ∾ *bedingungslose Übergabe;* the ∾ value *der Rückkaufswert*

survival n.: the ∾ of the fittest *das Übrigbleiben der Lebenskräftigsten*

suspense n.: to keep a person in ∾ *j.en in Spannung (Ungewißheit) halten*

suspension n.: the ∾ of hostilities *die Einstellung der Feindseligkeiten;* a ∾ of payment *eine Zahlungseinstellung, ein -aufschub;* a ∾(-)bridge *eine Hängebrücke*

sustain v.tr.: to ∾ a claim *einen Anspruch aufrechterhalten;* to ∾ comparison with a thing *einen Vergleich mit etwas aushalten;* to ∾ a severe contusion *eine schwere Quetschung davontragen;* to ∾ a defeat, a loss *eine Niederlage, einen Verlust erleiden;* ∾ing food *nahrhafte Speisen*

swallow¹ v.tr.: see 'affront, bait, camel, word'; he will ∾ anything you tell him *er nimmt alles, was Sie ihm sagen, als bare Münze (hin)*

swallow² n.: one ∾ does not make a summer (prov.) *eine Schwalbe macht noch keinen Sommer*

swamp v.tr.: I am ∾ed with letters *ich werde mit Briefen überschüttet (überschwemmt)*

swan I. n.: all his geese are ∾s (prov.) *jedem Narren gefällt seine Kappe; bei ihm ist immer alles besser als bei anderen;* the Swan of Avon *Shakespeare.* — **II.** v.i.: to go ∾ning, to ∾ around (sl.) *eine Erkundungsfahrt, eine Spritztour machen*

swank v.i. (colloq.): to ∾ *aufschneiden, prahlen*

swanky a. (colloq.): a ∾ dress *ein elegantes, großartiges Kleid*

sway I. v.i.: the branches ∾ in the wind *die Äste wiegen sich im Winde.* — **II.** v.tr.: he ∾s the audience with his words *er beeinflußt das Publikum durch seine Rede;* to ∾ the sceptre *das Zepter führen.* — **III.** n.: under the ∾ of *unter dem Einfluß (Bann) von;* to hold ∾ over *herrschen über*

swear I. v.tr.: to ∾ an oath *einen Eid leisten;* to ∾ a person in *j.en vereidigen;* to ∾ off drink *dem Trunk abschwören.* — **II.** v.i.: to ∾ at a person *auf j.en fluchen, ihn beschimpfen;* to ∾ by all that is sacred *Stein und Bein schwören;* to ∾ by a remedy *auf ein Heilmittel schwören;* to ∾ on the Book *auf die Bibel schwören;* to ∾ like a trooper *wie ein Landsknecht fluchen;* to ∾ to something *etwas beschwören;* to ∾ to a person *die Identität j.es beschwören*

sweat I. n.: by the ∾ of one's brow *im Schweiße seines Angesichts;* to be in a (all of a) ∾ (colloq.) *schwitzen, von Schweiß triefen, schweißgebadet sein;* he is in a terrible ∾ (in a cold ∾) about it *er ist in höchster Sorge darum;* I cannot stand the ∾ of it *ich kann die Plackerei nicht aushalten.* — **II.** v.i.: to ∾ at a job *bei einer Arbeit sich abschinden (abplacken);* he shall ∾ for it *er soll mir dafür büßen.* — **III.** v.tr.: to ∾ a person *j.en für einen Hungerlohn arbeiten lassen;* ∾ed clothes *Kleider, die für einen Hungerlohn angefertigt worden sind*

sweep I. v.i.: the wind ∾s across (or: over) the plain *der Wind fegt (streicht, peitscht) über die Ebene;* the plain ∾s away to the sea *die Ebene zieht sich bis zum Meere hin;* new brooms ∾ clean (prov.) *neue Besen kehren gut;* the cavalry ∾s down on the enemy *die Kavallerie stürzt sich auf den Feind;* a ∾ing remark *eine umfassende, weittragende Bemerkung;* a ∾ing success *ein durchschlagender Erfolg;* a ∾ing victory *ein vollständiger Sieg, ein Sieg auf der ganzen Linie.* — **II.** v.tr.: to ∾ the board *alle Einsätze gewinnen, über-*

all Sieger sein, alle Gewinne einstreichen; einen Bombenerfolg haben; the battery ∾s the approaches *die Batterie bestreicht die Zufahrtswege;* to ∾ a constituency *fast alle Stimmen in einem Wahlbezirk erhalten;* his eyes swept the horizon *seine Augen glitten forschend über den Horizont;* to ∾ the seas *die Meere nach allen Richtungen befahren; die Meere vom Feinde säubern;* he swept his hand across his forehead *er strich (fuhr) mit der Hand über die Stirn;* he swept his audience along with him *er riß seine Zuhörer mit sich fort;* to ∾ away the cobwebs *das Spinnengewebe (hin)wegfegen;* the audience were swept off their feet *die Zuhörer waren überwältigt (hingerissen, ganz weg);* the plague swept off thousands *die Pest raffte Tausende dahin;* to ∾ up the crumbs *die Krümel zusammenfegen.* — **III.** n.: with a ∾ of his arm *mit einer weit ausladenden Armbewegung;* a ∾ of mountain country *eine ausgedehnte Gebirgslandschaft;* the river makes a great ∾ to the left *der Fluß macht einen großen Bogen nach links;* a fine ∾ (carriage-∾) leads to the house *eine prächtige Auffahrt führt zum Hause;* within (beyond) the ∾ of human intelligence *innerhalb (außerhalb) des Bereiches menschlicher Erkenntnis;* give it a thorough ∾, ∾ up *fege es gründlich aus;* to make a clean ∾ *reinen Tisch machen*

sweet I. a.: the air is ∾ with thyme *es duftet lieblich nach Thymian;* is the meat still ∾? *ist das Fleisch noch gut?;* to keep the room clean and ∾ *das Zimmer fein sauber halten;* I like my tea ∾ *ich trinke Tee gern süß;* I gave him a ∾ one (sl.) *ich versetzte ihm einen gehörigen Schlag;* he has a ∾ temper *er ist ein liebenswürdiger Mann;* he has a ∾ tooth *er ißt gern Süßigkeiten, er ist ein Leckermaul;* at one's own ∾ will *gerade wie (wann) es einem paßt;* to be ∾ upon a person *in j.en verliebt sein;* I like ∾bread *ich esse gern Kalbsbröschen, -milch(er);* she is my ∾heart *sie ist mein Schatz (Liebling, Herzchen);* a bed of ∾ peas *ein Beet Gartenwicken, Spanischer Wicken.* — **II.** n.: no ∾ without sweat (prov.) *ohne Fleiß kein Preis;* would you like a ∾? *möchtest du einen Bonbon haben?;* the ∾ and the bitter (∾s and bitters) of life *die Freuden und Leiden des Lebens;* the ∾s of office, of success *die Annehmlichkeiten (Vorteile) des Amtes, des Erfolges*

swell I. v.i.: to ∾ like a turkey-cock *sich aufplustern, (sich) dicke tun;* his wrist began to ∾ (out, up) *sein Handgelenk begann anzuschwellen;* to ∾ with pride *sich aufblähen vor Stolz.* — **II.** v.tr.: the toad ∾ed himself out to the size of an ox *die Kröte blähte sich zu einem Ochsen auf;* items ∾ the total *einzelne Posten vermehren die Gesamtsumme;* he suffers from ∾ed head *er leidet an Einbildung, er ist ein aufgeblasener Kerl.* — **III.** n.: he is a great ∾ (colloq.) *er ist ein großer Stutzer;* what a ∾ you are! (colloq.) *du bist aber pikfein angezogen!;* I met some ∾s at the party (colloq.) *ich traf einige hohe Herren bei der Einladung (in der Gesellschaft);* he is a great ∾ at tennis (colloq.) *er ist eine Kanone im (beim) Tennis;* the ∾ of the sea *die Dünung des Meeres.* — **IV.** a. (colloq.): ∾ clothes *Staatskleider;* a ∾ pianist *ein hervorragender Klavierspieler;* in ∾ society *in der vornehmen Gesellschaft;* he looks very ∾ *er sieht sehr gut angezogen aus;* it was ∾ *es war prima (knorke)*

swift a.: to be ∾ of foot *schnellfüßig sein;* he is ∾ to anger *er gerät leicht in Zorn;* be ∾ to hear, slow to speak (Epistle of James, I, 19) *sei schnell zu hören, langsam aber zu reden*

swim I. v.i.: everything swam before his eyes *alles drehte sich ihm vor den Augen;* my head ∾s, I have a ∾ming in the head *mir schwindelt;* she swam into the room *sie schwebte ins Zimmer;* to ∾ to the bottom (like a stone, a tailor's goose) *untergehen, wie eine bleierne Ente schwimmen;* to ∾ with the tide (stream) *mit dem Strome schwimmen;* her eyes were ∾ming with tears *ihre Augen flossen über vor (sie schwamm in) Tränen.* — **II.** v.tr.: I cannot ∾ a stroke *ich kann keinen Schlag schwimmen;* to ∾ one's horse across a river *zu Pferde einen Fluß durchschwimmen.* — **III.** n.: I'm going for a ∾ (to have, to take a ∾) *ich gehe schwimmen;* to be in the ∾ *auf dem laufenden (eingeweiht) sein;* to get the ∾ of a thing *hinter etwas kommen*

swing I. v.i.: to ∾ at anchor *schwaien, schwojen, sich um den Anker drehen;* he shall ∾ for it (colloq.) *dafür soll er gehängt werden (baumeln);* to ∾ into line *einschwenken;* the door swung open (swung to) *die Tür flog auf, schlug zu;* he swung out of the room *er stürzte aus dem Zimmer;*

the general opinion has swung round *die allgemeine Meinung ist umgeschlagen;* the song has a ∾ing chorus *das Lied hat einen schwungvollen Refrain.* — **II.** v.tr.: to ∾ one's arms *die Arme schlenkern;* there is no room to ∾ a cat *man kann sich hier kaum umdrehen;* to ∾ the lead (sl.) *sich vom (vor dem) Dienst drücken.* — **III.** n.: to be in full ∾ *in vollem Gange (im Zuge) sein;* to get into ∾ *in Schwung kommen;* to get into the ∾ of a thing *sich mit einer Sache vertraut machen;* to give full ∾ to a thing, to let a thing have its ∾ *einer Sache freien Lauf lassen;* this tune ought to go with a ∾ *diese Melodie müßte schwungvoll gesungen werden;* to lose on the roundabouts what you make on the ∾s *hier verlieren, was man dort gewonnen hat*

swipe I. v.i.: to ∾ at a ball *einen Ball weitausholend (kräftig) schlagen.* — **II.** v.tr.: to ∾ a ball *einen Ball kräftig schlagen;* he ∾d my pen (sl.) *er klaute (stibitzte) meinen Federhalter.* — **III.** n.: to give a ball a ∾ *einen Ball kräftig schlagen*

switch I. n.: a double-∾ *eine Doppelweiche;* a two-way ∾ *ein Wechselschalter;* a ∾-back railway *eine Berg- und Talbahn;* a ∾-board *eine Schalttafel;* she wears a ∾ *sie trägt einen falschen Knoten (einen „Willi").* — **II.** v.tr.: I ∾ed my head round *ich drehte schnell den Kopf herum;* he ∾ed it out of my hand *er riß es mir aus der Hand;* the cow ∾es her tail *die Kuh schlägt mit dem Schwanz;* we ∾ed on to the Salzburg Festival *wir hörten die Radioübertragung von den Salzburger Festspielen;* to ∾ off the wireless *das Radio abstellen;* to ∾ on the light *das Licht anknipsen.* — **III.** v.i.: he ∾ed off to another subject *er sprang auf ein anderes Thema über*

swoop I. v.i.: the eagle ∾s down upon its prey *der Adler stößt (schießt) auf seine Beute herab.* — **II.** v.tr.: he ∾ed up the lot *er schnappte alles weg.* — **III.** n.: at one fell ∾ (Macbeth IV, 3, 219) *mit einem wilden Griff (Schlegel-Tieck)*

swop, swap I. v.tr.: never ∾ horses while crossing the stream (in midstream) *man soll im kritischen Augenblick keine Änderung versuchen;* shall we ∾ places? *sollen wir die Plätze tauschen?* — **II.** n. (colloq.): shall we try a ∾? *sollen wir einen Tausch versuchen?*

sword n.: to be at ∾'s points with a person *j.em feindlich gegenüberstehen, feindlich gesinnt sein;* to cross (to measure) ∾s *die Degen kreuzen;* to put to the ∾ *über die Klinge springen lassen;* to put up (to sheathe) one's ∾ *den Degen (das Schwert) einstecken;* to throw one's ∾ into the scale *sein Schwert in die Wagschale werfen*

swot I. v.i. (sl.): to ∾ at a task *ochsen (pauken, büffeln).* — **II.** v.tr.: to ∾ (swat) a fly *eine Fliege (er)schlagen, zerquetschen;* to ∾ up a subject *sich (dat.) ein Fach einpauken.* — **III.** n.: it is too much ∾ *es ist eine zu große Büffelei (Paukerei)*

T

T n.: to a ∾ *bis auf's Tüpfelchen;* he hit it off to a ∾ *er hat es bis aufs Haar genau getroffen;* that suits me to a ∾ *das paßt mir ausgezeichnet;* to cross the ∾s *peinlich genau sein; einen Punkt unterstreichen;* to be marked with a ∾ *als Dieb* (= thief) *bekannt sein*

ta n.: you must say ∾ (nursery, colloq.) *sag schön danke!;* ∾-∾ (colloq.) *auf Wiedersehen!*

tab I. n.: to keep a ∾ (∾s) on a person (thing) (colloq.) *j.en (etwas) ständig beobachten, kontrollieren, j.em auf die Finger sehen.* — **II.** v.tr.: (colloq.) to ∾ something *etwas ordnen, vermerken*

tabby n.: an old ∾ (fam.) *eine (alte) Klatschbase*

table I. n.: the Lord's ∾ *das heilige Abendmahl;* the multiplication ∾ *das Einmaleins;* the two ∾s, the ∾s of the law *die Gesetzestafeln, die zehn Gebote;* to be upon the ∾ *jedermann bekannt sein;* to keep the ∾ amused *die Tischgesellschaft unterhalten;* she keeps a good ∾ *sie führt eine gute Küche;* to lay the ∾ *den Tisch decken;* to lay a report on the ∾ *einen Bericht zurückstellen, verschieben;* to sit at ∾ *bei Tisch, beim Essen sitzen;* to sit down to ∾ *sich zu Tisch setzen;* to turn the ∾s on a person *den Spieß gegen j.en umdrehen;* the ∾s are turned *das Blatt (Blättchen) hat sich gewendet;* a ∾-spoon *ein Eßlöffel;* ∾-talk *Tischgespräch, leichte Unterhaltung.* — **II.** v.tr.: to ∾ a measure *einen Antrag auf den Tisch des Hauses legen, einen Antrag vorbringen*

tabloid n.: ∾ journalism *konzentrierte, sensationelle Zeitungsberichte*

tabula rasa n.: to make ∾ of something *mit etwas reinen Tisch machen, völlig aufräumen*

tace v.i.: ∾ is Latin for the candle (prov.) *schweig!*

tacit a.: with ∾ consent *mit stillschweigender Billigung*

tack I. n.: hard ∾ *Schiffszwieback;* soft ∾ *Brot, gutes Essen;* you are on the wrong ∾ *du bist auf dem Holzwege;* to get down to brass ∾s (colloq.) *zur Hauptsache kommen;* to get on a new ∾ *einen neuen Plan ersinnen.* — **II.** v.tr.: to ∾ a thing to (on to) another *etwas an eine andere Sache anhängen, -heften, -schließen.* — **III.** v.i.: he keeps on ∾ing *er ändert ständig sein Verhalten, er laviert*

tackle I. v.tr.: to ∾ an opponent *einen Gegner angreifen;* to ∾ a problem *ein Problem anpacken.* — **II.** v.i.: we must ∾ to it *wir müssen uns kräftig dranmachen.* — **III.** n.: fishing-∾ *Angelgerät;* shaving-∾ *Rasierzeug*

Taffy n.: (colloq.) a ∾ *ein Walliser*

tag I. n.: shoe ∾s *Schnürsenkel;* a Latin ∾ *ein bekannter lateinischer Ausspruch;* ∾ *(Kinderspiel) Nachlaufen.* — **II.** v.tr.: to ∾ the trunks *die Koffer mit Etiketten versehen.* — **III.** v.i.: to ∾ after someone, to ∾ around with someone *j.em überall(hin) nachlaufen*

tail I. n.: with his ∾ between his legs *ganz betreten, bedeppert, mit eingezogenem Schwanz, wie ein begossener Pudel;* he is ∾s up *er ist gut gelaunt, quietschvergnügt;* heads or ∾s *Kopf oder Wappen;* the sting is in the ∾ *das dicke Ende kommt nach;* to tread on the ∾s of a person's coat *j.en ärgern, beleidigen, reizen, ihm auf den Schlips (Schwanz) treten;* to turn ∾ *Reißaus nehmen, Fersengeld geben;* to twist a person's ∾ *j.en ärgern, reizen;* to wear ∾s *einen Frack tragen.* — **II.** v.tr.: to ∾ gooseberries *die Stiele von Stachelbeeren entfernen;* a detective is ∾ing him *ein Detektiv folgt ihm ständig.* — **III.** v.i.: to ∾ after a person *j.em dicht auf den Fersen folgen;* to ∾ away (∾ off) *abnehmen, allmählich kleiner werden;* a ship ∾s to the tide *ein Schiff steigt und fällt mit der Flut*

tailor I. n.: nine ∾s go to a man (prov.) *neun Schneider kommen auf einen Mann;* he rides like a ∾ *er reitet wie ein Mehlsack;* a ∾'s goose *ein Bügeleisen;* to swim like a ∾'s goose *untergehen, wie eine bleierne Ente schwimmen.* — **II.** v.tr.: a well-∾ed suit *ein gut gearbeiteter Anzug*

take I. v.tr.: see 'action, advantage, affront, aim, air, alarm, bad, bait, etc.'; England can ∾ it *England kann die Schläge schon aushalten;* I ∾ it to be a good thing *ich denke (finde), es ist etwas Gutes;* as I ∾ it *wie ich es verstehe (auffasse); meiner Meinung nach;* I'm going to ∾ it easy *ich werde mich nicht überanstrengen, werde mir die Sache bequem machen;* you may ∾ it from me *du kannst es mir glauben, du kannst es dir gesagt sein lassen;* it ∾s a strong man to do that *dazu gehört ein starker Mann;* it will ∾ you hours to do that *du wirst Stunden dazu brauchen;* to ∾ a back seat *in den Hintergrund treten;* that ∾s the cake (biscuit) (colloq.) *das übertrifft alles;* to ∾ the count (colloq.) *sterben;* to ∾ cover *in Deckung gehen;* to ∾ (to) flight *davonlaufen;* to ∾ fright *scheu werden;* ∾ heed of what I say *beachte meine Worte;* to ∾ (one's) orders from someone *Aufträge von j.em an-, entgegennehmen; j.em unterstellt sein;* to ∾ (Holy) Orders *Priester werden;* to ∾ the pledge *das Versprechen abgeben, keinen Alkohol mehr anzurühren;* to ∾ silk (legal) *King's Counsel werden;* to ∾ umbrage at something *etwas übelnehmen, über etwas beleidigt sein, Anstoß an etwas nehmen;* to ∾ a dim (or: poor) view of something (colloq.) *etwas mißbilligen;* to ∾ the wind out of someone's sails *j.em den Wind aus den Segeln nehmen; j.en dadurch seines Vorteils berauben, daß man ihm zuvorkommt und das tut, was der andere (zu tun) beabsichtigte.* — with prep. and adv.: to be ∾n aback *bestürzt, überrascht, verblüfft werden;* to ∾ along *mitnehmen;* to ∾ a thing amiss *etwas übelnehmen;* I will ∾ it at that *ich will es mal glauben;* to ∾ a person at his word *j.en beim Wort nehmen;* to ∾ a person by surprise *j.en überraschen (überrumpeln);* to ∾ a person by the throat *j.en an die Kehle (Gurgel) packen;* to ∾ down *niederschreiben;* to ∾ someone down a peg *j.es Stolz demütigen;* to ∾ a person for another *j.en für einen anderen halten, mit einem anderen verwechseln;* to ∾ a person for a fool *j.en für einen Narren halten;* to ∾ a thing for granted *etwas als (für) ausgemacht (selbstverständlich, erwiesen) annehmen;* to ∾ in a newspaper *eine Zeitung halten;* to ∾ a person in *j.en anführen (beschwindeln);* to ∾ a person in to dinner *j.en zu Tisch führen;* to ∾ something in good part *etwas gutwillig anerkennen, ohne beleidigt zu sein;* it was a great ∾-in *es war ein großer Schwindel;* to ∾ a thing in *eine Sache überschauen, verstehen;* to ∾ a thing in hand *etwas in die Hand nehmen, etwas unter-, übernehmen;* to ∾ in lodgers *Zimmer vermieten;* to ∾ in marriage *zur Frau nehmen;* to ∾ in sail *seine ehrgeizigen Pläne zurückschrauben, die Segel einziehen (fig.);* thou shall not ∾ the Name of the Lord thy God in vain *du sollst den Namen des Herrn deines Gottes nicht mißbrauchen;* he had ∾n it into his head *er hatte es sich in den Kopf gesetzt;* to ∾ into account *in Betracht ziehen;* to ∾ off one's hat to someone *j.en bewundern, vor ihm den Hut ziehen;* to ∾ oneself off *sich fortmachen;* to ∾ a person off *j.en nachmachen, ihn aufziehen, karikieren;* it was a clever ∾-off *es war eine geschickte Karikatur;* to ∾ a thing off a person's hands *j.em etwas abnehmen;* to ∾ on a bet *eine Wette annehmen;* to ∾ on a task *eine Aufgabe übernehmen;* to ∾ a person on *j.en in Dienst nehmen, einstellen;* to ∾ a person on at a game *zu einem Spiel mit j.em antreten;* we will ∾ the story on trust *wir werden (wollen) der Geschichte Glauben schenken;* to ∾ it out at tennis *sich durch Tennis Bewegung verschaffen;* the exertion took it out of me *die Anstrengung hat mich erschöpft;* I took it out in cigars and drinks *ich habe mich an Zigarren und Getränken schadlos gehalten;* to ∾ out a policy on one's life *eine Lebensversicherung abschließen;* to ∾ a person to task for a thing *j.en wegen einer Sache zur Rede stellen, ins Gebet nehmen, ihm die Leviten lesen, ihm aufs Dach steigen;* to ∾ up a job *eine Beschäftigung (Stelle) antreten;* to ∾ up one's quarters *sich irgendwo einquartieren;* to ∾ up the running *die Führung übernehmen, das Tempo angeben;* to ∾ up sailing *sich dem Segelsport widmen;* to ∾ up a person short *j.en unterbrechen;* it ∾s up all my time *es nimmt meine ganze Zeit in Anspruch;* to be ∾n up with a subject *mit einer Sache beschäftigt, in eine Sache vertieft sein;* to ∾ it upon oneself to do a thing *es übernehmen (es wagen), etwas zu tun;* he is quite ∾n with it *er ist ganz entzückt davon;* to be ∾n with malaria *an Malaria erkranken;* to be ∾n with sadness *von Trauer ergriffen werden.* — **II.** v.i.: the play will not ∾ *das Stück wird nicht ziehen;* that won't ∾ with me *damit wirst du bei mir kein Glück haben; das verfängt (zieht) bei mir nicht;* the vaccination did not ∾ *die Impfung war ohne Erfolg, ist nicht angegangen.* — with prep. & adv.: he ∾s after his father *er gleicht seinem Vater, er schlägt seinem Vater nach;* such faults do not ∾ from his credit as a historian *solche Fehler tun seiner Glaubwürdigkeit als Historiker keinen Abbruch;* to be ∾n ill of (with) a disease *krank sein, werden; an einem Leiden erkranken;* the plane ∾s off *das Flugzeug steigt auf;* don't ∾ on so *reg' dich nicht so auf, stell' dich nicht so an!;* to ∾ over from a person *j.en ablösen;* to ∾ to one's bed, legs, heels see 'bed, leg, heel'; he has ∾n to doing that *das hat er sich angewöhnt, er hat sich darauf gelegt;* to ∾ to drink *sich dem Trunk ergeben;* he has ∾n to the habit *er hat es sich (dat.) angewöhnt, er pflegt es zu tun;* to ∾ to a person *Gefallen an j.em finden, sich zu j.em hingezogen fühlen;* to ∾ to the road *Landstreicher werden;* to ∾ up with a fashion *eine Mode mitmachen;* to ∾ up with a person *mit j.em verkehren, anbändeln;* he ∾s well *er läßt sich gut photographieren, ist photogen.* — **III.** n.: the fishermen had a good ∾ *die Fischer hatten einen guten Fang*

taking I. n.: he was in a great ∾ (arch.) *er war in großer Aufregung.* — **II.** a.: she is very ∾ *sie ist sehr anziehend*

tale n.: and thereby hangs a ∾ (Shakespeare, As You like It, II, 7, 28) *und daran hängt ein Märlein (Schlegel);* to tell the ∾ *eine rührselige Geschichte erzählen, um Mitleid zu erwecken;* to tell ∾s (out of school) *klatschen, petzen;* that tells its own ∾ *das spricht für sich selbst;* I prefer to tell my own ∾ *ich ziehe es vor, meine eigene Version davon zu geben;* a ∾-bearer *eine Klatschbase;* dead men tell no ∾s (prov.) *tote Hunde beißen nicht*

talk I. v.i.: now you are ∾ing *jetzt redest du vernünftig; das lasse ich mir gefallen;* to ∾ big, tall *sich dicke tun, an-*

geben; to ∾ at a person *indirekt Bemerkungen gegen j.en machen, auf ihn sticheln;* ∾ing of meals, what time do you have supper? *da wir gerade von Mahlzeiten sprechen (zum Thema Mahlzeiten), wann eßt Ihr zu Abend?;* to ∾ over a plan *einen Plan ausführlich besprechen;* to ∾ through one's hat *übertreiben, prahlen, angeben, Unsinn reden;* ∾ up! *sprich lauter!* — **II.** v.tr.: to ∾ a person's head off *j.en durch vieles Reden ermüden; j.en dumm und dämlich reden;* he would ∾ the hind leg off a donkey *er redet dem Teufel ein Bein aus, er redet einen tot (dusselig);* he ∾s nineteen to the dozen *er schwatzt unaufhörlich (das Blaue vom Himmel herunter);* to ∾ shop *fachsimpeln;* to ∾ (cold) turkey (U.S.) *die nackte, ungeschminkte Wahrheit sagen;* I don't want to be ∾ed about *ich möchte nicht ins Gerede kommen;* to ∾ away the time *die Zeit verschwatzen;* to ∾ a person down *j.en durch Reden zum Schweigen bringen, niederschreien, unter den Tisch reden;* to ∾ a person over (round, up) *j.en überreden.* — **III.** n.: there is ∾ of building a bridge *es ist die Rede davon, daß eine Brücke gebaut wird (werden soll);* it will end in ∾ *es wird beim Reden bleiben;* to have a ∾ with a person *sich mit j.em unterhalten;* they are the ∾ of the town *sie bilden das Stadtgespräch*

talkies n.: to go to the ∾ *zum Tonfilm, ins Kino gehen*

talking-point n.: a ∾ *ein (Diskussions-) Thema*

talking-to n. (colloq.): to give someone a (good) ∾ *j.em ins Gewissen reden*

tall I. a.: how ∾ are you? *wie groß bist du?;* a ∾-boy *eine Kommode mit Aufsatz;* that is a ∾ order (colloq.) *das ist sehr viel verlangt;* a ∾ story (colloq.) *eine unglaubhafte Geschichte.* — **II.** adv.: to talk ∾ (colloq.) *prahlen, angeben.*

tally n.: to buy by the ∾ *im großen einkaufen.* — **II.** v.i.: the two stories ∾ with each other *die beiden Erzählungen stimmen (miteinander) überein.* — **III.** a.: to live ∾, to make a ∾ bargain *in Onkelehe leben*

tam-o'-shanter n.: to wear a ∾ *eine schottische Mütze (Art Baskenmütze) tragen*

tamper v.i.: the guard had been ∾ed with *die Wache war bestochen worden;* he ∾ed with the will *er hat an dem Testament herumgepfuscht (es gefälscht);* the lock had evidently been ∾ed with *offenbar hat j. versucht, das Schloß zu öffnen*

tan v.tr.: I'll ∾ his hide (colloq.) *ich werde ihn verprügeln*

tangent n.: to fly (to go off) at a ∾ *plötzlich vom Thema abspringen*

tangle I. n.: to be all in a ∾ *ganz verwickelt, verwirrt sein.* — **II.** a.: ∾-foot (sl.) *Alkohol, Whisky*

tansy n.: like a ∾ (arch.) *vollkommen, in bester Ordnung*

tantamount a.: his message was ∾ to a flat refusal *seine Botschaft lief auf eine glatte Weigerung hinaus*

tantrum n.: she is in (went into) her ∾s *sie hat ihren Koller (Rappel) bekommen, ist in Wut geraten*

tap[1] I. n.: it is an excellent ∾ *es ist ein ausgezeichnetes Gebräu;* I found him in the ∾ (∾-room) *ich fand ihn in der Schankstube;* beer on ∾ *Bier vom Faß.* — **II.** v.tr.: he ∾ped his claret (sl.) *er schlug ihn auf die Nase, daß sie blutete;* to ∾ a person for a thing *j.en um etwas angehen;* to ∾ telegraph wires, the telephone wire *Telegramme abfangen, Telefongespräche mithören*

tap[2] I. v.tr.: to ∾ a person on the shoulder *j.em auf die Schulter klopfen;* to ∾ a shoe *einen Flecken auf einen Schuh setzen.* — **II.** v.i.: to ∾ at the door *an die Tür klopfen.* — **III.** n.: I heard a ∾ at the door *ich hörte j.en an die Tür klopfen*

tape I. n.: red ∾ *Bürokratismus, Amtsschimmel;* to break (to breast) the ∾ *beim Wettlauf durchs Ziel gehen;* a ∾-measure *ein Bandmaß;* a ∾ worm *ein Bandwurm.* — **II.** v.tr.: I've got you ∾d *ich habe dich richtig eingeschätzt; ich weiß, was du willst;* to ∾ a book *ein Buch heften;* to ∾ off *mit einem Bandmaß ausmessen*

taper v.tr. & i.: to ∾ off *zuspitzen; spitz zulaufen*

tapis n.: to be (to come) on the ∾ *auf dem Tapet sein, aufs Tapet kommen, erörtert werden*

tar I. n.: he has a touch (or: lick) of the ∾-brush *er hat Negerblut in den Adern.* — **II.** v.tr.: to ∾ and feather *teeren und federn als Lynchjustiz;* they are both

∾red with the same brush *sie haben beide dieselben Fehler*

target n.: the coal ∾ was not reached (attained) *die geplante Kohlenförderung wurde nicht erreicht*

tart I. a.: a ∾ rejoinder *eine beißende, schroffe Antwort.* — **II.** n.: she is a ∾ (sl.) *sie ist eine Dirne*

Tartar n.: to catch a ∾ *an den Unrechten kommen, übel ankommen*

task I. n.: to set a person a ∾ *j.em eine Aufgabe stellen;* to take a person to ∾ for a thing *j.en wegen einer Sache zur Rede stellen, ins Gebet nehmen, ihm die Leviten lesen, ihm aufs Dach steigen.* — **II.** v.tr.: that ∾s his powers *das nimmt seine Kräfte in Anspruch*

taste n.: in good ∾ *geschmackvoll;* in bad ∾ *geschmacklos, unfein;* there is no accounting for ∾s (prov.) *über (den) Geschmack läßt sich nicht streiten;* to leave a bad ∾ in the mouth *einen üblen Nachgeschmack im Munde hinterlassen;* it is sweet to the ∾ *es schmeckt süß;* will you have a ∾ of this? *wollen Sie dieses mal probieren?;* he has a ∾ for ivory carvings *er hat eine Vorliebe für Elfenbeinschnitzereien*

tattoo n.: to beat the Devil's ∾ *ungeduldig mit den Fingern auf dem Tisch trommeln*

taxi n.: a ∾-dancer *ein(e) berufsmäßige(r) Tanzpartner(in) (in Tanzsälen)*

tea n.: that's not my cup of ∾ (sl.) *das ist nicht nach meinem Geschmack, daraus mache ich mir nichts;* (to have) high ∾ *eine Abendmahlzeit mit Tee und Fleischgerichten (einnehmen);* a storm in a ∾-cup *ein Sturm im Wasserglase;* a ∾-fight (colloq.) *eine Teegesellschaft, -schlacht*

team v.i.: to ∾ up with someone *mit j.em gemeinsam arbeiten*

tear[1] I. v.tr.: to ∾ one's hair *sich (dat.) die Haare raufen;* to ∾ someone off a strip (sl.) *j.en zurechtstauchen, anschnauzen;* that's torn it! (sl.) *da haben wir die Bescherung, den Salat;* to ∾ up *zerreißen, ausreißen (= zerren).* — **II.** v.i.: he tore down the hill *er raste den Berg hinunter;* he tore off *er rannte (raste) los.* — **III.** n.: the wear and ∾ *die natürliche Abnutzung*

tear[2] n.: in ∾s *unter Tränen;* to burst into ∾s *in Tränen ausbrechen*

teaser n. (colloq.): that is a ∾ *das ist eine schwierige Frage, eine harte Nuß*

teem v.i.: the book ∾s with blunders *das Buch strotzt (wimmelt) von Fehlern;* fish ∾ in these waters *es wimmelt von Fischen in diesen Gewässern*

teens n.pl.: she is in her ∾s, she is a teenager *sie ist zwischen 13 und 19*

teetotaller n.: he is a ∾ *er ist Abstinenzler*

telephone n.: are you on the ∾ ('phone)? *haben Sie Telefon?;* the ∾-exchange *das Fernsprechamt*

tell I. v.tr.: to ∾ one's beads *den Rosenkranz beten;* to ∾ a person his fortune *j.em wahrsagen;* he ∾s over his gold every night *er zählt jeden Abend sein Gold nach;* ∾ that to the horse-marines! *das kannst du deiner Großmutter erzählen!;* ∾ it not in Gath (joc. cf. 2 Samuel I, 20) *sag' kein Wort davon, häng es nicht an die große Glocke!;* to ∾ a lie, stories, tales, the truth, see 'lie[1], story, tale, truth'; ∾ me another! (sl.) *ach geh'! Unsinn!;* you're ∾ing me! (sl.) *das brauchst du mir nicht zu sagen (zu erzählen), das weiß ich schon längst;* to ∾ the tale *eine rührselige Geschichte erzählen, um Mitleid zu erwecken;* he told me of (about) his difficulties *er erzählte mir von seinen Schwierigkeiten;* you cannot ∾ the two apart, one from the other *man kann die beiden nicht unterscheiden;* to ∾ the votes *die Stimmen im Parlament zählen;* I can ∾ you, it is not so easy *ich kann dir sagen (versichern), es ist nicht so leicht;* I'll ∾ you what *ich will dir (et)was sagen;* I told you so *ich habe es dir ja gleich gesagt;* we were 15 men all told *wir waren im ganzen 15 Mann;* I was told off to get fuel *ich wurde abkommandiert, Brennmaterial zu holen;* to ∾ a person off (sl.) *j.en anschnauzen, abkanzeln, ihm aufs Dach steigen, den Marsch blasen;* I'll ∾ the world (sl.) *dessen bin ich (ganz) sicher!* — **II.** v.i.: every blow ∾s *jeder Schlag sitzt;* you never can ∾ *man kann nie wissen;* how can you ∾? *wie kannst du es wissen?;* for all we can ∾ *soviel wir wissen;* experience ∾s against it *die Erfahrung spricht dagegen;* that ∾s for his abilities *das spricht für seine Fähigkeiten;* the strain begins to ∾ on him *die Anstrengung beginnt, sich nachteilig auf ihn auszuwirken;* don't ∾ on me (childish) *verrate, verpetze mich nicht!*

telling I. a.: with ∾ effect *mit durchschlagendem Erfolg.* — **II.** n.: the story loses nothing in the ∾ *die Geschichte verliert nichts an Wert beim Lesen;* there's no ∾ what may happen *man kann nicht sagen, was geschehen wird*

telltale I. n.: she is a ∾ *sie ist eine Zwischenträgerin, Klatschbase;* the ∾ blushes *das verräterische Erröten*

temper I. v.tr.: to ∾ justice with mercy *Gerechtigkeit mit Gnade mildern;* God ∾s the wind to the shorn lamb (prov.) *Gott legt niemandem mehr auf, als er tragen kann;* a good-(a cross-)∾ed man *ein gut gelaunter, ein verdrießlicher Mensch.* — **II.** n.: a fit of ∾ *ein Zornesausbruch, Wutanfall;* to be in a ∾, out of ∾ *schlecht gelaunt, böse, zornig sein;* to be of placid ∾ *von sanftem Temperament sein;* I found him in a good ∾ *ich traf ihn in guter Laune;* to get into a ∾ *böse, zornig werden;* to keep (to control) one's ∾ *die Ruhe bewahren, ruhig bleiben;* to lose one's ∾ *böse, zornig, heftig werden;* to show one's ∾ *seine üble Laune zeigen*

temperance a.: a ∾ hotel *ein alkoholfreies Hotel;* the ∾ movement *die Abstinenz-, Blaukreuzbewegung*

ten n.: ∾ to one he forgets it *zehn zu eins: er vergißt es; er vergißt es totsicher;* the upper ∾ *die oberen Zehntausend*

tend v.i.: the road ∾s downwards *die Straße führt ins Tal;* it ∾s to the same effect *es zielt auf dieselbe Wirkung;* it will ∾ to make him careful *es wird dazu dienen, ihn vorsichtig zu machen*

tender[1] I. v.tr.: to ∾ money as payment *Geld als Bezahlung anbieten;* to ∾ an oath to a person *j.em einen Eid zuschieben;* to ∾ one's resignation *sein Rücktrittsgesuch einreichen;* to ∾ one's thanks *(j.em) seinen Dank aussprechen.* — **II.** v.i.: to ∾ for the execution of a work *ein Angebot auf Ausführung einer Arbeit einreichen, sich an einer Ausschreibung beteiligen.* — **III.** n.: to make a ∾ *einen Kostenanschlag einreichen;* legal ∾ *gesetzliches Zahlungsmittel*

tender[2] a.: of ∾ age *im zarten Alter;* ∾-hearted *gütig, weichherzig;* to be left to the ∾ mercies of one's enemies *seinen Feinden auf Gnade und Ungnade ausgeliefert sein;* to be ∾ of doing the wrong thing *sich fürchten (sich hüten), etwas Unrechtes zu tun;* to be ∾ of one's good name *auf seinen Ruf bedacht sein;* it is a ∾ subject *es ist ein heikles Thema*

tenner n. (colloq.): can you change me a ∾? *kannst du mir eine Zehnpfundnote wechseln?*

tenor n.: the even ∾ of his life *der (ruhige) Verlauf seines Lebens;* the ∾ of his speech *der Sinn (Inhalt, Ténor) seiner Rede*

tenterhooks n.: to be on ∾ *wie auf heißen Kohlen sitzen*

term I. n.: what are your ∾s? *welches sind Ihre Preise, Bedingungen?;* his ∾s are 10 shillings a lesson *er nimmt 10 Sh. für die Stunde;* not on any (upon no) ∾s *unter keiner Bedingung;* during ∾(-time) *während des Semesters;* on easy ∾s *zu günstigen Bedingungen;* the exact ∾s of the pact *der genaue Wortlaut des Vertrages;* in the most flattering ∾s *in den schmeichelhaftesten Ausdrücken;* it runs in the following ∾s *es lautet folgendermaßen;* inclusive ∾s *ein Preis, in dem alles eingeschlossen ist;* in plain (round) ∾s *rund herausgesagt;* he spoke in ∾s of approval *er äußerte sich beifällig darüber;* in ∾s of the Bible *in der Sprache der Bibel;* the ∾s of delivery *die Lieferungsbedingungen;* for a ∾ of five years *auf die Dauer von fünf Jahren;* his ∾ of office expired *seine Amtszeit ging zu Ende;* the ∾s of reference *der Untersuchungsbereich;* to be on good (bad, familiar, strained) ∾s with a person *mit j.em auf gutem (schlechtem, vertrautem, gespanntem) Fuße stehen;* we are not on visiting ∾s *wir stehen nicht auf Besuchsfuße;* we are not on speaking ∾s *wir sprechen nicht miteinander;* to bring a person to ∾s *j.en zwingen, Bedingungen anzunehmen;* to come to (to make) ∾s with a person *sich mit j.em einigen, vergleichen.* — **II.** v.tr.: he ∾ed it sheer robbery *er bezeichnete es als reinsten Raub*

terror n.: here comes this ∾ again (colloq.) *da kommt wieder diese Blage (dieses lästige Kind);* the king of ∾s (Job XVIII, 14) *der König des Schreckens, der Tod;* to strike a person with ∾, to strike ∾ into a person *j.em Schrecken einflößen;* ∾-stricken, ∾-struck *von Schrecken ergriffen*

test I. n.: it was a crucial ∾ *es war eine scharfe Prüfung, Feuerprobe;* success is not a fair ∾ *Erfolg ist kein gerechter Prüfungsmaßstab;* to apply a severe ∾ to a thing *etwas einer schweren Probe unterziehen;* to put a thing to the ∾ *etwas auf die Probe stellen;* to stand the ∾ *die Probe bestehen;* a ∾-match *ein internationales Kricketspiel;* a ∾-tube *ein Reagenzglas.* — **II.** v.tr.: to ∾ a thing *etwas prüfen, auf die Probe stellen;* that ∾s his powers of endurance *das stellt seine Ausdauer auf eine harte Probe;* ∾ed by *gemessen an*

testate a.: to die ∾ *mit Hinterlassung eines Testaments sterben*

testimonial n.: to give a person a ∾ *j.m ein Zeugnis ausstellen;* to present a person with a ∾ *j.em ein Ehrengeschenk überreichen*

testimony n.: in ∾ whereof *urkundlich, zum Zeugnis dessen;* to bear ∾ to a thing *von einer Sache Zeugnis ablegen;* to call a person in ∾ *j.en zum Zeugen aufrufen;* to produce ∾ to (of) a thing *Beweise für etwas erbringen*

tether I. n.: he was beyond (or: at the end of) his ∾ *er war am Ende seiner Kraft; er wußte nicht mehr ein noch aus.* — **II.** v.tr.: to ∾ a grazing animal to a post *ein weidendes Tier an einen Pfosten anbinden*

text n.: to stick to one's ∾ *bei der Sache bleiben, nicht abschweifen*

Thames n.pr.: he will never set the ∾ on fire *er hat das Pulver nicht erfunden*

than conj.: you are taller ∾ he is *du bist größer als er;* a man ∾ whom no one is better able to judge *ein Mann wie kein anderer befähigt, darüber zu urteilen*

thank I. v.tr.: ∾ God! *Gott sei Dank!;* would you like some more tea? ∾ you; no, ∾ you *möchten Sie noch etwas Tee? Bitte; nein, danke;* ∾ you for that ball *werfen Sie bitte den Ball her;* ∾ you for nothing (iron.) *dafür danke ich schönstens; ich danke für Obst und Südfrüchte;* I will ∾ you to shut the door *machen Sie gefälligst die Tür zu;* he may ∾ himself (he has only himself to ∾) for that *das hat er sich selbst zuzuschreiben;* you may ∾ your lucky stars that I came *du kannst von Glück sagen, daß ich gekommen bin.* — **II.** n.: ∾s, many ∾s; no ∾s *danke, bitte; vielen Dank; nein, danke;* ∾s be to God, ∾ Goodness, ∾ Heaven! *Gott sei Dank!;* small ∾s I got for it *ich habe wenig Dank dafür geerntet;* in ∾s for *zum Dank (als Dank) für;* ∾s to my foresight *dank meiner Voraussicht;* no ∾s to him though *obgleich es nicht ihm zu verdanken (nicht sein Verdienst) ist;* declined with ∾s *dankend abgelehnt (verbeten);* to give (to return) ∾s *Dank sagen, abstatten*

thankful a.: I'm ∾ he's gone *ich bin froh, daß er weg(gegangen) ist*

thankless a.: a ∾ task *eine undankbare Aufgabe*

that I. a.: he has ∾ confidence in his theory *er hat ein derartiges Zutrauen zu seiner Theorie;* he was wounded to ∾ degree that he resigned *er fühlte sich so verletzt, daß er zurücktrat;* ∾ house over there *das Haus da drüben.* — **II.** pron.: help me, ∾'s a dear *sei so lieb und hilf mir;* I lent, ∾ is to say, I gave him the money *ich borgte, d. h. schenkte, ihm das Geld;* ∾'s it, ∾'s right *so ist es recht, jawohl;* what was ∾ noise, what noise was ∾? *was war das für ein Lärm?;* so ∾'s ∾ *das wäre es, und damit Schluß, basta;* at ∾, he opened the door *darauf öffnete er die Tür;* he lost an arm, and the right arm at ∾ *er verlor einen Arm, und noch dazu den rechten;* I will take it at ∾ *ich will es mal glauben;* for all ∾, I like him *trotz alledem mag ich ihn gern;* I wouldn't give ∾ for it *ich gäbe nicht so viel (das, ein Fingerschnippen) drum;* don't talk like ∾ *rede nicht so;* to put this and ∾ together *eins zum anderen nehmen, seine Schlüsse ziehen, sich (dat.) etwas zusammenreimen;* to speak of this, ∾, and the other *von allen möglichen Dingen reden;* all (everything, much, the best) ∾ *alles (viel, das beste), was;* no one ∾ I knew *keiner, den ich kannte.* — **III.** adv.: I was ∾ angry, I could have struck him (colloq.) *ich war derartig (so) böse, ich hätte ihn schlagen können;* I will go ∾ far (colloq.) *soweit will ich gehen;* I have done ∾ much (colloq.) *soviel habe ich getan.* — **IV.** conj.: there is no doubt (∾) he meant it *er hat es zweifellos gemeint;* he withdrew (in order) ∾ the dispute might cease *er zog* *sich zurück, damit der Streit aufhörte;* not ∾ I have any objection *nicht, daß ich etwas dagegen hätte;* (O) ∾ I knew the truth! *wenn ich nur die Wahrheit wüßte!;* (O) ∾ ∾ were all! *wenn das nur alles wäre!;* now ∾ you know the address *jetzt, wo du die Adresse kennst*

thaw n.: a ∾ has set in *Tauwetter hat eingesetzt*

the I. def. art.: it is ∾ book of the day *es ist d a s Buch des Tages;* he is no relation of ∾ Browning *er ist nicht mit dem berühmten Browning verwandt.* — **II.** adv.: so much ∾ better (∾ worse) *um so besser (schlimmer);* ∾ more ∾ merrier *je mehr Personen, desto lustiger;* I am none (not any) ∾ better for the medicine *es geht mir keineswegs besser nach der Medizin;* I am none (not) ∾ more inclined to help him because he is poor *ich bin durchaus nicht geneigt, ihm zu helfen, bloß weil er arm ist;* one hope ∾ poorer *um eine Hoffnung ärmer*

theatre n.: the ∾ of war *der Kriegsschauplatz;* the operating ∾ *der Operationssaal*

then I. adv.: but ∾ I can't remember *aber andererseits kann ich mich nicht erinnern;* now and ∾ *dann und wann, hin und wieder, von Zeit zu Zeit;* on ∾ to new deeds *vorwärts denn zu neuen Taten;* all right ∾, well ∾ *nun gut denn;* there and ∾ *auf der Stelle, sofort;* ∾ it is so? *also doch?;* you know him ∾ *du kennst ihn also.* — **II.** conj.: ∾ it is no use your going *dann hat es keinen Zweck, daß du gehst;* now ∾! *nun denn, nun also, aber bitte.* — **III.** a.: the ∾ Duke *der damalige Herzog.* — **IV.** n.: by ∾ *inzwischen, bis dahin;* every now and ∾ *dann und wann, hin und wieder, von Zeit zu Zeit*

there I. adv.: ∾ arises the question *es (da) erhebt sich die Frage;* ∾ is, was, will be, etc. *es ist (gibt), war (gab), wird sein (wird geben) usw.;* ∾ is no trusting him *man kann ihm nicht trauen;* I have been ∾ before (sl.) *ich weiß Bescheid, ich kenne den Schwindel schon;* help me, ∾'s a dear, ∾'s a good boy *hilf mir, sei so lieb, du bist auch mein lieber Junge;* ∾ fell a deep silence *ein tiefes Schweigen trat ein;* ∾ it is, you see *da liegt eben die Schwierigkeit;* ∾ spoke a king *das war wie ein König gesprochen;* ∾ and then *auf der Stelle, sofort;* it was two years ago, ∾ or ∾abouts (t.o.t.) *es war vor etwa zwei Jahren;* it will come to £ 100, ∾ or ∾abouts *es wird sich auf ungefähr 100 Pfund stellen;* ∾ you are! *da haben Sie es ja;* he is not quite all ∾ (colloq.) *er ist nicht ganz bei Trost;* down (in, over, out, up) ∾ *da unten (dort drinnen, da drüben, da draußen, da oben);* that's neither here nor ∾ *das gehört nicht hierher, das hat nichts mit der Sache zu tun, hat wenig Bedeutung;* he got ∾ (sl.) *er hatte Erfolg (erreichte), was er wollte;* you ∾! *Sie da!* — **II.** int.: ∾!, what did I tell you? *da! siehst du? was habe ich dir gesagt?;* ∾, ∾, don't cry *sei nur ruhig, jetzt ist's gut, weine nicht;* so ∾! *da siehst du! da hast du's!*

thick I. a.: they are as ∾ as thieves (colloq.) *sie sind dicke Freunde;* that is a bit (rather, a little too) ∾ (sl.) *das geht etwas zu weit, ist zuviel des Guten, etwas happig;* blood is ∾er than water (prov.) *Blutsverwandtschaft ist das stärkste Bindemittel;* a ∾ voice *eine belegte (heisere) Stimme;* to lay it on ∾ (colloq.) *etwas dick auftragen, übertreiben;* he'll give me a ∾ ear (colloq.) *er wird mich ohrfeigen;* a ∾-skinned fellow *ein dickfelliger Bursche;* a ∾-skulled, ∾-witted fellow *ein dummer Bursche;* a ∾ 'un (sl.) *ein Pfund (Geld).* — **II.** n.: a cup of ∾ (sl.) *eine Tasse Kakao;* to be in the ∾ of it *mittendrin sein;* through ∾ and thin *durch dick und dünn.* — **III.** adv.: blows came ∾ and fast *ein Schlag folgte dicht auf den anderen;* to speak ∾ *undeutlich sprechen, eine schwere Zunge haben*

thicken v.i.: the plot ∾s (humorous) *die Verwicklung nimmt zu, der Knoten schürzt sich*

thief n.: to set a ∾ to catch a ∾ *den Bock zum Gärtner machen;* stop ∾! *haltet den Dieb!;* to be as thick as thieves *dicke Freunde sein;* thieves' Latin *(die) Gaunersprache*

thigh n.: to smite hip and ∾ (Judges XV, 8) *j.en vollständig besiegen*

thin I. a.: as ∾ as a wafer *hauchdünn;* to have (to get) the ∾ end of the stick *den kürzeren ziehen, schlecht bei etwas wegkommen (fahren);* to get in the ∾ end of the wedge *den ersten Anfang machen, erst mal in Gang kommen;* a ∾ excuse *eine fadenscheinige Ausrede;* a ∾ house (theatre) *ein spärlich (schwach) besuchtes Haus;* as ∾ as a lath *spindeldürr;* that's too ∾ *das ist zu kümmerlich, damit kommst du nicht durch;* through thick and ∾ *durch dick und dünn;* he had a ∾ time *es ging ihm schlecht;* a ∾-skinned person *eine zartfühlende, empfindliche Person;* a ∾ 'un (sl.) *eine Zehnschilling-Münze.* — **II.** v.tr.: to ∾ out seedlings *Sämlinge versetzen, dünnen.* — **III.** v.i.: his hair is ∾ning *sein Haar wird dünn (lichtet sich)*

thing n.: I know a ∾ or two about it *ich verstehe etwas davon;* the ∾ is to work harder *es heißt jetzt, schwerer arbeiten; es kommt jetzt darauf an, schwerer zu arbeiten;* that's the ∾! *das ist das Richtige (Gegebene), die Masche!;* it's the ∾ to do nowadays *es ist heute die Mode;* it is not the ∾ to do *das schickt sich nicht, das tut man nicht;* to get measles, of all ∾s! *ausgerechnet die Masern zu kriegen!;* I am not feeling at all the ∾ *ich fühle mich durchaus nicht wohl;* I shall do that the first ∾ in the morning *ich werde das morgen in aller Frühe, als erstes tun;* that's a foolish ∾ to do *es ist töricht, das zu tun;* one good ∾ about it was... *das einzige Gute daran war...;* he made a good ∾ of it *er verdiente gut daran; er hat die Sache zum Erfolg gebracht;* he has a ∾ about chickens (colloq.) *er hat eine fixe Idee über Hühner;* to do the handsome ∾ by a person *sich anständig (nobel) gegen j.en zeigen;* it's just the (very) ∾ we want *das ist gerade, was wir brauchen;* it's the latest ∾ in hats *es ist die letzte Neuheit in Hüten;* a little ∾ of mine I should like to read to you *ein kleines Gedicht (eine kleine Arbeit usw.) von mir, das (die) ich dir gern vorlesen möchte;* any old ∾ (colloq.) *irgendetwas, etwas x-beliebiges;* a dear old ∾ *eine liebe, gute Seele;* the one ∾ or other *das eine oder das andere;* for one ∾ *erstens einmal;* neither one ∾ nor the other *weder Fisch noch Fleisch;* taking one ∾ with another *im großen und ganzen;* the only ∾ now is to take a taxi *es bleibt uns nur übrig, eine Taxe zu nehmen;* poor ∾! *der, die Ärmste!;* it is the same old ∾ *es ist die alte Leier;* it comes to the same ∾ *es läuft auf dasselbe hinaus;* it is no small ∾ *es ist keine Kleinigkeit;* it is a strange ∾ that you cannot hold your tongue *es ist merkwürdig (sonderbar), daß du den Mund nicht halten kannst;* there is no such ∾ *so etwas gibt's gar nicht;* ∾s are beginning to look brighter *die Verhältnisse (Aussichten) bessern sich;* how are ∾s? *wie geht's? wie steht's?;* I am quite out of ∾s *ich bin vollkommen aus allem heraus;* books and ∾s *Bücher und dergleichen;* two good ∾s are better than one *doppelt genäht hält besser;* he has made a mess of ∾s *er hat die Sache verpfuscht (verhunzt);* pack up your ∾s *pack' deine Sachen (Brocken) zusammen;* he sees ∾s *er sieht Gespenster;* he takes ∾s too seriously *er nimmt alles zu ernst;* taking ∾s as they are at present *so wie die Sache im Augenblick steht;* the tea ∾s *das Teegeschirr;* as ∾s go (stand) *wie es in der Welt so geht; wie die Dinge liegen;* it is an understood ∾ *es ist eine Selbstverständlichkeit;* ∾s Italian *alles Italienische;* he is well versed in political ∾s *er weiß in der Politik gut Bescheid*

thingamy, thingumajig, thingumbob, thingummy n. (colloq.): to whom does that ∾ belong? *wem gehört das Dingsda?;* Mr. ∾ *Herr Dingsda (Dingskirchen)*

think I. v.tr.: to ∾ fit (proper, good, best) *es für passend (gut, das beste) halten;* the child thought no harm *das Kind dachte sich nichts Böses dabei;* I ∾ him a rich man *ich halte ihn für reich;* I ∾ it probable *ich halte es für wahrscheinlich;* I thought as much *das dachte ich wohl, das habe ich mir gedacht;* to ∾ out (up) a plan *einen Plan ausdenken;* to ∾ a thing over *sich (dat.) etwas überlegen, durch den Kopf gehen lassen;* to ∾ scorn of something *etwas verachten.* — **II.** v.i.: to ∾ that it may be true *wenn man bedenkt, daß es wahr sein könnte;* you are very polite, I don't ∾ (iron. sl.) *du bist wirklich sehr höflich, ich danke für deine Höflichkeit;* I should ∾ not *durchaus nicht (keineswegs); ich werde mich hüten, das fehlte mir noch;* I should ∾ so *das sollte (will) ich meinen;* to ∾ about a thing *über etwas nachdenken;* to ∾ of a person (thing) *an j.en (etwas) denken;* I couldn't ∾ of doing such a thing *so etwas käme mir überhaupt nicht in den Sinn, könnte mir nicht einfallen;* ∾ of my forgetting it *denk' dir nur, das hätte ich glatt vergessen;* I must be ∾ing of going *ich muß an das Weggehen denken;* to ∾ no small beer of it *eine hohe Meinung von etwas haben;* I ∾ better of him than to believe that *ich habe eine bessere Meinung* *von ihm, als daß ich glauben könnte, daß;* to ∾ better of it *es sich anders überlegen;* he ∾s little (nothing) of walking 30 miles a day *er macht sich (dat.) wenig (nichts) daraus, 30 Meilen am Tage zu gehen;* he ∾s much (no end) of it *er hält sehr viel davon;* he ∾s the world of you *er hält große Stücke auf dich, er denkt wunder(s) was von dir*

thinking n.: to my way of ∾ *meiner Meinung nach*

third a.: ∾ degree (Amer.) *Zwangsmaßnahme, um von (aus) j.em ein Geständnis zu erpressen;* ∾ party insurance (legal) *Haftpflichtversicherung;* a ∾-rater (colloq.) *ein erbärmlicher Typ*

thirst I. n.: to have a ∾ *Durst haben;* to quench one's ∾ *den Durst löschen.* — **II.** v.i.: to ∾ for (after) a thing *nach etwas dürsten*

thirsty a.: to be ∾ *Durst haben;* this is ∾ work *bei dieser Arbeit bekommt man Durst*

thirty n.: she is on the shady side of ∾ *sie ist aus dem Schneider (heraus), über 30 Jahre alt;* in the thirties of the last century *in den dreißiger Jahren des vergangenen Jahrhunderts*

this I. a.: ∾ afternoon, evening, morning *heute nachmittag, abend, morgen;* ∾ day, ∾ day week *heute, heute in acht Tagen;* one of these days *eines Tages;* I have been waiting ∾ half hour *ich warte schon eine halbe Stunde;* I know ∾ much, that the thing is absurd *soviel weiß ich, daß die Sache absurd ist;* (for) ∾ once *dieses eine Mal;* by ∾ time *mittlerweile, inzwischen;* I have been asking for it ∾ (these) three weeks *ich frage schon seit drei Wochen danach.* — **II.** pron.: to put ∾ and that together *eins zum anderen nehmen, seine Schlüsse ziehen, sich (dat.) etwas zusammenreimen;* to speak of ∾, that, and the other *von allen möglichen Dingen reden;* he ought to be ready by ∾ *er sollte inzwischen (mittlerweile) fertig sein;* it runs like ∾ *es lautet folgendermaßen*

thorn n.: to be a ∾ in a person's flesh (side) *j.em ein Dorn im Auge sein;* to be (to sit) on ∾s *wie auf heißen Kohlen (auf Nadeln) sitzen*

thorough I. a.: his work is seldom ∾ *er leistet selten gründliche Arbeit;* a ∾ change *eine völlige (vollkommene) Änderung;* he has caught a ∾ chill *er hat sich tüchtig erkältet;* he is a ∾ scoundrel *er ist ein vollendeter Schurke, Erzschurke.* — **II.** adv.: a ∾-bred *ein Vollblut;* no ∾fare *Durchfahrt verboten;* a ∾-going reform *eine durchgreifende Reform;* a ∾-paced rascal *ein ausgekochter (-gemachter, abgefeimter, durchtriebener) Schurke, ein Erzschurke*

though conj.: he finished first, ∾ he began last *er wurde (war) zuerst fertig, obwohl (obgleich) er zuletzt anfing;* it looks as ∾ he meant business *es sieht so aus, als ob er es ernst meinte;* even ∾ *selbst wenn;* what ∾ the way is long *was macht es, wenn auch der Weg lang ist;* he is sure to understand — ∾ you never know *er versteht es sicher — doch man kann nie wissen;* I did not expect such a lot ∾ *soviel erwartete ich denn doch nicht;* I wish you had told me ∾ *immerhin, ich wünschte, du hättest es mir gesagt*

thought n.: quick as ∾ *blitzschnell;* a penny for your ∾s! *(zu einem in Gedanken Versunkenen gesagt) ich gäbe was drum zu wissen, was Sie jetzt denken (ich möchte wissen, was du jetzt denkst)!;* on second ∾s *bei (nach) näherer Überlegung;* the wish is father to the ∾ (prov.) *der Wunsch ist der Vater des Gedankens;* to conceive a ∾ *einen Gedanken fassen;* cut it a ∾ shorter *schneide es etwas (eine Idee) kürzer;* to entertain (to harbour) a ∾ *einen Gedanken hegen, sich mit einem Gedunken tragen;* I didn't give it a ∾ *ich dachte gar nicht daran, ich beachtete es gar nicht;* I had no ∾ of offending him *ich dachte nicht daran, ihn zu beleidigen, ich wollte ihn gar nicht beleidigen;* I had some ∾s of doing so *mir kam der Gedanke (ich ging mit dem Gedanken um, ich dachte so halb und halb daran), es zu tun;* to take ∾ for *mit sich zu Rate gehen;* he takes no ∾ for tomorrow *er denkt nicht an morgen;* to turn one's ∾s to a thing *seine Gedanken einer Sache zuwenden*

thousand n.: a ∾ thanks *tausend Dank;* by the ∾ *zu tausenden, tausendweise;* not one in a ∾ would have done it *nicht einer unter Tausenden hätte das getan;* the ∾ and one small worries of life *die zahllosen kleinen Sorgen des Lebens*

thrash v.tr.: let us ∾ this matter out *laßt uns die Sache gründlich (von allen*

Seiten) durchsprechen; he got a good ∾ing *er bekam eine gehörige Tracht Prügel, er wurde tüchtig verdroschen*

thread I. n.: ∾ and thrum *Gutes und Schlechtes durcheinander;* to gather up the ∾s of a subject *die Unterabteilungen eines Gegenstandes nach Sonderbehandlung zu einander in Beziehung setzen;* he has not a dry ∾ on him *er hat keinen trockenen Faden am (auf dem) Leib;* his life hung by a slender (thin) ∾ *sein Leben hing an einem Fädchen;* to resume (to take up) the ∾ of a tale *den Faden einer Erzählung wieder aufnehmen;* ∾bare *fadenscheinig, abgetragen, schäbig.* — **II.** v.tr.: to ∾ beads *Glasperlen aufreihen;* to ∾ a needle *eine Nadel einfädeln;* to ∾ one's way through a crowd *sich durch eine Menge hindurchschlängeln, -winden*

Threadneedle n.prop.: the Old Lady of ∾ Street *die Bank von England*

threat n.: the ∾ fell on heedless ears *die Drohung blieb unbeachtet;* there is a ∾ of rain *Regen droht, es droht zu regnen;* it is a ∾ to peace *es ist eine Bedrohung des Friedens*

three I. a.: a ∾-decker *ein Roman in drei Bänden;* a ∾-cornered fight *ein Wahlkampf zwischen Kandidaten von drei Parteien;* ∾ halfpence *anderthalb Penny;* a ∾-lane road *eine Straße mit drei Fahrbahnen;* he is ∾ sheets in the wind (colloq.) *er ist betrunken;* the ∾ R's (reading, [w]riting, [a]rithmetic) *Lesen, Schreiben, Rechnen (als Grundlagen der Volksschulbildung).* — **II.** n.: the rule of ∾ *Regeldetri*

thrill I. v.tr.: his voice ∾ed the listeners *seine Stimme packte die Zuhörer, wühlte sie im Innern auf;* I was ∾ed by the play *das Stück packte mich im Innersten;* they were ∾ed with horror *sie waren von Schrekken ergriffen (erschüttert);* a ∾er *ein Schauerroman.* — **II.** v.i.: fear ∾ed through my veins *Furcht durchrieselte meine Adern.* — **III.** n.: a ∾ of joy *eine freudige Erregung;* it was a real ∾ *es war ein wirkliches Erlebnis*

throat n.: a clergyman's ∾ *Rachenentzündung durch vieles Sprechen;* he has a sore ∾ *er hat Halsschmerzen;* to clear one's ∾ *sich räuspern;* to cut a person's ∾ *j.em den Hals abschneiden;* to jump down a person's ∾ *j.em über den Mund fahren (ihm das Maul stopfen, ihn anfahren);* to lie in one's ∾ *das Blaue vom Himmel herunterlügen; lügen, daß sich die Balken biegen;* the words stuck in my ∾ *die Worte blieben mir im Halse stecken;* to take a person by the ∾ *j.en an die (der) Kehle (Gurgel) packen;* to thrust a thing down a person's ∾ *j.em etwas aufzwingen*

throe n.: in the ∾s of childbirth *in den Geburtswehen*

throne n.: to come (to raise, to succeed) to the ∾ *auf den Thron kommen, erheben, auf dem Throne folgen*

through I. prep.: from Monday ∾ Friday *von Montag bis einschließlich Freitag;* to get a thing ∾ hands *etwas fertig machen, vollenden;* all ∾ his life *sein ganzes Leben hindurch;* he concealed it ∾ shame *er verbarg es aus Schamhaftigkeit.* — **II.** adv.: are you ∾ with it? *bist du fertig damit?;* I'm ∾ with the affair *ich will mit der Sache nichts mehr zu tun haben;* the plan fell ∾ *aus dem Plan ist nichts geworden.* — **III.** a.: a ∾ train *ein durchgehender Zug*

throughout I. adv.: the timber is rotten ∾ *das Holz ist durch und durch faul.* — **II.** prep.: ∾ the century *das ganze Jahrhundert hindurch;* ∾ the country *durch das ganze Land*

throw I. v.tr.: see 'chest, cold (water), dust, kiss, light, money, party, sop'. — with prep. and adv.: to ∾ oneself at the head of a person *sich j.em an den Hals werfen;* to ∾ away an advantage *sich (dat.) einen Vorteil verscherzen;* to ∾ down the gauntlet (the glove) *j.en zum Kampf herausfordern, ihm den Fehdehandschuh hinwerfen;* to ∾ in one's lot with a person *das Schicksal mit j.em teilen, gemeinsame Sache mit ihm machen;* to ∾ a spanner in (to) the works *einen Plan vereiteln, j.em einen Knüppel zwischen die Beine werfen;* to ∾ a thing in a person's teeth *j.em etwas ins Gesicht schleudern, ihm etwas vorwerfen;* to ∾ something into the bargain *noch etwas dazugeben;* to ∾ off a cold *eine Erkältung loswerden;* that ∾s open the door to suspicion *das heißt dem Verdacht Tür und Tor öffnen;* his words threw me out *seine Worte verwirrten mich, brachten mich ganz durcheinander;* to ∾ out a feeler *einen Fühler ausstrecken;* I was ∾n out of work *ich wurde arbeitslos;* to ∾ one's bonnet (cap) over the windmill *sich einer Liebesaffäre hingeben, ohne Rücksicht auf die gesellschaftlichen Konventionen;* to ∾ a thing over *eine Sache aufgeben;* to ∾ up office *ein Amt niederlegen;* to ∾ up the sponge, to ∾ in the towel (boxing) *sich für besiegt erklären, sich geschlagen (den Kampf, das Spiel verloren) geben;* he threw himself (up)on the mercy of the court *er wandte sich (er appellierte an, verließ sich, baute auf) die Milde des Gerichts.* — **II.** v.i.: to ∾ back *Atavismus zeigen.* — **III.** n.: let me have a ∾ *laß mich mal werfen;* at a stone's ∾ from here *in Steinwurfweite (nur einen Katzensprung, in geringer Entfernung) von hier*

thrum n.: thread and ∾ *Gutes und Schlechtes durcheinander*

thrust I. v.tr.: he ∾ his fist into my face *er hielt mir die Faust unter die Nase;* he ∾s his nose into everything *er steckt seine Nase in alles hinein;* to ∾ a person through *j.en durchbohren;* he ∾ his way through the crowd *er bahnte sich den Weg durch die Menge.* — **II.** v.i.: the blow ∾ home *der Hieb saß;* to ∾ at a person with a dagger *mit einem Dolch nach j.em stoßen.* — **III.** n.: cut and ∾ *Hieb und Gegenhieb;* the cut and ∾ of a discussion *das Hin und Her einer Diskussion;* to parry the ∾ *den Hieb parieren (abwehren, auffangen)*

thumb I. n.: ∾s up! (sl.) *ausgezeichnet! famos! prima!;* his fingers are all ∾s *er ist sehr (schrecklich) ungeschickt, er hat zwei linke Hände;* to bite one's ∾ at a person (Shakespeare, Rom. & Jul. I, 1, 48) *j.en höhnisch herausfordern, verhöhnen;* to do a thing by rule of ∾ *etwas nach einfachen, praktischen Regeln bewerkstelligen;* to be under a person's ∾ *in j.es Gewalt sein; unter dem Pantoffel stehen;* a ∾-nail sketch *eine hastig, roh gezeichnete Skizze.* — **II.** v.tr.: to ∾ the pages of a book *die Seiten eines Buches beschmutzen;* to ∾ the piano *auf dem Klavier klimpern;* to ∾ one's way, a ride *durch Winken mit dem Daumen in die Fahrtrichtung ein Auto anhalten, um mitgenommen zu werden; trampen, „per Anhalter fahren"*

thump v.i.: to ∾ away (at, on) a thing *auf etwas draufloshämmern;* a ∾ing lie *eine faustdicke Lüge*

thunder n.: to steal a person's ∾ *j.es Ideen stehlen; j.em den Wind aus den Segeln nehmen;* a ∾bolt *ein Donnerkeil;* a ∾-clap *ein Donnerschlag;* a ∾-storm *ein Gewitter;* I was ∾-struck *ich war wie vom Donner gerührt, ich war ganz (einfach) baff*

Thunderer n.: the ∾ *(Jupiter, Zeus) der Spitzname der „Times"*

thundering (colloq.) **I.** a.: it's a ∾ nuisance *es ist verteufelt lästig.* — **II.** adv.: I was ∾ glad to get back *ich war heilsfroh zurückzugelangen*

thwart v.tr.: to ∾ a person's plans *j.es Pläne durchkreuzen (vereiteln), j.em einen Strich durch die Rechnung machen*

tick[1] **I.** v.tr.: to ∾ an item off in a list *einen Posten in einer Liste anhaken;* to ∾ a person off (sl.) *j.en anschnauzen, abkanzeln, ihm aufs Dach steigen, den Marsch blasen.* — **II.** n.: he came to (on the) ∾ *er kam auf den Glockenschlag, pünktlich*

tick[2] n. (colloq.): to buy goods on ∾ *Waren auf Pump kaufen*

ticket n.: the democratic ∾ *die Wahlliste, das Programm der demokratischen Partei (USA);* it is not quite the ∾ (colloq.) *es ist nicht ganz das Richtige, das schickt sich nicht;* to get one's ∾ (sl.) *seinen Entlassungsschein vom Militär erhalten;* to work one's ∾ *die Kosten der Überfahrt durch Arbeit ableisten;* a ∾-of-leave man *ein vorzeitig entlassener Sträfling*

tickle I. v.tr.: I was hugely ∾d (∾d to death) at the idea (colloq.) *der Gedanke machte mir einen Mords-, Heidenspaß*

tide I. n.: the ∾ has turned *das Glück (Blatt) hat sich gewendet;* that turned the ∾ *das gab den Ausschlag;* to go (to swim) with the ∾ *mit dem Strom schwimmen;* to stem the ∾ *die Flut eindämmen;* to work double ∾s *Tag und Nacht arbeiten, Doppelschicht machen.* — **II.** v.tr.: to ∾ a person over a difficulty *j.em über eine Schwierigkeit hinweghelfen.* — **III.** v.i.: I must ∾ over this difficulty *ich muß über diese Schwierigkeit hinwegkommen*

tidy a.: he left a ∾ sum behind him (colloq.) *er hinterließ eine hübsche Summe;* that was a ∾ day's work (colloq.) *das war eine anständige Tagesarbeit;* I am feeling pretty ∾ (colloq.) *ich fühle mich ziemlich wohl*

tie I. v.tr.: to ∾ a person to (down to) conditions *j.en an Bedingungen binden;* to ∾ up a parcel *ein Paket verschnüren;* he is ∾d to his mother's apron-strings *er ist ein Muttersöhnchen;* a ∾d house *ein Wirtshaus, das an eine bestimmte Brauerei gebunden ist.* — **II.** v.i.: to ∾ with a person *die gleiche Anzahl von Punkten im Spiel machen wie ein anderer, mit j.m gleichstehen.* — **III.** n.: the match was a ∾ *das Wettspiel endete unentschieden;* family ∾s, the ∾s of friendship *Familien-, Freundschaftsverpflichtungen;* the dog is often a ∾ *der Hund ist oft eine Last (eine Fessel)*

tight I. a.: as ∾ as a boiled owl (sl.) *sternhagelvoll, so blau wie ein Märzveilchen;* money is ∾ *Geld ist knapp;* to be in a ∾ corner (place, squeeze) *in der Klemme sein;* a ∾ squeeze *ein dichtes Gedränge;* a ∾ lass *ein schmuckes Mädel;* he is a ∾-fisted man, a ∾-wad (U.S. sl.) *er ist ein Geizhals (Geizkragen, Knicker);* a ∾-rope dancer (walker) *ein Seiltänzer;* water-∾ *wasserdicht.* — **II.** n.: acrobats in ∾s *Akrobaten in enganliegender Trikotkleidung.* — **III.** adv.: hold it ∾ *halte es fest!;* sit ∾ *bleib fest auf deinem Platz! gib nicht nach! bleib bei deiner Meinung!*

tile n.: he has a ∾ loose (sl.) *bei ihm ist eine Schraube los (locker), er hat einen Vogel (einen Sparren zu viel, zu wenig);* to go on the ∾s (colloq.) *(wie ein Kater auf den Dachziegeln) auf Liebesabenteuer ausgehen;* he is wearing a ∾ (colloq.) *er trägt eine Angströhre (einen Zylinder)*

tilt I. v.i.: to ∾ at the ring *Ringel stechen;* the table is apt to ∾ over *der Tisch kippt leicht über.* — **II.** v.tr.: to ∾ a cart *einen Karren stürzen (umkippen);* to ∾ a cask *ein Faß kippen.* — **III.** n.: to come (to run) full ∾ against a thing *in vollem Galopp (mit voller Wucht) gegen etwas (an)rennen*

timber n.: shiver my ∾s! (naut.) *etwa: da soll doch der Teufel dreinschlagen!*

time I. n.: the ∾ of the action is the 16th century *das Stück spielt im 16. Jahrhundert;* ∾ after ∾, ∾ and again *immer wieder;* close ∾ *Schonzeit;* I got there in ∾ enough to see him *ich kam dort früh genug an, um ihn zu sehen;* ∾, gentlemen! (in inns) *Feierabend, meine Herren!;* ∾s out of number *unzählige Male;* each, every ∾ *jedesmal;* the first, second, etc. ∾ *das erste, zweite usw. Mal;* it is high ∾ for you to go *es ist höchste Zeit, daß du gehst;* many a ∾ and oft *so manches liebe Mal;* most of the ∾ *die meiste Zeit;* she is near her ∾ *ihre Entbindung steht bevor;* now's your ∾ *jetzt ist die Gelegenheit günstig;* some ∾ about noon *etwa um Mittag;* the ∾s are out of joint (Hamlet I, 5) *die Welt ist aus den Fugen;* there is a ∾ for everything *Alles zu seiner Zeit;* ∾ and tide wait for no man (prov.) *eine verpaßte Gelegenheit kommt nicht so schnell wieder;* ∾ was when he owned two cars *die Zeit ist vorüber, als er zwei Autos besaß;* this ∾ tomorrow, next year *morgen, nächstes Jahr um diese Zeit;* three, four etc. ∾s running *dreimal, viermal, usw. hintereinander;* what ∾ is it? *wieviel Uhr ist es?;* all the (that) ∾ *die ganze Zeit;* at ∾s *von Zeit zu Zeit, zu-, bisweilen;* at a ∾ *auf einmal;* at such ∾s *bei solchen Gelegenheiten;* at the ∾ of writing *während ich schreibe;* one, two, etc. at a ∾ *einzeln, zu zweien usw.;* ten minutes at a ∾ *zehn Minuten lang hintereinander;* at all ∾s, at any ∾ *zu allen Zeiten, zu jeder Zeit;* at my ∾ of life *in meinem Alter;* at one ∾ we were good friends *wir waren einst gute Freunde;* at the same ∾ *gleichzeitig;* at this ∾ of day *um diese Tagesstunde, zu so später Stunde; bei unserem jetzigen Kulturstande;* to be behind ∾ *Verspätung haben;* behind the ∾s *rückständig;* between ∾s *in der Zwischenzeit;* by that ∾ *bis dahin, inzwischen;* by the ∾ he comes *bis (daß) er kommt;* for the ∾ being *für den Augenblick; bis jetzt, vorläufig;* from ∾ immemorial, out of mind *seit undenklichen Zeiten;* in ∾, in good ∾ *zur rechten Zeit, rechtzeitig;* in ∾ to come *in Zukunft;* in course of ∾ *im Laufe der Zeit;* in due ∾ *zur rechten Zeit;* all in good ∾ *alles zu seiner Zeit;* in the mean∾ *mittlerweile;* in the nick of ∾ *im richtigen Augenblick;* in no ∾ *im Handumdrehen, im Nu;* in one's own good ∾ *wenn es einem paßt;* on ∾, to ∾, up to ∾ *pünktlich;* out of ∾ *aus dem Takt;* till such ∾ as *bis, so lange als;* up to this ∾, the present ∾ *bis jetzt, bis heute;* once upon a ∾ there was a king *es war einmal ein König;* the ∾ is up *die Zeit ist abgelaufen;* to beat ∾ *den Takt schlagen;* I can bide my ∾ *ich kann ruhig abwarten;* to call ∾ *Feierabend bieten;* to comply with the ∾s *sich mit der Zeit abfinden, sich in* *die Zeit schicken;* to do ∾ *eine Gefängnisstrafe absitzen;* to fritter away the ∾ *die Zeit vergeuden;* to have the ∾ of one's life *es außerordentlich gut, so gut wie noch nie haben;* to have a good ∾ *es gut haben, sich amüsieren;* to have ∾ on one's hands *nichts zu tun, viel Zeit haben;* what a ∾ you'll have getting him home *es wird dich viel Mühe kosten, ihn nach Hause zu bringen;* to have no ∾ for someone, something (colloq.) *j.en, etwas mit Ungeduld, Mißbilligung betrachten;* to keep ∾ *Takt halten;* my watch keeps good ∾ *meine Uhr geht gut, richtig;* to kill ∾ *die Zeit totschlagen;* to know the ∾ of day *wissen, was die Glocke geschlagen hat;* my watch loses ∾ *meine Uhr geht nach;* to mark ∾ *auf der Stelle treten, abwarten;* to pass the ∾ of day *j.em guten Tag sagen;* to recover (to make up for) lost ∾ *verlorene Zeit ein-, nachholen;* so that's the ∾ of day *so sieht die Sache aus! das hast du also vor!;* I am pressed for ∾ *ich bin mit der Zeit im Druck;* to speak (to work) against ∾ *sehr schnell sprechen, arbeiten;* take your ∾ *laß dir nur Zeit;* it will take all your ∾ *es wird deine ganze Zeit, Kraft in Anspruch nehmen;* to take ∾ by the forelock *die Gelegenheit beim Schopfe fassen;* to waste one's ∾ *die Zeit verschwenden, vergeuden;* a ∾-honoured custom *eine altehrwürdige Sitte;* my watch is a good ∾-keeper *meine Uhr geht immer richtig, ist zuverlässig;* there is a ∾-lag between higher wages and increased prices *es gibt eine gewisse Zwischenzeit (einen gewissen Zeitraum) zwischen Lohnerhöhungen und Preissteigerungen;* a ∾-piece *eine kleine Standuhr;* a ∾-server *ein Achselträger, Heuchler, liebedienerischer Mensch;* a ∾-table *ein Fahr-, Stundenplan;* ∾-worn *abgenutzt.* — **II.** v.tr.: we ∾d our arrival for the following day *wir setzten unsere Ankunft für den folgenden Tag fest;* you must ∾ your blows *du mußt die richtige Zeit für deine Schläge wählen;* to ∾ a race *die Zeit eines Wettlaufs mit der Stoppuhr bestimmen;* the remark was well (ill) ∾d *das war eine Bemerkung zur rechten (unrechten) Zeit.* — **III.** v.i.: to ∾ with a person *mit j.em übereinstimmen*

tin I. n.: I have no ∾ (sl.) *ich habe kein Geld, keine Moneten, keinen Zaster;* a ∾ fish (sl.) *ein Torpedo;* a little ∾ god *ein eingebildeter, unbedeutender Mensch;* a ∾ hat (sl.) *ein Stahlhelm;* a ∾ Lizzie *Spitzname für einen Fordwagen, Blechkiste;* ∾ pan alley music (colloq.) *Schlagermusik;* a ∾-smith *ein Blechschmied;* to come down to ∾-tacks (sl.) *zur Sache kommen.* — **II.** v.tr.: to ∾ fruit *Obst in Büchsen einmachen*

tinker I. n.: I don't care a ∾'s cuss, damn *ich mache mir einen Dreck daraus;* I had an hour's ∾ at it *ich habe eine Stunde daran herumgeflickt.* — **II.** v.tr.: I just ∾ed it up *ich habe es nur zurechtgeflickt.* — **III.** v.i.: to ∾ at a thing *an etwas herumflicken, -pfuschen*

tip[1] I. n.: from ∾ to ∾ *von einer (Flügel)spitze zur anderen, von einem Ende zum anderen;* from ∾ to toe *von Kopf bis Fuß, vom Scheitel bis zur Sohle;* I had it on the ∾ of my tongue *mir schwebte es auf der Zunge;* on ∾toe *auf den Zehenspitzen.* — **II.** v.tr.: to ∾ a thing *etwas mit einer Spitze versehen*

tip[2] I. v.tr.: ∾ us a copper (sl.) *wirf (schmeiß) uns eine Kupfermünze zu;* ∾ us your fin (sl.) *gib mir deine Hand, reich' mir deine Flosse;* he ∾ped me a shilling *er gab mir einen Schilling als Trinkgeld;* you must ∾ the porter *du mußt dem Gepäckträger ein Trinkgeld geben;* to ∾ a person the traveller *j.em einen Bären aufbinden;* a ∾ and run raid *ein Überfall, nach dessen Ausführung man sofort davonläuft;* to ∾ the scales *die Wagschale sinken machen, überwiegen; den Vorrang behaupten;* you might have ∾ped me the wink (sl.) *du hättest mir einen Wink geben können;* ∾ us a yarn (sl.) *erzähle uns eine Geschichte;* to ∾ off a glass of wine *ein Glas Wein hinunterstürzen;* to ∾ a person off *j.en warnen;* to ∾ over (up) a cart *einen Karren stürzen (umkippen).* — **II.** v.i.: to ∾ over, up *umkippen.* — **III.** n.: I'll give you the straight ∾ *ich will dir den richtigen Tip (Wink) geben;* to give the waiter a ∾ *dem Kellner ein Trinkgeld geben;* to give a ∾ to a thing *etwas kippen;* to miss one's ∾ *sein Ziel, seinen Zweck verfehlen;* a ∾-up seat *ein Klappsitz*

tipsy a.: to get ∾ *sich betrinken, sich (dat.) einen Schwips antrinken*

tiptoe n.: to be on ∾ about (or: over) something *auf etwas sehr gespannt sein*

tire I. v.tr.: to ∾ a person to death (or: out) *j.en zu Tode (zum Sterben)* **ermüden,**

langweilen; I'm sick and ∾d of it *ich bin die Sache leid, ich habe es satt, die Sache hängt mir zum Halse heraus.* — **II.** v.i.: to ∾ with doing a thing *von etwas müde werden, ermatten*

tired a.: to be born ∾ (colloq.) *eine Abneigung gegen Arbeit haben, von Beruf müde sein*

tiresome a.: a ∾ job *eine ermüdende, lästige Arbeit;* how ∾! I've left my watch behind *wie ärgerlich! ich habe meine Uhr zu Hause gelassen*

tissue n.: it is a ∾ of lies *es ist ein Lügengewebe*

tit n.: ∾ for tat *wie du mir, so ich dir; Wurst wider Wurst*

tittle n.: not one jot or ∾ *nicht das kleinste bißchen, nicht eine Bohne*

to I. prep.: a) in the direction of place, person, thing, etc.: ∾ arms! *zu den Waffen!;* ∾ bed with you! *ins Bett mit dir!;* I told him ∾ his face *ich sagte ihm ins Gesicht;* a hand ∾ hand fight *ein Handgemenge;* I held it ∾ the light *ich hielt es ans Licht;* on a visit ∾ London *bei einem Besuch in London;* five minutes ∾ one *fünf Minuten vor eins;* it fluttered ∾ the pavement *es flatterte auf den Bürgersteig;* all ∾ no purpose *völlig vergebens;* on the way ∾ the station *auf dem Wege nach (zu) dem Bahnhof;* they fell ∾ work *sie machten sich an die Arbeit.* — b) as far as, not short of: he drank himself ∾ death *er trank (soff) sich zu Tode;* ∾ the end of the chapter *bis ans (zum) Ende des Kapitels;* ∾ all eternity *in alle Ewigkeit;* to fight ∾ the last gasp *bis zum letzten Atemzuge kämpfen;* it might run ∾ £ 5 *es könnte sich auf 5 Pfund stellen;* ∾ a man *bis auf den letzten Mann.* — c) comparison, ratio, reference: he compared him ∾ Shakespeare *er stellte ihn Shakespeare gleich;* corresponding ∾ *entsprechend;* inferior (superior) ∾ a thing *geringer als etwas, einer Sache überlegen;* ∾ all appearances *allem Anschein nach;* ∾ the best of one's knowledge *nach bestem Wissen;* ∾ the minute *auf die Minute;* I bet ten ∾ one *ich wette zehn gegen eins;* made ∾ order *auf Bestellung angefertigt;* ∾ his taste *nach seinem Geschmack;* nothing ∾ what it might be *nichts im Vergleich zu dem, was es sein könnte.* — d) introducing indirect object of verb, recipient, possessor, person or thing affected by the action, quality etc.: I am not accustomed ∾ that *daran bin ich nicht gewöhnt;* alive ∾ the necessity *der Notwendigkeit bewußt;* to have all ∾ oneself *alles für sich haben;* apply ∾ the secretary *wenden Sie sich an den Geschäftsführer;* it belongs ∾ me *es gehört mir;* explain it ∾ me *erkläre es mir;* here's ∾ your health *auf dein Wohl;* impervious ∾ argument *einer Beweisführung nicht zugänglich;* lend your knife ∾ him *leihe ihm dein Messer;* to listen ∾ reason *Vernunft annehmen;* obedient ∾ command *dem Befehle gehorsam;* pleasant ∾ the taste *angenehm im Geschmack;* ready ∾ his hand *griffbereit;* it seems ∾ me absurd *es erscheint mir absurd;* that's all there is ∾ it *das ist alles, damit wäre alles gesagt;* what's that ∾ you? *was macht dir das aus?;* would ∾ God! *wollte Gott!* — e) as sign of infinitive, expressing purpose, consequence, etc., limiting the meaning of adjective, or forming verbal noun: allow me ∾ remark *gestatten Sie mir zu bemerken;* he began ∾ sing *er begann zu singen;* he declines ∾ go *er weigert sich zu gehen;* it is difficult ∾ explain *es ist schwierig zu erklären;* he does it (in order) ∾ annoy me *er tut es, um mich zu ärgern;* I fail ∾ understand *ich kann nicht verstehen;* I had my work ∾ do *ich hatte meine Arbeit;* I had ∾ do my work *ich mußte meine Arbeit tun;* help me (∾) lift it *hilf mir, es aufzuheben;* it is ∾ be done *es ist zu machen;* be so kind as ∾ tell me *sei so freundlich und sag mir;* I know how ∾ do it *ich weiß, wie ich es machen soll;* he was made ∾ repeat it *man ließ ihn es wiederholen;* he was seen ∾ fall *man sah ihn fallen;* ∾ see is ∾ believe *Sehen heißt Glauben;* ∾ wit *das heißt, nämlich.* — f) as substitute for infinitive: I meant ∾ call but forgot ∾ *ich wollte vorsprechen, vergaß es aber;* you promised ∾ *du versprachst es.* — **II.** adv.: ∾ and fro *auf und ab, hin und her;* the door fell ∾ *die Tür schlug zu.* — **III.** n.: there was such a ∾-do (colloq.) *es gab eine große Aufregung*

toad n.: ∾-in-the-hole *Bratwurst in Pfannkuchenteig gebacken;* he is a ∾-eater *er ist ein Speichellecker*

toast I. n.: to have a person on ∾ *j.en in seiner Gewalt haben;* to give (to propose, to submit) the ∾ of a person *einen Trinkspruch auf j.en ausbringen.* — **II.** v.tr.: to ∾ a person *auf j.es Wohl trinken*

today I. adv.: ∾ week, a week ∾ *heute in einer Woche;* a week ago ∾ *heute vor acht Tagen.* — **II.** n.: ∾'s paper *die heutige Zeitung;* the writers of ∾ *die Schriftsteller der Gegenwart*

toe I. n.: on the light fantastic ∾ (Milton, L'Allegro) *im leichten Tanzschritt;* from top to ∾ *von Kopf bis Fuß, vom Scheitel bis zur Sohle;* to tread on a person's ∾s *j.em auf die Füße (Hühneraugen) treten;* to get a ∾-hold *eben (knapp) Fuß fassen, einen winzigen Stehplatz bekommen.* — **II.** v.tr.: to ∾ the line (mark, scratch) *sich zum Wettlauf am Start aufstellen;* to ∾ the line *sich den Parteivorschriften unterwerfen; sich gleichschalten, einfügen;* to ∾ a person *j.em einen Tritt versetzen;* to ∾ a shoe *einen Stiefel vorschuhen.* — **III.** v.i.: to ∾ in (out) *beim Gehen die Füße nach innen (außen) setzen*

toffee, toffy n.: he can't shoot for ∾ (colloq.) *er ist ein Schlumpschütze*

tog (sl.) **I.** n.: ∾s *Kleider.* — **II.** v.tr.: to ∾ oneself up *sich herausputzen*

together adv.: he would keep sober for weeks ∾ *(manchmal) blieb er wochenlang nüchtern*

toil I. v.i.: to ∾ at something *sich bei (mit) etwas abplacken (abschuften);* to ∾ up the hill *mühselig den Hügel hinaufsteigen.* — **II.** n.: in the ∾s of debt *in Schulden verstrickt.* — **III.** a.: ∾-worn *abgearbeitet;* ∾some *mühsam, -selig*

token n.: by this (the same) ∾ *als Beweis dafür, eben deshalb;* more by ∾ *um so mehr;* in ∾ of *als (zum) Zeichen von;* ∾ money *Privatgeld;* ∾ payment *Anzahlung als Schuldanerkennung;* a ∾ vote (Parl.) *Bewilligung eines Betrages, dessen Höhe pro forma (unverbindlich) genannt wird*

tom n.: a ∾boy *ein Wildfang, eine Range;* a ∾-cat *ein Kater;* Tom, Dick and Harry *Hinz und Kunz;* a ∾fool *ein Hansnarr;* there's more know Tom Fool than Tom Fool knows (prov.) *Sinn: berüchtigt sein ist keine Ehre;* Tom Thumb *Däumling, Zwerg*

tommy n.: Tommy Atkins *der britische Soldat;* don't talk such ∾ rot (sl.) *rede doch nicht so einen Blödsinn!*

ton n.: ∾s of people (colloq.) *riesig viele (eine Unmenge) Leute;* I have asked him ∾s of times (colloq.) *ich habe ihn unzählige Male (x-mal) gefragt*

tone v.i.: that ∾d down his anger, his excitement *das hat seinen Ärger, seine Aufregung gemildert (gemäßigt);* cold water ∾s up the muscles *kaltes Wasser stärkt die Muskeln*

tongs n.pl.: I would not touch him (it) with a pair of ∾ *ich würde ihn (es) nicht mit der Beißzange anfassen;* they went at him hammer and ∾ *sie gingen mit aller Macht auf ihn los*

tongue n.: on the ∾s of men *im Munde (Gerede) der Leute;* to keep a civil ∾ in one's head *höflich bleiben;* the confusion of ∾s *die babylonische Sprachverwirrung;* to have a fluent (ready) ∾ *fließend sprechen; geschwätzig sein;* a furred (dirty) ∾ *eine belegte Zunge;* the gift of ∾s *Sprachtalent;* the mother ∾ *die Muttersprache;* it was a slip of the ∾ *ich habe mich versprochen;* I had it on the tip of my ∾ *mir schwebte es auf der Zunge;* a dog gives (throws) ∾ *ein Hund bellt, gibt Laut;* to hold one's ∾ *den Mund halten;* to have lost one's ∾ *sprachlos sein;* to put out one's ∾ *die Zunge herausstrecken;* to speak with one's ∾ in one's cheek *ironisch, unaufrichtig sprechen;* to wag one's ∾ *indiskret, unaufhörlich schwatzen;* ∾s will wag *die Leute werden reden (schwätzen)*

too adv.: that's ∾ bad (colloq.) *Pech! zu dumm!;* it is ∾ delightful *es ist ganz entzückend;* it is ∾ good to be true *es ist zu schön, um wahr zu sein;* far ∾ many (much) *viel zu viele, viel zu viel;* it is really ∾ much of a good thing *es ist wirklich des Guten zuviel;* you're ∾ right (colloq.) *und ob du recht hast! du hast nur zu recht!;* I mean to do it ∾ *ich habe es wirklich fest vor;* it was achieved, ∾, at small cost *es wurde dazu (außerdem) mit geringen Kosten erreicht;* very nice, ∾ (colloq.) *sehr nett, prima!*

tooth n.: the child is cutting his teeth *das Kind zahnt;* to draw a person's teeth *j.en unschädlich machen;* to escape by the skin of one's teeth *mit knapper Not ent-*

kommen; to fight (to struggle) ∾ and nail *mit aller Kraft kämpfen;* to get one's teeth into a thing *eine Sache anpacken, sich in eine Sache einarbeiten;* to set one's teeth *die Zähne aufeinander-, zusammenbeißen;* to set a person's teeth on edge *j.en nervös machen, reizen;* to take the bit between one's teeth *störrisch, aufsässig werden;* in the teeth of violent opposition *angesichts (trotz) heftigen Widerstandes;* to cast (to fling, to throw) a thing in a person's teeth *j.em etwas ins Gesicht schleudern, ihm etwas vorwerfen;* to lie in one's teeth (archaic, jocular) *das Blaue vom Himmel herunterlügen; lügen, daß sich die Balken biegen;* long in the ∾ *alt, bejahrt;* armed to the teeth *bis an die Zähne bewaffnet;* to cut one's eye-(wisdom-)teeth *die Eck-, Weisheitszähne bekommen;* (fig.) *pfiffig, auf der Höhe sein;* he has a sweet ∾ *er ißt gern Süßigkeiten, er ist ein Leckermaul;* praise from the teeth outwards *unaufrichtiges Lob, bloßes Gerede;* a ∾-ful *ein kleiner Schluck;* ∾some *schmackhaft*

top¹ I. n.: the ∾s (colloq.) *die führenden Leute;* the ∾ of my ambition *mein höchster Ehrgeiz;* he came out ∾ of (in) the exam *er bestand als bester die Prüfung;* the ∾ of the milk (colloq.) *das Beste von allem;* the ∾ of the morning to you! (Irish) *schönen guten Morgen!;* he is at the ∾ of the ladder (or: tree) *er hat die höchste Stellung (im Amt, Beruf) erreicht;* he ran at the ∾ of his speed *er lief so schnell er nur konnte;* at the ∾ of the table *am Kopfende des Tisches;* at the ∾ of one's voice *aus voller Kehle, so laut wie möglich;* to feel on (the) ∾ of the world *sich obenauf fühlen;* from ∾ to toe *von Kopf bis Fuß, vom Scheitel bis zur Sohle;* I put it on ∾ of the cupboard *ich legte es oben auf den Schrank;* on the ∾ of it we got wet *wir wurden obendrein noch naß;* to go over the ∾ *aus dem Schützengraben zum Sturmangriff antreten;* to the ∾ of one's bent *nach Herzenslust, nach besten Kräften, bis zum Äußersten;* to come to the ∾ *sich auszeichnen:* to take the ∾ off the beer *die Blume (den Feldwebel) abtrinken.* — **II.** a.: ∾ boots *Schaftstiefel, Langschäfter;* to come out ∾ dog (sl.) *als Sieger hervorgehen;* to come out of the ∾ drawer (colloq.) *von guter Familie sein, aus guter F. stammen;* to wear a ∾ hat, a topper (colloq.) *einen Zylinderhut tragen;* it is ∾-heavy *es ist oben schwerer als unten;* a ∾-hole, ∾-notch performance (sl.) *eine erstklassige Aufführung;* he is a ∾sawyer (colloq.) *er ist ein hohes Tier;* at ∾ speed *mit höchster Geschwindigkeit.* — **III.** v.tr.: that ∾s everything *das übertrifft alles;* to ∾ one's part *seine Rolle vorzüglich spielen;* he ∾s six feet *er ist über sechs Fuß groß;* to ∾ off (up) a thing *etwas beendigen, einer Sache den letzten Schliff geben*

top² n.: to sleep like a ∾ *wie ein Dachs (Murmeltier, Ratz) schlafen*

topsy-turvy a.: to turn everything ∾ *das Oberste zu unterst kehren, alles auf den Kopf stellen*

torch n.: the ∾ of Hymen *die Liebesleidenschaft;* to carry the ∾ for someone *j.en bewundern oder lieben;* to hand on the ∾ *die Fackel (der Wissenschaft, Aufklärung usw.) weiterreichen*

torture n.: to put to the ∾ *auf die Folter spannen*

toss I. v.tr.: he was ∾ed by the bull *er wurde von dem Stier mit den Hörnern in die Luft geschleudert;* ∾ me the ball *wirf mir den Ball zu;* to ∾ (back) one's head *den Kopf zurück-, in den Nacken werfen;* to ∾ oars *die Riemen zum Gruß senkrecht in die Höhe strecken, die Riemen pieken;* to ∾ a pancake *einen Pfannkuchen durch Hochwerfen in der Pfanne wenden;* to ∾ a person in a blanket *(früheres Kinderspiel) j.en in einer Decke, die an den vier Ecken gehalten wird, hochwerfen und wieder auffangen;* I'll ∾ you for the seat *ich lose (knoble) mit dir um den Sitzplatz;* to ∾ a thing aside (away) *etwas achtlos fortwerfen (fortschmeißen);* to ∾ off a drink *ein Getränk in éinem Zuge hinunterstürzen;* to ∾ off a task *eine Aufgabe mühelos bewältigen (schmeißen);* to ∾ up a coin *eine Münze beim Losen hochwerfen.* — **II.** v.i.: the ship ∾es *das Schiff rollt;* to ∾ about in bed *sich im Bett herumwälzen;* let's ∾ up for it *wir wollen darum losen (knobeln).* — **III.** n.: with a contemptuous ∾ of the head *mit einem verächtlichen Zurückwerfen des Kopfes;* to take a ∾ *vom Pferd geworfen werden;* to win the ∾ *beim Losen gewinnen;* it is quite a ∾-up whether he comes or not *es ist sehr unbestimmt (hängt ganz vom Zufall ab), ob er kommt oder nicht*

tot¹ n.: a tiny ∾ *ein winziges Kerlchen;* a ∾ of whisky *ein Schlückchen Whisky*

tot² (colloq.) **I.** v.tr.: ∾ up these figures *addiere diese Zahlen, zähle sie zusammen.*— **II.** v.i.: it ∾s up to quite a lot *es beläuft sich auf eine ganz hübsche Summe*

total v.tr.: the visitors ∾ed several thousands *die Besucher zählten zusammen mehrere Tausend*

touch I. v.tr.: I couldn't ∾ the algebra paper *ich konnte mit der Algebraarbeit nichts anfangen;* I must not ∾ beer *ich darf kein Bier trinken (anrühren);* please ∾ the bell *klingeln Sie, bitte!;* prices have ∾ed bottom *die Preise haben den Tiefstand erreicht;* polish won't ∾ these candlesticks *Politur nützt nichts bei diesen Kerzenhaltern;* it was ∾-and-go whether we got past *es stand auf des Messers Schneide, ob wir vorbeikamen;* a ∾-and-go business *eine unsichere (riskante, brenzlige) Sache;* he ∾ed his hat *er berührte zum Gruß seinen Hut;* no one can ∾ him *ihm kommt keiner gleich; an ihn kann keiner tippen;* it ∾ed him to the heart (quick) *es rührte ihn bis ins Innerste;* that ∾ed him nearly *das ging ihm nahe;* he ∾ed me for £ 5 (sl.) *er hat mich um 5 Pfund angepumpt (angehauen);* they that ∾ pitch will be defiled (prov.) *wer Pech angreift, besudelt sich;* to ∾ the spot *den Finger auf die Wunde legen;* ∾ wood! *unberufen (toi! toi! toi!)!;* to be ∾ed by a thing *von etwas gerührt (ergriffen) sein;* it was a ∾ing story *es war eine rührende (ergreifende) Geschichte;* he is very ∾y *er ist sehr empfindlich, leicht reizbar;* he is ∾ed *er ist verrückt (verdreht);* the flowers are a little ∾ed with the east wind *die Blumen haben etwas unter dem Ostwind gelitten;* to ∾ in colours *Farben anbringen (auftragen);* to ∾ off a sketch *eine Skizze rasch entwerfen;* to ∾ up a photo *eine Aufnahme retuschieren.* — **II.** v.i.: to ∾ at a port *einen Hafen anlaufen;* to ∾ down at an airport *eine kurze Landung auf einem Flughafen machen;* the lecture ∾ed off a discussion *der Vortrag veranlaßte (verursachte) eine Diskussion;* to ∾ (up)on a subject *ein Thema berühren, auf einen Gegenstand zu sprechen kommen.* — **III.** n.: a ∾ of irony *ein Anflug von Ironie;* a ∾ of rheumatism *ein leichter Anfall von Rheumatismus;* a ∾ of salt *ein Körnchen Salz;* a ∾ of the sun *ein Sonnenstich;* a happy (sure) ∾ *ein glücklicher (sicherer) Griff;* to add (to give, to put) the finishing ∾es to a thing *die letzte Feile (Hand) an etwas legen;* a firm (light) ∾ on the piano *ein fester (leichter) Klavieranschlag;* it was a near ∾ *es ging nur mit knapper Not;* to give a person a ∾ *j.en berühren;* at a ∾ *bei einer leisen Berührung;* to get in(to) ∾ with a person *in Fühlung mit j.em kommen; (die) Verbindung mit j.em aufnehmen;* to keep in ∾ with a person *mit j.em in Fühlung bleiben;* it is cold to the ∾ *es fühlt sich kalt an;* to put to the ∾ *auf die Probe stellen*

toucher n.: (sl.) as near as a ∾ *um ein Haar*

tough I. a.: he is a ∾ customer *er ist ein grober Kunde, Grobian; ein eigensinniger, -williger Mensch;* I found it a ∾ job (colloq.) *ich fand es schwierig;* ∾ luck (colloq.) *Unglück, Pech.* — **II.** n.: he is a ∾ (U.S. sl.) *er ist ein Verbrecher, Raufbold, Rowdy*

tow n.: to have (to take) a person (a thing) in ∾ *j.en (etwas) im Schlepptau haben, ins Schlepptau nehmen*

towel n.: a lead ∾ *eine Bleikugel;* an oaken ∾ *eine Keule, ein Knüppel;* to throw in the ∾ (boxing) *sich für besiegt erklären, sich geschlagen (den Kampf, das Spiel verloren) geben;* a ∾-horse *ein Handtuchständer*

tower I. n.: a ∾ of strength *ein starker Hort.* — **II.** v.i.: he ∾s above his contemporaries *er ragt turmhoch über seine Zeitgenossen hervor;* he was in a ∾ing rage *er war fürchterlich wütend (fuchsteufelswild, er spuckte Gift und Galle)*

town n.: a man about ∾ *ein Lebemann;* a woman of the ∾ *eine Dirne;* the ∾ clerk *der Stadtdirektor;* ∾ and gown *Bürgerschaft und Studentenschaft (Oxford, Cambridge);* the ∾ hall *das Rat-, Stadthaus;* to be out of ∾ (Amer.) *verreist sein;* going to ∾ (Amer.) *durch etwas angenehm angeregt sein;* to paint the ∾ red *die ganze Stadt auf den Kopf stellen*

trace n.: to kick over the ∾s *über die Stränge schlagen*

track I. n.: the beaten ∾ *der ausgetretene Weg, das alte, gewohnte Gleis;* in one's ∾s *wie man geht und steht, auf der Stelle;* off the ∾ *entgleist; auf falscher Fährte, auf dem Holzweg;* I am on his ∾ *ich bin ihm auf der Spur;* to clear the ∾ *die*

Strecke freimachen; to cover up one's ∾s *seine Spuren verwischen;* to keep ∾ of a thing *den Verlauf, die Entwicklung einer Sache verfolgen;* to make ∾s (sl.) *ausreißen (abhauen, verduften);* to make ∾s for a thing (sl.) *etwas aufsuchen, einer Sache nachgehen;* to strike the ∾ *auf den Weg stoßen.* — **II.** v.tr.: to ∾ an animal *die Spur eines Tieres verfolgen;* to ∾ down (out) *aufspüren, ausfindig machen*

trade I. n.: the Board of Trade *das Handelsministerium;* he is a carpenter by ∾ *er ist Zimmermann von Beruf;* the foreign, home (domestic) ∾ *der Außen-, Innenhandel;* he is in ∾ *er ist Geschäftsmann, Gewerbetreibender;* Jack of all ∾s *Hans Dampf in allen Gassen;* a ∾ mark *eine Schutzmarke, ein Warenzeichen;* ∾ show *private Filmaufführung.* — **II.** v.tr.: to ∾ cigarettes for coffee *Zigaretten gegen Kaffee einhandeln (eintauschen).* — **III.** v.i.: to ∾ in wine *mit Wein Handel treiben (handeln);* to ∾ on a person's good nature *j.es Gutmütigkeit ausnutzen, auf j.es Gutmütigkeit spekulieren (reisen)*

trail I. n.: the ∾ of a meteor *der Schweif eines Meteors;* the slimy ∾ of a slug *die schleimige Spur einer Schnecke;* a ∾ of smoke *ein Rauchstreifen;* to blaze a ∾ *Pionierarbeit leisten;* to get on (off) the ∾ *auf die Spur kommen, die Spur verlieren.* — **II.** v.tr.: the man was ∾ing a cart *der Mann zog einen Karren hinter sich her;* to ∾ a criminal *einen Verbrecher verfolgen;* to ∾ one's coat *j.en herausfordern (reizen), j.n absichtlich beleidigen (ärgern)* — **III.** v.i.: his coat ∾ed on the ground *sein Rock schleifte auf dem Boden;* they ∾ed home *sie schleppten sich nach Hause*

trailer n.: a car with ∾ *ein Wagen mit Anhänger;* a film ∾ *Vorschau eines Filmes*

train I. v.tr.: to ∾ (up) a child in the way it should go *ein Kind in der richtigen Weise erziehen;* to ∾ a dog to jump through a hoop *einen Hund dressieren (abrichten), durch einen Reifen zu springen;* I shall ∾ it *ich fahre mit dem Zug (mit der Bahn);* he was ∾ed for the ministry *er wurde zum Geistlichen ausgebildet;* she is a ∾ed nurse *sie ist eine ausgebildete Krankenschwester.* — **II.** v.i.: to ∾ for a regatta *für eine Regatta trainieren.* — **III.** n.: a whole ∾ of admirers *ein ganzer Anhang von Bewunderern;* the ∾ of a comet *der Kometenschweif;* an unlucky ∾ of events *eine unglückliche Folge (Kette) von Ereignissen;* a ∾ of ideas *eine Gedankenfolge;* to bring (to have) in its ∾ *im Gefolge haben, nach sich ziehen, mit sich bringen;* to go (to travel) by ∾ *mit der Bahn (mit dem Zug) fahren (reisen);* to take ∾ for (to) a place *die Bahn (den Zug) nach einem Orte nehmen*

tramp I. v.i.: I heard him ∾ing about overhead *ich hörte ihn über mir herumtrampeln;* I have ∾ed up and down the whole day looking for you *ich bin auf der Suche nach dir den ganzen Tag herumgewandert.* — **II.** v.tr.: I have ∾ed the whole country *ich habe die ganze Gegend durchwandert (abgeklappert);* I had to ∾ it *ich mußte zu Fuß gehen.* — **III.** n.: he is a ∾ *er ist ein Landstreicher (Tippelbruder);* she is a ∾ *es ist ein Frachtdampfer ohne regelmäßige Reiseroute;* to be on the ∾ *auf (der) Wanderschaft sein*

translate v.tr.: kindly ∾ *drück' dich bitte in einfachen Worten aus;* to ∾ into German *ins Deutsche übersetzen;* to ∾ to Heaven (Bible) *in den Himmel versetzen (entrücken);* to ∾ a Bishop to another see *einen Bischof in eine andere Diozese versetzen;* I ∾d it as a protest *ich deutete es (faßte es auf) als Protest*

transpire v.i.: it ∾d that it was not true *es sickerte durch, daß es nicht wahr sei;* it ∾d (vulg.) *es geschah (ereignete sich)*

transport [træns'pɔ:t] **I.** v.tr.: to be ∾ed with joy, anger, fear *außer sich sein vor Freude, Wut, Furcht.* — **II.** n.: ['trænspɔ:t] he was in ∾s *er war außer sich vor Freude, er war freudetrunken;* in a ∾ of rage *außer sich vor Wut, in wütender Erregung, in rasender Wut*

trap n.: pack up your ∾s and be off *packe deine Siebensachen (zusammen) und verschwinde;* to set a ∾ *eine Falle stellen;* shut your ∾ (sl.) *halt's Maul! halt den Rand!*

trash n.: who steals my purse steals ∾ (Shakespeare, Othello, III, 3) *wer meinen Beutel stiehlt, nimmt Tand (Schlegel-Tieck)*

travel I. v.i.: to ∾ bodkin *eingequetscht zwischen zwei anderen Personen fahren (sitzen, reisen);* light ∾s faster than sound

Licht pflanzt sich schneller fort als Schall; to ∾ by car, land, rail, sea *mit dem Auto, zu Lande, mit der Bahn, zur See reisen;* to ∾ out of the record *vom Gegenstande abschweifen, nicht bei der Sache bleiben;* his eyes ∾led over the scene *seine Augen schweiften über den Schauplatz.* — **II.** v.tr.: he ∾led France from end to end *er durchreiste Frankreich von einem Ende zum anderen.* — **III.** n.: the ∾ of the piston *der Kolbenhub;* he has returned from his ∾s *er ist von seiner Reise zurückgekehrt;* books of ∾, ∾s *Reisebeschreibungen*

traveller n.: to tell a ∾'s tale *eine Räubergeschichte, Münchhausiade erzählen;* to tip a person the ∾ *j.em einen Bären aufbinden*

treacherous a.: the ice is ∾ *die Eisdecke hält nicht;* I have a ∾ memory *ich habe ein unzuverlässiges Gedächtnis*

tread I. v.i.: to ∾ awry *irren (von Personen), schief gehen (von Sachen);* to ∾ in a person's footsteps *j.es Beispiel folgen, in seine Fuß(s)tapfen treten;* to ∾ on air *im siebenten Himmel sein;* to ∾ on a person's corns (toes) *j.em auf die Hühneraugen treten;* to ∾ on a person's heels, see 'heel'. — **II.** v.tr.: to ∾ the boards (stage) *Schauspieler(in) sein;* to ∾ grapes *Trauben keltern;* to ∾ to measure *tanzen;* to ∾ underfoot *mit Füßen treten.* — **III.** n.: I recognized his heavy ∾ *ich erkannte seinen schweren Tritt*

treasure I. n.: my ∾ *mein Schatz;* the girl is a perfect ∾ (colloq.) *das Mädchen ist eine wahre Perle;* ∾ trove *ausgegrabener herrenloser Schatz.* — **II.** v.tr.: to ∾ up an insult *eine Beleidigung nicht vergessen*

treat I. v.tr.: to ∾ a sprained ankle *einen verstauchten Knöchel behandeln;* to ∾ a boy kindly *einen Jungen freundlich behandeln;* to ∾ a subject *ein Thema behandeln;* you must ∾ it as a joke *du mußt es als Scherz ansehen (auffassen, betrachten);* to ∾ a person for a cough *j.en wegen eines Hustens behandeln;* to ∾ a person to a thing *j.em etwas traktieren (spendieren);* I will ∾ myself this once *ich will mir einmal den Spaß leisten;* to ∾ a thing with care *etwas sorgfältig behandeln.* — **II.** v.i.: the book ∾s of the war *das Buch handelt von dem (vom) Krieg;* to ∾ with a person *mit j.em unter-, verhandeln.* — **III.** n.: it is a ∾ to hear him *es ist ein Hochgenuß, ihn zu hören;* this is my ∾ *dies geht auf meine Rechnung, diesmal bezahle ich;* to give a person a ∾ *j.em ein Fest bereiten;* to stand ∾ (colloq.) *die Zeche bezahlen*

tree I. n.: such as the ∾ is, such is the fruit *der Apfel fällt nicht weit vom Stamm;* he is at the top of the ∾ *er hat die höchste Stellung (im Amt, Beruf) erreicht;* to bark up the wrong ∾ *auf falscher Fährte, auf dem Holzwege sein;* to be up a ∾ *in Verlegenheit, in der Klemme sein;* a boot-∾ *ein Stiefelleisten;* a family ∾ *ein Stammbaum.* — **II.** v.tr.: to ∾ an animal *ein Tier auf einen Baum treiben;* to ∾ a person *j.en in Verlegenheit bringen;* to ∾ a boot *einen Stiefel auf den Leisten schlagen*

tremble I. v.i.: to ∾ all over *am ganzen Leib (Körper) zittern;* to ∾ at the thought, to think *bei dem Gedanken zittern;* I ∾ for his safety *ich zittere um seine Sicherheit;* his fate ∾d in the balance *sein Schicksal war in der Schwebe (ungewiß);* to ∾ with anger, excitement *vor Wut, Aufregung zittern.* — **II.** n.: there was a ∾ in her voice *ihre Stimme zitterte (bebte);* to be all of a ∾ (colloq.) *am ganzen Leibe (Körper) zittern*

trencher n.: he is a good ∾man *er ist ein tüchtiger Esser*

trespass v.i.: to ∾ against the law *ein Gesetz übertreten, sich gegen ein Gesetz vergehen, gegen ein Gesetz sündigen;* to ∾ upon a person's land *widerrechtlich fremdes Eigentum betreten;* to ∾ (up)on a person's preserves *sich in j.es Sonderinteressen mischen;* to ∾ (up)on a person's time *j.es Zeit über Gebühr in Anspruch nehmen*

trespasser n.: ∾s will be prosecuted *unbefugtes Betreten bei Strafe verboten!*

trial n.: by way of ∾ *versuchsweise, zur Probe;* on ∾ *auf Probe*; to be on (to stand, to undergo) ∾ for murder *unter Anklage des Mordes vor Gericht stehen;* to bring (to commit) a person to ∾ *j.en zur Aburteilung vor Gericht stellen;* you will find the boy a great ∾ *der Junge wird euch eine große Plage sein, sehr lästig fallen;* to give a thing a fair ∾ *einen ehrlichen Versuch mit etwas machen;* old age has many ∾s *das Alter bringt viele Beschwer-*

den; to make a ∾ of a thing *einen Versuch mit etwas machen;* to make a ∾ ascent, a ∾ trip (run) *einen Probeflug, eine Probefahrt machen;* a ∾ by battle (or: ordeal) *ein Gottesurteil;* a ∾ by jury *ein Verhör vor einem Geschworenengericht, eine Schwurgerichtsverhandlung;* a ∾ match *ein Ausscheidungsspiel*

tribute n.: the floral ∾s of her admirers *die Blumenspenden ihrer Bewunderer;* to be laid under ∾ *tributpflichtig sein;* to pay the ∾ of nature *der Natur seinen Tribut entrichten (zollen); sterben*

trice n.: in a ∾ *im Handumdrehen, im Nu*

trick I. n.: he is at his ∾s, full of ∾s *er macht dumme Streiche, steckt voller Streiche;* to be up to a person's ∾s *j.es Ränke (Schliche) durchschauen;* that will do the ∾ (sl.) *damit geht es, das tut es;* I shall soon get (learn) the ∾ of it *den Kniff werde ich bald heraushaben;* to have the ∾ of doing a thing *die Eigenart (die üble Angewohnheit) haben, etwas zu tun;* my dog knows no ∾s *mein Hund kann keine Kunststücke machen;* you can't teach an old dog new ∾s (prov.) *was Hänschen nicht lernt, lernt Hans nimmermehr; einem alten, ungeschickten Menschen kann man nichts mehr beibringen;* to play (to serve) a person a dirty (shabby, mean) dog's ∾, a dirty (etc.) ∾ on a person *j.em einen schmutzigen (schäbigen, gemeinen) Streich spielen;* my ace of hearts took (made, won) the ∾ *mein Herz Aß nahm (machte, gewann) den Stich;* to try one's ∾s on a person *j.en zu überlisten versuchen;* a ∾ cyclist *ein Kunstradfahrer; (scherzhaft) Psychiater;* the odd ∾ *der dreizehnte Stich beim Whist, wenn jede Partei sechs Stiche gemacht hat;* the whole bag of ∾s (sl.) *jeder Kniff, der ganze Kram;* the ∾s of the trade *die besonderen Geschäfts-, Kunstgriffe;* the ∾s of memory *die Tücken des Gedächtnisses.* — **II.** v.tr.: to ∾ a person into doing a thing *j.en dazu verführen (verlocken, verleiten), etwas zu tun;* to ∾ a person out of a thing *j.en um etwas betrügen (prellen);* to ∾ a thing out (up) *etwas schmücken (herausputzen)*

trifle I. n.: he seems a ∾ angry *er scheint ein wenig (etwas) böse zu sein;* the merest ∾ puts him out *die geringste Kleinigkeit ärgert ihn (bringt ihn außer Fassung, aus dem Konzept);* to dispute about ∾s *sich um Kleinigkeiten (Lappalien, des Kaisers Bart) streiten;* to spare a ∾ for a person *j.em eine Kleinigkeit ablassen;* to stand upon ∾s *auf Kleinigkeiten (Lappalien) Wert legen; ein Kleinigkeitskrämer (ein Korinthenkacker [derb]) sein;* he does not stick at ∾s *er gibt sich nicht mit Kleinigkeiten ab, ist nicht bange, hat keine Hemmungen.* — **II.** v.i.: to ∾ with a person (a thing) *mit j.em (einer Sache) tändeln, sein Spiel treiben;* he is not to be ∾d with *mit ihm ist nicht zu spaßen (fackeln).* — **III.** v.tr.: to ∾ away one's money (time) on an object *sein Geld (seine Zeit) für etwas verschwenden*

trifling I. a.: a ∾ error *ein geringfügiger (unbedeutender) Fehler.* — **II.** n.: no ∾ here *hier wird nicht gespielt (gespaßt, gefackelt)*

trigger n.: he is ∾-happy *er ist schießwütig*

trim I. a.: to have a ∾ appearance *nett (schmuck) aussehen.* — **II.** v.tr.: to ∾ a person's beard *j.em den Bart stutzen;* to ∾ a dish *eine Schüssel (ein Gericht) garnieren;* to ∾ a dress with lace *ein Kleid mit Spitze besetzen;* to ∾ a horse *ein Pferd putzen (striegeln);* to ∾ a person's jacket (colloq.) *j.em die Jacke vollhauen;* to ∾ a person (colloq.) *j.en zurechtstutzen (herunterputzen);* to ∾ one's sails accordingly (to the wind) *sich nach den Umständen richten, sich nach der Decke strecken;* a shoal of fish ∾s the shore *ein Fischschwarm folgt dicht der Küste;* to ∾ a wick *einen Docht putzen;* to ∾ off (away) the leaves *die Blätter abschneiden;* to ∾ a person out of his money *j.en um sein Geld betrügen (prellen);* to ∾ oneself up *sich ausstaffieren (herausputzen).* — **III.** v.i.: to ∾ *sich keiner Partei oder Meinung anschließen;* to ∾ with the times *sich den Zeiten anpassen.* — **IV.** n.: the ∾ of the hold (masts) *die für ein Schiff vorteilhafte Verstauung der Ladung, Mastenstellung;* to be in (out of) ∾ *in guter (schlechter) Ordnung (Verfassung) sein;* in fighting ∾ *gefechtsbereit;* I am in no ∾ for rough work *ich bin nicht in der Verfassung, grobe Arbeit zu leisten*

trip I. v.i.: his tongue ∾ped, he ∾ped with his tongue *er versprach (verhaspelte) sich;* we are all apt to ∾ *jeder irrt sich gelegentlich;* to ∾ along *dahintrippeln;* to ∾

over an obstacle *über ein Hindernis straucheln (stolpern)*; to catch a person ∾ping *j.en bei einem Fehler ertappen.* — **II.** v.tr.: to ∾ a person up *j.em ein Bein stellen, ihn zu Fall bringen; j.en bei einem Fehler ertappen.* — **III.** n.: to go on (to make, to take) a ∾ *einen Ausflug (Abstecher), eine Vergnügungsreise (Spritztour) machen*

tripe n.: that's all ∾ (sl.) *das ist alles Unsinn (Schund, Kitsch)*

trippers n.: the town is full of ∾s *die Stadt wimmelt von Touristen (Ausflüglern)*

Triton n.pr.: a ∾ among the minnows *ein Riese unter Zwergen; als Einäugiger unter den Blinden König (sein)*

trivet n.: as right as a ∾ *in schönster Ordnung, in bester Verfassung, sauwohl*

Trojan n.pr.: he fights like a ∾ *er kämpft wie ein Held;* he works like a ∾ *er arbeitet wie ein Pferd*

trooper n.: he swears like a ∾ *er flucht wie ein Landsknecht*

trot I. v.i.: now ∾ along (away, off) *nun troll' dich!* — **II.** v.tr.: to ∾ a person off his legs (to death) *j.en zu Tode hetzen;* to ∾ out an idea (an argument) *eine Idee (ein Argument) stolz vorbringen, anführen;* ∾ it out *sag' es doch, heraus mit der Sprache!* — **III.** n.: to put one's horse at a ∾ *sein Pferd in Trab setzen;* to go for a ∾ *einen kleinen Spaziergang machen, sich (dat.) die Beine vertreten;* to keep a person on the ∾ *j.en in Trab (im Gange, auf den Beinen) halten*

trouble I. v.tr.: to ∾ one's head about a thing *sich über etwas den Kopf zerbrechen;* don't let it ∾ you, don't ∾ your head about it *mach' dir darüber keine Sorgen; laß dir darüber keine grauen Haare wachsen;* I will ∾ you for the mustard *reichen Sie mir bitte den Senf;* I will ∾ you for his last exploit *ich bitte Sie, sich über seine letzte Heldentat zu äußern;* may I ∾ you to shut the door? *darf ich Sie bitten, die Tür zu schließen (zuzumachen)?;* I will ∾ you to translate this *Sinn: dies kannst du sicher nicht übersetzen;* a ∾d countenance *ein betrübtes, sorgenvolles Gesicht;* he has been ∾d about (with) money matters *er hat Geldsorgen gehabt;* to be ∾d with neuralgia *von Nervenschmerzen geplagt (heimgesucht) werden;* to fish in ∾d waters *im trüben fischen;* to pour oil on ∾d waters *Öl auf die Wogen gießen, die Gemüter beruhigen.* — **II.** v.i.: why should I ∾? *warum sollte ich mir die Mühe (die Umstände) machen?;* don't ∾ about it *reg' dich nicht darüber auf, mach' dir deswegen keine Sorgen;* don't ∾ to explain *gib dir keine Mühe, es zu erklären.* — **III.** n.: the ∾ is that *der Haken dabei ist, daß;* digestive ∾s *Verdauungsbeschwerden;* he is a great ∾ to his family *er ist ein großer Kummer für seine Familie;* the boy will be a great ∾ to you *der Junge wird dir eine große Last sein (dir sehr lästig fallen);* no ∾! *bitte sehr! keine Ursache!;* life is full of small ∾s *das Leben bringt viele Unannehmlichkeiten mit sich;* your ∾ is that you are too lenient *dein Fehler ist, daß du zu nachsichtig bist;* it is not worth the ∾ *es ist nicht der Mühe wert, es lohnt sich nicht der Mühe;* to ask (to look for) ∾ *den Streit (das Unglück) herausfordern;* to be in (to get into) ∾ *in Not (Verlegenheit) sein (geraten);* to be out of one's ∾s *aus der Verlegenheit (von den Sorgen) befreit sein;* to bring ∾ upon oneself *sich ins Unglück stürzen;* to get a girl into ∾ *ein Mädchen schwängern;* to get a person into ∾ *j.em Unannehmlichkeiten bereiten;* to give a person ∾ *j.em Mühe (Sorge, Umstände) machen;* I shall not put you to any ∾ *ich werde dich in keiner Weise belästigen, dir gar keine Scherereien machen;* to run to meet one's ∾s *sich im voraus Sorgen machen;* to save (to spare) a person ∾ *j.em die Mühe ersparen;* to stir up ∾ *Unruhe stiften;* you must take great ∾ to do it properly *du mußt dir große Mühe geben, es anständig zu machen;* he will not take the ∾ to write *er macht (nimmt) sich nicht die Mühe zu schreiben;* a ∾-maker *ein Unruhestifter;* a ∾-shooter (teleph., colloq.) *der Mann von der Störungsstelle*

trowel n.: to lay it on with a ∾ *dick auftragen, grob schmeicheln*

truant n.: to play ∾ *die Schule schwänzen*

truce n.: a ∾ to your compliments (archaic) *genug mit (Schluß mit, hör' auf mit, still mit) deinen Komplimenten;* the ∾ of God *der Gottesfrieden im Mittelalter;* the flag of ∾ *die Parlamentärflagge*

truck I. v.i.: to ∾ with a person for a thing *mit j.em etwas tauschen; mit j.em* *um etwas feilschen (schachern).* — **II.** v.tr.: to ∾ one thing for another *eine Sache gegen eine andere ein-, austauschen;* to ∾ wares *mit Waren hausieren gehen.* — **III.** n.: I have no ∾ with him *ich habe keine Gemeinschaft (keinen Verkehr, nichts zu tun) mit ihm;* I shall stand no ∾ (colloq.) *ich lasse mir nichts gefallen*

true I. a.: as ∾ as steel *(so) treu wie Gold;* (it is) ∾, it would cost more *es würde allerdings (freilich, zwar) mehr kosten;* that is ∾ of him das *trifft auf ihn zu;* ∾ to nature *naturgetreu;* my dreams have come ∾ *meine Träume haben sich erfüllt;* his words have come ∾ *seine Worte haben sich bewahrheitet;* he is a ∾-blue democrat *er ist ein waschechter Demokrat;* a ∾-bred animal *ein rasseechtes Tier;* my ∾-love *mein Schatz.* — **II.** adv.: to aim ∾ *genau zielen;* to breed ∾ *sich rasseecht vermehren;* tell me ∾ *sag mir wahrheitsgetreu*

truly adv.: ∾, I could hardly say *ich könnte wirklich (in der Tat) kaum sagen;* yours ∾, N.N. *Ihr ergebener N. N.;* that won't hurt your's ∾ (facet.) *das wird mir nicht wehtun*

trump I. n.: he is a ∾ (colloq.) *er ist ein Prachtkerl, -mensch;* to play one's ∾ card *den letzten (höchsten) Trumpf ausspielen;* to put a person to his ∾s *j.en zum Äußersten treiben, ihn zwingen, das letzte Mittel anzuwenden;* to turn up ∾s *sich als besser erweisen als erwartet; Glück (Dusel) haben.* — **II.** v.tr.: he ∾ed up an excuse *er machte (schwindelte) sich eine Entschuldigung zurecht*

trumpet n.: to blow one's own ∾ *sein eigenes Lob singen;* ∾ major *Stabstrompeter;* ear-(speaking-)∾ *Hör-, Sprachrohr*

trumpeter n.: to be one's own ∾ *sein eigenes Lob singen (ausposaunen)*

trunk n.: a ∾ call *ein Ferngespräch am Telefon;* ∾ hose *kurze Hosentracht des 16. und 17. Jahrhunderts*

trust I. n.: a position of ∾ *eine Vertrauensstellung;* he is our sole ∾ *er ist unsere einzige Hoffnung;* I have fulfilled my ∾ *ich habe meine Verpflichtung erfüllt;* to hold a thing in ∾ *eine Sache zu treuen Händen verwalten;* to put (to repose) ∾ in a person *sein Vertrauen auf j.en setzen;* to supply goods on ∾ *Waren auf Kredit liefern;* he takes everything on ∾ *er nimmt alles auf Treu und Glauben hin.* — **II.** v.tr.: you must not ∾ his words too much *du darfst seinen Worten nicht so sehr trauen, nicht so sehr auf seine Worte bauen;* ∾ him for (to do) that (iron.) *er ist gerade der Rechte dafür, das sieht ihm gerade ähnlich;* do not ∾ him with your car *vertraue ihm nicht dein Auto an, laß ihn nicht dein Auto fahren.* — **III.** v.i.: I ∾ you are not hurt *ich hoffe, Sie haben sich nicht verletzt;* we must ∾ to meeting someone who knows *wir müssen darauf vertrauen (uns darauf verlassen), j.en zu treffen, der es weiß;* it does not do to ∾ to memory for these things *es ist nicht gut (es geht nicht), sich hierbei auf sein Gedächtnis zu verlassen;* ∾ing you are all well, I remain — — — *in der Hoffnung, daß Ihr alle gesund (wohl) seid, verbleibe ich* — — —

truth n.: the ∾ is (to tell the ∾, ∾ to tell), I forgot all about it *ehrlich gesagt, ich habe es ganz vergessen;* are you telling the ∾? *sagst du auch die Wahrheit?;* to tell a person some home ∾s *j.em einige derbe, treffende Wahrheiten (gehörig die Wahrheit, Meinung) sagen;* the wheel is out of ∾ *das Rad hat einen Schlag;* children and fools tell the ∾ (prov.) *Kinder und Narren sagen die Wahrheit*

try I. v.tr.: to ∾ conclusions with a person *sich mit j.em messen;* that will ∾ his courage *das wird seinen Mut auf die Probe stellen;* to ∾ the door *die Tür zu öffnen versuchen;* to ∾ one's best *sein Bestes tun;* to ∾ one's eyes *die Augen überanstrengen;* to ∾ one's hardest *sich die größte Mühe geben;* to ∾ a fall *sich im Ringen messen, es aufnehmen mit;* to ∾ one's hand at a thing *etwas versuchen;* to ∾ one's luck *sein Glück versuchen;* his patience was sorely tried *seine Geduld wurde auf eine harte Probe gestellt;* to ∾ a person for murder *über j.en wegen Mordes zu Gericht sitzen;* to ∾ on clothes *Kleider anprobieren;* I shall ∾ it (out) on him first *ich probiere es zuerst bei ihm aus;* to ∾ it on with a person *j.en zu überlisten versuchen;* you can't ∾ it on with me *damit kannst du mir nicht kommen;* to ∾ a thing out *etwas probieren (ausprobieren);* to ∾ something out on the dog (colloq.) *j.en als Versuchskaninchen benutzen.* — **II.** v.i.: ∾ to (and) get it finished tonight *versuche, es heute abend fertigzustellen;* to ∾ back to a subject *auf* *ein Thema zurückgreifen, -kommen;* to ∾ for a post *sich um eine Stellung bemühen.* — **III.** n.: have a ∾ at it (colloq.) *versuch's doch einmal;* it was a ∾-on *es war ein Schwindelmanöver;* to give a thing a ∾-out *etwas ausprobieren*

trying a.: he is very ∾ *mit ihm ist schwer fertig werden;* under most ∾ circumstances *unter sehr schwierigen (mißlichen) Umständen*

tub n.: a tale of a ∾ *ein Ammenmärchen;* to have (to take) a ∾ *ein (Wannen)bad nehmen;* let every ∾ stand on its own bottom *jeder sorge für sich selbst;* to throw out a ∾ to a whale *ein Ablenkungsmanöver veranstalten, um einer drohenden Gefahr zu entgehen;* a ∾-thumper *ein lärmender (eifernder) Kanzelredner; vgl. rheinisch „Büttenredner"*

tube n.: to go by ∾ *mit der Untergrundbahn (U-Bahn) fahren*

tuck I. v.tr.: he ∾ed a few books under his arm *er klemmte sich ein paar Bücher unter den Arm;* a bird ∾s his head under his wing *ein Vogel steckt den Kopf unter den Flügel;* he ∾ed his legs under him like a tailor *er schlug die Beine unter sich wie ein Schneider;* to ∾ a thing away *etwas verstecken, verstauen;* to ∾ in the loose ends *die Enden einschlagen (umnähen);* to ∾ a child up in bed *die Bettdecken fest um ein Kind schlagen;* to ∾ a criminal up (sl.) *einen Verbrecher aufhängen;* to ∾ up one's shirt sleeves *die Hemdsärmel hochkrempeln.* — **II.** v.i.: to ∾ in (in at, into) food (colloq.) *beim Essen tüchtig einhauen.* — **III.** n.: to make a ∾ in the sleeves *eine Falte in die Ärmel legen (nähen);* it was a ∾-in, (-out) for us (sl.) *es war ein Festessen für uns;* the school ∾-shop *die Konditorei, wo (in der) die Schüler Gebäck und Süßigkeiten kaufen dürfen*

tucker[1] n.: she was dressed in her best bib and ∾ *sie trug ihren feinsten Staat*

tucker[2] v.tr.: (U.S. colloq.) to ∾ a person out *j.en ermüden*

tug I. v.tr.: to ∾ a vessel out of the harbour *ein Schiff aus dem Hafen schleppen;* to ∾ a subject into the discussion *ein Thema in die Debatte zerren.* — **II.** v.i.: to ∾ at a thing *heftig an etwas ziehen (zerren).* — **III.** n.: the parting was a ∾ *der Abschied fiel mir äußerst schwer;* he gave a ∾ at the bell *er zog heftig (zerrte, riß) an der Glocke;* I had a great ∾ to persuade him *ich hatte große Mühe, ihn zu überreden;* a ∾-of-war *ein Tauziehen; ein Entscheidungskampf*

tumble I. v.i.: he came tumbling along *er kam dahergestolpert, -getorkelt;* he ∾d down from his chair *er fiel (purzelte) von seinem Stuhl;* he ∾d home *er torkelte nach Hause;* I ∾d on him yesterday *ich stieß gestern zufällig auf ihn;* I didn't ∾ to it at once (colloq.) *ich kapierte es nicht sofort;* he ∾d up the stairs *er stolperte die Treppe hinauf.* — **II.** v.tr.: the sheets lay ∾d about on the floor *die Bettücher lagen in Unordnung (zerknittert, zerknüllt) auf dem Boden;* they ∾d us out of bed *sie warfen (schmissen) uns aus dem Bett.* — **III.** n.: things were all in a ∾ *alles war in großer Unordnung (alles war durcheinander);* I had a nasty ∾ *ich bin eklig gestürzt;* a rough-and-∾ fight *eine rohe (wüste) Schlägerei;* a ∾-down house *ein baufälliges Haus*

tune I. n.: that's the ∾ the old cow died of *das ist eine wahre Leichenmusik;* to pay the piper and call the ∾ (prov.) *die Kosten tragen, die Zeche bezahlen, und die Sache nach seinem Willen leiten (eigentlich: die Musikanten bezahlen und dann bestimmen, welches Lied gespielt werden soll);* to change one's ∾, to sing another ∾ *einen anderen Ton anschlagen, andere Saiten aufziehen;* give us a ∾ *spiel' uns etwas vor;* to strike up a ∾ *eine Melodie anstimmen;* the piano is out of ∾ *das Klavier ist verstimmt;* to be in (out of) ∾ with the surroundings *im Einklang (nicht im Einklang) mit der Umgebung stehen;* to sing in (out of) ∾ *rein (unrein) singen;* to dance to a ∾ *nach einer Melodie tanzen;* I had to pay to the ∾ of £ 5 *ich mußte die unverschämte (phantastische) Summe von 5 Pfund (sage und schreibe 5 Pfund) dafür bezahlen;* I ticked him off to every ∾ (sl.) *ich kanzelte ihn nach Strich und Faden ab.* — **II.** v.tr.: to ∾ a piano *ein Klavier stimmen;* the lark ∾s his song *die Lerche stimmt ihr Lied an;* to ∾ (a wireless-set) in to a station *einen Radioapparat auf eine Station einstellen;* to ∾ a person to a mood *j.en in eine Stimmung versetzen;* to ∾ a thing to the circumstances *etwas den Um-*

ständen anpassen; to ∾ up instruments *Instrumente höher stimmen;* to ∾ up a motor *einen Motor auf Touren bringen.* — **III.** v.i.: to ∾ with a thing *mit etwas im Einklang sein;* the band ∾d up *die Kapelle begann zu spielen (setzte ein);* the child ∾d up (facet.) *das Kind heulte los*

turf v.tr.: he was ∾ed out (sl.) *er wurde hinausgeworfen (-geschmissen, -gefeuert, -gepfeffert)*

Turk n.: to turn ∾ *böse, wild werden*

turkey n.: as red as a ∾-cock *puterrot;* he is a ∾-cock *er ist ein aufgeblasener Mensch, ein Wichtigtuer;* to talk (cold) ∾ (U.S.) *die nackte (ungeschminkte) Wahrheit sagen (deutsch, Fraktur reden)*

turn I. v.tr.: see 'attention, back, balance, brain, bullet, coat, etc.'. — with adv. and prep.: to ∾ a person adrift *j.en sich selbst überlassen, ihn seinem Schicksal preisgeben; ihn fortjagen;* to ∾ a person away *j.en abweisen;* to ∾ down the gas *das Gas klein stellen;* to ∾ down a proposal *einen Vorschlag ablehnen (-weisen); j.em einen Korb geben;* to ∾ everything upside down *das Oberste zu unterst kehren, alles auf den Kopf stellen;* he ∾s his toes in *er setzt seine Füße einwärts;* to ∾ the weeds in *das Unkraut eingraben;* to ∾ a thing into money *etwas zu Geld machen;* to ∾ water into wine *Wasser in Wein verwandeln;* to ∾ off a couple *ein Paar verheiraten;* to ∾ off a criminal *einen Verbrecher aufhängen;* to ∾ off the current (gas, light, water) *den Strom (das Gas, Licht, Wasser) abschalten (-drehen, -stellen);* to ∾ off a piece of work *eine Arbeit fertigbringen, -stellen;* to ∾ off a servant *einen Dienstboten entlassen;* to ∾ on the current (gas, light, water) *den Strom einschalten (das Gas, Licht, Wasser andrehen, -stellen);* to ∾ on the waterworks (sl.) *anfangen zu weinen (heulen);* to ∾ the tables on a person *den Spieß gegen j.en umdrehen;* to ∾ the cattle out *das Vieh auf die Weide treiben;* this factory ∾s out engines *diese Fabrik stellt Lokomotiven her;* to ∾ out the guard *die Wache herausrufen;* to ∾ out the light *das Licht ausmachen;* to ∾ a person out *j.en hinauswerfen;* I made him ∾ his pockets out (inside out) *ich ließ ihn die Taschen umkehren;* he ∾ed out his pupils good citizens *er schuf gute Staatsbürger aus seinen Schülern;* to ∾ out a room *ein Zimmer ausräumen, gründlich sauber machen;* she was elegantly ∾ed out (sl.) *sie war elegant aufgemacht (herausgeputzt);* ∾ out your toes *setze die Füße auswärts!;* to ∾ a person out of bed *j.en aus dem Bett werfen (schmeißen);* please ∾ over (abbr. p.t.o.) *bitte wenden!;* to ∾ over a new leaf *sich bessern, einen neuen Menschen anziehen;* to ∾ over a table *einen Tisch umwerfen;* to ∾ a thing over in one's mind *sich (dat.) etwas überlegen;* to ∾ a thing over to a person *j.em etwas übertragen;* this business ∾s over £ 1,000 a month *das Geschäft setzt monatlich 1000 Pfund um;* to ∾ a thing round *etwas umdrehen, -kehren;* to ∾ a person round one's (little) finger *j.en um den (kleinen) Finger wickeln;* to ∾ to account *verwerten, zunutze machen;* to ∾ everything topsy-turvy *das Oberste zu unterst kehren, alles auf den Kopf stellen;* to ∾ up a card *eine Karte aufdecken;* the sight ∾ed me up (vulg.) *bei dem Anblick wurde es mir übel;* to ∾ up one's nose at a thing *über etwas die Nase rümpfen;* the plough ∾ed up some skulls *der Pflug brachte einige Schädel ans Licht.* — **II.** v.i.: to ∾ Catholic (cold, pale, sour, traitor etc.) *katholisch (kalt, bleich, sauer, zum Verräter usw.) werden;* to ∾ Turk *böse, wild werden;* my head ∾s *mir wird schwindelig;* his head has ∾ed with success *der Erfolg ist ihm in den Kopf gestiegen;* my stomach ∾s *mir wird es übel, es kommt mir hoch;* the tap will not ∾ *der Hahn läßt sich nicht drehen;* the tide has ∾d *das Glück (Blatt) hat sich gewendet;* I don't know which way to ∾ *ich weiß nicht, was ich machen soll; ich geniere mich.* — with adv. and prep.: to ∾ about *sich umdrehen;* to ∾ against a person *sich gegen j.en wenden;* to ∾ aside (away) *sich abwenden;* to ∾ back *umkehren;* to ∾ in *zu Bett gehen;* it has ∾ed into a company *es hat sich in eine Gesellschaft verwandelt;* the road ∾s off to the right *der Weg biegt nach rechts ab;* everything ∾s on his answer *alles hängt von seiner Antwort ab;* he ∾ed on his heels *er drehte sich rasch (kurz) um;* to ∾ on a person *über j.en herfallen, ihn angreifen;* we shall see how things ∾ out *wir werden sehen, wie die Sache ausläuft;* the workers ∾ed out *die Arbeiter stellten die Arbeit ein (legten sie nieder);* only 15 men ∾ed out for duty *nur 15 Mann traten zum Dienst an;* I shall ∾ out early tomorrow *ich* *werde morgen früh (zeitig) aufstehen;* it has ∾ed out a fine evening *es ist noch ein schöner Abend geworden;* he ∾ed out to be a humbug *er erwies sich als Schwindler;* I hope it will ∾ out all right *ich hoffe, es wird alles gut gehen (klappen);* it ∾ed out a great success *es gestaltete sich zu einem großen Erfolg;* it ∾s out that he was never there *es stellt sich heraus, daß er nie dort war;* it ∾s out to be true *es erweist sich als wahr;* to ∾ over in bed *sich im Bett umdrehen;* the glass ∾ed over *das Glas fiel (kippte) um;* he ∾ed over to another party *er ging zu einer anderen Partei über;* he ∾ed round *er änderte seine Ansicht;* to ∾ to (adv.) (to work) *sich an die Arbeit machen;* all ∾ed to his advantage *alles schlug ihm zum Vorteil aus;* to ∾ to God in trouble *sich in der Not zu Gott hinwenden (bekehren);* water ∾s to ice *Wasser wird zu Eis;* my thoughts often ∾ed to the subject *ich habe mich oft in Gedanken mit dem Gegenstand beschäftigt;* to wait for something to ∾ up *darauf warten, daß sich etwas ereignet (bietet);* anything that may ∾ up *was sich gerade bietet;* he ∾ed up an hour late *er erschien eine Stunde zu spät;* it will ∾ up one of these days *es wird eines Tages zum Vorschein kommen;* he ∾ed up unexpectedly *er tauchte unerwartet auf.* — compounds with v.tr. and i.: a ∾coat *ein Abtrünniger, Achsel-, Mantelträger;* a ∾-key *ein Schließer im Gefängnis;* a ∾-out for duty *ein Antreten zum Dienst;* a ∾-out of employees *ein Streik der Angestellten;* a ∾-out of spectators *eine Versammlung von Zuschauern;* an elegant ∾-out *ein elegantes Gespann;* in fine ∾-out *hübsch hergerichtet, gut ausstaffiert;* the monthly ∾-out *die monatliche Produktion;* the yearly ∾over *der jährliche Umsatz;* a ∾pike *ein Schlagbaum;* the ∾-round of a ship *die Umschlagszeit eines Schiffes;* a ∾-screw *ein Schraubenzieher;* a ∾stile *ein Drehkreuz;* a ∾-table *eine Drehscheibe;* a terrible ∾-up *ein schrecklicher Tumult (Aufruhr).* — **III.** n.: the ∾ of an ankle *die Form (Gestalt) eines Knöchels;* the ∾ of the century *die Jahrhundertwende;* a ∾ of expression *eine Ausdrucksweise;* a ∾ of Fortune's wheel *ein Wechsel des Glücks;* a ∾ of a river *eine Krümmung (Windung) eines Flusses;* the ∾ of the scale *der Ausschlag beim Wiegen;* the ∾ of the sentence *die Bildung (der Wortlaut, die Tendenz) des Satzes;* a fine ∾ of speed *eine nette Geschwindigkeit;* a ∾ of work *eine Arbeitsleistung, ein Stück Arbeit;* one good ∾ deserves another (prov.) *eine Liebe ist der anderen wert;* it is my ∾ to watch *ich bin an der Reihe (dran) zu wachen;* it was now my ∾ to be angry *die Reihe war jetzt an mir, böse zu sein;* left (right, right about) ∾ *linksum! (rechtsum! rechtsum kehrt!);* short ∾s *kurze Auftritte im Varieté;* we worked ∾ and ∾ about *wir arbeiteten abwechselnd;* we dug by ∾s *wir gruben abwechselnd;* he went hot and cold by ∾s *ihm wurde abwechselnd heiß und kalt;* I shall hear you all in ∾ *ich werde euch alle der Reihe nach (einen nach dem anderen) anhören;* everything in its ∾ *alles zu seiner Zeit;* we took it in ∾s to work *wir arbeiteten abwechselnd;* the milk is on the ∾ *die Milch hat schon einen Stich;* the tide is on the ∾ *die Gezeit wechselt;* it is on the ∾ of twelve *es ist auf den Schlag zwölf Uhr;* to speak out of ∾ *außer der Reihe sprechen;* the meat is done to a ∾ *das Fleisch ist gerade richtig (tadellos) gebraten;* to be of a humourous ∾ *eine humorvolle Ader besitzen;* he did me a good (an ill) ∾ *er erwies (tat) mir einen guten (schlechten) Dienst;* to give a new ∾ to the argument *der Erörterung eine andere Wendung geben, ein neues Moment in die Erörterung bringen;* it gave me quite a ∾ (colloq.) *es erschreckte mich, es gab mir einen richtigen Schock;* to have a ∾ for a thing *einen Hang (eine Neigung) zu (einen Sinn für) etwas haben;* it did not serve my ∾ *es erfüllte meinen Zweck nicht;* we shall take ∾s *wir werden uns abwechseln;* you must take your ∾ *du mußt warten, bis du an der Reihe bist;* to take a ∾ in the garden *einen kurzen Spaziergang im (einen Bummel durch den) Garten machen;* the complaint took a bad ∾ (a ∾ for the better, worse) *das Leiden nahm eine Wendung zum Schlechten (zum Besseren, Schlechteren);* the road took a sudden ∾ to the left *die Straße bog plötzlich nach links ab*

turning n.: stop at the next ∾ *halten Sie an der nächsten Straßenecke;* take the second ∾ to the left *gehen Sie die zweite Straße links;* the matter has reached the ∾-point *die Sache hat den Wendepunkt erreicht;* it's a long lane that has no ∾ (prov.) *Alles hat ein Ende, einmal ändert sich das Glück*

turtle n.: to turn ∾ *kentern, umkippen*

twang n.: to speak with a nasal ∾ *eine näselnde Aussprache haben*

tweedledum and tweedledee n.: it is ∾ *es ist nur wenig Unterschied (es ist Jacke wie Hose, gehüpft wie gesprungen, Pott wie Deckel)*

twenty I. a.: I have told him ∾ times *ich habe es ihm x-mal gesagt.* — **II.** n.: in the twenties of the last century *in den zwanziger Jahren des vorigen Jahrhunderts*

twice adv.: he didn't think ∾ about doing it *er tat es ohne Bedenken, er überlegte es sich nicht lange;* he is ∾ the man (∾ as strong as) he was *er ist doppelt so stark wie zuvor;* he paid it in ∾ (colloq.) *er bezahlte es in zwei Raten*

twiddle I. v.tr.: to ∾ one's thumbs *die Daumen drehen, nichts tun (faulenzen).* — **II.** v.i.: to ∾ with a thing *mit einer Sache spielen*

twig I. n: as the ∾ is bent the tree is inclined (prov.) *früh krümmt sich, was ein Häkchen werden will;* to hop the ∾ (colloq.) *sterben, abkratzen;* to work the ∾ *mit der Wünschelrute arbeiten.* — **II.** v.tr.: I didn't ∾ it (colloq.) *ich habe es nicht kapiert*

twinkling n.: in the ∾ of an eye (of a bedpost) *im Augenblick, im Nu*

twirl I. v.tr.: to ∾ one's moustache *den Schnurbart drehen (zwirbeln);* to ∾ one's thumbs *die Daumen drehen, nichts tun (faulenzen).* — **II.** v.i.: to ∾ round *sich rasch umdrehen.* — **III.** n.: to add a ∾ to one's signature *die Unterschrift mit einem Schnörkel versehen*

twist I. n.: a ∾ of the wrist *Geschicklichkeit;* to give a thing a ∾ *einer Sache einen Dreh geben;* he has a curious ∾ *er ist merkwürdig verdreht (nicht ganz normal);* he had a tremendous ∾ (colloq.) *er hatte einen Mordsappetit;* to put a ∾ on a ball *einem Ball Drall (Effet) geben.* — **II.** v.tr.: features ∾ed with pain *schmerzverzerrte Züge;* to ∾ one's ankle *den Fuß umknikken;* to ∾ a person's arm *j.em den Arm umdrehen;* to ∾ one's way through the crowd *sich durch die Menge schlängeln;* to ∾ a person's words *j.em die Worte verdrehen;* to ∾ a piece off *ein Stück abdrehen*

twister n.: he is a ∾ *er ist ein Schwindler*

twit v.tr.: to ∾ a person with a fault *j.em einen Fehler vorwerfen;* to ∾ someone about (over) something *j.en wegen einer Sache aufziehen*

twitter n.: to be all of a ∾ (colloq.) *voller Aufregung sein*

two I. a.: a ∾ job man *ein Doppelverdiener;* ∾ heads are better than one (prov.) *vier Augen sehen mehr als zwei; frage bei schwierigen Dingen einen anderen um Rat;* one or ∾ people *ein paar Leute;* in ∾ ∾s, in ∾ shakes of a lamb's tail *in ganz kurzer Zeit, im Nu;* to have ∾ strings to one's bow *zwei Eisen im Feuer haben.* — **II.** n.: ∾ can play at that game *das kann ich auch, da hätte ich auch ein Wörtchen mitzureden;* ∾'s company, three's none (prov.) *zwei machen (bilden) ein Paar;* ∾ upon ten (i.e. two eyes on ten fingers) *man sehe ihm auf die Finger;* to cut in ∾ *entzweischneiden;* to put ∾ and ∾ together *aus einer Sache seine Schlüsse ziehen, sich (dat.) etwas zusammenreimen*

twopence n.: penny plain and ∾ coloured *billig und geschmacklos aufgemacht;* I don't care ∾ for it *ich mache mir nicht das geringste daraus;* to want ∾ in the shilling (sl.) *verrückt sein, einen Hau haben*

twopenny (tuppenny) **I.** a.: a ∾ (tuppennyha'penny) thing *eine wertlose, billige Sache.* — **II.** n.: tuck in your ∾ (at leap frog) *zieh' deinen Kopf (Schädel, „Ballon", „Dez") ein (beim Bockspringen)*

type I. n.: men of his ∾ *Männer seines Schlages;* to be true to ∾ *die charakteristischen Merkmale aufweisen;* to appear in ∾ *im Druck erscheinen;* to be in ∾ *abgesetzt, druckfertig sein;* in bold ∾ *im Fettdruck*

U

U. n.: it's all U.P. (sl.) *es ist alles aus*

ugly a.: as ∾ as sin *(pott)häßlich;* an ∾ customer *ein garstiger, gemeiner Mensch;* an ∾ duckling *ein Kind (eine Sache), das (die) sich besser entwickelt, als man gedacht hätte;* to cut up ∾ (colloq.) *grob, bedrohlich werden*

ulterior a.: an ∾ motive *tiefere Beweggründe, Hintergedanken*

ultimo (ult.) n.: your letter of the 5th ∾ *Ihr Brief vom 5. letzten Monats*

umbrage n.: to take ∾ at *Anstoß nehmen an*

umpteen a. (colloq.): ∾ times *mehrmal(s), x-mal*

unawares adv.: to take (to catch) someone ∾ *j.en überraschen*

unbeaten a.: to follow an ∾ track *einem unbetretenen Pfad folgen; einen eigenen, unerforschten Weg gehen*

unbeknown (unbeknownst) adv.: ∾ to me *ohne mein Wissen*

unbend I. v.tr.: to ∾ a bow *einen Bogen entspannen.* — **II.** v.i.: to ∾ over a book *sich durch Lesen entspannen;* he ∾s in company *er taut auf (wird freundlich) in Gesellschaft*

unbosom v.tr.: to ∾ oneself *seine Sorgen (Gedanken) j.em anvertrauen; j.em sein Herz ausschütten*

unbridled a.: ∾ rage *zügellose Wut*

unburden v.tr.: to ∾ oneself (one's soul) to someone *sein Herz j.em gegenüber erleichtern (befreien)*

uncertain I. a.: a lady of ∾ age (facet.) *eine ältere (auf „Jung" aufgemachte) Frau;* an ∾ temper *eine schwankende Laune;* ∾ weather *unsicheres Wetter.* — **II.** n.: void for ∾ (jur.) *ungültig wegen Unklarheit*

uncle n.: my watch is at ∾'s *meine Uhr ist im Pfandhaus;* to talk to a person like a Dutch ∾ *j.en väterlich zurechtweisen*

uncover I. v.tr.: to ∾ a wound *den Verband von einer Wunde abnehmen;* to ∾ a plot *ein Komplott aufdecken.* — **II.** v.i.: he ∾ed as we passed *er nahm den Hut ab (er grüßte), als wir vorbeigingen.* — **III.** a.: an ∾ agent *ein Geheimagent*

unction n.: Extreme Unction *die Letzte Ölung;* he spoke with ∾ *er sprach mit Salbung (Inbrunst, Pathos, heuchlerisch);* he did it with ∾ *er tat es mit Behagen*

under I. prep.: ∾ a person's nose *j.em vor der Nase;* ∾ the rose *im Vertrauen;* ∾ age *minderjährig;* ∾ one's breath *flüsternd, leise;* ∾ cover *in Deckung;* ∾ the cover of darkness *unter dem Schutze der Dunkelheit;* ∾ this cover *beiliegend;* ∾ chloroform *in der Narkose;* to be ∾ a cloud *unter Verdacht stehen, übel beleumdet sein;* to be ∾ consideration *erwogen, erörtert werden;* to be ∾ a mistake *sich im Irrtum befinden;* to be ∾ repair *in Reparatur sein;* ∾ sentence of death *zum Tode verurteilt;* ∾-the-table *heimlich, illegal, ungesetzlich;* ∾ treatment *in Behandlung;* ∾ way *auf dem Wege;* to be (a bit) ∾ the weather (colloq.) *etwas deprimiert (nicht ganz auf der Höhe) sein.* — **II.** adv.: to knuckle ∾ (colloq.) *nachgeben, klein beigeben;* ∾privi-ledged persons *Menschen, welche an den üblichen kulturellen und sozialen Vorteilen keinen Anteil haben, arme Menschen*

underhand a.: to act in an ∾ way *heimlich, unehrlich handeln*

undies (abbr. underclothes, fam.) n.: *(Frauen) Leib-, Unterwäsche*

understand v.tr.: am I to ∾ that you refuse? *soll ich etwa annehmen, daß du dich weigerst?;* do I ∾ you to say? *willst du etwa damit sagen?;* no one could ∾ that from my words *niemand konnte das meinen Worten entnehmen;* he gave me to ∾, I was given to ∾ *er gab mir zu verstehen, mir wurde zu verstehen gegeben;* I understood that doors open at 7.30 *ich nahm an, daß um halb acht geöffnet wurde;* be it understood *wohlverstanden!;* it is understood *es ist ausgemacht, selbstverständlich;* the verb must be understood *das Zeitwort muß sinngemäß ergänzt werden;* we must not be understood *wir dürfen nicht dahin verstanden werden;* have I made myself understood? *habe ich mich verständlich gemacht?;* now ∾ me *nun versteh' mich recht, ich warne dich*

understanding n.: to have a good ∾ with a person *in gutem Einvernehmen mit j.em stehen;* to come to an ∾ with someone *sich mit j.em verständigen;* on the ∾ that *unter der Voraussetzung (Bedingung), daß*

undertake I. v.tr.: to ∾ a post, a responsibility *ein Amt, eine Verantwortung übernehmen, sich dazu verpflichten.* — **II.** v.i.: to ∾ to do something *sich mit etwas befassen;* I cannot ∾ that it will be a success *ich kann mich nicht dafür verbürgen, daß es erfolgreich sein wird*

undertaker n.: he is an ∾ *er ist Leichenbestatter*

undesirous a.: to be ∾ of something *etwas nicht begehren, es nicht wünschen*

undo v.tr.: to ∾ a knot *einen Knoten lösen, aufmachen;* we are undone *wir sind ruiniert, es ist aus mit uns;* all my work is undone *meine ganze Arbeit ist zugrunde gerichtet (verloren, hin);* to come undone *auf-, losgehen;* to leave nothing undone to help a person *nichts unterlassen (alles tun), um j.em zu helfen;* the work is still undone *die Arbeit ist noch ungeschehen, unvollendet;* what is done cannot be undone *getan ist getan, es kann nichts rückgängig gemacht werden*

unearthly a.: why call me at this ∾ hour? (colloq.) *warum weckst du mich zu dieser nachtschlafenden Zeit?*

unfreeze v.tr.: to ∾ controls on industry *wirtschaftliche Zwangsmaßnahmen aufheben*

unholy a. (colloq.): they were kicking up an ∾ row *sie machten einen Heidenlärm*

unhinged a.: his mind is ∾ *sein Geist ist verwirrt*

unity n.: to be at ∾ with a person *mit j.em übereinstimmen;* to dwell together in ∾ *einträchtig zusammenwohnen*

unparliamentary a.: ∾ language *Schimpfworte, Beleidigungen*

unruly a.: the ∾ member (James, III, 1) *die Zunge*

unseasonable a.: an ∾ remark *eine unangebrachte, unpassende Bemerkung;* ∾ weather *ungewöhnliches Wetter (der Jahreszeit nicht entsprechend)*

unseen n.: the ∾ *die unsichtbare (übernatürliche) Welt;* a Latin ∾ *eine nicht vorbereitete (nicht vorher durchgearbeitete) Lateinarbeit (Übersetzung)*

unstuck v.tr.: it came ∾ (sl.) *die Sache ging schief*

unscramble v.tr.: to ∾ a secret message *einen Geheimbericht entziffern (dechiffrieren)*

unwrung a. (old fash.): my withers are ∾ by the argument *das Argument (der Beweis) läßt mich kalt*

up I. adv.: examples of ∾ (adv.) in connection with verbs are given under the verbs in question *Beispiele mit „up" (adv.) in Verbindung mit Verben werden unter den betreffenden Verben gebracht;* ∾!, ∾ with it!, ∾ with you *auf!, auf damit!, auf mit dir!;* ∾ to date *modern, zeitgemäß;* (to ∾date a book *ein Buch der Neuzeit gemäß umarbeiten);* ∾ to now, ∾ to the present *bis jetzt;* ∾ there *dort oben;* it is all ∾ with him *mit ihm ist es aus;* as far ∾ as *bis hinauf nach;* his blood is ∾ *es kocht in ihm, sein Blut ist in Wallung geraten;* corn is ∾ *Korn steht hoch im Preis;* three floors ∾ *drei Stockwerke, Treppen hoch;* the game is ∾ *das Spiel ist aus, die Sache ist verloren;* to be a hundred, three, ∾ *100 Punkte auf der Gewinntafel verzeichnet haben, 3 Punkte voraus sein;* with a better jockey ∾ *mit einem besseren Jockei im Sattel;* Parliament is ∾ *das Parlament tagt nicht;* the whole of the west is ∾ *der ganze Westen ist in Aufruhr;* what is ∾? *was gibt's? was ist los?;* to be ∾ and about (∾ and doing) *wieder auf den Beinen, tätig sein;* to be ∾ against a hard job, to be ∾ against it *einer schwierigen Arbeit gegenüberstehen; Schwierigkeiten vor sich haben;* to look for a thing ∾ and down *überall nach etwas suchen;* to be well ∾ in mathematics *in Mathematik sehr bewandert sein, gut Mathematik können;* it is not ∾ to much *es ist nicht viel wert, nicht viel daran;* to be ∾ to a person, a thing *j.em, einer Sache gewachsen sein;* what are you ∾ to there? *was machst du da?;* he is not ∾ to travelling *er ist nicht reisefähig;* it is ∾ to us to do so *es ist an uns, es zu tun.* — **II.** prep.: to climb ∾ a ladder, hill etc. *eine Leiter, einen Hügel usw. hinaufklettern;* to be ∾ the pole (spout, tree) (colloq.) *in der Klemme sein;* to sail ∾ the river *flußaufwärts segeln, fahren;* he lives further ∾ the road *er wohnt weiter oben in der Straße.* — **III.** a.: an ∾ train *ein nach der Hauptstadt (London) fahrender Zug.* — **IV.** n.: the ∾s and downs *das Auf und Ab;* the ∾s and downs of life *die Wechselfälle des Lebens.* — **V.** v.i.: (humor., colloq.) he ∾ed with his fists, stick *er erhob seine Fäuste, seinen Stock*

upbraid v.tr.: to ∾ a person with (for) a fault *j.em einen Fehler vorwerfen, ihn wegen eines Fehlers ausschelten*

update v.tr.: to ∾ a report *einen Bericht nach dem neuesten Stand der Dinge ergänzen*

upper **I.** a.: to gain (to get) the ∾ hand *die Oberhand gewinnen;* to keep a stiff ∾ lip *Mut zeigen, beharrlich bleiben;* ∾ bracket tax-payers, employees *Angehörige höherer Steuergruppen, Angestellte im gehobenen (höheren) Dienst;* he has something wrong in his ∾ storey (colloq.) *er ist nicht ganz richtig im Oberstübchen.* — **II.** n.: the ∾s *das Oberleder;* to be (down) on one's ∾s *heruntergekommen, in Not oder Bedrängnis sein*

uppermost adv.: I said whatever came ∾ *ich sagte, was mir gerade einfiel*

ups-a-daisy (upsy-daisy) int.: etwa: *hoppla! (wenn ein Kind fällt)*

upset[1] **I.** v.tr.: to ∾ a glass *ein Glas umstoßen, umwerfen;* the news quite ∾ him *die Nachricht brachte ihn ganz außer Fassung;* he ate something that ∾ him *er aß etwas, das ihm schlecht bekam;* it ∾ all our plans *es warf unsere ganzen Pläne über den Haufen, machte uns einen Strich durch die Rechnung.* — **II.** v.i.: the carriage fell into a ditch and ∾ *der Wagen stürzte in einen Graben und schlug um.* — **III.** n.: the carriage had an ∾ *der Wagen schlug um*

upset[2] a.: the ∾ price *der Vorbehalts-, Einsatzpreis (bei Versteigerung)*

upshot n.: what will be the ∾ of it? *was wird dabei herauskommen?;* the ∾ of the matter was ——— *das Ende (Resultat) der Sache (das Ende vom Lied) war* ———

upside-down **I.** adv.: everything was ∾ *alles war drunter und drüber, stand auf dem Kopf;* to turn a thing ∾ *etwas auf den Kopf stellen.* — **II.** a.: an ∾ arrangement *eine verkehrte Ordnung*

upsides adv.: to be ∾ with a person *auf gleichem Fuße mit j.em stehen;* to get ∾ with a person *gegen j.en den Spieß umdrehen, ihm etwas heimzahlen*

upstage a.: to be ∾ *hochnäsig, eingebildet sein*

upwards adv.: I found ∾ of 40 specimens *ich fand mehr als 40 Exemplare*

uptake n.: to be quick (slow) in the ∾ *etwas schnell begreifen (schwer von Begriff sein, eine lange Leitung haben)*

urge **I.** v.tr.: to ∾ a horse *ein Pferd antreiben;* to ∾ someone to come *j.en dringend auffordern zu kommen;* to ∾ upon someone the need of being careful *j.em die Notwendigkeit der Vorsicht nahelegen (nachdrücklich betonen, ans Herz legen).* — **II.** n.: I have an ∾ to travel *ich habe den (inneren) Drang (den dringenden Wunsch) zu reisen*

urgency n.: it is a matter of great ∾ *die Sache drängt (eilt) sehr;* the ∾ of poverty *die Bedrückung der Armut*

urgent a.: the matter is ∾ *die Sache drängt (eilt);* an ∾ demand *eine dringliche Forderung;* to be in ∾ need of a thing *etwas dringend nötig haben;* he was ∾ with me for (to disclose) further particulars *er drang um weitere Einzelheiten in mich*

use **I.** n.: once a ∾, and ever a custom (prov.) *jung gewohnt, alt getan;* according to ∾ and custom *nach Gebrauch und Sitte;* for the ∾ of *zum Gebrauch für, von;* what is the ∾ of crying? *was hat es für einen Zweck zu weinen?;* to find a ∾ for a thing *für etwas eine Anwendungsmöglichkeit finden;* he lost the ∾ of his left arm *er verlor die Kraft (Fähigkeit), seinen linken Arm zu gebrauchen;* to make ∾ of a thing *von etwas Gebrauch machen, etwas anwenden;* you may make ∾ of my name *du darfst dich auf mich berufen (beziehen);* he taught me the ∾ of a file *er lehrte mich, eine Feile zu gebrauchen;* it is (of) no ∾ talking, to talk, talking is no ∾ *Reden hat keinen Zweck, ist zwecklos;* there is no ∾ in saying so *es ist nutz-, zwecklos, es zu sagen;* I have no ∾ for it *ich kann es nicht gebrauchen, habe nichts dafür übrig;* to be of great ∾ *von großem Nutzen, sehr dienlich sein;* to be no longer in ∾ *nicht mehr gebraucht werden, nicht mehr üblich sein;* to bring into ∾ *in Anwendung bringen;* to get (to go, to fall, to pass) out of ∾ *außer Gebrauch kommen, ungebräuchlich werden, veralten;* to put a thing to a good ∾ *etwas mit Nutzen, nützlich anwenden.* — **II.** v.tr.: to ∾ a thing *etwas anwenden, benutzen, gebrauchen, handhaben;* may I ∾ your name? *darf ich mich auf dich berufen (beziehen)?;* he has ∾d me like a dog *er hat mich wie einen Hund behandelt;* ∾ your loaf (sl.) *überleg' mal, Köpfchen!;* to ∾ up all the wood *das ganze Holz auf-, verbrauchen.* — **III.** v.i.: I ∾d to take the bus *ich pflegte, den Omnibus zu nehmen, ich fuhr früher mit dem Omnibus;* he ∾d not (didn't ∾) to answer *er pflegte nicht zu antworten, er antwortete gewöhnlich nicht;* he does not come as often as he ∾d to *er kommt nicht so oft wie früher*

used pred. a.: I am not ∾ to it *ich bin nicht daran gewöhnt;* I am not ∾ to being called a liar *ich bin nicht gewöhnt, ein Lügner genannt zu werden;* I have become (got) ∾ to it *ich habe mich daran gewöhnt*

useful a.: he gave me some ∾ hints *er gab mir einige nützliche Winke;* he must make himself generally ∾ *er muß sich allgemein nützlich machen;* it was a pretty ∾ achievement *es war eine höchst ehrenwerte Leistung;* to be pretty ∾ at a thing *sich gut auf etwas verstehen*

utmost I. a.: to the ∾ ends of the earth *bis zum entferntesten (weitesten) Teile der Erde;* the ∾ praise *das höchste Lob;* with the ∾ accuracy *mit äußerster Genauigkeit.* — **II.** n.: I trust him to the ∾ *ich vertraue ihm aufs Äußerste;* to the ∾ of one's power *nach besten Kräften;* to do one's ∾ *sein möglichstes tun*

utter I. a.: in ∾ misery *im äußersten Elend;* in ∾ darkness *völlig im Dunkeln;* an ∾ stranger *ein Wildfremder;* an ∾ rascal *ein regelrechter (ausgekochter) Schurke.* — **II.** v.tr.: to ∾ thoughts *Gedanken ausdrücken;* to ∾ false money (coin) *falsches Geld in Umlauf bringen*

utterance[1] n.: to find ∾ in *Ausdruck finden in;* to give ∾ to one's thoughts *seinen Gedanken Ausdruck geben;* the gift of ∾ *die Gabe der Rede (Sprache);* his public ∾s *seine öffentlichen Reden*

utterance[2] n.: to fight to the ∾ *bis zum bitteren Ende (Äußersten) kämpfen*

V

vacancy n.: to fill (up) a ∾ *eine freie, unbesetzte Stelle ausfüllen;* to look into (to stare at) ∾ *ins Leere blicken, ins Blaue starren*

vacant a.: the house is still ∾ *das Haus steht noch leer, ist unbewohnt;* he has been granted ∾ possession of the house *das Haus wird für ihn frei gemacht;* a ∾ smoking-compartment *ein leeres, unbesetztes Raucherabteil;* it will amuse your ∾ hours *es wird dich in den Freistunden amüsieren;* to apply for a ∾ post *sich um eine freie, unbesetzte Stelle bewerben;* his mind seems to be completely ∾ *er scheint ganz geistlos zu sein;* to be given up to ∾ frivolities *sich faden Vergnügungen hingeben;* he recieved the news with a ∾ stare (look) *er nahm die Nachricht mit einem ausdrucklosen (leeren) Blick auf*

vagrant a.: a ∾ musician *ein fahrender Musikant;* to indulge in ∾ speculations *sich unruhigen, sprunghaften Vermutungen hingeben*

vain a.: a ∾ boast *eine eitle Prahlerei;* a ∾ distinction *ein nichtiger Unterschied;* a ∾ effort *ein fruchtloses, vergebliches Bemühen;* she is ∾ of her beauty *sie bildet sich auf ihre Schönheit etwas ein;* it was in ∾ that we protested, we protested in ∾ *wir protestierten vergebens (umsonst);* to take a person's name in ∾ *j.es Namen mißbrauchen, unnütz im Munde führen*

valid a.: a ∾ reason (objection) *ein triftiger, zwingender Grund (Einwand);* the marriage was declared ∾ *die Ehe wurde für gültig erklärt*

value I. n.: the face ∾ of a note *der Nennwert einer Banknote;* the precise ∾ of a word *die genaue Bedeutung eines Wortes;* the surplus ∾ *der Mehrwert;* to be of great ∾ to a person *j.em von großem Wert sein;* to get good ∾ for one's money *etwas preiswert kaufen;* to give someone good ∾ *j.en reell bedienen;* to place (to set) a high ∾ on a thing *hohen (großen) Wert auf etwas legen.* — **II.** v.tr.: a ∾d friend *ein geschätzter Freund;* I do not ∾ that a brass farthing *ich lege nicht einen Pfennig Wert darauf;* I should ∾ the whole thing at £ 2,000 *ich würde das Ganze auf 2000 Pfund schätzen (taxieren);* he ∾s himself on his conversational powers *er bildet sich auf seine Unterhaltungsgabe viel ein*

vamp[1] v.tr.: to ∾ the accompaniment to a tune *die Begleitung zu einer Melodie improvisieren;* to ∾ up an article *einen Artikel zusammenstoppeln, aufbessern*

vamp[2] n.: she is a ∾ *sie ist eine Abenteurerin, Nepperin*

van n.: in the ∾ of civilisation *an der Spitze der Zivilisation*

vanity n.: the vanities of life *die Hohlheiten des Lebens;* a ∾ bag *eine Damenhandtasche;* Vanity Fair (Bunyan, Thackeray) *Jahrmarkt der Eitelkeit; die sündhafte Welt;* injured ∾ *verletzte Eitelkeit*

variance n.: to have a ∾ with a person *mit j.em Streit haben;* to be at ∾ with *uneinig, uneins sein mit; im Widerspruch stehen mit (zu);* to set at ∾ with *uneinig machen, entzweien; in Widerspruch setzen mit (zu)*

variety n.: for the sake of ∾ *zwecks Abwechslung, abwechslungshalber;* a ∾ of hats *eine Reihe (eine große Menge, eine Auswahl) von Hüten;* for a ∾ of reasons *aus verschiedenen Gründen;* a ∾ of patterns *verschiedenartige Muster;* this ∾ of lily *diese Abart von Lilien*

vehicle n.: he used the press as ∾ for his political opinions *er benutzte die Presse als Vermittlerin für seine politischen Ansichten;* I will not be used as a ∾ of your resentment *du kannst deinen Ärger nicht an mir auslassen*

veil I. n.: beyond the ∾ *im Jenseits;* under the ∾ of religion *unter dem Deckmantel der Religion;* to draw a ∾ over a subject *die Erörterung eines Themas vermeiden;* to raise the ∾ *den Schleier lüften;* to take the ∾ *den Schleier nehmen, Nonne werden.* — **II.** v.tr.: with ∾ed resentment *mit verschleiertem, getarntem Ärger*

vein n.: to be in the ∾ for something *zu etwas aufgelegt sein;* to be in the ∾ for giving *bei Geberlaune sein;* to be of a humorous ∾ *eine humorvolle Ader besitzen*

velvet I. n.: to be (to stand) on ∾ (colloq.) *gegen Verlust gesichert sein, glänzend dastehen.* — **II.** a.: with an iron hand in a ∾ glove *mit äußerer Milde Unbeugsamkeit verschleiernd;* the ∾ paw *das Samtpfötchen der Katze (als Sinnbild der durch Liebenswürdigkeit verschleierten Grausamkeit)*

vengeance n.: to exact (to take, to wreak) ∾ on a person *an j.em Rache nehmen (üben), sich rächen;* to lay oneself open to (a person's) ∾ *(j.es) Rache ausgeliefert sein;* to play the ∾ with a person *j.em verteufelt (übel) mitspielen;* he is a demagogue with a ∾ *er ist im übelsten Sinne ein Demagoge;* this is punctuality with a ∾ *das ist Pünktlichkeit im höchsten Grade, in höchster Potenz;* they belaboured him with a ∾ *sie verprügelten ihn ganz gehörig, daß es nur so eine Art hatte;* he lays it on with a ∾ *er übertreibt ganz fürchterlich*

vent I. n.: to find ∾ for a thing *für etwas einen Ausweg finden;* to give ∾ to one's anger on a person *seinem Zorn gegen j.en Luft machen; seinen Zorn an j.em auslassen;* to give ∾ to one's feelings *seinen Gefühlen freien Lauf lassen.* — **II.** v.tr.: to ∾ one's anger on a person *seinen Zorn an j.em auslassen;* she ∾ed all her venom on us *sie verspritzte all ihr Gift an uns*

venture I. n.: at a ∾ *aufs Geratewohl, auf gut Glück;* to draw a bow at a ∾ *auf den Busch klopfen;* to put a thing to a ∾ *etwas auf gut Glück hin wagen (riskieren);* he failed in all his ∾s *alles, was er unternahm, schlug fehl.* — **II.** v.tr.: nothing ∾ nothing win (have) *wer nicht wagt, gewinnt nicht;* to ∾ one's life for a cause *sein Leben für eine Sache wagen (aufs Spiel setzen);* I shall not ∾ an opinion *ich werde keine Meinung äußern.* — **III.** v.i.: I did not ∾ to call him *ich wagte nicht, ihn zu rufen;* I ∾ to differ from you *ich erlaube mir (bin so frei), eine andere Meinung als Sie zu haben;* I shall ∾ (up)on a protest *ich werde es wagen zu protestieren;* will you ∾ on a piece of cake? *wollen Sie es mit einem Stück Kuchen versuchen?*

verdict n.: the ∾ of the public was in its favour *die öffentliche Meinung war dafür;* an open ∾ *ein unentschiedener Urteilsspruch;* the jury brought in (delivered, gave, returned) a ∾ of guilty (not guilty, acquittal) *die Geschworenen erkannten auf schuldig (nicht schuldig, Freisprechung);* to pass one's ∾ on a thing *sein Urteil über etwas abgeben*

verge I. n.: on the ∾ of *am Rande, an der Grenze von;* he was on the ∾ of betraying his secret *er war nahe daran, sein Geheimnis zu verraten;* he is on the ∾ of seventy *er ist nahe an (nahezu) siebzig.* — **II.** v.i.: the now verging sun *die jetzt sinkende Sonne;* to ∾ on brown *ins Braune gehen;* his eccentricity ∾s on insanity *seine Überspanntheit grenzt an Wahnsinn;* to ∾ to a close *sich dem Ende nähern*

verse n.: to cap ∾s *um die Wette Verse hersagen unter Berücksichtigung gewisser*

Vorschriften bezüglich Anfangsbuchstaben, Endreim usw.; to give chapter and ∾ for a thing *etwas genau belegen;* to turn a Latin ∾ *einen lateinischen Vers machen;* a ∾-monger *ein Verseschmied*

versed a.: to be well ∾ in a subject *in einem Stoff gut bewandert sein*

very I. a.: in the ∾ act *auf frischer Tat;* at, from the ∾ beginning *gleich zu Anfang, von Anfang an;* the ∾ day *an demselben Tag;* this ∾ day *noch heute;* that is the ∾ devil *das ist rein zum Totärgern;* to the ∾ end *ganz bis ans Ende;* a ∾ fool *ein ausgemachter Narr;* the ∾ idea *der bloße Gedanke (allein, schon der Gedanke);* their ∾ look *schon ihr Blick, ihr Blick allein;* give me only a ∾ little *gib mir nur ein ganz klein wenig;* you are the ∾ man I want *dich kann ich gerade gebrauchen;* his ∾ servants did not obey him *selbst (sogar) seine Diener gehorchten ihm nicht;* in his ∾ presence *direkt in seiner Gegenwart.* — **II.** adv.: the ∾ best thing *das Allerbeste;* a ∾ dazzling effect *eine sehr verwirrende Wirkung;* it is my ∾ own *es gehört mir allein;* a ∾ pained (pleased, surprised, troubled) expression *ein sehr schmerzvoller (froher, überraschter, besorgter) Ausdruck;* ∾ well *nun gut*

vessel n.: a blood-∾ *ein Blutgefäß;* a chosen ∾ (Acts IX, 15) *ein ausgewählt(es) Rüstzeug;* the weaker ∾ (1 Peter, III, 7) *das schwächere Werkzeug, Geschlecht: das Weib;* the ∾s of wrath (Rom. IX, 22) *die Gefäße des Zorns*

vested a.: ∾ interests *fest begründete (althergebrachte) Rechte (Interessen);* power is ∾ in his hands *die Macht liegt in seinen Händen*

vet v.tr.: to have an animal ∾ted *ein Tier vom Tierarzt behandeln lassen;* he has been ∾ted (colloq.) *er ist auf Herz und Nieren (auf seine politische Zuverlässigkeit) geprüft worden;* to ∾ a book (colloq.) *ein Buch revidieren, verbessern*

veto I. n.: to interpose (to put) one's ∾ on a proposal *sein Veto gegen einen Vorschlag einlegen.* — **II.** v.tr.: the President ∾ed the bill *der Präsident legte sein Veto gegen den Gesetzesantrag ein*

vex v.tr: how ∾ing! *wie ärgerlich!;* a ∾ed question *eine Streitfrage, Doktorfrage*

vial n.: to pour out the ∾s of wrath (cf. Rev. XV, 7) *Rache nehmen, seinen Zorn auslassen*

vie v.i.: to ∾ with a person for a thing *mit j.em um etwas wetteifern;* to ∾ with a person in politeness (in being polite) *es mit j.em an Höflichkeit aufnehmen*

view I. n.: a superb ∾ *eine prächtige Aussicht;* at first ∾ *auf den ersten Blick;* it passed from our ∾ *es entschwand unserem Blick;* in ∾ of recent developments *angesichts, in Anbetracht der (in Hinblick, mit Rücksicht auf die) jüngsten Entwicklungen;* we came in ∾ of the castle *wir erblickten das Schloß; wir konnten vom Schloß aus gesehen werden;* to have in ∾ *im Auge haben, beabsichtigen;* to keep in ∾ *im Auge behalten, berücksichtigen;* he stood in full ∾ of the crowd *er war den Blicken der Menge voll ausgesetzt;* in my ∾ *nach meiner Ansicht;* to come into ∾ *in Sicht kommen, sichtbar werden;* to be on ∾ *zu sehen, zu besichtigen, ausgestellt sein;* to the ∾ *vor allen Augen, öffentlich;* to lose to ∾ *aus den Augen verlieren;* it is plain to ∾ *es ist gut sichtbar;* with a ∾ to (of) doing a thing *mit der Absicht, etwas zu tun;* with a ∾ to the vacant post *mit einem Auge auf die freie Stelle;* I cannot fall in with your ∾s *ich kann deinen Ansichten (Absichten) nicht beipflichten (zustimmen);* the cat has ∾s **on** (upon) the larder *die Katze hat Absichten auf die Speisekammer;* to get a general ∾ of a subject *einen allgemeinen Überblick über ein Gebiet erhalten;* does this meet your ∾s? *entspricht das deinen An-, Absichten?;* to take ∾s of a place *Aufnahmen von einem Ort machen;* he took (held) the ∾ that ——— *er vertrat den Standpunkt, daß* ———; to take a bright ∾ of something *etwas in rosigem Lichte betrachten;* to take a different (favourable, grave) ∾ of the situation *die Lage anders (günstig, ernst) beurteilen;* to take a high ∾ of a thing *eine hohe Meinung von etwas haben;* I'm taking the long ∾ *ich denke auf lange Sicht;* to take a poor (dim) ∾ of something (colloq.) *etwas mißbilligen, keinen Gefallen an etwas finden;* as seen from the bird's-eye ∾ *aus der Vogelschau gesehen;* from this point of ∾ *von diesem Gesichtspunkte (Standpunkte) aus;* the ∾-finder *der Sucher am photographischen Apparat;* a private ∾

(film) *eine private Vorführung;* ∾ halloo! *Ausruf des Jägers beim Erscheinen des Fuchses auf der Parforcejagd;* a ∾ of life *eine Lebensanschauung.* — **II.** v.i.: to ∾ (colloq.) *ein Fernsehprogramm ansehen*

vine n.: to dwell under one's ∾ and fig-tree (I Kings, IV, 25) *die Freuden eines eigenen Heims genießen*

virtue n.: by ∾ of a thing *kraft (vermöge) einer Sache;* in ∾ of a thing *infolge (auf Grund) einer Sache;* it has the ∾ of being adjustable *es hat den Vorzug, umstellbar zu sein;* to make a ∾ of necessity *aus der Not eine Tugend machen;* a woman of easy ∾ *eine untugendhafte Frau*

visit I. n.: to be on a ∾ *auf, zu Besuch sein;* to pay a person a ∾, a ∾ to a person *j.em einen Besuch abstatten (machen).* — **II.** v.tr.: to ∾ the sins upon a person *die Sünden an j.em heimsuchen;* to ∾ a person with salvation *j.en mit Erlösung beglücken, segnen*

visiting a.: he is not on my ∾ list *er ist kein Freund von mir;* to be on ∾ terms with someone *mit j.em auf Besuchsfuß stehen, mit ihm verkehren*

voice I. n.: the still small ∾ *das Gewissen;* she is not in ∾ *sie ist nicht bei Stimme;* with one ∾ *einstimmig;* to find ∾ in *Ausdruck finden in;* to give ∾ to one's joy *seiner Freude Ausdruck geben (verleihen);* I have no ∾ in the matter *ich habe keinen Einfluß auf die Sache (bei der Sache nichts zu sagen);* to lift up one's ∾ *seine Stimme erheben.* — **II.** v.tr.: to ∾ a thought *einen Gedanken äußern*

void I. n.: an aching ∾ *eine schmerzliche Leere;* to fill the ∾ *die Lücke ausfüllen.* — **II.** a.: to be ∾ of a thing *einer Sache ermangeln, etwas nicht besitzen;* to be ∾ of sense *ohne Sinn, sinnlos sein;* null and ∾ *null und nichtig;* the post fell ∾ *die Stelle wurde frei*

vote I. n.: a ∾ of confidence *ein Vertrauensvotum;* the casting ∾ *die entscheidende, ausschlaggebende Stimme;* the floating ∾ *die Stimme der Parteilosen;* the Labour ∾ *die Stimmen der Arbeiterpartei;* a straw ∾ *eine Probeabstimmung;* to cast a ∾ *eine Stimme abgeben;* to give one's ∾ to (for) a person *j.em seine Stimme geben;* to have a ∾ *(das) Stimmrecht haben, stimmberechtigt sein;* to put to the ∾ *zur Abstimmung bringen;* to take a ∾ *eine Abstimmung vornehmen.* — **II.** v.i.: to ∾ for (against) a measure *für (gegen) einen Antrag stimmen;* to ∾ that it should be done *dafür stimmen, daß es gemacht wird;* I ∾ (that) we go *ich schlage vor (bin dafür), wir gehen.* — **III.** v.tr.: to ∾ Labour *für die Arbeiterpartei stimmen;* to ∾ a large sum *eine große Summe bewilligen;* it was ∾d a failure *es wurde allgemein als mißlungen hingestellt;* to ∾ a measure down *einen Antrag ablehnen*

vulgar a.: the ∾ era *die christliche Zeitrechnung;* a ∾ error *ein gewöhnlicher, häufig vorkommender Fehler;* a ∾ fraction (math.) *ein gemeiner (gewöhnlicher) Bruch;* the ∾ tongue *die Landessprache;* a ∾ expression *ein gemeiner (derber) Ausdruck;* a ∾ taste *ein gemeiner (niedriger, unfeiner) Geschmack*

W

wad I. n.: a ∾ of cotton-wool *ein Wattebausch;* a ∾ of notes *ein Päckchen (Stoß) Banknoten;* he made a ∾ (colloq.) *er verdiente viel Geld;* a tight-∾ (U.S. sl.) *ein Geizhals, Geizkragen (Knicker).* — **II.** v.tr.: he is well ∾ded with conceit *er besitzt eine gute Portion Einbildung*

wade v.i.: to ∾ into a thing *etwas energisch angreifen;* to ∾ through a book *sich mühsam durch ein Buch hindurcharbeiten*

wafer n.: as thin as a ∾ *hauchdünn*

waffle v.i. (sl.): to ∾ *schwafeln, viel reden, Unsinn reden*

wag[1] I. v.tr.: to ∾ one's finger at a person *j.em mit dem Finger drohen;* a dog ∾s his tail *ein Hund wedelt mit dem Schwanz;* the tail ∾s the dog *das bedeutungsloseste Mitglied einer Gesellschaft (Partei) hat zu sagen.* — **II.** v.i.: to set beards (chins, jaws, tongues) ∾ging *ein Gerede aufbringen;* let them ∾! *laß sie reden!;* how ∾s the world? *wie geht's in der Welt?* — **III.** n.: to give a ∾ of the tail *mit dem Schwanze wedeln*

wag[2] n.: he is a bit of a ∾ *er ist ein kleiner Spaßvogel, Witzbold;* to play the ∾ (sl.) *die Schule schwänzen*

wage[1] n.: the ∾s of sin is death (Rom. VI, 23) *der Tod ist der Sünde Lohn;* at a

∾ (∾s) of £ 1 a week *zu einem Wochenlohn von 1 Pfund;* a living ∾ *ein auskömmlicher Lohn*

wage² v.tr.: to ∾ war with (against, upon) a country *mit einem (gegen ein) Land Krieg führen;* to ∾ (effective) war upon a thing *einer Sache (wirksam) zu Leibe gehen*

wag(g)on n.: by ∾ *per Achse;* by the ∾-load *waggonweise;* to hitch one's ∾ to a star *höhere Ziele haben;* to be on the (water) ∾ *vorübergehender Abstinenzler sein*

waifs and strays n.: *Abfälle, Überreste; heimatlose, verwahrloste Kinder*

Wain n.: the ∾ (Charles's, Arthur's ∾) *der große Bär*

wait I. v.i.: ∾ and see *abwarten und Tee trinken;* everything comes to those who ∾ *Warten lohnt sich immer, mit Geduld und Spucke fängt man eine Mucke;* to ∾ at table *bei Tisch bedienen;* to ∾ for a person (thing) *auf j.en (etwas) warten;* he always has to be ∾ed for *er ist immer unpünktlich;* to ∾ upon a person *j.en bei Tisch bedienen; einem Vorgesetzten seine Aufwartung machen;* to ∾ on a person with a thing *j.em mit etwas aufwarten;* to ∾ up for a person *aufbleiben, bis j. kommt;* to keep a person ∾ing *j.en warten lassen;* the work is ∾ing to be done *die Arbeit läßt noch auf sich warten;* a lord-, lady-in-∾ing *ein diensttuender Kammerherr, eine Hofdame.* — **II.** v.tr.: don't ∾ dinner for me *warte nicht mit dem Essen auf mich;* you must ∾ my convenience *du mußt warten, bis es mir genehm ist (paßt);* he is ∾ing his opportunity *er wartet die Gelegenheit ab.* — **III.** n.: the ∾s *von Haus zu Haus ziehende Weihnachtssänger;* I had a long ∾ for the train *ich mußte lange auf den Zug warten;* to lie (lay) in ∾ for a person *j.em auflauern, einen Hinterhalt legen*

wake¹ I. v.i.: to ∾ from (out of) a dream *aus einem Traum erwachen;* to ∾ up to a thing *sich einer Sache bewußt werden;* ∾ up there! *aufgewacht!* — **II.** v.tr.: to ∾ a corpse *bei einer Leiche wachen;* to ∾ snakes *in ein Wespennest stechen;* to ∾ a person up *j.en wecken, aufrütteln.* — **III.** n.: to hold ∾ over a corpse *die Totenwache halten*

wake² n.: the ∾ of a ship *das Kielwasser eines Schiffes;* to follow in the ∾ of a person (thing) *in den Fußstapfen (auf den Spuren) j.es (einer Sache) folgen;* an explosion followed in the ∾ *eine Explosion erfolgte unmittelbar darauf*

walk I. v.i.: a ghost ∾s *ein Gespenst geht um, es spukt;* to ∾ after the flesh *sich sinnlichen Genüssen ergeben;* to ∾ after (before, with) God *vor dem Herrn wandeln, ein gottgefälliges Leben führen;* to ∾ away from a person *j.en leicht hinter sich lassen (übertreffen);* to ∾ into a person (colloq.) *j.en beschimpfen, verprügeln;* to ∾ into food (colloq.) *tüchtig einhauen ins Essen;* to ∾ off (away) with a thing *etwas mitgehen heißen, stehlen;* to ∾ on air *im siebenten Himmel sein;* to ∾ out on someone (colloq.) *j.en im Stich lassen; j.en in einer unangenehmen Lage zurücklassen;* our cook ∾s out with a sailor *unsere Köchin hat ein Verhältnis mit einem Matrosen;* ∾ing out dress (mil.) *Ausgeh-, Paradeuniform;* to make someone ∾ Spanish *j.en entlassen;* to ∾ through one's part *seine Rolle hersagen, ohne dabei zu spielen oder zu mimen;* ∾ up, ladies and gentlemen *nur hereinspaziert, meine Damen und Herren;* he is a ∾ing dictionary *er ist ein wandelndes Lexikon;* a ∾ing gentleman, lady *ein Statist, eine Statistin;* he got his ∾ing papers (ticket) *er bekam seine Entlassungspapiere;* a ∾ing tour *eine Fußwanderung.* — **II.** v.tr.: to ∾ the boards *Schauspieler(in) sein;* to ∾ the chalk *auf dem Kreidestrich gehen können, nüchtern sein;* to ∾ a horse *ein Pferd im Schritt führen (reiten);* to ∾ the hospitals *als Medizinstudent die klinischen Semester machen;* to ∾ the plank *(von Seeräubern) gezwungen sein, über die Schiffsplanke zu gehen und so zu ertrinken;* to ∾ the streets *Prostituierte werden (sein);* the might of Him that ∾ed the waves (Milton, Lycidas) *die Macht des Herrn, der auf den Wogen wandelte;* the policeman ∾d him off *der Polizist (Schutzmann) führte ihn ab;* to ∾ a person off his legs *j.en todmüde machen.* — **III.** n.: in all ∾s of life *in allen Lebensstellungen (Berufen);* it is quite a ∾ *es ist ein gutes Stück zu gehen;* to go at a ∾ *im Schritt gehen;* to go for (to take) a ∾ *einen Spaziergang machen, spazieren gehen;* I recognized him by his ∾ *ich erkannte ihn an seinem Gang;* a ∾-out *ein Streik, eine*

Arbeitsniederlegung; to give a person a ∾-over *j.en ohne Kampf (ohne zu spielen) gewinnen lassen;* a rope-∾ *eine Seilerbahn;* a sheep-∾ *eine Schafweide;* a walkie-talkie *ein kleiner, tragbarer Radiosender und -empfänger*

wall I. n.: ∾s have ears *Wände haben Ohren;* they were fighting with their backs to the ∾ *sie waren in großer Bedrängnis (in die Enge getrieben);* to give a lady the ∾ *eine Dame auf der sauberen, ungefährdeteren Seite des Bürgersteigs an der Häuserreihe gehen lassen (daher: höflich sein);* the weakest goes to the ∾ *der Schwächste wird an die Wand gedrückt;* to run one's head against a ∾ *mit dem Kopf gegen die Wand rennen, mit dem Kopf durch die Wand wollen;* to take the ∾ of a person *j.en nicht auf der sauberen, ungefährdeteren Seite des Bürgersteigs an der Häuserreihe gehen lassen;* to be up against a brick ∾ *nicht mehr weiter können;* to see through a brick ∾ *durch eine Mauer hindurchsehen, einen übernatürlichen Scharfblick haben;* to be ∾-eyed *auf einem Auge blind sein.* — **II.** v.tr.: to ∾ in *mit einer Mauer umgeben;* to ∾ up a passage *einen Durchgang zumauern*

wallop v.tr. (sl.): to ∾ a person *j.en verprügeln, verdreschen, vermöbeln;* a ∾ping fellow *ein Mordskerl;* a ∾ping lie *eine faustdicke Lüge*

wallow v.i.: he is ∾ing in money *er schwimmt im Gelde*

walnut n.: to discuss a thing over the ∾s and wine *etwas beim Dessert (Nachtisch) besprechen*

wander I. v.i.: to ∾ from the subject *vom Thema abschweifen;* his mind is (wits are) ∾ing *er faselt, redet irre;* the Wandering Jew *der Ewige Jude.* — **II.** v.tr.: to ∾ the world through *die Welt durchwandern*

wane I. v.i.: a waning moon *ein abnehmender Mond.* — **II.** n.: to be on the ∾ *abnehmen, verfallen*

wangle v.tr. (sl.): I ∾d that all right *das habe ich mal fein gedeichselt (gedreht, geschoben);* to ∾ a thing out of a person *j.m etwas ablotsen*

want I. v.i.: waste not, ∾ not (prov.) see 'waste'; I don't ∾ to go *ich will nicht gehen;* let him ∾ for nothing *laß es ihm an nichts mangeln (fehlen); laß ihm nichts abgehen;* it ∾s something of perfection *die letzte Vollkommenheit fehlt;* he is a little ∾ing *er ist etwas geistesschwach;* it was found ∾ing *es wurde zu leicht befunden;* he is ∾ing in judgement *es fehlt (mangelt) ihm an Urteilskraft;* he is ∾ing to a sense of duty *es fehlt ihm an Pflichtbewußtsein;* he was ∾ing to the occasion *er war der Lage nicht gewachsen.* — **II.** v.tr.: I ∾ it done *ich möchte es getan haben;* it ∾s careful handling *es bedarf sorgfältiger Behandlung;* he ∾s judgement *es fehlt (mangelt) ihm an Urteilskraft;* it ∾s half a minute of the hour *es fehlt eine halbe Minute an der vollen Stunde;* I ∾ some sugar *ich möchte etwas Zucker haben (ich brauche, benötige etwas Zucker);* the boy ∾s the whip (to be whipped) *der Junge verdient Prügel;* I ∾ you to try *ich möchte (wünsche), daß du es versuchst;* he is ∾ed by the police *er wird von der Polizei gesucht;* you are ∾ed on the 'phone *du wirst am Telefon verlangt.* — **II.** n.: ∾ is a severe teacher *Bedürftigkeit (Armut, Not) ist eine strenge Lehrmeisterin;* wilful waste makes woeful ∾ (prov.) see 'waste'; to meet (to supply) a (long-felt) ∾ *ein Bedürfnis befriedigen, einem Bedürfnis abhelfen;* a man of few ∾s *ein bedürfnisloser Mensch;* for ∾ of a thing *in Ermangelung einer Sache, aus Mangel an etwas;* to be in ∾ of a thing *etwas bedürfen (benötigen, brauchen), nötig haben*

wanting prep.: ∾ honesty, nothing can be done *ohne Ehrlichkeit kann nichts gemacht werden;* all ∾ one *alle bis auf einen*

war I. n.: all's fair in love and ∾ (prov.) *in der Liebe und im Krieg ist alles erlaubt;* a civil ∾ *ein Bürgerkrieg;* the dogs of ∾ *die Furien des Krieges;* a man-of-∾ *ein Kriegsschiff;* the sinews of ∾ *Geld (die Seele des Krieges);* the theatre of ∾ *der Kriegsschauplatz;* a tug-of-∾ *ein Tauziehen;* to be at ∾ with a country, person *mit einem Lande Krieg führen; mit j.em auf Kriegsfuß stehen;* he has been in the ∾s *er ist arg mitgenommen, ramponiert worden;* to carry the ∾ into the enemy's country *den Krieg ins Feindesland tragen, zum Gegenangriff vorgehen;* to declare ∾ upon a country *einem Lande den Krieg erklären;* to drift into ∾ *in den Krieg treiben (schliddern);* to go to ∾ with a country *Krieg mit einem Lande anfangen;* to go to the ∾s *als Soldat dienen;* to levy ∾ against (upon) a country *zum Krieg gegen ein Land schreiten, die Waffen gegen ein Land ergreifen;* to make (to wage) ∾ on (against) a country *gegen ein Land Krieg führen;* on ∾ footing *auf Kriegsstärke;* like an old ∾-horse *wie ein alter Haudegen (Kampfhahn);* the War Office *das Kriegs- (Verteidigungs-)ministerium;* in full ∾-paint *in voller Kriegsbemalung (vollem Staat).* — **II.** v.tr.: to ∾ resistance down *den Widerstand niederkämpfen.* — **III.** v.i.: to ∾ against (on, with) a country *gegen ein Land Krieg führen;* they are ∾ring principles *es sind widerstreitende Grundsätze*

ward I. n.: a ∾ in Chancery *ein Kanzleigerichtsmündel;* a casual ∾ *ein Obdachlosenasyl;* a hospital ∾ *eine Krankenhausstation;* to be in (under) ∾ *unter Vormundschaft stehen;* to keep watch and ∾ see 'watch'; to put a person in ∾ *j.en gefangensetzen.* — **II.** v.tr.: to ∾ off a blow, danger *einen Schlag parieren, eine Gefahr abwenden*

warm I. a.: a ∾ friend *ein intimer Freund;* a ∾ man *ein reicher Mann;* a ∾ partisan *ein eifriger, leidenschaftlicher Anhänger (Parteigänger);* it was ∾ work *es war schwere Arbeit, ein harter Kampf;* ∾ with wine *vom Wein erhitzt (durchglüht);* to grow ∾ *warm werden, sich erhitzen;* to make it (things) ∾ for a person *j.em die Hölle heißmachen.* — **II.** v.tr.: it is wine to ∾ the heart *es ist ein herzerfreuender, köstlicher Wein;* to ∾ a person's jacket *j.em die Jacke vollhauen;* a house-∾ing party *eine Einzugsfeier, ein Einzugsschmaus.* — **III.** v.i.: he ∾ed (∾ed up) to his subject *er wurde bei seinem Thema allmählich wärmer;* the room is ∾ing up *das Zimmer wird wärmer.* — **IV.** n.: I must give it another ∾ first *ich muß es erst nochmals aufwärmen;* I must have a ∾ *ich muß mich wärmen*

wart n.: to paint a thing with all its ∾s *etwas mit allen Fehlern malen*

wash I. v.tr.: would you like to ∾ your hands? *diskrete Frage, ob man zur Toilette gehen möchte;* to ∾ one's hands of a thing *seine Hände in Unschuld waschen; mit einer Sache nichts mehr zu tun haben wollen;* to ∾ one's dirty linen in public *seine schmutzige Wäsche in der Öffentlichkeit waschen;* to ∾ ashore *ans Land spülen (schwemmen);* to ∾ away (off, out) a stain *einen Fleck durch Waschen entfernen;* to ∾ a thing down *etwas gründlich abwaschen;* to ∾ beef down with ale *Rindfleisch mit Bier hinunterspülen;* he looks ∾ed out (colloq.) *er sieht erschöpft, verkatert aus;* the play was a ∾-out (sl.) *das Stück war eine Niete, ein Reinfall, ein Fiasko;* you can ∾ that out (sl.) *du kannst das vergessen, außer Betracht lassen;* to ∾ up the plates *die Teller spülen.* — **II.** v.i.: that argument won't ∾ *das Argument ist nicht stichhaltig (zieht nicht);* that material ∾es well *dieser Stoff ist waschecht;* I must ∾ before dinner *ich muß mich vor dem Essen waschen;* she ∾es for her living *sie verdient sich als Waschfrau ihr Brot;* the stain will ∾ out *der Fleck geht in der Wäsche heraus;* I must ∾ up *ich muß aufwaschen (spülen).* — **III.** n.: his talk was all ∾ (colloq.) *was er sagte, war nur Gewäsch;* this tea is mere ∾ *dieser Tee ist ein dünnes Gesöff;* it will come out in the ∾ (colloq.) *es wird am Ende gut;* I must get (have) a ∾ *ich muß mich waschen;* give it a good ∾ *wasch es gut aus;* I have a big ∾ tomorrow *ich habe morgen große Wäsche;* to send the linen to the ∾ *die Wäsche zur Wäscherei schicken*

waste I. a.: to lay ∾ *verwüsten, -heeren;* to lie ∾ *brachliegen;* a ∾-paper basket *ein Papierkorb.* — **II.** v.tr.: ∾ not, want not (prov.) *spare in der Zeit, so hast du in der Not;* to ∾ one's breath *in den Wind reden;* a wasting disease *eine aufzehrende Krankheit;* to ∾ one's time *seine Zeit vergeuden.* — **III.** v.i.: to ∾ away *abnehmen, verfallen, dahinschwinden.* — **IV.** n.: the garden runs to ∾ *der Garten verwildert;* the opportunities are let run to ∾ *die Gelegenheiten (Chancen) werden nicht genutzt;* wilful ∾ makes woeful want (prov.) *leichtsinniges Verschwenden bringt bittere Not*

waster n.: he is a ∾ *er ist ein Tunichtgut (Taugenichts)*

watch I. n.: to pass as a ∾ in the night *bald vergessen werden;* to be on the ∾ for a thing *auf der Lauer nach etwas sein;* to keep ∾ and ward *strenge Wache halten;* I must set my ∾ *ich muß meine Uhr stellen.* — **II.** v.tr.: if you don't ∾ it *wenn du nicht aufpaßt;* to ∾ one's time *den richtigen Augenblick abwarten;* a ∾ed pot never boils (prov.) *ein Topf, auf dessen Kochen man wartet, kocht nie; man soll Geduld* *haben, sich nicht aufregen;* I had him ∾ed by detectives *ich ließ ihn durch Detektive beobachten.* — **III.** v.i.: ∾ and pray *wachet und betet!;* to ∾ for an opportunity *auf eine Gelegenheit lauern*

water I. n,: to be in deep ∾(s) *in Not sein;* to be of the first ∾ *vom reinsten Wasser, erstklassig sein;* to be in low ∾ *knapp bei Kasse sein;* between wind and ∾ *an einer verwundbaren, verfänglichen Stelle;* that brings the ∾ to my mouth *das läßt mir das Wasser im Munde zusammenlaufen;* to cast one's bread upon the ∾s *Gutes tun, ohne Dankbarkeit oder Vorteil zu erwarten;* to cross the ∾s *übers Meer fahren;* to drink the ∾s of forgetfulness (Hesiod) *aus dem Strom der Vergessenheit trinken;* to drink the ∾s at a spa *in einem Badeort Brunnen trinken;* I feel like a fish out of ∾ *ich fühle mich nicht in meinem Element, ich komme mir ganz verlassen, komisch vor;* to fish in troubled ∾s *im trüben fischen;* much ∾ has flowed under the bridges (under the mill) *eine geraume Zeit ist vergangen, vgl. bis dahin fließt viel Wasser den Rhein hinunter;* you can't get ∾ out of a stone (prov.) *wo nichts ist, hat selbst der Kaiser sein Recht verloren;* to get into hot ∾ *sich in die Nesseln setzen; in (des) Teufels Küche geraten;* to go through fire and ∾ for a person *für j.en durch's Feuer gehen;* to hold ∾ *wasserdicht sein;* that argument won't hold ∾ *das Argument ist nicht stichhaltig, steht auf schwachen Füßen;* to keep one's head above ∾ *sich über Wasser halten;* to make (to pass) ∾ *Wasser lassen, urinieren;* to pour oil on troubled ∾s *Öl auf die Wogen gießen; die Gemüter beruhigen;* to spend money like ∾ *verschwenderisch (sehr flott) mit dem Gelde sein;* still ∾s run deep (prov.) *stille Wasser sind tief;* to throw cold ∾ on a plan *von einem Vorhaben abraten, abschrecken;* to travel by ∾ *zu Wasser, zur See reisen;* written in (on) ∾ *in Sand geschrieben;* ∾ bewitched *sehr dünner Tee, stark gewässerte geistige Getränke;* ∾ of life *geistige Erleuchtung;* ∾proof, ∾tight *wasserdicht;* to keep in ∾tight compartments *streng gesondert halten;* to be on the ∾-wag(g)on *vorübergehender Abstinenzler sein;* to turn on the ∾works (sl.) *anfangen zu weinen (zu heulen).* — **II.** v.tr.: to ∾ flowers *Blumen (be)gießen;* a ∾ing-can *eine Gießkanne;* to ∾ down the horrors of a story *das Gräßliche einer Geschichte abschwächen.* — **III.** v.i.: it makes my mouth ∾ *da läuft mir das Wasser im Munde zusammen;* a ∾ing place *ein Badeort*

Waterloo n.pr.: to meet one's ∾ *eine vernichtende Niederlage erleiden*

wave I. v.tr.: to ∾ one's arms *mit den Armen fuchteln;* to ∾ a flag *eine Fahne schwenken;* to ∾ one's hand to a person *j.em zum Gruß mit der Hand winken;* to ∾ a person farewell *j.em ein Lebewohl zuwinken;* to ∾ a person aside (away) *j.en beiseitewinken;* to ∾ a thing aside (away) *etwas abweisen, ablehnen.* — **II.** v.i.: to ∾ in the wind *im Winde wehen (flattern);* to ∾ to a person *j.em zuwinken.* — **III.** n.: a ∾ of the hand *ein Wink mit der Hand;* the might of Him that walked the ∾s see 'walk'

wax[1] v.i.: a ∾ing moon *ein zunehmender Mond;* to ∾ fat, old, merry, etc. *dick, alt, fröhlich usw. werden;* to ∾ and wane *zunehmen und abnehmen*

wax[2] n.: to be in (to get into) a ∾ *aufgebracht (böse, zornig) werden, hochgehen;* a man of ∾ *ein Mustertyp;* to have a nose of ∾ *gefällig, entgegenkommend, leicht beeinflußbar sein*

way I. n.: where there's a will there's a ∾ see 'will'; the ∾ of the world *der Gang (Lauf) der Welt;* the good old ∾s *die guten alten Sitten;* to ask a person the (one's) ∾ *j.en nach dem Wege fragen;* to be the only ∾ to do (of doing) it *die einzige Möglichkeit sein, es zu tun;* to be at the parting of the ∾s *am Scheidewege sein (stehen);* that is the ∾ to do it *so muß es gemacht werden;* that is always the ∾ with you *so ist es immer mit dir;* it is not my ∾ to desert people *es ist nicht meine Art (Gewohnheit), Leute im Stich zu lassen;* it is no ∾ inferior to it *es steht der Sache in keiner Weise (keineswegs) nach;* it is often the ∾ with foreigners *das hat man oft (es ist oft so) bei Ausländern;* to beg one's ∾ *sich durchbetteln;* to clear the ∾ *den Weg freimachen;* I shall do it any ∾ *ich tue es auf jeden Fall;* he does his work anyway *er arbeitet nachlässig;* I shall do it one (some) ∾ or other *ich werde es auf irgendeine Weise tun;* to feel one's ∾ *sich durch Tasten zurechtfinden; vorsichtig vorgehen;* I feel the same ∾ about it *das ist auch mein Gefühl (meine Meinung) darüber;* to find the (one's) ∾ *sich zurechtfinden;* to find ∾s and means *Mittel und Wege finden;* the ship gathers (loses) ∾ *das Schiff kommt in (verliert an) Fahrt;* to give ∾ to a passion *einer Leidenschaft nachgehen;* the rope gave ∾ *das Seil gab nach, riß;* to go the ∾ of the earth (of all flesh, of nature) *den Weg alles Fleisches gehen, sterben;* to go one's ∾s *fort-, weggehen;* this (a little of this) goes a long ∾ *dieses hält lange vor, ist sparsam im Gebrauch;* I find (that) a little of him goes a long ∾ (colloq.) *ich werde seine Gesellschaft schnell leid (seiner Gesellschaft bald überdrüssig);* that will go a long ∾ towards reconciling him *das wird viel dazu beitragen, ihn zu versöhnen;* kindness goes a long ∾ with him *Güte wirkt sehr bei ihm;* to go (to take) one's own ∾ *seinen eigenen Weg einschlagen;* I shall go some ∾ to meet you in that matter *ich komme dir in der Angelegenheit entgegen;* you can't have it both ∾s *du kannst es nicht einmal so und einmal so haben wollen;* he has a little ∾ of leaving his bills unpaid *er hat so eine Art (die üble Angewohnheit), seine Rechnungen nicht zu bezahlen;* to have no ∾ of doing a thing *keine Möglichkeit haben, etwas zu tun;* have it your own ∾ *mach', was du willst! meinetwegen! du sollst recht haben!;* to have (to get) one's own ∾ *seinen Willen bekommen (kriegen);* to have the right of ∾ *das Durchgangs-, Vorfahrtsrecht haben;* he has a wonderful ∾ with children *er versteht es glänzend, mit Kindern umzugehen;* he has a wonderful ∾ with him *er hat eine wunderbare Art an sich;* I know his little ∾s *ich kenne seine Schliche (so seine Art);* to lead the ∾ *führen, vorangehen;* he lives somewhere London ∾ *er wohnt irgendwo in der Nähe von London;* to lose one's ∾ *sich verirren, sich verlaufen;* to make ∾ for a person *j.em Platz machen;* to make the best of one's ∾ *sich beeilen;* I'm making no (head)∾ in the matter *ich komme in der Angelegenheit nicht vorwärts;* to make (to win) one's (one's own) ∾ *seinen Weg machen, vorwärtskommen; sein Glück machen;* to mend one's ∾s *sich bessern;* to pave the ∾ *den Weg ebnen;* to pay one's ∾ *ohne Schulden weiterkommen;* to see one's ∾ to do a thing *in der Lage (berechtigt) sein, etwas zu tun;* to stop the ∾ *den Weg versperren;* to take one's ∾ to (towards) a place *sich nach einem Orte aufmachen;* to work one's ∾ *sich durcharbeiten, die Reisekosten, das Studium durch Arbeit verdienen.* — with prep.: he lives across the ∾ *er wohnt gegenüber;* by the ∾ *nebenbei bemerkt;* he is by ∾ of knowing everybody *er kennt alle Welt;* I travelled by ∾ of London *ich fuhr über London;* not by a long ∾ *noch lange nicht;* in a ∾ *in beschränktem Maße, nicht ganz, einigermaßen;* a lion in the ∾ *ein (meist eingebildetes) Hindernis;* once in a ∾ *ab und zu einmal, ausnahmsweise;* to be (to stand) in the ∾ *im Wege sein (stehen), hemmen, stören;* to get in the ∾ *in den Weg treten, hindern;* to get into the ∾ of doing a thing *sich einarbeiten; sich daran gewöhnen, etwas zu tun;* to put a person in the ∾ of doing a thing *j.em Gelegenheit geben (ihn in die Lage versetzen), etwas zu tun;* to set a person in the ∾ of doing a thing *j.en anleiten, etwas zu tun;* to stand in the ancient ∾s *altmodisch sein, von Neuerungen nichts wissen wollen;* to be in a bad ∾ *übel dran sein;* in the ∾ of business *auf dem üblichen Geschäftswege;* she's in the family ∾ (colloq.) *sie ist schwanger;* to be in a great ∾ *sehr aufgeregt sein;* to be in the grocery ∾ *in der Kolonialwarenbranche sein;* philosophy is not (does not come, fall, lie) in my ∾ *Philosophie ist nicht mein Gebiet (Fach), liegt mir nicht;* we are all in the same ∾ *wir sind alle in derselben Lage;* he is a capitalist in a small ∾ *er ist in kleinem Umfange Kapitalist;* to live in a small ∾ *bescheiden leben;* he is not a bad fellow in some ∾s *er ist in mancher Beziehung kein übler Kerl;* have you anything in the stationery ∾, in the ∾ of stationery? *haben Sie etwas an Schreibwaren?;* it is a long ∾ off perfection *es ist lange nicht vollkommen;* he is on the ∾ *er ist auf dem Wege, er kommt gleich;* that argument is quite out of the ∾ *das Argument ist völlig abwegig;* an out-of-the-∾ corner *ein abgelegener Winkel;* it is nothing out of the ∾ *es ist nichts Ungewöhnliches;* to get out of the ∾ *zur Seite treten, den Weg freigeben;* to get out of the ∾ of doing a thing *das Geschick, etwas zu tun, verlieren; sich etwas abgewöhnen;* to go out of the (one's) ∾ to do a thing *sich (dat.) besondere Mühe geben, etwas zu tun;* to put oneself out of one's ∾ to help a person *sich persönlichen Unannehmlichkeiten aussetzen, um j.em zu helfen;* he lives over the ∾ *er wohnt gegenüber;* to be (to get) under ∾ *in Fahrt sein, kommen.* — with adv.: a long ∾ about *ein Umweg;* the ∾ back (home) *der Rück-, Heimweg;* the ∾ in, out *der Ein-, Ausgang;* a long ∾ off *weit entfernt;* a ship has ∾ on *das Schiff ist in Fahrt.* — **II.** adv.: ∾ back in the desert *weit dahinten in der Wüste;* ∾ back in the Middle Ages *weit zurück im Mittelalter;* ∾ down south *weit unten im Süden;* ∾ off from all civilisation *weit weg von aller Zivilisation;* ∾ up in the mountains *hoch oben im Gebirge*

weal n.: ∾ and (or) woe *Wohl und Wehe;* the common (general, public) ∾ *das Gemeinwohl*

wear I. v.tr.: to ∾ one's heart upon one's sleeve *das Herz auf der Zunge haben (tragen), seine Gefühle nicht verheimlichen können;* to ∾ a person in one's heart *j.en im Herzen tragen;* he ∾s his years well *er hat sich für sein Alter gut gehalten, er sieht noch jugendlich aus;* a worn (well-worn) joke *ein alter, uralter Witz;* worn to a shadow with care *vor Sorgen nur noch der Schatten seines einstigen Selbst sein; zum Skelett abgemagert;* to ∾ away (down, off, out) a thing *etwas abnutzen, abtragen;* to ∾ down (out) one's welcome *unwillkommen werden durch zu häufiges Besuchen (durch zu langes Bleiben).* — **II.** v.i.: this material won't ∾ *dieser Stoff hält sich nicht (ist nicht sehr haltbar);* this material ∾s well (badly) *dieser Stoff ist sehr haltbar (nicht haltbar);* a person ∾s well *j. hält sich gut, sieht jugendlich aus;* clothes ∾ to one's shape *Kleider passen sich im Tragen der Figur an;* to ∾ away (down, off, out) *sich abnutzen, sich abtragen;* my headache wore off *meine Kopfschmerzen verschwanden;* time ∾s on *die Zeit schreitet fort;* the exertion ∾s on me *die Anstrengung ermüdet mich (nimmt mich mit);* to ∾ through the day *den Tag irgendwie totschlagen.* — **III.** n.: the coat I have in ∾ *der Rock, den ich trage;* silk is in general (the only) ∾ *Seide wird allgemein getragen, ist die große Mode;* my Sunday ∾ *meine Sonntagskleider;* there is a great deal of (no) ∾ in it *es läßt sich gut (schlecht) tragen;* it is the worse for ∾ *es ist sehr abgetragen (verschlissen);* he looks the worse for ∾ *er sieht stark mitgenommen aus;* ∾ and tear *die natürliche Abnutzung*

weasand n. (arch.): to slit a person's ∾ *j.em die Kehle durchschneiden*

weasel n.: to catch a ∾ asleep *einen sehr Wachsamen dennoch überrumpeln; einen Gerissenen hintergehen;* a ∾-word *ein zweideutiges Wort*

weather I. n.: the Clerk of the ∾ *der Wettergott;* to be under the ∾ (colloq.) *etwas deprimiert, nicht ganz auf der Höhe sein;* under stress of ∾ *durch das schlechte Wetter gezwungen;* to make good (bad) ∾ *auf gutes (schlechtes) Wetter stoßen;* to make heavy ∾ of a thing *etwas anstrengend (beschwerlich, mühsam) finden;* ∾-beaten *vom Wetter beschädigt; abgehärtet, wetterhart;* a ∾cock *ein Wetterhahn, eine Windfahne; ein wetterwendischer Mensch;* the ∾-forecast *die Wettervoraussage, der Wetterbericht.* — **II.** a.: on the ∾ beam (bow, quarter) of a ship *auf der Luvseite eines Schiffes;* to keep one's ∾ eye open *gut aufpassen;* to have the ∾ gage (gauge) of a thing *einer Sache gegenüber im Vorteil sein.* — **III.** v.tr.: to ∾ a gale *einen Sturm überstehen, Schwierigkeiten überwinden.* — **IV.** v.i.: to ∾ *verwittern*

wedge n.: to get in the thin edge (or: end) of the ∾ *einen schwachen Anfang machen, den ersten Schritt tun*

weed n.: ill ∾s grow apace (prov.) *Unkraut vergeht nicht;* the Indian (soothing) ∾ *der Tabak*

weeds n.pl.: she is wearing widow's ∾ *sie trägt einen Witwenschleier*

week n.: a ∾ of Sundays *eine Ewigkeit;* ∾ in ∾ out *Woche für Woche;* today ∾ *heute in acht Tagen;* to knock a person into the middle of next ∾ *j.en im hohen Bogen hinauswerfen*

weep v.i.: to come home by Weeping Cross *Reue empfinden*

weigh I. v.tr.: to ∾ anchor *den Anker lichten;* to ∾ one's words *seine Worte wägen;* to ∾ one thing against (with) another *eine Sache gegen eine andere abwägen;* one good argument ∾s down six bad ones *ein gutes Argument wiegt sechs schlechte auf;* to be ∾ed down with cares *von Sorgen niedergedrückt sein;* to ∾ a jockey in, out *einen Jockei vor und nach dem Rennen wiegen;* to ∾ out butter *Butter auswiegen.* — **II.** v.i.: when did you ∾ last? *wann hast* *du dich zuletzt gewogen?;* it ∾s little (nothing, etc.) *es wiegt wenig (nichts, usw.);* it ∾s heavy upon me *es lastet schwer auf mir;* a jockey ∾s in, out *ein Jockei läßt sich vor und nach dem Rennen wiegen;* to ∾ in with an argument *ein Argument triumphierend vorbringen;* the point that ∾s with him *der Punkt, der bei ihm Gewicht hat (von Einfluß, ausschlaggebend ist)*

weight I. n.: what is your ∾? *wieviel wiegst du?;* he is twice your ∾ *er ist zweimal so schwer wie du;* to be of great ∾ (to carry, have great ∾) with a person *bei j.em viel wiegen, bedeuten, gelten;* to give due ∾ to a thing *einer Sache volle Bedeutung schenken, etwas würdigen;* to throw one's ∾ about (colloq.) *sich wichtig machen (sich wichtig, dicke tun);* it was a ∾ off my mind *mir fiel ein Stein vom Herzen;* to lose in ∾ *an Gewicht verlieren, abnehmen;* to pull one's ∾ *tüchtig rudern; sich anstrengen, sein bestes hergeben;* to put the ∾ *die Kugel stoßen;* to put on ∾ *an Gewicht zunehmen;* a paper-∾ *ein Briefbeschwerer.* — **II.** v.tr.: to ∾ the scales in favour of a person *etwas für j.en in die Waagschale werfen;* to be ∾ed with cares *von Sorgen belastet (bedrückt) sein*

weird I. n.: to dree one's ∾ *sein Schicksal ertragen;* a ∾ affair *eine eigenartige, seltsame Geschichte;* the ∾ sisters *die Schicksalschwestern*

welcome I. int.: ∾ home! *willkommen zu Hause, in der Heimat!* — **II.** n.: a hearty ∾ is the best cheer (prov.) *ein freundliches Gesicht ist das beste Gericht;* to bid a person ∾ *j.en willkommen heißen;* to find a ready ∾ *freundlich aufgenommen werden;* to wear out (to outstay) one's ∾ see 'wear'. — **III.** v.tr.: to ∾ a person, a thing *j.en willkommen heißen, etwas begrüßen.* — **IV.** a.: as ∾ as snow in harvest *höchst unwillkommen;* you are ∾ to your opinions *meinetwegen kannst du denken, was du willst;* (you are) ∾! *nichts zu danken! gern geschehen! bitte sehr!;* you are ∾ to any service I can do *ich stehe dir ganz zu Diensten;* you are ∾ to take what steps you please *es steht dir frei, alle Schritte zu unternehmen, die du willst*

well[1] v.i.: to ∾ forth (out, up) *hervorquellen, hervorsprudeln;* tears ∾ed up to her eyes *Tränen traten ihr in die Augen*

well[2] **I.** adv.: ∾ begun is half done (prov.) *frisch gewagt ist halb gewonnen;* it was ∾ done of you to come *du tatest gut daran, zu kommen;* ∾ into the night *bis tief in die Nacht;* to be ∾-off (∾-to-do) *wohlhabend sein;* to be ∾-off for a thing *gut mit etwas versehen sein;* ∾ on in life *in vorgeschrittenem Alter;* ∾ met *gut, daß ich dich treffe (du kommst mir wie gerufen);* he is ∾ past forty *er ist weit über vierzig;* I wish I were ∾ out of it *ich wünschte, ich wäre glücklich aus der Sache (ich hätte die Sache hinter mir);* to be ∾ up in the list *hoch oben in der Liste stehen;* to be ∾ up in a matter *in einer Sache gut bewandert sein;* to come off ∾ *Glück, Erfolg haben, sich auszeichnen;* it speaks ∾ for his discipline *es spricht für seine Disziplin;* to stand ∾ with a person *mit j.em gut stehen, bei j.em gut angeschrieben sein;* he is a Christian as ∾ *er ist noch dazu ein Christ;* clothes as ∾ as food *sowohl Kleider als auch Nahrung;* I may as ∾ be hanged for a sheep as a lamb *wenn schon, denn schon;* you might as ∾ throw your money away *du könntest ebensogut dein Geld wegwerfen.* — **II.** a.: all's ∾ that ends ∾ (prov.) *Ende gut, alles gut;* perhaps it is just as ∾ *vielleicht ist es gut so;* that is all very ∾ *das ist alles ganz schön (schön und gut);* if you choose to take my advice, ∾ and good *wenn du meinem Rate folgen willst, schön und gut.* — **III.** n.: let (leave) ∾ alone *misch' dich nicht unnötig ein, laß' es gut sein!;* to wish a person ∾ *j.em alles Gute wünschen.* — **IV.** int.: ∾, I never! *nein, so was!;* ∾ then, let us say no more about it *nun gut (na schön), sagen wir nichts mehr davon;* ∾, who was it? *nun, wer war es?*

west adv.: to be ∾ of a place *westlich von einem Orte liegen;* to go ∾ (sl.) *sterben, abkratzen, verloren-, hops-, flötengehen*

wet I. a.: the country is ∾ *in dem Lande herrscht kein Alkoholverbot;* ∾ to the skin *naß bis auf die Haut, patschnaß;* a ∾ bob *ein Schüler in Eton, der Wassersport treibt;* a ∾ blanket *ein Dämpfer; kalter Wasserstrahl; ein Spielverderber (Miesmacher);* a ∾-nurse *eine Amme.* — **II.** v.tr.: to ∾ a bargain *ein Geschäft durch einen Trunk bekräftigen;* to ∾ one's whistle *die Kehle anfeuchten, eins hinter die Binde gießen.* — **III.** n.: he's a ∾ *er ist ein Gegner* *des Alkoholverbots;* I'm longing for a ∾ (sl.) *ich sehne mich nach einem Trunk*

whack I. v.tr.: to ∾ (up) things on the square (colloq.) *Sachen ehrlich teilen;* a ∾ing big piece (sl.) *ein ganz gehöriges Stück;* to get a good ∾ing *eine tüchtige Tracht Prügel bekommen;* to be ∾ed to the wide (sl.) *erschöpft, ermattet sein.* — **II.** n.: to go ∾s (sl.) *zu gleichen Teilen gehen;* I have had my ∾ of pleasure (sl.) *ich habe meinen Teil Vergnügen gehabt;* let me have (take) a ∾ at it (sl.) *laß mich mal versuchen*

whale n.: very like a ∾ (Hamlet, III, 2, 399) *ganz wie ein Walfisch; eine ironische Zustimmung zu einer absurden Behauptung;* to be a ∾ at (for) a thing (colloq.) *auf einem Gebiet sehr gut, eine Kanone sein;* to be a ∾ on a thing (colloq.) *auf etwas ganz versessen sein;* to throw a sprat to catch a ∾ *mit der Wurst nach der Speckseite werfen*

what pron.: I know ∾ *ich habe einen Gedanken (eine Idee), ich weiß was;* I'll tell you ∾ *ich will dir was sagen;* he knows ∾'s ∾ *er ist nicht auf den Kopf gefallen; er weiß, was los ist; er ist im Bilde; er weiß, wo Barthel den Most holt;* to tell a person ∾'s ∾ *j.em zeigen, was eine Harke ist;* ∾ about (of) this? *wie steht's hiermit?;* Mr. ∾-d'ye-call-him ∾'s-his-name *Herr Dingsda, Dingskirchen;* he gave him ∾ for (sl.) *er hat's ihm gründlich gesteckt, ihm tüchtig den Kopf gewaschen, ihn gehörig verprügelt;* ∾ ho! *hallo!;* ∾ if we were to try? *wie wäre es, wenn wir es versuchten?;* and ∾ not *und was nicht alles;* a ∾-not *eine Etagere;* ∾ through we are poor *was macht's, daß wir arm sind; und wenn wir auch arm sind;* ∾ with drink and ∾ with fright *teils vor Betrunkenheit und teils vor Schreck;* ∾'s yours? *was möchtest du trinken?*

wheedle v.tr.: to ∾ a person into doing a thing *j.en beschwätzen, etwas zu tun;* to ∾ a thing out of a person *j.em etwas abschwatzen, ablotsen*

wheel I. n.: the ∾ has come full circle (Shakespeare, K. Lear, V. 3) *die gerechte Vergeltung ist eingetreten;* the ∾s of life *die Vorgänge (Kräfte) des Lebens;* ∾s within ∾s *verwickelte Verhältnisse;* a fly on the ∾ *j., der seinen Einfluß überschätzt;* the man at the ∾ *der Steuermann;* right ∾, left ∾ *rechts schwenkt!, links schwenkt!;* to break a butterfly on the ∾ *mit Kanonen nach Spatzen schießen;* free ∾ *Freilauf;* I'm going by ∾ *ich fahre mit dem Rad;* everything is going on ∾s *alles geht glatt (wie geschmiert);* to put (to set) one's shoulder to the ∾ *kräftige Anstrengungen machen, sich ernstlich an die Arbeit machen;* to put a spoke in a person's ∾ *j.es Pläne durchkreuzen, j.em einen Knüppel zwischen die Beine werfen;* to take the ∾ *das Steuerrad ergreifen;* to turn a ∾ *ein Rad schlagen;* a ∾barrow *ein Schiebkarren.* — **II.** v.tr.: to ∾ a cart *einen Karren schieben (rollen, fahren);* I'm going to ∾ it *ich fahre mit dem Rad.* — **III.** v.i.: to ∾ round *sich plötzlich umdrehen, umschwenken, seine Meinung ändern*

when adv.: say ∾! *sag, wenn ich aufhören soll! (beim Eingießen)*

whereabouts n.: to know a person's ∾ *wissen, wo j. wohnt, wo er zu finden ist*

wherewithal n.: he has not the ∾ to do it *dazu fehlt ihm das Geld*

while I. n.: the whilst *derweil, während der Zeit;* all the (this) ∾ *die ganze Zeit über;* between ∾s *zuweilen, dann und wann;* for a ∾ *eine Zeitlang;* for a long ∾, this long ∾ past *seit langem;* in a little ∾ *bald;* mean∾ *mittlerweile;* once in a ∾ *gelegentlich, dann und wann;* quite a ∾ *eine ganze Zeit;* it is worth ∾, worth my ∾ *es ist der Mühe wert, es lohnt sich;* I shall make it worth your ∾ *ich werde es dir vergelten, du sollst nicht dabei zu kurz kommen.* — **II.** v.tr.: to ∾ away the time *sich (dat.) die Zeit vertreiben*

whip I. v.tr.: a ∾ping boy *ein Prügeljunge, -knabe;* to ∾ the cat (sl.) *sich betrinken, blauen Montag machen;* ∾ped cream *Schlagsahne;* that ∾s creation *das übertrifft alles;* to ∾ the devil (the old gentleman) round the post (stump) *etwas auf unehrliche Weise, auf Umwegen erreichen;* to ∾ in party members *Parteimitglieder einpeitschen, zur Abstimmung zusammentrommeln;* to ∾ off (on) one's coat *den Rock hastig ausziehen (überwerfen, anziehen);* to ∾ on (or: up) a horse *ein Pferd mit der Peitsche antreiben;* to ∾ out a knife *ein Messer aus der Tasche reißen;* to ∾ up a thing *etwas schnell an sich reißen, aufraffen.*

— **II.** v.i.: she ∾ped away (off) to France *sie riß aus (entwetzte) nach Frankreich;* to ∾ round *sich schnell umdrehen;* he ∾ped upstairs *er stürzte (sauste, flitzte) die Treppe hinauf.* — **III.** n.: he is a good (poor) ∾ *er kutschiert (fährt) gut (schlecht);* a party ∾, ∾per-in *ein Einpeitscher einer Partei;* a five-line ∾ *eine fünfmal unterstrichene, sehr dringliche Aufforderung des Einpeitschers, zur Abstimmung zu erscheinen;* to ride ∾ and spur *Hals über Kopf reiten;* his veins stood out like ∾-cord *seine Venen traten wie Stricke hervor;* to have the ∾ hand of a person *j.en in der Gewalt haben;* to make (to take up) a ∾-round *(auf der Stelle) eine Geldsammlung machen (veranstalten)*

whipper-snapper n.: a little ∾ *ein Knirps, Dreikäsehoch*

whirl I. v.tr.: to ∾ one's stick *den Stock wirbelnd schwingen.* — **II.** v.i.: my head ∾s *mir schwindelt;* a ∾ing dervish *ein tanzender Derwisch;* to ∾ about (round) *sich schnell umdrehen, sich drehen;* the carriage ∾ed away *der Wagen rollte fort.* — **III.** n.: my thoughts are in a ∾ *die Gedanken schwirren mir im Kopf herum;* to sow the wind and reap the ∾wind *(den) Wind säen und Ungewitter (Sturmwind) ernten* (Hos. VIII, 7)

whirligig n.: the ∾ of time *der Strudel, sausende Webstuhl der Zeit*

whisk I. v.tr.: she went ∾ing a cane *sie schlug mit einem Rohrstock um sich:* he was ∾ed across the Channel in an aeroplane *er wurde eiligst über den Kanal geflogen;* the waiter ∾ed my plate away *der Kellner nahm schnell meinen Teller fort.* — **II.** v.i.: a mouse ∾s into its hole *eine Maus huscht in ihr Loch;* he ∾ed off (away) *er flitzte weg.* — **III.** n.: with a ∾ of the tail *mit einer schnellen Bewegung des Schwanzes*

whiskers n.: that joke has ∾ (sl.) *der Witz hat so einen Bart;* that was all my ∾ (sl.) *das war alles Unsinn (Mumpitz, Quatsch)*

whisper n.: in a pig's ∾ *sehr schnell, im Nu*

whistle I. v.i.: to ∾ down the wind *in den Wind schlagen, unbeachtet lassen, aufgeben;* you may ∾ for it *darauf kannst du lange warten;* to ∾ for one's money *das Geld in den Schornstein schreiben;* to let a person go ∾ *j.es Wünsche nicht berücksichtigen.* — **II.** n.: to pay for one's ∾ (colloq.) *eine Liebhaberei, eine Marotte teuer bezahlen;* to wet one's ∾ see 'wet'

whit n.: it is every ∾ as good *es ist genau so (ebenso) gut;* no (not a, never a) ∾ better *nicht im geringsten (kein Jota) besser*

white a.: see 'elephant, feather, flag, heat, horse, lie, sheet, slave'; a ∾-collar worker *ein Büroangestellter (im Gegensatz zum Handwerker);* a ∾-headed boy *ein Günstling, Liebling;* a ∾ man *ein anständiger, ehrlicher Kerl;* a ∾ night *eine schlaflose Nacht;* as ∾ as a sheet *so weiß wie ein Laken, wie die Wand, kreidebleich*

whodunit n. (sl.): he writes ∾s (who done it?) *er schreibt Detektivgeschichten*

wholesale I. n.: to sell by ∾ *en gros verkaufen.* — **II.** a.: a ∾ dealer *ein Grossist, Großhändler;* a ∾ slaughter took place *ein Massenabschlachten fand statt.* — **III.** adv.: to buy (to sell) ∾ *en gros einkaufen (verkaufen)*

whoopee n. (sl.): to make ∾ *ein Gaudi machen*

whop v.tr. (sl.): to ∾ a person, give a person a good ∾ping *j.en gehörig verprügeln, durchhauen;* a ∾ping lie (whopper) *eine faustdicke Lüge*

why I. int.: ∾, of course, that was it *ei natürlich, das war es;* ∾, a child could answer that *das könnte ja ein Kind beantworten;* if silver will not do, ∾, we must try gold *wenn es mit Silber nicht geht, müssen wir es eben mit Gold versuchen.* — **II.** n.: the ∾s and wherefores *das Wie und Warum*

wide I. a.: a ∾ boy (sl.) *ein schlauer Kerl.* — **II.** adv.: ∾ apart *weit getrennt, auseinander;* ∾ awake *hellwach, auf der Hut;* a ∾-awake *ein breitrandiger Schlapphut;* far and ∾ *weit und breit;* ∾ of the mark *weit vom Ziel ab;* ∾ of the truth *weit von der Wahrheit entfernt; hinausgehend über die Grenzen.* — **III.** n.: broke to the ∾ (colloq.) *vollkommen bankrott;* dead (done) to the ∾ *total besoffen*

wife n.: all the world and his ∾ see 'world'; a mid∾ *eine Hebamme;* an old wives' tale *ein Ammenmärchen*

wig I. n.: there will be ∾s on the green *es wird eine Schlägerei (Rauferei) geben.* — **II.** v.tr.: to give a person a good ∾ging *j.en tüchtig ausschimpfen, abkanzeln*

will I. v.aux.: boys ∾ be boys *Jungens sind nun mal Jungens;* he ∾ have his smoke *er kann das Rauchen nicht lassen;* I ∾ not be caught again *ich lasse mich nicht noch einmal fangen, dabei ertappen;* he would sit there for hours *er pflegte stundenlang dort zu sitzen, er saß oft stundenlang da;* a would-be gentleman *einer, der sich als feiner Herr ausgibt, der gern ein feiner Herr sein möchte.* — **II.** v.tr.: to ∾ one's money to a hospital *sein Geld einem Krankenhaus vermachen;* to ∾ oneself into contentment *sich zur Zufriedenheit zwingen.* — **III.** n.: where there's a ∾ there's a way (prov.) *wo ein Wille ist, ist auch ein Weg;* at ∾ *nach Belieben;* of one's own free ∾ *freiwillig, aus freien Stücken;* to do a thing with a ∾ *etwas energisch, mit Lust und Liebe tun;* to make one's ∾ *sein Testament machen*

willing a.: to be ∾ to do a thing *willens (bereit) sein, etwas zu tun;* to flog (to spur) a ∾ horse *offene Türen einrennen, j.en unnötig drängen*

willow n.: to handle the ∾ *den Kricketschläger führen;* to wear the ∾ *den Verlust, die Abwesenheit einer geliebten Person betrauern*

willynilly adv.: he had to do it ∾ *er mußte es wohl oder übel tun, ob er wollte oder nicht, nolens volens*

win I. v.tr.: to ∾ the day (the field) *den Sieg davontragen;* to ∾ one's goal *sein Ziel erreichen;* to ∾ golden opinions *die allgemeine Achtung der Menschen gewinnen;* to ∾ one's spurs *die Sporen erlangen, sich die Sporen verdienen;* to ∾ the toss *beim Münzenhochwerfen das Los gewinnen;* to ∾ one's way *seinen Weg machen, sich durchsetzen;* it will ∾ him many friends *es wird ihm viele Freunde bringen;* to ∾ someone to agree *j.en überreden, zuzustimmen;* to ∾ someone to one's side *j.en für sich gewinnen.* — **II.** v.i.: to ∾ hands down (colloq.) *spielend siegen;* to ∾ free (clear, out, through) *sich durchsetzen, siegen, ans Ziel kommen*

wind¹ I. n.: between ∾ and water *an einer verwundbaren, verfänglichen Stelle;* a capful of ∾ *eine vorübergehende Brise;* it is an ill ∾ that blows nobody any good (prov.) *kein Unglück ist so groß, es trägt ein Glück im Schoß;* in the ∾'s eye, in the teeth of the ∾ *gegen den Wind;* to break ∾ *Winde lassen;* to cast (to fling, to throw) to the ∾s *in den Wind schlagen;* a rumour gets (takes) ∾ *ein Gerücht kommt auf, verbreitet sich;* to get the ∾ of a person *j.em einen Vorteil abgewinnen;* to get ∾ of a thing *Wind von einer Sache bekommen; etwas erfahren;* to get the ∾ up (sl.) *Angst, Dampf bekommen;* to hang in the ∾ *in der Luft, in Ungewißheit schweben;* to hit a person in the ∾ *j.en vor den Bauch stoßen, daß ihm die Luft ausgeht;* to know how (which way) the ∾ blows (lies) *wissen, woher der Wind weht;* to put the ∾ up a person (sl.) *j.em Angst, einen Schrecken einjagen;* to raise the ∾ *Geld auftreiben;* let me recover my ∾ *laß mich wieder zu Atem kommen;* to sail (to be) close to the ∾ *sich an der Grenze des Erlaubten oder des Schicklichen bewegen;* to scatter to the four ∾s of heaven *in alle vier Winde zerstreuen;* a slant of ∾ *eine günstige Brise;* to sow the ∾ and reap the whirl∾ see 'whirlwind'; to take the ∾ out of a person's sails *j.em den Wind aus den Segeln nehmen;* to whistle down the ∾ see 'whistle'; he is a ∾bag *er ist ein Windbeutel, Schwätzer;* it is a ∾fall *es ist Fallobst; ein unerwartetes Glück;* to fight ∾mills *gegen Windmühlen anrennen;* to throw one's cap over the ∾mill *jede Vorsicht (Vernunft) außer acht lassen;* to get to the ∾ward of a person *j.em einen Vorsprung abgewinnen, ein Schnippchen schlagen.* — **II.** v.tr.: the hounds ∾ed the fox *die Hunde witterten den Fuchs;* to ∾ the horses *die Pferde verschnaufen lassen;* I am quite ∾ed *ich bin ganz außer Atem, ich kann nicht mehr japsen*

wind² I. v.i.: a ∾ing staircase *eine Wendeltreppe;* a path ∾s along (down, up) the river *ein Pfad schlängelt sich am Fluß entlang (den Fluß hinunter, hinauf);* a creeper ∾s round a tree *eine Kletterpflanze schlingt (windet) sich um einen Baum;* a company ∾s up *eine Gesellschaft liquidiert;* he wound up by declaring (with the words) *er schloß mit der Erklärung (mit den Worten).* — **II.** v.tr.: to ∾ cotton off (on) a reel *Garn ab-, aufspulen;* he wound himself (his way) into my confidence *er schlich* *(schmeichelte) sich in mein Vertrauen ein;* to ∾ a person round one's little finger *j.en um den (kleinen) Finger wickeln;* the administration needs ∾ing up *die Verwaltung muß angespornt (angetrieben, aufgemuntert, aufgerüttelt) werden;* to ∾ up a clock *eine Uhr aufziehen;* he is ∾ing himself up for an effort *er ermannt sich zu einem Versuch;* to ∾ up a piece of string *ein Stück Kordel aufwickeln;* he wound up his speech *er schloß seine Rede;* expectation was wound up to the highest pitch *die Erwartung war aufs höchste gestiegen*

window n.: he has a bow ∾ (sl.) *er hat einen Schmerbauch;* he has (puts) all his goods in the ∾ *er ist oberflächlich, hinter ihm steckt nichts*

wine n.: Adam's ∾ *Trinkwasser, Gänsewein;* good ∾ needs no bush (prov.) *gute Ware lobt sich selbst;* new ∾ in old bottles (Matth. IX, 17) *Most in alten Schläuchen;* over the walnuts and the ∾ see 'walnut'; to be in ∾ *angeheitert, betrunken sein*

wing I. n.: to be on the ∾ *im Fluge, in Bewegung sein;* to clip a person's ∾s *j.em die Flügel beschneiden;* to come on the ∾s of the wind *mit Windeseile kommen;* to lend (to add) ∾s to a thing *etwas beflügeln, beschleunigen;* to take ∾ *zu fliegen beginnen;* money takes to itself ∾s *das Geld verschwindet schnell;* to take under one's ∾ *unter seine Fittiche nehmen.* — **II.** v.tr.: to ∾ an arrow *einen Pfeil mit Federn versehen;* to ∾ a bird *einen Vogel flügellahm schießen;* a bird ∾s its flight to its nest *ein Vogel nimmt seinen Flug zum Nest;* fear ∾ed his steps *die Angst beflügelte seine Schritte*

wink I. v.i.: to ∾ at a thing *ein Auge bei einer Sache zudrücken;* to ∾ to (at) a person *j.em zublinzeln;* like ∾ing *im Nu.* — **II.** v.tr.: to ∾ one's eyes *mit den Augen blinzeln.* — **III.** n.: I could not get a ∾ of sleep, I did not sleep a ∾ all night *ich habe die ganze Nacht kein Auge zugetan;* to take forty ∾s *ein Schläfchen (Nickerchen) machen;* to tip a person the ∾ (colloq.) *j.em einen Wink geben*

wipe I. v.tr.: to ∾ a person's eye (sl.) *j.em zuvorkommen, ihn übervorteilen, beschummeln, über's Ohr hauen;* to ∾ the floor with a person *j.em eine demütigende Niederlage beibringen;* to ∾ away (off, out, up) a thing *etwas weg- (aus-, auf)wischen;* the whole race was ∾d out *die ganze Rasse wurde ausgerottet.* — **II.** v.i.: he ∾d at me with his sword *er führte einen weit ausholenden Schlag mit dem Schwert gegen mich.* — **III.** n.: he fetched him a ∾, took a ∾ at him (sl.) *er wischte ihm eins aus;* give this plate a ∾ *wisch' diesen Teller ab;* I've lost my ∾ (vulg.) *ich habe mein Taschentuch (derb: meine Rotzfahne) verloren*

wire I. n.: by ∾ *telegraphisch;* a live ∾ *ein elektrisch geladener Draht; eine äußerst energische, ungestüme Person;* to pull the ∾s *der Drahtzieher sein;* to send a ∾ *ein Telegramm schicken.* — **II.** v.tr.: ∾ me the result *telegraphiere mir das Ergebnis.* — **III.** v.i.: he was ∾d for *man ließ ihn telegraphisch holen;* to ∾ to a person *j.em telegraphieren;* to ∾ in (sl.) *sich dahinterklemmen, ins Geschirr legen*

wise[1] I. a.: where ignorance is bliss, 'tis folly to be ∾ (Thom. Gray) *wo Unkenntnis ein Segen, ist es töricht, weise zu sein;* as ∾ as before *so klug wie vorher;* none the ∾r *um nichts klüger (gescheiter);* to be penny ∾ and pound foolish *am unrechten Ende sparen;* a ∾ crack (sl.) *eine kurze, prägnante Bemerkung;* a ∾ saw *ein alter (weiser) Spruch;* a ∾ woman (arch.) *eine weise Frau, Wahrsagerin, Hexe;* to be (to get) ∾ to a thing (sl.) *von etwas Kenntnis haben, eine(r) Sache gewahr werden;* to put a person ∾ to a thing (sl.) *j.en über etwas unterrichten, aufklären;* a word to the ∾ *laß dir raten, wenn du klug bist.* — **II.** v.tr.: to ∾ up a person (sl.) *j.en über etwas unterrichten (aufklären).* — **III.** v.i.: to ∾ up to a thing (sl.) *sich über etwas unterrichten (aufklären)*

wise[2] n.: in solemn ∾ (arch.) *in feierlicher Weise;* in no ∾ *auf keine Weise;* in some (any) ∾ *auf irgendeine Weise, irgendwie;* on this ∾ *auf diese Weise*

wish I. v.tr.: to ∾ a person at the devil (further, farther) *j.en zum Teufel (weit fort) wünschen;* I ∾ you joy of it (iron.) *viel Vergnügen!* — **II.** v.i.: I ∾ I were at home *ich wünschte, ich wäre zu Hause;* there is nothing left to be ∾ed for *es ist alles nach Wunsch gegangen.* — **III.** n.: the ∾ is father to the thought *der Wunsch ist der Vater des Gedankens;* if ∾es were horses beggars might ride (prov.) *vom Wünschen* *ist noch niemand reich geworden;* with all good ∾es *mit herzlichen Glückwünschen (Grüßen)*

wishful a.: ∾ thinking *fromme Wünsche*

wish-wash n.: this soup is mere ∾ *diese Suppe ist das reinste Spülwasser;* he only talks ∾ *er redet nur Gewäsch*

wishy-washy a.: a ∾ drink *ein labberiges Gesöff;* ∾ talk *seichtes Gerede, Gewäsch*

wit I. v.i.: to ∾ *das heißt, nämlich;* God wot (arch.) *Gott weiß, weiß Gott.* — **II.** n.: he is a ∾ *er ist ein Witzbold;* he has his ∾s about him *er hat seine fünf Sinne beisammen;* to be at one's ∾'s end, at the end of one's ∾s *mit seinem Verstand am Ende sein; nicht ein noch aus wissen; sich nicht mehr auskennen;* to drive a person out of his ∾s *j.en verrückt machen;* to frighten a person out of his ∾s *j.em einen Todesschreck einjagen;* to keep one's ∾s about one *auf der Hut sein;* to live by one's ∾s *sich geschickt (gewissenlos) durch's Leben schlagen; von der Hand in den Mund leben;* to set one's ∾s to a problem *sich an die Lösung eines Problems machen*

with prep.: ∾ all his learning *bei (trotz) all' seiner Gelehrsamkeit;* it is holiday time ∾ us *bei uns sind Ferien;* it rests ∾ you to decide *die Entscheidung liegt bei dir;* he is down ∾ fever *er liegt mit Fieber danieder;* he is stiff ∾ cold *er ist steif vor Kälte;* he trembles ∾ fear *er zittert vor Furcht;* to part ∾ a thing *sich von etwas trennen;* to differ ∾ a person *anderer Meinung als j. sein*

withers n.pl.: our ∾ are unwrung (Hamlet, III, 2) *das betrifft uns nicht, geht uns nichts an, läßt uns kalt (Schlegel: unsere Haut ist gesund)*

within I. adv.: to go (to stay) ∾ *ins Haus gehen, drinnen bleiben.* — **II.** n.: as seen from ∾ *von innen gesehen.* — **III.** prep.: ∾ an ace of *um ein Haar, beinahe;* ∾ call (reach, sight) *in Ruf-, Reich-, Sichtweite;* to stay ∾ doors *im, zu Hause bleiben;* he is running ∾ himself *er läuft, ohne sich sonderlich anzustrengen;* ∾ a year of his death *noch ein Jahr nach, vor seinem Tode*

witness I. n.: a ∾ for the crown, prosecution *ein Belastungszeuge;* a ∾ for the defence *ein Entlastungszeuge;* in ∾ of *zum Zeugnis von;* to bear ∾ to (of) a thing *von etwas Zeugnis ablegen;* to call to ∾ *als Zeugen anrufen;* the ∾-box *die Zeugenbank.* — **II.** v.tr.: his nervous manner ∾ed his guilty conscience *seine Nervosität bezeugte sein schlechtes Gewissen;* to ∾ a document *eine Urkunde unterschriftlich beglaubigen;* I ∾ed the event *ich war Zeuge des Ereignisses, ich sah es mit eigenen Augen.* — **III.** v.i.: to ∾ for (against) a person *für (gegen) j.en Zeugnis ablegen;* to ∾ to an event *ein Ereignis bezeugen*

wizard a. (sl.): it was ∾ *es war herrlich, wunderbar, prima*

woe n.: weal and ∾ see 'weal'; ∾ is me! *wehe mir!;* ∾ worth the day *verflucht sei der Tag!;* ∾begone *vergrämt, betrübt aussehend;* ∾ betide you *wehe dir!*

wolf I. n.: as greedy (hungry) as a ∾ *gierig (gefräßig, hungrig) wie ein Wolf; mit wahrem Wolfshunger;* a ∾ in sheep's clothing *ein Wolf in Schafskleidern;* to cry ∾ *blinden Lärm schlagen;* to have (to hold) the ∾ by the ears *in der Klemme sein; nicht ein noch aus können;* to keep the ∾ from the door *sich vorm Verhungern bewahren.* — **II.** v.tr.: to ∾ down one's food *das Essen gierig herunterschlingen*

wonder I. n.: the ∾ is that *man muß sich wundern, daß;* you are punctual for a ∾ *du bist merkwürdigerweise pünktlich;* a nine days' ∾ *eine Sensation;* no (small, what) ∾ he didn't come *kein (was) Wunder, daß er nicht kam;* to do (to work) ∾s *Wunder tun, bemerkenswerten Erfolg haben;* to promise ∾s *goldene Berge versprechen.* — **II.** v.i.: I ∾ he came *ich wundere mich (bin erstaunt), daß er kam;* can you ∾ at it? *wunderst du dich darüber?;* I ∾ at you *ich muß mich doch sehr über dich (dein Benehmen) wundern;* I ∾ to myself *ich wundere (frage) mich im stillen, vergebens;* I ∾! *das möchte ich gern wissen!;* I ∾ when, where, whether, who, why *ich möchte wissen wann, wo, ob, wer, warum, usw.*

wood n.: he cannot see the ∾ for the trees *er sieht den Wald vor lauter Bäumen nicht;* don't halloo till you are out of the ∾ *frohlocke nicht zu früh;* we are not yet out of the ∾ *wir sind noch nicht außer Gefahr, über den Berg;* touch ∾! *unberufen!;* wine from the ∾ *Wein vom Faß*

wool n.: dyed in the ∾ *durchtrieben, ausgekocht;* much cry and little ∾ *viel Geschrei und wenig Wolle;* to draw (to pull) the ∾ over a person's eyes *j.em Sand in die Augen streuen, ihn hinters Licht führen;* to go for ∾ and come home shorn *das Gegenteil von etwas Erstrebtem erreichen; in seinen Absichten stark enttäuscht werden;* keep your ∾ on (sl.) *nur keine Aufregung!;* to lose one's ∾ (sl.) *in die Wolle geraten;* ∾gathering *zerstreut, Zerstreutheit*

word I. n.: it was a ∾ and a blow *es wurde gleich zugeschlagen;* my ∾ for it *auf mein Wort, mein Wort darauf;* a ∾ in a person's ear *ein Wort im Vertrauen;* a ∾ in (out of) season *ein Wort zur rechten (unrechten) Zeit; ein angebrachtes (unangebrachtes) Wort;* a ∾ with you *nur ein paar Worte!;* ∾s are but wind *Worte sind leerer Schall;* to take a person at his ∾ *j.en beim Wort nehmen;* at these ∾s *bei diesen Worten;* by ∾ of mouth *mündlich;* it is too silly for ∾s *es ist unsagbar töricht;* to translate ∾ for ∾ *Wort für Wort, wörtlich übersetzen;* in a ∾ *mit éinem Wort, kurz und gut;* in other ∾s *mit anderen Worten;* to put into ∾s *in Worte kleiden;* a man of his ∾ *ein Mann von Wort;* on (with) the ∾ he went away *bei dem Wort (als er das hörte,) ging er fort;* to hang on a person's ∾s *j.em aufmerksam zuhören;* to lead to ∾s *zu Streitigkeiten führen;* to suit the action to the ∾ *die Tat dem Worte folgen lassen;* upon my ∾! *auf mein Wort! mein Gott! nein, so was!;* to play upon ∾s *ein Wortspiel machen;* big ∾s *große, prahlerische Worte;* fair (fine, soft) ∾s butter no parsnips (prov.) *Redensarten sind billig; schöne Worte machen den Kohl nicht fett;* to give a person one's good ∾ for a post *j.en für eine Stelle empfehlen;* to say a good ∾ for a person *für j.en ein gutes Wort einlegen;* hard ∾s break no bones *Schimpfe tut nicht so weh wie Prügel;* high (hot) ∾s *zornige Worte;* a household ∾ *ein allgemein bekannter Ausspruch, ein Alltagswort;* it is the last ∾ in wireless sets *es ist die letzte Errungenschaft in Radioapparaten;* mum's the ∾ *schweig! nichts gesagt!;* sharp's the ∾! *mach schnell! dalli!;* vain ∾s *leere (eitle) Worte, Versprechungen;* to be as good as one's ∾ *zu seinem Worte stehen;* his ∾ is as good as his bond *sein Wort gilt soviel wie seine Unterschrift;* to bring (to send) ∾ *Nachricht bringen, senden;* to coin a ∾ *ein Wort prägen;* to drop a ∾ *ein Wort fallen lassen;* to eat one's ∾s *seine Worte zurücknehmen (widerrufen) müssen; zu Kreuze kriechen;* to give (to pledge, to pass) one's ∾ *sein Wort geben, verpfänden;* to give the ∾ for (to do) a thing *das Zeichen zu etwas geben;* I have also a ∾ to say in the matter *in der Angelegenheit habe ich auch etwas mitzureden;* he hasn't a ∾ to throw at a dog *er ist ein ungeselliger, hochmütig schweigsamer Mensch; er hat kein Wort für einen übrig, er ist sehr unzugänglich;* I should like to have a ∾ with him *ich möchte ein paar Worte mit ihm reden;* to have (to bandy) ∾s with a person *sich mit j.em streiten;* to leave ∾ *Nachricht (Bescheid) hinterlassen;* to make no ∾s about a matter *keine Worte über eine Angelegenheit verlieren;* to put in a ∾ *ein Wort einfließen lassen;* to put in a ∾ for a person *für j.en ein gutes Wort einlegen;* to swallow one's ∾s *seine Worte zurücknehmen;* you may take my ∾ for it *du kannst es mir glauben;* to torture ∾s *Worte verdrehen.* — **II.** v.tr.: a cautiously ∾ed protest *ein vorsichtig (ab)gefaßter Protest*

work I. n.: he is at ∾ (he has got to ∾) at last *er ist endlich bei der Arbeit, hat sich endlich an die Arbeit gemacht;* it is all in the day's ∾ *das bringt die gewöhnliche Tagesarbeit mit sich;* all ∾ and no play, makes Jack a dull boy (prov.) *zuviel Arbeit und zuwenig Spiel macht dumm;* to be out of ∾ *arbeitslos sein;* to set to ∾ *sich dranmachen, etwas zu tun;* he has his ∾ cut out for him *er hat ein tüchtiges Stück Arbeit vor sich;* many hands make light ∾ (prov.) *viele Hände machen der Arbeit bald ein Ende;* you have made sad ∾ of it *du hast etwas Schönes angerichtet;* to make short ∾ of a thing *kurzen Prozeß (nicht viel Umstände) mit etwas machen;* he has not done a stroke of ∾ *er hat keinen Strich (Schlag) gearbeitet;* this is thirsty ∾ *bei dieser Arbeit bekommt man Durst;* to give a person the ∾s (sl.) *j.en gehörig zwischennehmen, rauh anpacken, schleifen;* there is something wrong with the ∾s *an dem (Uhr)werk ist etwas nicht in Ordnung;* the defense ∾s are impregnable *die Verteidigungswerke sind uneinnehmbar;* a glass ∾s *eine Glashütte, -fabrik;* this ∾aday world *diese Welt des Alltags;* the ∾house *das Armenhaus;* an ill ∾man quarrels with his tools (prov.) *ein schlechter Handwerker schimpft auf sein Werkzeug;* a ∾manlike achievement *eine kunstgerechte, fachmännische Leistung;* we are God's (of God's) ∾manship *wir sind Gotteswerk;* a ∾shop *eine Werkstatt.* — **II.** v.tr.: to ∾ the audience into enthusiasm *die Zuhörer in Begeisterung versetzen;* he ∾s the bus from A. to B. *er fährt den Bus von A. nach B.;* it is ∾ed by electricity *es wird elektrisch betrieben:* to ∾ a change *eine Veränderung hervorbringen (herbeiführen);* to ∾ one's fingers (oneself) to the bone for a person *sich für j.en abschinden;* I will ∾ it if I can (sl.) *ich werde die Sache schon deichseln (drehen);* to ∾ one's jaws *mit den Kinnbacken arbeiten, die Kinnbacken bewegen;* to ∾ one's knife through a thing *mit dem Messer durch etwas dringen;* to ∾ a machine *eine Maschine bedienen;* to ∾ a mine *ein Bergwerk ausbeuten;* to ∾ the oracle in one's favour *zu seinem Vorteil hinter den Kulissen arbeiten;* to ∾ a person to death *j.en zu Tode hetzen (arbeiten);* to ∾ a plan *einen Plan ausführen;* to ∾ the ropes *eine Sache heimlich leiten (bewerkstelligen);* to ∾ one's way see 'way'; a worm ∾s its way into (out of) the soil *ein Wurm bohrt sich in den (aus dem) Boden;* to ∾ one's will upon a person *j.em seinen Willen aufzwingen;* to ∾ wonders see 'wonder'; to ∾ double tides *Tag und Nacht arbeiten, Doppelschicht machen.* — with adv.: to ∾ in a thing *etwas hineinarbeiten, einfügen;* he ∾s off his bad temper on his servants *er läßt seine üble Laune an seinen Dienern aus;* I ∾ed off my old things on him *ich wurde meine alten Sachen an ihn los;* to ∾ out a mine *ein Bergwerk abbauen;* to ∾ out a sum *eine Rechenaufgabe lösen;* to ∾ oneself (a person) up into a rage *sich (j.en) in Wut bringen, hineinsteigern;* to ∾ up a subject for an examination *sich (dat.) einen Stoff für eine Prüfung einpauken.* — **III.** v.i.: it won't ∾ *es geht nicht;* the pump will not ∾ *die Pumpe funktioniert nicht;* let the remedy ∾ *laß das Mittel sich auswirken.* — with prep. & adv.: he is ∾ing against time *er strengt sich an, um zur festgesetzten Zeit fertig zu werden;* to ∾ at a thing *an etwas arbeiten;* to ∾ away on *drauflosarbeiten;* the fire is ∾ing down (up) *das Feuer greift nach unten (oben) um sich;* the screw has ∾ed loose *die Schraube hat sich gelockert;* my headache is ∾ing off *meine Kopfschmerzen vergehen allmählich;* the sum will not ∾ out *die Rechenaufgabe geht nicht auf;* the wind has ∾ed round *der Wind hat sich gedreht;* to ∾ to rule *als Ersatz für offenen Streik streng nach den Vorschriften arbeiten und dadurch die Leistung mindern;* to ∾ upon a person *auf j.en einwirken, ihn bearbeiten;* he is hard to ∾ with *mit ihm ist schwer arbeiten*

working I. n.: the ∾s of conscience *die Regungen des Gewissens;* the ∾ of an engine *die Bewegung (der Gang) eines Motors;* the ∾s of his face *seine Gesichtsbewegungen;* the ∾s of his mind *seine Gedankengänge;* the ∾s of a mine, quarry *die Teile eines Bergwerkes, eines Steinbruches.* — **II.** a.: a ∾ basis *eine Arbeitsbasis;* ∾ capital *Betriebs-, Geschäftskapital;* a ∾ day *die tägliche Arbeitszeit;* a ∾ drawing *ein Bauplan;* ∾ expenses *Betriebskosten;* ∾ hours *Arbeitsstunden;* ∾ load *Höchstbelastung;* a ∾ majority (parl.) *eine arbeitsfähige Mehrheit;* ∾ method *Arbeitsverfahren;* in ∾ order *im (richtigen) Gang, in Ordnung;* ∾ power *Leistungsfähigkeit;* a ∾ party *eine Arbeitsgemeinschaft*

world n.: the ∾, the flesh and the devil *weltliche (fleischliche, sündige) Gelüste;* the ∾ of letters *die gelehrte Welt;* it is a ∾ too wide *es ist viel zu weit;* ∾ without end *in Ewigkeit;* all the ∾'s a stage (As You Like It, II, 7) *die ganze Welt ist Bühne (Schlegel);* all the ∾ and his wife were there *alle Welt (alles, was Beine hatte, was etwas auf sich hält) war dort;* she is all the ∾ to me *sie ist mein ein und alles;* it will do you all the good in the ∾ *es wird dir alles denkbare Gute tun;* it is for all the ∾ as if *es ist genau so, als ob;* he is for all the ∾ like his father *er gleicht genau seinem Vater;* from all over the ∾ *aus aller Herren Ländern;* the other (the next) ∾ (the ∾ to come) *das Jenseits;* to begin the ∾ *ins Leben (ein)treten;* to bring a child into the ∾ *ein Kind zur Welt bringen;* to carry the ∾ before one *einen außerordentlichen Erfolg haben;* I would not do it for the ∾ (to gain the whole ∾) *ich täte es um alles in der Welt nicht;* dead to the ∾ *völlig betrunken;* I would give the ∾ to know *ich gäbe alles in der Welt (wer weiß nicht was), um zu wissen;* to give a book to the ∾ *ein Buch veröffentlichen;* how goes the ∾ with you? *wie geht es dir?;* to know (to see) the ∾ *welterfahren sein, die Welt kennenlernen;* to let the ∾ slide *die Ereignisse ihren Gang nehmen lassen;* to live out of the ∾ *jede Gesellschaft meiden;* she's something out of the (this) ∾ (colloq.) *sie ist etwas ganz Außerordentliches, etwas Wunderbares;* to make the best of both ∾s *weltliche und geistliche Interessen in Einklang bringen;* to make a noise in the ∾ *Aufsehen erregen, viel besprochen werden;* there's no reason in the ∾ for it *es besteht kein vernünftiger (nicht der geringste) Grund dafür;* all's right with the ∾ *es ist alles herrlich auf der Welt;* to take the ∾ as it is (as one finds it) *sich mit den gegebenen Verhältnissen abfinden;* he thinks the ∾ of you *er hält große Stücke auf dich, denkt wunder was von dir;* who, how, what, etc., in the ∾ was it? *wer, wie, was, usw., in aller Welt war es?*

worm I. n.: even a ∾ will turn (prov.) *auch ein Wurm krümmt sich, wenn er getreten wird;* food for ∾s *tot;* ∾-eaten *wurmstichig, veraltet.* — **II.** v.tr.: to ∾ a garden bed *ein Beet von Würmern befreien;* to ∾ oneself into a person's favour *sich in j.es Gunst einschmeicheln;* to ∾ oneself (one's way) through the bushes *sich durch die Büsche schlängeln;* to ∾ a secret out of a person *j.em ein Geheimnis entlocken, die Würmer aus der Nase ziehen.* — **III.** v.i.: to ∾ into (out of) *sich hinein-, herauswinden, -schlängeln*

worry I. v.tr.: a dog worries a cat *ein Hund würgt eine Katze;* to ∾ oneself (to be worried) about a thing *sich über etwas ärgern, aufregen, um etwas ängstigen;* to ∾ a person *j.en ärgern, aufregen, plagen, belästigen;* to ∾ a person to do a thing *j.em zusetzen, etwas zu tun;* to ∾ a person's life out *j.em ständig zusetzen, ihn ständig quälen;* to ∾ a person out of a thing *j.en durch Quälen um etwas bringen; davon abbringen, etwas zu tun;* to ∾ a problem out *ein Problem bis zur Lösung immer wieder vornehmen (anpacken);* to ∾ the sword *beim Fechten den Gegner durch kleine, rasche Bewegungen beunruhigen.* — **II.** v.i.: I should ∾! (colloq.) *das regt mich nicht auf (läßt mich ganz kalt);* to ∾ along *sich mühsam durchschlagen (hinquälen).* — **III.** n.: the worries and cares of life *die Aufregungen und Sorgen des Lebens*

worse I. a.: so much the ∾ *um so schlimmer;* ∾ luck! *leider; unglücklicherweise! so ein Pech!;* to be the ∾ for drink *etwas betrunken sein;* to be (to look) the ∾ for wear see 'wear'; I am none (little) the ∾ for it *die Sache hat mir nicht (wenig) geschadet;* your coat would be none the ∾ for a cleaning *dein Rock könnte eine Reinigung gut vertragen, eine Reinigung würde deinem Rock wahrhaftig nichts schaden;* the situation is getting ∾ and ∾ *die Lage wird immer schlechter, schlimmer;* and to make it (matters) ∾ *und zu allem Unglück, um das Unglück voll zu machen.* — **II.** adv.: to be ∾ off *schlechter, schlimmer daran sein;* to fare ∾ *es schlechter, schlimmer haben;* to think none the ∾ of a person *nicht geringer von j.em denken.* — **III.** n.: from bad to ∾ *immer schlimmer, aus dem (vom) Regen in die Traufe;* for better or for ∾ *zum Schaden oder Vorteil, was auch geschehe;* a change for the ∾ *eine Wendung zum Schlechteren, Schlimmeren;* to have (to get) the ∾ *schlechter fahren (wegkommen), den kürzeren ziehen;* to put a person to the ∾ *j.em einen Schaden zufügen, eine Niederlage beibringen*

worst I. a.: the best things are ∾ to come at (prov.) *gut Ding will Weile haben.* — **II.** n.: if the ∾ comes to the ∾ (at the ∾) *im schlimmsten Fall, wenn alle Stricke reißen;* to see a person at his ∾ *j.en von seiner schlechtesten Seite kennenlernen;* do your ∾ *mach', was du willst! sieh zu, wie du fertig wirst!;* to get (to have) the ∾ of it *besiegt werden, den kürzeren ziehen;* we are prepared for the ∾ *wir sind aufs schlimmste gefaßt.* — **III.** v.tr.: the enemy was ∾ed *der Feind wurde besiegt (geschlagen)*

worth I. a.: a bird in the hand is ∾ two in the bush (prov.) *ein Sperling in der Hand ist besser als eine Taube auf dem Dach;* the game is not ∾ the candle *die Sache lohnt nicht;* it is not ∾ doing (mentioning. speaking of, etc.) *es ist nicht wert, getan zu werden (nicht erwähnenswert, der Rede wert usw.);* he died ∾ a million *er hinterließ eine Million;* it is not ∾ powder and shot *es ist keinen Schuß Pulver wert;* he is not ∾ his salt *er ist* *seines Lohnes nicht wert, er taugt nichts;* I shall make it ∾ your while see 'while'; a ∾while experiment *ein lohnendes Experiment;* I give you (you must take) this for what it is ∾ *ich erzähle dir dies, ohne mich für die Wahrheit verbürgen zu können;* my opinion for what it is ∾ *meine unmaßgebliche Meinung;* you must run for all you are ∾ *du mußt laufen, was du Beine hast;* he spent all he was ∾ on it *er gab sein ganzes Vermögen dafür aus.* — **II.** n.: a man of great ∾ *ein verdienstvoller Mann;* money can buy money's ∾ *für Geld ist alles zu haben;* a ha'porth *etwas im Werte von einem halben Penny;* that was a good (bad) penny∾ *das war ein gutes (schlechtes) Geschäft;* give me a shilling's ∾ of stamps *geben Sie mir für einen Shilling Freimarken;* to get one's money's ∾ *auf seine Kosten kommen*

worthy I. a.: a ∾ adversary *ein würdiger, ebenbürtiger Gegner;* the labourer is ∾ of his hire *der Arbeiter ist seines Lohnes wert;* to be ∾ of praise *des Lobes würdig sein, Lob verdienen;* a praise∾ thing *eine lobenswerte Sache;* I asked the ∾ rustic *ich fragte den biederen Mann.* — **II.** n.: an Elizabethan ∾ *ein elisabethanischer Ehrenmann;* a village ∾ *eine Dorfgröße*

wow n.: (U.S. sl.) the play was a ∾ *das Stück war ein Bombenerfolg*

wowser n.: (Austral.) he is a ∾ *er ist ein bigotter Eiferer*

wrap I. v.tr.: the affair is ∾ped in mystery *die Angelegenheit ist in Geheimnis gehüllt;* ∾ it in paper *wick(e)le es in Papier ein;* she ∾ped her shawl closer about (round) her *sie legte (schlug) ihren Schal enger um sich;* to ∾ up a parcel *ein Paket einwickeln, -packen;* she is ∾ped up in her child *sie geht in ihrem Kinde auf.* — **II.** v.i.: mind you ∾ up well if you go out *zieh dich ja warm an, wenn du ausgehst.* — **III.** n.: she threw a ∾ round her *sie warf sich (dat.) einen Morgenrock (Bademantel) um*

wreak v.tr.: to ∾ one's anger (rage) upon a person *seine Wut an j.em auslassen, sein Mütchen an j.em kühlen;* to ∾ one's thoughts upon expression *nach passenden Worten suchen;* to ∾ vengeance upon a person *an j.em Rache üben*

wring I. v.tr.: to ∾ out clothes *Kleider auswringen;* his clothes are ∾ing wet *seine Kleider sind patschnaß;* to ∾ a person's hand *j.em bewegt die Hand drücken;* to ∾ one's hands *die Hände ringen;* to ∾ the neck of a chicken *einem Huhn den Hals ab-, umdrehen;* to ∾ money out of a person *von j.em Geld erpressen;* a face wrung with pain *ein schmerzentstelltes, -verzerrtes Gesicht;* he has wrung the words from their true meaning *er hat den wahren Sinn der Worte entstellt.* — **II.** n.: he gave my hand a ∾ *er drückte mir bewegt die Hand;* give these clothes a ∾ *wringe diese Kleider aus*

wrinkle[1] **I.** v.tr.: he ∾d his forehead *er runzelte die Stirn;* he ∾d (up) his nose at it *er rümpfte die Nase darüber.* — **II.** v.i.: this material ∾s *dieser Stoff (zer)knittert (zerknautscht) leicht.* — **III.** n.: his face is full of ∾s *sein Gesicht ist voller Falten (Runzeln)*

wrinkle[2] n.: he is full of ∾s *er kennt jeden Kniff;* he gave me (put me up to) a ∾ or two *er gab mir manch nützlichen Tip*

write I. v.i.: that's nothing to ∾ home about (colloq.) *dessen brauchst du dich nicht zu rühmen, darauf brauchst du nicht so stolz zu sein;* I shall ∾ off at once *ich schreibe sofort;* I shall ∾ off for it *ich schreibe darum, bestelle es.* — **II.** v.tr.: ∾ me down as an ass *ich bin ein großer Esel gewesen;* he ∾s a good hand *er hat eine schöne Handschrift;* you must ∾ your name down (out) in full *du mußt deinen Namen ganz ausschreiben;* how does he ∾ himself? *wie schreibt er sich?;* to ∾ a play down *ein Stück in der Presse herunterreißen;* to ∾ shares down *den Nennwert von Aktien herabsetzen;* to ∾ a thing down *etwas nieder-, aufschreiben;* his name is written in the Book of Life *sein Name ist auf der Liste der Geretteten;* written in (on) water see 'water'; to ∾ off a debt *eine Schuld abschreiben;* to ∾ off a poem *ein Gedicht schnell (leicht) abfassen, herunterschreiben;* he has written himself out *er hat sich ausgeschrieben;* you must ∾ it out fair (out over again) *du mußt es ins Reine schreiben, nochmal abschreiben;* I must ∾ up my diary *ich muß mein Tagebuch vervollständigen;* to ∾ up a film *einen Film in der Presse herausstreichen;* a journalist ∾s up an incident *ein Journalist berichtet ausführlich über einen Vorfall*

writer n.: ∾'s cramp, palsy *Schreibkrampf*

wrong I. a.: the ∾ answer *die falsche (unrichtige, verkehrte) Antwort;* I am ∾ *ich habe unrecht (habe mich geirrt);* my liver is (has gone, has got) ∾ *meine Leber ist nicht in Ordnung;* stealing is ∾ *Stehlen ist eine Sünde;* I can prove you ∾ *ich kann beweisen, daß du unrecht hast;* something is ∾ with him *mit ihm ist etwas nicht in Ordnung;* your watch is ∾ *deine Uhr geht falsch (verkehrt);* what's ∾ with a cup of tea? (colloq.) *wie wäre es mit einer Tasse Tee?;* to be in the ∾ box *auf dem Holzwege sein;* to get hold of the ∾ end of the stick *die Sache falsch auffassen (mißverstehen);* to be the ∾ side out *schlechter Laune (übel gelaunt) sein;* to be born on the ∾ side of the blanket *ein uneheliches Kind sein;* to be on the ∾ side of forty *über vierzig sein;* you'll laugh on the ∾ side of your mouth soon *dir wird bald das Lachen vergehen;* he always does the ∾ thing *er macht immer alles falsch (verkehrt);* to go (to take) the ∾ way *den falschen (verkehrten) Weg einschlagen;* to go the ∾ way to work *etwas verkehrt anfangen;* to go down the ∾ way *in die falsche (unrechte) Kehle geraten;* to rub a person up the ∾ way *j.en reizen, ärgern;* to take a thing the ∾ way *etwas übelnehmen.* — **II.** adv.: to answer ∾ *falsch (verkehrt) antworten;* to go ∾ *fehlgehen; vom Wege der Tugend abweichen, auf Abwege geraten;* to get in ∾ with a person (colloq.) *j.es Mißfallen, -gunst erregen;* to get a person in ∾ (colloq.) *j.en in Mißkredit bringen.* — **III.** n.: the difference between right and ∾ *der Unterschied zwischen Recht und Unrecht;* two ∾s cannot make a right *Unrecht bleibt Unrecht;* to do ∾ *Unrecht tun, sündigen;* the king can do no ∾ *der König kann nicht Unrecht tun;* to do ∾ to a person *j.en ungerecht behandeln;* you do me ∾ *du verleumdest mich;* you were both in the ∾ *Ihr hattet beide unrecht;* to put a person in the ∾ *j.en ins Unrecht setzen.* — **IV.** v.tr.: to ∾ a person *j.em Unrecht tun, j.en ungerecht behandeln*

wrought p.p. of work: ∾ iron *Schmiedeeisen;* he is in a highly ∾-up state *er ist hochgradig nervös*

wry a.: to draw (to pull) a ∾ face (mouth) *ein schiefes Gesicht (Maul) ziehen*

Y

yank v.tr. (sl.): to ∾ out a loose tooth *einen losen Zahn mit einem Ruck herausziehen*

yarn n.: to spin a ∾ *eine (Abenteuer-, Wunder-) Geschichte erzählen, ein Garn spinnen; aufschneiden, lügen*

year n.: all the ∾ round *das ganze Jahr (hin)durch;* at this time of ∾ *zu dieser Jahreszeit;* by the ∾ *jahresweise, jährlich;* ∾ by ∾ *Jahr für Jahr;* ∾ in ∾ out *jahrein jahraus;* every other (second) ∾ *alle zwei Jahre;* one ∾ with another *ein Jahr ins andere gerechnet;* he earns £ 2,000 a ∾ *er verdient 2000 Pfund im Jahre (jährlich);* this ∾'s wine *der diesjährige Wein;* a two-∾ old *ein zwei Jahre altes Pferd;* at two ∾s old (of age) *im Alter von zwei Jahren;* a ∾ ago *vor einem Jahr;* a ∾-long struggle *ein Kampf, welcher ein ganzes Jahr (jahrelang) dauerte;* many ∾s (of) training *eine langjährige Ausbildung;* after five ∾s' absence *nach einer Abwesenheit von fünf Jahren;* for ∾s (to come) *auf (viele) Jahre hinaus;* I have not seen him for ∾s *ich habe ihn seit Jahren (jahrelang) nicht gesehen;* in a ∾'s time *in einem Jahr;* of late (in recent) ∾s *in den letzten Jahren;* with the ∾s *mit den Jahren;* it is 25 ∾s this August since we married *in diesem August sind es 25 Jahre her, daß (seit) wir heirateten;* it may be ∾s yet *darüber können noch Jahre vergehen;* the ∾s of discretion *gesetztes, mündiges Alter (14 Jahr nach engl. Recht);* in the Year of Grace 1958 *im Jahr des Heiles 1958;* a leap-∾ *ein Schaltjahr;* that happened in the ∾ 1 (dot) (colloq.) *das ist vor vielen Jahren (vor X-Jahren) passiert;* he is in ∾s (young in ∾s) *er ist alt, betagt (jung an Jahren);* he is young for his ∾s *er ist jung für sein Alter;* he bears his ∾s well *er ist für sein Alter recht rüstig*

yearn v.i.: to ∾ for (after) a home *sich nach einem Heime sehnen;* to ∾ to do a thing *danach schmachten (verlangen, sich sehnen), etwas zu tun;* to ∾ towards (to) a person *sich zu j.em hingezogen fühlen*

yeasty a.: a ∾ conscience *ein unruhiges Gewissen;* a ∾ fellow *ein oberflächlicher Bursche, Schwätzer;* ∾' talk *Schaumschlägerei*

yellow a.: a ∾ back *ein billiger Schundroman;* ∾ Jack *das gelbe Fieber;* the sere and ∾ leaf *das Greisenalter:* a ∾ look *ein eifersüchtiger (neidischer, argwöhnischer) Blick;* the ∾ press *die chauvinistische Hetzpresse;* to wear ∾ stockings *eifersüchtig sein;* a ∾ streak *ein feiger Zug*

yen n. (sl.): to have a ∾ for something *sich nach etwas sehnen*

yeoman n.: this coat has seen (done) ∾'s service *dieser Rock hat guten (nützlichen) Dienst getan*

yes-man n.: a ∾ *ein Ja-sager, Schmarotzer*

yet I. adv.: ∾ again *nochmals;* is he ∾ alive? *lebt er noch?;* I gave him another and ∾ another chance *ich gab ihm immer wieder Gelegenheit (Gelegenheit über Gelegenheit);* a ∾ more difficult task *eine noch schwierigere Aufgabe;* the largest ∾ found *die größten bisher gefundenen;* strange and ∾ true *seltsam und doch wahr;* as ∾ *bis jetzt (bislang, bisher);* is he dead ∾? *ist er schon tot?;* need you go ∾? *mußt du schon gehen?;* haven't you heard ∾? *hast du noch nicht gehört?;* it will not happen just ∾ *es tritt nicht gerade jetzt ein;* much ∾ remains to be done *es bleibt noch viel zu tun übrig;* there is one ∾ missing *einer (eine, eines) fehlt noch;* I seem to see him ∾ *ich sehe ihn immer noch vor mir;* it is not time ∾ *es ist noch nicht Zeit;* I will be even with you ∾ *ich rechne schon noch mit dir ab;* it may be years ∾ *es kann noch Jahre dauern.* — **II.** conj.: ∾ what is the use of it all? *jedoch (doch), was nützt das alles?*

yield I. v.tr.: the land ∾s good crops *das Land bringt gute Ernten hervor;* to ∾ a fortress *eine Festung übergeben;* to ∾ the palm to a person *sich (für) geschlagen, übertroffen bekennen;* to ∾ a point in the debate *in der Diskussion einen Punkt zugeben;* to ∾ precedence to a person *j.em den Vorrang einräumen;* to ∾ oneself prisoner *sich gefangengeben;* the business ∾s a good profit *das Geschäft bringt einen guten Gewinn ein, wirft einen guten Gewinn ab;* to ∾ consent *einwilligen;* to ∾ up the ghost *den Geist aufgeben.* — **II.** v.i.: the town ∾ed at once *die Stadt ergab sich sofort;* to ∾ to superior force *der Übermacht weichen;* to ∾ to none in *keinem nachstehen an;* to ∾ to persuasion *sich überreden lassen;* to ∾ to pressure *dem Druck nachgeben;* the disease ∾s to treatment *die Krankheit wird durch Behandlung besser;* the field ∾s poorly (well) *das Feld liefert einen schlechten (guten) Ertrag.* — **III.** n.: the ∾ of the year *der Jahresertrag*

yoke I. n.: the ∾ of public opinion *der Druck (Zwang) der öffentlichen Meinung;* a ∾ of oxen *ein Paar Ochsen;* the ∾ of a shirt *das Schulterstück eines Hemdes;* to submit to (to pass under) the ∾ *sich dem Joche beugen, unter das Joch kommen;* my ∾fellow, ∾-mate *mein,-e Lebensgefährte,-in; Arbeitsgenosse,-in.* — **II.** v.tr.: to ∾ an animal *ein Tier anspannen (anschirren);* to ∾ a pair in marriage *ein Paar ehelich verbinden.* — **III.** v.i.: to ∾ together (with) a person *zusammenarbeiten, -passen;* they do not ∾ well *sie passen nicht gut zueinander*

Yorkshire n.pr.: to come ∾ over (on, to put ∾ on) a person *j.en betrügen, beschwindeln;* I'se ∾ too *ich bin so schlau wie du, mich kannst du nicht beschwindeln*

young n.: an animal is with ∾ *ein Tier ist trächtig*

yourself pron.: how's ∾? (colloq.) *wie geht's selbst?;* you are not quite ∾ tonight *du bist heute Abend nicht ganz auf der Höhe;* be ∾! (colloq.) *reiß' dich zusammen!;* by ∾ *allein, ohne Hilfe;* you must see for ∾ *du mußt selbst sehen*

you've had it! interj. (sl.): *die Chance (Gelegenheit) ist vorbei!*

Z

zenith n.: it is at its (has reached its) ∾ *es ist auf dem Höhepunkt, hat den Höhepunkt (Gipfel) erreicht*

zero n.: ∾ hour is 6 a.m. *X-Zeit ist sechs Uhr morgens;* to be at ∾ *auf dem tiefsten Punkt sein, den Tiefstand erreicht haben;* to sink to ∾ *auf den Nullpunkt fallen (sinken)*

zest n.: it adds (gives) ∾ to it *es verleiht der Sache Würze, erhöht den Genuß;* he entered into it with great ∾ *er beteiligte sich mit großem Eifer daran*

zip n.: the ∾ of a bullet *das Pfeifen einer Kugel;* he did it with ∾ *er tat es energisch, mit Schwung;* a ∾-fastener (∾per) *ein Reißverschluß*

ziss n. (colloq.): to take (to have) a ∾ *ein Schläfchen machen*

ADDENDA

acid n.: the ∾ test *Prüfung auf Herz und Nieren, Feuerprobe*

anybody n.: ∾'s guess *reine Vermutung*

arty-crafty adj.: (colloq.) *künstlerisch aufgemacht (Gegenstand), künstlerisch, aber unpraktisch, kunstgewerblich*

ash n.: to sit in sackcloth and ∾es *in Sack und Asche Buße tun;* to turn to dust and ∾es *erfolglos sein, sich zerschlagen*; to win (bring) back the ∾es *die Niederlage wettmachen (nur im Kricketvergleichskampf Englands gegen Australien)*

back n.: to put one's ∾ into anything *sich kräftig anstrengen, sich abmühen*

back-room boy n.: (colloq.) *Fachmann (bes. in geheimer Forschung)*

backwards adv.: to know something ∾ *etwas vollkommen beherrschen, etwas im Schlaf können*

band wag(g)on n.: to climb (jump, get) on (aboard) the ∾ *,mitlaufen', zur erfolgreichen Partei umschwenken*

ban-the-bomb adj.: *zugunsten der atomaren Abrüstung*

bat n.: to carry one's ∾ (Cricket) *bei Spielende ungeschlagen sein*

boffin n.: (colloq.) *Wissenschaftler, der (im Auftrag der Regierung) an einem Geheimprojekt arbeitet*

boot n.: he's getting too big for his ∾s *er wird pompös, bombastisch*

Bow Bells n.: to be born within the sound of ∾ *ein waschechter Londoner (Cockney) sein (Kirche St. Mary le Bow in der City von London)*

bread-line n.: a ∾ *Schlange von Bedürftigen (an die Nahrungsmittel verteilt werden)*; to live near the ∾ *ein ärmliches Leben führen*

bug v.tr./i.: to ∾ a room (colloq.) *Zimmer mit einem versteckten Mikrophon versehen (zwecks Spionage)*

built-in adj.: the ∾ safeguards of our constitution against tyranny *die in unserer Verfassung vorgesehenen (eingebauten) Sicherungsmaßnahmen gegen Tyrannei*

built-up adj.: a ∾ area *bebautes Gelände*

bumf, bumph n.: (sl.) *Toilettenpapier, Papierkram (verächtlich für Akten, Formblätter, Reklame usw.)*

candid camera n.: *Miniaturkamera, mit der man j.en heimlich photographieren kann*

clear n.: to be in the ∾ *schuldlos, unbelastet (Gewissen), frei (von Schulden) sein*

clueless adj.: (colloq.) *ahnungslos, ohne einen Schimmer*

corner-boy n.: *Rowdy*

crackers adj.: (Am. sl.) to drive (send) someone ∾ *j.en zum Wahnsinn treiben*

crumble v.i.: that's the way the cookie ∾s (Am. prov.) *es ist reine Glückssache, Schicksal*

cuff n.: off the ∾ statement *Feststellung ohne Gewähr, aus dem Stegreif*

curate n.: like the ∾'s egg (good in parts) *teils gut, teils schlecht*

dig v.tr.: (sl.) *gern haben, genießen, aufmerksam zuhören, wahrnehmen*

drop n.: at the ∾ of a hat (Am. colloq.) *prompt, bei jeder passenden und unpassenden Gelegenheit*

egghead n.: *(oft verächtlich) Intellektueller*

eye n.: to be easy on the ∾ (sl.) *hübsch anzusehen sein*

fab adj.: (sl.), (fabulous) *fantastisch*

fat n.: to live on one's ∾ *von Vorrat, Reserven leben*

feather-bedding n.: (colloq.) *Verwöhnung, Verweichlichung, staatliche Subventionen;* the ∾ of industry *Anstellung unnötiger Arbeitskräfte (auf Verlangen einer Gewerkschaft)*

flat-footed adj.: (colloq.) to catch someone ∾ *j.en überrumpeln, j.en auf frischer Tat, bei einer offensichtlichen Lüge, ertappen*

folksy adj.: (iron.) *volkstümelnd, volkstümlerisch*

foot-loose adj.: *frei, ungebunden, unbeschwert*

free adj.: all for ∾ *gratis und franko*

fringe I. n.: the ∾s of civilization *die Randzonen der Zivilisation*; ∾ benefits *Sozialleistungen (Urlaub, Kinderzulagen usw.)*; the lunatic ∾ (colloq.) *die Übereifrigen,*

Hundertfünfzigprozentigen, Extremisten; **II.** adj.: ∾ behaviour *unorthodox, kaum innerhalb der Grenzen des Gesetzes, ‚am Rande der Legalität‘*

good adv.: people who never had it so ∾, are busy having it so ∾ *Leute denen es niemals vorher so gut gegangen ist*

green light n.: (colloq.) he got the ∾ *er bekam die Erlaubnis (zur Durchführung eines bestimmten Vorhabens)*

groove n.: in the ∾ (sl.) *im richtigen Fahrwasser;* to get (fall) into a ∾ *in Routine verfallen*

ground n.: common ∾ *unbestritten*; to cover much ∾ *(Bericht usw.) umfassend sein, viel behandeln, (Arbeit, Diskussion) gut weiterkommen*; to cut the ∾ from under someone's feet *j.en in die Enge treiben*

hair n.: to let one's ∾ down (sl.) *sich gehen lassen, zwanglos sein;* to a ∾ *haargenau;* to make one's ∾ curl (colloq.) *das Blut (in den Adern) erstarren lassen*

ham adj.: (colloq.) ∾ actor *dilettantischer Schauspieler*; ∾ radio *Amateursender*; ∾-fisted *ungeschickt*

handout n.: (sl.) *Almosen (für Bettler), Broschüre, Werbezettel, Erklärung für die Presse*

hep adj.: (sl.) he is ∾ to anything *er versteht alles*; to put someone ∾ to a thing *j.en in etwas einweihen*

high-jump n.: (sl.) he's for the ∾ *er wird gehängt*

hoop n.: to go through the ∾ (colloq.) *etwas Schlimmes über sich ergehen lassen, bes. den Bankrott erklären*

jam n.: a ∾ session *frei improvisierter Jazz*; in a ∾ *in der Klemme, mißliche Lage*; money for ∾ *ein außergewöhnliches Geschenk, großes Glück*

keep up v.i.: to ∾ with the Joneses *mit den Nachbarn schritthalten, hinter den anderen nicht zurückbleiben*

kite n.: to fly a ∾ (fig.) *einen Versuchsballon steigen lassen, sich durch Wechselreiterei Geld oder Kredit beschaffen*

knot n.: to tie oneself in ∾s *sich verwickeln, verheddern, sich umbringen vor Beflissenheit*

leaden-footed adj.: a ∾ comparison *ein Vergleich, der hinkt*

long-range adj.: ∾ plans *Planung auf weite Sicht*

market n.: to be in the ∾ for *etwas kaufen wollen, Bedarf haben an*; to be on the ∾ *zum Verkauf angeboten werden*; to come into the ∾ *auf den Markt kommen*; to place (put) on the ∾ *auf den Markt bringen*; sale in the open ∾ *freier Verkauf*; ∾ for future delivery *Terminmarkt*; to play the ∾ *an der Börse spekulieren*

mickey n.: (sl.) to take the ∾ out of someone *j.en verspotten, verhohnepiepeln*; a M∾ Finn *Schlaf-, Betäubungstrunk*

monkey I. n.: a ∾ (sl.) £500 *(fünfhundert Pfund)*; ∾ business (colloq.) *Gaunerei, Schwindel*; to throw a ∾ wrench into something (colloq.) *etwas durcheinander bringen*; to have a ∾ on one's back (sl.) *rauschgiftsüchtig sein*; **II.** v.i. to ∾ about *herumpfuschen, herumspielen*

nasty adj.: a ∾ bit of work *ein unangenehmer, (boshafter) Mensch*; to turn ∾ *gehässig, unverschämt werden*

off-balance adj.: (colloq.) it caught him ∾ *er war nicht darauf gefaßt*

off-beam adj.: (colloq.) this belief is right ∾ *diese Meinung ist falsch, unlogisch*

off-beat adj.: (colloq.) ∾ thinking *eine ungewöhnliche, ausgefallene Denkweise*

overegg v.tr.: (colloq.) to ∾ the cake *des Guten zuviel tun*

package deal n.: *ein Koppelungsgeschäft*; (fig.) *das Schlechte mit dem Guten in Kauf nehmen*

paid p.part. of pay v.tr./i.: to put ∾ to something (colloq.) *etwas verhindern, beenden*

panhandle v.tr./i.: (colloq.) *betteln, ‚schnorren‘*

pansy n.: (colloq.) *weibischer junger Mann, Homosexueller*

pinhead n.: (colloq.) *Dummkopf*

pinta n.: (colloq.) *(ungefähr) ein halber Liter Milch*

pint-sized adj.: (colloq.) *‚Taschenformat‘ (verächtlich)*

pipeline n.: goods which are in the ∾ *Sachen unterwegs (zur Lieferung)*; the number of houses in the ∾ at the present time *die Zahl der zur Zeit im Bau befindlichen Häuser*

play down v.tr.: *gering veranschlagen, in den Hintergrund rücken, etwas verharmlosen*

ploy n.: *Beschäftigung, Tätigkeit, eine ‚Masche‘ (um Eindruck zu machen)*

queer n.: *Homosexueller*

raise v.tr. to ∾ the wind (colloq.) *eine Anleihe aufnehmen*; to ∾ a laugh *Gelächter hervorrufen*; to ∾ hell (the roof) *einen*

Spektakel machen; to ∾ land (naut.) *Land sichten*; to ∾ a point *etwas zur Sprache bringen*

ratrace n.: *Fahrradtreterei (für Geld, Macht oder Karriere), erbarmungsloses Wettrennen zum Erfolg*

river n.: to sell someone down the ∾ (sl.) *j.en völlig im Stich lassen*

rock v.tr.: to ∾ the boat (fig.) *die Sache ins Wanken bringen*

rubber-stamp v.tr.: to ∾ a decision (colloq.) *zustimmen, ohne viel zu überlegen*

sacred adj.: a ∾ cow (humor.) *eine unantastbare, sakrosankte Sache*

sandboy n.: as happy as a ∾ *(nur in dieser Redewendung) kreuzfidel, sehr lustig*

score I. n.: to have no idea what the ∾ is *keine Ahnung davon haben, wie es wirklicht steht*; **II.** v.tr.: to ∾ off someone (colloq.) *j.em eins auswischen, j.en überlisten*

slant I. n.: to take a ∾ at (colloq.) *einen Seitenblick werfen auf*; to give a Russian ∾ to the project *dem Unternehmen eine russische Tendenz geben;* **II.** v.tr./i.: *Nachrichten usw. ‚färben', frisieren (zu einem bestimmten Zweck oder für ein bestimmtes Publikum)*

snob n.: ∾ appeal *Anziehungskraft für Snobs*; ∾ value *von gesellschaftlichem Wert, wertvoll für Angeber*

soap opera n.: *rührselige Hörspiel- oder Fernsehserie (z. B. von Seifenfirmen zu Werbungszwecken finanziert)*

soft-pedal v.tr./i.: (sl.) *kleinlaut machen, j.em einen Dämpfer aufsetzen, etwas abmildern, weniger laut vorbringen, abdämpfen*

spark v.tr.: to ∾ (off) a myth *ein Märchen in die Welt setzen*

square adj.: (sl.) *altmodisch, spießbürgerlich*

stag v.i.: (sl.) *in neu ausgegebenen Aktien spekulieren*

swinging adj.: (colloq.) *vital, lebensfroh,* heiter

taper off v.i.: (colloq.) purchases of grain will now ∾ *Getreideeinkäufe werden jetzt langsam abnehmen*

tear-jerker n.: (colloq.) *Schnulze (rührseliges Lied, Theaterstück, Buch usw.)*

Teddy-boy n.: *Halbstarker (in England)*

tick v.i. (colloq.) what makes him ∾ *was ihn antreibt, in Schwung hält*

top I. n.: big ∾ *Zirkus Zelt*; he's ∾s (sl.) *er ist Klasse;* to blow one's ∾ (colloq.) *vor Ärger in die Luft gehen, seinem Zorn Luft machen*; **II.** v.tr./i.: to ∾ up a glass *ein Glas bis zum Rande wieder auffüllen*

uppercrust n.: (sl.) *die oberen Zehntausend*

with it prep.: (sl.) *auf Draht, schwer auf der Höhe*

wrong adj.: adv.: to get on the ∾ side of a person, to get in ∾ with him, *es mit j.em verderben*; to get someone in ∾ (sl.) *j.en in Mißkredit bringen* (with someone)

Ronald Taylor / Walter Gottschalk

A German-English Dictionary of Idioms

Idiomatic and Figurative German Expressions with English Translations

4. Auflage, 598 Seiten, Linson, Hueber-Nr. 6216

6000 deutsche Redewendungen mit idiomatischen englischen Übersetzungen. Bei der Fülle der gebotenen englischen Entsprechungen kann der deutsche Benutzer des Bandes jeweils leicht diejenige aussuchen, die sich ihrer Form und ihrem Wesen nach am besten in den jeweiligen Zusammenhang einfügt. Zur Veranschaulichung ist den deutschen Ausdrücken jeweils ein Übungssatz mit englischer Übertragung beigefügt.

John Leyton

Modern English Vocabulary in Narrative Form

With 2000 Translated Idioms

5., verbesserte Auflage, 244 Seiten, kartoniert, Hueber-Nr. 2084

Dieses locker und humorvoll geschriebene Buch bietet eine nach Sachgruppen gegliederte Darstellung des modernen englischen Wortschatzes in Erzählform. Alle Bereiche des englischen Lebens sind erfaßt, und an jedes Kapitel schließt sich eine Sammlung der wichtigsten Idioms aus dem betreffenden Themenkreis an.

Peter F. McDonald – Juan C. Sager

The Languages of English Journalism

Hueber Hochschulreihe, Bd. 29, 192 Seiten, kart., Hueber-Nr. 2177

Dieses materialreiche Arbeitsbuch vermittelt dem Studierenden über exemplarisches Lesen und gesteuerte Analyse von Originaltexten eine bewußte Kenntnis von Textsorten und sprachlichen Registern der englischen Presse und implizit der geschriebenen Gegenwartssprache überhaupt. Neben einer Schulung des Leseverstehens und systematischer Wortschatzerweiterung wird die Fähigkeit vermittelt, bestimmte Textarten selbständig zu produzieren.

MAX HUEBER VERLAG ISMANING

Hans-Wilhelm Klein / Wolf Friederich

Englische Synonymik

Für Studierende und Lehrer

4., völlig neu bearbeitete und erweiterte Auflage, 920 Seiten, Linson, Hueber-Nr. 2032

Diese völlig neu bearbeitete Ausgabe der „Englischen Synonymik" berücksichtigt in vollem Umfang sämtliche Eigenheiten des modernen englischen Sprachgebrauchs. Sämtliche Vokabeln werden ausschließlich in Englisch definiert und mit englischen Originalbeispielen, meist aus der Literatur, belegt.

Armin Blass / Wolf Friederich

Englischer Wortschatz in Sachgruppen

Mit Anhang: Aussprache und unregelmäßige Plurale

10. Auflage, 141 Seiten, kartoniert, Hueber-Nr. 2077

Aus dem auch für den Kundigen kaum übersehbaren Wortschatz des Englischen sind hier etwa 10 000 Wörter und Ausdrücke als breite Grundlage ausgewählt worden. Die Neubildungen der jüngsten Vergangenheit und der Gegenwart wurden ebenso wie der amerikanische Sprachgebrauch berücksichtigt. Der Anhang enthält eine Zusammenstellung der unregelmäßigen Plurale sowie eine Liste der Wörter mit Ausspracheschwierigkeiten.

Clemens Gruber

Wörterbuch der Werbung und des Marketing

Dictionary of Advertising and Marketing
Englisch-Deutsch/Deutsch-Englisch

312 Seiten, kartoniert, Hueber-Nr. 6312

Dieses Wörterbuch enthält insgesamt ca. 9000 Einträge zur Terminologie des Sach- und Berufsfeldes Werbung und Marketing. Aus den Grenzgebieten, die die Werbung berühren – Druckwesen, Fotografie, Public Relations, Design usw. – wurde eine möglichst umfassende Auswahl getroffen.

MAX HUEBER VERLAG ISMANING

Notizen

Notizen